THE CANADIAN YEARBOOK OF INTERNATIONAL LAW

2005

ANNUAIRE CANADIEN DE DROIT INTERNATIONAL

The Canadian Yearbook of International Law

VOLUME XLIII   2005   TOME XLIII

Annuaire canadien de Droit international

Published under the auspices of
THE CANADIAN BRANCH, INTERNATIONAL LAW ASSOCIATION
AND
THE CANADIAN COUNCIL ON INTERNATIONAL LAW

Publié sous les auspices de
LA SECTION CANADIENNE DE L'ASSOCIATION DE DROIT INTERNATIONAL
ET
LE CONSEIL CANADIEN DE DROIT INTERNATIONAL

UBC Press
VANCOUVER / TORONTO

Printed in Canada on acid-free paper ∞

ISBN 978-0-7748-1359-4
ISSN 0069-0058

Canadian Cataloguing in Publication Data

The National Library of Canada has catalogued this publication as
follows:

*The Canadian yearbook of international law — Annuaire canadien de
droit international*

> Annual.
> Text in English and French.
> "Published under the auspices of the Canadian Branch,
> International Law Association and the Canadian Council on
> International Law."
> ISSN 0069-0058

> 1. International Law — Periodicals.
> I. International Law Association. Canadian Branch.
> II. Title: Annuaire canadien de droit international.
> JC 21.C3   341'.05   C75-34558-6E

Données de catalogage avant publication (Canada)

*Annuaire canadien de droit international — The Canadian yearbook of
international law*

> Annuel.
> Textes en anglais et en français.
> "Publié sous les auspices de la section canadienne de
> l'Association de droit international et le Conseil canadien de
> droit international."
> ISSN 0069-0058

> 1. Droit international — Périodiques.
> I. Association de droit international. Section canadienne.
> II. Conseil canadien de droit international.
> III. Titre: The Canadian yearbook of international law.
> JC 21.C3   341'.05   C75-34558-6E

UBC Press
University of British Columbia
2029 West Mall
Vancouver, BC V6T 1Z2
(604) 822-3259
www.ubcpress.ca

The Board of Editors, the Canadian Branch of the International Law Association, the Canadian Council on International Law, and the University of British Columbia are not in any way responsible for the views expressed by contributors, whether the contributions are signed or unsigned.

Les opinions émises dans le présent *Annuaire* par nos collaborateurs, qu'il s'agisse d'articles signés, ne sauraient en aucune façon engager la responsabilité du Comité de rédaction, de la Section canadienne du Conseil canadien de droit international ou de l'Université de la Colombie-Britannique.

Communications to the *Yearbook* should be addressed to:

Les communications destinées à l'*Annuaire* doivent être adressées à:

THE EDITOR, THE CANADIAN YEARBOOK OF INTERNATIONAL LAW
FACULTY OF LAW, COMMON LAW SECTION
UNIVERSITY OF OTTAWA
57 LOUIS PASTEUR
OTTAWA, ONTARIO K1N 6N5 CANADA

Contents / Matière

Notes and Comments / Notes et commentaires

Chronique de Droit international économique en 2004 / Digest of International Economic Law in 2004

Canadian Practice in International Law / Pratique canadienne en matière de droit international

Cases / Jurisprudence

Book Reviews / Recensions de livres

THE CANADIAN YEARBOOK OF INTERNATIONAL LAW

2005

ANNUAIRE CANADIEN DE DROIT INTERNATIONAL

La négociation de la convention de l'UNESCO sur la protection et la promotion de la diversité des expressions culturelles

IVAN BERNIER

En octobre 2003, la Conférence générale de l'UNESCO confiait au Directeur général le mandat de soumettre à sa prochaine session (octobre 2005) un rapport préliminaire accompagné d'un avant-projet de convention sur la protection de la diversité des contenus culturels et des expressions artistiques.[1] Peu de temps après, le Directeur général constituait un groupe international multidisciplinaire de quinze experts indépendants chargés de lui adresser des suggestions et des avis sur l'élaboration de l'avant-projet de convention.[2] Au terme de trois rencontres qui se sont échelonnées de décembre 2003 à mai 2004, le groupe des experts indépendants transmit au Directeur général le texte d'un avant-projet de convention sur la protection de la diversité des contenus culturels et des expressions artistiques que celui-ci fit immédiatement circuler auprès des États membres afin de recueillir leurs commentaires

Ivan Bernier, Professeur émérite, Faculté de droit, Université Laval. Auteur et éditeur de nombreux articles et ouvrages traitant du rapport entre commerce et culture, il était invité en 2003 par le Directeur Général de l'UNESCO à faire partie d'un groupe d'experts indépendants en vue de l'élaboration d'un avant-projet de convention internationale concernant la protection de la diversité des contenus culturels et des expressions artistiques

1 UNESCO, Conférence générale, Réunion intergouvernementale d'experts sur l'avant-projet de convention sur la protection de la diversité des contenus culturels et des expressions artistiques, Rés. 32C/34, Opportunité de l'élaboration d'un instrument normatif international concernant la diversité culturelle, 17 octobre 2003, disponible en ligne à: <http://portal.unesco.org/culture/fr/file_download.php/626c288f150cbd3e071230e4ef40329Fr-Resolution32C34-conf201-5.pdf> (dernière visite: le 6 septembre 2006).

2 UNESCO, Culture, Réunions d'experts indépendants, disponible en ligne à: <http://portal.unesco.org/culture/fr/ev.php-URL_ID=21903&URL_DO=DO_TOPIC&URL_SECTION=201.html> (dernière visite: le 5 septembre 2006).

et observations écrites jusqu'à la mi-novembre 2004. Par la même occasion, il convoquait une première session de la Réunion inter-gouvernementale d'experts destinée à avancer l'élaboration de l'avant-projet de convention en vue de faire rapport à la Confé-rence générale à sa trente-troisième session. Trois rencontres fu-rent nécessaires pour mener à bonne fin les négociations. Au terme de la troisième et dernière session, les représentants de plus de 130 pays ont approuvé à la quasi-unanimité le libellé final d'un avant-projet de convention et recommandé à la Conférence géné-rale son adoption à la trente-troisième session, en octobre 2005. Mais ce résultat, qualifié de moment historique par plusieurs délé-gations dans leur déclaration de clôture, fut dénoncé avec vigueur par les États-Unis, ces derniers allant jusqu'à affirmer, dans une déclaration rendue publique par leur ambassade à Paris, que le texte de convention proposé était profondément défectueux parce qu'il concernait le commerce plutôt que la culture, qu'il était en conséquence hors de la compétence de l'UNESCO et que son adop-tion ne pourrait que compromettre la réputation de l'UNESCO à titre d'organisation internationale responsable. Comment en est-on arrivé à ce résultat? C'est ce que nous allons chercher à voir dans les pages qui suivent en examinant le déroulement de cha-cune des trois sessions de négociations et en remontant le cours des évènements qui ont conduit par la suite à l'adoption de la Con-vention par la Conférence générale.

LA PREMIÈRE SESSION: UNE SESSION DE RECONNAISSANCE ET D'OBSERVATION

La première session de la Réunion intergouvernementale d'ex-perts sur l'avant-projet de convention s'est tenue du 20 au 24 sep-tembre 2004. Dans son allocution d'ouverture, le Directeur général de l'UNESCO, M. Koïchiro Matsuura, souligna combien cette pre-mière étape de négociation était importante pour l'Organisation. Il ajouta: "Je souhaite que cette première rencontre soit l'occasion d'un véritable débat à l'échelle internationale sur la question cru-ciale que pose la protection et la promotion de la diversité des expressions culturelles dans le monde d'aujourd'hui."[3] Dans les

---

[3] UNESCO, Directeur général, *Discours de M. Koïchiro Matsuura à l'occasion de la première réunion intergouvernementale sur la préparation de l'avant-projet de convention sur la protection de la diversité des contenus culturels et des expressions artistiques*, Doc. DG 2004/126, à la p. 2 disponible en ligne à: <http://unesdoc.unesco.org/images/0013/001364/136453f.pdf>, (dernière visite: le 5 septembre 2006).

faits, cette première session n'a peut-être pas donné lieu à un véritable débat, comme le souhaitait le Directeur général de l'UNESCO, mais elle a mis en place les éléments essentiels à la tenue de celui-ci. On mettra ici plus particulièrement en lumière son apport concret à l'instauration d'une dynamique de négociation.

Quatre développements sont intervenus durant cette session qui ont marqué le cours futur de la négociation. Le premier développement a trait à la mise en place de la structure de négociation elle-même, c'est-à-dire à l'élection du Président de la Réunion intergouvernementale d'experts, à la formation du Bureau de direction ainsi qu'à la constitution d'un Comité de rédaction composé de vingt-quatre membres. Il n'est pas sans intérêt de les examiner de plus près afin de voir leurs implications pour la suite de la négociation. Le second développement est lié à l'apparition, lors du débat sur l'avant-projet, de conceptions assez différentes du type de convention à mettre en place. Ces conceptions, même si elles n'exprimaient pas des positions définitives sur le contenu de la Convention, n'en demeuraient pas moins de nature à influencer de façon importante la suite du débat en l'entraînant dans des directions parfois assez opposées. Le troisième développement réside dans l'acceptation pratiquement unanime par les États de l'avant-projet de convention des experts indépendants comme une base de discussion utile et leur accord pour travailler à partir de celui-ci. Ce consensus, un des rares qui ressorte de la première session de travail des experts gouvernementaux, a donné à la négociation un cadre normatif qui devait contribuer à recentrer le débat lorsque celui-ci s'engageait dans des directions trop divergentes. Enfin, un dernier développement important pour la suite des négociations a été la mise en évidence du besoin de préciser certains enjeux de base de la Convention. Mais pour mieux comprendre la nature de ces développements, il est nécessaire de revenir brièvement sur chacun d'eux.

LA MISE EN PLACE DE LA STRUCTURE DE NÉGOCIATION

La mise en place de la structure de négociation s'est effectuée en deux temps. Il y a d'abord eu l'élection du Président de la Réunion intergouvernementale d'experts et la constitution du Bureau de direction la toute première journée de la Réunion, puis ensuite, sur la base d'une décision de ce dernier, la formation deux jours plus tard du Comité de rédaction.

Dans toute négociation, le poste le plus important à combler est celui de président de conférence car le succès des négociations

dépendra pour une part substantielle de l'autorité de ce dernier et
de son habilité dans la conduite des discussions. Il n'est donc pas
surprenant que ce poste soit souvent convoité et que son choix
fasse presque toujours l'objet de discussions préalables entre les
États. Dans le cas présent, ce choix ne semble pas avoir soulevé de
difficultés sérieuses. Proposée officiellement au nom du Groupe
africain (groupe 6) par le représentant de Madagascar, l'élection
de M. Kader Asmal de l'Afrique du Sud au poste de Président de
conférence a été appuyée par les représentants d'Oman, du Mexique, des États-Unis, de l'Afghanistan et du Sri Lanka au nom des
cinq autres groupes. Dans son discours lors de la session d'ouverture, M. Asmal a fait preuve d'une remarquable compréhension
des enjeux de la négociation, rappelant entre autres que si la liberté d'expression et la libre circulation des idées et des connais-
sances constituaient les bases de tout effort en vue de promouvoir
et de protéger la diversité des expressions culturelles, il n'en demeurait pas moins qu'en l'absence d'expressions culturelles multiples et distinctes, il ne pouvait y avoir de véritable dialogue
interculturel. Conjuguant fermeté et humour, M. Asmal s'est avéré
dans les faits un président particulièrement soucieux d'efficacité, à
tel point que la première session, qui devait durer originalement
du 20 au 25 septembre 2004, s'est clôturée un jour plus tôt que
prévu. Pareil résultat, remarquable lorsqu'on considère que cent
trente-deux États membres, dix-neuf OIG et vingt ONG/OING ont
participé à cette rencontre et que près d'une centaine d'interventions orales ont été faites dans le cadre des discussions, augurait
bien pour la suite de la négociation. Mais on pouvait regretter cependant que, compte tenu du temps disponible, des efforts supplémentaires n'aient pas été faits en vue d'établir des liens entre
les différentes opinions exprimées, car l'on s'est effectivement re-
trouvé à la fin de la session avec un ensemble de points de vue
assez disparates qui pouvaient parfois coïncider mais dont il était
difficile de tirer quelque conclusion que ce soit relativement à
l'existence ou non d'un consensus. L'impression qui se dégage
de cette première Réunion en fait est que les États, soit parce
qu'ils n'étaient pas suffisamment prêts ou soit parce qu'ils considéraient qu'ils n'avaient pas assez de temps pour s'exprimer (pas
moins de quarante-cinq ont même senti le besoin de fournir un
texte écrit en complément de leur présentation orale), se sont con-
tentés d'exposer sommairement leurs vues et d'observer pour le
reste ce que les autres avaient à dire.

En ce qui concerne le Bureau de direction, il fut convenu qu'il devait veiller de façon générale au bon déroulement de la négociation dans le respect de la procédure établie. Appelé à évaluer sur une base régulière les progrès réalisés, il devait être en mesure d'intervenir, en particulier lorsque des difficultés survenaient. De ce point de vue, il constituait un rouage important de la négociation. Le Bureau tel que constitué comprenait, outre le Président de la Réunion, un rapporteur dont le rôle était de noter le contenu des discussions lors des séances plénières pour en donner un compte rendu une fois les séances terminées. On comptait typiquement sur le Rapporteur pour mettre une cohérence dans les discussions et en tirer les conclusions qui s'imposaient. Il était prévu également que le Rapporteur officierait en tant que ressource technique pour le Comité de rédaction afin de refléter les instructions de la Plénière. Dans cette fonction, le Rapporteur, assisté du Secrétariat, était appelé à travailler en étroite collaboration avec le Président de la Réunion et le Bureau de direction. Quatre vice-présidents complétaient le Bureau, pour un total de six postes qui devaient être pourvus en respectant les exigences en matière de représentation géographique. Le poste de Rapporteur fut confié à M. Artur Wilczynski du Canada et les quatre postes de vice-président aux représentants de la Tunisie, de Ste-Lucie, de la Lituanie et de la République de Corée. Durant la première Réunion des experts gouvernementaux, le Bureau s'est réuni à plusieurs reprises pour traiter de questions liées essentiellement au déroulement du débat et à la structuration de la suite de la négociation. La décision la plus importante qu'il fut amené à prendre lors de ces rencontres est sans aucun doute celle de mettre sur pied un comité de rédaction.

Le Comité de rédaction était appelé à jouer un rôle crucial dans l'élaboration du texte de la Convention. Son mandat, tel que défini par le Bureau et transmis à la Plénière, prévoyait qu'il serait composé de quatre membres par groupe électoral régional et serait assisté du Secrétariat de l'UNESCO. Il lui revenait plus spécialement de traduire en langage concret et en termes juridiques les instructions de la Plénière soumises par le Président. Ce dernier pouvait demander au Comité de rédaction des recommandations linguistiques, de styles ou de formulation d'options au cas où la Plénière n'atteindrait pas un consensus. Sa tâche dans un tel contexte pouvait s'avérer délicate et c'est pourquoi, dans un souci de transparence, il a été précisé dans son mandat que les observateurs seraient admis aux travaux du Comité. La composition du Comité était relativement équilibrée dans la mesure où elle reflétait assez bien les principales tendances qui se sont exprimées durant le débat relativement au type de convention souhaité. Pour mémoire, il peut être utile de rappeler ici que les vingt-quatre États représentés sur le Comité de rédaction, soit quatre par groupe électoral régional, étaient les suivants: (groupe 1) la Finlande, la France, la Suisse et les États-Unis; (groupe 2) l'Arménie, la Croatie, la Hongrie et la Russie; (groupe 3) la Barbade, le Brésil, le Costa Rica et l'Équateur; (groupe 4) la Chine, l'Inde, le Japon et la Corée; (groupe 5) le Bénin, le Nigeria, Madagascar et le Sénégal; (groupe 6) l'Algérie, le Liban, l'Arabie Saoudite et les Émirats arabes unis.

Il était prévu que le Directeur général de l'UNESCO convoquerait la première réunion du Comité de rédaction en décembre 2004, après avoir reçu les commentaires écrits des États membres, et que le Comité élirait alors son Président et déciderait de son programme de travail en tenant compte des échéances établies par la Conférence générale. Sa première tâche était de soumettre à l'intention de la session suivante de la Plénière une version révisée de l'avant-projet de convention des experts independents incorporant les commentaires écrits des États membres. Toutes les propositions du Comité de rédaction devaient être soumises à la Plénière pour approbation. Le Comité pouvait se réunir en même temps que la Plénière et recevait ses instructions de son Président; mais il pouvait aussi se réunir entre les sessions de la Plénière. Il restait à voir comment un comité de rédaction aussi large allait fonctionner dans la pratique. Dans la mesure où trois de ses membres faisaient partie de l'Union européenne (la France, la Finlande et la Hongrie), il fallait attendre en outre que soit connu le rôle que cette dernière entendait jouer dans la négociation pour savoir ce qu'il adviendrait de la participation de ceux-ci aux travaux du Comité de rédaction. Selon la réponse apportée, la dynamique de travail au sein du Comité pouvait s'en trouver modifiée.

LES DIFFÉRENTES CONCEPTIONS CONCERNANT LE TYPE DE CONVENTION À METTRE EN PLACE

Sauf circonstances exceptionnelles, la négociation d'une convention implique la réconciliation de points de vue parfois assez différents concernant le contenu de la convention. Les différences les plus importantes concernent généralement l'objet précis, la portée des engagements et le niveau de contrainte de la convention. Dans le cas présent, de telles différences de vues se sont manifestées très rapidement lors de l'examen, chapitre par chapitre, de l'avant-projet de convention des experts indépendants. Trois conceptions distinctes concernant le type de convention souhaité pouvaient déjà, au terme de la première session, être identifiées à cet égard sur la base des commentaires oraux ou écrits des États membres.

La première conception, qui ralliait de façon assez lâche une majorité des États qui se sont exprimés lors du débat, accueillait favorablement dans ses grandes lignes l'avant-projet de convention, même si elle questionnait certains aspects de celui-ci et suggérait des modifications et des ajouts. Elle se prononçait en faveur d'un instrument juridique contraignant, égal en valeur aux autres accords internationaux, qui reconnaîtrait la spécificité des produits culturels ainsi que le droit des États de mettre en œuvre des mesures de préservation et de promotion de leurs expressions culturelles tout en demeurant ouvert aux autres expressions culturelles. Cet instrument juridique inciterait ces mêmes États à prendre les mesures nécessaires en vue de préserver et promouvoir leurs propres expressions culturelles et les engagerait à renforcer concrètement la coopération pour le développement dans le domaine culturel. Afin que la Convention ne demeure pas lettre morte et puisse évoluer avec le temps, elle se montrait également favorable à l'incorporation d'un mécanisme de suivi et d'un mécanisme de règlement des différends, pourvu que l'on évite toute lourdeur bureaucratique et que les mécanismes en question demeurent peu coûteux. Enfin, on peut considérer comme un élément caractéristique de cette première conception le fait que les États qui la défendaient considéraient important que la négociation procède dans les meilleurs délais.

La deuxième conception était partagée par un nombre restreint d'États, mais cet apparent désavantage était compensé en bonne partie par l'importance économique et la cohésion idéologique des États en question. Tout en acceptant que l'avant-projet vise principalement la question des contenus culturels et des expressions artistiques et en reconnaissant le bien-fondé et la pertinence de plusieurs de ses dispositions (en particulier les dispositions relatives à la coopération pour le développement), cette conception entretenait de sérieuses réserves sur plusieurs aspects importants de l'avant-projet de convention. Ces réserves concernaient d'abord le champ d'application de la Convention qui était considéré trop axé sur les biens et services culturels et sur la protection des expressions culturelles et pas suffisamment sur la promotion de la diversité culturelle ainsi que sur l'ouverture aux autres cultures.

Elles concernaient aussi: le droit souverain des États d'adopter des mesures pour protéger et promouvoir la diversité des expressions culturelles sur leur territoire, jugé potentiellement incompatible avec les engagements des parties à l'Organisation mondiale du commerce (OMC); l'engagement des États signataires à promouvoir les objectifs et les principes de la Convention dans les autres enceintes internationales et de se consulter à cette fin, jugé dangereux; les mécanismes de suivi et de règlement des différends, qui devraient être réduits à leur plus simple expression sinon éliminés parce qu'inappropriés en matière culturelle; les accords de coproduction et le traitement de préférence pour les pays en développement, considérés incompatibles avec les engagements des parties à l'OMC; et enfin l'article sur les relations avec les autres instruments internationaux qui devait, à leurs yeux, établir clairement que la Convention demeurerait conforme en tout temps aux autres accords internationaux. De façon générale, le modèle de convention envisagé en était un où les moyens de réaliser les objectifs fixés au plan international étaient axés davantage sur le dialogue et la coopération que sur une réglementation contraignante. Enfin, il faut souligner que les États qui s'identifiaient plus particulièrement à cette conception de la Convention étaient aussi ceux qui faisaient valoir qu'il n'était pas essentiel que la convention soit adoptée en 2005 et qu'il fallait prendre le temps nécessaire pour établir des consensus et donc faire attention aux échéances trop courtes.

Une troisième conception de la Convention soutenue par un nombre très limité d'États questionnait la pertinence de l'avant-projet de convention des experts indépendants pour le motif qu'il était trop centré sur la protection et la promotion de la diversité des expressions culturelles. Elle proposait plutôt un instrument juridique d'une portée plus large qui mettrait l'accent sur le respect du droit des États d'adopter des politiques qui reflètent leurs croyances, sur l'amélioration du respect interculturel ainsi que sur le développement de valeurs communes. Cette conception, qui remettait en cause implicitement le mandat initialement confié au Directeur général de l'UNESCO par la Conférence générale, ouvrait la porte à un élargissement du champ d'application de la Convention plus en rapport avec la promotion de la diversité culturelle au sens large qu'avec la promotion et la protection de la diversité des expressions culturelles.

L'existence de ces trois points de vue distincts concernant le type de convention que l'UNESCO devrait adopter pouvait difficilement, dans le contexte d'une négociation axée sur la recherche d'un consensus, ne pas avoir d'impact sur le résultat de la négociation. Cela n'a rien d'exceptionnel et c'est précisément à travers la négociation que s'opère normalement un rapprochement de ces différents points de vue et qu'une convention respectueuse des préoccupations de l'ensemble des membres peut être conclue. Mais une telle situation laissait malgré tout entrevoir un danger. Si la négociation, en effet, devait aboutir à un texte qui ne soit rien d'autre que le plus petit commun dénominateur de l'ensemble des demandes formulées par les États membres, s'il devait en résulter un accord reflétant une série de compromis politiques n'ayant pas vraiment de signification légale et que la diversité des expressions culturelles en ressorte affaiblie plutôt que renforcie, alors il y avait risque qu'elle s'avère un échec. Toutefois, ce risque se trouvait atténué du fait que la négociation était entreprise à partir d'un texte de base qui avait déjà sa propre structure et sa propre logique, comme nous le verrons maintenant.

L'AVANT-PROJET DE CONVENTION DES EXPERTS INDÉPENDANTS COMME BASE DE NÉGOCIATION

Ainsi que le soulignait le Rapporteur dans son rapport oral au terme de la première session, les délégations avaient reconnu que l'avant-projet de convention des experts indépendants constituait une base valable de discussion et un instrument utile pour faciliter le débat à l'étape du processus intergouvernemental.[4] De fait, l'ensemble du débat s'est déroulé lors de cette première session sur la base de cet avant-projet. Plus important encore, le mandat confié au Comité de rédaction précisait que le texte révisé de convention que celui-ci devait soumettre à la deuxième session serait basé sur l'avant-projet de convention des experts indépendants tout en incorporant à celui-ci les commentaires écrits soumis par les États membres.

L'utilisation de l'avant-projet en question comme base du texte révisé de convention pour la session de la Plénière a eu pour conséquence immédiate de structurer le débat autour d'une certaine

---

4 UNESCO, *Rapport oral du Rapporteur, M. Artur Wilczynski, à la session de clôture de la première session de la Réunion intergouvernementale d'experts sur l'avant-projet de convention sur la protection de la diversité des contenus culturels et des expressions artistiques* (25 Septembre 2004) à la p. 3, disponible en ligne à: <http://portal.unesco.org/culture/admin/file_download.php/oralrepintergov.pdf?URL_ID=25964&filename=1112602551 3 oralrepintergov.pdf&filetype=application%2Fpdf&filesize=152202&name=oralrepintergov.pdf&location=user-S/> (dernière visite: le 6 septembre 2006).

conception de la Convention qui avait déjà sa structure et sa logique propre, même si les États demeuraient totalement libres en
théorie de faire ce qu'ils voulaient du texte proposé, y compris le
transformer en profondeur ou le rejeter pour repartir sur une toute
autre base. Mais à en juger par les commentaires formulés par les
délégations lors du débat sur l'avant-projet, il était déjà évident au
terme de la première session que la structure de base, de même
qu'une partie substantielle des dispositions de l'avant-projet, de-
meureraient dans le projet de convention finalement adopté, soit
telles quelles, soit modifiées dans leur formulation ou encore com-
plétées par d'autres dispositions. Les dispositions de l'avant-projet
concernant la coopération pour le développement, par exemple,
ou encore celles concernant l'éducation et la société civile semblaient là pour demeurer, même si des améliorations leur seraient
vraisemblablement apportées. Là où le texte de l'avant-projet sou-
levait des problèmes plus importants, certaines pistes de solution
concernant les modifications à apporter avaient déjà été proposées. Comme on peut le voir, l'avant-projet des experts indépendants agissait comme un mécanisme intégrateur des différentes
conceptions de la convention qui avait cours, même s'il était lui-
même appelé à ressortir transformé de la négociation.

DES ENJEUX À CLARIFIER POUR QU'UN VÉRITABLE DÉBAT AIT LIEU

Les enjeux en question concernaient plus spécialement trois questions dont le traitement dans l'avant-projet des experts indépendants demeurait encore ambigu si l'on en juge par les commentaires
des États sur ce dernier, soit: (1) l'objet propre de la Convention;
(2) le rapport de la Convention avec les autres accords internationaux; (3) le caractère contraignant de la Convention.

Aux termes du mandat confié par la Conférence générale au
Directeur général de l'UNESCO, la Convention devait porter sur
"la protection de la diversité des contenus culturels et des expressions artistiques." L'avant-projet de convention préparé par les experts indépendants et présenté par le Directeur général pour
discussion lors de la première session était effectivement intitulé:
"Avant-projet de convention sur la protection de la diversité des
contenus culturels et des expressions artistiques." L'objet propre
de la Convention, tel qu'envisagé dans l'avant-projet, n'était donc
pas la protection de la diversité culturelle entendue au sens large
(comme englobant des aspects aussi divers que l'ensemble des traits
distinctifs qui caractérisent une société ou un groupe, ou si l'on

veut la culture entendue dans un sens sociologique, les droits culturels, le patrimoine culturel sous toutes ses formes, le développement culturel, les droits d'auteur, l'expression culturelle, le multiculturalisme, les droits linguistiques), mais bien plutôt la protection d'un aspect précis de cette diversité culturelle qui est la diversité des contenus culturels et des expressions artistiques.

Toutefois, malgré le titre donné à l'avant-projet, on retrouvait dans le texte même de ce dernier des références assez nombreuses à la diversité culturelle qui laissaient sous-entendre que l'objet précis de la Convention pourrait être plus large. De telles références à la diversité culturelle entendue dans un sens large pouvaient avoir leur place dans une convention sur la protection de la diversité des contenus culturels et des expressions artistiques mais à la condition que le lien entre les deux soit bien compris. Or, cela n'était malheureusement pas le cas, ainsi qu'il ressort de nombreux commentaires sur l'avant-projet formulés par les États lors de la première rencontre où ces derniers parlent de la Convention comme si elle avait pour objet propre la préservation de la diversité culturelle.[5] La confusion concernant l'objet propre de la convention atteignit un point tel durant la discussion que le Président jugea opportun de demander à l'UNESCO une clarification du mandat de négociation. Dans sa réponse, le Sous-directeur général pour la culture, M. Mounir Bouchenaki, rappela les débats qui avaient entouré la décision de la Conférence générale à l'automne 2003 d'aller de l'avant avec la négociation d'une convention portant spécifiquement sur "la protection de la diversité des contenus culturels et des expressions artistiques" et expliqua que c'est sur la base de ce mandat tout à fait clair que le travail en vue d'en arriver à une convention avait été entrepris depuis.

En ce qui concerne le rapport de la Convention avec les autres accords internationaux, le débat sur cette question lors de la première session fut loin d'être concluant. Il faut dire que l'avant-projet

---

5 C'est ainsi que dans les commentaires généraux de la première journée de la Réunion, on présente la Convention comme un "instrument utile de promotion de la diversité culturelle," on espère que la Convention constituera "l'un des piliers juridiques de la diversité culturelle," on suggère que la Convention "insiste sur la promotion de la diversité culturelle" ou on énumère les conditions pour qu'une "convention sur la diversité culturelle" ne devienne pas encore une autre convention dépourvue d'effet concret. Ce qui n'empêche pas d'autres États de souligner que l'objet propre de la Convention est la diversité des contenus culturels et des expressions artistiques ou de demander que le contenu culturel apparaisse "comme le thème central et le fil conducteur de la convention."

de convention n'aidait pas véritablement à le résoudre en offrant deux variantes sur le sujet (article 19). La variante A se lisait ainsi:

1. Rien, dans la présente Convention, ne peut être interprété comme portant atteinte aux droits et obligations des États parties au titre de tout instrument international existant relatif aux droits de propriété intellectuelle auxquels ils sont parties.
2. Les dispositions de la présente Convention ne modifient en rien les droits et obligations découlant pour un État partie d'un accord international existant, sauf si l'exercice de ces droits ou le respect de ces obligations causait de sérieux dommages à la diversité des expressions culturelles ou constituaient pour elle une sérieuse menace.

La variante B de l'avant-projet de convention quant à elle se lisait ainsi:

Rien, dans la présente Convention, ne modifie les droits et obligations des États parties au titre d'autres instruments internationaux existants.

Parmi les États qui se prononcèrent sur la question, une majorité se déclara favorable à la variante A, mais ce choix était souvent accompagné de remarques qui laissaient entrevoir une certaine hésitation sur la façon de régler le problème. Une minorité substantielle, par ailleurs, opta en faveur de la variante B, mais avec des commentaires qui laissaient sous-entendre que des précisions supplémentaires pourraient être nécessaires. Entre les tenants de la variante A et les tenants de la variante B, l'opposition était assez marquée et on sentait que pour les uns comme pour les autres, l'enjeu était majeur. Plusieurs États, par ailleurs, refusèrent de se prononcer en faveur de l'une ou de l'autre option en faisant valoir qu'il était trop tôt pour faire un choix ou qu'ils ne disposaient pas de suffisamment d'informations pour ce faire. Enfin, symptôme manifeste d'une difficulté à saisir les implications des choix offerts, plus d'un tiers des États présents lors de la première session s'abstinrent de se prononcer sur la question. Ainsi, au terme de la première rencontre, on se retrouvait avec un débat qui prenait une importance croissante au plan politique, mais dont les enjeux, paradoxalement, demeuraient encore mal compris. Un examen plus approfondi de ce qui était véritablement en cause derrière ce débat s'imposait de toute évidence.

Durant le débat sur l'avant-projet de convention lors de la première session bon nombre d'interventions soulignèrent la nécessité d'arriver à une convention efficace qui aurait un caractère contraignant. Plusieurs États, il est vrai, exprimèrent des préoccupations relativement à la lourdeur et au coût des mécanismes de mise en œuvre et de règlement des différends proposés, mais la plupart n'en souhaitaient pas moins le maintien de tels mécanismes sous une forme ou une autre. Certains États, par contre, questionnèrent sérieusement la nécessité de doter la Convention de mécanismes de mise en œuvre et de règlement des différends pour le motif que cela n'était pas approprié dans le domaine culturel. Dans l'ensemble, une conviction générale sembla se dégager qu'il était trop tôt pour prendre position sur le sujet, les engagements précis des parties aux termes de la Convention n'étant pas encore connus. Mais si la question du caractère contraignant de la Convention ne paraissait pas trop préoccuper encore les membres de l'UNESCO au terme de la première session, il en allait différemment de certaines organisations non gouvernementales, qui voyaient dans celle-ci un élément absolument fondamental de la Convention. C'est le cas, par exemple, de la Fédération internationale des droits de l'Homme, qui précisait dans son commentaire écrit sur l'avant-projet que le seul moyen d'assurer l'effectivité de la Convention était de doter celle-ci d'un mécanisme de règlement des différends équivalent à celui de l'OMC, c'est-à-dire d'un mécanisme d'arbitrage obligatoire accompagné de sanctions, et qu'à défaut de ce faire, la Convention risquait de tomber dans le verbalisme. Il en va de même de l'Institut international du théâtre qui, dans ses remarques, commentaires et observations concernant l'avant-projet de convention, signalait que l'absence d'un régime de sanctions était susceptible de provoquer un déséquilibre par rapport à d'autres traités, notamment des traités commerciaux, qui prévoyaient un tel régime. De là à conclure qu'en l'absence d'un tel mécanisme, la Convention, privée de toute effectivité, deviendrait rapidement lettre morte, il n'y avait qu'un pas que ces ONGs semblaient prêtes à franchir.

Dans l'ensemble, la première session de la Réunion des experts gouvernementaux sur l'avant-projet de convention a surtout contribué à mettre en place les éléments essentiels à la tenue d'un véritable débat "sur la question cruciale que pose la protection et la promotion de la diversité des expressions culturelles dans le monde d'aujourd'hui," pour reprendre les mots du Directeur général de l'UNESCO.[6] Mais en même temps, elle a fait ressortir des

---

6 Voir *supra* note 3.

divergences parfois assez marquées sur cette question et mis en évidence l'importance de clarifier les enjeux sous-jacents qui demeuraient encore mal compris.

LA DEUXIÈME SESSION: UNE BATAILLE DE TRANCHÉE

Au terme de la première session de la Réunion des experts gouvernementaux sur l'Avant-projet de convention sur la diversité des contenus culturels et des expressions artistiques, le mandat avait été donné au Comité de rédaction nouvellement constitué, assisté du Secrétariat de l'UNESCO, de préparer un texte révisé de convention basé sur l'avant-projet soumis par le Directeur général et incorporant à celui-ci les commentaires écrits et les propositions d'amendements soumis par les États membres, le texte en question devant servir de point de départ pour la seconde session. Une première réunion du Comité de rédaction se tint effectivement du 14 au 17 décembre 2004 en vue de proposer, à partir des commentaires adressés, "des formulations en langage juridique clair qui ne trahissent aucune voix tout en tentant d'en saisir l'essence," ainsi que le suggérait le Directeur général dans son allocution de bienvenue.[7] Mais la tâche devait s'avérer beaucoup plus ardue qu'envisagé.

D'entrée de jeu, certains problèmes déjà prévisibles après la première session ont entravé le fonctionnement du Comité lors de cette première rencontre. La taille du Comité (vingt-quatre membres), les différentes interprétations des membres quant au mandat de ce dernier ainsi que leur propension à défendre des positions nationales et enfin la quantité et la diversité considérables des commentaires et suggestions d'amendements transmis, ont entraîné un questionnement sur la méthode de travail qui a duré jusqu'à la fin de la rencontre. Il faut dire, à la décharge du Comité, que cette première réunion avait quelque chose d'un peu expérimental en ce sens que c'était la première fois, dans la pratique de l'UNESCO, qu'un comité d'États membres était chargé de synthétiser les commentaires écrits de l'ensemble des membres, ce rôle

---

7 Voir UNESCO, *Discours de M. Koïchiro Matsuura à l'occasion de la deuxième session de la Réunion d'experts intergouvernementaux sur l'avant-projet de convention internationale concernant la protection de la diversité des contenus culturels et des expressions artistiques*, Doc. DG/2005/018, 31 janvier 2005, en ligne: http://unesdoc.unesco.org/images/0013/001384/138466f.pdf (dernière visite: le 5 septembre 2006).

ayant traditionnellement été assigné au Secrétariat qui remettait subséquemment le résultat de son travail à l'Assemblée plénière. Une question en particulier a opposé les membres tout au long des discussions, celle de savoir de quelle façon en arriver à une formulation juridique claire qui ne trahisse aucune voix. Pour certains, une formulation juridique susceptible de contribuer à l'avancement des travaux ne pouvait se réaliser sans modifier ou éliminer certaines suggestions ou options, en d'autres termes sans négocier. Pour d'autres, il ne pouvait être question de négocier avant que la Plénière n'ait d'abord pris connaissance de l'ensemble des options, et en tout état de cause, la négociation ne relevait pas du mandat du Comité de rédaction. En dernier ressort, il fut convenu que le Comité allait simplement transmettre à la Plénière une liste synthétisant toutes les options ainsi que des remarques de nature à faciliter le travail de la Plénière, remarques tendant essentiellement à dégager les grandes tendances en ce qui concerne les options. Ce mode de fonctionnement devait permettre d'accélérer suffisamment le travail (après la première journée de travail, le Comité n'en était toujours qu'à l'article 1) pour qu'un projet de texte révisé contenant une série d'options issues des contributions des États, de même que les remarques du Comité de rédaction concernant le titre et les articles 1 à 11, soit présenté aux membres.

Le résultat du cette première rencontre de Comité de rédaction a malgré tout été perçu par la plupart des observateurs comme plutôt décevant dans la mesure où à peine un tiers de l'avant-projet révisé a été effectivement discuté par celui-ci. Néanmoins, il faut reconnaître qu'en plus d'avoir diminué très substantiellement le nombre d'options à considérer par la Plénière grâce au travail de synthèse effectué par le Secrétariat, le Comité de rédaction avait permis, à travers ses débats, de mettre en évidence certaines ambiguïtés concernant son rôle ainsi que sa méthode de travail, ambiguïtés qui demandaient à être clarifiées avant le début de la seconde session de la Réunion des experts gouvernementaux. Malheureusement, les mêmes problèmes devaient resurgir dès la première journée de la seconde session de la Réunion des experts gouvernementaux et affecter par la suite le rythme de travail ainsi que le résultat de celle-ci. Pour permettre de bien comprendre la contribution de cette dernière au progrès de la négociation, nous nous pencherons successivement sur la méthode de travail utilisée durant les travaux, sur les résultats atteints au terme de la rencontre et enfin sur les questions qui demeuraient encore en suspens.

LA MÉTHODE DE TRAVAIL

Après les allocutions de bienvenue du Directeur général et du Président du Conseil exécutif, la seconde session démarra avec un exposé du Président de la Réunion intergouvernementale d'experts sur la méthode de travail. Celui-ci suggéra d'abord, pour accélérer le travail, la création au besoin de groupes informels dont la mission serait d'examiner les questions les plus importantes et les plus controversées en vue de faire ressortir les principales options défendues par les membres en Assemblée plénière, les groupes en question devant lui faire rapport. Ensuite, le Président proposa de structurer le débat en Plénière autour des trois thèmes suivants: (1) le cadre conceptuel de la convention (qui inclurait, outre le titre, les objectifs, les principes, les définitions et le champ d'application); (2) le cadre politique de la Convention, qui couvrirait l'ensemble des dispositions relatives aux droits et obligations des membres et aux liens avec les autres instruments internationaux; (3) le cadre juridique et administratif de la Convention, qui se pencherait sur les dispositions relatives aux mécanismes de suivi et de règlement des différends ainsi qu'aux clauses finales. Avant d'aborder le thème premier, toutefois, le Président proposa de procéder immédiatement à l'examen des questions dites "transversales," c'est-à-dire des questions susceptibles de se soulever de façon récurrente tout au long de l'examen de l'avant-projet révisé. Ces questions étaient le plus souvent liées à l'utilisation de certains termes et expressions qui ne faisaient pas consensus. C'est à partir de cet exposé sommaire de la méthode de travail, complété par un rappel des objectifs de la négociation et du rôle spécifique du Comité de rédaction ainsi que par des explications sur le texte de l'avant-projet révisé que s'enclencha le débat proprement dit. Mais à peine lancé, celui-ci devait donner lieu à plusieurs interventions de la part des membres concernant la méthode de travail, lesquelles allaient se poursuivre durant une bonne partie de la seconde session et forcer le Président à revenir sur le sujet à plusieurs reprises. Un tel développement, non dépourvu de risques pour la suite de la négociation, demande des explications. Aussi nous est-il apparu utile, pour mieux comprendre la dynamique qui sous-tend ce développement, de revenir sur trois questions qui ont alimenté du début jusqu'à la fin de la seconde session le débat sur la méthode de travail.

Le problème de la méthode de négociation

En ouvrant le débat sur le thème 1 (le cadre conceptuel de la Convention), le Président avait explicitement demandé que l'on traite d'abord des questions transversales, donnant comme exemple des questions relatives à l'utilisation de termes tels que "contenus culturels et expressions artistiques," "expressions culturelles," "protection" et "biens et services culturels." Mais le premier État à intervenir, la Thaïlande, demanda que l'on commence par les définitions de l'article 4. Cette intervention fut suivie ensuite de celle du Pérou qui demanda que l'on commence par le titre, de celle du Canada qui demanda que l'on commence par les objectifs énumérés à l'article 1, de celle de l'Arabie saoudite qui exprima le souhait que l'on revienne au titre, de celle des États-Unis qui suggéra que l'on revienne aux questions transversales, de celle du Japon qui insista pour que l'on parle dans le titre de diversité culturelle plutôt que de diversité des expressions culturelles, et ainsi de suite, jusqu'à ce que le Maroc soulève une question d'ordre demandant que l'on clarifie l'objet du débat, suivi en cela par un certain nombre d'autres États. En réponse à ces demandes d'éclaircissement des membres concernant l'objet exact du débat, le Président, déclara simplement qu'il revenait à l'Assemblée plénière de décider comment elle entendait procéder. En l'absence d'une directive précise, les Membres délaissèrent l'étude des questions transversales pour concentrer leurs interventions sur le titre de la Convention ainsi que sur les objectifs de l'article 1. En d'autres mots, la stratégie de clarification des questions transversales au tout début des négociations fut implicitement abandonnée.

Ceci étant, il fallait s'attendre à ce que ces mêmes questions refassent surface tout au long de la négociation, ce qui ne manqua pas de se produire. Elles refirent leur apparition plus spécialement dans le cadre des discussions du Comité de rédaction et des groupes de travail informels où elles donnèrent lieu à de multiples interventions relatives entre autres à l'utilisation de crochets et des notes de bas de page, ralentissant ainsi de façon marquée le travail de ces derniers. Le résultat est que tout au long de la seconde session, on a assisté en Assemblée plénière à des débats structurés de façon plutôt lâche, dépourvus de perspective et peu propices à de véritables négociations. Les interventions s'enchaînaient de façon souvent décousue, se contentaient dans bien des cas d'exprimer un choix parmi les diverses options proposées et, qui plus est, justi-fiaient rarement les choix en question. Dans un tel contexte, le risque était grand de prendre l'arbre pour la forêt, c'est-à-dire de perdre de vue le fait que derrière les débats sur les mots et les for-mules se profilaient des différences de points de vue fondamen-tales quant au type de convention à adopter.

Le rôle respectif des groupes informels, du Comité de rédaction et de l'Assemblée plénière, ou la question du lieu de la négociation

Dès la fin de la première journée de discussion au sein de l'As-semblée plénière, un groupe informel fut créé par le Président en vue de dégager les éléments essentiels du débat sur le titre et les objectifs. Ce dernier devait faire rapport dès la reprise des travaux de l'Assemblée plénière le lendemain matin. Toutefois, le rapport transmis verbalement le lendemain matin souleva plus de problèmes qu'il n'en réglait. Le rapport en tant que tel était plutôt succinct (il ne couvrait que le titre et les paragraphes (a) et (c) de l'article (1). Immédiatement après la présentation de celui-ci, plusieurs États intervinrent pour mettre en doute la légitimité et la pertinence du groupe, faisant valoir que celui-ci empiétait sur le rôle du Comité de rédaction sans en avoir le caractère représentatif. D'autres États répliquèrent en faisant valoir que le Président était autorisé en vertu des règlements à constituer des groupes de travail et que si le man-dat d'un groupe de travail n'était pas clair, il suffisait de le préciser. Derrière ces interventions, toutefois, un autre type de critique se faisait jour relatif au contenu et au fonctionnement du groupe. Pour un certain nombre d'États, en effet, le rapport du Groupe de travail, particulièrement sur le titre, ne reflétait pas les principales tendances observées dans le débat de l'Assemblée plénière la jour-née précédente.[8]

Ce débat sur le rapport du tout premier Groupe de travail ne prit fin que lorsque le Président intervint pour préciser le rôle respectif des groupes de travail, du Comité de rédaction et de l'Assemblée plénière. Celui-ci expliqua que le Groupe de travail devait assister l'Assemblée plénière en réduisant les différends entre les déléga-

---

8 Deux des trois options proposées par le Groupe de travail concernant le titre faisaient référence à la "diversité culturelle" plutôt qu'à la "diversité des conte-nus culturels et des expressions artistiques," qui était la formulation la plus lar-gement utilisée durant la Plénière. Dans les commentaires transmis par les États en novembre 2004, seulement trois des seize options proposées utilisaient l'ex-pression "diversité culturelle."

tions et en réduisant les options. Il ne remplaçait pas le Comité de rédaction qui conservait son mandat et son statut. Les questions contentieuses ne pouvaient pas être réglées par le Comité de rédaction car c'est à l'Assemblée plénière qu'il revenait d'identifier les solutions avec l'aide du Groupe de travail. Mais ces explications ne devaient pas satisfaire plusieurs États qui revinrent à la charge pour demander que l'on donne un mandat élargi au Comité de rédaction afin que celui-ci soit en mesure de négocier. Le Président intervint à nouveau alors pour mettre fin à ce débat. Il se dit d'accord pour accorder une plus grande flexibilité au Comité de rédaction mais en insistant sur le fait que l'on ne pouvait transférer au Comité de rédaction toutes les questions de fond. En réponses aux plaintes à l'effet qu'il n'y avait pas de véritable négociation, il suggéra que les États se rencontrent de façon informelle pour négocier.

Dans les jours qui suivirent, le Président dû, malgré tout, intervenir à plusieurs reprises pour expliquer le mandat du Comité de rédaction. Le vendredi 4 février, après avoir fait rapport sur le travail de ce dernier la soirée précédente, il souligna le peu de progrès réalisé et se plaignit du fait que le processus au sein du Comité était trop lourd et trop lent. Il répéta à cette occasion les règles qui devaient guider l'action du Comité, à savoir: (1) que si une directive de la Plénière était claire, alors elle devait se refléter dans la proposition que le Comité de rédaction préparait; (2) que si un État voulait remettre en question une directive de la Plénière, alors il devait le faire en plénière et non au Comité de rédaction; (3) que les séances du Comité de rédaction n'étaient pas le lieu des débats de fond: c'était en plénière que se discutaient ces questions. Le lundi 7 février, ayant constaté que les travaux du Comité de rédaction ne progressaient toujours pas convenablement, il reprit ses explications en se plaignant cette fois du fait que les délégués nationaux au sein du Comité étaient davantage préoccupés de défendre leurs positions nationales que de chercher à transcrire le consensus émergeant au sein de la Plénière. Mais le mercredi 9 février, le Brésil se plaignait encore au sein du Comité de rédaction du fait que certaines dispositions de l'article 6 étaient substantiellement atténuées à l'encontre de la volonté clairement exprimée de la Plénière. Dans les derniers jours de la session, des rencontres informelles prirent place entre certains États ou groupes d'États en vue de favoriser des rapprochements, mais sans résultats très apparents, du moins si l'on en juge par les discussions en plénière et par les textes provenant du Comité de rédaction, toujours parsemés de multiples crochets.

Le recours aux crochets et aux notes, ou la question de l'utilisation
de la procédure comme instrument de négociation

Bien que la question de l'utilisation des crochets et des notes ait été soulevée pour la première fois dans le cadre du Groupe de travail informel sur le titre et l'article 1 de l'avant-projet de convention révisé, comme nous l'avons vu précédemment, c'est surtout dans le cadre des travaux du Comité de rédaction que la question fut discutée et cela souvent avec beaucoup de passion. Elle devait revenir pratiquement chaque jour pendant la majeure partie de la première semaine de négociation (et encore durant les derniers jours de la seconde semaine) et c'est avec une frustration croissante que le Président s'évertua à clarifier celle-ci.

Dans les tout premiers jours, c'est le principe même du recours aux crochets et aux notes qui fut d'abord contesté. C'est ainsi que le 2 février, lors de l'examen par le Comité de rédaction de l'article 1(a), la Suisse intervint pour souligner qu'il existait un mandat clair de la Plénière et qu'il fallait trouver une solution à partie des instructions fournies; l'utilisation de crochets ne devait donc pas être considérée. Cette intervention en entraîna une autre de la part des États-Unis qui déclarèrent qu'à leur avis, le Comité avait pleine autorité pour suggérer l'insertion de crochets. Sur ce, le Président du Comité intervint pour suggérer qu'il serait peut-être préférable d'expliquer les différences de vues au lieu d'utiliser les crochets. Mais les États-Unis revinrent à la charge en affirmant que la pratique constante de l'UNESCO avait été l'utilisation des crochets au lieu des notes en bas de page. Et le débat continua ainsi avec des interventions entre autres du Bénin, qui se prononça en faveur de l'utilisation des crochets et contre les notes en bas de page, de l'Inde qui souligna que la technique des notes en bas de page était plus complexe que celle des crochets, du Président du Comité qui, après s'être prononcé en faveur de la méthode des notes, posa la question de savoir s'il y avait lieu d'utiliser la méthode des crochets, du Brésil, qui expliqua que les crochets devaient être utilisés pour indiquer clairement où sont les différences d'opinion, de la Russie qui se déclara en faveur des notes en bas de page, du Costa Rica, également en faveur des notes en bas de page et totalement opposé à l'utilisation des crochets et du Japon, qui diplomatiquement proposa l'utilisation à la fois des crochets et des notes ne bas de page. L'Équateur ayant poursuivi le débat en affirmant que les notes en bas de page étaient beaucoup plus parlantes que les crochets, le Président profita de l'occasion pour faire part à nouveau de sa préférence pour les notes en bas de page. Mais après avoir entendu le Sénégal reprendre l'idée qu'il n'y avait pas lieu de se priver de l'une ou l'autre méthode, il décida finalement que les crochets et les notes en bas de page pourraient être utilisés selon les circonstances. Dès lors, la porte était grande ouverte à une utilisation extensive de ces deux techniques afin de préserver des points de vue minoritaires face aux choix majoritairement exprimés au sein de l'Assemblée plénière et clairement véhiculés dans les instructions du Président au Comité de rédaction.

Dès le 4 février, de nouveaux débats surgirent au sein du Comité de rédaction à propos de l'utilisation des crochets et des notes. Pendant près de deux heures, les membres du Comité s'interrogèrent sur l'opportunité de conserver le terme "librement" dans la formulation proposée de l'article 1(d) qui présentait ainsi un des objectifs de la Convention: "créer les conditions au sein desquelles les cultures puissent librement évoluer et interagir." Pour éviter d'avoir à recourir à des crochets, le Président décida en dernier ressort de renvoyer la question à la Plénière avec deux options. Immédiatement après, un nouveau débat s'engagea sur l'utilisation de crochets à propos de l'article 1(e) qui se lisait, dans sa version originale largement favorisée par la Plénière et transmise telle quelle au Comité de rédaction, de la façon suivante: "encourager le dialogue entre les cultures et les civilisations afin d'assurer des échanges culturels plus intenses et mieux équilibrés entre les pays du monde." Le débat était à peine engagé que les États-Unis intervinrent pour faire valoir qu'ils s'objectaient au texte original et qu'ils souhaitaient utiliser des crochets, qui constituaient une technique de négociation parfaitement acceptable, pour indiquer leur désaccord avec l'expression "plus intenses et mieux équilibrés." Le Rapporteur intervint alors pour souligner que les instructions explicites de la Plénière étaient de garder l'expression "plus intenses et mieux équilibrés." Les États-Unis revinrent à la charge avec leur demande qui fut refusée par plusieurs pays. Finalement, un compromis permettant d'éviter le recours aux crochets fut trouvé lorsque les membres du Comité acceptèrent que l'expression "plus intenses et mieux équilibrés" se lisent "plus intenses et équilibrés."

Ce dernier débat au sein du Comité de rédaction entraîna, comme on pouvait s'y attendre, une réaction de la part du Président Asmal le lendemain matin, 5 février. Celui-ci manifesta son impatience devant le fait que le Comité de rédaction avait passé plus de deux heures à discuter de termes et de concepts qui n'avaient pas été discutés dans la Plénière. Il demanda que l'utilisation des crochets soit réservée aux termes et expressions ayant une importance réelle dans le débat et suggéra que dans les cas où la signification d'un concept demandait à être clarifiée par la Plénière, cela soit indiqué dans les notes en bas de page. Un peu plus tard, ce même jour, le Président revint encore sur cette question de l'utilisation des crochets pour rappeler que celle-ci était permise si un article présentait une seule recommandation et qu'un mot ou expression de cette recommandation posait une question "vitale" à une délégation. Lors de la seconde semaine de négociations, de nouveaux accrochages sur l'utilisation des crochets survinrent, notamment en ce qui concerne le droit de les utiliser pour une disposition entière. À la toute fin de la rencontre, le Président de l'Assemblée plénière devait lui-même revenir, dans sa revue du travail accompli durant la seconde session, sur le sujet en constatant, au vu des nombreux crochets et notes de bas de pages qui parsemaient le texte, qu'il existait encore de sérieuses différences de points de vue sur la Convention qui demandaient à être comblées.

Ainsi qu'on puisse le constater, le débat sur l'utilisation des crochets et des notes aura accaparé un temps anormalement long durant cette seconde session. Dans un contexte où de sérieuses différences de perspectives sur la Convention, pour reprendre les termes du Président, se manifestaient, cela était pratiquement inévitable: le recours aux crochets et aux notes devenait alors le seul moyen de forcer la prise en considération de points de vue minoritaires. À l'examen, on constate effectivement que cette technique de négociation a été utilisée de façon prépondérante par des États dont le point de vue, sur des questions qu'ils jugeaient importantes, avait reçu un appui clairement minoritaire en Assemblée plénière. Mais avec la multiplication de ce type d'interventions, un nouveau risque se faisait jour: celui que le vœu majoritaire de l'Assemblée plénière soit perdu de vue.

LE RÉSULTAT AU TERME DE LA SECONDE SESSION

Il est relativement facile de se faire une idée de base du travail accompli durant la deuxième session à partir du texte "composite" de l'avant-projet de convention sur la diversité des contenus culturels et des expressions artistiques qui accompagne le Rapport préliminaire envoyé par le Directeur général de l'UNESCO aux Membres le 3 mars 2005.[9] Le texte en question, comme le souligne

---

9 UNESCO, *Avant-projet de convention sur la protection de la diversité descontenus culturels et des expressions artistiques,* 3 mars 2005, Doc. clt/cpd/2005/conf.203/6,

le Rapport préliminaire, reflétait l'état d'avancement des travaux et illustrait les progrès réalisés aussi bien que le travail qui restait à accomplir.[10] Il comportait trois parties élaborées à des degrés divers, soit la Partie I, qui présentait le résultat des travaux du Comité de rédaction (les articles 1 à 11 sauf l'article 8 toujours en discussion), la Partie II qui présentait le résultat des travaux du Groupe de travail informel sur la Section III.2 (les nouveaux articles 12, 13, 14 et 15 qui traitaient de la coopération internationale) et enfin la Partie III qui présentait les commentaires de l'Assemblée plénière sur les dispositions restantes (l'article 8, l'ancien article 15, les anciens article 13 et 19, les articles 20 à 23 et 25 à 34). L'Assemblée plénière s'était déjà penchée sur la quasi-totalité des dispositions de l'avant-projet révisé, à l'exception du préambule et de l'article 24 avec ses deux annexes; toutefois, il lui restait à prendre position sur les questions transversales qui faisaient l'objet de crochets et de notes de bas de page, ainsi que sur un certain nombre de questions pas encore réglées et susceptibles de donner lieu à de sérieux débats. Le Comité de rédaction, pour sa part, était nettement moins avancé et se devait d'accélérer le pas pour ne pas retarder indûment le travail de l'Assemblée. Somme toute, le résultat de cette seconde session, si l'on envisage strictement l'ampleur du travail accompli, demeurait convenable, même si on aurait peut-être pu espérer mieux.

Au travail accompli durant la seconde session, il faut ajouter par ailleurs celui réalisé postérieurement par le Président Asmal à la demande de l'Assemblée plénière, soit la préparation d'un texte "consolidé" composé des projets de dispositions recommandés par le Comité de rédaction, et pour les parties restantes du texte, de ses propres propositions élaborées à la lumière des directives spécifiques de la Plénière en utilisant le cas échéant des options ou des notes en bas de page afin de prendre en compte différentes approches nécessitant un examen ultérieur.[11] Ce texte, rendu public en même temps que le texte "composite," peut être considéré comme faisant partie du travail accompli par la seconde session. Dans les faits, non seulement il complète les parties restantes du texte mais il revient aussi, dans un souci de cohérence et de clarté,

---

aux pp.13-48, disponible en ligne à: <http://unesdoc.unesco.org/images/0013/001387/138765f.pdf> (dernière visite: le 5 septembre 2006).

[10] *Ibid.*, à la p. 15, par. 47.

[11] Voir UNESCO, Doc. 171 EX/INF.18 (21 avril 2005), appendice 2, à la p. 2.

sur un certain nombre de formulations recommandées par le Comité de rédaction. Selon le Directeur général, ces deux textes devaient "être lus ensemble et de manière complémentaire."[12]

Au terme de cette seconde session, il demeurait cependant difficile de se faire une idée claire du type de convention en voie d'élaboration. Trop de dispositions avaient un contenu qui n'était pas encore suffisamment fixé pour qu'il soit possible de porter un jugement définitif à cet égard. C'était le cas en particulier des dispositions qui incorporaient des termes et expressions entre crochets tels que "protection," "biens et services culturels" ou encore "expressions culturelles" qui étaient toujours en discussion.[13] Même si le texte consolidé établi par le Président Asmal éliminait l'ensemble des crochets et notes de bas de page, cela ne signifiait pas, comme le soulignait le Président lui-même, que les mots concernés avaient finalement été acceptés. C'était le cas aussi de dispositions comme celles relatives aux relations avec les autres instruments, qui faisaient toujours partie des questions en suspens, tout comme c'était le cas des dispositions qui n'avaient reçu qu'une approbation de principe sans que le détail de celles-ci ne soit abordé, comme celles relatives aux organes et mécanismes de suivi, ou qui n'avaient toujours pas été considérées par l'Assemblée plénière, comme celles relatives au règlement des différends. Bien que des solutions aient été apportées dans ces derniers cas par le texte consolidé du Président Asmal, celles-ci n'avaient pas encore été considérées par l'Assemblée plénière. Dans ces conditions, toute prédiction relativement au type de convention susceptible d'émerger des négociations au terme du processus demeurait difficile.

La troisième session: Le dénouement

La troisième session, comme devait le rappeler le Président Asmal dans son allocution d'ouverture, constituait la phase la plus critique du processus de négociation devant conduire à l'adoption

---

12 Voir UNESCO, Doc. EX/INF.18 (21 avril 2005), appendices 1 et 2 du *Rapport du Directeur général sur l'état d'avancement du projet de convention sur la protection de la diversité des contenus culturels et des expressions artistiques* (annexe 3 du document 171 ex/44) à la p. 1, disponible en ligne à: <http://unesdoc.unesco.org/images/0013/001392/139257f.pdf> (dernière visite: le 6 septembre 2006).

13 On peut se faire une idée du problème en considérant que dans les seuls articles 1 à 11 (ceux examinés par le Comité de rédaction), les termes "expressions culturelles" reviennent à plus d'une trentaine de reprises, "protection" à dix-huit reprises et "biens et services culturels" à huit reprises.

du projet de convention que l'on désirait soumettre pour adoption lors de la trente-troisième Conférence générale de l'UNESCO. Bien que productive, en effet, la session précédente n'avait pas permis de compléter l'examen de l'ensemble du texte et sur plusieurs points importants, il n'y avait toujours pas de convergence. Manifestement, le résultat souhaité ne pouvait être atteint si la négociation procédait de la même façon que lors de la seconde session; une méthode de travail plus efficace devait être adoptée. Il apparaissait important en particulier de sortir le débat du Comité de rédaction pour le ramener au niveau de l'Assemblée plénière et de faciliter la prise de décision en isolant graduellement les questions les plus controversées. Mais pour introduire de tels changements, le Président Asmal devait bénéficier d'un important support au sein de l'Assemblée plénière.

Avant le début de la troisième session, l'ampleur de ce support n'était pas nécessairement évidente. Considérant la réaction très critique des États-Unis lors de la sortie du nouveau texte consolidé établi par le Président Asmal, bon nombre d'observateurs s'attendaient à ce que la question du texte à utiliser comme base de discussion pour la troisième session soit soulevée et âprement débattue dès le départ. Dans les jours qui précédèrent l'ouverture de la session, plusieurs délégations se réunirent selon leur appartenance géographique ou linguistique pour discuter de leur position sur le sujet. Dans son discours d'ouverture, le Directeur général, M. Matsuura, fit prudemment référence au "rapport composite" qu'il décrivit comme "un texte synthèse de positions consensuelles et des discussions à mener" et au "texte consolidé," qu'il décrivit comme "un texte sans crochet ni option fondé sur des propositions de rapprochement des points de vues." Or, si la question du texte de référence fut bien soulevée d'entrée de jeu par les États membres, ce fut pour louanger le texte du Président Asmal et suggérer de façon quasi-unanime que ce dernier serve de base pour la poursuite de la discussion. Le Costa Rica au nom du Groupe des 77, le Canada au nom du Groupe des ambassadeurs francophones, le Luxembourg au nom de l'Union européenne, le Mexique au nom de l'Amérique latine et des Caraïbes, la Chine, la Suisse, la Norvège, le Vietnam, le Brésil, l'Inde, l'Andorre, l'Arabie saoudite, la Nouvelle-Zélande, la Russie et le Bénin saluèrent à tour de rôle le texte du Président, le qualifiant de cohérent et d'équilibré et souhaitant en faire leur texte de discussion. Certains États, toutefois, tout en se ralliant au texte du Président, soulignèrent que l'autre texte devait rester à la portée de la main pour être consulté. Ce fut le cas, entre autres, du Maroc, de l'Australie et du Japon, ce dernier se montrant plus réservé à l'égard du texte consolidé. Les États-Unis, enfin, dirent regretter que les recommandations du Comité de rédaction n'aient pas été prises en comptes et que plusieurs des concepts entre crochets aient été révisés dans le texte consolidé du Président Asmal. En dernier ressort, le texte consolidé fut donc retenu comme base de discussion, sans écarter pour autant la possibilité d'utiliser le texte composite comme référence au besoin. Dans les faits, on ne devait guère plus faire référence à ce dernier dans la suite de la négociation. L'autorité et le prestige du Président Asmal ressortirent nettement renforcés de ce débat, ce qui ouvrit la porte à une initiative déterminante en ce qui concerne la méthode de travail.

Le président Asmal, dans son allocution d'ouverture, se montra plus directif qu'il l'avait été lors de la seconde session sur ce point. Le débat, annonça-t-il, se ferait par grands thèmes: préambule, objectifs et principes, champ d'application et définitions, droits et obligations y compris la coopération internationale, relations avec les autres instruments, organes de la Convention, clauses finales y compris les annexes sur le règlement des différends. Les délégations qui souhaitaient proposer des amendements au texte consolidé devraient le faire par écrit et suffisamment à l'avance pour que le Bureau de direction puisse les prendre en considération. Ce dernier les examinerait et conviendrait des suites à leur donner. Les propositions mineures, de style et sans impact sur le fond seraient traitées par le Bureau. Celles sur le fond seraient soumises à la Plénière; si personne ne les soutenait, elles seraient rejetées sans appel. Les décisions pourraient être soumises au vote mais dans la mesure du possible elles devraient être prises par voie de consensus. Le Président devait également préciser, en ouvrant le débat sur le premier thème, que les questions transversales seraient abordées au moment opportun, c'est-à-dire pour la majorité d'entre elles, lors de l'examen des définitions.

Mais paradoxalement, le changement le plus important, l'élimination du Comité de rédaction, passa pratiquement inaperçu tant celui-ci parut aller de soi. Dans sa présentation de la méthode de travail, le Président lui-même ne fit aucune référence au rôle du Comité de rédaction, ce qui était plutôt surprenant considérant le rôle de premier plan que celui-ci avait joué lors de la seconde session. Dès la reprise des travaux, il devint vite évident que le Comité de rédaction était écarté au profit de l'Assemblée plénière qui était appelée ainsi à exercer un contrôle plus direct sur la rédaction.

Même les États-Unis, qui avaient utilisé avec profit le Comité de rédaction pour défendre leurs vues lors de la seconde session, ne réagirent pas à ce changement. Il faut dire que les réticences du Comité de rédaction à suivre les directives de l'Assemblée plénière, sa difficulté à trancher dans les débats entre la majorité et la minorité et son efficacité très relative ne militaient pas pour son maintien.

Ces changements contribuèrent à accélérer l'examen des différentes dispositions du texte consolidé du Président Asmal. La majeure partie de ces dispositions fut approuvée assez rapidement, parfois avec modifications, parfois sans modification. La stratégie d'isoler les questions les plus contentieuses pour les discuter au moment approprié portât fruit. De sa propre initiative ou à la suggestion des Parties, le Président n'hésita pas à constituer des groupes de travail afin de faciliter un rapprochement entre les Parties sur ces questions, ce qui contribua à rassurer les États qui défendaient des positions minoritaires sur celles-ci. Cinq groupes furent ainsi constitués pour traiter des questions suivantes: la définition des "activités, biens et services culturels" ainsi que celle des "expressions culturelles" et d'"industries culturelles"; l'alinéa 8 du préambule (les savoirs traditionnels); l'article 20 (relations avec les autres instruments internationaux); l'article 25 (règlement des différends); et enfin l'article 30 (régimes constitutionnels fédéraux). À deux occasions, toutefois, le Président refusa d'accéder à des demandes de constitution d'un groupe de travail. Ce fut le cas lorsque les États-Unis, insatisfait de l'évolution du débat sur l'article 5(1), soulevèrent un point de procédure pour demander la constitution d'un groupe de travail comprenant des avocats en raison de la complexité des problèmes soulevés. Cette demande fut écartée par le Président qui souligna que ces questions devaient être traités par les représentants des États désignés et non par des avocats. Ce fut le cas également lorsque le Japon, en réaction à une demande à l'effet que le débat sur l'article 5(1) soit reporté après la discussion sur l'article 20 étant donné les liens entre ces deux questions, demanda la constitution d'un groupe de travail indépendant sur l'article 5(1); cette demande fut implicitement rejetée lorsque le Président se prononça en faveur du report.

Le rôle assigné aux groupes de travail était clair: ils devaient chercher à réaliser un consensus sur les questions qui leur étaient soumises. À défaut d'y arriver dans les délais impartis, ils étaient dessaisis de leur mandat et les questions revenaient devant l'Assemblée plénière pour décision. C'est ainsi que le tout premier Groupe de travail créé, celui sur les définitions des termes "activités, biens et services culturels," "expressions culturelles" et "industries culturel-les," n'ayant pu parvenir à un accord lorsque l'Assemblée plénière aborda l'article 4 sur les définitions, se trouva dessaisi de son man-dat au profit de cette dernière qui procéda aussitôt à l'examen des amendements soumis par écrits sur cet article.[14] Deux autres groupes spéciaux, soit ceux sur l'alinéa 7 bis du préambule (devenu l'alinéa 8 du préambule dans la version finale) et sur l'article 30 (régimes constitutionnels fédéraux) furent en mesure de propo-ser à l'Assemblée plénière des solutions de compromis qui furent effectivement retenues par cette dernière. Le groupe sur l'article 25 proposa lui aussi une solution de compromis à l'Assemblée plénière sur la question du règlement des différends mais cette solution devait subséquemment être revue à le demande d'un nom-bre substantiel d'États et ne fut finalement acceptée, telle que mo-difiée, qu'après qu'on l'eut accompagnée d'une clause autorisant une partie signataire à se désengager, au moment de la ratification, du mécanisme de règlement des différends envisagé (conciliation à la demande d'une seule partie).

Toute autre fut l'expérience du Groupe de travail chargé de trou-ver une solution de compromis sur l'article 20 (relations avec les autres instruments internationaux). La tâche n'était pas facile car l'article 20, ainsi qu'il était devenu évident depuis le tout début de la négociation, était au cœur du conflit qui opposait la majorité à la minorité sur le projet de convention. Ce Groupe de travail, dont la création avait été annoncée dès la troisième journée de la ren-contre (vendredi, 27 mai) n'avait toujours pas réussi à produire un texte susceptible de rapprocher les Parties le lundi soir 30 mai. Lors de l'ouverture de l'Assemblée plénière, le 31 mai, le Prési-dent Asmal convoqua le groupe pour une session de travail sous sa direction. Le lendemain, 1er juin, le Président était en mesure d'annoncer un accord au sein du Groupe de travail sur l'article 20 et invita le Canada et la Finlande, à titre de co-présidents du groupe, à présenter le résultat de celui-ci. Le nouveau texte fut décrit comme un tout, un "paquet" qu'il était difficile de modifier sans mettre en péril le très large consensus réalisé. Un long débat s'ensuivi au cours duquel pas moins de cinquante-six délégations intervinrent. Au terme de cet échange, une large majorité des dé-légations se prononcèrent en faveur du texte proposé. Certaines

---

[14] Ceci n'empêcha pas la prise en compte par la Conférence générale de certaines propositions issues du Groupe de travail alors même qu'elles n'avaient pas été soumises par écrit comme amendements.

délégations dirent avoir obtenu l'accord de leur capitale seulement après de longues discussions. D'autres se dirent d'accord avec le texte proposé mais en ajoutant qu'elles souhaitaient y apporter des amendements mineurs. La délégation américaine, toutefois, se déclara en désaccord avec le texte proposé et demanda que les discussions se poursuivent jusqu'à ce qu'un texte satisfaisant soit trouvé, à défaut de quoi les États-Unis se présenteraient à la Conférence générale avec un autre texte pour l'article 20. Le Président Asmal décida alors de réunir à nouveau le Groupe de travail sous sa direction pendant le déjeuner.

Durant cette rencontre, les propositions d'amendement qui avaient été soumises par les États-Unis, le Sénégal, l'Afrique du Sud, l'Andorre et le Mexique furent discutées. Certaines délégations soulignèrent d'entrée de jeu que toute modification au texte proposé devait être écartée à défaut de quoi la notion d'un texte de compromis constituant un tout risquait d'être remise en cause. D'autres délégations suggérèrent que l'on distingue entre les amendements techniques, qui ne changeaient pas le sens du texte, et les amendements de substance. Le Président intervint alors pour annoncer qu'il procéderait sur la base de la seconde option. Écartant temporairement l'amendement américain, considéré comme un amendement de fond, il procéda d'abord à l'examen de l'amendement de l'Andorre qui fut adopté après une courte discussion mais donna lieu par la suite à des remarques du Japon et des États-Unis à l'effet que l'amendement en question pouvait changer le sens du paragraphe 1(b) de l'article 20. Les autres amendements furent rejetés à l'exception de celui de l'Afrique du Sud qui accepta de le retirer. Revenant finalement à l'amendement des États-Unis, le Président, après avoir écouté les explications de ces derniers et les commentaires d'un certain nombre d'États, décréta que celui-ci introduisait un important déséquilibre dans le texte proposé par le Groupe de travail et décida que le temps était venu de retourner en Assemblée plénière afin de trancher la question.

À l'ouverture de l'Assemblée plénière, le lendemain, 2 juin, le Président Asmal demanda au Rapporteur de faire lecture de la nouvelle version de l'article 20 incluant l'amendement de l'Andorre. Puis immédiatement après, il demanda si l'Assemblée plénière voulait adopter le texte en question. Aucune opposition ne se manifestant, le Président déclara le texte adopté, ce qui déclencha immédiatement les applaudissements de la salle. Mais les États-Unis soulevèrent immédiatement un point d'ordre pour souligner que le texte n'était pas final car l'amendement qu'ils avaient proposé

n'avait toujours pas été discuté alors qu'il avait reçu un certain support et, qu'en conséquence, ils voulaient voir le texte en question
discuté lors de la Conférence générale. Cela impliquait la soumis-
sion à la Conférence générale d'un texte de la Convention proposant deux versions distinctes de l'article 20. Un certain nombre
d'États intervinrent par la suite pour dire qu'ils avaient certains
problèmes avec l'article 20 et annoncer qu'ils réservaient donc leur
position sur cet article. Revenant alors sur la demande des États-
Unis, le Brésil déclara qu'il était totalement opposé à l'idée d'avoir
deux options sur l'article 20: selon ce dernier, tout le monde avait
fait des compromis pour arriver au texte sur la table et maintenant
une délégation voulait son propre texte; ceci n'était pas juste. À ce
stade du débat, plusieurs délégations intervinrent pour demander
que l'on passe au vote. Malgré l'objection des États-Unis qui réité-
rèrent qu'un vote n'était pas approprié car il n'y avait pas de consensus sur l'article 20, le Président demanda qui était en faveur
d'avoir deux options. Seuls l'Argentine, les États-Unis, l'Australie
et l'Israël acquiescèrent, toutes les autres délégations se pronon-
çant contre la proposition américaine. Il fut donc décidé qu'une
seule version de l'article 20 irait à la Conférence générale, soit
celle du Groupe de travail telle que modifiée par l'amendement
d'Andorre. Le débat prit fin avec la demande des États-Unis que
leur objection formelle à la décision du Président de passer au vote
ainsi qu'au texte adopté soit enregistrée. Le Président répondit
que toutes les objections formelles seraient intégrées au rapport
du Directeur général à la Conférence générale. Le résultat du débat, qualifié de moment historique par plusieurs délégations dans
leur déclaration de clôture, fut dénoncé avec vigueur par les États-
Unis, ces derniers allant jusqu'à affirmer, dans une déclaration rendue publique par leur ambassade à Paris, que le texte de convention
proposé était profondément défectueux parce qu'il concernait le
commerce plutôt que la culture, qu'il était en conséquence hors
de la compétence de l'UNESCO et que son adoption ne pourrait
que compromettre la réputation de l'UNESCO à titre d'organisation internationale responsable.

Cette description sommaire du déroulement de la négociation
lors de la troisième session appelle quelques observations. D'abord,
le fait déterminant qui a permis de dénouer l'impasse dans laquelle
s'était engagée la négociation au terme de la seconde session a été
la décision du Président, appuyé en cela par l'Assemblée plénière,
de jouer un rôle plus direct dans le déroulement de la négociation.
Confrontés à une volonté très ferme des représentants américains

qui exigeaient que tout consensus autour du projet de convention se fasse aux conditions fixées par les États-Unis, le Président et l'Assemblée plénière ont refusé d'entériner une interprétation du consensus qui aurait abouti, dans les faits, à donner un droit de veto à une ou à quelques Membres pour adopter plutôt, comme ligne de conduite, la recherche de l'unanimité dans la mesure du possible et, à défaut, l'appui d'une large pluralité des États membres tel que déterminé par le vote. Deuxièmement, la mise au rancart du Comité de rédaction et le recours aux groupes de travail pour donner une dernière chance à la négociation d'aboutir en cas d'impasses ont permis de cerner de plus en plus la nature de l'opposition entre la majorité et la minorité, ramenant celle-ci en dernier ressort à la question du lien entre la Convention et les autres accords internationaux, plus particulièrement les accords de l'OMC. Enfin, le compromis réalisé sur cette dernière question à l'article 20 peut être considéré comme l'expression du consensus général de l'Assemblée plénière sur la Convention elle-même, pratiquement tous les États ayant appuyé celui-ci.

L'EXAMEN DU PROJET DE CONVENTION PAR LA CONFÉRENCE GÉNÉRALE

Le jugement très critique exprimé par les États-Unis à l'encontre du projet de convention entériné lors de la troisième session donnait clairement à entendre que ces derniers n'avaient pas dit leur dernier mot sur le sujet. De fait, entre la date de clôture de la troisième session et la date d'ouverture de la Conférence générale de l'UNESCO, le 3 octobre 2005, les États-Unis intervinrent à plusieurs reprises et dans différents contextes dans le but de justifier leur opposition au projet de convention issu de la rencontre des experts gouvernementaux et de faire obstacle à l'adoption de ce dernier par la trente-troisième Conférence générale. Mais les pays désireux de voir le projet de convention en question adopté par la Conférence générale ne sont pas demeurés en reste et ont euxmêmes procédé à des consultations en vue d'empêcher la réouverture de la négociation qui s'était terminée le 3 juin 2005 et d'assurer l'adoption de la Convention dès octobre 2005.[15] Deux évènements

---

15 De telles rencontres informelles de consultations s'organisèrent assez tôt, comme par exemple à l'occasion de la cinquante-cinquième session du Conseil permanent de la Francophonie, qui eut lieu le 30 juin 2005. Elles se sont multipliées par la suite jusqu'à l'ouverture de la Conférence générale en octobre 2005.

en particulier ont marqué la bataille d'arrière-garde menée par les États-Unis durant cette période. Le premier est intervenu dans le cadre de l'OMC, le second, dans le cadre de l'UNESCO.

Le 25 août 2005, une réunion informelle était organisée à la demande d'un certain nombre de Membres de l'OMC qui souhaitaient que le Directeur général soumette des commentaires à l'UNESCO sur leurs préoccupations concernant les effets de la Convention sur les négociations de l'OMC. Une soixantaine de pays participèrent à cette rencontre qui donna lieu à des échanges animés. Deux points de vue opposés s'exprimèrent, soit celui des promoteurs d'une telle rencontre, au premier chef les États-Unis, qui firent part de leurs critiques ou réserves à l'égard de la Convention, et celle d'une majorité des participants satisfaits de la Convention qui s'opposèrent à ce que l'OMC communique un point de vue non sollicité sur la Convention à l'UNESCO. En dernier ressort, le Directeur général de l'OMC se rangea à cette position.

Le second évènement eut lieu lors de la 172ème session du Conseil exécutif de l'UNESCO, en septembre 2005, lorsque fut débattu le rapport du Directeur général sur l'avant-projet de convention. Le 23 septembre, les membres de la Commission du programme et des relations extérieures du Conseil furent saisis d'un projet d'amendement du Canada, signé par cinquante pays, visant l'ajout d'un nouveau paragraphe à la recommandation faite par le Directeur général au Conseil exécutif concernant l'avant-projet de convention, recommandation qui se lisait originalement ainsi:

Le Conseil exécutif,

1. Ayant à l'esprit la résolution 32/34,
2. Rappelant les décisions 169/3.7.2 et 171 EX/19,
3. Ayant examiné le document 172 EX/20,
4. Soulignant que les experts gouvernementaux ont rempli leur mandat, qui était "d'avancer l'élaboration de l'avant-projet de convention afin de faire rapport à la Conférence générale à sa 33e session" conformément à la décision 169 EX/3.7.2.,
5. Prend note du texte de l'avant-projet, adopté par la troisième session de la Réunion intergouvernementale d'experts, tenue au Siège du 25 mai au 3 juin 2005, qui sera examiné par la Conférence générale, à sa 33ème session, en application de la résolution 32 C/34

Le nouveau paragraphe proposé par le Canada se lisait pour sa part de la façon suivante:

6. Recommande que la Conférence générale, à sa 33ème session, considère ledit avant-projet comme un projet de convention et l'adopte en
tant que convention de l'UNESCO.

En proposant ainsi que ce qui avait été décrit jusqu'alors comme
un avant-projet de convention soit dorénavant considéré par la
Conférence générale comme un projet de convention et en demandant que celui-ci soit adopté comme convention de l'UNESCO,
l'amendement canadien coupait court en pratique à toute possibilité que la Conférence générale renvoie la question à sa prochaine
session, en 2007, en espérant qu'un accord se réalise entre temps
sur le texte d'un projet de convention. Comme il fallait s'y attendre, les États-Unis se sont vigoureusement opposés à cet amendement, insistant sur le fait que le texte n'était pas prêt pour adoption
et que l'UNESCO cherchait à procéder trop rapidement. Ils ont
demandé qu'un vote formel soit pris sur celui-ci. Finalement, c'est
par cinquante-trois voix en faveur, une voix contre (celle des États-
Unis) et une abstention (celle de l'Australie), que le projet d'amendement canadien fut adopté par la Commission du programme et
des relations extérieures.

Six jours plus tard, le 29 septembre, le rapport de cette dernière
était présenté aux membres du Conseil exécutif pour adoption. À
cette occasion, les États-Unis demandèrent, en s'appuyant sur l'article 47 du règlement intérieur, que la recommandation concernant l'avant-projet de convention (et notamment son paragraphe
6) soit adoptée séparément des autres points du rapport. Ce faisant, il devenait plus facile pour eux de demander par la suite une
discussion de fond sur le sixième paragraphe. Après un court débat, le Président du Conseil exécutif demanda le vote sur la motion
des États-Unis de surseoir à la recommandation. Par cinquante-
cinq voix contre et une en faveur (les États-Unis), la motion fut
rejetée. Mais les États-Unis revinrent immédiatement à la charge
en proposant un amendement au sixième paragraphe qui se lisait
de la façon suivante: "Recommande à la Conférence générale, à sa
33ème session, d'examiner le texte de cet avant-projet en tant que
projet de convention et d'envisager de l'adopter comme convention de l'UNESCO." Un nouveau débat s'ensuivit au cours duquel
pratiquement tous les membres qui intervinrent se prononcèrent
contre la démarche des États-Unis, manifestement agacés par l'in-
sistance de ces derniers. Au bout du compte, la proposition fut reti-
rée et l'on procéda au vote sur la recommandation telle qu'adoptée

par le Comité: par cinquante-trois voix pour, une contre et une abstention, celle-ci fut entérinée et transmise en l'état à la Conférence générale.

La Conférence générale s'ouvrit le 3 octobre par les discours du Président du Conseil exécutif et du Directeur général. Suivirent après l'examen d'un certain nombre de points préalables tels que le Rapport du Comité de vérification des pouvoirs à la Conférence générale, l'adoption de l'ordre du jour, l'élection du président et des vice-présidents de la Conférence générale, ainsi que des présidents, vice-présidents et rapporteurs des commissions et comités. Le lendemain, 4 octobre, débuta le débat de politique générale où tous les sujets pouvaient être abordés par les Membres. Celui-ci fut marqué par une attaque en règle des États-Unis contre le fait que l'Union européenne était habilitée à parler durant la Conférence au nom des États membres. Aux yeux des États-Unis, il s'agissait là d'un dangereux précédent qu'il fallait à tout prix éviter. Mais pour plusieurs autres Membres, la demande américaine visait surtout à diviser l'Union européenne sur la question du projet de convention sur la protection et la promotion de la diversité des expressions culturelles. La demande donna lieu à un vif débat au terme duquel un vote fut pris pour ou contre l'intervention de la Commission européenne dans les débats de la Conférence générale. Par 158 voix en faveur, une contre et une abstention, le droit d'intervention de la Commission fut confirmé.

Le même jour, la Secrétaire d'État des États-Unis, Condoleeza Rice, faisait parvenir aux ministres des Affaires étrangères des pays membres de l'UNESCO une lettre dans laquelle elle exprimait sa profonde inquiétude concernant le projet de convention sur la protection et la promotion de la diversité des expressions culturelles. Elle présentait cette dernière comme ambiguë à plusieurs égards et susceptible d'être utilisée à des fins protectionnistes et demandait d'appuyer les États-Unis dans leur demande de retarder l'adoption du projet de convention pour permettre la poursuite des négociations jusqu'à ce que ces lacunes aient été corrigées. Une note sur les modifications que les États-Unis jugeaient essentielles fut mise en circulation le même jour par la délégation américaine à l'UNESCO; entre autres articles visés par ces modifications, on retrouvait les articles 5, 6, 7, 8, 18, 19, 20, 21, 23 et 24 de la Convention. Ces deux initiatives ne semblent pas avoir donné lieu à des résultats très concrets, si ce n'est qu'un certain nombre de journaux firent état dans leurs pages de la lettre de la Secrétaire d'État Condoleeza Rice, et que l'Organisation internationale de la Francophonie, dans une note rendue publique le lendemain, répondit point par point aux arguments de la note américaine.

Le 10 octobre, le Président de la Commission IV, à la demande des États-Unis, organisa une "rencontre informelle" afin de permettre aux Membres de discuter avec les représentants américains de la Convention. Ces derniers, déplorant le fait que les États-Unis n'aient pas eu véritablement la chance de se faire entendre, exposèrent à nouveau les arguments américains à l'encontre du projet de convention. Une vingtaine de pays participèrent à cette rencontre. La plupart réagirent en faisant valoir que le texte de la Convention tenait déjà largement compte des inquiétudes américaines. Une seconde réunion, organisée le lendemain par les États-Unis dans le même but, n'attira que six États et prit fin rapidement. Aux yeux de la plupart des observateurs, toutefois, il était clair que les États-Unis ne baisseraient pas les bras et chercheraient à profiter du débat au sein de la Commission IV pour bloquer le processus d'adoption.

Dans les jours qui précédèrent l'examen du projet de convention par la Commission IV, une information circula à l'effet que les États-Unis présenteraient plusieurs amendements à la Convention. De fait, les travaux de la Commission IV sur le projet de Convention débutèrent avec l'annonce, par le Président, que les États-Unis avaient soumis pas moins de vingt-huit amendements, lesquels ne seraient abordés toutefois qu'après avoir donné la chance aux délégations qui le souhaitaient d'intervenir sur le projet de convention. À la suggestion du Président, les délégations représentées par leurs ministres prirent la parole en premier (une quinzaine de ministres intervinrent), puis les autres délégations qui avaient demandé à intervenir suivirent (quelque soixante-dix délégations). Le Royaume-Uni, parlant au nom des vingt-cinq États membres de l'Union européenne ainsi qu'au nom de la Bulgarie, de la Croatie, de la Roumanie et de la Turquie, se dit d'avis que la Convention était équilibrée et qu'elle constituait un cadre valable pour la protection et la promotion de la diversité des expressions culturelles. Le Costa Rica, au nom du Groupe des 77, et le Panama, au nom du GRULAC (groupe électoral comprenant les pays de l'Amérique latine ainsi que des Caraïbes), intervinrent également en faveur de la Convention. L'Inde fit savoir qu'elle considérait la Convention comme un jalon de l'histoire de l'UNESCO, qu'elle l'appuyait sans réserves et qu'elle espérait son adoption. Le Japon, pour sa part, se déclara ravi qu'on soit parvenu à un projet de convention et dit souhaiter l'adoption de celui-ci par la Conférence générale; il ajouta qu'il déposerait un projet de résolution pour le bénéfice de tous une fois la convention adoptée. Les États-Unis enfin reprirent leurs arguments à l'effet que la Convention était erronée et incompatible avec les obligations de l'UNESCO. Ils insistèrent sur le fait que la rapidité de la négociation de la Convention avait été une barrière au consensus et firent valoir que non seulement la qualité du texte en souffrait mais que les conséquences de l'adoption d'un texte aussi erroné seraient graves.

Après cette première phase, où la parole était donnée aux diverses délégations, la Commission entama l'examen des amendements proposés par les États-Unis. Certains de ces amendements étaient relativement inoffensifs et d'autres auraient probablement pu être accepté après négociation mais la majorité reflétait les exigences incontournables des États-Unis. Pour la majorité des Membres, il était clair que si l'on commençait à discuter de chacun de ces amendements, comme le souhaitaient les États-Unis, on rouvrait la négociation et on empêchait à toute fin pratique l'adoption du projet de convention par la Conférence générale. Dès le départ, l'examen des amendements donna lieu à un imbroglio concernant la façon de procéder. En réponse à une demande d'éclaircissement à cet égard, le conseiller juridique de l'UNESCO indiqua qu'il y avait deux manières de procéder pour l'examen des amendements: soit le Président prenait le "pouls" de l'Assemblée sur les amendements, soit on procédait par vote en bonne et due forme sur chacun d'entre eux. Mais il était nécessaire de procéder au vote si une délégation en faisait la demande formelle. Pour les premiers amendements, le Président demanda simplement qui était en faveur sans demander qui était contre ou qui s'abstenait. Mais les États-Unis s'objectèrent à cette façon de procéder et demandèrent que l'on reprenne le vote en procédant dans les formes, c'est-à-dire en comptant les oui, les non ainsi que les abstentions. Comme l'UNESCO n'était pas équipée pour procéder au décompte des voix de façon électronique, on procéda à main levée, ce qui exigea près d'une heure trente. Pour chacun des vingt-huit amendements, le résultat fut à peu de choses près le même: la très vaste majorité des voix contre, deux ou trois en faveur et quatre ou cinq abstentions. Au terme de cet exercice, il ne restait plus qu'à voter sur le projet de convention. Le résultat final fut 151 pour, deux contre (les États-Unis et l'Israël) et deux abstentions (l'Australie et le Kiribati).

La Commission procéda ensuite à l'examen du projet de résolution soumis par le Japon et appuyé par l'Afghanistan relatif au projet de convention.[16] Le texte de la résolution en question se lisait comme suit:

La Conférence générale,
1. Exprimant sa satisfaction suite à l'adoption de la Convention sur la protection et la promotion de la diversité des expressions culturelles,
2. Consciente du fait que cette Convention a trait au domaine de la culture, l'UNESCO, étant la seule agence responsable de la culture au sein du système des Nations Unies, s'attend à son entrée en vigueur et souhaite qu'elle soit mise en œuvre d'une façon efficace et judicieuse, s'inscrivant avec cohérence dans le cadre du dispositif des instruments internationaux,
3. Invite le Président du Comité intergouvernemental de la Convention à mettre à disposition de tous les États membres les rapports établis en application de l'article 23.6 de la Convention avec tous les États membres de l'UNESCO ;
4. Exprime sa confiance quant au fait que la Convention soit mise en œuvre de manière cohérente avec les principes et les objectifs de l'Acte constitutif de l'UNESCO.

Après examen (le débat, plutôt court, fut marqué par une proposition d'amendement des États-Unis qui fut rejetée à la quasi-unanimité), la Commission, par la voie d'un vote à main levée, recommanda celle-ci à la Conférence générale pour adoption.

D'un point de vue juridique, la question se pose de savoir si cette résolution a un impact quelconque sur la Convention. En droit international, il est généralement admis que les résolutions n'ont pas de force obligatoire mais qu'elles peuvent parfois avoir une valeur normative lorsqu'il peut être démontré que telle était la volonté des parties qui l'ont adoptée.[17] Si la discussion et l'adoption de la résolution japonaise ont eu lieu dans le cadre du débat sur le même point 8.3 de l'ordre du jour de la Commission IV (Avant-projet de convention sur la protection de la diversité des contenus culturels et des expressions artistiques et Rapport du Directeur

---

16 UNESCO, Conférence générale, Commission IV, *Projet de résolution du Japon*, Doc.33 C/COM.IV/DR.3 Rev. (17 octobre 2005), disponible en ligne à: <http://unesdoc.unesco.org/images/0014/001414/141427f.pdf> (dernière visite: le 6 septembre 2006).

17 Cour internationale de justice, Avis du 8 juillet sur la *Licéité de la menace ou de l'emploi d'armes nucléaires*, à la p.70.

général à ce sujet), il n'en demeure pas moins que la résolution en tant que telle ne fait pas partie de la Convention et que l'on se trouve en présence de deux textes juridiquement distincts dont le caractère contraignant diffère. Il ne fait pas de doute à cet égard qu'en cas de conflit entre le texte de la Convention et le texte de la résolution, la Convention l'emporterait.[18] Mais en cas de doute sur l'interprétation à donner à la Convention, la résolution du Japon pourrait-elle influencer cette interprétation ? Si la réponse à cette question n'est pas claire d'un point de vue juridique, force est d'admettre que d'un point de vue politique, la pression serait forte pour qu'il en soit ainsi.

Le rapport transmis par la Commission IV proposait à la Conférence générale d'adopter l'avant-projet de convention sur la protection de la diversité des contenus culturels et des expressions artistiques en tant que Convention de l'UNESCO sur la protection et la promotion de la diversité des expressions culturelles tel que contenu à l'Annexe V du document 33 C/23 et proposait également à la Conférence générale d'adopter le projet de résolution présenté par le Japon. Cette dernière étape devait être franchie le 20 octobre. La Convention était dès lors ouverte à la ratification des États.

CONCLUSION

La négociation de la *Convention sur la protection et la promotion de la diversité des expressions culturelles* aura suscité un intérêt et une tension facilement palpables tant parmi les Membres de l'UNESCO qu'au sein du Secrétariat de l'Organisation elle-même, et ce tout au long des trois sessions de négociations ainsi qu'à l'occasion de l'examen du projet de convention par la Commission IV de la Conférence générale. Un nombre record de Membres et d'observateurs non-gouvernementaux ont été impliqués et c'est à plusieurs reprises dans des salles combles que les débats se sont poursuivis. Lors de l'examen du projet de convention par la Commission IV, en octobre 2005, il fallut même suspendre temporairement les débats pour permettre l'accès à une salle plus vaste. Manifestement, cette négociation qui abordait de front la problématique de l'interface commerce/culture touchait à une question très sensible.

---

[18] Une telle contradiction pourrait être invoquée par exemple dans le cas du paragraphe 3 de la résolution qui vient modifier la portée de l'article 23.6 de la Convention.

Deux visions distinctes de l'interface commerce/culture s'affrontaient autour de cette question, reflets elles-mêmes de la double nature des produits culturels, à la fois produits échangés dans le commerce et langage de communication sociale. Ces deux visions, avec leur logique propre, sont également légitimes. L'UNESCO est tout aussi en droit, d'un point de vue culturel, de se préoccuper des répercussions de la mondialisation de l'économie et de la libéralisation des échanges sur la préservation et le développement des expressions culturelles que l'OMC est en droit, d'un point de vue commercial, de se préoccuper des répercussions des mesures mises de l'avant dans une convention sur la préservation et la promotion de la diversité des expressions culturelles. À moins donc que les États membres de l'UNESCO acceptent que les préoccupations culturelles soient moins importantes que les préoccupations commerciales, la solution à ce problème de gouvernance au plan international ne pourra consister dans l'affirmation pure et simple de la prépondérance de la perspective commerciale sur la perspective culturelle. Il faut donc trouver une solution qui soit respectueuse à la fois de l'une et de l'autre perspective.

Malheureusement, tout au long de la négociation, les États-Unis ont défendu le point de vue que les préoccupations culturelles ne devaient en aucun cas l'emporter sur les préoccupations commerciales et ont adopté à cet égard une position que l'on peut qualifier à juste titre d'intransigeante. Sur le plan stratégique, ils ont utilisé tous les moyens de procédure possibles pour faire en sorte que leurs exigences soient reconnues. Jusqu'à la fin, ils ont présenté ces exigences comme incontournables et essentielles à la réalisation d'un consensus, s'octroyant ainsi, dans les faits, un droit de veto. Conscients que la vaste majorité des États n'appuyait pas ce point de vue, ils ont cherché en même temps par tous les moyens à retarder la négociation. Dès 2003, lors du débat sur l'ouverture d'une négociation portant sur la protection de la diversité des contenus culturels et des expressions artistiques, ils avaient fait valoir qu'une telle convention était prématurée et qu'il était nécessaire de procéder à des études afin de déterminer si elle répondait à des besoins réels. Ils ont repris ce point de vue tout au long de la négociation et jusque dans les derniers moments du débat sur la convention lors de la Conférence générale de 2005.

Mais phénomène remarquable, cette opposition déterminée des États-Unis n'a pu triompher de la volonté toute aussi déterminée de la vaste majorité des Membres de disposer le plus rapidement possible d'un instrument international destiné à assurer la protection et la promotion de la diversité des expressions culturelles et qui placerait la culture sur un pied d'égalité avec les autres instruments internationaux. Au terme de négociations ardues où chacun a dû faire des concessions, cette vaste majorité des membres a considéré que le projet de convention finalement approuvé reflétait un très large consensus et a exprimé le désir que celui-ci soit entériné par la Conférence générale comme convention de l'UNESCO. Plusieurs États partageaient certaines des préoccupations des États-Unis et la vaste majorité aurait souhaité que ces derniers signent cette Convention. Mais pratiquement aucun n'était prêt à accepter qu'un seul Membre puisse dicter le contenu de la Convention. S'il est des conclusions qui peuvent être tirées de cette négociation, c'est d'abord et avant tout que la volonté politique, lorsqu'elle s'appuie sur la conviction et le courage, peut parfois triompher d'obstacles en apparence insurmontables et que la gouvernance internationale peut difficilement se construire sur une vision réductrice des besoins humains.

Summary

Negotiation of the UNESCO Convention on the Protection and Promotion of the Diversity of Cultural Expressions

Since its beginning in September 2004, the negotiation of the Convention on the Protection and Promotion of the Diversity of Cultural Expressions has raised a great deal of interest and even tension among UNESCO member states. A record number of members and non-governmental observers have been involved, and, on many occasions, the debates have taken place in overflowing rooms. During the study of the draft convention by Commission IV, on 17 October 2005, the debate even had to be temporarily suspended in order to find a larger room. Obviously, the negotiations, which addressed head on the problem of the interface between trade and culture, dealt with a very sensitive matter. On 20 October 2005, the convention was finally adopted by the UNESCO General Conference (148 votes for, two against, and four abstentions). Considered to be a historical moment by several delegations in their closing declaration, the results of this decision was vigorously denounced by the United States. It went so far as to assert, in a declaration made public by the US embassy in Paris, that the proposed convention was deeply flawed since it dealt with trade rather than culture and that it therefore fell outside UNESCO jurisdiction. How was such a result achieved? This article attempts to clarify these issues, following the negotiation step by step as well as the dynamic that led to the ultimate result.

Sommaire

La négociation de la convention de l'UNESCO sur la protection et la promotion de la diversité des expressions culturelles

La négociation de la Convention sur la protection et la promotion de la diversité des expressions culturelles, qui a débuté en septembre 2004, a suscité dès le départ un intérêt considérable et même une certaine tension parmi les États membres de l'UNESCO. Un nombre record d'États et d'observateurs non gouvernementaux y ont pris part; à plusieurs reprises, c'est dans des salles combles que les débats se sont poursuivis. Manifestement, cette négociation qui abordait de front la problématique de l'interface commerce/ culture touchait à une question très sensible. Le 20 octobre 2005, la Conférence générale de l'UNESCO adoptait finalement (par 148 voix contre deux et quatre abstentions) le texte de la convention qui est maintenant ouvert pour ratification par les membres. Mais ce résultat, qualifié de moment historique par plusieurs délégations dans leur déclaration de clôture, a été dénoncé avec vigueur par les États-Unis, ces derniers allant jusqu'à affirmer, dans une déclaration rendue publique par leur ambassade à Paris, que le texte de convention proposé était profondément défectueux parce qu'il concernait le commerce plutôt que la culture et qu'il était de ce fait hors de la compétence de l'UNESCO. Comment en est-on arrivé à ce résultat? C'est la question explorée dans le présent article, en examinant le déroulement de chacune des trois séances de négociation et en remontant le cours des événements qui ont conduit à l'adoption de la Convention par la Conférence générale.

The Role for Human Rights Obligations in Canadian Extradition Law

JOANNA HARRINGTON

Extradition is the surrender from one state to another, on request, of persons accused or convicted of committing a serious crime in the jurisdiction of the state requesting the extradition. While governed primarily within Canada by the terms of the Extradition Act[1] and the Canadian Charter of Rights and Freedoms,[2] extradition is also a matter of treaty law and of international law more generally, given that the act of surrendering an individual from one state to another is ultimately the sovereign act of a willing state. I make this point clearly at the outset since many in Canada classify extradition, incorrectly in my view, as a matter of criminal law.[3] This viewpoint is also odd given the importance of treaties to

Joanna Harrington is associate professor in the Faculty of Law at the University of Alberta. Appreciation is extended by the author to the Fellows of Gonville and Caius College at the University of Cambridge for generously supporting her doctoral work on extradition and human rights through the award of a W.M. Tapp Studentship in Law. Appreciation is also extended to Professors Grant Huscroft and John Law for their helpful comments on an earlier draft.

[1] Extradition Act, S.C. 1999, c. 18, as amended.

[2] Canadian Charter of Rights and Freedoms, Part I of the Constitution Act, 1982, being Schedule B to the Canada Act 1982 (U.K.), 1982, c. 11 [Charter].

[3] The *Canadian Abridgment* and the indices to the *Supreme Court Reports*, for example, classify extradition as a matter of criminal law, while many respected international law texts identify extradition as a matter of public international law (often under the heading of jurisdiction). The criminal law process, and its associated burden of proof, kicks in after an extradition, albeit that the offence underlying an extradition request must be criminal in nature. Extradition has been recognized as part of international law since at least the 1960s, with India's Satya Bedi and Australia's Ivan Shearer writing their doctoral theses on the subject at Utrecht and Northwestern respectively. See S.D. Bedi, *Extradition in International Law and Practice* (Rotterdam: Bronder-Offset, 1966); and I.A. Shearer, *Extradition in International Law* (Manchester: Manchester University Press, 1971). For

extradition — treaties being a recognized and significant source of international law. Although a state may choose to extradite as a matter of courtesy or goodwill, most states prefer to conduct their extradition relations on a treaty basis so as to secure some guarantee of future reciprocity. An extradition treaty thus brings into force an obligation to extradite upon request under international law, provided the terms and conditions of the treaty are met, including any terms providing protection for the rights of the individual wanted for extradition. It is understood that Canada is a party to some fifty bilateral extradition treaties and a further ten multilateral treaties containing extradition provisions for certain crimes of international concern.[4]

But alongside this network of extradition treaties to which Canada is a party lie a network of human rights treaties to which Canada has also agreed to be bound. These human rights treaties are just as binding under international law as an extradition treaty, with the most relevant treaties being the International Covenant on Civil and Political Rights (ICCPR),[5] which has bound Canada since 1976, and the UN Convention against Torture and Other Cruel, Inhuman or Degrading Treatment or Punishment (UNCAT), which has been binding on Canada since 1987.[6] Viewed from an international law

---

extradition's current inclusion in several leading texts on international law, see A. Aust, *Handbook of International Law* (Cambridge: Cambridge University Press, 2005) at 264–68, I. Brownlie, *Principles of Public International Law*, 6th edition (New York: Oxford University Press, 2003) at 312–14, J. Dugard, *International Law: A South African Perspective*, 2nd edition (Kenwyn: Juta and Company, 2000) at 155–79, H.M. Kindred et al., *International Law: Chiefly as Interpreted and Applied in Canada*, 6th edition (Toronto: Emond Montgomery, 2000) at 547–59, and M.N. Shaw, *International Law*, 5th edition (Cambridge: Cambridge University Press, 2003) at 610–11.

4 This tally was provided by the government of Canada to the Organization of American States (OAS) in 2004 as part of an OAS review of "Mutual Legal Assistance in Criminal Matters and Extradition," available online at <http://www.oas.org/juridico/MLA/en/can/en_can-ext-gen-g8iag.html> (15 August 2006).

5 International Covenant on Civil and Political Rights, 16 December 1966, 999 U.N.T.S. 171, (1967) 6 I.L.M. 368, Can. T.S. 1976 No. 47 (in force 23 March 1976; accession by Canada 19 May 1976) [ICCPR]. Canada's treaty ratification record can now be verified online using the government of Canada's treaty information website at <http://www.treaty-accord.gc.ca/> (15 August 2006).

6 Convention against Torture and Other Cruel, Inhuman or Degrading Treatment or Punishment, 10 December 1984, 1465 U.N.T.S. 85, (1984) 23 I.L.M. 1027, Can. T.S. 1987 No. 36 (in force 26 June 1987; ratification by Canada 24 June 1987) [UNCAT].

perspective, these human rights treaties should serve to supplement the safeguards already found in the extradition treaties by recognizing the universal application of certain human rights guarantees, including the rights to fair treatment and a fair trial. It has also become clear, since the landmark judgment of the European Court of Human Rights in *Soering v. United Kingdom*,[7] that a treaty-based human rights obligation can also form the basis for holding a sending state responsible under international law for any foreseeable violations of an individual's rights in the requesting state, leading to much discussion in the early and late 1990s on the role for human rights considerations in matters of extradition.[8]

But while one can find reference in Canadian extradition case law to the extradition jurisprudence of the European organs operating under the authority of a treaty not binding on Canada,[9] one is hard-pressed to find more than a passing reference to the ICCPR, a treaty guaranteeing essentially the same rights that has bound Canada for thirty years. In the various challenges to extradition at-

7 *Soering v. United Kingdom*, Judgment of 7 July 1989, Series A, No. 161, (1989) 11 E.H.R.R. 439 and (1989) 29 I.L.M. 1063 [*Soering*] (concerning the extradition, without assurances, of a German citizen from the United Kingdom to the United States in circumstances where there was a real risk he would spend many years in deplorable conditions on death row awaiting his execution). For an early discussion of the import of the *Soering* case published in Canada, see S.A. Williams, "Extradition to a State That Imposes the Death Penalty" (1990) 28 Can. Y.B. Int'l L. 117 at 130–38 and 148–53.

8 See S. Breitenmoser and G.E. Wilms, "Human Rights v. Extradition: The *Soering* Case" (1990) 11 Mich. J. Int'l L. 845; J. Quigley, "The Rule of Non-Inquiry and the Impact of Human Rights on Extradition Law" (1990) 15 N.C. J. Int'l L. & Comm. Reg'n 401; C. van den Wyngaert, "Applying the European Convention on Human Rights to Extradition: Opening Pandora's Box?" (1990) 39 Int'l & Comp. L.Q. 757; O. Lagodny, "Human Rights and Extradition" (1991) 62 Rev. I.D.P. 45; D.K. Piragoff and M.V.J. Kran, "The Impact of Human Rights Principles on Extradition from Canada and the United States: The Role of National Courts" (1992) 3 Crim. L. Forum 225; M.P. Shea, "Expanding Judicial Scrutiny of Human Rights in Extradition Cases after *Soering*" (1992) 17 Yale J. Int'l L. 85; S.A. Williams, "Human Rights Safeguards and International Cooperation: Striking the Balance" (1992) 3 Crim. L. Forum 191; J. Dugard and C. van den Wyngaert, "Reconciling Extradition with Human Rights" (1998) 92 Am. J. Int'l L. 187; and P. Michell, "Domestic Rights and International Responsibilities: Extradition under the Canadian Charter" (1998) Yale J. Int'l L. 141.

9 (European) Convention for the Protection of Human Rights and Fundamental Freedoms, 4 November 1950, 213 U.N.T.S. 221, E.T.S. No. 5 (in force 3 September 1953) [ECHR].

tempted in Canada, scant attention is paid by the courts to Canada's human rights obligations as treaty obligations, particularly when compared to the value placed on respecting Canada's extradition treaty obligations. All too often, extradition is seen as a matter of comity or respect for Canada's international relations,[10] but without recognition that this respect should also extend to Canada's treaty engagements with the international community in the field of human rights. This is not to say, however, that human rights considerations play no role in Canadian extradition law. As will be shown in this review of Canada's extradition jurisprudence over the past thirty years, human rights have carved out a role, as supported by the Charter. This review also suggests that the role for human rights in extradition may include the right to a fair trial as well as fair treatment rights.

The problem, however, is that the threshold for invoking the Charter as a ground for refusing an extradition request on human rights grounds remains high, with the jurisprudential test for its application resting heavily on a subjective evaluation as to whether the requested extradition "shocks the conscience" of Canadians. Canadian extradition law may, however, gain some benefit in terms of both coherence and guidance if a role akin to that accorded to Charter rights was given to Canada's (rather than Europe's) international human rights treaty obligations, such that both were considered in the balancing approach that governs a decision to extradite from Canada. According such a role to an international human rights treaty would help unify the law in this area, particularly given the inevitable intersection of international and domestic law in extradition matters, while also affording equal treatment to all of Canada's treaty obligations relevant to extradition. Such an approach would also make clear that an extradition treaty is no more binding, nor more legitimate, than a human rights treaty, and, as international law-making instruments, both should be respected as such when Canada considers an extradition request.

---

10 See *United States of America v. Burns*, [2001] 1 S.C.R. 283 at para. 72 [*Burns*]; *Kindler v. Canada (Minister of Justice)*, [1991] 2 S.C.R. 779 at 844; and *Argentina v. Mellino*, [1987] 1 S.C.R. 536 at 551. See also A.W. La Forest, "The Balance between Liberty and Comity in the Evidentiary Requirements Applicable to Extradition Proceedings" (2002) 28 Queen's L.J. 95 (with the title reflecting the importance attached to comity in Canadian extradition law).

Canadian Statutory Regime for Extradition

Extradition from Canada is governed primarily by the 1999 Extradition Act,[11] which works in tandem with an extradition treaty between Canada and a requesting state.[12] The Act assumes primacy because of the long-standing rule that treaties must be incorporated into Canadian law to have domestic effect,[13] although this rule is weakening, at least with respect to human rights treaties, given the Supreme Court of Canada's decision in *Baker v. Canada*, holding that "the values" of an unincorporated international human rights treaty "may help inform the contextual approach to statutory interpretation and judicial review."[14] Canada's current Extradition Act came into force on 17 June 1999, repealing the previous Extradition Act[15] as well as the Fugitive Offenders Act,[16] which was concerned with the rendition of individuals between Commonwealth countries. Canada no longer applies a different regime for extradition to and from Commonwealth states

---

11 Extradition Act, *supra* note 1. Commentary on the Act's provisions can be found in G. Botting, *Canadian Extradition Law Practice* (Toronto: Lexis-Nexis, 2005); and E.F. Krivel et al., *A Practical Guide to Canadian Extradition* (Toronto: Carswell, 2002). Sadly, the former leading text, *La Forest's Extradition to and from Canada*, is now out of date: A.W. La Forest, *La Forest's Extradition to and from Canada*, 3rd edition (Aurora: Canada Law Book, 1991).

12 Canada does not ordinarily extradite to non-Commonwealth states unless there is an extradition treaty in place with the requesting state, although the statutory regime does permit the making of a specific agreement "for the purpose of giving effect to a request for extradition in a particular case." Extradition Act, *supra* note 1 at s. 10(1). Extradition on a case-by-case basis was also permitted by proclamation under Part II of the former Extradition Act, but used sparingly. See J.-G. Castel and S.A. Williams, "The Extradition of Canadian Citizens and Sections 1 and 6(1) of the Canadian Charter of Rights and Freedoms" (1987) 25 Can. Y.B. Int'l L. 263 at 265; and Krivel et al., *supra* note 11 at para. 2.2(c).

13 *Canada (A-G) v. Ontario (A-G)*, [1937] A.C. 326 (P.C.). As explained in *United States of America v. Allard (No. 2)*, [1991] 1 S.C.R. 861 at 865 [*Allard (No. 2)*], "extradition does not exist by virtue of customary international law. Rather extradition takes place in accordance with the [then] *Extradition Act*, R.S.C. 1985, c. E-23, and pursuant to section 3 of the Act, with the provisions of the applicable treaty."

14 *Baker v. Canada*, [1999] 2 S.C.R. 817 at para. 70.

15 Extradition Act, R.S.C. 1985, c. E-23.

16 Fugitive Offenders Act, R.S.C. 1985, c. F-32.

and now designates these countries as extradition partners under the 1999 Act.[17]

Canada's statutory regime for extradition is largely a copy of the British scheme of 1870, which initiated the use of a generalized act that could be readily applied to incorporate both current and future treaties into domestic law.[18] The British Act was used initially in Canada, but, after some confusion, Canada passed its own Extradition Act in 1877.[19] The 1877 Act has since served as the nucleus of Canadian extradition law, requiring little amendment until 1992,[20] when changes were made to clarify the Charter jurisdiction of extradition judges and streamline the appeal process,[21] and, again in 1999, when the Act was repealed and replaced by a new statute. While the 1999 reforms retain the basic structure of extradition, they also intend to modernize and simplify the law by revising the evidentiary requirements so as to alleviate difficulties often faced when extraditing to civil law countries and by removing the list approach used to specify extraditable crimes so as to accommodate more readily new forms of criminal activity.[22] The 1999 reforms also addressed duplication concerns between extradition and refugee proceedings and extended the Act's application to include the surrender of individuals to international criminal tribunals.[23]

---

[17] Extradition Act, *supra* note 1 at s. 9(1) and Schedule.

[18] Extradition Act, 1870 (U.K.), 33 & 34 Vict., c. 52.

[19] As explained by La Forest J. in *McVey v. United States of America*, [1992] 3 S.C.R. 475 at 509.

[20] An Act to Amend the Extradition Act, S.C. 1992, c. 13. Minor amendments were made in 1882, 1886, 1909, and 1985.

[21] As discussed in *United States of America v. Kwok*, [2001] 1 S.C.R. 532 [*Kwok*], a case concerning the extradition of a Canadian citizen to the United States on charges of conspiracy to traffic heroin.

[22] The problem with the list approach is that it requires a statutory amendment as new crimes arise, and delays in doing so can jeopardize Canada's extradition relations, as illustrated in *Allard (No. 2)*, *supra* note 13, where Canada had to refuse a US request for two hijackers in 1969 because hijacking was not listed as an extraditable offence until 1976. To avoid this problem, and still meet the need for double criminality, extraditable crimes are now described in terms of the severity of their punishment.

[23] Canada, Department of Justice, "Canada's Proposed New Extradition Act," press release (5 May 1998).

Pursuant to the legislative scheme, extradition responsibilities with respect to a request for surrender from Canada are divided between an extradition judge and the Minister of Justice, with the minister having the ultimate decision-making authority.[24] The process begins at a preliminary phase where the Minister of Justice, after receiving an extradition request from an extradition partner, is required to ensure that the preconditions with respect to the severity of the punishment for the alleged offence are met.[25] If so, the minister issues an authority to proceed, triggering the judicial phase (or "committal phase") of the extradition process.[26] It is the task of the judge to hold an extradition hearing to determine whether the evidence is sufficient to justify committing the requested individual for surrender,[27] a role often described as "a modest one,"[28] although it should be noted that the Act permits an extradition judge to include with the order "any report that the judge thinks fit."[29] The committal order is, however, only the first step towards securing a fugitive's extradition from Canada. Once made, the extradition process enters its executive phase, with the actual order for surrender being a personal and admittedly political decision of the Minister of Justice,[30] made after weighing the fugitive's

---

[24] Since this division of responsibilities was also part of the previous statutory scheme, now clarified under the 1999 Extradition Act, the jurisprudence associated with the former Act remains relevant.

[25] Extradition Act, *supra* note 1 at ss. 3(1)(a) and 3(3).

[26] *Ibid.* at s. 15.

[27] *Ibid.* at s. 29(1). See also *United States of America v. Ferras; United States of America v. Latty,* 2006 SCC 33 [*Ferras*].

[28] *Argentina v. Mellino,* [1987] 1 S.C.R. 536 at 553; *United States of America v. Lépine,* [1994] 1 S.C.R. 286 at para. 10; *United States of America v. Dynar,* [1997] 2 S.C.R. 462 at para. 120; and *United States of America v. Yang* (2001), 56 O.R. (3d) 52 at para. 47 (C.A.). However, as Sopinka J. noted in *Lépine* at para. 33: "It seems inconsistent with the approach to the interpretation of the Act ... stressing the importance of the hearing to the rights of the individual and then to proceed to interpret the content of that hearing as ever-increasingly 'modest'."

[29] Extradition Act, *supra* note 1 at s. 38(1)(c). The Attorney General of Canada has conceded that this report could be used by the judge to address concerns. See *Canada (A.G.) v. Fulfillment Solutions,* [2005] B.C.J. No. 2794 at para. 113.

[30] Section 40(1) of the Extradition Act, *supra* note 1, stipulates that "[t]he Minister may, within a period of 90 days after the date of a person's committal to await surrender, personally order that the person be surrendered to the extradition partner."

submissions against Canada's international obligations.[31] It is also the minister's responsibility to consider the human rights record of the requesting state[32] — a point expressly accepted by the parliamentary secretary to the Minister of Justice during the Act's passage through Parliament,[33] presumably on behalf of the minister who did not take part in the debates.

This increased awareness of extradition's human rights dimension has also prompted a curtailment of the scope of the minister's discretion under the 1999 Act with respect to the decision to surrender that was not seen under the previous regime.[34] A prime example is section 44(1)(b) of the 1999 Extradition Act, which requires the minister to refuse surrender if satisfied that

the request for extradition is made for the purpose of prosecuting or punishing the person by reason of their race, religion, nationality, ethnic origin, language, colour, political opinion, sex, sexual orientation, age, mental or physical disability, or status or that the person's position may be prejudiced for any of those reasons.[35]

This discrimination clause is more widely cast than in most extradition treaties, which typically name only race, religion, nationality, and political opinion as grounds. Canada, however, opted for a broader clause, with its initial version drawing upon[36] the wording of the discrimination clause proposed by the UN Model Treaty on Extradition, a non-binding distillation of best practices and

---

[31] *Idziak v. Canada (Minister of Justice)*, [1992] 3 S.C.R. 631 at 658 [*Idziak*].

[32] This responsibility was acknowledged in the department's press release issued when the proposed Act was tabled in Parliament: "Canada's Proposed New Extradition Act," *supra* note 23.

[33] "The Minister of Justice, on the other hand, will have the responsibility for assessing the foreign legal system to ensure that human rights are respected and a fair trial will be provided in the requesting state." Canada, *H.C. Debates*, 36th Parl., 1st Sess., vol. 135, No. 135 at 9006 (8 October 1998) (Eleni Bakopanos, Lib.).

[34] Under the former Extradition Act, the only statutory restrictions on a minister's discretion to extradite were those concerning political offences. Extradition Act, R.S.C. 1985, c. E-23, ss. 21 and 22.

[35] Extradition Act, *supra* note 1 at s. 44(1)(b).

[36] As acknowledged in Canada, *H.C. Debates*, 36th Parl., 1st Sess., vol. 135, No. 135 at 9006 (8 October 1998) (Eleni Bakopanos, Lib.). See also Canada, *H.C. Debates*, 36th Parl., 1st Sess., vol. 135, No. 162 at 10592 (30 November 1998) (Peter Adams, Lib.).

aspirations.[37] This wording was then expanded further by amendments made at the committee stage of the parliamentary process to ensure that the provision's breadth matched that of the equality guarantees found in both international human rights instruments[38] and Canada's Charter.[39] The 1999 Extradition Act also requires the minister to refuse surrender if satisfied that it "would be unjust or oppressive having regard to all the relevant circumstances,"[40] a provision taken from the former Fugitive Offenders Act[41] and now made applicable to all extraditions.

Section 46 of the Act further requires the minister to refuse surrender where a prosecution is statute-barred,[42] where the offence is one of a military character,[43] and where the offence is one of a political character.[44] However, with respect to the political offence exception, the 1999 Act also attempts to curtail its scope by giving pre-eminence to any multilateral treaty that obliges Canada to extradite, while also specifying that certain crimes of violence cannot be considered political, including murder, manslaughter,

---

[37] UN Model Treaty on Extradition, adopted by the General Assembly on 14 December 1990 by Resolution 45/116, UN Doc. A/RES/45/116 (1990), reprinted in (1991) 30 I.L.M. 1407. For commentary, see A.T.H. (Bert) Swart, "Refusal of Extradition and the United Nations Model Treaty on Extradition" (1992) 23 Netherlands Y.B. Int'l L. 75. The template has since been modified by the adoption of "Complementary Provisions to the Model Treaty on Extradition" by the General Assembly on 12 December 1997 by Resolution 52/88, UN Doc. A/RES/52/88 (1997).

[38] Canada, *H.C. Debates*, 36th Parl., 1st Sess., vol. 135, No. 162 at 10598 (30 November 1998) (Daniel Turp, PQ).

[39] Canada, *H.C. Debates*, 36th Parl., 1st Sess., vol. 135, No. 162 at 10592 (30 November 1998) (Peter Adams, Lib.).

[40] Extradition Act, *supra* note 1 at s. 44(1)(a). This discretion accorded to the minister is not open to judicial review. *Dai v. Canada (Minister of Justice)*, 2006 BCCA 179 [*Dai*].

[41] Fugitive Offenders Act, *supra* note 16 at s. 16. The origins of the "unjust and oppressive" clause can be traced back to the British scheme for rendition found in the Fugitive Offenders Act, 1881, 44 & 45 Vict., c. 69, s. 10. Recent cases have, incorrectly in my view given the provision's history, combined this statutory ground for refusing extradition with the constitutional ground of fundamental justice. *United States of America v. Reumayr* (2003), 176 C.C.C. (3d) 377 at para. 19 (B.C.C.A.), cited in *United States of America v. Fordham*, 2005 BCCA 197 at para. 13.

[42] Extradition Act, *supra* note 1 at s. 46(1)(a).

[43] *Ibid.* at s. 46(1)(b).

[44] *Ibid.* at s. 46(1)(c).

hostage-taking, and the use of explosives.[45] These specific exemptions, however, may not apply to Canada's bilateral extradition relations, as the Act accords primacy to the terms of a bilateral treaty,[46] and, as Canada has noted,[47] most of its bilateral extradition treaties provide a mandatory ground of refusal for political offences. However, for terrorist offences, these bilateral treaties must now be read with the obligation imposed on all UN member states by the Security Council "to ensure ... that claims of political motivation are not recognized as grounds for refusing requests for the extradition of alleged terrorists."[48]

As for discretionary grounds for refusing surrender, the 1999 Extradition Act codifies several familiar exceptions, including those for double jeopardy, *in absentia* convictions, and pending proceedings in Canada.[49] The Act also specifies that the minister "may" refuse surrender if the offence underlying the extradition request is one punishable by death in the requesting state.[50] This approach marked a move away from the usual requirement for refusal to be predicated on the absence of assurances[51] but was offset by the clear intention on the part of the government to retain ministerial discretion in death penalty extradition cases.[52] This discretion has since

---

[45] *Ibid.* at s. 46(2).

[46] Section 45(1) of the Extradition Act, *supra* note 1, provides that "[t]he reasons for the refusal of surrender contained in a relevant extradition agreement, other than a multilateral extradition agreement, or the absence of reasons for refusal in such an agreement, prevail over sections 46 and 47."

[47] See Canada's report to the OAS, *supra* note 4 at 4.

[48] UN Security Council Res. 1373, UN SCOR, 56th Sess., 4385th mtg, UN Doc. S/Res/1373 (2001) at operative paras. 3(f) and 3(g).

[49] Extradition Act, *supra* note 1 at s. 47.

[50] *Ibid.* at s. 44(2).

[51] See, for example, Article 6 of the Canada-US Extradition Treaty, 3 December 1971, 1041 U.N.T.S. 57, Can. T.S. 1976 No. 3 (in force 22 March 1976), as amended by an exchange of notes done on 28 June 1974 and 9 July 1974, and by protocols signed on 11 January 1988 and 12 January 2001, which stipulates that "[w]hen the offense for which extradition is requested is punishable by death under the laws of the requesting State and the laws of the requested State do not permit such punishment for that offense, extradition may be refused unless the requesting State provides such assurances as the requested State considers sufficient that the death penalty shall not be imposed, or, if imposed, shall not be executed."

[52] Canada, *H.C. Debates*, 36th Parl., 1st Sess., vol. 135, No. 135 at 9006 (8 October 1998) (Eleni Bakopanos, Lib.). This retention of discretion later led to a failed attempt in the Senate by Liberal members Jerry Grafstein and Serge Joyal to

been curtailed by the Supreme Court of Canada's decision of 2001 that such an assurance is required in all but the exceptional case.[53] The 1999 Extradition Act also introduces a new optional exception for extradition concerning persons under the age of eighteen where the law in the requesting state differs from the fundamental principles of Canada's approach to youth criminal justice.[54]

The Extradition Act also confirms that the minister's discretion can be exercised in ways other than simply for or against surrender. Section 40(3) expressly stipulates that the minister "may" seek any assurances that he or she considers appropriate from the extradition partner and "may" attach any conditions he or she considers appropriate to the order of surrender. While these options were previously available to the minister prior to 1999, as illustrated by their use in 1976,[55] 1992,[56] and 1996,[57] the absence of an express authorization in the former Extradition Act led some to question the minister's authority to attach such conditions.[58]

---

make the death penalty a mandatory ground of refusal. J. Aubry, "Liberals Turn Down Free Vote on Extradition Bill," *Vancouver Sun*, 6 May 1999, at A11.

[53] See the discussion in *Burns, supra* note 10. However, an assurance is not required when the requesting state has advised Canada that the death penalty is not available for the offences underlying the extradition request. *Dai, supra* note 40.

[54] Extradition Act, *supra* note 1 at s. 47(c), as amended by the Youth Criminal Justice Act, S.C. 2002, c. 1, s. 190.

[55] Canada secured the 1976 extradition of Leonard Peltier to the United States with a death penalty assurance. Canada, Department of Justice, "Release of Materials Concerning the Extradition of Leonard Peltier," press release (15 October 1999). For further comment on the *Peltier* extradition, see note 67 in this article.

[56] In February 1992, assurances were given to secure the extradition of Leo Robert O'Bomsawin to Florida to stand trial for murder. Canada apparently sought assurances because of concerns that O'Bomsawin, as an Abenaki Indian, was more likely to receive the death penalty than if he was white. J.F. Burns, "Canada Wins U.S. Extradition Deal," *New York Times*, 14 February 1992, at A3; and W. Claiborne, "Murder Suspect Tests U.S.-Canada Extradition Act," *Washington Post*, 29 November 1991, at A38.

[57] In February 1996, Canada required Mexico to agree, "in writing and in advance," to four conditions before extraditing an openly gay man to stand trial for murder due to hostility shown by Mexican authorities towards homosexuals. Canada, Department of Justice, "Minister of Justice Orders Surrender of Dennis Hurley to Mexico," press release (27 February 1996). In October 1996, Canada sought both death penalty and speedy trial assurances from the Philippines. Canada, Department of Justice, "Minister of Justice Orders Surrender of Rodolfo Pacificador to the Republic of the Philippines," press release (23 October 1996).

[58] See, for example, *United States of Mexico v. Hurley* (1997), 35 O.R. (3d) 481 (C.A.), leave to appeal discontinued 30 September 1997 [*Hurley*].

Given the supremacy of constitutional law, the decisions made by both the judiciary and the executive in the extradition process are open to challenge on Charter grounds, although such challenges are best raised after the minister has made the order to surrender.[59] However, because extradition is ultimately a matter of executive discretion, albeit now limited by the 1999 reforms, Canadian courts have often held that a minister's decision to extradite is entitled to deference.[60] Such deference works well with the government's stated objective for enacting the 1999 Extradition Act, namely to "prevent Canada from becoming a safe haven for fugitives," although this should be balanced with the other stated objective of "enhanc[ing] protections and safeguards for persons who are the subject of an extradition request."[61] As a result, all fugitives challenging their extradition from Canada must present a compelling case concerning the feared violation of their Charter rights in the requesting state if they are to override the courts' deference to the executive in extradition matters — a point illustrated by this review of Canada's extradition jurisprudence.

CANADIAN JURISPRUDENCE ON EXTRADITION

Canada's courts have long accepted that a degree of trust must be accorded to states seeking surrender under a treaty, especially in regard to the treatment to be accorded to the individual once surrendered to the foreign state.[62] This view is based on an assumption that Canada would not risk its own good name by entering into treaties with states whose justice systems do not warrant such trust,

---

59 This point is well illustrated by the *Jamieson* case where two applications for judicial review were brought, one before and one after the minister had exercised his discretion, resulting in two different judgments by the same court on the same facts. *United States of America v. Jamieson (No. 1)* (1992), 73 C.C.C. (3d) 460 (Qué. C.A.) [*Jamieson (No. 1)*]; and *United States of America v. Jamieson (No. 2)* (1994), 93 C.C.C. (3d) 265 (Qué. C.A.) [*Jamieson (No. 2)*].

60 See *Kwok*, *supra* note 21 at paras. 93 and 94.

61 "Canada's Proposed New Extradition Act," *supra* note 23. Upon the Act's coming into force, the minister of justice proclaimed: "Our message is clear—Canada will not be a safe haven for fugitives from justice." Canada, Department of Justice, "New Extradition Act Comes into Force," press release (18 June 1999).

62 *Re Burley* (1865), 1 C.L.J. 34 at 50, reiterated by La Forest J. in *Canada v. Schmidt*, [1987] 1 S.C.R. 500 at 516. See also *Re Rosenberg* (1918), 28 Man. R. 439 at 445 (C.A.): "It would be an insult to a friendly state to entertain any doubt as to the justice of its courts or the good faith with which it will observe the provisions of the treaty."

even though changes could well have taken place within the partner state after the treaty's conclusion. Moreover, trust is often not enough for the protection of human rights, no matter how honourable the intentions of the initial treaty-makers, leading to challenges to extradition in domestic courts on various human rights grounds.

Such challenges arose in Canada initially within the context of *habeas corpus* proceedings and then, after the creation of the Federal Court,[63] within judicial review proceedings, with later cases invoking the liberty and fair hearing provisions of the 1960 Canadian Bill of Rights in support.[64] Yet the courts were careful to draw a distinction between an extradition hearing and a full-blown trial on the subject of guilt or innocence, noting that in the latter, the absence of legal rights, such as a right to cross-examination, might well be a breach of fairness and justice requirements, but that this was not the case with an extradition hearing.[65] It was the view of the courts that the liberty interests of the individual had been adequately protected by the inclusion of a judicial phase in the proceedings leading to extradition,[66] with any further concerns about fairness to be raised within the jurisdiction of the requesting state. Such caution, equally applicable to the application of the Canadian Bill of Rights guarantees to extradition, also extended beyond unfair trial claims to claims of arbitrary detention, inequality, and cruel and unusual treatment, with the courts again expressing reluctance for fear of giving Canada's internal guarantees extraterritorial effect.[67]

---

63 Federal Court Act, S.C. 1970, c. 1. See also *Puerto Rico (Commonwealth) v. Hernandez*, [1975] 1 S.C.R. 228 [*Hernandez*], concerning a US request for the extradition of a student political activist accused of murdering a police officer during a campus riot.

64 Section 1(a) of the Canadian Bill of Rights, S.C. 1960, c. 44, protects the "right of the individual to life, liberty, security of the person and enjoyment of property, and the right not to be deprived thereof except by due process of law," while section 2(e) provides that no federal law shall be construed or applied so as to "deprive a person of the right to a fair hearing in accordance with the principles of fundamental justice for the determination of his rights and obligations."

65 *Armstrong v. Wisconsin*, [1973] F.C. 437 at 443 (C.A.), leave to appeal denied, (1973) 32 D.L.R. (3d) 265 n (S.C.C.) [*Armstrong*]. At issue was a US request for the extradition of an opponent of the Vietnam War accused of bombing university buildings in which he believed war-related research was taking place.

66 *Hernandez*, *supra* note 63 at 245 (Laskin J. dissenting on other grounds), cited with approval in *United States of America v. Dynar*, [1997] 2 S.C.R. 462 at para. 121.

67 See, for example, *United States of America v. Peltier*, Vancouver Reg. No. 760176, 18 June 1976 (B.C.S.C.); *Re Peltier*, Court File No. T-1327-76, 27 October 1976 (Fed. C.A.), concerning a US request for the extradition of an Aboriginal leader

Since the enactment of the Charter, further attempts have been made to prevent extradition on these same grounds, with the earliest cases reaching the Supreme Court of Canada in 1987. However, with each attempted challenge, the court has adopted a highly deferential standard of review, placing much emphasis on the importance of international cooperation in criminal matters, respect for comity as between nations, and the need to recognize the executive's experience and expertise in foreign affairs, notwithstanding the fact that the law assigns responsibility for extradition, presumably for a reason, to the Minister of Justice and not the Minister of Foreign Affairs. Nevertheless, so great was the deference accorded to the executive that it was not until 2001 that a challenge was successful before the highest court,[68] although the result was swayed by reasons inapplicable to extradition outside the death penalty context (notably, the finality of death). However, before any firm conclusions can be made as to the role for human rights guarantees in Canadian extradition law, it is worth examining Canada's key jurisprudential developments both before and after the dramatic turnaround of 2001.

EARLY CHARTER JURISPRUDENCE ON EXTRADITION

Any examination of the Charter's impact on extradition must begin with the 1987 trilogy of *Canada v. Schmidt*,[69] *Argentina v.*

---

for the murder of FBI agents at a South Dakota reservation. Peltier was surrendered to the United States in December 1976 and convicted at trial in 1977. A post-surrender appeal to the Supreme Court of Canada was dismissed 22 June 1989. *United States of America v. Peltier*, [1989] S.C.C.A. No. 207. But the case continues to attract concern in Canada and abroad with many believing that Peltier's extradition was secured by false affidavits procured by the US authorities. A Canadian departmental review of the file was ordered in 1994, with the results and the conclusion that Peltier had been lawfully extradited being released to the public in 1999. See "Release of Materials Concerning the Extradition of Leonard Peltier," *supra* note 55. Peltier, now in his sixties, continues to serve two consecutive life sentences in an American penitentiary, while concerns about his extradition persist. K. Lunman, "MPs Call for Probe of Peltier Extradition," *Globe and Mail*, 20 November 2002, at A6. See also D.L. Martin, "Unredressed Wrong: The Extradition of Leonard Peltier from Canada," in Susan C. Boyd et al., eds., *(Ab)Using Power: The Canadian Experience* (Halifax: Fernwood, 2001), 214; and D.L. Martin, "Extradition, The Charter and Due Process: Is Procedural Fairness Enough?" (2002) S.C.L.R. (2d) 161 at 172–80.

68 Some challenges were initially successful before the Québec courts, as discussed later in this article, but subsequently over-turned by the Supreme Court of Canada.

69 *Canada v. Schmidt*, [1987] 1 S.C.R. 500 [*Schmidt*].

Mellino,[70] and *United States of America v. Allard and Charette.*[71] Released on the same day, these three cases aptly illustrate the view then taken by the Supreme Court of Canada with respect to the role for Charter rights in matters of extradition from Canada. In all three decisions, challenges to extradition based on section 11 of the Charter failed. Section 11 provides that "any person charged with an offence" has certain specific rights, including the right "to be tried within a reasonable time" (section 11(b)) and "if finally acquitted of the offence, not to be tried for it again" (section 11(h)). The three challenges also indirectly invoked section 7, a more general provision, which provides that "[e]veryone has the right to life, liberty and security of the person and the right not to be deprived thereof except in accordance with the principles of fundamental justice." By its very terms, this is a right that contemplates a valid rights-denial, and, since a decision to extradite clearly involves a deprivation of liberty, the real issue of substance is whether the deprivation of liberty by way of extradition has taken place "in accordance with the principles of fundamental justice."

Schmidt concerned the requested extradition of a woman to the state of Ohio to face a state charge of child stealing when she had already been charged and acquitted of the federal crime of kidnapping. Under US law, the Ohio charge was considered a separate and distinct offence, since unlike kidnapping, it did not require proof of a ransom or reward, and so the federal acquittal did not bar prosecution on the state charge.[72] In Canada, however, *Schmidt* invoked in aid the protection against double jeopardy guaranteed by section 11(h) of the Charter, as well as section 7 of the Charter, given the impact of extradition on her liberty. Writing for the majority, La Forest J. dismissed the appeal, holding that while the Charter applied to extradition proceedings taking place in Canada, the specific guarantees in section 11 did not, since this section was never intended to govern criminal proceedings that would later take place outside Canada. La Forest J. bolstered this conclusion by noting that some of the specific section 11 rights, such as that guaranteeing the right to a jury trial, do not exist in countries with which Canada has extradition treaties.[73]

---

[70] *Argentina v. Mellino,* [1987] 1 S.C.R. 536 [*Mellino*].

[71] *United States of America v. Allard and Charette,* [1987] 1 S.C.R. 564 [*Allard*].

[72] See further, *Schmidt, supra* note 69 at 506–8.

[73] *Ibid.* at 519.

Section 7 was also held to be of no assistance, although La Forest J. did conclude that in some circumstances the manner in which the foreign state will deal with a fugitive on surrender might be such that the surrender would violate the principles of fundamental justice. He cited a European human rights case in support, even though Canada is not a party to this particular treaty regime.[74] Torture was given as the concrete example, but La Forest J. also added that

[s]ituations falling far short of this may well arise where the nature of the criminal procedures or penalties in a foreign country sufficiently shocks the conscience as to make a decision to surrender a fugitive for trial there one that breaches the principles of fundamental justice enshrined in section 7.[75]

A caution, however, was also added, with La Forest J. expressing concern about the impact on the effectiveness of extradition if Canada imposed its constitutional standards of judicial administration on a requesting state. He thus concluded that judicial intervention in extradition cases was to be "limited to cases of real substance"[76] and "compelling situations bearing in mind that the executive has the first responsibility in this area."[77] He also warned of the negative message such intervention would send with respect to the suspected motives and actions of both Canada and the requesting state.[78]

In dissent, Lamer and Wilson JJ. agreed with the disposition of the appeal[79] but took issue with La Forest J.'s conclusions concerning the applicability of section 11. For Lamer J., an extradition hearing was akin to a preliminary inquiry in a domestic criminal case and so section 11 should apply,[80] whereas Wilson J.'s point of

---

74 *Ibid.* at 522. The European case was *Altun v. Federal Republic of Germany*, 3 May 1983, No. 10308/83, (1984) 36 D.R. 236, (1984) 7 E.H.R.R. 154, decided by the now-abolished European Commission on Human Rights.

75 *Ibid.*

76 *Ibid.* at 523.

77 *Ibid.* at 526.

78 *Ibid.* at 526–27. Humanitarian considerations, however, eventually won out, with the Minister of Justice subsequently refusing to surrender Schmidt because she was seriously ill. La Forest, *supra* note 11 at 209.

79 But on the basis that the two offences were not the same. *Schmidt, supra* note 69 at 531 (Lamer J.) and 534 (Wilson J.).

80 *Ibid.* at 530.

departure was on the issue of the Charter's extraterritorial effect. In Wilson J.'s view, refusing to commit a fugitive for extradition because of a Charter violation did not give the Charter extraterritorial effect since the effect of the violation was felt in Canada, in the Canadian extradition proceedings, albeit with repercussions abroad.[81] She thus concluded "somewhat tentatively"[82] that the extraditee would have been entitled to the protection of section 11(h).

Similar positions were taken in the companion case of *Mellino*, concerning the extradition from Canada to Argentina of a man charged with the murder of his wife. Mellino, however, relied on section 11(b) of the Charter, guaranteeing protection against unreasonable delay, as well as the fundamental justice aspect of section 7. He based his claim on the fact that this was his second extradition proceeding, the first having been stayed some seventeen months earlier after Argentina had failed to supply the necessary documentation. Mellino's claim was initially successful, but, on appeal, the Supreme Court of Canada held, as it had done in *Schmidt*, that section 11 had no application to extradition proceedings[83] and further held that section 7 was of no assistance since there had been no clear abuse of process.[84] La Forest J., again writing for the majority, noted that "since an extradition is not a trial, new proceedings may be initiated on the same or new evidence."[85] He also noted that during the seventeen-month period before the second extradition request, Mellino was free and there was no evidence that he had been harassed or interfered with by officials or that his defence was prejudiced by the lapse of time.[86] Lamer and Wilson JJ. again reiterated their position in *Schmidt* that section 11 should apply to extradition proceedings,[87] but Wilson J. disagreed with Lamer J.'s position regarding the source of the delay. For Lamer J., the source was irrelevant whereas for Wilson J. any delay relied on under section 11(b) had to be caused by the Canadian, rather than the Argentinean, authorities.[88]

---

[81] *Ibid.* at 532–33.

[82] *Ibid.* at 535.

[83] *Mellino, supra* note 70 at 547.

[84] *Ibid.* at 550.

[85] *Ibid.*

[86] *Ibid.*

[87] *Ibid.* at 559 (Lamer J.) and 561 (Wilson J.).

[88] *Ibid.* at 560 (Lamer J.) and 562 (Wilson J.).

The third case of the 1987 trilogy also concerned the issue of delay. It arose within the context of a US request for the extradition of two former members of the Front de liberation du Québec (FLQ) who had allegedly hijacked an American airplane to Cuba in 1969.[89] Although the American authorities were made aware of the fugitives' presence in Canada in 1979, no extradition request was made until 1984, thereby providing the factual basis for the argument that this unexplained delay of five years infringed section 11(b) of the Charter. This argument was initially successful in the Québec courts but not on appeal to the Supreme Court of Canada, where a majority held that section 11(b) could not apply to the activities of a foreign government.[90] While the court appeared to accept that there had been an unreasonable delay attributable to the US authorities, it expressly presumed that the two accused would receive a fair trial in the United States, suggesting that the appropriate forum in which to raise the delay argument was before the US trial judge after surrender.[91]

As for the fundamental justice guarantee found in section 7 of the Charter, La Forest J. found no circumstances in the case to establish that the accused would face a situation that was "simply unacceptable."[92] He further explained that the discretion to surrender a fugitive rests primarily with the executive, and, while the courts have the right to review this decision by virtue of their responsibility to uphold the Constitution, they must exercise this role with caution in light of the international obligations involved.[93] In dissent, Lamer J. held that the delay of five years, if unexplained by either the Canadian or American authorities, was an "abuse of the extradition process taking place in Canada" and therefore a violation of the guarantee in section 7 that liberty will only be denied in accordance with the principles of fundamental justice.[94] Wilson J., in a separate opinion, agreed that an argument could be made

---

[89] After returning to Canada from Cuba in 1979, Allard and Charette served time in prison for their roles in the FLQ bombings of the 1960s, a terrorist campaign aimed at achieving Québec's independence. "U.S. Denied Extradition in FLQ Hijacking Case," *Toronto Star*, 30 June 1987, at A23.

[90] *Allard, supra* note 71 at 571 (La Forest J.).

[91] *Ibid.*

[92] *Ibid.* at 572.

[93] *Ibid.* at 572–73.

[94] *Ibid.* at 574.

under section 7 but reiterated her position that the delay had to be attributed to the Canadian authorities to establish a violation.[95]

Two years later, in the combined cases of *United States of America v. Cotroni* and *United States of America v. El Zein*,[96] the Supreme Court of Canada addressed a third ground for challenging extradition under the Charter — that of nationality. The cases arose within the context of an American request to prosecute two Canadian citizens for drug trafficking when all of the related activities had taken place in Canada.[97] In light of their Canadian nationality, the two accused invoked the protection of section 6(1) of the Charter, which provides that "[e]very citizen of Canada has the right to enter, remain in or leave Canada." But the view of a majority of the Supreme Court of Canada was that while extradition was certainly a *prima facie* infringement of a citizen's right to remain in Canada, it was redeemed under section 1 of the Charter as "a reasonable limit prescribed by law as can be demonstrably justified in a free and democratic society," given the need for international cooperation for the suppression of the drug trade, thus making *Cotroni* the first significant Supreme Court of Canada pronouncement on the application of the Charter's general limitation clause to extradition.[98]

---

95 *Ibid.* at 576. Allard and Charette would later avoid extradition to the United States by way of a unanimous ruling by the Court on the grounds that a fugitive may only be extradited for acts recognized in Canada as crimes at the time of commission. Hijacking was not recognized as an offence in Canada until 1972 and was not included in Canada's list of extraditable offences until 1976. *Allard (No. 2), supra* note 13. Canada's Justice Department responded by making a rare application to rehear the case, but this was unsuccessful.

96 *United States of America v. Cotroni; United States of America v. El Zein*, [1989] 1 S.C.R. 1469 [*Cotroni*].

97 One of the accused was the well-known mafia boss, Frank Cotroni, whose family is said to control several rackets in Québec and has been linked to the powerful Bonnanno crime family in New York. Cotroni had been convicted in the United States for drug smuggling in 1975, but was paroled after serving four years of a fifteen-year sentence. He was later convicted in Canada of manslaughter in relation to the 1981 killing of a former associate, turned police informant, in Montréal and was in prison at the time of the US indictment and extradition request. Cotroni is also famous as perhaps the only mobster to have authored a cookbook, the preface to which hints at his past. See F. Cotroni, *Cuisine des souvenirs et recettes* (Montréal: Trécarré, 2003).

98 A majority of the court had suggested in *obiter* in *Schmidt*, *supra* note 69 at 520, that the extradition of a Canadian citizen accused of committing crimes in another jurisdiction was not an unjustified infringement of section 6(1), relying on the Ontario Court of Appeal's decision in *Re Federal Republic of Germany and Rauca* (1983), 4 C.C.C. (3d) 385 at 404 (Ont. C.A.) [*Rauca*], but the *Cotroni*

The accepted test for the application of section 1 is that set down in *R. v. Oakes.*[99] This test requires that the impugned legislation have a sufficiently important objective so as to justify overriding a constitutionally protected right and, second, that the means for achieving that objective be proportional in three respects: namely, that there must be a rational connection between the measure and the objective; that the measure should infringe the right or freedom as little as possible; and that the effects of the measure on the right should be proportional to the attainment of the objective. According to La Forest J., again for the majority, the objectives of extradition were clearly of a pressing and substantial concern and warranted what he viewed as a limited interference with the section 6(1) right to remain. Canada's extradition practices had, in La Forest J.'s view, "been tailored as much as possible for the protection of the liberty of the individual."[100] But he was also of the view that "[a]s against this somewhat peripheral Charter infringement must be weighed the importance of the objectives sought by extradition [namely] the investigation, prosecution, repression and punishment of both national and transnational crimes for the protection of the public."[101]

As for the argument that extradition was unreasonable in circumstances where a prosecution could take place in Canada, La Forest J. took the view that there was a sufficient link with the United States in this case to warrant that country's conduct of the prosecution, opining that it was "often better that a crime be prosecuted where its harmful impact is felt and where the witnesses and the persons most interested in bringing the criminal to justice reside."[102] He also declined to create "a general exception [to extradition] for a Canadian citizen who could be charged in Canada" on the grounds that "it would, in [his] view, interfere unduly with the objectives of extradition,"[103] fearing problems would be caused by a lack of evidence. For La Forest J., the key consideration in such cases was whether due weight had been accorded to the section

---

case was the first to require the court to address the section 6(1) argument directly since the acts were committed in Canada and could be prosecuted in Canada.

[99] *R. v. Oakes*, [1986] 1 S.C.R. 103.

[100] *Cotroni, supra* note 96 at 1490.

[101] *Ibid.*

[102] *Ibid.* at 1488.

[103] *Ibid.* at 1494.

6(1) right, with no violation arising if the Canadian authorities had assured themselves that prosecution in Canada was not a realistic option.[104] Thus, the majority preserved the flexibility granted to the Department of Justice in deciding whether, when dealing with crimes with a cross-border dimension, to pursue a prosecution in Canada or to support one in the United States, with the latter usually leading to lengthier terms in prison.[105]

The two dissenting members of the court took issue with this approach. For Wilson J., extradition was a reasonable limit where a Canadian citizen committed an offence within the territorial boundaries of a foreign state (as in *Schmidt*), but it was not a reasonable limit where the wrongful conduct took place wholly within Canada and constituted an offence for which the citizen could be charged and prosecuted in Canada.[106] Sopinka J. concurred with Wilson J.'s conclusion and reasons but noted in a separate dissenting opinion his concern about the characterization of the infringement as peripheral in light of the fact that Canadian citizens could be extradited to countries where systems are radically different than Canada's and where the laws provide none of the traditional protections for persons charged.[107] La Forest J. had, however, addressed this argument with the view that "[i]t was not for this Court to pass upon the validity of the laws of other countries," although he did admit, as he had done in *Schmidt*, that there was a potential role for judicial review where an extraditee faced a penalty that would constitute cruel and unusual punishment.[108]

THE *KINDLER* AND *NG* EXTRADITIONS

Having apparently exhausted the opportunities for challenge provided by sections 6 and 11 of the Charter, individuals facing

---

[104] *Ibid.* at 1498.

[105] A ministerial order for Cotroni's surrender was subsequently made in 1990 to take effect upon the completion of his Canadian prison sentence. A year later, however, Cotroni consented to his extradition, satisfying US desires for an earlier trial given the effect of time on witness memory, on the condition that he be returned later to Canada: "Mob Figure Agrees to Extradition to U.S.," *Toronto Star*, 27 February 1991, at A14. Cotroni was later convicted for drug trafficking and served a Canadian prison sentence until 2002. "Mafia Boss Cotroni Linked to Bonnannos; Death Marks End of an Era in Canadian Crime," *Hamilton Spectator*, 18 August 2004, at A10.

[106] *Cotroni, supra* note 96 at 1509.

[107] *Ibid.* at 1517–18.

[108] *Ibid.* at 1501.

extradition turned to the protection afforded specifically by section 12 against harsh treatment or punishment[109] as a new means of challenging extradition decisions on human rights grounds. Section 7 again served to bolster these claims. The leading example of this type of challenge, and the court's reaction, can be found in the companion cases of *Kindler v. Canada (Minister of Justice)*[110] and *Reference re Ng Extradition*,[111] where the Supreme Court of Canada was asked to determine whether the extradition of two fugitives to the United States to face the death penalty violated sections 12 or 7 of the Charter. By a narrow margin, the court held that the decision to extradite infringed neither the protection against cruel and unusual punishment nor the guarantee of fundamental justice and dismissed the appeals.[112]

The factual circumstances of *Kindler* and *Ng* are similar. In *Kindler,* the United States sought the extradition of an American citizen who had been convicted of first-degree murder, conspiracy to commit murder, and kidnapping in Pennsylvania, after killing an accomplice in a burglary who had planned to testify against him. The jury had made a recommendation in favour of the death penalty, but Kindler had escaped to Canada before its formal imposition. In *Ng,* the United States sought the extradition of a British subject, but American resident, who had been charged in California with multiple counts of murder that, upon conviction, would likely result in the imposition of the death penalty. Ng, however, had escaped from custody before trial and so, unlike Kindler, still enjoyed the presumption of innocence. A crucial element in both cases was

---

109 Section 12 of the Charter provides that "[e]veryone has the right not to be subjected to any cruel and unusual treatment or punishment."

110 *Kindler v. Canada (Minister of Justice),* [1991] 2 S.C.R. 779 [*Kindler*].

111 *Reference re Ng Extradition,* [1991] 2 S.C.R. 858 [*Ng*]. The decision in *Ng,* however, is essentially rendered in *Kindler, supra* note 110.

112 For commentary, see A. Manson, "*Kindler* and the Courage to Deal with American Convictions" (1992) 8 Crim. R. (4th) 68; J.W. O'Reilly, "Case Comment: *Ng* and *Kindler*" (1992) 37 McGill L.J. 873; J. Pak, "Canadian Extradition and the Death Penalty: Seeking a Constitutional Assurance of Life" (1993) 26 Cornell Int'l L. J. 239; W.A. Schabas, "*Kindler* and *Ng*: Our Supreme Magistrates Take a Frightening Step into the Court of Public Opinion" (1991) 51 Rev. du B. 673; and A.J. Spencer, "Fugitive Rights: The Role of the Charter in Extradition Cases" (1993) 51 U. of T. Fac. of L. Rev. 54. See also S.A. Williams, "Extradition and the Death Penalty Exception in Canada: Resolving the *Ng* and *Kindler* Cases" (1991) 13 Loyola L.A. Int'l & Comp. L.J. 799 (written before the judgments of the Supreme Court).

Article 6 of the Canada-US Extradition Treaty, which gives Canada the authority to make extradition conditional on the receipt of assurances from the United States that the death penalty shall not be imposed or, if imposed, shall not be executed.[113] However, in both *Kindler* and *Ng*, the Minister of Justice declined to exercise this option, ordering surrender without ever seeking an assurance and prompting challenges on Charter grounds.

In a close decision, comprised of four separate opinions, the Supreme Court of Canada dismissed Kindler's (and thus Ng's) challenge to extradition. La Forest and McLachlin JJ. wrote the majority opinions, each receiving the concurrence of L'Heureux-Dubé and Gonthier JJ., while Sopinka and Cory JJ. wrote the dissents, both joined by Lamer C.J.C. There is little difference between the majority opinions of McLachlin and La Forest JJ., with both holding that the minister's decision to extradite without first seeking a death penalty assurance did not infringe the Charter.

In regard to section 12, both McLachlin and La Forest JJ. held that the provision was inapplicable to extradition matters since the punishment, even if cruel and unusual, would be imposed by a foreign state, not by Canada.[114] According to McLachlin J., "to apply section 12 directly to the act of surrender to a foreign country where a particular penalty may be imposed, is to overshoot the purpose of the guarantee and to cast the net of the Charter broadly in extraterritorial waters."[115] Section 12 was thus held to be inapplicable to extradition, although the majority did accept that it could have an indirect effect as an underlying value or factor of influence in determining whether extradition infringed the fundamental justice guarantee in section 7.[116]

The real question was therefore whether extradition without assurances violated section 7. Using the tests developed in *Schmidt* and *Allard* in 1987, the majority found no violation since it was not clear that the extradition of a fugitive to face the death penalty would shock the conscience of Canadians or lead Canadians to conclude that the situation faced by the fugitive was simply unacceptable,[117] notwithstanding the fact that Canada was a *de facto*

---

113 Canada-US Extradition Treaty, *supra* note 51.

114 *Kindler, supra* note 110 at 831 (La Forest J.) and 846 (McLachlin J.).

115 *Ibid.* at 846.

116 *Ibid.* at 831 (La Forest J.) and 847 (McLachlin J.).

117 *Ibid.* at 832 (La Forest J.) and 852 (McLachlin J.).

abolition state.[118] In support of this conclusion, McLachlin J. noted that there was no clear consensus in Canada that capital punishment was morally abhorrent or absolutely unacceptable[119] and that public opinion polls showed considerable support for the return of the death penalty for certain offences.[120] She also pointed out that both fugitives were being sought for crimes involving brutal murders by a requesting state whose legal system was the product of a democratic government and included a bill of rights.[121] She also stated expressly that extradition without assurances was "not out of step with the international community," although on this point, she erroneously equated the standing of a European Commission decision with that of a binding judgment of the European Court of Human Rights.[122]

McLachlin J. did, however, acknowledge that in some cases the unconditional surrender of a fugitive to face the death penalty might sufficiently shock the national conscience so as to require the minister to seek an assurance that the penalty will not be imposed. But she also warned that if such assurances were to become mandatory in every case, Canada might become a safe haven for America's criminals seeking to avoid the death penalty.[123] She failed to note, however, that Canada would only become a safe haven if the United States refused to give an assurance — a situation contrary to a long

---

[118] Canada carried out its last execution in 1962 and abolished the death penalty for most offences in 1976, although the penalty remained potentially available for military offences until 1998. See Criminal Law Amendment Act (No. 2), S.C. 1976, c. 105 and An Act to Amend the National Defence Act, S.C. 1998, c. 35, ss. 24–28. On the history of the death penalty in Canada, see R. Harvie and H. Foster, "Shocks and Balances: *United States v. Burns*, Fine-Tuning Canadian Extradition Law and the Future of the Death Penalty" (2005) 40 Gonzaga L.R. 293 at 308–12.

[119] Both McLachlin and La Forest JJ. drew attention to the fact that only four years prior, a resolution to reinstate capital punishment had narrowly escaped adoption in the House of Commons. *Kindler, supra* note 110 at 852 and 832.

[120] *Ibid.* at 852.

[121] *Ibid.*

[122] After referring to the commission's 1984 decision in *Kirkwood v. United Kingdom*, No. 10479/83, (1984) 37 C.D. 158 and the court's 1989 judgment in *Soering, supra* note 7, McLachlin J. stated: "The fact that two tribunals reached different views on not dissimilar cases illustrates the complexity of the issue and supports the view that courts should not lightly interfere with executive decisions on extradition matters." *Kindler, supra* note 110 at 856. This statement does not acknowledge that commission decisions could be appealed to the court.

[123] *Ibid.* at 852–53.

history of past cases involving European,[124] South American,[125] and even Canadian[126] requests for assurances. Ten years later, the Supreme Court of Canada would unanimously accept that "[a] state seeking to prosecute a serious crime is unlikely to decide that if it cannot impose the ultimate sanction — the death penalty — it will not prosecute at all."[127]

In his separate opinion, La Forest J. agreed with McLachlin J. but laid greater emphasis on the brutality of Kindler's and Ng's crimes. According to La Forest J., the issue to be determined was whether it shocked the conscience to surrender individuals who have been charged with the "worst sort of crimes" to face capital prosecution in the United States.[128] He thus concluded that absent mitigating circumstances, unconditional extradition for the "worst sort of crimes" did not offend the Charter. As for the death penalty *per se*, La Forest J. not only acknowledged the trend towards its abolition but also noted the absence of an international norm against its use and invoked the non-binding UN Model Treaty on Extradition as support for a state retaining discretion in death penalty extradition cases.[129]

For the dissenting members of the court, however, this case was about the death penalty, which all three viewed as cruel and unusual and thus contrary to section 12. Sopinka J., however, preferred to rest his judgment on section 7, holding that extradition without first seeking assurances was tantamount to Canadian acceptance of a punishment that, if carried out in Canada, would clearly violate the Charter,[130] while Cory J. decided the case directly under section

---

[124] After losing on this issue in *Soering, supra* note 7, the United States responded with the provision of an assurance, as confirmed in R.B. Lillich, "The Soering Case" (1991) 85 Am. J. Int'l L. 128 at 141. See also Schabas, *supra* note 112 at 678. The court has since recognized that European states routinely request assurances, albeit with the suggestion that this was a new practice. *Burns, supra* note 10 at para. 138.

[125] A practice long established. See J.S. Reeves, "Extradition Treaties and the Death Penalty" (1924) 18 Am. J. Int'l L. 298.

[126] "Release of Materials Concerning the Extradition of Leonard Peltier," *supra* note 55. These materials, released in 1999, confirm that Canada in 1976 required a death penalty assurance to secure Peltier's extradition.

[127] *Burns, supra* note 10 at para. 138.

[128] *Kindler, supra* note 110 at 835–36.

[129] *Ibid.* at 834.

[130] *Ibid.* at 792.

1 2.[131] Marshalling support from various international developments in the struggle to abolish the death penalty, Cory J. took the view that any government that extradited a fugitive to face what he viewed as a penalty "repugnant to any belief in the importance of human dignity"[132] would have to accept responsibility for the ultimate consequence of that extradition. To argue that the punishment was inflicted by a foreign state, and thus not Canada's action, was in his view "an indefensible abdication of moral responsibility,"[133] and he concluded by holding that the violation could not be justified as reasonable under section 1, viewing the "safe haven" rationale as an *in terrorem* argument lacking any evidentiary basis.[134]

Within hours of the court's judgment, the government of Canada responded positively[135] and swiftly, sending both Kindler and Ng to the United States that very day[136] and without heed to a request from the UN Human Rights Committee to stay the extraditions pending the resolution of international proceedings.[137] Canada would later be found in violation of its international human rights treaty obligations in the *Ng* case, but not in *Kindler*,[138] because the method of execution used in California at the time was poisonous gas.[139] Gas causes a great deal of suffering, and, thus,

---

[131] *Ibid.* at 824.

[132] *Ibid.* at 815.

[133] *Ibid.* at 824.

[134] *Ibid.* at 825.

[135] "When the decision was announced in the House of Commons, members of … [the] government applauded vigorously." D. Marain, "Canada Sends Accused Killer Ng Back to US," *Los Angeles Times*, 27 September 1991, at A3. This is hardly surprising given the government's receipt of over 100,000 letters from Canadians, urging Ng's extradition. A. Sachs, "A Fate Better Than Death," *Time*, 4 March 1991, at 52.

[136] Marain, *supra* note 135; K. Bishop, "Canada Extradites Suspect in California Slayings," *New York Times*, 27 September 1991, at A16; and "Two American Fugitives Whisked out of Canada," *The Record (Kitchener-Waterloo)*, 27 September 1991, at A3.

[137] See further J. Harrington, "Punting Terrorists, Assassins and Other Undesirables: Canada, the Human Rights Committee and Requests for Interim Measures of Protection" (2003) 48 McGill L.J. 55 at 84.

[138] Kindler would, however, later successfully challenge his death sentence in the Philadelphia courts on the grounds that the jury instructions had been flawed. *Kindler v. Horn*, 291 F.Supp. 2d 323 (E.D.Pa. 2003).

[139] *Kindler v. Canada*, UN Doc. CCPR/48/D/470/1991 (views adopted 30 July 1993), later published in *Report of the Human Rights Committee*, UN Doc.

the committee was of the view with respect to *Ng* that Canada was in violation for extraditing without assurances in circumstances where it was reasonably foreseeable that Ng would be subjected to cruel and unusual treatment on surrender.[140] However, Canada, having already extradited Ng, was in no position to remedy the violation, and the committee's views on Canadian extradition law, albeit non-binding, have escaped even a mention in all subsequent extradition decisions of the Supreme Court of Canada, notwithstanding the attention brought to them by an unsuccessful application for leave to appeal on the very ground of Canada's violation in *Ng* at the international level.[141] The international proceedings in *Kindler* and *Ng* have not, however, been overlooked elsewhere, with *both* the domestic and international decisions being mentioned by the South African Constitutional Court in its landmark judgment on the constitutionality of the death penalty.[142]

SHORT SHRIFT FROM THE SUPREMES: THE SECOND EXTRADITION
TRILOGY

Five years later, on 19 March 1996, a nine-member Supreme Court of Canada released a second trilogy on Charter challenges

---

A/48/40 (1993), vol. II, annex XII.U, 98 I.L.R. 426, (1993) 14 H.R.L.J. 307 and (1994) 1 I.H.R.R. 98 [*Kindler*]; and *Ng v. Canada*, UN Doc. CCPR/49/D/469/1991 (views adopted 5 November 1993), later published in *Report of the Human Rights Committee*, UN Doc. A/49/40 (1994), vol. II, annex IX.CC, 98 I.L.R. 479, (1994) 15 H.R.L.J. 149 and (1994) 1 I.H.R.R. 161 [*Ng*]. The views in *Kindler* have since been overturned by the Human Rights Committee in *Judge v. Canada*, UN Doc. CCPR/C/78/D/829/1998 (views adopted 5 August 2003), later published in *Report of the Human Rights Committee*, UN Doc. A/58/40 (2003), vol. II, annex V.G, (2003) 42 I.L.M. 1214 and (2004) 11 I.H.R.R. 125.

140 After numerous delays and a change in venue as a result of the pre-trial publicity, Ng was convicted of eleven counts of first-degree murder in 1999 and sentenced to death. "Killer Charles Ng Sentenced to Death," *Los Angeles Times*, 1 July 1999, at A3. He currently resides on death row in San Quentin State Prison awaiting the assignment of counsel to pursue an appeal of his sentence. D.J. Saunders, "Justice Delayed (and Delayed and Delayed)," *San Francisco Chronicle*, 2 November 2004, at B9.

141 *R. v. Hanson*, [1994] O.J. No. 102 (C.A.), leave to appeal denied, [1994] S.C.C.A. No. 112.

142 *State v. Makwanyane* (1995), (3) S.A. 391 (C.C.). See also the discussion of both sets of proceedings in S.A. Williams, "Extradition from Canada since the Charter of Rights," in J. Cameron, ed., *The Charter's Impact on the Criminal Justice System* (Scarborough: Carswell, 1996), 387.

to extradition,[143] with each case concerning the extradition of alleged drug offenders to the United States to face mandatory minimum prison sentences much harsher than those imposed in Canada.[144] The trilogy consisted of three surprisingly short one-sentence unanimous judgments with no discussion of the issues — a manner of delivery that presumably must have been intended to send a message about the high threshold required to overturn an extradition decision. The brevity is astonishing in light of the division of opinion in the courts below, involving three of Canada's most respected appellate courts and which at the very least suggested that there was an argument to be addressed.[145] But, in two of the three cases, the Supreme Court simply dismissed the appeals for the reasons given by the majority of the court below, while in the third, the court set aside the appeal court's decision in order to restore the order for extradition. The discussion begins with the third case, *United States of America v. Jamieson*,[146] where for the first time in Canada, a provincial appeal court had denied a request for extradition on the grounds that it would amount to cruel and unusual treatment.[147]

Jamieson concerned the requested surrender of a young first-time offender who had sold a small amount of cocaine to an undercover police officer in Michigan and now faced the prospect of a twenty-

---

[143] *United States of America v. Ross*, [1996] 1 S.C.R. 469 [*Ross*]; *United States of America v. Whitley*, [1996] 1 S.C.R. 46 [*Whitley*]; and *United States of America v. Jamieson*, [1996] 1 S.C.R. 465 [*Jamieson*].

[144] Mandatory minimum sentences are also problematic on human rights grounds because they provide no opportunity for judicial consideration of any mitigating circumstances. The Summer/Fall 2001 issue of volume 39 of the *Osgoode Hall Law Journal* is devoted to the topic of mandatory minimum sentencing, as is issue 2 of volume 18 (2004) of the *Notre Dame Journal of Law, Ethics and Public Policy*. See also J. Harrington, "The Challenge to the Mandatory Death Penalty in the Commonwealth Caribbean" (2004) 98 Am. J. Int'l L. 126.

[145] The Supreme Court of Canada did not even call on lawyers for the Department of Justice to present arguments. S. Bindman, "Fugitives Face Long Terms," *Hamilton Spectator*, 17 June 1996, at A2.

[146] For comment, see J.D. McCann, "The Role of the Canadian Charter in Canadian Extradition Law" (1997) 30 Cornell Int'l L.J. 139.

[147] The same appellate court had previously denied an extradition request on grounds of Canadian nationality in *Cotroni, supra* note 96. For comment, see A. Costi, "Le refus d'extrader dans les affiares 'Zein' et 'Cotroni': Decision deraisonable ou violation des obligations internationals du Canada?" (1986) 20 Revue Juridique Themis 485.

year minimum sentence[148] — a sentence viewed by the *Washington Post* as "the toughest of its kind in the United States."[149] Such a sentence, it was argued, was so excessive and disproportionate from a Canadian perspective that it justified judicial intervention — an argument with which the Québec Court of Appeal, by two votes to one, initially disagreed,[150] but later accepted, again by two votes to one, on the basis that the decision to surrender violated Jamieson's rights under section 7 of the Charter, as seen in light of the protection against cruel and unusual treatment in section 12, since section 12 could not be applied directly.[151] For the majority, Fish J.A., then of the Québec Court of Appeal and now of the Supreme Court of Canada, held that the situation faced by Jamieson was so "shocking and fundamentally unacceptable to our society" that it met the tests established in *Schmidt* and *Kindler*,[152] given that such a sentence, if imposed in Canada, would violate the Charter, especially section 12.[153] Although he recognized that the Supreme Court of Canada had found section 12 to have no application in cases of extradition, Fish J.A. justified his use of section 12's jurisprudence as a relevant consideration in the application of section 7,[154] concluding that in this case, the decision to surrender offended "the Canadian sense of what is fair, right and just, even bearing in mind the foreign justice system and considerations of comity and security, and according due latitude to balance the conflicting considerations."[155]

---

148 Michigan case law made it clear that Jamieson stood no realistic chance of establishing substantial and compelling reasons for departing from the minimum sentence. *Jamieson (No. 2)*, *supra* note 59 at 280–83 (Fish J.A.); and *Jamieson (No. 1)*, *supra* note 59 at 472–73 (Proulx J.A.).

149 A. Swardson, "Québec Court Finds a U.S. Drug Sentence Shocking to Canadian Sensibility," *Washington Post*, 2 September 1994, at A13.

150 See *Jamieson (No. 1)*, *supra* note 59, leave to appeal denied, (1992) 73 C.C.C. (3d) vi (S.C.C.).

151 See *Jamieson (No. 2)*, *supra* note 59. For comment, see J. Leeson, "Refusal to Extradite: An Examination of Canada's Indictment of the American Legal System" (1996) 25 Georgia J. Int'l & Comp. L. 641.

152 *Ibid.* at 278.

153 *Ibid.* The Supreme Court of Canada had ruled in *Smith v. R.*, [1987] 1 S.C.R. 1045, that a mandatory minimum sentence of seven years for a narcotics offence was excessive and a violation of the constitutional guarantee to protection against cruel and unusual punishment.

154 *Ibid.* at 278–79.

155 *Ibid.* at 280, applying *Kindler*, *supra* note 110.

In dissent, Baudouin J.A. held that the decision to surrender was not unacceptable to the Canadian conscience. Although he put on record his view of the Michigan law as being "severe, even very severe, and ... the reflection of a repressive philosophy which would probably be considered outdated in our country,"[156] Baudouin J.A. also accepted expressly that the law had been enacted by democratically elected representatives to deal with a serious drug problem.[157] He also heeded the caution expressed by McLachlin J. in *Kindler* that a court should be extremely circumspect in reviewing decisions of the executive in matters of extradition, given the executive's pre-eminent position in foreign relations.[158] These reasons were later endorsed by the Supreme Court of Canada, which overturned the majority's decision "essentially for the reasons of Baudouin J.A."[159] and restored the order in favour of Jamieson's surrender. Although it was not stated, this decision echoed that of La Forest J. in *Cotroni* who had dismissed an earlier minimum-sentencing argument on the grounds that "[i]t is not for this Court to pass upon the validity of the laws of other countries."[160]

Accompanying the *Jamieson* decision was the decision in *Ross v. United States of America*,[161] where again the Supreme Court of Canada was faced with a split decision from the court below, albeit that this time the majority had opted for extradition. On the facts, however, Ross had an arguable case of injustice. A Canadian citizen, Ross had jumped bail in Florida after learning that his associates in a cocaine buy had, through plea arrangements, received reduced sentences in return for implicating him. This left Ross with no opportunity to make a similar bargain and he fled to Canada where he was eventually found and committed for extradition. In his submissions to the Minister of Justice, Ross offered to plead guilty to charges in Canada in relation to his conduct in Florida, knowing that the likely sentence in Canada was five years rather than the mandatory mini-

---

156 *Ibid.* at 268.

157 *Ibid.* at 269.

158 *Ibid.* at 268.

159 *Jamieson, supra* note 143. This decision has since been used to deny an extradition challenge where the extraditee faced "an admittedly harsh sentence" in the United States of two consecutive sentences of sixty years. *Gwynne v. Canada (Minister of Justice)* (1998), 103 B.C.A.C. 1 at para. 28, leave to appeal denied, [1998] 1 S.C.R. ix [*Gwynne*].

160 *Cotroni, supra* note 96 at 1501.

161 *Ross, supra* note 143.

mum of fifteen years under Florida law.[162] This offer was, however, rejected by the minister, and an order for surrender was issued.

On appeal, Ross challenged the constitutionality of the surrender order on two distinct grounds. The first related to the minimum sentence of fifteen years, which Ross argued was "simply unacceptable" given that his co-conspirators received a five-year and a suspended sentence respectively for working with the authorities to facilitate his arrest and conviction. The second ground of attack was that as a Canadian, Ross had a right to remain in Canada under the Charter and any infringement of this right had to be justified.

Taylor J.A., with the concurrence of Finch J.A., for the majority, dismissed Ross's appeal on both grounds. In his view, there was nothing in the past case law to suggest that the imposition of a more severe punishment in a requesting state would by itself render extradition as contrary to the Charter.[163] Noting that the consequences of drug trafficking in Florida were more serious than in Canada and that Ross had voluntarily gone to Florida, thus submitting himself to its laws, Taylor J.A. concluded that Ross did not face a situation that was simply unacceptable,[164] nor did he find the situation unconscionable or shocking so as to constitute an unjustifiable breach of Ross's citizenship rights under section 6.[165] The fact that Ross would receive a greater sentence than his co-accused was disregarded since Canada also engaged in a practice of reducing sentences for cooperants, and, on the issue of Ross's offer to plead guilty to charges in Canada, Taylor J.A. concluded that this was not a good reason for refusing extradition since the only justification proffered was to enable Ross to secure a less severe punishment.[166]

Finch J.A. agreed but used his opinion to record his criticism of the tests enunciated in *Allard, Schmidt,* and *Kindler,* noting how hard it was to assess "such imponderable concepts as the public conscience, the Canadian conscience, or the values of the Canadian community."[167] It seemed "to come down to a question of whether

---

162 *Ross v. United States of America* (1994), 93 C.C.C. (3d) 500 (B.C.C.A.) at 515 (Lambert J.A.) and 533 (Taylor J.A.). Unlike in *Jamieson,* evidence was led to suggest that the sentence could be reduced by satisfactory performance in prison.

163 *Ibid.* at 534.

164 *Ibid.*

165 *Ibid.* at 535.

166 *Ibid.* at 536.

167 *Ibid.* at 537.

the judges are shocked, outraged, or find unacceptable the foreign law or sentencing regime,"[168] and, with reference to the division of judicial opinion in *Jamieson*, Finch J.A. took the view that a foreign law could not be found shocking, outrageous, or simply unacceptable when judges hold contrary, but reasoned, views on such a question.[169] He thus suggested that a clear case leading to unanimity, "or something very close to it,"[170] was required to establish a violation of section 7, with torture again being the only clear example.

In dissent, Lambert J.A. held that the surrender of a Canadian citizen who was prepared to plead guilty in Canada to offences as serious as those in Florida and arising from the same set of facts was simply unacceptable, given the minimum sentence to which he would be exposed. In his view, the fifteen-year sentence in Florida, like the twenty-year sentence at issue in *Jamieson*, was neither proportionate by Canadian standards nor fair given the much-reduced sentences of Ross's co-conspirators.[171] However, for Lambert J.A., the crucial element in this case was Ross's Canadian citizenship. Applying the test set down in *Cotroni*, Lambert J.A. concluded that prosecution in Canada was a realistic option, particularly since Ross was prepared to plead guilty,[172] and, therefore, there was no justification for overriding Ross's right as a citizen to remain in Canada. The Supreme Court of Canada, however, disagreed and in a one-line judgment dismissed Ross's appeal, "substantially for the reasons of Taylor J.A."[173]

The third case of the trilogy, *Whitley v. United States of America*,[174] also concerned the surrender of an alleged drug trafficker to the United States, but with a twist. In this case, Canada had first charged the accused and then withdrawn the charges in order to facilitate his prosecution in the United States, presumably knowing that the likely punishment was a fifty-year jail term, given the American use of mandatory minimum sentences. Whitley was allegedly the key actor in an organized attempt to import 1,100 pounds of marihuana through the United States and into Canada. In challenging

168 *Ibid.* at 538.

169 *Ibid.*

170 *Ibid.* at 539.

171 *Ibid.* at 516.

172 *Ibid.* at 524.

173 *Ross, supra* note 143.

174 *Whitley, supra* note 143.

the validity of his extradition, Whitley argued that his surrender would violate both his right, as a citizen, to remain in Canada and his right to fundamental justice. The Ontario Court of Appeal, however, unanimously disagreed, holding that Whitley's surrender would not unreasonably infringe section 6(1) of the Charter since there were no grounds to suggest that the Minister of Justice had erred in law, disregarded relevant facts, or reached a decision that was unreasonable.[175] While Laskin J.A., for the court, acknowledged that some of the factors — such as Whitley's nationality, the intended country for distribution, and the nationality of the police force directing the investigation — favoured a Canadian prosecution, he also noted that other factors — such as the availability and location of the evidence, and the jurisdiction with the most comprehensive case — favoured extradition.[176] Seeing the case as largely a challenge to the exercise of prosecutorial discretion, a right rarely interfered with by Canadian courts,[177] Laskin J.A. gave no significance to the withdrawal of the Canadian charge, given the reasonableness of the conclusion that prosecution in the United States would be a more effective option. He also noted that Whitley's position was similar to that of the appellants in *Cotroni* where the Supreme Court of Canada had found no Charter violation.[178]

As for the section 7 argument, in which Whitley tried to make use of the comparably "soft" nature of marihuana under Canadian law, Laskin J.A. paid heed to the caution in *Kindler* that extradition should only be refused where the penalties in the foreign state shocked the conscience, were simply unacceptable, or were fundamentally unjust, and concluded that the minister had applied the correct principles in rejecting Whitley's argument against surrender. According to Laskin J.A.,

the allegations, if proven, paint a picture of the appellant supervising a large and a sophisticated international operation, in which he stood to make a substantial profit. The appellant has an extensive prior criminal

---

175 *Whitley v. United States of America* (1994), 20 O.R. (3d) 794 (C.A.) at 811 [*Whitley 1994*].

176 *Ibid.*

177 Although in criminal cases, the courts have a residual discretion to remedy an abuse of the court's process this discretion is invoked in only "the clearest of cases," defined to amount "to conduct which shocks the conscience of the community and is so detrimental to the proper administration of justice that it warrants judicial intervention." *R. v. Power*, [1994] 1 S.C.R. 601 at 615–16 [*Power*].

178 *Whitley 1994*, *supra* note 175 at 812.

record including convictions for trafficking and possession for the purpose of trafficking. I do not think in the light of these considerations, that the sentences the appellant faces in the [United States] are so grossly disproportionate to the gravity of the alleged offences that they can be said to be fundamentally unjust.[179]

Laskin also dismissed any comparison to *Jamieson* on the basis that Whitley was not a young first-time offender who was trafficking a small amount.[180] Whitley's subsequent appeal to the Supreme Court of Canada was equally unsuccessful, with the entire judgment of the court being: "The appeal is dismissed, substantially for the reasons of Laskin J.A."[181]

Yet, despite such short shrift from the Supreme Court of Canada, the court felt inclined to release another extradition judgment only a few weeks later, emphasizing its reluctance to interfere with the Canadian strategy of cooperation with US authorities in the prosecution of cross-border drug crimes.[182] The judgment is known as *United States of America v. Leon*,[183] and it concerned a challenge to extradition on the basis of sections 6(1) and 7 of the Charter, again arising from the withdrawal of charges in Canada to facilitate a Canadian citizen's extradition to the United States to stand trial on the same charges but with much harsher penalties given the American use of mandatory minimum sentences. On appeal, however, Leon also alleged that the Canadian prosecutorial authorities had threatened him with extradition if he did not plead guilty to the Canadian charge,[184] thus making, in Leon's view, his extradition fundamentally unjust. The Ontario Court of Appeal, however, readily dismissed this claim, holding that the suggestion "amounted to no more than a plea bargaining offer" and did not connote the degree of improper notice or bad faith that would violate the conscience of the community.[185] The court also easily dismissed Leon's right-to-remain claim, reading the facts as showing that Leon had

---

[179] *Ibid.* at 813.

[180] *Ibid.*

[181] *Whitley, supra* note 143.

[182] Within three months of the March 1996 rulings, six fugitives had been surrendered and another forty were being sought from Canada who faced mandatory minimum sentences in the United States. Bindman, *supra* note 145.

[183] *United States of America v. Leon*, [1996] 1 S.C.R. 888 [*Leon*].

[184] *United States of America v. Leon* (1995), 96 C.C.C. (3d) 568 (Ont. C.A.) at 574.

[185] *Ibid.* at 575.

committed discrete and separate acts of misconduct in both the United States and Canada,[186] and thus prosecution in one would not bar prosecution in the other. Leon's case was thus distinguishable from *Cotroni* where the same conduct constituted the criminal offence in both jurisdictions, which, in turn, raised the Charter obligation to consider whether prosecution in Canada was not a realistic option.[187]

On further appeal to the Supreme Court of Canada, the sole issue for consideration was whether the conduct of the Canadian prosecutorial authorities was so egregious that the extradition should be stayed.[188] Having found no misconduct or bad faith on the part of the Canadian authorities, the Supreme Court of Canada dismissed the appeal, characterizing the suggestion to plead guilty as "no more than an offer that may have been made with the best of intentions based upon the longer sentence the appellant might face in the United States."[189] In doing so, the court in essence confirmed the flexibility it had granted the Canadian government since *Cotroni* as between pursuing a Canadian prosecution or cooperating with one in the United States.

2001: THE TURNING POINT FOR CHARTER CHALLENGES TO EXTRADITION

In the 1980s and 1990s, the Supreme Court of Canada maintained such a high threshold for challenging a surrender order under the Charter that no challenge before it was ever successful. In 2001, however, the court's jurisprudence reached a turning point, marked by the decision in *Burns v. United States of America*[190] concerning the extradition of two Canadian citizens to stand trial for murder in Washington state. Washington state is a death penalty jurisdiction, but, as with *Kindler* and *Ng*, the Canadian Minister of Justice chose not to seek an assurance with respect to the death penalty and ordered the accused to be surrendered.[191] This order was then challenged on the grounds that the unconditional extradition of two

---

186 *Ibid.*

187 *Cotroni, supra* note 96 at 1498.

188 *Leon, supra* note 183 at para. 1.

189 *Ibid.* at para. 10.

190 *Burns, supra* note 10.

191 Canada, Department of Justice, "Extradition of Atif Ahmad Rafay and Glen Sebastian Burns to the United States of America," press release (12 July 1996).

Canadian citizens, aged eighteen at the time of the murders, to face the death penalty would shock the Canadian conscience and thus violate sections 6(1), 7, and 12 of the Charter.

The British Columbia Court of Appeal, by two votes to one, appeared to agree, directing the minister to seek assurances on the basis that a Canadian citizen, if forced out of the country and put to death, could not exercise his right of return guaranteed by section 6(1) of the Charter.[192] Thus, a nationality exception to extradition to face the death penalty was carved out. Donald J.A. had recognized the precedential value of *Kindler* but held that a citizen was entitled to consider his own country a safe haven.[193] While weak in reasoning,[194] but understandable given the foreclosure of alternatives by binding precedent, the Court of Appeal's decision likely served to gain a foothold in the docket of the Supreme Court of Canada, and, after some delay including a rehearing after changes in the court's membership,[195] a final decision was released on 15 February 2001.

In a unanimous decision, written by "the court" ten years after *Kindler* and *Ng*, the Supreme Court of Canada held that the unconditional extradition of the two accused to face the death penalty would violate the Charter's guarantee of fundamental justice, thus agreeing with the result but not the reasons of the court below. The court recognized its own "historically exercised restraint in the judicial review of extradition decisions"[196] as well as the need to be "extremely circumspect" to avoid undue interference with the executive.[197] It also confirmed that it is generally for the minister, and not the court, to balance on a case-by-case basis the various

---

[192] *United States of America v. Burns* (1997), 116 C.C.C. (3d) 524 (B.C.C.A.) at para. 31.

[193] *Ibid.* at para. 54.

[194] After all, a life sentence without parole would also frustrate a citizen's right of return to Canada.

[195] The government sought leave to appeal the decision in 1997 because of a concern that a requirement to seek assurances "may serve as a serious limitation on ministerial discretion." Canada, Department of Justice, "Attorney General of Canada Seeks Leave to Appeal to the Supreme Court of Canada," press release (18 July 1997). The first hearing of the appeal took place on 22 March 1999. A rehearing took place on 23 May 2000, following the retirements of Lamer C.J.C. and Cory J. and the appointments of Arbour and Le Bel JJ.

[196] *Burns, supra* note 10 at para. 36.

[197] *Ibid.*

factors for and against extradition with assurances,[198] but then held that "such assurances are constitutionally required in all but exceptional cases"[199] (without defining what constitutes an exceptional case). "The availability of the death penalty, like death itself, open[ed] up a different dimension,"[200] with the judgment's opening reference and subsequent discussion of several wrongful convictions in Canada suggesting that the court was especially concerned with death's irreversible nature and the possibility of error. "An accelerating concern about potential wrongful convictions" is later identified in the judgment as "a factor of increased weight."[201]

But the decision in *Kindler* posed a problem, especially to a court so reluctant to overturn its own jurisprudence that it still claimed that Kindler was rightly extradited.[202] How does one draw a distinction between the accused in *Burns,* who murdered family members for money, and Kindler, a man who murdered his accomplice and witness to his crime? The court, however, expressly affirmed the correctness of *Kindler* and *Ng,* recognizing that the "balancing approach" adopted therein allowed for the possible existence of circumstances that could constitutionally vitiate an order for surrender.[203] Such circumstances might include "the youth, insanity, mental retardation or pregnancy of a fugitive"[204] or when "the punishment is so extreme that it ... overwhelms the rest of the analysis,"[205] although the court was careful to emphasize the need to proceed case by case. With respect to the death penalty, however, the court now found it "difficult to avoid the conclusion that in the Canadian view of fundamental justice, capital punishment is unjust,"[206] noting the existence of an international trend towards its

---

[198] *Ibid.* at para. 8.

[199] *Ibid.* at para. 8 and again at para. 65.

[200] *Ibid.* at para. 38.

[201] *Ibid.* at para. 95 ff.

[202] *Ibid.* at para. 144. Many, however, view *Burns* as effectively overruling *Kindler* (see, for example, R. Haigh, "A *Kindler,* Gentler Supreme Court? The Case of *Burns* and the Need for a Principled Approach to Overruling" (2001) 14 S.C.L.R. (2d) 139) — a position with which the court now agrees (see *R. v. Henry,* [2005] 3 S.C.R. 609 at para. 44).

[203] *Burns, supra* note 10 at paras. 64–65.

[204] *Ibid.* at para. 68.

[205] *Ibid.* at para. 69.

[206] *Ibid.* at para. 84.

abolition.[207] To extradite without assurances was thus viewed as contrary to fundamental justice, with the arguments in favour of assurances having become stronger since *Kindler*.[208] The court found no pressing or substantial purpose for the minister's refusal to seek assurances that would justify a breach of the Charter.[209]

As for the section 12 claim that extradition without assurances violates the Charter's prohibition on cruel and unusual treatment, the court again confirmed that this provision could not be invoked in an extradition proceeding given the concern about giving the Charter extraterritorial effect. This time, however, the court addressed the *Soering* judgment of the European Court of Human Rights with more care,[210] recognizing its support for engaging the responsibility of the sending state when there is a real risk of torture or inhuman or degrading treatment in the requesting state. But the court was reluctant to overturn settled jurisprudence that the proper place for the state responsibility debate was section 7, making a weak argument that the linkage between Canada's actions and the foreign state's infliction of the punishment was not strong enough to invoke section 12 when there were "many potential outcomes other than capital punishment."[211] This is an odd statement in a judgment focused expressly on capital punishment. It is also interesting that the court makes no mention of the views of the UN Human Rights Committee in the *Kindler* and *Ng* cases,[212]

---

[207] The court also drew support from concerns in the United States about the death penalty's imposition, including concerns expressed after the hearing of the case and thus without submissions by counsel. *Ibid.* at para. 105 ff.

[208] *Ibid.* at para. 131.

[209] Within a month of the decision, an assurance was provided by the US prosecutor, securing the surrender of the two accused. M. Dunn, "Ottawa Set to Extradite Fugitives," *London Free Press,* 10 March 2001, at A10. Both were convicted of murder in May 2004 and sentenced to three consecutive life terms. T. Johnson and H. Castro, "Rafay, Burns are Convicted of Murder," *Seattle Post-Intelligencer,* 27 May 2004, at A1; S.J. Green, "Burns, Rafay Sentenced to Three Life Terms," *Seattle Times,* 23 October 2004, at B2.

[210] *Soering, supra* note 7. Compare *Burns, supra* note 10 at para. 53 to *Kindler, supra* note 110 at 856. *Soering* is also discussed in *Burns* at paras. 119 and 137. For a comparison of *Kindler* and *Soering,* written prior to *Burns,* see A. Mori Kobayashi, "International and Domestic Approaches to Constitutional Protections of Individual Rights: Reconciling the *Soering* and *Kindler* Decisions" (1996) 34 Am. Crim. L. Rev. 225.

[211] *Burns, supra* note 10 at para. 54.

[212] *Kindler* and *Ng,* both *supra* note 139.

given Canada's long-standing membership by treaty in this UN regime. Various treaties were cited to support the recognition of an "international trend" towards the abolition of the death penalty, but not two concrete cases involving Canada before an international tribunal in which Canada has participated since 1976.[213]

Two months later, in yet another extradition trilogy,[214] the Supreme Court of Canada halted the extradition of four Canadian citizens wanted in the United States on fraud charges because of a statement made by the US prosecutor threatening the accused with sexual violence if they contested their extradition. The specific threat was that the accused would serve "longer sentences under much more stringent conditions" than their co-conspirators who had returned to the United States voluntarily and thus "would become the boyfriend of a very bad man" if they waited out their extradition.[215] The Supreme Court of Canada agreed with the lower courts that to commit the accused for surrender in such circumstances would shock the Canadian conscience so as to constitute a breach of either section 7 or the common law doctrine of abuse of process. But the court's reasons weaken the precedential value of this trilogy for establishing a human rights exception to extradition on the basis of treatment to be accorded to an extraditee in a foreign state since the real focus was on the impact of the statements on the fairness of the judicial proceedings in Canada. As explained by Arbour J. for the court,

[t]he issue at this stage is not whether the appellants will have a fair trial if extradited, but whether they are having a fair extradition hearing in light of the threats and inducements imposed upon them, by those involved in requesting their extradition, to force them to abandon their right to such a hearing. The focus of the fairness issue is thus the hearing in Canada.[216]

---

213 See further J. Harrington, "The Absent Dialogue: Extradition and the International Covenant on Civil and Political Rights" Queen's Law Journal (forthcoming).

214 *United States of America v. Cobb*, [2001] 1 S.C.R. 587 [*Cobb*]; *United States of America v. Schulman*, [2001] 1 S.C.R. 616; and *United States of America v. Tsioubris*, [2001] 1 S.C.R. 613. A fourth case concerning different facts was also heard with these appeals and its judgment was released concurrently. *Kwok, supra* note 21.

215 *Cobb, supra* note 214 at para. 8. Concern was also expressed about remarks made by a US judge about their sentences, although the court (at para. 17) found these statements to be somewhat ambiguous.

216 *Ibid.* at para. 33.

Arbour J. thus confirmed that any concerns about the fairness of the US proceedings would have to be raised in the proceedings before the minister, although she did suggest in *obiter* that it was for the minister, *and the courts upon judicial review,* to consider whether the accused "will face a possibly unfair trial, or an unfair sentencing hearing in the United States, or whether, if convicted and sentenced to imprisonment, they will be subject to sexual violence as predicted, indeed as prescribed, by the attorney prosecuting the case against them."[217] In this case, however, no such determination was needed since the stay of proceedings issued by the extradition judge, and confirmed by the highest court, meant that there was no committal order in place to trigger the executive stage.

FUTURE HUMAN RIGHTS GROUNDS FOR CHALLENGING EXTRADITION

Despite the highest court's ready dismissal of the mandatory sentences trilogy in 1996,[218] Canada's provincial appellate courts continue to hear claims that the disparity between Canadian and American prison sentences, including the use of consecutive rather than concurrent sentences and the lack of parole or early release, are grounds for invoking the "shock the conscience" or "simply unacceptable" exception to unconditional extradition.[219] This claim is pressed strongly when the fugitive is older and the sentence is lengthy — the argument being that such a sentence is in effect a death sentence. Challenges have also been made with respect to the lack of credit in US sentencing regimes for pre-surrender custody, including the lack of enhanced credit when such time is served in harsh conditions,[220] even though Canada does not itself guarantee

---

[217] *Ibid.* at para. 42 [emphasis added].

[218] Followed a year later by the denial of leave to appeal a one-page ruling by the Ontario Court of Appeal that stated without qualification that "it is not a violation of s. 7 rights to surrender the appellant to the United States to face a mandatory minimum sentence for a drug offence." *United States of America v. Johnson,* [1997] O.J. No. 3778, leave to appeal denied, [1997] S.C.C.A. No. 578.

[219] See, for example, *United States of America v. Bonamie* (2001), Alta. L.R. (3d) 252 (C.A.); *United States of America v. Reumayr* (2003), 176 C.C.C. (3d) 377 (B.C.C.A.), leaves to appeal denied, [2005] S.C.C.A. No. 474 and [2005] S.C.C.A. No. 520 [*Reumayr*]; *United States of America v. J.H.K.* (2002), 165 C.C.C. (3d) 449 (Ont. C.A.), leave to appeal denied, [2002] S.C.C.A. No. 501 [*J.H.K.*]; and *United States of America v. D.P.R.* (2003), 185 O.A.C. 345.

[220] As the Ontario Court of Appeal recognized with reference to the Toronto (Don) Jail, "crowded and adverse conditions [are] all too typical of holding jails." *Adam*

such credit, preferring to decide the matter on a case-by-case basis.[221] Prison conditions are also another potential area for future challenge — a situation that is hardly surprising given that it was the harsh conditions on Virginia's death row, and not the death penalty *per se*, that grounded the violation found so long ago by the European Court of Human Rights in *Soering*.[222] However, to date, all such claims in Canada have been unsuccessful, despite some recognition by the courts of the harshness of both American prison sentences[223] and American prisons.[224]

Similar challenges are also percolating at the international level. In one such case, an escaped fugitive known as Weiss faced a prison sentence of 845 years on return to the state of Florida, with the possibility of a reduction to 711 years for good behaviour, as well as pecuniary penalties in excess of US $248 million. After he was caught in Austria, Weiss initially challenged his extradition in the Austrian courts and then made an application to the European Court of Human Rights. He later withdrew this application[225] in order to take his case to the UN Human Rights Committee in Geneva, claiming that his punishment was both "exceptional and grotesque." The committee, however, was able to side-step the merits

---

v. United States of America (2003), 64 O.R. (3d) 268 at para. 5 (C.A.) [*Adam*] — a situation made worse by the length of time spent in such jails awaiting an extradition decision.

221 As noted by the court in *Adam*, *ibid.* at para. 34 and endorsed by the Supreme Court of Canada in *Ferras*, *supra* note 27 at para. 90. However, in *United States of America v. Johnson* (2002), 62 O.R. (3d) 327, the Ontario Court of Appeal did hold that the minister must consider this time as a factor to balance.

222 *Soering*, *supra* note 7. The court has since held that poor conditions of detention, even in states suffering economic difficulties, violate the European treaty's absolute prohibition on degrading treatment. *Kalashnikov v. Russia*, No. 47095/99, E.C.H.R. 2002-VI, (2003) 36 E.H.R.R. 34.

223 See *Reumayr*, *supra* note 219 at para. 29 and *J.H.K.*, *supra* note 219 at para. 42.

224 Southin J.A. in dissent in *Gwynne*, *supra* note 159, would have refused extradition on the ground that the conditions in Alabama prisons were so appalling when combined with the length of sentence as to be fundamentally unacceptable. She, and two other justices, have since confirmed in a subsequent case that the Alabama prison conditions were "inhumane." *Reumayr*, *supra* note 219 at para. 28. See also *États-Unis d'Amérique c. Chipitsyn* (17 June 1999) (Qué. C.A.), leave to appeal denied, [1999] C.S.C.R. no. 432. For an American perspective in regard to women and juvenile prisoners, see D.J. Sharfstein, "Human Rights beyond the War on Terrorism: Extradition Defenses Based on Prison Conditions in the United States" (2002) 42 Santa Clara L. Rev. 1137.

225 *Weiss v. Austria*, No. 74511/01 (13 June 2002).

of his claim on the grounds that the conviction and sentencing were not yet final, pending the outcome of a re-sentencing process set to take place in the United States after extradition.[226] But while the extradition took place, the promised re-sentencing never did,[227] putting into question past presumptions about the reliability of extradition on assurance to the United States.

But the emerging ground of challenge that has had some success before the lower courts is one related to the right to a fair trial, rather than to fair treatment, thus returning extradition law full circle to the due process claims of the 1970s.[228] The latest ground of challenge concerns the admission of evidence in an extradition hearing that is neither first hand nor sworn but, nonetheless, permitted by the "record of the case" approach now embraced by the Extradition Act.[229] Since such evidence is ordinarily inadmissible under Canadian law, the argument has been made that its admission at an extradition hearing violates the "fundamental justice" aspect of the section 7 guarantee,[230] although some courts have remedied this by reading in a requirement for reliability.[231] However, in the leading case of *United States of America v. Yang*,[232] in which the Ontario Court of Appeal examined fully the origins of the new provisions and the difficulties caused by the previous rule that evidence had to be presented in the form of sworn affidavits by persons with first-hand knowledge, it was held that the new eviden-

---

[226] *Weiss v. Austria*, UN Doc. CCPR/C/77/D/1086/2002 (views adopted 3 April 2003), later published in *Report of the Human Rights Committee*, UN Doc. A/58/40 (2003), vol. II, annex V.FF and (2003) 10 I.H.R.R. 685.

[227] B. Zagaris, "US Court Denies US Government Weiss Re-sentence Motion Despite Austrian Conditions" (2002) 18(10) Int'l Law Enforcement Rep. 402.

[228] See *Armstrong, supra* note 65 and the associated discussion.

[229] Extradition Act, *supra* note 1 at ss. 32–34.

[230] For a fuller argument as to why the new evidentiary provisions are contrary to principles of fundamental justice, see A.W. La Forest, "The Balance between Liberty and Comity in the Evidentiary Requirements Applicable to Extradition Proceedings" (2002) 28 Queen's L.J. 95. In my view, however, the very balancing of liberty against comity long associated with Canadian extradition law is problematic on the grounds that a right to liberty should not be qualified by a mere principle of international comity. Liberty and comity are not equivalent in status and any desire for comity or friendship between nations cannot justify the impairment of a right as fundamental as liberty in a Charter scheme that operates according to a standard of minimal impairment.

[231] See *Bourgeon v. Canada (Attorney General)* (2000), 187 D.L.R. (4th) 542 (Ont. S.C.).

[232] *United States of America v. Yang* (2001), 56 O.R. (2d) 52 (C.A.) [*Yang*].

tiary rules met "the basic demands of justice" within the extradition context.[233] The court was also of the view that "if we are prepared to countenance a trial of persons, including our own citizens, in jurisdictions with very different legal systems from our own, it is open to Parliament to design an extradition procedure that, with appropriate safeguards, accommodates these differences."[234]

The *Yang* decision has since been followed by several appellate courts in Canada, initially with the presumed concurrence of the Supreme Court of Canada, since it had consistently denied leave on this point.[235] However, in October 2004, leave to appeal was granted in two cases from Ontario challenging the *Yang* decision,[236] with a third case from British Columbia, *United States of Mexico v. Ortega*, receiving leave to appeal a related issue in October 2005.[237] It is worth noting that the lower court in *Ortega* was of the view that "international standards can be an indicator of fundamental justice requirements,"[238] although the court then failed to recognize

---

233 *Ibid.* at para. 43.

234 *Ibid.*

235 *United States of America v. Wacjman*, [2002] Q.J. No. 5097 (C.A.), leave to appeal denied, [2003] S.C.C.A. No. 89; *Germany (Federal Republic) v. Ebke* (2003), 173 C.C.C. (3d) 261 (N.W.T. C.A.), leave to appeal denied, [2003] S.C.C.A. No. 178; *United States of America v. Scott*, [2003] O.J. No. 5377 (C.A.), leave to appeal denied, [2004] S.C.C.A. No. 288; *United States of America v. Drysdale (appeal by Manningham)* (2004), 183 C.C.C. (3d) 133 (Ont. C.A.), leave to appeal denied, [2004] S.C.C.A. No. 305; and *United States of America v. McDowell* (2004), 183 C.C.C. (3d) 149 (Ont. C.A.), leave to appeal denied, [2004] S.C.C.A. No. 325. See also *Netherlands v. Clarkson* (2000), 146 C.C.C. (3d) 482 (B.C.C.A.), leave to appeal denied, [2000] S.C.C.A. No. 482 (30 November 2000), concerning similar evidentiary requirements in the extradition treaty rather than the statute.

236 *United States of America v. Ferras* (2004), 183 C.C.C. (3d) 119 (Ont. C.A.); and *United States of America v. Latty* (2004), 183 C.C.C. (3d) 126 (Ont. C.A.). These appeals were heard on 17 October 2005. A judgment combining the two appeals was released by the Supreme Court of Canada on 21 July 2006. See *Ferras, supra* note 27.

237 *United States of Mexico v. Ortega*, (2005) 253 D.L.R. (3th) 237 (C.A.), leave to appeal granted 20 October 2005, [2005] S.C.C.A. No. 292. *Yang, supra* note 232, was distinguished in *Ortega* as being focused on the reliability of evidence under section 32(1)(a) rather than the certification of evidence under section 32(1)(b). The Supreme Court of Canada released its judgment in *Ortega* on the same day as its judgments in *Ferras* and *Latty* (noted above) and in conjunction with another British Columbia case focussing on the certification of extradition evidence. See *United Mexican States v. Ortega; United States of America v. Fiessel*, 2006 SCC 34.

238 *United States of Mexico v. Ortega*, (2004) 183 C.C.C. (3d) 75 (B.C.S.C.) at para. 32.

that the *Yang* decision accords in broad terms with international human rights law, which generally grants a wide margin of appreciation to national laws of evidence to accommodate the various differences among states.[239] Thus, it cannot be assumed that a greater role for international human rights law in the balancing approach to extradition automatically secures a "win" for the individual involved. Sometimes, states benefit from international human rights law.[240] However, a flagrant denial of the right to a fair trial in a requesting state would bar extradition under international human rights law,[241] and should too under Canadian extradition law, notwithstanding the presumption that a fair trial will be held in the requesting state.[242]

As this article went to press, the Supreme Court of Canada released its decision in the Ontario and British Columbia cases that were essentially appealing aspects of *Yang*, finding in favour of a *prima facie* case requirement at the committal or judicial stage of the extradition process. This means that "before a person can be extradited, there must be a judicial determination that the requesting state has established a *prima facie* case that the person sought committed the crime alleged and should stand trial for it,"[243] with the obligations of fundamental justice (in the section 7 sense) requiring "an independent and impartial judicial determination on

---

239 See, for example, *Schenk v. Switzerland*, 12 July 1988, Series A, No. 140, (1991) 13 E.H.R.R. 242 at para. 46: "While Article 6 of the Convention guarantees the right to a fair trial, it does not lay down any rules on the admissibility of evidence as such, which is therefore primarily a matter for regulation under national law." For recent confirmation of this principle, see *Storck v. Germany*, 16 June 2005, No. 61603/00 (ECtHR) at para. 134.

240 See also J. Harrington, "How Canadian Lawyers Can Contribute to the Effectiveness of the UN Human Rights Committee," in *The Measure of International Law: Effectiveness, Fairness and Validity: Proceedings of the 31st Annual Conference of the Canadian Council on International Law, Ottawa, October 24-26, 2002* (London: Kluwer Law International, 2004), 132.

241 The flagrant denial test with respect to the right to a fair trial and extradition can be found in *Soering, supra* note 7 at para. 113. This test was recently confirmed by the European Court of Human Rights, sitting as a Grand Chamber, in *Mamatkulov and Askarov v. Turkey*, 4 February 2005, Nos. 46827/99 and 46951/99, (2005) 41 E.H.R.R. 25, (2005) 44 I.L.M. 759 at paras. 86–91.

242 As La Forest J. stated in *Mellino, supra* note 70 at 558: "Our courts must assume that he will be given a fair trial in the foreign country. Matters of due process *generally* are to be left for the courts to determine at the trial there as they would be if he were to be tried here" [emphasis added].

243 *Ferras, supra* note 27 at para. 20.

the facts and evidence on the ultimate question of whether there is sufficient evidence to establish the case for extradition."[244] An extradition judge is thus empowered, through the court's reading of the Extradition Act in conjunction with section 7, to "evaluate the evidence, including its reliability, to determine whether the evidence establishes a sufficient case to commit."[245] It is worth noting for further study that this position differs from developments in Europe, where common law countries have moved away from the *prima facie* case requirement in extradition to enhance cooperation.

Yet, even before this recent decision, it could be noted that the fair trial assumption in extradition law was already waning, as evidenced by the Ontario Court of Appeal's decision in *Canada (Minister of Justice) v. Pacificador* (leave to appeal denied by the Supreme Court of Canada), overturning a minister's decision to surrender where an assurance had been obtained from the requesting state with the intention of securing a trial for the accused within one year of surrender.[246] According to the Court of Appeal, there were no grounds for the minister's reliance on the assurance given the suspension of proceedings in the requesting state and significant delays in the trial of the co-accused, despite two requests for further submissions from the minister as to why she was satisfied with the assurance.[247] The intended extradition of Rodolfo Pacificador to the Philippines to stand trial for the 1986 assassination of his father's political opponent was thus found to have contravened the Charter's guarantee of fundamental justice — a ruling with which the Supreme Court of Canada either agreed or did not find so wrong in law as to justify an appeal.

As for Pacificador, he remains in Canada where he is seeking asylum as a refugee on grounds of political affiliation, the Federal Court of Canada having overturned the dismissal of his claim by the Immigration and Refugee Appeal Board in favour of a new hearing.[248] Yet despite denying the claim, the board had, as summarized by the Federal Court of Canada, "found that the judicial system of the Philippines is corrupt, as a whole" and that "several

---

[244] *Ibid.* at para. 34.

[245] *Ibid.* at para. 41.

[246] *Canada (Minister of Justice) v. Pacificador*, [2002] S.C.C.A. No. 390 (20 February 2003).

[247] *Canada (Minister of Justice) v. Pacificador* (2002), 60 O.R. (3d) 685 (C.A.).

[248] *Pacificador v. Canada (Minister of Citizenship and Immigration)*, [2003] F.C. 1462.

aspects of that state's prosecution of Pacificador were tainted with corruption and interference, including bribery and coercion of witnesses, and politically motivated pressures";[249] thus putting into question the very assumption underlying Canada's extradition jurisprudence that Canada only treats with nations worthy of its trust. In this case, however, the desire to extradite Pacificador, who entered Canada in October 1987, had been a "significant factor" behind Canada's conclusion of an extradition treaty with the Philippines in late 1989.[250] Interestingly, in October 2004, a Filipino court acquitted Pacificador's father of the 1986 murder but found his lawyer and security men guilty, while also implicating Rodolfo Pacificador as the mastermind behind the killing.[251]

The Role for Human Rights in Canadian Extradition

Traditionally, a state's decision to extradite has been made within the context of a treaty relationship between two or more states. Upon receiving an extradition request, the surrendering state would look to the relevant treaty and enabling statute to determine whether there was an obligation to extradite. If the request was in conformity with the terms of the treaty as transformed by statute, the surrendering state was in principle under a legal duty to extradite, absent the provision of exceptions or grounds for refusal, such as in the case of political offenders. However, most of the traditional treaty-based exceptions to extradition have state interests rather than individual interests as their prime concern, although this is a matter of some debate,[252] and none provide for a comprehensive exception to extradition on the basis of a state's responsibility to protect an individual's human rights. Individuals facing extradition have therefore looked to other sources to support a human rights exception to extradition, and, in Canada, they have relied on the provisions of the Charter, which largely embody Canada's human rights obligations under both constitutional and international law.

Extradition proceedings are clearly subject to the Charter. This includes the hearing before the extradition judge as well as the

---

249 *Ibid.* at para. 73.

250 As recognized by the Ontario Court of Appeal in *Pacificador* (Ont. C.A.), *supra* note 247 at para. 7.

251 N.P. Burgos, "Pacificador Cleared of Javier Murder," *Philippine Daily Inquirer,* 13 October 2004, at 1.

252 See, for example, van den Wyngaert, *supra* note 8; and Swart, *supra* note 37.

exercise of ministerial discretion in favour of surrender,[253] the latter being the focus of this work. However, as the Supreme Court of Canada has often emphasized, the Charter does not apply to a foreign state,[254] and its provisions cannot be used to dictate how criminal proceedings in another state are to be conducted.[255] Successful challenges to extradition must therefore focus on Canada's actions, demonstrating a sufficient causal connection between the Canadian decision to extradite and the future treatment of the offender in the foreign state. This avoids the conclusion that the Charter has extraterritorial effect in exceptional circumstances and, instead, views the Charter as taking effect within Canada's jurisdiction, to a decision by the Canadian Minister of Justice, based on knowledge held by Canadian officials, which has serious repercussions abroad.

Such an approach to sending state responsibility accords with that taken by the European Court of Human Rights under the (European) Convention for the Protection of Human Rights and Fundamental Freedoms (ECHR)[256] since 1989[257] and by the UN Human Rights Committee under the International Covenant on Civil and Political Rights (ICCPR)[258] since 1993.[259] Yet despite the similarities between the Charter, the ECHR, and the ICCPR — a connection that was recognized as being relevant to extradition by Jean-Gabriel Castel and Sharon Williams writing in this journal almost twenty years ago[260] — the Supreme Court of Canada insists on taking a less discrete, and potentially more subjective, approach with respect to the grounds for such a challenge. Intervention is limited to cases of fundamental injustice, whatever that may truly mean, due to a concern that to do otherwise might all too easily place Canada in the position of violating its international obligations, by which the court has meant its extradition obligations and not its human rights obligations.

---

[253] *Cobb, supra* note 214 at para. 24, relying on *Burns* and *Schmidt.*

[254] *R. v. Cook*, [1998] 2 S.C.R. 597 at paras. 23–48 (concerning the use of evidence obtained abroad after an extradition from the United States to Canada).

[255] *Schmidt, supra* note 69 at 518.

[256] ECHR, *supra* note 9.

[257] *Soering, supra* note 7.

[258] ICCPR, *supra* note 5.

[259] *Kindler* and *Ng*, both *supra* note 139.

[260] See Castel and Williams, *supra* note 12 at 271–77.

Canada, however, is party to both extradition treaties and human rights treaties, with both the ICCPR and the Convention against Torture and Other Cruel, Inhuman or Degrading Treatment or Punishment (UNCAT)[261] having been ratified by Canada long after the conclusion of an extradition treaty with the United States, its most frequent extradition partner. Presumably, the executive intended these treaty obligations to work together since it did not withdraw from one to ratify the other, nor make reservations contrary to this assumption.[262] Yet nowhere in Canada's extradition jurisprudence is there an attempt to reconcile these treaty obligations as treaty obligations, and, instead, the court focuses on a narrow conception of comity and respect as compliance with an extradition obligation owed to another state and not with the human rights treaty obligations owed to many states, if not the entire international community, for rights of a universal nature.

Nevertheless, as recognized by the court since 1987, there are circumstances where "the manner in which the foreign state will deal with the fugitive on surrender, whether that course of conduct is justifiable or not under the law of that country, may be such that it would violate the principles of fundamental justice to surrender an accused."[263] To succeed, an extraditee must show that the impending treatment in the foreign state sufficiently shocks the Canadian conscience or is simply unacceptable according to a balancing test that takes into account a number of factors, including the nature of the foreign treatment, the quality of the foreign justice system, as well as considerations of comity, security, and deference to the executive in matters of foreign affairs. The court has also accepted that a fugitive's age and mental capacity may also be relevant considerations.[264] Yet, to date, this test has only had an impact in capital cases,[265] and only then after a decade of debate and a

---

[261] ICCPR, *supra* note 5; and UNCAT, *supra* note 6.

[262] The changes to the Canada-U.S. Extradition Treaty prompted by the revision of Canada's Extradition Act in 1999 also illustrate the possibility of treaty amendment: *supra* note 51.

[263] *Schmidt, supra* note 69 at 522.

[264] *Burns, supra* note 10 at para. 68, reflecting the position taken in *Soering, supra* note 7.

[265] With the exception of *Pacificador, supra* note 246, although the requesting state involved had reinstated the death penalty, prompting Canada to seek an assurance. See "Minister of Justice Orders Surrender of Rodolfo Pacificador to the Republic of the Philippines," *supra* note 57.

series of Canadian miscarriages of justice heightening the court's sensitivity to error. The intimidation cases are more akin to an abuse of process complaint arising within the Canadian proceedings, albeit the fact that the source of the intimidation has come from abroad, while the cases concerning mandatory minimum sentences have prompted a strict hands-off approach from the court under the rubric of prosecutorial discretion. Clearly, the threshold has been set very high for a successful challenge, with great deference being accorded to the role of the executive.

It is also clear from reviewing Canada's extradition jurisprudence that other provisions of the Charter are supposed to offer no direct assistance, including the protection offered specifically by section 12 against cruel and unusual treatments or punishments. This seems odd, given that the values underlying section 12 may contribute to the balancing test under section 7, but the provision itself cannot be invoked directly because to do so would ostensibly give the Charter an extraterritorial effect. This does not make sense. The European position is that state responsibility accrues for a surrender to face *torture* on the basis of the *torture* provision in the applicable human rights instrument. Faced with such clarity, Canada's rejection of this approach is difficult to understand, particularly since the very example given since *Schmidt* to justify intervention is precisely the kind of harm that section 12 is intended to address. If all Charter rights are equal, as suggested by the absence of any hierarchy in the Charter's text, Canada's highest court has simply failed to explain why it is better, and intra-territorial, to halt an extradition to face future acts of torture in a foreign state on the grounds of the more ephemeral "fundamental justice" than on the grounds in section 12. Canadian extradition law also loses the benefit of the guidance offered by cases decided under section 12, and its equivalent in foreign and international jurisdictions, as to what circumstances will constitute a real or foreseeable risk of torture or cruel, inhuman, or degrading treatment in the foreign state so as to bar surrender and rests instead on a court's subjective analysis of what is fundamentally unjust.[266]

As for the penalties considered to be sufficiently shocking, they include torture (as decided since *Schmidt*), the death penalty, stoning

---

[266] Others have also called for the direct application of section 12 in extradition challenges, invoking in support the analysis of Cory J. in *Kindler*. See R.J. Currie, "Charter without Borders? The Supreme Court of Canada, Transnational Crime and Constitutional Rights and Freedoms" (2004) 27 Dalh. L.J. 235.

to death for the crime of adultery, and the chopping off of hands for theft (as stated in *Burns*), although none serve as an absolute bar to surrender. In an effort to respect *stare decisis* and reconcile its own case law, the court has made it clear that extradition to face the death penalty, as well as extradition to face the death row phenomenon,[267] may still be possible in an exceptional case,[268] and a year later, albeit in a deportation case, the full court unanimously extended this approach to torture. In *Suresh v. Canada*,[269] which concerned the desired deportation of a Sri Lankan of Tamil descent believed to be engaged in activities supporting terrorism, the court held that deportation to face torture is "*generally* unconstitutional"[270] because the balancing undertaken under section 7 "will *usually* come down against expelling a person to face torture elsewhere."[271] This is a shocking conclusion given that the clear import of Canada's treaty obligations in the field of international human rights is to foreclose such a possibility absolutely.[272] Canada had also been reminded by the UN Human Rights Committee of its obligation "never to expel, extradite, deport or otherwise remove a person to a place where treatment or punishment that is contrary to Article 7 [of the ICCPR][273] is a substantial risk."[274] Yet, the court

---

267 While the court has now accepted, unlike in *Kindler*, that the administration of the death penalty inevitably leads to lengthy delays and an associated psychological trauma, it has also held that "the death row phenomenon is not a controlling factor in the section 7 balance." *Burns, supra* note 10 at paras. 121–23. It remains, however, "a relevant consideration," with La Forest J. conceding in *Kindler, supra* note 110 at 838, with a nod to *Soering, supra* note 7, that "there may be situations where the age or mental capacity of the fugitive may affect the matter."

268 Comparative European jurisprudence would suggest that this is no longer the case now that Canada has acceded, as of 25 November 2005, to the Second Optional Protocol to the International Covenant on Civil and Political Rights, Aiming at the Abolition of the Death Penalty, 29 December 1989, GA Res. 44/128, UN Doc. A/44/49 (1989) at 207 (in force 11 July 1991). This factor was not in existence for consideration in *Burns, supra* note 10.

269 *Suresh v. Canada*, [2002] 1 S.C.R. 3 [*Suresh*].

270 *Ibid.* at paras. 1 and 5 [emphasis added].

271 *Ibid.* at para. 58 [emphasis added].

272 As recognized in *Suresh, ibid.* at paras. 67–68 and para. 75.

273 ICCPR, *supra* note 5.

274 See *Concluding Observations of the Human Rights Committee: Canada*, UN Doc. CCPR/C/79/Add.105 (7 April 1999) at para. 13.

has held that an exceptional discretion to deport to torture does exist.[275]

Legal rights, as protected by section 11 of the Charter, also remain directly inapplicable to extradition,[276] although here the court has buttressed its conclusion by noting that some section 11 rights, by their very terms, are inapplicable, such as the right to trial by jury. Yet why the non-application of one part of section 11 should bar the application of all other parts is an issue not adequately addressed by the court,[277] and this is regrettable since the sub-parts of section 11, in contrast with the broadly worded fundamental justice guarantee, set out specifically what are considered to be the components of a fair trial within a criminal context. A more flexible approach would allow the courts to apply the section 11 guarantees so as to benefit from the guidance offered by their associated jurisprudence, with section 1 remaining available to alleviate any concerns that section 11's application would bar extradition simply because a foreign trial procedure differed from that used in Canada.

It is likely that the equality guarantee in section 15 of the Charter is also of no direct application to extradition. As yet, the Supreme Court of Canada has not had the opportunity to make this pronouncement, but it was the view of the Ontario Court of Appeal when it considered a claim of future persecution on grounds of sexual orientation flowing from the extradition of an openly gay man to Mexico for the murder of his partner.[278] In dismissing the application of section 15, the court explained that such persecution, if it were to occur, would not be attributable to any decision or act on the part of the minister but to the actions or inactions of the Mexican authorities, thus dismissing the argument that it was the minister's decision to extradite that placed the extraditee at risk of persecution.[279] This ruling, however, conflicts with an earlier

275 *Suresh, supra* note 269 at paras. 76–78.

276 *Schmidt, supra* note 69; *Mellino, supra* note 70; and *Allard, supra* note 71.

277 As noted by Spencer, *supra* note 112 at 70. La Forest's need for consistency in application seems inconsistent with his suggestion that the extradition context requires a slightly different approach to the Charter from that taken in domestic criminal matters.

278 *Hurley, supra* note 58.

279 *Ibid.* at paras. 44–45. The minister had, however, already recognized the climate of hostility towards homosexuals in Mexico and granted the extradition on condition of certain protections. See "Minister of Justice Orders Surrender of Denis Hurley to Mexico," *supra* note 57.

ruling by the Ontario Court of Appeal, suggesting that while section 7 includes the equality rights of section 15 within the ambit of fundamental justice, it would be better to address the validity of a discrimination claim by reference to the specific provision and not to the more general language of section 7.[280]

Fugitives with Canadian citizenship may, however, have an additional provision on which to base a human rights challenge to extradition, namely the protection afforded to mobility rights by section 6(1) of the Charter, which provides that "every citizen of Canada has the right to enter, remain in and leave Canada." This challenge, in essence, reflects a desire to create a nationality exception to extradition, which is a ground for refusing extradition commonly provided for by treaty[281] and often exercised by civil law countries as they typically refuse to extradite their own nationals. Common law countries, however, operate on the assumption that extradition applies to all persons, regardless of nationality, unless the relevant extradition treaty expressly provides otherwise.[282] When the Charter first came into force, there was some discussion[283] about the possibility of a Charter-mandated nationality exception emerging under Canadian law, but, since that time, the courts have made it clear that this exception, while possible, is not easily obtained.

The jurisprudential position is that although the surrender of a citizen to a foreign state does infringe section 6(1),[284] it is an infringement justified as reasonable and thus permissible under the Charter.[285] Even in the more difficult cases, such as *Cotroni*, where there is the opportunity to prosecute the Canadian in Canada for the same criminal conduct, the courts have shown a reluctance to interfere, albeit that there is now a requirement to show that prosecution in Canada is not a realistic option.[286] This test, however, is easily met unless an equally effective prospect of prosecution has

---

280 *Republic of the Philippines v. Pacificador* (1993), 14 O.R. (3d) 321 at 338 (C.A.), leave to appeal on other grounds denied, [1994] 1 S.C.R. x (28 April 1994).

281 See Shearer, *supra* note 3 at 94–131.

282 See further Castel and Williams, *supra* note 12 at 266–68.

283 *Ibid.*

284 As first established in *Rauca, supra* note 98, and endorsed by La Forest J. in *Schmidt, supra* note 69 at 520 as follows: "Section 6 was not raised in this case, though Schmidt is a Canadian citizen, no doubt because her counsel believed, as I do, that it was properly disposed of in the *Rauca* case."

285 *Cotroni, supra* note 96.

286 *Ibid.* at 1497–98.

been unjustifiably and improperly abandoned.[287] Moreover, as demonstrated in the series of extradition challenges concerning the use of mandatory minimum sentences in the United States, this requirement is neutered by the expressly proclaimed "high degree of deference" afforded to prosecutorial discretion,[288] which, in effect, closes the door to a successful section 6 challenge.[289] The concern, however, remains that the court's jurisprudence enables the Canadian government to work in tandem with a foreign state to secure indirectly a penalty for a fugitive that is either unconstitutional or unavailable in Canada.

CONCLUSION

For many years, the real stumbling block to securing a human rights exception to extradition from Canada was the high degree of deference accorded by the courts to the executive in matters of foreign affairs, based on an assumption that Canada does not enter into extradition relations with states unworthy of its trust. But not all states deserve such trust, even those with which we may have treated many years ago, and, on this aspect, I submit that the courts should operate on the basis of a rebuttable presumption. As for the issue of deference, clearly "much less" is now required for ministerial decisions concerning the violation of constitutional rights,[290] albeit that the only right applicable in an extradition challenge remains what has become a right *to* fundamental justice, which, in essence, combines elements of section 7 with section 12. This is problematic since, while the values underlying other rights, identified as being fundamental by their inclusion in the Charter, can contribute to the balancing approach, the associated case law guiding the proper application of these rights is of no application. It also limits the consideration of comparative and international jurisprudence decided on grounds with more specificity than the ephemeral "fundamental justice," although it is a welcome development that the general tenor of Canada's extradition jurisprudence now reflects, in application as well as in theory, the principle

---

287 *Kwok, supra* note 21 at para. 61.

288 As stated in *Kwok, supra* note 21 at para. 93, citing *Burns, supra* note 10; *Idziak, supra* note 31; *Whitley, supra* note 175; *Schmidt, supra* note 69; *Gwynne, supra* note 159; and *Power, supra* note 177.

289 See *Leon, supra* note 183; *Power, supra* note 177; and *Kwok, supra* note 21.

290 *Kwok, supra* note 21 at para. 94.

long established elsewhere that holds a sending state responsible for real and foreseeable risks to an individual's rights in a receiving state.

But the high threshold imposed by the court for invoking this protection leads to the ironic conclusion that a fugitive's best chance of securing a role for human rights protections in matters of extradition remains with the Minister of Justice who has the power, as now confirmed by its express inclusion in the Extradition Act, to impose conditions on the requesting state, including the requirement to provide assurances. To secure greater consistency in the use of conditional extradition, Canada's domestic and international human rights obligations, including those sourced by treaty, need to be recognized as having a guiding role to play in determining the appropriate response to an extradition request.[291] Canada has in fact acknowledged this role, at least when one arm of the Canadian bureaucracy speaks abroad, as evidenced by Canada's submission in the international proceedings in *Ng* that the Minister of Justice must consider the terms of the Charter *and the ICCPR* within the Canadian extradition process.[292] Canada's courts, however, have yet to hold Canada accountable domestically to ensure such consideration. The ICCPR has been identified by the United Nations as one of twenty-five treaties to be singled out as being basic to a comprehensive international legal framework.[293] Given its importance, and Canada's freely given consent to be bound to the protection of the rights it identifies as universally fundamental, extradition treaty obligations should not be the only consideration marshalled by counsel and considered by the courts when valuing comity between nations in extradition decisions.

---

[291] A similar call for the court to make greater reference to international human rights material was made by Michell, *supra* note 8 at 229.

[292] *Ng, supra* note 139 at para. 8.4. See also *Cox. v. Canada*, UN Doc. CCPR/C/52/ D/539/1993 (views adopted 31 October 1994), published in *Report of the Human Rights Committee*, UN Doc. A/50/40 (1995), vol. II, annex X.M, 114 I.L.R. 347, (1994) 15 H.R.L.J. 410, (1995) 2 I.H.R.R. 307 at para. 5.4. Canada has since assured the committee that "the Minister of Justice takes into consideration the protection afforded by the Covenant in decisions on extradition requests that raise the issue of the death penalty." *Fourth Periodic Reports of States Parties Due in 1995: Canada* (Addendum), UN Doc. CCPR/C/103/Add.5 (15 October 1997) at para. 44.

[293] *Millennium Summit Multilateral Treaty Framework: An Invitation to Universal Participation* (New York: United Nations, 2000).

Sommaire

Le rôle des obligations en matière de la protection de la personne en droit canadien de l'extradition

Afin d'assurer une plus grande coopération entre les États dans la mise en application du droit pénal, le Canada a adhéré à un réseau de traités d'extradition. Le Canada a aussi accepté d'être lié par un réseau parallèle de traités sur les droits de la personne. Étant donné la nature intrinsèquement internationale de l'extradition et l'interconnexion des obligations du Canada en vertu des traités sur les droits de la personne et en vertu de sa Charte des droits et libertés, l'on aurait pu croire que les obligations internationales du Canada en matière de la protection des droits humains joueraient un rôle dans la mise en œuvre des protections garanties par la Charte afin de protéger les droits d'une personne menacée d'extradition du Canada, même si le seuil requis pour invoquer ces dispositions reste élevé. Si l'étude de la jurisprudence canadienne des trente dernières années en matière d'extradition confirme que les droits humains ont aujourd'hui leur place en droit canadien de l'extradition, très peu d'attention a été accordée aux obligations internationales du Canada en vertu des traités sur les droits de la personne en tant qu'obligations fondées sur un traité au moment de décider s'il y a lieu d'ordonner l'extradition lors de la réception d'une demande valide. L'auteure soutient que si l'on tenait compte des obligations internationales du Canada en matière des droits humains et de ses obligations nationales en vertu de la Charte, nous serions mieux en mesure d'assurer un juste équilibre des droits et des obligations en jeu, en pesant bien toutes les dispositions fondées sur un traité qui sont pertinentes en matière d'extradition.

Summary

The Role for Human Rights Obligations in Canadian Extradition Law

To secure greater inter-state cooperation in criminal law enforcement, Canada has entered into a number of extradition treaties. Yet alongside this network of extradition treaties lies a network of human rights treaties to which Canada has also agreed to be bound. Given the inherently international nature of extradition, and the interconnection between Canada's human rights treaties and its obligations under the Canadian Charter of Rights and Freedoms, one would have thought that Canada's international human rights obligations might play some role in bolstering the protection afforded by the Charter to the rights of an individual facing extradition from Canada, even if the threshold for invoking the latter remains high. And yet, while a review of Canada's extradition jurisprudence for the past thirty years confirms that a role for human rights has emerged in Canadian extradition law, scant attention has been paid to Canada's international human rights treaty obligations as treaty obligations when deciding whether to extradite upon receiving a valid request. The author argues that if Canada's international human rights obligations were considered, along with Canada's domestic Charter obligations, greater guidance would be made available as to the appropriate balance of rights and obligations at stake, while also affording equal treatment to all of the treaty obligations relevant to extradition.

Coming in from the Shadow of the Law: The Use of Law by States to Negotiate International Environmental Disputes in Good Faith

CAMERON HUTCHISON

Increasingly, international law obliges states to negotiate *in good faith* environmental disputes that arise in connection with the use and protection of shared or common property natural resources — that is, watercourses, fisheries, and migratory species. Typically, the obligation is for states to reconcile the rights of use of a source state, on the one hand, with the rights of protection of an affected state or, alternatively, the obligations of protection of both source and affected states, on the other (referred to as "competing rights" hereinafter). Articulation of this duty to negotiate in good faith has been vague, and, perhaps as a consequence, disputes have been protracted or have gone unresolved. Part of the problem may be that states do not know how to interpret their competing rights in the resource. If the interaction of competing rights remains unclear, we may expect that states will have difficulty achieving shared understandings to help reconcile their different interests in the resource. If states are to avoid the pitfalls of rights indeterminacy, including self-serving legal argument that undermines the prospect of resolution, international legal doctrine must clarify the manner in which states can more exactly interpret the relationship between competing rights.

This article explores the facilitative potential of international authoritative soft law[1] to good faith negotiation where rights and

Cameron Hutchison is an assistant professor at the University of Alberta's Faculty of Law. The article is based on the author's completed S.J.D. dissertation (University of Toronto). The author would like to thank Jutta Brunnée (in particular), Lorne Sossin, Karen Knop, and Andrew Green for their comments and feedback on earlier versions of this work. This article is dedicated to the memory of my brother Scott, who was an ardent believer in peace and justice. Any errors are my own.

[1] In this article, I use "international authoritative soft law" to mean law that, while not necessarily formally binding on parties to a dispute, possesses attributes —

obligations of resource use and protection are broadly stated and their relationship to one another is unclear. Our understanding of the relevance, sources, and use of law in the negotiation process contributes to whether law functions to facilitate or frustrate dispute resolution. The duty to negotiate in good faith, as part of the international law of cooperation, must acknowledge the inevitability of legal disputes arising, ensure that these disputes are cooperatively managed by states, and seek guidance from international authoritative soft law to assist in dispute resolution. On this last point, states should look to international authoritative soft law to explicate, integrate, and reconcile the legitimate interests within their competing rights, according to prescribed legitimacy criteria. By way of example, I focus on international watercourse law and show how the Convention on the Law of Non-Navigational Uses of International Watercourses (Watercourses Convention)[2] could be used to resolve a lingering dispute in the *Case Concerning the Gabčíkovo-Nagymaros Project (Hungary v. Slovakia).*[3]

Duty to Negotiate Environmental Disputes in Good Faith

The obligation to negotiate environmental disputes in good faith in connection with shared or common property natural resources — watercourses, high seas fisheries, and migratory species — has gained prominence in recent years in both international case law and treaty law.[4] The essential nature of the obligation is for the

---

namely the product of a process that is inclusive of the international community of states — that make it persuasive within negotiation discourse. See discussion at notes 66–90 and accompanying text.

2   Convention on the Law of Non-Navigational Uses of International Watercourses, (1996) 36 I.L.M. 719 [Watercourses Convention].

3   *Case Concerning the Gabčíkovo-Nagymaros Project (Hungary v. Slovakia)*, [1997] I.C.J. Rep. 92 (25 September) [*Gabčíkovo-Nagymaros*].

4   Cases include *Lac Lanoux Arbitration (Spain v. France)* (1957) 24 I.L.R. 101 (Arbitral Tribunal) [*Lac Lanoux*]; *Fisheries Jurisdiction Case (Spain v. Canada)*, [1974] I.C.J. Rep. 3 [*Fisheries Jurisdiction*]; *Gabčíkovo-Nagymaros, supra* note 3; *United States – Import Prohibition of Shrimps and Certain Shrimp Products*, WTO Doc. WT/DS58/ AB/R (12 October 1998) [*Shrimp-Turtle*]; and *Southern Bluefin Tuna Cases (Zealand v. Japan; Australia v. Japan)*, Provisional Measures, ITLOS No. 3 and 4 (1999). Treaties include Watercourses Convention, *supra* note 2 at sections 3(5) and 17; UN Convention on the Law of the Sea, (1982) 21 I.L.M. 1261, Articles 61, 62, 63, and 118 [LOSC]; UN Agreement Relating to the Conservation and Management of Straddling Fish Stocks and Migratory Fish Stocks, (1995) 34 I.L.M. 1542, Article 8(2) [Fish Stocks Agreement]. On the distinction between shared and

parties to make good faith efforts to strive towards agreement that reconciles their competing rights of use and protection.[5] Little substantive guidance has been offered beyond the concept of reasonableness, as a derivative of the principle of good faith, to manage states' appreciation of their rights[6] or, in the alternative, that states use to compromise and engage in meaningful negotiations.[7] However, it is unclear from these pronouncements what constitutes a legitimate expression of rights in the negotiation circumstances, upon which reasonableness, compromise, or meaningful negotiation can be based. Furthermore, tribunals have mystically referred to the applicability of law and legal norms to the negotiation process, perhaps implying that law can facilitate agreement that achieves the appropriate balance between use and protection.[8]

In many cases, when states negotiate, a lack of legal guidance may not be a problem since states will have incentives to settle or

---

common property natural resources, the former has been described as "a limited form of community interest, usually involving a small group of states in geographic continuity, who exercise shared rights over the resources in question," for example, shared watercourses, while "common property resources, such as fisheries or mammals on the high seas, occur in areas beyond national jurisdiction where the resource is open to the use of all states and cannot be appropriated to the exclusive sovereignty of any state." P. Birnie and A. Boyle, *International Law and the Environment* (Oxford: Oxford University Press, 2002) at 139 and 141. The distinction is one without a difference for the purpose of this article, and I will refer to the term "shared natural resources" in relation to both.

5 *Gabčíkovo-Nagymaros, supra* note 3 at para. 141. While efforts are to be strong, there is no obligation to conclude an agreement. See *Lac Lanoux, supra* note 4 at 140; and *United States – Import Prohibitions of Certain Shrimp and Shrimp Products,* Recourse to Article 21.5 of the DSU by Malaysia, WTO Doc. WT/DS58/AB/RW (2001) at para. 123–24.

6 In *Shrimp-Turtle, supra* note 4 at para. 158, rights of environmental protection are to be exercised reasonably when it affects a treaty obligation (of nondiscriminatory market access). In *Gabčíkovo-Nagymaros, supra* note 3 at para. 142, the International Court of Justice (ICJ) referred to the principle of good faith in Article 26 of the Vienna Convention on the Law of Treaties, (1969) 8 I.L.M. 689 [Vienna Convention]: "The principle of good faith obliges the Parties to apply [the treaty] in a reasonable way and in such a manner that its purpose can be realized."

7 *Gabčíkovo-Nagymaros, supra* note 3 at para. 141 (bargaining is to be "meaningful"); and *Lac Lanoux, supra* note 4 at 140 (conflicting interests in a shared watercourse to be reconciled "by mutual concessions").

8 *Fisheries Jurisdiction, supra* note 4 at para. 69 ("an equitable solution derived from the applicable law"); *Gabčíkovo-Nagymaros, supra* note 3 at para. 141 (parties to find an agreed solution that takes into account "norms of international environmental law and the principles of the law of international watercourses").

may arrive at a cooperative political solution. Yet when parties cannot resolve their dispute, how are states to understand the nature of their rights or, more to the point, the interaction of seemingly opposed rights of use and protection, when they negotiate in good faith? This may present a real problem when states engage in legal discourse to support their competing interests in the shared resource — legal indeterminacy can lead to self-serving interpretation of law and thus frustrate dispute resolution. Conversely, when there is an authoritative body of rules to resolve the interpretation of rights, there is less room for legal distortion.[9] In other words, the more determinate the rules, the more narrow the bounds within which legal discourse can take place *in good faith*. The challenge taken up in this article is to understand law in a way that helps shape the parameters of legal debate in negotiations.

The obligation demands that the principle of good faith is to regulate negotiation. Yet what constitutes good faith legal argument in this process? The principle of good faith may be understood to mean different things in different legal contexts, even in international law.[10] Without a strong facilitative principle of good faith, we might expect states to have difficulty in achieving agreement in light of the considerable barriers discussed next. Since the duty to negotiate in good faith is an obligation of cooperation and is specifically concerned with states reaching agreement in difficult circumstances, the principle of good faith should point to a "close link that exists between the obligation itself and its performance."[11] In other words, the *obligation* to strive for agreement should be

---

[9] J.K. Irvin, "The Role of Law in the Negotiated Settlement of International Disputes" (1969) 3 Vanderbilt International 58 at 70 (where there is "a sophisticated and large body of applicable legal rules of law, decisions based on such law, whether made by adjudicators or negotiators, would be easier and distortion of legal arguments would be more difficult").

[10] Under the Vienna Convention, *supra* note 6, for example, good faith may mean simply that states not act in bad faith, for example, the prohibition against inducing states to conclude a treaty by fraudulent conduct under Article 49. Or good faith may have more proactive content, such as Article 26, which requires treaty obligations to be performed in good faith, meaning a reasonableness standard. See *Gabčíkovo-Nagymaros, supra* note 3.

[11] S. Rosenne, *Developments in the Law of Treaties 1945-1986* (Cambridge: Cambridge University Press, 1989) at 175 (referring to the general role of good faith in decision-making, whether in a second or third-party context). For more discussion on this point, see C. Hutchison "The Duty to Negotiate International Environmental Law Disputes in Good Faith" (2006) 2 McGill Int'l J. Sustainable Development L. & Pol'y [forthcoming].

performed through cooperative state behaviours, including the manner in which states interpret and advance their legal rights in bargaining. Good faith legal argument cannot be wholly self-serving to the rights of individual states but must also accommodate the rights of other states in the process of legal discourse. This accommodation process need not occur in a vacuum but instead can be facilitated by international authoritative soft law.

PROBLEMS OF INTERNATIONAL ENVIRONMENTAL COOPERATION

It is essential to our understanding of how law should work within good faith negotiation to appreciate the formidable barriers to meeting the imperatives of environmental protection. In light of these impediments, the law of international environmental protection relies heavily on the principle of good faith (discussed earlier), cooperative procedural mechanisms (discussed in this section), and also soft legal norms (discussed later in this article) to meet its objectives.

CHALLENGES AND LEGAL RESPONSES

Many variables affect the difficulty and tenor of international negotiations,[12] although environmental negotiations tend to labour under added layers of complexity. Two features that typically impede progress towards agreement are scientific uncertainty as to the causes, effects, and risks of environmental problems and the complexity of social choice or the balancing of costs and benefits between source and affected states. Effective responses to environmental degradation usually rely on two additional factors, which also complicate negotiations, the need for preventative approaches and the need for collaborative solutions between states.

First, the science of environmental protection — that is, uncovering the full dimensions of degradation, identifying the sources, predicting the effects, and ascertaining the effective and feasible solutions — is not only made up of extremely complex issues but also its negotiations are often hampered by a lack of scientific knowledge,

---

12 For example, the number and types of actors involved, the number and complexity of issues under consideration, the structure and timelines within which negotiations occur, and the strategies and approaches that parties may employ. For a general overview of these issues, see B. Starkey, M. Boyer, and J. Wilkenfeld, *Negotiating a Complex World: An Introduction to International Negotiation* (Lanham, MD: Rowman and Littlefield, 1999).

information, and consensus on these points.[13] Indeed, it may be difficult to establish the scope of negotiations — what to negotiate about — without "a widely shared scientific consensus on the nature of the problem and its solutions."[14] The corollary is that scientific uncertainty results in a greater likelihood of inaction, as states may question the need for costly remedial measures for a problem that some may perceive as inflated or non-existent. Even when the parties engage in an attempt to address the problem, one party's solution may, in the face of uncertain science, appear just as feasible as one that is advanced by another.[15] Studies also reveal that uncertainty leads to a tendency towards self-interested arguments, misrepresentation of information, and the ensuing erosion of trust between the negotiating parties.[16]

Second, environmental issues weigh the benefits of human activities and costs of controlling them against probable environmental impacts.[17] Polluters may be asked to institute immediate and costly measures for the benefit of uncertain long-term gains for future generations.[18] In these circumstances, there is a tendency on the part of political leaders, not to mention the short-term agendas of economic actors, to postpone unpopular and "unprofitable" action.[19] In the transboundary context, this balancing of interests occurs between source and affected state, where the refusal of the source state to take costly remedial measures to the detriment of an affected state's environmental interest is the crux of the controversy.

Third, the nature of environmental protection typically demands preventative solutions. Traditional legal concepts of liability for damages accruing to victims of environmental damage are largely

---

[13] See, e.g., G. Sjostedt, "Preface," in G. Sjostedt, ed., *International Environmental Negotiations* (Newbury Park: Sage, 1993) at xiv.

[14] A. Hurrell and B. Kingsbury, eds., *The International Politics of the Environment: Actors, Interests and Institutions* (Oxford: Clarendon Press, 1992) at 19.

[15] See G.O. Faure and J.Z. Rubin, "Organizing Concepts and Questions," in G. Sjostedt, ed., *International Environmental Negotiation* (Newbury Park: Sage, 1993), 22.

[16] A.E. Tenbrunsel, "Trust as an Obstacle in Environmental-Economic Disputes" (1999) 42 Am. Behavioural Scientist 1354.

[17] C. Cooper, "The Management of International Environmental Disputes in the Context of Canada-US Relations: A Survey and Evalutation of Techniques and Mechanisms" (1986) 24 Can. Y.B. Int'l L. 252.

[18] Sjostedt, *supra* note 13 at xiv.

[19] See R.E. Benedick, "Perspectives of a Negotiation Practitioner," in Sjostedt, ed., *supra* note 13, 220.

impractical since there are large evidentiary hurdles of proving causation between source and effect.[20] Liability mechanisms may be ineffective since after-the-fact solutions, while difficult to quantify as damages, will usually be inadequate as measured against actual environmental restoration. More than that, some environmental problems threaten to be irreversible in their potential effects if preventative measures are delayed beyond a critical point.[21] Thus, preventative measures are infinitely more suited to environmental protection than *ex post facto* solutions.

Fourth, the need for international negotiation on the environment presupposes the existence of an environmental problem that demands joint or multiple state actions. These collective state efforts may be indispensable for shared natural resource conservation, where several nations have contributed to pollution or resource over-exploitation. Without collaboration, a tragedy of the commons scenario arises wherein no state has the incentive to abate if others are not prepared to do likewise.[22] States may be faced with the very real prospect of serious and irreversible environmental damage when cooperative approaches are not harnessed to address environmental protection. However, the controversies elicited by information scarcity and asymmetrical costs and benefits often mean that perpetrating states simply do not consent to treaty commitments on environmental protection, thus frustrating collaborative solutions.[23]

International environmental legal doctrine works within these negotiation constraints and focuses on cooperative procedural mechanisms to generate environmental knowledge and promote early inter-state interaction to address environmental concerns. These procedural obligations in3clude information sharing to help diagnose environmental dangers, notification to affected states of possible environmental risks, and consultation between states to explore alternatives to environmentally sensitive projects.[24] These

---

[20] R. Bilder "The Settlement of Disputes in the Field of the International Law of the Environment" (1976) 144 Rec. des Cours 155. As well, international environmental problems often involve multiple victims and multiple sources.

[21] Benedick, *supra* note 19 at 219, referring to projected effects of climate change.

[22] Bilder, *supra* note 20 at 154.

[23] Or states "free ride" on costly environmental protection regimes. See L.E. Susskind, *Environmental Diplomacy: Negotiating More Effective Global Agreements* (Oxford: Oxford University Press, 1994) at 18–24.

[24] Rio Declaration on Environment and Development, 13 June 1992, (1992) 31 I.L.M. 874 [Rio Declaration], Principle 19: "States shall provide prior and timely

cooperative obligations have been coined "dispute avoidance mechanisms."[25]

Cooperation is a central principle in international environmental law and lies at the heart of many of its rules. Cooperation in international law has been defined as

[marking] the effort of States to accomplish an object by joint action, where the activity of a single State cannot achieve the same result. Thus, the duty to cooperate means the obligation to enter into such coordinated action so as to achieve a specific goal. The significance and value of cooperation depends upon its goal.[26]

This definition captures the fact that specific duties of cooperation are tied to the purposes they are to serve. As we will see in the case study next, procedural norms of international environmental cooperation can be ineffective when there is not substantive guidance in the process. The goal of the duty to negotiate in good faith is to achieve agreement on use and protection of shared natural resources in difficult circumstances and, by necessity, must imply a high level of cooperation to achieve this purpose.[27]

---

notification and relevant information to potentially affected States on activities that may have a significant adverse transboundary environmental effect and shall consult with those States at an early stage and in good faith." According to P. Sands, *Principles of International Environmental Law*, 2nd edition (Cambridge: Cambridge University Press, 2003), Principle 19 is part of customary international law.

25 Obligations of information exchange, prior notification, and consultation are viewed as dispute avoidance mechanisms, "designed to increase cooperation generally, identify potential conflicts as they are emerging, build confidence between the parties, or otherwise assist in allowing the parties to avoid and prevent disputes before they arise." D. Hunter, J. Salzman, and D. Zaelke, *International Environmental Law and Policy* (New York: Foundation, 1998) at 495–96.

26 R. Wolfrum, "International Law of Cooperation," in *Encyclopedia of Public International Law*, volume 2 (Amsterdam: Elsvier, 1995), 1242.

27 The duty to negotiate in good faith as an obligation of cooperation is clear from the case law listed in note 4), though its precise nature has been noted to be unclear. See P.M. Dupuy, "The Place and Role of Unilateralism in Contemporary International Law" (2000) 11 Eur. J. Int'l L. 23: "The relationship between the obligation to cooperate and the obligation to negotiate remains to be clarified, with the latter in reality appearing as one of the translations of the former, certainly the most immediate one." See also S. McCaffrey, *The Law of International Watercourses, Non Navigable Uses* (Oxford: Oxford University Press, 2001) at 402, who refers to the *Lac Lanoux* arbitration: "[T]he tribunal also illustrates

GABČÍKOVO-NAGYMAROS DISPUTE

The *Gabčíkovo-Nagymaros* dispute stemmed from a 1977 treaty between Hungary and (now) Slovakia to construct a system of locks on the Danube River. The stated goals of the treaty were hydroelectricity production, improved navigation, and flood prevention, and they called for the building of two series of locks, one at *Gabčíkovo* on Slovak territory along a thirty-one-kilometre bypass canal and another at Nagymaros on Hungarian territory, to comprise "a single and indivisible operational system of works."[28] The project required the building of three dams: first, at Dunakaliti to divert 95 per cent of the Danube River into the bypass canal that would feed *Gabčíkovo*; second, at *Gabčíkovo*, which was located in the middle of the canal, to regulate water level and generate hydroelectric power; and, third, at Nagymaros, 100 kilometres downstream of the canal, to produce further hydroelectric power and to regulate powerful water releases from *Gabčíkovo* at peak consumption periods. Hungary was responsible for the works at both Dunakiliti and Nagymaros. Importantly, the Treaty Concerning the Construction and Operation of the Gabčíkovo-Nagymaros System of Locks (1977 Treaty) contained broadly worded provisions for the protection of water quality, nature, and fishing interests to be implemented through a technical joint contractual plan that was negotiated over the years.[29] The treaty made no provision for termination, and dispute settlement was ultimately referable to the governments of the two countries.

---

how a state could be shown to break its obligation to cooperate, when cooperation takes the specific form of negotiating in good faith with a view to reaching an agreement."

28 The cost, construction, and operation of the project were to be borne in equal measure by the parties. *Gabčíkovo-Nagymaros, supra* note 3 at para. 18.

29 Treaty Concerning the Construction and Operation of the Gabčíkovo-Nagymaros System of Locks, 32 I.L.M. 1247 (1993) [1977 Treaty], Article 15: The parties "shall ensure, by means specified in the joint contractual plan, that the quality of the water in the Danube is not impaired as a result of the construction and operation of the System of Locks." Article 19: The parties "shall, through the means specified in the joint contractual plan, ensure compliance with the obligations for the protection of nature arising in connection with the construction and operation of the System of Locks." Article 20: The parties are to "take appropriate measures within the framework of their natural investments, for the protection of fishing interests in conformity with the *Convention Concerning Fishing in the Waters of the Danube*."

By the spring of 1989, work on the *Gabčíkovo* sector was substantially completed, while Hungary's progress on Nagymaros lagged far behind.[30] The environmental consequences of the project became the source of increasing public and scientific apprehension in Hungary in the late 1980s.[31] Fears were raised that the operation of Gabčíkovo at peak power mode could gravely threaten the primary drinking water supply to Budapest (by necessitating the building of the Nagymaros dam) and could also result in serious impairment of groundwater quality and the extinction of fluvial flora and fauna in the area adjacent to Dunakiliti.[32] Notwithstanding the preliminary nature of the science on these concerns, Hungary suspended and later abandoned work on the Nagymaros portion in 1989.[33] Hungary also proceeded to suspend work at Dunakiliti, which rendered impossible the operation of the Gabčíkovo power plant under the original plan.

Slovakia was anxious to proceed with the project, given its significant investment of US $2.3 billion by this time and its need for this important source of energy for its economic development.[34] Slovakia's position was that an agreement should be negotiated on ecological guarantees for the project on the basis that Hungary would immediately commence preparatory work at Dunakiliti. Furthermore, it proposed the negotiation of a separate agreement limiting or excluding the peak power mode at Gabčíkovo but also insisted on construction of Nagymaros within a fifteen-month extended time frame to permit environmental impact studies.[35] Should Hungary continue to breach the treaty, Slovakia indicated it would proceed with a "provisiona" solution to "prevent further losses."[36] Hungary, for its part, proposed a treaty with Slovakia to complete its portion of Gabčíkovo (with environmental protection guarantees) in exchange for the relinquishing of peak power operation at Gabčíkovo and the abandonment of the Nagymaros works.[37]

---

[30] *Gabčíkovo-Nagymaros, supra* note 3 at para. 31. The Gabčíkovo sector was 70–95 per cent complete on various projects.

[31] *Ibid.* at para. 32.

[32] *Ibid.* at para. 40.

[33] *Ibid.* at para. 35. The study of environmental impacts was not certain and would require "time-consuming studies."

[34] *Ibid.* at 225, per Vereshchetin J. (dissenting).

[35] *Ibid.* at para. 37.

[36] *Ibid.* at para. 61.

[37] *Ibid.* at para. 37.

Negotiations failed, and Slovakia eventually implemented a provisional solution (Variant C), which involved unilateral diversion of the Danube on Slovak territory upstream of Dunakiliti, including a dam, which would divert water into the Gabčíkovo canal. The plan, however, did not address Hungarian concerns of ecological damage to the old riverbed of the Danube, which would henceforth receive only 5 per cent of its original flow. Construction of the Variant C dam began in November 1991.[38] In May 1992, Hungary unilaterally terminated the 1977 Treaty, specifying Slovakia's refusal to suspend Variant C.[39] Implementation of Variant C was stepped up during the autumn of 1992, resulting in a diversion of 80–90 per cent of the Danube River waters into the canal feeding the Gabčíkovo power plant.[40]

In April 1993, both parties signed a special agreement referring the dispute before the International Court of Justice (ICJ). The main findings of the court's 1997 judgment were:

- Hungary's suspension and abandonment of works at Nagymaros and Dunakiliti breached the 1977 Treaty inasmuch as it rendered completion of the Project as a "single and indivisible" undertaking impossible;[41]
- Slovakia violated Hungary's right to equitable utilization of the Danube as a shared watercourse by putting Variant C into operation;[42] and
- termination of the treaty by Hungary was invalid.[43]

Notwithstanding the serious breaches committed by each party — abandonment and suspension of essential works by Hungary and illegal unilateral diversion by Slovakia — which *de facto* had brought the treaty to an end and fundamentally changed the nature of the project, the court upheld the 1977 Treaty and imposed on the parties a duty to negotiate in good faith its multiple objectives.[44] The

---

38 This may have marked the point of no return in terms of a negotiated outcome, according to Fleischhauer J. *Ibid.* at 209.

39 *Ibid.* at para. 91.

40 *Ibid.* at para. 65.

41 *Ibid.* at para. 48.

42 *Ibid.* at para. 78.

43 *Ibid.* at para. 89 ff.

44 See C.P.R. Romano, *The Peaceful Settlement of International Environmental Disputes: A Pragmatic Approach* (The Hague: Kluwer, 2000) at 259–60. The author notes

ICJ reasoned that the 1977 Treaty was a framework agreement that envisioned ongoing negotiations to meet its varied objectives. In the court's view, none of the treaty's objectives — whether energy production, improved navigation, or environmental protection — had been given absolute priority over the others, notwithstanding the apparent emphasis given to construction of the locks and energy production.[45] The court imposed on the parties an obligation to negotiate the multiple objectives of the 1977 Treaty, "keeping in mind that all of them should be fulfilled."[46] The task for the parties was to find a solution that would take account of the treaty objectives "in a joint and integrated way, as well as the norms of international environmental law and the principles of the law of international watercourses."[47]

The impasse in this case occurred in 1989 when Hungary insisted on suspending works pending further environmental studies while, at the same time, Slovakia pushed for completion of the project with provision for ecological protection modifications along the way. Hungary grounded its claim on a possibility of dire ecological and environmental consequences that required further study. Slovakia's reply was that Hungary's apprehensions could have been remedied through modifications to the plan. Slovakia further maintained that no agreement had yet been made on peak power operation at Gabčíkovo and, in any event, that Hungary's fears related only to "operating conditions of an extreme kind."[48] Meanwhile, Slovakia had a considerable investment and strong economic interest in completing the project.

The parties, convinced of the urgent and opposed imperatives they were facing and likely believing that they had valid legal grounds, reached a stalemate once their respective positions were formed. In restoring the 1977 Treaty, the ICJ implicitly offered what might have been a reasonable resolution to the dispute:

---

the "dogged defense" of the 1977 Treaty, notwithstanding the "continuous and reciprocal disregard" by both parties. However, upholding of a treaty was to be expected since the parties under the *compromis* put the focus on the 1977 Treaty.

[45] *Gabčíkovo-Nagymaros, supra* note 3 at para. 135. But see Romano, *ibid.* at 249. While the 1977 Treaty did not establish a priority for any one objective, "even a superficial reading of it showed the primacy of the hydroelectric element over the others."

[46] *Gabčíkovo-Nagymaros, supra* note 3 at para. 139.

[47] *Ibid.* at para. 141.

[48] *Ibid.* at para. 44.

Not only did Hungary insist on terminating construction at Nagymaros, but [Slovakia] stated, on various occasions in the course of negotiations, that it was willing to consider a limitation or even exclusion of operation at peak hour mode. In the latter case the construction of the Nagymaros dam would have become pointless. The explicit terms of the Treaty itself were therefore in practice acknowledged by the parties to be negotiable.[49]

The court communicated that the parties should have mutually accommodated each other's legitimate interests — Slovakia's economic interest and investment in proceeding with a modified project and Hungary's preventative approach to protect the drinking water supply of its capital city.

SOME LESSONS LEARNED

This case illustrates the complexity of international environmental negotiations. Hungary's concern for environmental protection rested on uncertain science, yet the magnitude of the risk, at least in the case of Budapest's drinking water supply, was severe (scientific uncertainty and the need for prevention). Slovakia's development needs were also compelling, particularly since they had invested vast sums of money into the project. The costs and benefits of either proceeding with the project as planned or cancelling it outright were highly asymmetrical (social costs). The interests of each party ultimately presented as zero sum solutions, and the parties resorted to antagonistic measures to achieve their seemingly irreconcilable ends. The governing law to the dispute — the 1977 Treaty — was not facilitative to dispute resolution since the rights and obligations contained therein were broad and indeterminate and depended on ongoing negotiations to meet its multiple objectives.

Norms of procedural cooperation, on their own, can be inadequate for solving complex and potentially costly environmental problems when they do not yield a political solution. Faced with crushing economic costs or dire environmental consequences, states may adopt reactive and defensive postures that usually result in failed negotiations. The reactions run the spectrum of self-serving legal argument, intransigence, and, when all else fails, recourse to

---

49 *Ibid.* at para. 138. While the proposed dams and canals were the subject of the 1977 Treaty, peak power operation was not in the treaty but could be negotiated under joint contractual plan that implemented the technical requirements of the treaty obligations.

unilateral state action.[50] These responses create antagonism and distrust in the other side, making resolution highly unlikely. The central point addressed in the next section is whether law, properly understood by the parties, could have helped reconcile these interests in the watercourse.

Relevance, Sources, and Use of Law

To summarize thus far, the law of international environmental cooperation emphasizes the need for states to work together to achieve shared goals of environmental protection. Specific obligations of cooperation are generally of a procedural nature and, as demonstrated in *Gabčíkovo-Nagymaros*, are not always successful. As an obligation of cooperation, the duty to negotiate in good faith demands strong efforts by states to strive towards agreement on use and protection. The principle of good faith activates a nexus between the efforts of states and the goal of agreement. Yet it is not clear how interacting rights are to be managed by states within this cooperative process. This section will propose an understanding of the function of law within international environmental negotiations. It will be suggested that soft legal norms express norms and goals of cooperation that reflect emerging concerns of the international community of states. On this basis, and under certain conditions, states should be receptive to international authoritative soft law instruments that help define existing rights when they negotiate in good faith.

RELEVANCE OF LAW

The way that law is conceived by states in international negotiations has fundamental consequences for whether law functions as a facilitative tool towards, or as an impediment against, agreement. A pure adjudicative model sees law as a body of binding rules

---

[50] R. Bilder, "The Role of Unilateral State Action in Preventing International Environmental Injury" (1981) 14 Vand. J. Transnat'l L. 53, defines unilateral state action as "any action which a state takes solely on its own, independent of any express co-operative arrangement with any other state or international institution." On the negative effects of unilateral measures on state cooperation, see L. Boisson de Chazournes, "Unilateralism and Environmental Protection: Issues of Perception and Reality of Issues" (2000) 11 Eur. J. Int'l L. 320, suggesting they lack legitimacy based on their individualistic nature [judge in its own cause] and tend to be a hegemonic weapon of powerful states.

ultimately enforceable through a third party arbiter.[51] To the extent that law is viewed as relevant under this approach, parties negotiate in the "shadow of the law," meaning their prospects of success, should the matter be litigated.[52] However, since recourse to adjudication is exceedingly rare in international law, particularly for environmental disputes, what role, if any, can law play in second party negotiation? In a horizontal legal system, absent a court of compulsory jurisdiction in most circumstances, the influence of law must be viewed in the context of interaction between states.

States often justify their positions, or alter their conduct, based on the persuasive force of legal argument of other states or international institutions. In their influential work, *The New Sovereignty*, Abraham Chayes and Antonia Handler Chayes advance that compliance with international law is best promoted through a process of justificatory discourse and persuasion between states, with law setting the parameters of debate.[53] In regime settings, non-complying states by practical necessity must give reasons for their conduct, leading to an iterative process of "justificatory discourse."[54] The

---

51 See J. Collier and A.V. Lowe, *The Settlement of Disputes in International Law: Institutions and Procedures* (Oxford: Oxford University Press, 1999) at 8: "[T]he disputing parties perceptions of the strength of their respective legal arguments is a major factor influencing the outcome of the negotiations or the decision to move from negotiation to some other form of dispute settlement."

52 States generally do not consent to the compulsory jurisdiction of international courts and tribunals, preferring instead to preserve their freedom of action and maintain control over the outcome of dispute resolution. In environmental disputes, there are added reasons not to go to court. See Birnie and Boyle, *supra* note 4 at 178–79.

53 A. Chayes and A. Handler Chayes, *The New Sovereignty: Compliance with International Regulatory Agreements* (Cambridge, MA: Harvard University Press, 1995). The starting point of this work is that states do not tend to intentionally flout their legal commitments but, to the extent that they do not comply, it is frequently related to problems of incapacity, ambiguity in treaty language, and/or transitional (or temporal) factors.

54 *Ibid.* at 25–26. The concept of "justificatory discourse" resembles the requirement of "rational discussion" with respect to good faith negotiation in Canadian labour relations law. One corollary of rational discussion is that parties justify the negotiating positions that they take. The premise here is that parties can meaningfully negotiate and more likely reach agreement if they engage in a rational discussion, as opposed to hard bargaining. An employer or union cannot during good faith bargaining, for example, insist on their own interpretation of the law and refuse to discuss other interpretations. See *Adams Canadian Labour Law*, looseleaf (Aurora: Canada Law Book, 2003) at 10–93 ff; and B. Adell, "The Duty to Bargain in Good Faith: Its Recent Development in Canada,"

role of legal norms in the compliance process envisioned by the Chayeses is critical in defining "the methods and terms of the continuing international discourse in which states seek to justify their actions."[55] However, these norms are not presumed to be clear and self-guiding in any given circumstance but, instead, rely on discursive interpretation by the parties to clarify the meaning of the rules.[56] Law is seen as a process of interpretation and argumentation moving towards common understandings in the scenario presented.[57] In the final analysis, "jawboning" together with good legal argument is persuasive (and bad legal argument is not), and this combination promotes compliance. The need of states to achieve their goals as members in good standing of the international community is ample incentive for states to comply with regime norms.[58] Even outside of regime settings, states employ legal argument to justify positions and to persuade other parties, and they will do so on the basis of soft law. Soft law's lack of formal status, in other words, is not determinative of its influence in negotiations.[59]

---

paper presented at the twenty-eighth Annual Conference of the McGill University Industrial Relations Centre, March 1980, Queens University Industrial Relations Centre, No. 48.

[55] Chayes and Handler Chayes, *supra* note 53 at 8.

[56] *Ibid.* at 12.

[57] *Ibid.* at 122.

[58] *Ibid.* at 26–27. The success of the managerial process is assured through the "new sovereignty," where states, if they are to realize their own interests in an interdependent world, must "submit to the pressures of international regulation" in order to maintain their membership in good standing within regimes and in the international community.

[59] See D. Bodansky, "Symposium: Customary (and Not So Customary) International Environmental Law" (1995) 3 Ind. J. Global Leg. Stud. 105, who argues that it is better to view international environmental norms not as how states behave but in how states speak to one another. This "declarative law" acts as "evaluative standards used by states to justify their actions and to criticize the actions of others" (at 115). Recognizing the dearth of third-party dispute resolution in international law, Bodansky views inter-state negotiation as the forum for declarative law and in this context (as opposed to adjudication) the legal status of a norm is not critical to its influence. In this regard, it has been documented in several cases that emanation of soft law norms from accepted channels has facilitated the resolution of international disputes. Others have also noted that the form of the instrument is not determinative of its influence. See C. Chinkin, "Normative Development in the International Legal System," in D. Shelton, ed., *Commitment and Compliance: The Role of Non-Binding Norms in the International Legal System* (Oxford: Oxford University Press, 2000) at 37; D. Shelton, "Law, Non

Law as persuasion is a starting point for harnessing the constructive potential of law for dispute settlement. Another premise that must be challenged is the connotation of the concept of "dispute" in international law. The international law definition of "dispute" is "a disagreement over a point of law or fact, a conflict of legal views or interests between two persons."[60] This definition, by itself, does not pose any conceptual barriers to a constructive role of law in the negotiation process. In setting a threshold for adjudication, it merely recognizes the reality that factual and legal disputes between states can and do occur. But the term "dispute" in international legal doctrine, including the law of watercourses, connotes an adversarial process culminating in adjudication.[61] This is the wrong framework to start from. When disputes do arise, there is no inherent reason why they should be treated by states in an adversarial or contentious manner. For reasons already discussed, cooperative approaches to dispute resolution are what is needed. Instead of characterizing disputes as anathema to the law of environmental protection — that is, dispute avoidance — it is better, and more accurate, to conceptualize the negotiation of disputes as a specific and more demanding duty within the law of cooperation.

SOURCES OF LAW

As technically binding sources, international law consists primarily of treaty law and customary law.[62] These are binding sources of law in the sense that the rules they prescribe must be followed by

---

Law and the Problem of 'Soft Law,'" in Shelton, ed., *ibid.* at 11; and J. Brunnée and S.J. Toope, "The Changing Nile Basin Regime: Does Law Matter?" (2002) 43 Harv. Int'l L.J. 148.

60 *Mavrommatis Palestine Concession*, (1924) P.C.I.J. (Ser. A) No. 2, 12.

61 Draft Articles on the Law of the Non-Navigational Uses of International Watercourses, *infra* note 80, Article 7(2), which requires consultation when an affected state is caused significant harm despite the exercise of due diligence, indicates that when consultations fail to lead to a solution, the Article 33 dispute settlement procedures (including negotiation) will apply. See also A. Tanzi and M. Arcari *The United Nations Convention on the Law of International Watercourses* (The Hague: Kluwer Law, 2001) at 123. The term "consultation" is employed in Article 6(2) since it was believed "negotiation" necessitated the existence of a dispute possibly requiring dispute settlement procedures, when instead dispute avoidance was the aim of the provision.

62 Statute of the International Court of Justice, in I. Brownlie. ed., *Basic Documents in International Law*, 3rd edition (Oxford: Clarendon Press, 1983) at 387. Article

states in good faith. Briefly, treaty obligations are signified by mandatory commitments detailed in a written document between states.[63] International custom requires both the objective element of widespread *state practice* and the subjective belief by states that the rule is binding — that is, *opinio juris*.[64] Generally speaking, the lengthy time periods involved garnering evidence of sufficiently widespread state practice and *opinio juris* makes reliance on custom ill-suited to emerging areas such as international environmental law.[65] In the shared watercourse context, the few customary rules that exist are indeterminate in their meaning and in their relationship to one another, much like the rights of use and obligations of protection in the 1977 Treaty in the *Gabčíkovo-Nagymaros* case. Authoritative soft law can serve as an interpretive aid in these situations of broadly expressed rights and obligations.

Persuasive Attributes of Authoritative Soft Law

Soft scientific facts, high costs, and hard choices explain the proliferation of "soft law" commitments undertaken by states in the area of international environmental protection. The term "soft law" has been described as a social norm that is somewhere between legally binding in the strict sense and mere political or moral commitment.[66] It is associated with a kind of law that serves, in the minds

---

38(1) also refers to general principles of law and, as subsidiary sources, judicial decisions, and the teachings of highly qualified publicists.

63 "Treaty" is defined as "an international agreement concluded between States in written form and governed by international law, whether embodied in a single instrument or in two or more related instruments and whatever its particular designation. Vienna Convention, *supra* note 4, Article 2(1)(a).

64 Custom need not be based on universal state practice and *opinio juris*, but there should be widespread participation including states whose interests are specially affected. I. Brownlie, *Principles of Public International Law*, 5th edition (London: Clarendon Press, 1998) at 6.

65 It is possible though not common, however, for custom to arise within a short period provided certain stringent conditions are met. See *Case Concerning North Sea Continental Shelf (Federal Republic of Germany v. Denmark; Federal Republic of Germany v. Netherlands)*, [1969] I.C.J. Rep. 3 (20 February) at para. 73.

66 D. Thurer, "Soft Law," in *Encyclopedia of Public International Law*, volume 4 (Amsterdam: Elsevier, 2000), 452. See also Chinkin, *supra* note 59 at 30, which provides a more comprehensive list of law that may be considered soft law: articulation in a non-binding form; terms that are vague and imprecise; the declaring body lacks international law-making authority; law directed at non-state actors; law without a "corresponding theory of responsibility"; and law based on voluntary

of some, as a questionable basis for legal obligation.[67] Yet certain kinds of soft law articulations — that is, those that emanate from a fair process that is representative of the international community of states — *prima facie* have strong persuasive value when states negotiate in the absence of clear treaty or customary rules, notwithstanding their non-binding status.

In a substantive sense, soft international environmental law occurs when states undertake qualified treaty commitments (for example, to reduce pollution "as appropriate" or "where possible"). Here, soft law accomplishes a number of specific purposes in connection with environmental protection.[68] It allows states to undertake qualified substantive obligations to protect the environment when there is a lack of will or knowledge (such as scientific uncertainty) to do more. It thus serves as a first step towards the creation or development of "hard" obligations, as knowledge, feasible options, and political will are gathered.[69] In form, soft law obligations may be inferred from the nature of the instrument or legal articulation. The Rio Declaration on Environment and Development is an example of a legal instrument that employs mandatory wording but is considered non-binding on states.[70] Other examples include authoritative statements of legal rules by the International Law Commission, which I discuss in the next section.

Fundamentally, the recourse to soft international environmental law reflects an imperative to act on international problems in a manner that is flexible, to reflect the diversity of state needs and capabilities, and, incrementally progressive, to reflect growing

---

adherence or non-judicial means of enforcement. See also A. Boyle, "Some Reflections on the Relationship of Treaties and Soft Law" (1999) 48 I.C.L.Q. 901, which identifies three possible meanings: soft law as non-binding; soft law as principles, not rules; and soft law as law that is not enforceable through binding dispute resolution.

[67] Indeed, some writers have rejected as oxymoron the possibility of law as not being coextensive with legal obligation. See Thurer, *supra* note 66 at 456.

[68] See D. Shelton, *supra* note 59 at 12–13; Chinkin, *supra* note 59 at 30–31 and 41; and A. Kiss, "Commentary and Conclusions," in Shelton, ed., *supra* note 59, 237. Some other purposes of soft law are to avoid domestic legislative and constitutional barriers to treaty ratification and/or permit ease of amendment or termination and to elaborate upon hard law obligations.

[69] Where there is uncertainty in technical knowledge, soft law is an appropriate means "to formulate shared expectations at a lower level." Thurer, *supra* note 66 at 453.

[70] Rio Declaration, *supra* note 24.

consensus regarding problems and possible solutions.[71] Christine
Chinkin captures the essence of the need and purpose of soft law
in relation to formal sources:

The complexity of international legal affairs has outpaced traditional
methods of law-making, necessitating management through international
organizations, specialized agencies, programmes, and private bodies that
do not fit the paradigm of Article 38(1) of the Statute of the ICJ [that is,
treaties and custom]. Consequently, the concept of soft law facilitates international cooperation by acting as a bridge between the formalities of
law making and the needs of international life by legitimizing behaviour
and creating stability.[72]

Daniel Thurer echoes this view by positing that soft law norms, in a
horizontal legal order, provide a compromise position between state
sovereignty (based on treaty and customary rules) and the need to
establish a basis for international cooperation and stability.[73] Among
the features that Thurer identifies with soft law is that it generally
expresses common expectations and is "characterized by a certain
proximity to the law and above all by its capacity to produce certain
legal effects."[74]

Soft law embodies many of the attributes that make law persuasive in international negotiations, namely formality, authoritative-
ness, ability to elicit an obligation of obedience, and ability to serve
as a basis for criticism.[75] First, soft law possesses formality in the
sense that it is the product of intense negotiations and acts as "declarative law" between states in the negotiation process. Accordingly,
soft law has a legitimacy and authority beyond its non-binding status. Second, the creation of soft law through fair and accepted procedures that reflect the will of the international community of states
can give it an authority that is indistinguishable in its effects from
binding rules. Third, soft law elicits an obligation of obedience, at

---

[71] Soft law does this in a way that traditional forms of law-making — that is, custom
and hard treaty commitments — are incapable of addressing, for example, in
the way soft law influences state behaviour, sets negotiating agendas, and sup-
plements and shades existing obligations. Chinkin, *supra* note 59 at 41.

[72] *Ibid.* at 42.

[73] Thurer, *supra* note 66 at 453.

[74] *Ibid.* at 454.

[75] These criteria of law's persuasive attributes are from Chayes and Handler Chayes,
supra note 53 at 116.

least with respect to consenting states.[76] The point is concretely illustrated in *Commonwealth of Australia v. State of Tasmania*, where the soft law wording of the Convention for the Protection of the World Cultural and Natural Heritage — that states "shall endeavour" to protect natural heritage — was held by the Australian Court of Appeal to be an obligation of good faith performance.[77] Fourth, soft law can clearly serve as a basis for criticism when it is not followed. Soft law may be viewed as "evaluative standards" or "standards of good conduct," which, when not adhered to, may expose recalcitrant states to criticism. Chinkin elaborates this concept, suggesting that soft law

has both a legitimizing and delegitimizing direct effect: it is extremely difficult for even a State that rejected some instrument of soft law to argue that behaviour in conformity with it by those who accept it is illegitimate ... the legitimacy of a previously existing norm of international law may be undermined by emerging principles of soft law.[78]

In sum, soft law may carry a "formal" and authoritative quality as a result of the process through which it is articulated. Furthermore, and as a result of its authoritative quality, it can also serve as a basis for criticism when its "standards" are not followed. These attributes of law endow soft law norms with the capacity to persuade when the conditions of legitimacy, discussed further in this article, are favourable. Finally, whatever one's view of the "legality" of soft law, it has *de facto* practical relevance to negotiation:

Soft law, as well as law in the strict sense, provides a means to determine politics by the establishment of principles. When a legal solution to a

---

[76] Thurer, *supra* note 66 at 457: "[T]he principle of good faith ... has the effect that expectations produced by [soft law] are legally protected insofar as they are justified by the conduct of the parties concerned."

[77] *Commonwealth of Australia v. The State of Tasmania*, (1983) 158 C.L.R. 1 (Australian Supreme Court). Convention for the Protection of the World Cultural and Natural Heritage, 11 I.L.M. 1358 (1972).

[78] C.M. Chinkin, "The Challenge of Soft Law: Development and Change in International Law" (1989) 38 I.C.L.Q. at 866. See also O. Schachter, *Sharing the World's Resources* (New York: Columbia University Press, 1977) at 3–4: "Whether or not they [referring to declarations, charters and resolutions of UN organizations] are accepted as international legal rules, they are likely to engender expectations about future patterns of international distribution, and, in some cases, to delegitimize traditional norms which would otherwise be regarded as authoritative."

specific problem in international relations cannot be reached, extralegal norms [meaning soft law] often provide a practical substitute or a basis for developing legally binding norms.[79]

On a theoretical and practical level then, soft law does have attributes that make it persuasive within the process of negotiation.

Watercourses Convention

Strictly speaking, the Watercourses Convention is a treaty and would not be characterized as soft law. However, the term soft law is used here to include legal instruments that are generated through, or representative of, a fair and inclusive process that reflects the will of the international community of states *although it may not be binding on the disputing parties.* In 1994, and after thirty-five years of preparation, the International Law Commission (ILC) released its Final Draft Articles on the Non-Navigable Uses of International Watercourses (Draft Articles on Watercourses). This comprehensive work on the law of international watercourses was subsequently adopted in treaty form, without substantial change, as the Watercourses Convention.[80] Since these instruments are substantially the same, I refer throughout to the Watercourses Convention but draw heavily from the important work of the ILC — that is, the ILC draft articles and commentary.

One source of *prima facie* persuasive soft law is this authoritative work of the ILC, which is a permanent subsidiary body of the UN General Assembly charged with the codification and progressive development of international law.[81] "Codification" under the Statute of the International Law Commission is defined as "the more

---

[79] Thurer, *supra* note 66 at 459. See also R. Baxter, "International Law in 'Her Infinite Majesty'" (1980) 29 I.C.L.Q. 565 (soft law as establishing a legal framework to guide negotiations).

[80] Draft Articles on the Law of the Non-Navigational Uses of International Watercourses, International Law Commission 46th Session, *Yearbook of the International Law Commission* (1994), volume 2, Part 2, in A. Watts, ed., *The International Law Commission 1949-1998*, volume 2 "The Treaties," Part II (Oxford: Oxford University Press, 1999) at 1332 [Draft Articles on Watercourses]. The Watercourse Convention was adopted through the UN General Assembly "without substantially departing from" the final ILC articles.

[81] Statute of the International Law Commission, Article 13(1)(a) of the Charter of the United Nations, in M.R. Anderson et al., eds., *The International Law Commission and the Future of International Law* (London: British Institute of International and Comparative Law, 1998), 55 [ILC Statute].

precise formulation and systematisation of rules of international law where there has already been extensive State practice, precedent and doctrine," whereas "progressive development" means subjects not yet regulated or in which law has been insufficiently developed through state practice.[82] The ILC is comprised of experts in international law who *de facto* act in an individual, rather than in a representative, capacity. As well, ILC membership reflects the "main forms of civilisation and the principal legal systems of the world."[83]

As former ICJ Judge Schwebel comments, the ILC deliberations consist of an extensive scholarly and systematic analysis of state practice, jurisprudence, and doctrine in codifying and developing legal principles.[84] In light of these efforts, it is not surprising that "(m)any of its codifications have become widely regarded as authoritative statements of the law and relied on by international courts, international organisations, and governments."[85] The thorough work of five rapporteurs over a quarter of a century in the area of non-navigable uses of international watercourses gives the ILC's Draft Articles on Watercourses, in the opinion of one study, "an authority which is likely to endure."[86] Yet the commission's success in instigating a deliberative and authoritative process for codification may also contribute to its weakness in progressively developing the law.[87] In other words, its slow apolitical procedures do not make it amenable to the dynamic negotiation process of law-making in fast changing areas such as international environmental law.[88] Thus, while the ILC's comprehensive and impartial study of a subject area

---

[82] ILC Statute, *ibid.*, Article 15.

[83] *Ibid.*, Article 8. See also M.R. Anderson and C. Wickremasinghe, "Introduction," in Anderson et al., eds., *supra* note 81 at xv.

[84] S.M. Schwebel, "The Influence of the International Court of Justice on the Work of the International Law Commission and the Influence of the Commission on the Work of the Court," in *Making Better International Law: The International Law Commission at Fifty* (New York: United Nations, 1998) at 161. See also ILC Statute, *supra* note 81, Articles 16 and 17.

[85] Birnie and Boyle, *supra* note 4 at 22. And indeed, the ICJ in the *Gabčíkovo-Nagymaros* case, *supra* note 3, explicitly relied on the work of the ILC in four areas of law: treaties, state succession, state responsibility, and international watercourses.

[86] A.E. Boyle and A.V. Lowe, "Report of the Study Group on the Future Work of the International Law Commission," in Anderson et al., eds., *supra* note 81 at 14.

[87] *Ibid.* at 22–23

[88] *Ibid.*

of law gives its work a unique authoritative quality, the rather clinical nature of its processes may tend towards a conservative picture of the law.

Exclusive reliance on treaty and customary law is not an accurate reflection of how states negotiate in connection with emerging concerns and interests of environmental protection. Soft law instruments can serve as reference points in identifying the goals of international cooperation or a "communality of purpose," which reflects increasing global interdependencies.[89] Soft law is "eminently suitable for resolution of disputes through negotiation" and "may provide a framework of expectations that could be utilized in negotiations to reach an adjustment of a dispute."[90] In soft law, we may identify not only the goals of international cooperation but also the norms applicable to achieving these goals. The principle of good faith that closely connects state efforts and the goal of negotiated agreement set a parallel nexus between authoritative soft law and the goals of international cooperation. In other words, good faith efforts to achieve agreement can, and should, be directly informed by the objectives and norms of authoritative soft law instruments. The more difficult question is how this is to be done.

USE OF LAW: THE LEGITIMACY OF INTERESTS WITHIN RIGHTS

When rights and obligations are unclear in meaning or intention and are in need of interpretation, authoritative soft law can be harnessed to establish the legitimacy of interests within established rights and to assist in the process of their reconciliation. This approach offers the advantage of a discourse that is more functional for the negotiation process.

Problem of Rights

A competing rights approach to international environmental dispute resolution, without more, tells us little about the specific interests at stake for the parties and how these relate to one another

---

[89] G. Handl "A Hard Look at Soft Law" (1988) 82 A.S.I.L. Proc. 371. Soft law can be an expression of emerging notions of public international order — a basis for establishing "legitimate international concern" in areas that were previously the exclusive domain of state sovereignty. Further, soft law reflects a paradigm shift of "communality of purpose" as a result of deepening global interdependencies in international security, environmental, and economic matters.

[90] C.M. Chinkin, in Handl, *supra* note 89 at 391.

during negotiations. As already mentioned, tribunals have indicated that state rights in these situations are to be interpreted and exercised reasonably. But the notion of reasonableness does not assist when there is no shared meaning of the concept among states of the international community.[91] More objective is the idea that the interpretation of rights may be assisted by looking to state practice in the international community, thus, discretion "can be structured ... and rendered more predictable, by careful analysis of international practice or by explicit recognition of relevant criteria in treaties or other instruments."[92] State practice is indeed a helpful criterion, but, even still, a more probing inquiry is needed to determine the nature and interaction of rights in any given negotiation scenario.

One possibility is to precisely identify the specific interests in play during negotiations. Practically speaking, states "activate" their specific interests at stake during negotiations that are derivative of rights and obligations. In the absence of specific treaty rules, these interests may be legitimized with reference to authoritative soft law. A focus on legitimate interests, as established through a wider conception of law, can reduce confusion and ward off self-interested interpretation that otherwise emerges from the expression of broad rights. Consideration for the interests of states in shared watercourses was indicated in *Lac Lanoux Arbitration (Spain v. France)*, where the tribunal observed that,

according to the rules of good faith, the upstream state is under the obligation to take into consideration the various interests involved, to seek to give them every satisfaction compatible with the pursuit of its own interests, and to show that in this regard it is genuinely concerned to reconcile the interests of the other riparian State with its own.[93]

---

[91] M. Byers, "Abuse of Rights" (2002) 47 McGill L.J. 417, referring to reasonableness standard in international law, "(c)onstructing a hypothetical 'man on the Clapham omnibus' requires a degree of cultural and situational commonality that has traditionally not been present among many of the states that make up the international community."

[92] Birnie and Boyle, *supra* note 4 at 146–47, referring to the principle of equitable utilization of watercourses. Interpreting the exercise of rights on the basis of state practice was also suggested by Sir Hersh Lauterpacht in the context of discussing the limits placed on rights under abuse of right doctrine. See Brownlie, *supra* note 62 at 296 and 305.

[93] *Lac Lanoux, supra* note 4 at 150.

Cooperative reconciliation of interests in the watercourse is the essential nature of the principle of equitable utilization of a shared watercourse (discussed later in this article), but it may be unclear what constitutes a *legally* significant interest that is captured by the right and how this interest is to be reconciled with competing *legally* significant interests. A legal approach to identifying interests within rights — what I will call legitimate interests — can be harnessed through authoritative soft law instruments.

Identifying Legitimate Interests

Theories of legitimacy in international law may help determine the nature of, and interaction between, specific interests at play in shared natural resource disputes. Thomas Franck proposes four indicators that advance the legitimacy of legal norms: determinacy, or the ability of the norm to convey a clear meaning; coherence, or consistency of the content and practice of the rule with other rules (that is, whether it treats likes alike or at least exceptions as coherent); symbolic validation, or the asserting of a rule's authority through repetitive practice or ritual; and adherence, or the relationship to secondary rules of recognition, for example, treaty and custom.[94] The greater the degree to which a norm embodies these attributes, according to Franck, the more it will be considered legitimate and exert a compliance pull on states.

However, the last two legitimacy criteria are not entirely convincing. In discussing symbolic validation, Franck makes the point that the "law accords a particular veneration to rules which have stood the test of time."[95] Yet, in fact, much of international environmental law modifies the established rules of resource use that have stood the test of time. Legal argument based on this criterion, at least in the environmental context, would not be responsive to current concerns that seek to modify established rules. Furthermore, adherence emphasizes the connection of norms with treaty and customary law, thus negating the possibility of soft law as signalling emerging concerns that are relevant to the negotiation process.[96]

---

[94] T.M. Franck, *Fairness in International Law and Institutions* (Oxford: Clarendon Press, 1995) at 30–45.

[95] *Ibid.* at 37.

[96] On this last point, it is interesting to note that Franck's discussion of the draft Watercourse Convention (as it then was) suggests that there "is no reason why these standards (of the convention) cannot be applied just as effectively as standards found in more traditional normative rules." *Ibid.* at 75.

The theory of Lon Fuller offers a critical building block for developing a more convincing theory of legitimacy, including the identification of legitimate interests, for international environmental negotiations. Fuller views law as a constant mutually generative process of construction between the governed and the governing with the aim of achieving purposive goals.[97] Although law's purposive goals remain largely aspirational to Fuller, law has a more immediate and less lofty aim of imposing duties on actors within the system.[98] In other words, "certain conditions need to be in place to allow human beings to pursue their purposes through law" and without this legitimacy, law creation is fundamentally flawed.[99] This morality of duty, as Fuller calls it, establishes "minimum standards of appropriate conduct that make life in society possible."[100] Fuller identifies eight criteria that could indicate a failure in law-making: a failure to make rules, a failure to publicize rules, the making of retroactive laws, a failure to make comprehensible rules, making rules that contradict with one another, creating rules that make compliance impossible, changing rules so often that required conduct becomes unclear and there is inconsistency between stated rules and their administration in practice.[101]

Brunnée and Toope's interactional international theory borrow from Fuller's eight internal criteria for legality and applies them to the legitimacy and persuasiveness of legal norms within regimes:

In an interactional theory of law, law can be distinguished from other forms of social normativity by the specific type of rationality apparent in the internal processes that make law possible. This rationality is dependent upon reasoned argument, reference to past practice and contemporary social aspirations, and the deployment of analogy. The conditions of internal morality ensure that rules are compatible with one another, that they ask reasonable things of the people to whom they are directed, that they are transparent and relatively predictable, and that officials treat known rules as shaping their exercise of discretion. When these conditions are met,

---

[97] Discussed in J. Brunnée and S.J. Toope, "International Law and Constructivism: Elements of an Interactional Theory of International Law" (2000) 39 Colum. J Transnat'l L. 45.

[98] *Ibid.* at 54.

[99] *Ibid.* at 53.

[100] *Ibid.* at 54.

[101] L. Fuller, *The Morality of Law*, 2nd edition (New Haven, CT: Yale University Press, 1969) at 33 ff.

when this particular rationality is evident, law will tend to attract its own adherence. It will be viewed as legitimate, possessing the capacity to generate moral commitment. Interactional legal theory treats bindingness as an internal quality of the subjects (and creators) of the legal system; bindingness becomes self-bindingness.[102]

To restate, it is the internal characteristics of legal norms that give them their legitimacy, these being that:

- [t]he rules are transparent and relatively predictable;
- [o]fficial action is congruent with known rules;
- [t]he rules are compatible with one another; and
- [t]he rules ask reasonable things of the parties.[103]

The legitimacy of legal norms, according to Brunnée and Toope, does not depend on formal consent or conventional notions of bindingness.[104] One appeal of these legitimacy criteria is that they posit an explanation for the normative role that non-binding "soft law" clearly does play in international law-making. The transparency of a norm is not necessarily tied to treaty or customary law, but it can hold persuasive value on the authoritative basis of its creation. The legitimacy of a norm does not depend on its status as custom but can be advanced when it is shown to reflect an emerging state practice. Perhaps most importantly for negotiation, this approach to legitimacy is responsive to current concerns and realities of the international community of states — that is, does the norm ask reasonable things of the parties?

The ability of legal norms to meet these criteria establishes their persuasiveness as good legal argument in the process of justificatory discourse during negotiation. Yet what constitutes good legal argument may not be obvious since "the various legitimacy requirements will not necessarily point law-makers in the same direction."[105] There may be a tension, for example, between the reasonableness of what law asks, on the one hand, and the predictability and transparency of rules, on the other hand, which requires law-makers to

---

102 Brunnée and Toope, *supra* note 97 at 56.

103 J. Brunnée, "COPing with Consent: Law-Making under Multilateral Environmental Agreements" (2002) 15 Leiden J. Int'l L. 36.

104 J. Brunnée and S.J. Toope, "Persuasion and Enforcement: Explaining Compliance with International Law" (2002) 13 Finnish Y.B. Int'l L. 273.

105 Brunnée, *supra* note 103 at 44.

strike a balance.[106] Still, the stronger the adherence to these criteria, the more persuasive will be the rule.[107]

The legitimacy criteria of Brunnée and Toope need to be modified for pre-regime negotiation scenarios where there is an absence of easily identifiable norms. The first criterion becomes, in our context, how *obviously applicable* the norm is to a negotiation scenario? Treaty commitments on the subject matter will obviously be most applicable, but recent authoritative soft law instruments may supplement treaties when the latter are unclear in their meaning. To maintain legitimacy in this kind of scenario, however, soft law must be reasonably clear in how it resolves the controversy between the parties, otherwise it adds nothing.[108] Second, the fact that the negotiating states (or, in their absence, other states) adhere to the norm *in actual practice* in similar cases imbues the norm with legitimacy. However, one should not confuse this criterion with the threshold of state practice that is required to establish a rule of customary international law. Emerging state practice, especially in tandem with the other legitimacy criteria, may be enough to persuasively establish the legitimacy of the norm. Third, authoritative soft law must be compatible with existing rules between the parties — that is, formal rights and obligations, otherwise they may serve to confuse matters and will not be convincing. Fourth, norms must resonate with the negotiation "facts" or dilemma with which the parties are grappling. I therefore suggest that the legitimacy of a norm, and, thus, its persuasiveness, will increase in positive correlation to the following factors:

- How obviously applicable are the norms to the negotiation scenario and how clear is the meaning of these rules (transparency and clarity)?
- Do the negotiating states and other states in similar situations follow these norms (past state practice)?
- Are norms compatible with existing norms of the negotiating states?
- Do the norms ask reasonable things in relation to the circumstances?

---

[106] *Ibid.* "Frequently, they will be in a dynamic relationship and will require lawmakers to strike a balance between them."

[107] *Ibid.* at 46.

[108] I do not include here the criterion of "relative predictability" since the arduous process of negotiation between a global community of states ensures that these instruments do not arise frequently.

How might this theory of norms apply to international watercourse negotiations? Assuming the absence of clear treaty rules, authoritative rules in the Watercourses Convention can be persuasively invoked by parties to advance, and reconcile, legitimate interests. First, as discussed earlier, the Watercourses Convention is the product of a fair, inclusive, and deliberative process, and it possesses unique authority in international watercourse law. It follows that the convention would be a natural reference point for states to negotiate their competing interests in a shared watercourse. Furthermore, the convention is reasonably clear in explicating the interests contained within these rights and how these are to be integrated or reconciled. Second, the Watercourses Convention, owing to the means by which it was created, provides strong evidence of state practice of the international community. States, of course, may look at other examples of state practice (including, most importantly, their own), but the Watercourses Convention can be of presumptive importance. Third, determining compatibility with existing norms means looking at the existing formal rules, whether treaty or custom, in order to assess compatibility with an authoritative soft law instrument. Where rights and obligations are broad and unclear, the Watercourses Convention can explicate relevant interests contained within those rights, integrate them when they are in tension, and, if integration is not possible, may even reconcile opposed interests. The integration and reconciliation of relevant social, environmental, and economic interests in the rules of the Watercourses Convention accord added legitimacy to the instrument.

Based on these first three criteria, the Watercourses Convention may *prima facie* hold a high degree of legitimacy — it lays out transparent rules reflecting state practice, which interpret broad treaty or customary rules. The degree to which these new rules correspond to the factual imperatives in which the parties find themselves is the most important factor in determining their legitimacy and, thus, their persuasive value. In other words, where an interest that "asks reasonable things" corresponds to an authoritative legal articulation, its persuasive value will be undeniable in negotiations. For example, the greater the urgency or seriousness of the environmental threat and the stronger its correlation to the legitimacy of soft law, the more persuasive will be the claim to a legitimate interest in environmental protection that must be effectively accommodated in the negotiated outcome.

GABČÍKOVO-NAGYMAROS REVISITED

By way of illustration, this section attempts to apply the above theory of legitimate legal rules to the *Gabčíkovo-Nagymaros* case — a dispute that remains unresolved to this day. The intention is to illustrate how states might use an authoritative soft law instrument to resolve disputes in good faith in the absence of detailed treaty rules between them — this being the situation between Hungary and Slovakia around the time of the ICJ's judgment. I will first discuss the Watercourses Convention in some detail and then discuss its application towards a possible resolution of the impasse.

WATERCOURSES CONVENTION

Customary international law recognizes both a right of equitable (though not necessarily equal) use for riparian states to a shared watercourse as well as a right of states to be free of environmental harm caused by other states.[109] Prior to the Watercourses Convention, the scope of the principle of equitable utilization in relation to environmental protection was unclear, including its relationship to the "no significant harm" principle. The Watercourses Convention explicates, integrates, and ultimately reconciles legitimate interests in the watercourse.[110]

Equitable Utilization

The principle of equitable and reasonable utilization is formulated in Article 5 of the Watercourses Convention, as follows:

5(1) Watercourse States shall in their respective territories utilize an international watercourse in an equitable and reasonable manner. In particular, an international watercourse shall be used and developed by watercourse States with a view to attaining optimal and sustainable utilization thereof

---

109 On equitable utilization, see Article 5 of Watercourses Convention, *supra* note 2, and ILC commentary in Draft Articles on Watercourses, *supra* note 80 at 1352 ff, in particular para. (8). On the no significant harm principle, see Principle 2 of the Rio Declaration, *supra* note 24.

110 Expression is given to environmental protection, though in the view of some writers, it does not go far enough in incorporating international environmental law. See E. Hey, "The Watercourses Convention: To What Extent Does It Provide a Basis for Regulating Uses of International Watercourses? (1998) 7 R.E.C.I.E.L. 291.

and benefits therefrom, taking into account the interests of the water-course States concerned, consistent with adequate protection of the watercourse.

5(2) Watercourse States shall participate in the use, development and protection of an international watercourse in an equitable and reasonable manner. Such participation includes both the right to utilize the watercourse and the duty to cooperate in the protection and development thereof, as provided in the present Convention.

This provision goes further than a customary right of equitable utilization by indicating the objective of "optimal and sustainable utilization" consistent with "adequate protection of the watercourse." "Sustainable use," according to the ILC commentary, means that watercourse development and management are to be pursued in an "integrated manner," taking into account long- and short-term planning needs, and "should incorporate environmental, economic and social considerations."[111] Adequate protection has a broad meaning, including protection of the watercourse ecosystem.[112] There is a significant procedural component, in that equitable participation of states is seen as being integral to achieving equitable utilization.[113] States are not to make "blind assessments"

---

[111] Draft Articles on Watercourses, *supra* note 80 at 1353. Sustainable use, while referred to in the article's commentary, was included in the text of the Watercourse Convention. One criticism of this formulation of sustainable use is that it is not specific enough in its requirements. States therefore have much discretion in giving effect to sustainable use. Furthermore, when states dispute conflicting uses, the question becomes not whether the use is sustainable, but sustainable for what purpose? See Birnie and Boyle, *supra* note 4 at 89 and 318.

[112] Draft Articles on Watercourses, *supra* note 80 at 1353. Adequate protection of the watercourse is broadly defined to include conservation, water-related disease, or security concerns as well as issues such as regulating flow and controlling floods. A specific application of adequate protection is Article 20, which formulates an obligation to "individually or jointly, protect and preserve the ecosystems of international watercourses" (at 1397). This essentially requires states to "shield" international watercourse ecosystems from harm or damage. The duty to "preserve" is made principally in relation to freshwater ecosystems in "pristine and unspoiled condition." The duty to protect and preserve ecosystems assists in ensuring the continued viability of freshwater ecosystems as life support systems, "thus providing an essential basis for sustainable development" (at 1397). The standard of Article 20 is one of due diligence.

[113] *Ibid.* at 1353–54. Equitable participation "flows from, and is bound up with, the rule of equitable utilization."

of equitable utilization of a watercourse without cooperative duties of information sharing, consultation, and negotiation. [114]

Article 6 of the Draft Articles on Watercourses provides a non-exhaustive list of factors that states are to consider in determining equitable and reasonable utilization:

- Geographic, hydrographic, hydrological, climatic, ecological and other factors of a natural character;
- The social and economic needs of the watercourse States concerned;
- The population dependent on the watercourse in each watercourse State;
- The effects of the use or uses of the watercourses in one watercourse State on other watercourse States;
- Existing and potential uses of the watercourse;
- Conservation, protection, development and economy of use of the water resources of the watercourse and the costs of measures taken to that effect;
- The availability of alternatives, of comparable value, to a particular planned or existing use.[115]

Paragraphs (b) to (f) signal some of the interests that states may have in the watercourse, including conservation and protection of the watercourse. Article 6(3) informs that the "weight given to each

[114] *Ibid.* at 1354. Optimal use "implies attaining maximum possible benefits for all watercourse states and achieving the greatest possible satisfaction of all their needs, while minimizing the detriment to, or unmet needs of, each" and "the attainment of optimal utilization and benefits entails cooperation between watercourse states through their participation in the protection and development of the watercourse." "[T]he failure of a state to negotiate and cooperate in good faith with its co-riparians in order to co-ordinate their respective interests … will make it difficult for that State to claim that its planned or actual use is 'optimal' and, therefore, equitable under Article 5 of the Convention." Tanzi and Arcari, *supra* note 61 at 109, suggest that the goal of optimal utilization in Article 5 implies a duty of cooperation. "Obviously, then, for a state to ensure that its own use is equitable or reasonable, it must be provided with a variety of kinds of data and information by its co-riparians," otherwise it would be forced to make a "blind assessment." McCaffrey, *supra* note 27 at 342. "[T]he obligation of equitable and reasonable utilization depends ultimately on good faith and ongoing cooperation between the states concerned" (at 343). See also Article 6(2), which requires states shall "when the need arises, enter into consultations in a spirit of cooperation."

[115] Draft Articles on Watercourses, *supra* note 80 at 1362. "[P]rotection" is used in the same sense as stated in note 112 of this article; "conservation" is defined as measures relating to conservation and management, degradation of water

factor is to be determined by its importance in comparison with that of other relevant factors" and "all relevant factors are to be considered together and a conclusion reached on the basis of the whole." No priority is given to any particular criterion, thus preserving the equal right of all riparian states to use and share the watercourse.[116] Importantly, where a conflict of use arises that is not governed by agreement or custom, it is to be resolved with reference to Article 5–7 "with special regard being given to the requirement of vital human needs."[117] The commentary to the ILC Draft Articles on Watercourses elaborates vital human needs to mean "special attention is to be paid to providing sufficient water to sustain human life, including both drinking water and water required for the production of food in order to prevent starvation" and thus appears to integrate social concerns.[118]

No Significant Harm Principle

The no significant harm principle prohibits a state from using its territory in such a way as to cause harm to the environment of another state.[119] Formulations of the rule have set thresholds of harm at various levels, such as "significant," "appreciable," or "serious" harm. In earlier discussions within the ILC, a strict liability "no appreciable harm" rule was proposed,[120] making the protection of the environment essentially non-negotiable if the affected party so chose. However, the standard in the convention is one of due diligence, as codified under Article 7:

7(1) Watercourse States shall, in utilizing an international watercourse in their territories, take all appropriate measures to prevent the causing of significant harm to other watercourse States.

7(2) Where significant harm nevertheless is caused to another watercourse State, the States whose use causes such harm shall, in the absence of agreement to such use, take all appropriate measures, having due regard for

---

quality, and supraotably pollution), as well as to living resources, flood control, erosion, sedimentation, and salt water intrusion.

116 Tanzi and Arcari, *supra* note 61 at 124.

117 Draft Articles on Watercourses, *supra* note 80, Article 10(2).

118 *Ibid.* at 1379, the commentary cross-references this to Article 6(1)(b).

119 Principle 2 of Rio Declaration, *supra* note 24.

120 I. Kaya, *Equitable Utilization: The Law of the Non-Navigational Uses of International Watercourses* (Aldershot, UK: Ashgate, 2003) at 157.

the provisions of articles 5 and 6, in consultation with the affected State, to eliminate or mitigate such harm and, where appropriate, to discuss the question of compensation.

The ILC commentary defines the standard of due diligence to mean

a diligence proportioned to the magnitude of the subject and to the dignity and strength of the power which is to exercise it; and such care as governments ordinarily employ in their domestic concerns. The obligation of due diligence contained in article 7 sets the threshold for lawful State activity. It is not intended to guarantee that in utilizing an international watercourse significant harm would not occur. It is an obligation of conduct, not an obligation of result.[121]

Where significant harms result, despite due diligence efforts and consideration of all of the relevant circumstances through a process of consultation and negotiation, it should be tolerated by states.[122] The convention therefore appears to "authorize" the causing of

---

[121] Draft Articles on Watercourses, *supra* note 80 at 1365. One writer attributes to due diligence "a minimum standard of conduct … usually measured by an emerging set of procedural rules on the conduct of States," which includes, in the watercourse context, exchange of information, notification of planned measures as well as consultation and negotiation. See Xue Hanquin, *Transboundary Damage in International Law* (Cambridge: Cambridge University Press, 2003) at 165–75. *Gabčíkovo-Nagymaros, supra* note 3 at para. 140, infers a duty to continually monitor the environmental impacts of projects, which arguably may form a part of due diligence in watercourse law. The case cannot be viewed as definitively staking out a place for the "no significant harm" rule *vis-à-vis* equitable utilization. Some commentators, however, take the view that the court implicitly rejected priority to the rule. The ICJ in *Gabčíkovo-Nagymaros* rejected Hungary's "invitation to apply a no harm rule," stating that the court made a number of references to general international law. McCaffrey, *supra* note 27 at 359. The court did not endorse the principle in its decision, "giving no credibility to the notion of the existence of a 'no significant harm' rule that qualifies the principle of equitable utilization." C.B. Bourne, "The Case Concerning the Gabčíkovo-Nagymaros Project: An Important Milestone in International Water Law" (1997) 8 Y.B. Int'l Envtl. L. 10.

[122] McCaffrey, *supra* note 27 at 379, concludes that for the no significant harm obligation to be breached, three conditions must be met: significant harm must result; the acting state must have been capable of preventing the harm by other conduct; and the conduct must be unreasonable in all the circumstances (at 367). He emphasizes "significant harm" as a threshold that triggers discussions (whether consultations or negotiations) to review the extent of the harm and whether it is reasonable for the affected state to insist on being free from the harm. Environmental harm forms part of equitable balancing only where harm

significant harm if it cannot be prevented by due diligence efforts and if it results from a process of equitable balancing. The ILC commentary does, however, make the qualification that significant harm to human health and safety is "inherently inequitable and unreasonable" and, in the view of many ILC members, other forms of "extreme harm" would very likely be illegal as well.[123]

A specific application of the no significant harm principle, in cases of pollution, is provided in Article 21(2):

> Watercourse States shall, individually and, where appropriate, jointly, pre-vent, reduce and control the pollution of an international watercourse that may cause significant harm to other watercourse States or to their environment, including harm to human health or safety, to the use of the waters for any beneficial purpose or to the living resources of the water-course. Watercourse States shall take steps to harmonize their policies in this connection.

The ILC commentary implies no significant harm of pollution as a due diligence standard, and many commentators interpret it as such.[124] Importantly, while the convention reconciles no significant harm within equitable utilization, it does not invalidate environ-mental protection as a legitimate interest. It is only when harm or environmental degradation cannot be avoided, after consideration of all legitimate interests in the watercourse *and* the exercise of due diligence, that the Watercourses Convention will allow it, sub-ject to an exception of significant human health and safety effects.

---

is less than "significant" or where harm is significant but unavoidable even through the exercise of due diligence. Birnie and Boyle, *supra* note 4 at 309–10. See J. Brunnee and S.J. Toope, "Environmental Security and Freshwater Resources: Ecosystem Regime Building" (1997) 91 Am. J. Int'l L. 26, who add an extra element of procedural caution, suggesting a shifting of the burden in that even where significant harm will result despite the exercise of due dili-gence, the use will be "*prima facie* inequitable."

123 Draft Articles on Watercourses, *supra* note 80 at 1368.

124 "[T]he obligation to prevent pollution that may cause significant harm includes the duty to exercise due diligence to prevent the threat of such harm." And, later in the same paragraph, reduce and control pollution is said to relate to cases where pollution of the watercourse already exists, indicating "a general willingness to tolerate even significant pollution harm, provided that the water-course State of origin is making its best efforts to reduce the pollution to a mutually acceptable limit." *Ibid.* at 1403. See also Brunnée and Toope, *supra* note 122 at 63; Birnie and Boyle, *supra* note 4 at 307; and McCaffrey, *supra* note 27 at 386.

NEGOTIATING LEGITIMATE INTERESTS

The indeterminate relationship between rights of use and obligations of environmental protection in the 1977 Treaty make the *Gabčíkovo-Nagymaros* case a situation where the Watercourses Convention could usefully advance the negotiation process. In this section, an attempt is made to use the convention to reconcile the *main* legitimate interests advanced in this case. The convention *explicates* rights by providing a transparent articulation of legitimate state interests within those rights. Furthermore, the convention provides a reasonably well-integrated account of international watercourse law, in light of the economic, social, and environmental interests that it balances and, on this basis, instructs states on how to integrate these interests and, where this is not possible, how to reconcile them. The convention envisages that states will accomplish this through a process of cooperation and, where appropriate, good faith negotiation.

The Watercourses Convention explicates the interests involved in the use and protection of shared watercourses. The development of the watercourse to improve economic circumstances in Slovakia is a recognized legitimate interest of equitable use, in particular, of Article 6(b) on "the social and economic needs" of a watercourse state. Protection of the drinking water supply of Budapest qualifies as a legitimate interest under Article 6(f) on "conservation," Article 7 on "no significant harm," and Article 10(2) on "vital human needs." The first question is whether states are exercising due diligence, which invites consideration of the community standards of care (in the domestic context) as well as a response proportionate to the environmental risk presented by the use. This standard is meaningful and may, in cases of uncertain science, include the sharing of information, the institution of environmental safeguards, or the monitoring of impacts in cases of scientific uncertainty.

Where harm may result despite due diligence, the parties are to negotiate the integration of their interests as set out in Articles 5, 6, and 7. Parties are under an obligation to reassess whether the use is equitable, taking into account the seriousness of the environmental consequence, the degree of risk, the social and economic cost of delay of economic activity, the feasibility of alternative measures, as well as the cost of preventative solutions. The implication here is that the parties are to look at cost-effective alternatives to achieve similar development ends that accommodate protection concerns. A balance is struck between the needs of use and the importance of protection with the parties discussing ways in which both objectives can be realized. This balance is also suggested by the concept of sustainable use in the commentary, which asks the parties to look at watercourse development in an "integrated manner," incorporating environmental, social, and economic considerations.

When an integrated solution cannot be achieved, the convention reconciles use with protection of the resource in different ways depending on the circumstances of the case. Generally, reconciliation of the no significant harm principle within equitable utilization suggests that environmental protection as the objective of negotiations may, in certain situations, be compromised by a caveat of permissible significant harm in exceptional cases. One hypothetical situation envisaged by the drafting committee of the Watercourses Convention gives a flavour of the high threshold envisaged. In this example, a hydroelectric dam that would provide hundreds of thousands of people with electric power should prevail over the recreational fishing interests of a few hundred people that would be destroyed by the dam's construction.[125]

However, protection of the watercourse may also be given priority over utilization. Concerns of human health and safety are given preference of consideration in equitable balancing under Article 7, as are vital human needs in conflict of use situations under Article 10(2), suggesting their priority in equitable balancing. If, in the *Gabčíkovo-Nagymaros* case, the parties cannot reconcile their interests through an integrated solution — for example, appropriate environmental safeguards to protect drinking water supply — Hungary's priority claim could be supported on two bases. First, a threat to the drinking water supply would qualify as harm to human health and safety, which is "inherently inequitable." Second, drinking water is explicitly identified as a vital human need under Article 10(2), which takes priority in a conflict of use situation.

To convincingly establish this priority, Hungary would have to demonstrate, pursuant to Article 15, that the risk of harm presents as more than just a "mere possibility."[126] This standard, while not

---

[125] From Kaya, *supra* note 120 at 161–62.

[126] Draft Articles on Watercourses, *supra* note 80 at 1389. The notified state, under Article 15, is to communicate its findings, and provide detailed explanations should it conclude the planned measure *would* be inconsistent with Article 5 (equitable utilization) or Article 7 (the no harm rule). Importantly for cases of scientific uncertainty, the ILC commentary suggests that the word "would" is used rather than "might" because "the notified state must conclude that a violation of articles 5 or 7 is more than a mere possibility."

demanding, requires at least some scientific proof of the risk. The parties are in the best position to set a reasonable time period within which scientific proof of harm must be established in the circumstances, but, if they cannot agree, the notifying state may proceed with the measure after six months and subject to its obligations under Articles 5 and 7.[127] This mandate suggests that states must negotiate in good faith and accommodate reasonable requests to extend delayed implementation of the measure to allow for the parties, as circumstances warrant, to gather more information and agree to an acceptable resolution. The seriousness of this risk in this case would suggest a significant period in which to generate scientific information.

Therefore, specific interests of economic development and of environmental protection under the Watercourses Convention are to be cooperatively accommodated and integrated by riparian states. Where this is not possible, and the choice is between development and human health and safety, the latter may take priority. In the absence of a feasible "integrated" solution, one reasonable option would be to exclude peak power operation at the Gabčíkovo dam, thus making the construction of Nagymaros unnecessary and the concern of the ensuing effects on drinking water no longer an issue. This solution is consistent with the convention and "asks reasonable things" of the parties (and also accords with the ICJ's implicit solution mentioned earlier). There is, in other words, a resonance between the law, the facts, and the solution that is highly persuasive. Beyond these parameters, which are set out in the convention, the parties are to tailor specific implementation of their solution based on the facts before them, in good faith.

CONCLUSIONS

The international law of environmental cooperation engages a number of procedural mechanisms, of which the duty to negotiate in good faith is one, to help ensure the goal of appropriate environmental protection measures in the circumstances of each case. A large body of international environmental soft law, both procedural and substantive in nature, exists to serve as a basis for international negotiations to achieve these goals. The principle of good faith should instruct states to heed authoritative soft law norms — to act as a catalyst, if you will — so that environmental protection

[127] *Ibid.* at 1392 (commentary to Article 17).

goals can be advanced or, at least, appropriately considered in the difficult circumstances of environmental negotiations. The purpose of this article has been to show how states might better understand the nature of their rights and obligations in good faith negotiation, using prescribed legitimacy criteria when rights and obligations between them are unclear. Authoritative soft law instruments that are the product of a fair and inclusive process of international negotiation, such as the Watercourses Convention, can have a very high correlation to legitimacy criteria in these situations. This instrument instructs that, within negotiations, states activate legitimate interests in shared resources that are to be co-operatively integrated and, if necessary, reconciled. The approach that is offered applies equally to other environmental negotiations, for example, straddling fish stocks management[128] or trade disputes involving endangered species.[129] In most negotiation scenarios,

---

128 The Fish Stocks Agreement, *supra* note 4, was adopted by consensus including all major distant water and coastal fishing states. Birnie and Boyle, *supra* note 4 at 673. There were fifty-two ratifications as of May 2005. See <http://www.un. org/Depts/los/reference_files/chronological_lists_of_ratifications. htm#AgreementfortheimplementationoftheprovisionsoftheConvention relatingtotheconservationandmanagementofstraddlingfishstocksandhighly migratoryfishstocks> (26 June 2005). Article 7 of the Fish Stocks Agreement explicates legitimate interests in fish stocks conservation.

129 One legal issue that is still unresolved in the international trade jurisprudence is whether rights of environmental protection under Article XX of the General Agreement on Tariffs and Trade, 30 October 1947, 55 U.N.T.S. 194, can be asserted outside of a state's jurisdiction — that is, whether the right to take measures under Article XX(g) "relating to the conservation of exhaustible natural resources if such measures are made effective in conjunction with restrictions on domestic production or consumption" extends to environmental protection concerns outside of a state's jurisdiction. In two cases, *United States – Restrictions on Imports of Tuna*, 39 GATT B.I.S.D. 155 (1993), reprinted in 30 I.L.M. 1594 (1991), panels came to different conclusions on the issue. In *Shrimp-Turtle*, *supra* note 4 at para. 133, the Appellate Body held that, because the sea turtle species being regulated occur at times within US waters, "there is a sufficient jurisdictional nexus between the migratory and endangered marine populations involved and the United States for the purposes of Article XX (g)." A wider conception of law, as advanced through legitimacy criteria, may help resolve this controversy. Widely ratified global conservation treaties identify a legitimate interest of the international community in endangered species protection, regardless of location, as a matter of common concern, for example, the preamble to the Convention on Biological Diversity, (1992) 31 I.L.M. 822 [CBD], identifies the conservation of biological diversity as "a common concern of humankind" (at preamble, recital 3). The Convention on International Trade in Endangered Species of Wild Fauna and Flora, (1973) 12 I.L.M. 1085, recognizes that wild fauna and flora must be protected for future generations

authoritative international soft law can explicate legitimate interests and may even provide cues to resolution, making them instrumental to shaping the parameters of negotiated debate.

The criteria suggested as a basis for the persuasive advancement of norms within negotiation — transparency and clarity, compatibility of norms, past state practice, and asking reasonable things — are not necessarily tied to the usual conceptions of binding rules of international law — that is, treaty and custom. Still, the suggestion that soft legal norms have legal relevance and effect in international law is widely acknowledged — even international tribunals use soft law for this purpose.[130] The approach offered in this article is different only in the attempt to present a more elaborate and convincing view as to how states use soft law to interpret broad rights and obligations.

The simplified example of *Gabčíkovo-Nagymaros* was chosen for illustration purposes, though we may suppose that the identification and accommodation process of legitimate interests even in these circumstances is not a self-guiding process. No discourse-based approach to negotiated dispute resolution can possibly do this. Authoritative soft law instruments nonetheless can assist in narrowing and shaping the parameters of debate in a way that might not otherwise be the case.

It is true that cooperation may succeed or fail in meeting environmental protection objectives depending, ultimately, on the will of states.[131] Yet the more encouraging news is that states do not

---

and lists most migratory sea turtles as "species threatened with extinction" (at preamble, recital 1). The Convention on Conservation on the Conservation of Migratory Species of Wild Animals, (1980) 19 I.L.M. 15 [CMS Convention], recognizes that wild animals are to be conserved for "the good of mankind" and for future generations (at preamble, recital 1 and 2).

130 See *Shrimp-Turtle, supra* note 4 at para. 130. The Appellate Body looked to modern international environmental treaties and instruments, most of which the United States was not a party to — LOSC, *supra* note 4; CMS Convention, *supra* note 129; CBD, *supra* note 129; and Agenda 21, 13 June 1992, UN Doc. A/CONF. 151/26 (1992) — to support an interpretation of exhaustible natural resources as including living natural resources.

131 Francesco Orrego Vicuna, *The Changing International Law of High Seas Fisheries* (Cambridge: Cambridge University Press, 1999) at 2–3: "Important as cooperation is, it nonetheless rests on weak grounds since it assumes a degree of good will and spirit of accommodation that is not always available among highly competitive entities ... In addition this co-operative approach has been one of the important flaws in the historical experience of international law (of high seas fisheries)."

generally oppose the principle of cooperation but rather react unilaterally to protect their legitimate interests in the face of failed negotiations.[132] One reason that negotiations may fail is that states do not know how to interpret their competing rights in a resource because international legal doctrine does not tell them how. A more developed articulation of good faith negotiation can have widespread effect in setting standards by which states are to behave and understand their rights. In areas of intense natural resource scarcity, like shared watercourses, such understandings are sorely needed.

Sommaire

Le droit sort de l'ombre: son utilisation par les États pour négocier de bonne foi le règlement de différends environnementaux internationaux

De plus en plus le droit international oblige les États à négocier de bonne foi en matière des différends environnementaux qui surgissent concernant l'utilisation et la protection des ressources naturelles qui sont partagées ou qui constituent un bien commun, par exemple, les cours d'eau, les pêcheries et les espèces migratoires. Cette obligation de négocier de bonne foi est encore formulée en termes flous, ce qui explique probablement que les négociations se prolongent ou que les différends demeurent irrésolus. Le problème, nul doute, réside en partie dans le fait que les États ne savent pas comment interpréter leurs droits concurrents à ces ressources. L'article explore le potentiel facilitateur des directives non impératives qui font autorité en droit international en matière de la négociation de bonne foi lorsque les droits et les obligations en matière de l'utilisation et de la protection des ressources sont énoncés de façon large et que les rapports entre l'un et l'autre sont ambigus. Dans ce contexte, notre compréhension de la pertinence, des sources et de l'utilisation du droit dans la procédure de négociation déterminera notre capacité d'utiliser le droit afin de faciliter ou de nuire à la résolution de différends. Dans le cadre de l'interaction discursive entreprise de bonne foi, les États devraient prendre en ligne de compte les directives non impératives qui font autorité en droit international afin d'expliquer, d'intégrer et de réconcilier leurs intérêts légitimes dans le contexte de leurs droits et obligations concurrents, en conformité avec le critère de légitimité énoncé.

---

[132] States acting unilaterally are rarely opposed to the principle of multilateralism. Bilder, *supra* note 50 at 91.

Summary

Coming in from the Shadow of the Law: The Use of Law by States to Negotiate International Environmental Disputes in Good Faith

International law increasingly obliges states to negotiate in good faith environmental disputes that arise in connection with the use and protection of shared or common property natural resources — that is, watercourses, fisheries, and migratory species. Articulation of this duty to negotiate in good faith has been vague, and, perhaps as a consequence, disputes have been protracted or have gone unresolved. Part of the problem may be that states do not know how to interpret their competing rights in the resource. This article explores the facilitative potential of international authoritative soft law to good faith negotiation where rights and obligations of resource use and protection are broadly stated and their relationship to one another is unclear. In this context, our understanding of the relevance, sources, and use of law in the negotiation process contributes to whether law functions to facilitate or frustrate dispute resolution. Through discursive interaction undertaken in good faith, states should look to international authoritative soft law to explicate, integrate, and reconcile their legitimate interests within their competing rights and obligations, according to prescribed legitimacy criteria.

Murder as a Crime against Humanity at the Ad Hoc Tribunals: Reconciling Differing Languages

CHILE EBOE-OSUJI

INTRODUCTION — DIFFERING LANGUAGES

The English texts of the Statutes of the International Criminal Tribunals for Rwanda (ICTR Statute) and for the former Yugoslavia (ICTY Statute) uniformly give the respective tribunals jurisdiction over murder as a crime against humanity.[1] Yet where the English texts speak of "murder," the French versions speak of

---

Chile Eboe-Osuji, LL.M., of the Bar of Ontario; Barrister at Borden, Ladner, Gervais LL.P.; formerly senior legal officer, International Criminal Tribunal for Rwanda; formerly prosecution counsel, International Criminal Tribunal for Rwanda; formerly head legal officer in the Appeals Chamber, International Criminal Tribunal for Rwanda. This article draws from a book in progress. The views expressed in this article are purely those of the author, except where the context clearly indicates otherwise.

[1] The English text of Article 3 of the Statute of the International Criminal Tribunal for Rwanda, UN Doc. S/RES/955 (8 November 1994) [ICTR Statute], provides: "The International Tribunal for Rwanda shall have the power to prosecute persons responsible for the following crimes when committed as part of a widespread or systematic attack against any civilian population on national, political, ethnic, racial or religious grounds: (a) murder; (b) extermination; (c) enslavement; (d) deportation; (e) imprisonment; (f) torture; (g) rape; (h) persecutions on political, racial and religious grounds; (i) other inhumane acts." For its part, Article 5 of the Statute of the International Criminal Tribunal for the Former Yugoslavia, UN Doc. S/RES/827 (25 May 1993) [ICTY Statute], provides as follows: "The International Tribunal shall have the power to prosecute persons responsible for the following crimes when committed in armed conflict, whether international or internal in character, and directed against any civilian population: (a) murder; (b) extermination; (c) enslavement; (d) deportation; (e) imprisonment; (f) torture; (g) rape; (h) persecutions on political, racial and religious grounds; (i) other inhumane acts."

"*assassinat.*"[2] This distinction has provoked legal thought. To lawyers from the common law world, whose juridical language is invariably English, the element of *mens rea* for the crime of murder recognizes a range of faulty minds — from premeditation, at the higher end, down to "wicked and corrupt disregard of the lives and safety of others."[3] Section 316 of the Criminal Code of Nigeria[4] — appearing in identical terms as section 302 of the Criminal Code of Queensland, Australia[5] — is probably illustrative of this range of

[2] The French text of Article 3 of the ICTR Statute, *supra* note 1, provides: "Le Tribunal international pour le Rwanda est habilité à juger les personnes responsables des crimes suivants lorsqu'ils ont été commis dans le cadre d'une attaque généralisée et systématique dirigée contre une population civile quelle qu'elle soit, en raison de son appartenance nationale, politique, ethnique, raciale ou religieuse: (a) assassinat; (b) extermination; (c) réduction en esclavage; (d) expulsion; (e) emprisonnement; (f) torture; (g) viol; (h) persécutions pour des raisons politiques, raciales et religieuses; (i) autres actes inhumains." And the French text of Article 5 of the ICTY Statute, *supra* note 1, provides as follows: "Le Tribunal international est habilité à juger les personnes présumées responsables des crimes suivants lorsqu'ils ont été commis au cours d'un conflit armé, de caractère international ou interne, et dirigés contre une population civile quelle qu'elle soit: (a) assassinat; (b) extermination; (c) réduction en esclavage; (d) expulsion; (e) emprisonnement; (f) torture; (g) viol; (h) persécutions pour des raisons politiques, raciales et religieuses; (i) autres actes inhumains."

[3] As the ICTY Trial Chamber noted in *Prosecutor v. Delalić & Ors (Judgment)*, "[a]t common law, the term 'malice' is often utilised to describe the necessary additional element that transforms a homicide from a case of manslaughter to one of murder. Yet again, however, there is a strong danger of confusion if such terminology is transposed into the context of international law, without explanation of its exact meaning. Malice does not merely refer to ill will on the part of the perpetrator of the killing, but extends to his intention to cause great bodily harm or to kill without legal justification or excuse and also "denotes a wicked and corrupt disregard of the lives and safety of others." In most common law jurisdictions, the *mens rea* requirement of murder is satisfied where the accused is aware of the likelihood or probability of causing death or is reckless as to the causing of death. In Australia, for example, knowledge that death or grievous bodily harm will *probably* result from the actions of the accused is the requisite test. Under Canadian law, the accused is required to have a simultaneous awareness of the probability of death and the intention to inflict some form of serious harm, and this is also the position in Pakistan." *Prosecutor v. Delalić & Ors (Judgment)* (16 November 1998), Case no. IT-96-21-T (ICTY Trial Chamber) at para. 434 [*Delalić*].

[4] Nigerian Criminal Code (1916), Cap. 77 of the Laws of the Federation of Nigeria 1990. See <http://www.nigeria-law.org/Criminal%20Code%20Act-PartV.htm#Chapter%2027> (30 July 2006).

[5] See <http://www.legislation.qld.gov.au/LEGISLTN/CURRENT/C/CriminCode.pdf> (30 July 2006).

mens rea for murder in the common law world. Section 316 of the Nigerian Criminal Code provides as follows:

Except as hereinafter set forth, a person who unlawfully kills another under any of the following circumstances, that is to say:

(1) if the offender intends to cause the death of the person killed, or that of some other person;
(2) if the offender intends to do to the person killed or to some other person some grievous harm;
(3) if death is caused by means of an act done in the prosecution of an unlawful purpose, which act is of such nature as to be likely to endanger human life;
(4) if the offender intends to do grievous harm to some person for the purpose of facilitating the commission of an offence which is such that the offender may be arrested without warrant, or for the purpose of facilitating the flight of an offender who has committed or attempted to commit any such offence:
 i. if death is caused by administering any stupefying or overpowering things for either of the purposes last aforesaid;
 ii. if death is caused by wilfully stopping the breath of any person for either of such purposes;

is guilty of murder. In the second case it is immaterial that the offender did not intend to hurt the particular person who is killed. In the third case it is immaterial that the offender did not intend to hurt any person. In the last three cases it is immaterial that the offender did not intend to cause death or did know that death was likely to result.[6]

---

6 The murder provisions of the Tanzanian Penal Code, Cap. 16 of 1945, are also interesting to note. Section 196 provides: "Any Person who of malice aforethought causes the death of another person by an unlawful act or omission is guilty of murder." And section 200 defines malice aforethought as follows: "Malice aforethought shall be deemed to be established by evidence proving any one or more of the following circumstances: — (a) an intention to cause the death of, or to do grievous harm to, any person, whether such person is the person actually killed or not; (b) knowledge that the act or omission causing death will probably cause the death of or grievous harm to some person, whether such a person is the person actually killed or not, although such knowledge is accompanied by indifference whether death or grievous bodily harm is caused or not, or by a wish that it may not be caused; (c) an intent to commit a felony; (d) an intention by the act or omission to facilitate the flight or escape from custody of any person who has committed or attempted to commit a felony."

Similar provisions appear in the Canadian Criminal Code's provisions on murder. The code classifies homicide into "culpable homicide" and "not culpable homicide"[7] — either of which may be caused directly or indirectly.[8] There are three types of culpable homicide: murder, manslaughter, or infanticide.[9] And then the code describes murder as follows:

229. Culpable homicide is murder

(a) where the person who causes the death of a human being
  (i) means to cause his death, or
  (ii) means to cause him bodily harm that he knows is likely to cause his death, and is reckless whether death ensues or not;
(b) where a person, meaning to cause death to a human being or meaning to cause him bodily harm that he knows is likely to cause his death, and being reckless whether death ensues or not, by accident or mistake causes death to another human being, notwithstanding that he does not mean to cause death or bodily harm to that human being; or
(c) where a person, for an unlawful object, does anything that he knows or ought to know is likely to cause death, and thereby causes death to a human being, notwithstanding that he desires to effect his object without causing death or bodily harm to any human being.

230. Culpable homicide is murder where a person causes the death of a human being while committing or attempting to commit high treason or treason or an offence mentioned in section 52 (sabotage), 75 (piratical acts), 76 (hijacking an aircraft), 144 or subsection 145(1) or sections 146 to 148 (escape or rescue from prison or lawful custody), section 270 (assaulting a peace officer), section 271 (sexual assault), 272 (sexual assault with a weapon, threats to a third party or causing bodily harm), 273 (aggravated sexual assault), 279 (kidnapping and forcible confinement), 279.1 (hostage taking), 343 (robbery), 348 (breaking and entering) or 433 or 434 (arson), whether or not the person means to cause death to any human being and whether or not he knows that death is likely to be caused to any human being, if

(a) he means to cause bodily harm for the purpose of
  (i) facilitating the commission of the offence, or

---

[7] Criminal Code of Canada, R.S.C. 1985, c. C-46, s. 222(2).
[8] *Ibid.* at section 222(1).
[9] *Ibid.* at section 222(4).

(ii) facilitating his flight after committing or attempting to commit the offence, and the death ensues from the bodily harm;
(b) he administers a stupefying or overpowering thing for a purpose mentioned in paragraph (*a*), and the death ensues therefrom; or
(c) he wilfully stops, by any means, the breath of a human being for a purpose mentioned in paragraph (*a*), and the death ensues therefrom.

To the same effect, in America, paragraph 210.2 of the Model Penal Code provides as follows:

(1) Except as provided in Section 210.3(1)(b), criminal homicide constitutes murder when:

(a) it is committed purposely or knowingly; or
(b) it is committed recklessly under circumstances manifesting extreme indifference to the value of human life. Such recklessness and indifference are presumed if the actor is engaged or is an accomplice in the commission of, or an attempt to commit, or flight after committing or attempting to commit robbery, rape or deviate sexual intercourse by force or threat of force, arson, burglary, kidnapping or felonious escape.[10]

This sampling of common law jurisdictions from North America to Australia, through Africa, clearly shows that, in this legal system, the *mens rea* for murder does capture a range of conducts beyond the premeditation to kill another human being. The French law equivalent of murder in this broader sense would have been *meurtre*, which simply means "the act of voluntarily causing the death of another."[11] The French law notion of "*assassinat*," which is the notion appearing in the French texts of the tribunals' statutes, is equivalent only to the premeditated kind of murder or "first degree

---

[10] Paragraph 210.3 of the Model Penal Code makes provision in respect of manslaughter. It provides as follows: "(1) Criminal homicide constitutes manslaughter when: (a) it is committed recklessly; or (b) a homicide which would otherwise be murder is committed under the influence of extreme mental or emotional disturbance for which there is reasonable explanation or excuse. The reasonableness of such explanation or excuse shall be determined from the viewpoint of a person in the actor's situation under the circumstances as he believes them to be."

[11] J. Bell, S. Boyron, and S. Whittaker, *Principles of French Law* (1998) at 242. More specifically, Article 221–21 of the New Penal Code of France provides: "Le fait

murder" as it is popularly known in America[12] and Canada.[13] This notion of murder, of course, suggests something narrower. It might be interesting to note that in Canada, a common law country in which English and French are the official national languages, with all of the national legislation drafted accordingly, section 229 of the Canadian Criminal Code refers to "murder" in English and "*meurtre*" in French. There is no species of culpable homicide known as "*assassinat.*" Premeditated murder (described as *assassinat* in France) is described in the French version of the Canadian Criminal Code as "*meurtre au premier degré,*" which is defined as follows: "Le meurtre au premier degré est le meurtre commis avec préméditation et de propos délibéré."[14]

Differing Views from the Bench

Between the ICTY and the ICTR, this variation in the English and the French texts of the statutes has generated considerable judicial debate. It all started with the ICTR case of *Prosecutor v. Akayesu (Judgment),*[15] which was the very first judgment of the Rwanda tribunal in a contested case. The Trial Chamber considered the variation briefly and held, in the end, that the difference resulted from a translation error. They then resolved the variation in favour of the English text, which they held to be more consistent with developments in customary international law. In the words of the chamber,

[t]he Chamber notes that article 3(a) of the English version of the Statute refers to "Murder," whilst the French version of the Statute refers to "Assassinat." Customary International Law dictates that it is the act of

---

de donner volontairement la mort à autrui constitue un meurtre. Il est puni de trente ans de reclusion criminelle."

[12] See Bell, Boyron, and Whittaker, *supra* note 11; A. Deysine, ed., *Dictionnaire de l'anglais économique et juridique et du commerce inter*national (1996) at 256. One notes the striking similarity between this provision and the language of Article 221-23 of the New Penal Code of France, which describes "*assassinat*" as follows: "Le meurtre commis avec préméditation constitue un assassinat. Il est puni de la réclusion criminelle à perpetuité."

[13] See Criminal Code of Canada, *supra* note 7 at section 231.

[14] (Murder is first degree murder when it is planned and deliberate). *Ibid.* at section 231(2).

[15] *Prosecutor v. Akayesu (Judgment)*, (2 September 1998) Case no. ICTR-96-4 (International Criminal Tribunal for Rwanda (ICTR), Trial Chamber I, composed of Judges Kama, Aspegren, and Pillay) at paras. 588 and 589 [*Akayesu*].

"Murder" that constitutes a crime against humanity and not "Assassinat." There are therefore sufficient reasons to assume that the French version of the Statute suffers from an error in translation.[16]

Having so decided, the chamber proceeded to provide the following definition of murder for purposes of crimes against humanity:

The Chamber defines murder as the unlawful, intentional killing of a human being. The requisite elements of murder are:

1) the victim is dead;
2) the death resulted from an unlawful act or omission of the accused or a subordinate;
3) at the time of the killing the accused or a subordinate had the intention to kill or inflict grievous bodily harm on the deceased having known that such bodily harm is likely to cause the victim's death, and is reckless whether death ensues or not.[17]

In two subsequent cases,[18] the Trial Chamber I followed the decision that was made in *Akayesu*.

In their own turn, Trial Chamber II in *Prosecutor v. Kayishema and Ruzindana (Judgment)*[19] departed from the position of Trial Chamber I in *Akayesu*. The *Kayishema and Ruzindana* Trial Chamber essentially held that as much as it may indeed be the case that customary international law favours the concept of "murder" — and not "*assassinat*" — for the purposes of crimes against humanity,[20] the chamber was still faced with a statute that expressed itself

---

16 *Ibid.* at para. 588.

17 *Ibid.* at para. 589.

18 *Prosecutor v. Rutaganda (Judgment)*, (6 December 1999) Case no. ICTR-96-3 (ICTR Trial Chamber I, composed of Judges Kama, Aspegren, and Pillay) at para. 79; and *Prosecutor v. Musema (Judgment)* (27 January 2000) Case no. ICTR-96-13 (ICTR Trial Chamber I, composed of Judges Kama, Aspegren, and Pillay) at para. 214.

19 *Prosecutor v. Kayishema and Ruzindana (Judgment)* (21 May 1999) Case no. ICTR-95-01 (ICTR Trial Chamber II, composed of Judges Sekule, Ostrovsky, and Khan) at paras. 137–40 [*Kayishema and Ruzindana*].

20 The *Kayishema and Ruzindana* Trial Chamber, *supra* note 19, did eventually question the position that customary international law favours murder rather than *assassinat* as the prevailing notion of homicide as a crime against humanity. According to them, "the ICTR and ICTY Statutes did not reflect customary international law at the time of drafting. This is evident by the inclusion of the need for armed conflict in the ICTY Statute and the inclusion of the requirement that the crimes be committed with discriminatory intent in the ICTR Statute" (at

as having been made in English and French, both being equally
authoritative, and in which the "drafters chose to use the term
assassinat rather than *meurtre* [in the French text]," while employing the term "murder" in the English text. In the circumstances,
the Trial Chamber saw no need to resolve the disparity in favour of
one language, as was done in *Akayesu*. The principal judicial solution lies, rather, in ascertaining the notion of murder that both
texts have in common. This common denominator is the premeditated type of murder — for "murder" as understood in the English-
speaking legal world also includes premeditated murder (the
equivalent of "*assassinat*"), while "*assassinat*" means only premeditated murder in the French system.[21] Following through with this
reasoning, the Trial Chamber opined that any ambiguity in a penal
provision must be resolved in favour of an accused. In this case,
since the requirement to establish premeditation in murder is more
favourable to the accused than the requirement to prove murder
with a lesser form of *mens rea*, the chamber reasoned that premeditated murder was the applicable notion of homicide in the context.[22] Ultimately, reasoned the chamber, both the English notion
of murder and the French concept of "*assassinat*" ought to be reflected in the application of the judicial mind to the notion of
crimes against humanity. And the Trial Chamber's formula for
doing so follows this reasoning: "When murder is considered along
with *assassinat* the Chamber finds that the standard of *mens rea* required is intentional and premeditated killing. The result is premeditated when the actor formulated his intent to kill after a cool
moment of reflection. The result is intended when it is the actor's
purpose, or the actor is aware that it will occur in the ordinary
course of events."[23]

Having so reasoned, the Trial Chamber enunciated the following
definition of murder in the context of crimes against humanity:

---

para. 138). This indeed is a curious case of mixing apples and oranges, for the
Akayesu Trial Chamber did not say that every concept contained in the provision on crimes against humanity reflects the position of customary international law, so as to engage the point about discriminatory intent versus the
context of armed conflict. The point with which the *Akayesu* Trial Chamber was
dealing was murder versus *assassinat*, as reflecting customary international law.

[21] *Ibid.* at para. 138.

[22] *Ibid.* at para. 139.

[23] *Ibid.*

The accused is guilty of murder if the accused, engaging in conduct which is unlawful:

1) causes the death of another;
2) by a premeditated act or omission;
3) intending to kill any person or,
4) intending to cause grievous bodily harm to any person.

Essentially then, for the *Kayishema and Ruzindana* Chamber, murder entails unlawful death resulting from an intention to kill or cause grievous bodily harm.[24]

In *Prosecutor v. Bagilishema (Judgment)*, a differently constituted Trial Chamber I simply concurred with the earlier-mentioned *Kayishema and Ruzindana* formulation, without further discussion.[25]

For their part, the ICTY judges appear uniformly to have resolved themselves in favour of the *Akayesu* proposition.[26] As was observed by a Trial Chamber in *Prosecutor v. Kordić (Judgment)*:

Although there has been some controversy in the International Tribunal's jurisprudence as to the meaning to be attached to the discrepancy between the use of the word "murder" in the English text of the Statute and the use of the word "*assassinat*" in the French text, it is now settled that premeditation is not required. Most recently, the *Blaškić* Trial Chamber

---

24 The chamber does not specifically discuss whether the victim must be the same person intended to be killed or caused grievous bodily harm, although the chamber's language does speak of the intention to kill or cause grievous bodily harm to "any person."

25 *Prosecutor v. Bagilishema (Judgment)* (7 June 2001) Case no. ICTR-95-1A (ICTR Trial Chamber I, composed of Judges Møse, Gunawardana, and Güney) at paras. 84 and 85.

26 See *Prosecutor v. Jelesić (Judgment)*, (14 December 1999) Case no. IT-95-10-T (ICTY Trial Chamber) at paras. 35 and 51; *Prosecutor v. Kupreškić (Judgment)* (14 January 2000) Case no. IT-95-16 (ICTY Trial Chamber) at paras. 560 and 561; *Prosecutor v. Blaškić (Judgment)* (3 March 2000) Case no. IT-95-14 (ICTY Trial Chamber) at paras. 216 and 217; *Prosecutor v. Kordić (Judgment)* 28 February 2001 Case no. IT-95-14/2 (ICTY Trial Chamber) at paras. 235 and 236 [*Kordić*]; *Prosecutor v. Krstić (Judgment)* (2 August 2001) Case no. IT-98-33 (ICTY Trial Chamber) at para. 485; *Prosecutor v. Kvočka (Judgment)* (2 November 2001) Case no. IT-98-30/1 (ICTY Trial Chamber) at paras. 132 and 136; *Prosecutor v. Vasiljević (Judgment)* (28 November 2002) Case no. IT-98-32 (ICTY Trial Chamber) at para. 205; *Prosecutor v. Naletilić & Anor (Judgment)*, (31 March 2003) Case no. IT-98-34 (ICTY Trial Chamber) at paras. 248 and 249 [*Naletilić*]; and *Prosecutor v. Stakić (Judgment)* (31 July 2003) Case no. IT-97-24 (ICTY Trial Chamber) at paras. 584–7 and 631 [*Stakić*].

held that "it is murder (*"meurtre"*) and not premeditated murder (*"assassinat"*) which must be the underlying offence of a crime against humanity."[27]

The constituent elements of a murder do not appear to be controversial. In order for an accused to be found guilty of murder, the following elements need to be proved:

- the death of the victim;
- that the death resulted from an act or omission of the accused or his subordinate; and
- that the accused or his subordinate intended to kill the victim or to cause grievous bodily harm or inflict serious injury in the reasonable knowledge that the attack was likely to result in death.

These elements are similar to those required in connection to wilful killing under Article 2 and murder under Article 3 of the statute, with the exception that in order to be characterized as a crime against humanity a murder must have been committed as part of a widespread or systematic attack against a civilian population.[28]

Another ICTY case of note is the case of *Prosecutor v. Stakić*. In this case, an ICTY Trial Chamber first considered the definition of murder under Article 3 of the ICTY Statute, dealing with the war crime of violations of the laws or customs of war, as a settled notion. As the chamber observed,

[t]he definition of murder as a violation of the laws or customs of war is now settled in the jurisprudence of the ICTR and the ICTY which holds that the death of the victim must result from an act or omission of the accused committed with the intent either to kill or to cause serious bodily harm in the reasonable knowledge that it would likely result in death.[29]

The chamber next considered that "murder" means the taking of the life of another person in circumstances equating *"meurtre"* in French law and *"mord"* in German law.[30] It is perhaps interesting to

---

27 *Kordić, supra* note 26 at para. 235.

28 *Ibid.*

29 *Stakić, supra* note 26 at para. 584. It should probably be noted here that this was the definition of murder as a crime against humanity as formulated in *Akayesu, supra* note 15.

30 *Stakić, supra* note 26 at para. 586: "The Trial Chamber finds that in the context of Article 3 of the Statute 'murder' means taking another person's life. If murder

note here that in providing for the crime of violation of the laws or customs of war, Article 3 of the ICTY Statute does not expressly mention murder in the list of crimes specifically enumerated there.[31] Naturally, the list is non-exhaustive. Still, it is worth noting that the judges have read "murder" — the equivalent of "*meurtre*" and not "*assassinat*" — into this list. This development is particularly impor-tant in this discussion, given that no other provision in the ICTY Statute is expressed in terms of "murder," apart from Article 5, which provides for murder as a crime against humanity.[32] Article 2

---

is conceived in the narrow sense only, ordinary killings, namely the taking of another person's life without any additional subjective or objective aggravating elements, do not fall under the Article. This Trial Chamber believes, however, that murder should be equated to killings, that is *meurtre* in French law and *Mord* in German law."

[31] According to the ICTY Statute, *supra* note 1, Article 3: "The International Tribu-nal shall have the power to prosecute persons violating the laws or customs of war. Such violations shall include, but not be limited to: (a) employment of poi-sonous weapons or other weapons calculated to cause unnecessary suffering; (b) wanton destruction of cities, towns or villages, or devastation not justified by military necessity; (c) attack, or bombardment, by whatever means, of unde-fended towns, villages, dwellings, or buildings; (d) seizure of, destruction or wilful damage done to institutions dedicated to religion, charity and education, the arts and sciences, historic monuments and works of art and science; (e) plunder of public or private property."

[32] This is to be contrasted with the only war crimes provision in the ICTR Statute, *supra* note 1, Article 4, which specifically lists murder — with the French version listing *meurtre* — as a war crime. The English version provides as follows: "The International Tribunal for Rwanda shall have the power to prosecute persons committing or ordering to be committed serious violations of Article 3 common to the Geneva Conventions of 12 August 1949 for the Protection of War Vic-tims, and of Additional Protocol II thereto of 8 June 1977. These violations shall include, but shall not be limited to: (a) Violence to life, health and physical or mental well-being of persons, in particular murder as well as cruel treatment such as torture, mutilation or any form of corporal punishment; (b) Collective punishments; (c) Taking of hostages; (d) Acts of terrorism; (e) Outrages upon personal dignity, in particular humiliating and degrading treatment, rape, en-forced prostitution and any form of indecent assault; (f) Pillage; (g) The pass-ing of sentences and the carrying out of executions without previous judgement pronounced by a regularly constituted court, affording all the judicial guaran-tees which are recognized as indispensable by civilised peoples; (h) Threats to commit any of the foregoing acts." And the French version provides: "Le Tribu-nal international pour le Rwanda est habilité à poursuivre les personnes qui commettent ou donnent l'ordre de commettre des violations graves de l'Article 3 commun aux Conventions de Genève du 12 août 1949 pour la protection des victimes en temps de guerre, et du Protocole additionnel II auxdites Conven-tions du 8 juin 1977. Ces violations comprennent, sans s'y limiter: (a) Les

of the ICTY Statute,[33] the other war crimes provision, does indeed specify "wilful killing" — expressed in the French version as "*homicide intentionnel*" — in its own list of war crimes. This, however, does not necessarily mean murder. Certainly, all murder is intentional or wilful homicide. Yet not all intentional homicide is murder, for manslaughter is intentional homicide,[34] especially when resulting

---

atteintes portées à la vie, à la santé et au bien-être physique ou mental des personnes, en particulier le meurtre, de même que les traitements cruels tels que la torture, les mutilations ou toutes formes de peines corporelles; (b) Les punitions collectives; (c) La prise d'otages; (d) Les actes de terrorisme; (e) Les atteintes à la dignité de la personne, notamment les traitements humiliants et dégradants, le viol, la contrainte à la prostitution et tout attentat à la pudeur; (f) Le pillage; (g) Les condamnations prononcées et les exécutions effectuées sans un jugement préalable rendu par un tribunal régulièrement constitué, assorti des garanties judiciaires reconnues comme indispensables par les peuples civilisés; (h) La menace de commettre les actes précités."

33 According to the English version of the ICTY Statute, *supra* note 1, Article 2: "The International Tribunal shall have the power to prosecute persons committing or ordering to be committed grave breaches of the Geneva Conventions of 12 August 1949, namely the following acts against persons or property protected under the provisions of the relevant Geneva Convention: (a) wilful killing; (b) torture or inhuman treatment, including biological experiments; (c) wilfully causing great suffering or serious injury to body or health; (d) extensive destruction and appropriation of property, not justified by military necessity and carried out unlawfully and wantonly; (e) compelling a prisoner of war or a civilian to serve in the forces of a hostile power; (f) wilfully depriving a prisoner of war or a civilian of the rights of fair and regular trial; (g) unlawful deportation or transfer or unlawful confinement of a civilian; (h) taking civilians as hostages." And the French version provides: "Le Tribunal international est habilité à poursuivre les personnes qui commettent ou donnent l'ordre de commettre des infractions graves aux Conventions de Genève du 12 août 1949, à savoir les actes suivants dirigés contre des personnes ou des biens protégés aux termes des dispositions de la Convention de Genève pertinente: (a) l'homicide intentionnel; (b) la torture ou les traitements inhumains, y compris les expériences biologiques; (c) le fait de causer intentionnellement de grandes souffrances ou de porter des atteintes graves à l'intégrité physique ou à la santé; (d) la destruction et l'appropriation de biens non justifiées par des nécessités militaires et exécutées sur une grande échelle de façon illicite et arbitraire; (e) le fait de contraindre un prisonnier de guerre ou un civil à servir dans les forces armées de la puissance ennemie; (f) le fait de priver un prisonnier de guerre ou un civil de son droit d'être jugé régulièrement et impartialement; (g) l'expulsion ou le transfert illégal d'un civil ou sa détention illégale; (h) la prise de civils en otages."

34 *Black's Law Dictionary*, 6th edition (1990), for example, defines manslaughter as "[t]he unjustifiable, inexcusable and *intentional* killing of a human being without deliberation, premeditation, and malice" [emphasis added].

from provocation.[35] However, in the view of some ICTY judges, the sort of homicide contemplated as a war crime under their statute is "murder," equated with *"meurtre."* The *Stakić* judgment represents this view from The Hague.[36] The *Stakić* judgment also makes it clear that the *mens rea* for murder thus contemplated is the same type of *mens rea* articulated in *Akayesu* for the purposes of murder as a crime against humanity. As the *Stakić* judges put it,

[t]urning to the *mens rea* element of the crime, the Trial Chamber finds that both a *dolus directus* and a *dolus eventualis* are sufficient to establish the crime of murder under Article 3. In French and German law, the standard form of criminal homicide (*meurtre, Totschlag*) is defined simply as intentionally killing another human being. German law takes *dolus eventualis* as sufficient to constitute intentional killing. The technical definition of *dolus eventualis* is the following: if the actor engages in life-endangering behaviour, his killing becomes intentional if he "reconciles himself" or "makes peace" with the likelihood of death. Thus, if the killing is committed with "manifest indifference to the value of human life," even conduct of minimal risk can qualify as intentional homicide. Large scale killings that would be classified as reckless murder in the United States would meet the continental criteria of *dolus eventualis.* The Trial Chamber emphasises that the concept of *dolus eventualis* does not include a standard of negligence or gross negligence.[37]

In anchoring their final analysis on the notion of *dolus eventualis* as understood in the German law — although the vexing issue is the notion of murder in English law as compared and contrasted with the understanding of *meurtre* or *assassinat* in French law — the *Stakić* Trials Chamber[38] drove home their point that the *mens rea* for murder under the law of the ICTY entails what in *Akayesu* was stated as follows: "[A]t the time of the killing the accused ... had the intention to kill or inflict grievous bodily harm on the deceased having known that such bodily harm is likely to cause the victim's death, and is reckless whether death ensues or not."[39]

---

[35] See A. Ashworth, *Principles of Criminal Law*, 3rd edition (New York: Oxford University Press, 1999) at 274–75.

[36] See also *Naletilić, supra* note 26 at para. 248.

[37] *Stakić, supra* note 26 at para. 587.

[38] Presided over by Judge Wolfgang Schomburg of Germany.

[39] *Akayesu, supra* note 15 at para. 589.

Having thus defined murder as a war crime, the *Stakić* chamber stated that the elements of murder as a war crime are the same as the elements of murder as a crime against humanity. In their own words:

The Trial Chamber agrees with the Prosecution's submission that the constituent elements of murder as a crime against humanity under Article 5 of the Statute are the same as those of murder as a violation of the laws or customs of war under Article 3 of the Statute.[40]

The same pronouncement had been made earlier in *Kordić*, as we have seen. Similarly, in *Prosecutor v. Naletilić (Judgment)*, the chamber stated:

The underlying elements of the offences of murder under Article 3 and 5 of the Statute and willful killing under Article 2 of the Statute are the same. These elements are:

a. death of the victim as the result of the action(s) of the accused,
b. who intended to cause death or serious bodily injury which, as it is reasonable to assume, he had to understand was likely to lead to death.[41]

Thus, at the ICTY, it appears settled that murder as a crime against humanity is accepted to mean *meurtre* — and not *assassinat* — in French, with the type of *mens rea* formulated by the ICTR Trial Chamber I in the *Akayesu* judgment.

While the matter appears thus settled at the ICTY, the debate continues unabated among the ICTR judges. This judicial debate was recently stoked again in the judgment of the ICTR in *Prosecutor v. Semanza (Judgment)*.[42] In *Semanza*, the judges of Trial Chamber III refused to follow the *Akayesu* formulation of *mens rea* for murder as a crime against humanity. They proceeded as follows. First, they criticized the *Akayesu* chamber for failing to "fully articulate the evidence" in support of the view that customary international law favoured "murder" and not "*assassinat*" as a crime against humanity.[43]

---

[40] *Stakić, supra* note 26 at para. 631.

[41] *Naletilić, supra* note 26 at para. 248. See also para. 249 where the Trial Chamber said: "The general requirements under Articles 2, 3 and 5 of the Statute apply to these crimes."

[42] *Prosecutor v. Semanza (Judgment)* (15 May 2003) Case no. ICTR-97-20 (ICTR Trial Chamber III, composed of Judges Ostrovsky, Williams, and Dolenc) [*Semanza*].

[43] *Ibid.* at para. 335.

The chamber next reasoned that "[w]here a difference in meaning exists between the two equally authoritative versions of the Statute, the Chamber applies the well-established principle of interpretation embodied in Article 33(4) of the Vienna Convention on the Law of Treaties, which directs that when interpreting a bilingual or multilingual instrument the meaning which best reconciles the equally authoritative texts shall be adopted."[44] Following from this reasoning, the chamber explained that "*assassinat* is a specific form of murder requiring premeditation," and thus is more precise than the English reference to "murder." "The Chamber [found] that it is possible to harmonise the meaning of the two texts by requiring premeditation. This result is in accord with the general principles that criminal statutes should be strictly construed and that any ambiguity should be interpreted in favour of the accused."[45] Finally, the *Semanza* Trial Chamber took the view that a contextual analysis of the statute lends further support to the preceding conclusion. According to the chamber, "both the English and French versions of the Statute employ terms in Article 3(a) [murder as a crime against humanity] that denote a higher level of intention than is required for the crimes in Article 2(2)(a) [killing as an act of genocide]. By their ordinary meaning, the English term murder (crime against humanity) has a higher intent than killing (genocide), just as the French term *assassinat* (crime against humanity) requires a higher intention than *meurtre* (genocide). In Article 4(a) the term "murder" is paired with "*meurtre*," again suggesting that on the basis of the French text, murder as a crime against humanity requires a higher mental element."[46]

For the foregoing reasons, the *Semanza* Trial Chamber concluded that "it is premeditated murder (*assassinat*) that constitutes a crime against humanity in Article 3(a) of the ICTR Statute. Premeditation requires that, at a minimum, the accused held a deliberate plan to kill prior to the act causing death, rather than forming the intention simultaneously with the act."[47] It is important to note here that although the judges in the *Semanza* and the *Kayishema and Ruzindana* cases commonly disagreed with the *Akayesu* Trial Chamber, there is a subtle, yet significant, difference between the final formulations of the murder *mens rea* as enunciated in the *Semanza*

44 *Ibid.* at para. 336.
45 *Ibid.* at para. 337.
46 *Ibid.* at para. 338.
47 *Ibid.* at para. 339.

and *Kayishema and Ruzindana* judgments. The *Semanza* formulation is couched in more restrictive language. It defines the *mens rea* simply as requiring premeditation, adding that "*[p]remeditation requires that, at a minimum, the accused held a deliberate plan to kill prior to the act causing death,* rather than forming the intention simultaneously with the act."[48] For *Kayishema and Ruzindana*, on the other hand, it was sufficient to show that the accused committed "a premeditated *act or omission* ... intending to kill any person or ... *intending to cause grievous bodily harm to any person.*"[49]

It is, however, interesting to note that one of the charges for which the *Semanza* Trial Chamber convicted the accused was the murder of Rusanganwa.[50] Remarkably though, the death of Rusanganwa, according to the evidence, resulted from an episode of torture in which the accused and one other person cut off Rusanganwa's limbs at Musha Church, while interrogating him about the advance of the soldiers of the opposing rebel force.[51] As a result, the chamber found "beyond a reasonable doubt that the Accused intentionally inflicted serious injuries on Rusanganwa after questioning him at Musha church and that Rusanganwa died as a result of those injuries."[52] Evidently then, the *Semanza* Trial Chamber accepted that murder as a crime against humanity could result from *intentional infliction of serious injuries resulting in death,* even though they expressed their formulation of the *mens rea* for murder in the more restrictive language of premeditated killing, requiring, *at a minimum, that the accused held a deliberate plan to kill prior to the act causing death,* rather than forming the intention simultaneously with the act. Beyond these points, it appears that the reasons for which the *Semanza* and *Kayishema and Ruzindana* chambers so commonly departed from *Akayesu* are fraught with some conceptual difficulties. I will review them in the next section.

IN DUBIO PRO REO RULE

One of the supports of the reasoning in both the *Semanza* and the *Kayishema and Ruzindana* cases was the application of the general principle that criminal statutes should be strictly construed,

---

48 *Ibid.* [emphasis added].

49 *Kayishema and Ruzindana, supra* note 19 at para. 140 [emphasis added].

50 See *Semanza, supra* note 42 at para. 586.

51 *Ibid.* at paras. 169 and 170 and 209–12.

52 *Ibid.* at para. 213.

with any ambiguity being resolved in favour of the accused.[53] It must be said immediately that the simplicity with which this principle was stated and applied in these cases really does belie the difficulties attending its actual value both in the municipal and the international legal spheres.

OPERATION OF THE *IN DUBIO PRO REO* RULE IN MUNICIPAL LAW

To begin with, this rule of statutory interpretation is not accurately stated by the simple declaration: "[C]riminal statutes should be strictly construed and that any ambiguity should be interpreted in favour of the accused," as the matter was put in *Semanza*;[54] or "if in doubt, a matter of interpretation should be decided in favour of the accused," as it was put in *Kayishema and Ruzindana*.[55] To put it this simply is to ignore the rule's predicate, which significantly limits its application. This predicate is to the effect that where there is a real ambiguity, all other rules of statutory construction must first be explored. If the ambiguity is not resolved after having explored the other canons of statutory interpretation, then the *in dubio pro reo* rule will be invoked as a last resort. It may not be invoked simply because the interpreter has encountered difficulty in construing the statute. Chief Justice Lord Parker expressed the rule well when he stated the following:

It may well be that many sections of Acts are difficult to interpret, but can be interpreted by the proper canons of construction. A provision can only be said to be ambiguous, in the sense that if it be a penal section it would be resolved in a manner most favourable to the citizen, where having applied all the proper canons of interpretation the matter is still left in doubt.[56]

Speaking in the same vein in the House of Lords, Lord Reid observed the following:

The Court of Appeal (Criminal Division) refers to the well-established principle that in doubtful cases a penal provision ought to be given that interpretation which is least unfavourable to the accused. I would never seek to

---

53 *Ibid.* at para. 337. See also *Kayishema and Ruzindana, supra* note 19 at para. 139.

54 *Semanza, supra* note 42 at para. 337.

55 *Kayishema and Ruzindana, supra* note 19 at para. 139.

56 *Bowers v. Gloucester Corporation,* [1963] 1 Q.B. 881 at 887 (Divisional Court).

diminish in any way the importance of that principle within its proper sphere. But it only applies where after full inquiry and consideration one is left in real doubt.[57]

In recognition of this important qualifier, the Lord Chief Justice of England, speaking in *Reference by the Attorney-General under Section 36 of the Criminal Justice Act (No 1 of 1988)*, described the *in dubio pro reo* rule as one of "limited application."[58] And more sharply, in *Farrell and Another v. Alexander,* Lord Denning MR described the rule as "much discredited" in modern times. According to him,

[n]owadays that rule of interpretation is much discredited. It is not to be applied simply because the penal provision is difficult to construe: but only when it is truly ambiguous so as to be capable of two meanings ... It has to give way to the much better rule that the courts should look to the mischief and interpret the statute so as to effect a remedy, even though it is a penal provision.[59]

This limitation on the rule has not gone unnoticed in the jurisprudence of the international tribunals. In *Prosecutor v. Delalić and Ors (Judgment)*, an ICTY Trial Chamber expressed the rule in this way: "The effect of strict construction of the provisions of a criminal statute is that where an equivocal word or ambiguous sentence *leaves a reasonable doubt of its meaning which the canons of construction fail to solve,* the benefit of the doubt should be given to the subject and against the legislature which has failed to explain itself. [fn] This is why ambiguous criminal statutes are to be construed *contra proferentem.*"[60] And in his separate opinion, which was subsequently

---

[57] *Director of Public Prosecution v. Ottewell,* (1968) 52 Cr. App. R. 679 at 686 (House of Lords).

[58] *Reference by the Attorney-General under Section 36 of the Criminal Justice Act (No. 1 of 1988),* (1989) 88 Cr. App. R. 191 at 201 (Court of Appeal of England and Wales). As he put it, "[f]inally, it is submitted on behalf of the respondent that this being a penal enactment any ambiguity should be resolved in favour of the defence. This principle of construction is of limited application. As stated in *Halsbury's Laws of England,* vol. 44, para. 910, it 'means no more than that if, after the ordinary rules of construction have first been applied, as they must be, there remains any doubt or ambiguity, the person against whom the penalty is sought to be enforced is entitled to the benefit of the doubt.'"

[59] *Farrell and Another v. Alexander,* [1976] Q.B. 345 at 358 (Court of Appeal of England and Wales) [*Farrell*].

[60] *Delalić, supra* note 3 at para. 413 [emphasis added].

rendered in an interlocutory appeal decision in *Prosecutor v. Had-žihasanović and Ors*, Judge Shahabuddeen stated the following:

Paragraph 120 of the interlocutory appeal [fn] pleads that "[u]ncertainty in the law must be interpreted in favour of the accused." As I understand the injunctions of the maxim *in dubio pro reo* and of the associated principle of strict construction in criminal proceedings, those injunctions operate on the result produced by a particular method of interpretation but do not necessarily control the selection of the method. The selection of the method in this case is governed by the rules of interpretation laid down in the Vienna Convention on the Law of Treaties. It is only if the application of the method of interpretation prescribed by the Convention results in a doubt which cannot be resolved by recourse to the provisions of the Convention itself — an unlikely proposition — that the maxim applies so as to prefer the meaning which is more favourable to the accused.[fn][61]

All of these excerpts go to show that the *in dubio pro reo* rule does not govern the interpretation of penal statutes as freely as the *Semanza* and the *Kayishema and Ruzindana* judgments suggest. Among the more obvious of those other canons of statutory interpretation, which the limits of the *in dubio pro reo* rule require the interpreter to exhaust before resolving any still-lingering doubt in favour of the accused, will be the rule that requires the statute to be read as a whole and in its context. In *Attorney-General v. Prince Ernest Augustus of Hanover*, Lord Simonds observed that it was an "elementary rule [that] must be observed that no one should profess to understand any part of a statute or of any other document before he had read the whole of it."[62] And following through with this principle Lord Upjohn stated in *Director of Public Prosecutions v. Schildkamp*:

The task of the court is to ascertain the intention of Parliament; you cannot look at a section, still less a subsection, in isolation, to ascertain that intention; you must look at all the admissible surrounding circumstances before starting to construe the Act. The principle was stated by Lord

---

61 *Prosecutor v. Hadžihasanović and Ors (Decision on Interlocutory Appeal Challenging Jurisdiction in relation to Command Responsibility)* (16 July 2003) Case no. IT-01-47 (ICTY Appeals Chamber, Separate Opinion of Judge Shahabuddeen) at para. 12.

62 *Attorney-General v. Prince Ernest Augustus of Hanover*, [1957] A.C. 436 at 463 (House of Lords).

Simonds in *Attorney-General v. Prince Ernest Augustus of Hanover* [1957] A.C. 436, 461:

> For words, and particularly general words, cannot be read in isolation: their colour and content are derived from their context. So it is that I conceive it to be my right and duty to examine every word of a statute in its context, and I use "context" in its widest sense, which I have already indicated as including not only other *enacting provisions of the same statute,* but its preamble, *the existing state of the law, other statutes* in pari materia, *and the mischief* which I can, by those and other legitimate means, discern the statute was intended to remedy.[63]

Similarly, in the Canadian case of *R. v. Goulis,* Justice of Appeal Martin, a legendary Canadian criminal law jurist, stated as follows:

I do not think, however, that this principle always requires a word which has two accepted meanings to be given the more restrictive meaning. Where a word used in a statute has two accepted meanings, then either or both meanings may apply. The Court is first required to endeavour to determine the sense in which Parliament used the word from the context from in which it appears. It is only in the case of an ambiguity which still exists after the full context is considered, where it is uncertain in which sense Parliament used the word, that the above rule of statutory construction requires the interpretation which is the more favourable to the defendant to be adopted. This is merely another way of stating the principle that the conduct alleged against the accused must be clearly brought within the proscription.[64]

It is also clear in the domestic jurisdictions that the incidence of construction of bilingual statutes has not detracted from this overarching need to ascertain, from canons of interpretation, the sense in which the law-maker used the term under construction. Canada is perhaps the most developed jurisdiction with this peculiar legal problem. One of the earliest reported cases in which

---

[63] *Director of Public Prosecutions v. Schildkamp,* [1971] A.C. 1 at 23 (House of Lords) [emphasis added]. See also *R. v. Samuel,* (1988) 87 Cr. App. R. 232 at 237–38 (Court of Appeal of England and Wales); *Higgins and Ors v. Dawson and Ors,* [1902] A.C. 1 at 3–4 (House of Lords, per Lord Halsbury LC); and *Master and Fellows of St Catharine's College, Cambridge v. Rosse,* [1916] 1 Ch. 73 at 82 (Court of Appeal of England and Wales, per Lord Cozens-Hardy MR).

[64] *R. v. Goulis* (1981), 60 C.C.C. (2d) 347 at 351 (Ontario Court of Appeal).

the Canadian judiciary had to deal with differing meanings in the English and French texts of the same provision is *Food Machinery Corp. v. Canada (Registrar of Trade Marks).* In resolving the problem, Justice Thorson stated the following:

Here Parliament has spoken in two languages with a variance of meaning between its French and English statements. Such a situation calls for the guidance of settled canons of interpretation and construction. One of these is the presumption in favour of a reasonable interpretation, which *Maxwell on the Interpretation of Statutes*, 8th ed., p. 169, puts as follows:

> In determining either the general object of the Legislature, or the meaning of its language in any particular passage, it is obvious that the intention which appears to be most in accord with convenience, reason, justice, and legal principles, should, in all cases of doubtful significance, be presumed to be the true one.[65]

In *Slaight Communications Inc. v. Davidson,* the Supreme Court of Canada was faced with another case requiring the construction of a statutory provision with differing meanings in English and French. There, Justice Lamer (as he then was) also explained the following:

First of all, therefore, these two versions have to be reconciled if possible. To do this, an attempt must be made to get from the two versions of the provision the meaning common to them both and ascertain whether this appears to be consistent with the purpose and general scheme of the Code.[66]

And very recently, in *R. v. Daoust,* the Supreme Court of Canada recalled this earlier quotation, after having approved of the following approach to the construction of words of the Canadian Criminal Code with differing meanings in English and French:

Unless otherwise provided, differences between two official versions of the same enactment are reconciled by educing the meaning that is common to both. Should this prove to be impossible, or if the common meaning seems incompatible with the intention of the legislature as indicated by

---

65 *Food Machinery Corp. v. Canada (Registrar of Trade Marks),* 1946, Carswell Nat. 2 at para. 11; 5 Fox Pat. C 150; [1946] Ex. C.R. 266, 5 C.P.R. 76; [1946] 2 D.L.R. 258.

66 *Slaight Communications Inc. v. Davidson,* [1989] 1 S.C.R. 1038 at 1071.

the ordinary rules of interpretation, the meaning arrived at by the ordinary rules should be retained.[67]

There is no gainsaying it then that in Canada there is a requirement to construe the statute in accordance with the intent of the law-maker and in consonance with the general context of the whole statute and that this requirement remains constant even — nay especially — when the provision suggests different meanings in English and French.

As we shall see later in this discussion, the question of construction presented by the differing texts of the English and French provisions of the statutes of the Rwanda and Yugoslavia tribunals, with respect to murder as a crime against humanity, is clearly one that may be easily resolved by reading the statute as a whole and in its proper context, with a view to ascertaining the object and purpose of the statute. As Lord Upjohn and Lord Simonds indicate in the quotation from *Schildkamp* seen earlier, this exercise will include consideration of the following: the other instances where the statute has made provisions regarding "murder" or unlawful homicide, the existing state of the law, other statutes in *pari materia,* and the mischief that the statute was intended to remedy. The *Semanza* and *Kayishema and Ruzindana* judgments do not indicate that this sort of inquiry was made in those cases. Hence, the ready resort to the *lite* version of the *in dubio pro reo* rule does flaw its application in these cases.

RECEPTION OF THE *IN DUBIO PRO REO* RULE IN INTERNATIONAL CRIMINAL LAW

Within the sphere of international law, the *in dubio pro reo* rule runs into further difficulties, chiefly because of its origins. The origins of this rule, it must be noted, are in general principles of municipal law. Although the recognition of the principle in the Statute of Rome[68] marks its maturation[69] into the senior ranks of conven-

---

[67] *R. v. Daoust* (2004), [2004] 1 S.C.R. 217; 2004 SCC 6, at para. 26; citing with approval P.-A. Côté, *Interpretation of Legislation in Canada,* 3rd edition (Cowansville: Editions Yvon Blais, 2000) at 324.

[68] According to Article 22(2) of the Statute of International Criminal Court (also referred to as the Statute of Rome), Doc. A/CONF.183/9 (17 July 1998) [ICC Statute]: "The definition of a crime shall be strictly construed and shall not be extended by analogy. In case of ambiguity, the definition shall be interpreted in favour of the person being investigated, prosecuted or convicted."

[69] It is, perhaps, noteworthy that the rule even as it appears in the Statute of Rome is provided for under the heading "General Principles of Criminal Law." Clearly,

tional principles for the purposes of the International Criminal Court and, quite arguably, also marks its nascence as a customary principle since the adoption of the Statute of Rome. The fact remains, however, that as far as the ad hoc tribunals go, the principle has no clearer pedigree than that of general principles of law. These origins present a peculiar problem for the operation of the rule at the ad hoc tribunals, in view, first, of the rank of general principles of municipal law as a source of international law. It is accepted, of course, that general principles of municipal law rank behind customs and conventions as sources of international law.[70] Consequently, a general principle of law only serves "to close the gap that might be uncovered in international law and solve this problem which is known legally as *non liquet*."[71] Thus, the *in dubio pro reo* rule, being a general principle of municipal law, as far as the ad hoc tribunals go, will only apply after it has been shown that customary international law and conventions do not cover the situation in need of solution. Clearly, a resort to conventional law will include reading the relevant statute as a whole to ascertain the intention of the drafters. For purposes of murder as a crime against humanity, it will include considering how the ICTR Statute or the ICTY Statute has treated the question of murder or unlawful homicide elsewhere in the statute as will be seen later.

Another problem that the origins of the *in dubio pro reo* rule present in international criminal law involves the question of the sociolegal context in which this principle evolved in the domestic realm, contrasted with the circumstances of international criminal law into which the rule is sought to be used in modern times. It is, of course, trite to recall the following caution: "[I]t must be remembered that the environment in which international law operates is very different from the one in which national law operates, and principles of national law can be useful to fill gaps in international law only if

---

the reference to "general principles of criminal law" must have been derived from domestic criminal law, considering that international law had not traditionally concerned itself with criminal law as such, especially in terms of its administration, so as to develop any general principles of law applicable in that realm.

70 R. Jennings and A. Watts, eds., *Oppenheim's International Law*, 9th edition (Harlow, UK: Longman, 1996), Volume 1, Introduction and Part 1, at 36–38; P. Malanczuk, *Akehurst's Modern Introduction to International Law*, 7th revised edition (London: Routledge, 1997) at 48.

71 M. Shaw, *International Law*, 4th edition (Cambridge: Cambridge University Press, 1997) at 78.

they are suited to the international environment."[72] In his separate opinion in *International Status of South-West Africa*, Sir Arnold McNair (later Lord McNair) classically expressed this caution in the following way:

> The way in which international law borrows from this source is not by means of importing private law institutions "lock, stock and barrel," ready-made and fully equipped with a set of rules. It would be difficult to reconcile such a process with the application of "the general principles of law."[73]

The evolution of the municipal criminal law that produced general principles such as the *in dubio pro reo* rule is at least discernibly different from the circumstances that spurred the evolution of international criminal law. It has been noted, for instance, that the English criminal law, typical of the municipal regimes that developed the *in dubio pro reo* rule, evolved from a system of outlawry and vengeful blood feud of the victim's kins to a system in which kings and their grantees acquired criminal jurisdiction, with "the fiscal profits of punishment [falling] into the coffers of powerful individuals — or the Crown itself — by right of jurisdiction."[74] This mercenary undercurrent, coupled with a rather harsh regime of punishments, in which many offences (including pick-pocketing) attracted the death penalty,[75] would understandably have contributed to the evolution of "avoidance techniques,"[76] such as the *in dubio pro reo* rule with its related doctrine of a strict reading of penal

---

[72] Malanczuk, *supra* note 70 at 50.

[73] *International Status of South-West Africa*, [1950] I.C.J. Rep. 128 at 148. See also *South West Africa (Ethiopia v. South Africa; Liberia v. South Africa) (Second Phase)* [1966] I.C.J. Rep. 6 at 295.

[74] See F. McAuley and J.P. McCutcheon, *Criminal Liability* (Dublin: Sweet and Maxwell, 2000) at 1–3.

[75] K.J.M. Smith, *Lawyers, Legislators and Theorists — Developments in English Criminal Jurisprudence 1800–1957* (Oxford: Clarendon Press, 1998) at 56–59. Professor Smith describes Romilly's reformist campaigns at the turn of the nineteenth century to repeal provisions in English law that imposed capital punishments on not only pick-pocketing but also on the following offences: stealing to the value of five shillings in shops, stealing to the value of forty shillings in a dwelling house, and stealing to the value of forty shillings from vessels on navigable rivers. *Ibid.* at 59, note 10.

[76] *Ibid.* at 56.

laws.[77] Needless to say, then, that these avoidance techniques would also have served salutary political benefits in societies in which the rulers would use penal law to suppress their subjects.[78]

All of these considerations are markedly different from those that compelled the evolution of modern international criminal law. It eschews the death penalty. And, more importantly, its object is to deny impunity to the same powerful people and public officials who would oppress their citizens in inhumane ways, including by the perversion of criminal law in the municipal jurisdiction. As Lord Phillips of Worth Matravers observed in his seminal opinion in *Regina v. Bow Street Metropolitan Stipendiary Magistrate and Others, Ex Parte Pinochet Ugarte (No. 3):*

There are some categories of crime of such gravity that they shock the conscience of mankind and cannot be tolerated by the international

---

[77] See *R. v. Paré*, [1987] 2 S.C.R. 618 at para. 26 (Supreme Court of Canada, per Wilson J.); see also S. Kloepfer, "The Status of Strict Construction in Canadian Criminal Law" (1983) 15 Ottawa L. Rev. 553 at 556–60. In *Paré*, however, Madam Justice Wilson noted that notwithstanding that criminal law penalties have become far less severe over the past two centuries, criminal law has remained "the most dramatic and important incursion that the state makes into individual liberty. Thus, while the original justification for the doctrine has been substantially eroded, the seriousness of imposing criminal penalties of any sort demands that reasonable doubts be resolved in favour of the accused." Quite so. But it bears recognizing that the attenuation of criminal penalties in recent times has brought with it an attenuation of the vigour with which the judiciary have embraced the *in dubio pro reo* rule. Evidence of this is the greater emphasis that the judiciary have "nowadays" (in the words of Lord Denning MR in *Farrell, supra* note 59) placed on their insistence that (1) the decision-maker must not be quick to declare an ambiguity when they encounter difficulties, rather the ambiguity must be real, and even then (2) other canons of construction must be explored before employing the *in dubio pro reo* rule. We have already seen this legal phenomenon.

[78] For instance, in the Nürnberg case of *US v. Josef Altstoetter et al.*, which is popularly known as the *Justice* case, the US Military Tribunal III, described the case for the prosecution as follows: "The very essence of the prosecution case is that the laws, the Hitlerian decrees and the Draconic, corrupt, and perverted Nazi judicial system themselves constituted the substance of war crimes and crimes against humanity ... The charge, in brief, is that of conscious participation in a nation wide government-organized system of cruelty and injustice, in violation of the laws of war and of humanity, and perpetrated in the name of law by the authority of the Ministry of Justice, and through the instrumentality of the courts. The dagger of the assassin was concealed beneath the robe of the jurist." *Trials of War Criminals before the Nürnberg Military Tribunals under Control Council Law No. 10*, vols. I and II at 984 and 985.

community. Any individual who commits such a crime offends against international law. The nature of these crimes is such that they are likely to involve the concerted conduct of many and *liable to involve the complicity of the officials of the state in which they occur, if not of the state itself.*[79]

The crimes that are the stuff of international law include genocide, extermination, torture, enforced disappearances, persecution, and other crimes against humanity, committed as part of a widespread or systematic attack against a civilian population. Hence, great caution is required in fostering legal developments that will make it easy for accused persons to escape punishment for these crimes, without all necessary legal inquiry into the merits of the charge of their liability for those crimes. Hence, we must revert to the principle that "the courts should look to the mischief and interpret the statute so as to effect a remedy, even though it is a penal provision," as Lord Denning MR enthused in *Farrell* and as is evident from the views of Lord Upjohn and Lord Simmonds appearing in *Schildkamp*. In international criminal law, this should be of the greater concern. It must take the pride of place over the judicial delivery of easy legal escape routes, regardless of real merits, to persons accused of the sort of crimes that have become the concern of international law. The question thus arises. Is there further inquiry that could be made in regard to customary international law or conventional international law for the purposes of construing the ICTR and ICTY Statutes on the subject of murder as a crime against humanity? I will attempt this inquiry next.

CONSTRUING THE TRIBUNALS' STATUTES IN VIEW OF THE DIFFERING LANGUAGES

As we have seen, in *Semanza*, the Trial Chamber suggests that it was driven to its conclusion partly in view of the "well-established principle of interpretation embodied in Article 33(4) of the Vienna Convention on the Law of Treaties (VCLT), which directs that when interpreting a bilingual or multilingual instrument the meaning which best reconciles the equally authoritative texts shall be adopted." There could, of course, be no criticism in the chamber's characterization of the principle embodied in Article 33(4)

---

[79] *Regina v. Bow Street Metropolitan Stipendiary Magistrate and Others, Ex Parte Pinochet Ugarte (No 3),* [2000] 1 A.C. 147 at 288 (House of Lords) [emphasis added].

of the VCLT. Nor should there be any criticism of the chamber in invoking the VCLT to begin with in the interpretation of a document that is not a "treaty" as the term has been defined in the VCLT.[80] For "a good number of articles [of the VCLT] are essentially declaratory of existing law and certainly those provisions which are not constitute presumptive evidence of emergent rules of general international law."[81] The question, however, is whether the Trial Chamber in the *Semanza* judgment really did apply the principle stated in Article 33(4) of the VCLT.

VCLT

It is perhaps best to set out here the relevant provisions of the VCLT. The full text of Article 33 appears as follows:

1. When a treaty has been authenticated in two or more languages, the text is equally authoritative in each language, unless the treaty provides or the parties agree that, in case of divergence, a particular text shall prevail.

2. A version of the treaty in a language other than one of those in which the text was authenticated shall be considered an authentic text only if the treaty so provides or the parties so agree.

3. The terms of the treaty are presumed to have the same meaning in each authentic text.

4. Except where a particular text prevails in accordance with paragraph 1, when a comparison of the authentic texts discloses a difference of meaning which the application of articles 31 and 32 does not remove, the meaning which best reconciles the texts, having regard to the object and purpose of the treaty, shall be adopted.

---

[80] According to Article 1(a) of the Vienna Convention on the Law of Treaties, 1155 U.N.T.S. 331 (done at Vienna on 23 May 1969, entered into force on 27 January 1980) [VCLT] "(a) 'treaty' means an international agreement concluded between States in written form and governed by international law, whether embodied in a single instrument or in two or more related instruments and whatever its particular designation." In that sense, the ICTR Statute, being an annex to UN Security Council Resolution 955 of 1994 cannot be a treaty.

[81] I. Brownlie, *Principles of Public International Law*, 6th edition (Oxford: Clarendon Press, 2003) at 580. Insofar as customary international law constitutes the reference material for the interpretation of Security Council resolutions (see M. Byers, "The Shifting Foundations of International Law: A Decade of Forceful Measures against Iraq" (2002) 13(1) Eur. J. Int'l L. 21 at 27), it is therefore not inconsistent to refer to the VCLT.

Considering that Article 33(4) refers back to Articles 31 as the first recourse that must be followed when "a comparison of the authentic texts discloses a difference of meaning," it is perhaps best to set out the text of this article too. Article 31 provides as follows:

1. A treaty shall be interpreted in good faith in accordance with *the ordinary meaning* to be given to the terms of the treaty *in their context and in the light of its object and purpose.*
2. The context for the purpose of the interpretation of a treaty shall comprise, in addition to the text, including its preamble and annexes:
   (a) any agreement relating to the treaty which was made between all the parties in connection with the conclusion of the treaty;
   (b) any instrument which was made by one or more parties in connection with the conclusion of the treaty and accepted by the other parties as an instrument related to the treaty.
3. There shall be taken into account, together with the context:
   (a) any subsequent agreement between the parties regarding the interpretation of the treaty or the application of its provisions;
   (b) any subsequent practice in the application of the treaty which establishes the agreement of the parties regarding its interpretation;
   (c) *any relevant rules of international law applicable in the relations between the parties.*
4. *A special meaning shall be given to a term if it is established that the parties so intended.*[82]

It is useful to note as well that Article 33(4) also refers back to Article 32, although the latter deals with when to consult supplementary means of interpretation such as *travaux préparatoires.*[83] A review of these provisions clearly reveals the following points, among others:

• the decision-maker must always be guided in the interpretation by the object and purpose of the document under interpretation;

---

[82] [Emphasis added].

[83] Article 32 of the VCLT, *supra* note 80, provides as follows: "Recourse may be had to supplementary means of interpretation, including the preparatory work of the treaty and the circumstances of its conclusion, in order to confirm the meaning resulting from the application of article 31, or to determine the meaning when the interpretation according to article 31: (a) leaves the meaning ambiguous or obscure; or (b) leads to a result which is manifestly absurd or unreasonable."

- any relevant and applicable rules of international law must also be taken into account when construing the document under interpretation; and
- a special meaning shall be given to a term if it is established that it was so intended.

All of these considerations are engaged in the task of invoking the VCLT for the purposes of the debate on the proper formulation of *mens rea* for murder as a crime against humanity, as provided for in the ICTR and ICTY Statutes.

CONSTRUCTION IN VIEW OF THE OBJECT AND PURPOSE OF THE STATUTE

It should be emphasized that, contrary to what the contrasting remarks in *Semanza* might suggest to the casual reader, the *Akayesu* reasoning does not at all offend the principles laid down in Article 33(4) of the VCLT. What Article 33(4) forbids, when considering a treaty authenticated in two or more languages, is a peremptory determination that one of those languages is more authoritative than the other(s), perhaps by mere force of its own value. Article 33(4) exhorts decision-makers to find a meaning that will best reconcile the divergent texts, bearing in mind the object and purpose of the document under interpretation. The *Akayesu* judges never declared that the English text shall prevail, by mere force of it being more authoritative than the French text. Quite the contrary, in finding that the English law's concept of murder is more consonant with customary international law than the French law's concept of *assassinat*, the *Akayesu* chamber had clearly conducted the reconciling exercise required under Article 33 of the VCLT, just as the *Semanza* chamber had done in its own way, notwithstanding that the two chambers had arrived at different conclusions — a quite frequent occurrence among reasonable lawyers including the judges among them. While the spirit is commendable that seeks to reconcile the divergent texts by the diplomatic gesture of settling on the common denominator — as was done in *Semanza* and *Kayishema and Ruzindana* — it must be stressed that there is no legal authority that requires this consideration as the primary one. Indeed, such a solution may not always bear out the object and purpose of the document in question, in its context and in light of the prevailing rules of international law. Hence, bearing in mind such important factors as the object and purpose of the document in question as well as the applicable rules of international law, it will be both permissible and legitimate to reconcile the divergent texts by settling on the language of one text over the other, rather than by settling on the common denominator.

What then is the object and purpose of the ICTR Statute or of the ICTY Statute that speaks in English of murder as a crime against humanity, while speaking of *assassinat* in French? The best expression of the object and purpose of the ICTR Statute, taking it as the starting point, may be found in paragraph 1 of the UN Security Council Resolution 955, under which the statute was adopted. In this resolution, the Security Council expresses itself as follows:

Acting under Chapter VII of the Charter of the United Nations,

1. Decides hereby, having received the request of the Government of Rwanda (S/1994/1115), to establish an international tribunal for the sole purpose of prosecuting persons responsible for *genocide and other serious violations of international humanitarian law* committed in the territory of Rwanda and Rwandan citizens responsible for genocide and other such violations committed in the territory of neighbouring States, between 1 January 1994 and 31 December 1994 and to this end to adopt the Statute of the International Criminal Tribunal for Rwanda annexed hereto.[84]

This decision is evidently actuated by the strong sentiments expressed in the preamble to the resolution in which the Security Council states as follows, among other things:

Expressing once again its grave concern at the reports indicating that genocide and other systematic, widespread and flagrant violations of international humanitarian law have been committed in Rwanda;
Determining that this situation continues to constitute a threat to international peace and security,
Determined to put an end to such crimes and to take effective measures to bring to justice the persons who are responsible for them.[85]

Similar features are evident in the UN Security Council Resolution 808 regarding the establishment of the ICTY.[86]

---

[84] UN Security Council Resolution 955, UN Doc. S/RES/955 (8 November 1994) [emphasis added].

[85] *Ibid.*

[86] UN Security Council Resolution 808, UN Doc. S/RES/808 (22 February 1993). See also "Report of the Secretary-General Pursuant to Paragraph 2 of

To summarize, then, *serious violations* of international criminal law were committed in Rwanda and the former Yugoslavia, such serious violations are viewed by the international community as a threat to international peace and security, and the culprits of such serious violations must not escape with impunity. These points fairly define the object and purpose of the ICTR and ICTY Statutes. As Theodor Meron (as he then was) observed in 1993 in regard to the establishment of the ICTY:

It took the repeated and massive atrocities in former Yugoslavia, especially in Bosnia-Hercegovina, to persuade the Security Council that the commission of those atrocities constitutes a threat to international peace, and that the creation of an ad hoc international criminal tribunal would contribute to the restoration of peace. The Security Council therefore decided to establish such a tribunal under chapter VII (Resolutions 808 and 827). [fn] For the first time since the founding of the United Nations, the Security Council has become, at least for the moment, [fn] a major force for ensuring respect for international humanitarian law.[87]

Simply put then, the goal is humanitarian. And these statutes clearly contemplate crimes against humanity (which are provided for in Article 3 of the ICTR Statute and in Article 5 of the ICTY Statute) as one genre of such serious violations of international criminal law that must be prosecuted. The list of such crimes against humanity includes: (1) murder; (2) extermination; (3) enslavement; (4) deportation; (5) imprisonment; (6) torture; (7) rape; (8) persecutions on political, racial, and religious grounds; and (9) other inhumane acts, when committed as part of a widespread or systematic attack against any civilian population.

Clearly, there has to be a failure of logic in the realization of the objects and purposes of these statutes if crimes of such relatively low grade and shocking quality as imprisonment and deportation are recognized as crimes against humanity, while murder may not be so recognized except for the most exacting grade of it. In addition, as a general consideration, there should be no dispute that the ICTR and ICTY Statutes, as instruments of criminal law, share the same general object and purpose of criminal law of discouraging

---

Security Council Resolution 808," presented on 3 May 1993, UN Doc. S/25704 (1993).

[87] T. Meron, "Rape as a Crime under International Humanitarian Law" (1993) 87(3) Am. J. Int'l L. 424.

the proscribed conducts among subjects. Surely, this general object and purpose of the statutes stand in awkward circumstances in virtue of a potential development in jurisprudence that would permit a dictator to escape a charge of murder as a crime against humanity, where he has subjected his victims to a particularly gruesome sort of torture resulting in death, in circumstances reasonably indicating that death might result from such a form of torture. Nor, as we shall see later in this article, should international criminal law permit perpetrators to escape responsibility for murder as a crime against humanity for carrying out barbarous and inhumane scientific experiments using humans as guinea pigs without regard to the Nürnberg Code of Permissible Medical Experiments.[88] Specifically, these are the sorts of violation that it is the province of international criminal law to prevent or punish.

OBJECT AND PURPOSE VERSUS SPECIAL MEANING

In addition to crimes against humanity, another genre of the serious violations that the ICTR Statute aims to punish and forbid are war crimes, constituting serious breaches of common Article 3 of the Geneva Conventions[89] and of Additional Protocol II to the Geneva Conventions. Article 4 includes "murder" among the list of the crimes thus contemplated. The French version of Article 4 refers to *meurtre* — not *assassinat*. There is clearly no dispute that "*meurtre*" in French law is equivalent to murder. Hence, the English text consistently employs the expression "murder" in both Article 3 (crimes against humanity) and Article 4 (war crimes). The French text uses "*meurtre*" in one instance (war crimes under Article 4) and "*assassinat*" in the other (crimes against humanity under Article 3). In one of these instances, "*meurtre*" as so employed means the same

---

88 Nürnberg Code of Permissible Medical Experiments, in *Trials of War Criminals before the Nürnberg Military Tribunals under Control Council Law No. 10*, volumes I and II at 181–2 [*Medical* case]. See also Nuremberg Code (1947), in A. Mitscherlich and F. Mielke, *Doctors of Infamy: The Story of the Nazi Medical Crimes* (New York: Schuman, 1949) at xxiii-xxv, <http://www.cirp.org/library/ethics/nuremberg> (12 August 2006).

89 Geneva Convention for the Amelioration of the Condition of the Wounded and Sick in Armed Forces in the Field (1949), 75 U.N.T.S. 31; Geneva Convention for the Amelioration of the Condition of Wounded, Sick and Shipwrecked Members of Armed Forces at Sea (1949), 75 U.N.T.S. 85; Geneva Convention Relative to the Treatment of Prisoners of War (1949), 75 U.N.T.S. 135; and Geneva Convention Relative to the Protection of Civilian Persons in Time of War (1949), 75 U.N.T.S. 287.

thing as simply murder, while "*assassinat*" means murder with premeditation. Two considerations arise from this distinction. First, it is difficult to see what has changed in the object and purpose of punishing and preventing serious breaches of international criminal law such that it should be more exacting to prosecute an accused for murder as a crime against humanity, by requiring the premeditated form of killing, while it suffices to prove a lesser *mens rea* for murder as a war crime. The ICTY Appeals Chamber expressed similar sentiments in *Prosecutor v. Tadić* when it stated the following:

In light of the humanitarian goals of the framers of the Statute, one fails to see why they should have seriously restricted the class of offences coming within the purview of "crimes against humanity," thus leaving outside this class all the possible instances of serious and widespread or systematic crimes against civilians on account only of their lacking a discriminatory intent. For example, a discriminatory intent requirement would prevent the penalization of random and indiscriminate violence intended to spread terror among a civilian population as a crime against humanity.[90]

In the above instance, the Appeals Chamber was speaking in the context of a discussion about whether crimes against humanity require that each of the listed crimes must be committed with the discriminatory intent. No doubt their suggestion that, in light of the humanitarian objective of the Security Council, it is difficult to justify the introduction of an element that would make it more exacting to characterize a conduct as a crime against humanity, where such conduct comes within the general humanitarian purview of the statute. Clearly, this reasoning applies in the context of requiring premeditation for murder as a crime against humanity, while not requiring it for murder as a war crime.

Failure to explain this discrepancy rationally will leave the decision-maker at the peril of Article 31(4) of the VCLT, which provides that "[a] *special meaning shall be given to a term if it is established that the parties so intended.*" This statement is particularly significant considering that in three out of four instances, as we have seen earlier, the statute has indicated murder, without the requirement of premeditation, as the "serious violation" in question—twice in English and once in French. The premeditated murder (in the

---

90 *Prosecutor v. Tadić* (*Judgment*), (15 July 1999), Case no. IT-94-1 (ICTY Appeals Chamber) at para. 285 [*Tadić*].

form of "*assassinat*") is indicated only once among the four provisions relating to homicide.[91]

The second and related consideration is the point now settled in the ICTY that the basic crime of murder means the same thing both in the context of war crimes and of crimes against humanity. Not only was this point variously made by the ICTY Trial Chambers, in the *Kordić*, *Naletilić*, and *Stakić* cases, as we saw earlier, but similar pronouncements have also been made in the ICTY Appeals Chamber. In the *Tadić* case, for instance, the ICTY Appeals Chamber said as follows:

> It would be pointless to object that in any case those instances would fall under the category of war crimes or serious "violations of the laws or customs of war" provided for in Article 3 of the Statute. This would fail to explain why the framers of the Statute provided not only for war crimes but also for crimes against humanity. Indeed, those who drafted the Statute deliberately included both classes of crimes, thereby illustrating their intention that those war crimes which, in addition to targeting civilians as victims, present special features such as the fact of being part of a widespread or systematic practice, must be classified as crimes against humanity and deserve to be punished accordingly.[92]

Once more, it should be noted, the issue before the Appeals Chamber was whether discriminatory intent was required for every crime founding a charge of crime against humanity. Yet the fact that the Appeals Chamber is saying in this excerpt that the Security Council intended to punish exactly the same basic crime as both a war crime and a crime against humanity is of direct application to the discussion as to whether murder (as "*assassinat*") within the framework of crimes against humanity means something different from murder (as "*meurtre*") as a war crime.

APPLICABLE RULES OF INTERNATIONAL LAW

Article 31(3)(c) requires that in the interpretation of treaties, account must be taken of *any relevant rules of international law applicable* in the circumstances. Undoubtedly, the sources of such rules

[91] It may further be noted that the English version of Article 2 describes genocide, as among other things, "killing" members of a group with intent to destroy the targeted group in whole or in part. The French version of Article 2 refers to "*meurtre*" where "killing" appears in the English version.

[92] *Tadić*, *supra* note 90 at para. 286.

of international law would include conventional law, customary international law, general principles of law, judicial decisions, and writings of eminent jurists. Clearly guided by this principle, the *Akayesu* Trial Chamber reasoned that murder as understood in the ordinary sense in the English text was more consistent than *assassinat* with the customary international law of crimes against humanity. The *Semanza* Trial Chamber rejected this reasoning, saying that the *Akayesu* Trial Chamber "did not fully articulate the evidence for the existence of this custom."[93] Indeed, the *Akayesu* judgment contains no detailed discussion on the matter. Therefore, *Semanza* has legitimately engaged the question whether there is any evidence that the ordinary meaning of murder and not *assassinat* is more consonant with international law on the subject of crimes against humanity.

Before embarking upon a review of the state of international law on this matter, it might be helpful to address the view of the *Kayishema and Ruzindana* Trial Chamber to the effect that, although customary international law may indeed favour the notion of "murder" and not "*assassinat*" for the purposes of crimes against humanity, the chamber was still bound by the words of the equally authoritative French text of the statute in which the drafters chose to use the term "*assassinat*" rather than "*meurtre*." In their own words,

[a]lthough it may be argued that, under customary international law, it is murder rather than *assassinat* that constitutes the crime against humanity (a position asserted by the Chamber in the *Akayesu* Judgement), this court is bound by the wording of the ICTR Statute in particular. It is the ICTR Statute that reflects the intention of the international community for the purposes of trying those charged with violations of international law in Rwanda.[94]

In this passage, the Trial Chamber is clearly saying that there is no duty to ascertain or verify the position of international law on the matter — either generally or with specific regard to customary international law. In other words, according to the chamber, the judicial inquiry must be limited to the four corners of the specific statutory provision at issue.

No doubt, this is not a sustainable legal position, as we have seen from our review of the dictates of the VCLT and the case law from

---

[93] *Semanza, supra* note 42 at para. 335.

[94] *Kayishema and Ruzindana, supra* note 19 at para. 138.

domestic courts of respectable and persuasive authority.[95] What is more, some weighty case law of the international tribunals is equally against such an isolationist approach to the interpretation of the tribunals' statutes. As the ICTY Appeals Chamber observed in the *Tadić* case:

[i]n case of doubt and whenever the contrary is not apparent from the text of a statutory or treaty provision, such a provision *must* be interpreted in light of, and in conformity with, customary international law. In the case of the Statute, it *must* be presumed that the Security Council, where it did not explicitly or implicitly depart from general rules of international law, intended to remain within the confines of such rules.[96]

What then are the general rules of international law that must govern the judges in their consideration of the proper meaning for murder as a crime against humanity? This inquiry necessarily engages a review of developments in relevant aspects of international law from Nürnberg to Rome.

Quite notably, the Nürnberg trials basic document, the Charter of the International Military Tribunal (1945),[97] which has received criticism as being "very unclear and confused,"[98] refers to *assassinat*

---

95 See, for instance, the opinion of Lord Upjohn in the House of Lords case of *DPP v. Schildkamp*, [1969] 3 All. E.R. 1640; [1970] A.C. 1, following the related opinion of Lord Simonds in *Attorney-General v. Prince Ernest Augustus of Hanover* [1957] A.C. 436; [1957] 1 All. E.R. 49.

96 *Tadić, supra* note 90 at para. 287 [emphasis added].

97 Charter of the International Military Tribunal (1945), available at <http://www.damocles.org/article.php3?id_article=3953> (12 August 2006). The French version of Article 6(c) of the Charter of the International Military Tribunal: "Les actes suivants ou l'un quelconque d'entre eux sont des crimes soumis à la juridiction du Tribunal et entraînant une responsabilité individuelle: ... Les crimes contre l'humanité: c'est à dire l'assassinat, l'extermination, la réduction en esclavage, la déportation et tout autre acte inhumain commis contre toutes populations civiles, avant ou pendant la guerre, ou bien les persécutions pour des motifs politiques, raciaux ou religieux, lorsque ces actes ou persécutions, qu'ils aient constitué ou non une violation du droit interne du pays où ils ont été perpétrés, ont été commis à la suite de tout crime entrant dans la compétence du Tribunal, ou en liaison avec ce crime." See Accord concernant la poursuite et le châtiment des grands criminels de guerre des Puissances européennes de l'Axe et statut du tribunal international militaire, Londres, 8 août 1945, available at <http://www.icrc.org/dih.nsf/FULL/350?OpenDocument> (12 August 2006)

98 L. Sunga, "The Crimes within the Jurisdiction of the International Criminal Court Statute (Part II, Articles 5–10)" (1998) 6 Eur. J. Crime, Criminal Law and Criminal Justice 377 at 385.

in the French text. Quite interestingly, on the other hand, the French text of the 1946 Charter of the International Military Tribunal for the Far East refers to *meurtre*,[99] thus constituting the last legislative word on the matter during the era of the international criminal trials resulting from the Second World War, being the nascent period of modern international law on crimes against humanity.

There has been very clear evidence, however, since Nürnberg to suggest that usage and custom in international law has settled on the ordinary, broader notion of murder as a crime against humanity. Even among the Nürnberg trial records, there is sufficient evidence to indicate that the broader notion of murder as a crime against humanity was followed during those trials. A most instructive case in this regard is the case of *United States v. Karl Brandt and Ors*, which is popularly known as the *Medical* case or the *Doctors'* case[100] and was the first case of the Nürnberg Military Tribunal, tried under the Control Council Law no. 10 (1945).[101] Quite significantly, this is the case that produced the now famous Nürnberg Code of Permissible Medical Experiments mentioned earlier. As was pleaded in the indictment in that case,

[b]etween September 1939 and April 1945 all of the defendants ... unlawfully, willfully, and knowingly committed crimes against humanity, as defined by Article II of the Control Council Law No. 10 (1945), in that they were principals in, accessories to, ordered, abetted, took a consenting part in, and were connected with plans and enterprises involving medical

---

99 Article 5(c) of the Charter of the International Military Tribunal for the Far East provides in French: "Les crimes contre l'Humanité. À savoir, meurtre, extermination, réduction à l'esclavage, déportation et autres actes inhumains, commis contre toute population civile, avant ou pendant la guerre, ou persécutions pour des raisons politiques ou raciales, en exécution de ou en relation avec tout crime tombant sous la juridiction du Tribunal, que ce soit ou non en violation de la législation intérieure du pays où fut perpétré le crime. Les chefs, organisateurs, instigateurs et complices participants à l'élaborations ou à l'exécution d'un plan commun ou à un complot en vue de commettre l'un quelconque des crimes énoncés, sont responsables de tous actes accomplis par toute personne en exécution dudit plan." J.-P. Bazelaire and T. Cretin, *La justice pénale internationale: Son évolution, son avenir de Nuremberg á La Haye* (2000), Annexe 3.

100 *United States v. Karl Brandt and Ors*, in *Medical* case, *supra* note 88.

101 It should be recalled that the purposes of the Control Council Law no. 10 was expressed in the preamble as "[i]n order to give effect to the terms of the Moscow Declaration of 30 October 1943 and the London Agreement of 8 August 1945, and the Charter issued pursuant thereto and in order to establish a uniform legal basis in Germany for the prosecution of war criminals and other similar offenders, other than those dealt with by the International Military Tribunal."

experiments, without the subjects' consent, upon German civilians and nationals of other countries, in the course of which experiments the defendants committed *murders*, brutalities, cruelties, tortures, atrocities, and other inhuman acts.[102]

The said medical experiments included the following:[103]

- *Freezing experiments* — experiments carried out to investigate the most effective means of treating persons who had been severely chilled or frozen. In one series of such experiments, the subjects were forced to remain in a tank of ice water for periods of up to three hours. Extreme rigour developed in a short time. Numerous victims died in the course of these experiments. After the survivors were severely chilled, re-warming was attempted by various means. In another series of these experiments, the subjects were kept naked outdoors for several hours at temperatures below freezing point.
- *Malaria experiments* — in order to investigate immunization for, and treatment of, malaria, healthy concentration camp inmates were infected by mosquitoes or by injections of extracts of the mucous glands of mosquitoes. After having contracted malaria, the subjects were treated with various drugs to test their relative efficacy. Over 1,000 involuntary subjects were used in these experiments. Many of the victims died.
- *Epidemic jaundice experiments* — some victims died in experiments to investigate the causes of, and inoculations against, epidemic jaundice. The victims were deliberately infected with epidemic jaundice.
- *Lost gas or mustard gas experiments* — in order to investigate the most effective treatment of wounds caused by lost gas (commonly known as mustard gas), wounds deliberately inflicted on the subjects were infected with lost gas. Some of the subjects died as a result of these experiments.
- *Sulphanilamide experiments* — these involved experiments to investigate the effectiveness of sulphanilamide. Wounds deliberately inflicted on the experimental subjects were infected with bacteria such as streptococcus, gas gangrene, and tetanus. Circulation of blood was interrupted by tying off blood vessels at both ends of the wound to create a condition similar to that of a

---

102 See *Medical* case, *supra* note 88 at para. 11.

103 See *ibid.* at paras. 6, 7, 11, and 12.

battlefield wound. Infection was aggravated by forcing wood shavings and ground glass into the wounds. The infection was treated with sulphanilamide and other drugs to determine their effectiveness. Some subjects died as a result of these experiments.

- *Spotted fever or typhus experiments* — these involved experiments to investigate the effectiveness of spotted fever and other vaccines. Numerous healthy inmates were deliberately infected with spotted fever virus in order to keep the virus alive — over 90 per cent of the victims died as a result. Other healthy inmates were used to determine the effectiveness of different spotted fever vaccines and of various chemical substances. In the course of these experiments, 75 per cent of the selected number of inmates were vaccinated with one of the vaccines or nourished with one of the chemical substances and, after a period of three to four weeks, were infected with spotted fever germs. The remaining 25 per cent were infected without any previous protection in order to compare the effectiveness of the vaccines and the chemical substances. As a result, hundreds of those experimented upon died.
- *Experiments with poison* — to investigate the effect of various poisons upon human beings. The poisons were secretly administered to experimental subjects in their food. The victims died as a result of the poison or were killed immediately in order to permit autopsies. In or about September 1944, experimental subjects were shot with poison bullets and suffered torture and death.

In the judgment of the US Military Tribunal 1 in the *Medical* case, sixteen of the twenty-three defendants were convicted. Seven were acquitted. All but one of the sixteen convicts were convicted of crimes against humanity as charged — including murder — in consequence of the deaths arising from these experiments. There was no suggestion in the judgment that murder in these circumstances must only entail the premeditation to kill the victim. Speaking generally of the experiments, the tribunal found as follows:

Judged by any standard of proof the record clearly shows the commission of war crimes and crimes against humanity substantially as alleged in counts two and three of the indictment. Beginning with the outbreak of World War II criminal medical experiments on non-German nationals, both prisoners of war and civilians, including Jews and "asocial" persons, were carried out on a large scale in Germany and the occupied countries.[104]

---

[104] *Ibid.*

...

All of the experiments were conducted with unnecessary suffering and injury and but very little, if any, precautions were taken to protect or safeguard the human subjects from the possibilities of injury, disability, or death. In every one of the experiments the subjects experienced extreme pain or torture, and in most of them they suffered permanent injury, mutilation, or death, either as a direct result of the experiments or because of lack of adequate follow-up care.[105]

It is particularly instructive that a number of the convicts were convicted upon a theory of omission, as superiors, to intervene and stop the human experiments than for actual execution of the experiments. Siegfried Handloser was one such convict. He was a professional soldier, who received his commission in the Medical Services of the German Army. He eventually rose to the position of chief of the Wehrmacht Medical Service.[106] The tribunal found that he had actual knowledge of the following experiments in the course of which deaths had resulted to some of the experimental subjects: the freezing experiments;[107] the sulphanilamide experiments;[108] the typhus experiments;[109] as well as the malaria, the lost gas, and the epidemic jaundice experiments.[110] Basing itself on the doctrine of command responsibility, the tribunal found Handloser responsible for crimes against humanity. In the tribunal's own words:

In connection with Handloser's responsibility for unlawful experiments upon human beings, the evidence is conclusive that with knowledge of the frequent use of non-German nationals as human experimental subjects, he failed to exercise any proper degree of control over those subordinated to him who were implicated in medical experiments coming within his official sphere of competence. This was a duty which clearly devolved upon him by virtue of his official position. Had he exercised his responsibility, great numbers of non-German nationals would have been saved from *murder*. To the extent that the crimes committed by or under his authority were not war crimes *they were crimes against humanity.*[111]

105 *Ibid.* at 183.

106 *Ibid.* at 199.

107 *Ibid.* at 201.

108 *Ibid.* at 202.

109 *Ibid.* at 206.

110 *Ibid.* at 206–7.

111 *Ibid.* at 207 [emphasis added].

Consequently, the tribunal found Handloser guilty of counts 2 and 3 of the indictment[112] and sentenced him to imprisonment for the "full term and period of [his] natural life."[113]

It is specifically enlightening that the tribunal entered into no discussion suggesting that the deaths resulting from these experiments needed to result from a premeditation to kill the subjects in order to qualify as a crime against humanity, given that the French version of murder as a crime against humanity under the Nürnberg Charter is indicated as *assassinat*. This is especially significant since the tribunal's characterization of these deaths as murder would have been hard to sustain under a requirement of *premeditated* killing, where death resulted from a regimen of experiments in which the ultimate objective was to save the lives of the victims albeit by default of having a successful experiment, as is evidenced by the fact that some, if not a majority, of the subjects survived. *A fortiori*, harder still to sustain would have been the finding of criminal responsibility on the part of Handloser, as a superior, for those *murders*. In short, the theory of *mens rea* upon which these convictions is based was not premeditated killing but simply that of "wicked and corrupt disregard of the lives and safety of others."

The Nürnberg cases inspired much work at the United Nations International Law Commission (ILC) after the Second World War on the subject of crimes against humanity.[114] In 1950, the commission adopted its Principles of International Law Recognized in the Charter of the Nürnberg Tribunal and in the Judgment of the Tribunal. Principle VI recognized murder, among other violations, as a crime against humanity, being a crime under international law.[115] Next, in 1954, the commission produced the first Draft Code of Offences against the Peace and Security of Mankind. This draft code included "[i]nhumane acts such as murder, extermination, enslavement deportation or persecutions, committed against any civilian population on social, political, racial, religious or cultural grounds."[116]

---

[112] *Ibid.*

[113] *Ibid.* at 298.

[114] United Nations, *Report of the International Law Commission on the Work of Its Forty-Eighth Session 6 May–26 July 1996*, UN General Assembly, 51st Session, Supp. no. 10, Doc. UNGAOR (A/51/10) (1996) at 94, para. 2 [*Report of Its Forty-Eighth Session*].

[115] Where committed in execution of, or in connection with, any crime against peace or any war crime as specified in the principles.

[116] "[B]y the authorities of a State or by private individuals acting at the instigation or with toleration of such authorities." See Article 2(11) of the Draft Code of

In 1996, the commission produced the Draft Code of Crimes against the Peace and Security of Mankind (Draft Code). In Article 18, murder was, once more, included among the list of crimes against humanity.[117] In their 6 May–26 July 1996 report, the commission made the following commentary with respect to murder as a crime against humanity as provided for in the 1996 Draft Code:

Murder is a crime that is clearly understood and well defined in the national law of every State. This prohibited act does not require any further explanation. Murder was included as a crime against humanity in the Nürnberg Charter (article 6(c)), Control Council Law No. 10 (article II, paragraph c), the Statutes of the International Criminal Tribunals for the former Yugoslavia (article 5) and Rwanda (article 3) as well as the Nürnberg Principles (Principle VI) and the 1954 draft Code (article 2, paragraph 11).[118]

It should be noted here that the *Akayesu* Trial Chamber based themselves on this commentary in finding that murder and not *assassinat* is more consistent with customary international law.[119] Thus, it may not be entirely correct to suggest, as was done in *Semanza*, that their claim of consonance of murder with customary international law was a bald assertion devoid of evidence.

In stating that "murder," as used in all of the documents referred to in the ILC commentary appearing earlier in this article, is a crime that is clearly understood and well defined in the national law of every state, thus requiring no further explanation, there is no doubt that the commission is indicating that murder is to be understood in the ordinary sense—and not in the narrow sense of only premeditated homicide. This point is clearly driven home when the French version of Article 18 of the 1996 Draft Code refers to "*le meurtre*" and not "*assassinat*." And referring once more to "*le meurtre*" in the French version of their commentary (quoted earlier) in the 1996 report, the commission states the following:

Offences against the Peace and Security of Mankind, 1954, UN GAOR Supp. (No. 9) at 11, UN Doc. A/2693 (1954).

117 When committed in a systematic manner or on a large scale and instigated or directed by a government or by any organization or group.

118 *Report of Its Forty-Eighth Session, supra* note 114 at 48, para. 7.

119 See *Akayesu, supra* note 15 at para. 587.

Le meurtre est un crime qui, dans le droit national de tous les Etats, a une signification claire et bien définie. Cet acte prohibé n'appelle pas de plus amples explications. Le meurtre figure au nombre des crimes contre l'humanité cités dans le statut du Tribunal de Nuremberg (art. 6 c)), dans la Loi No 10 du Conseil de contrôle (art. II, c)), dans les statuts des tribunaux pénaux internationaux pour l'ex-Yougoslavie (art. 5) et pour le Rwanda (art. 3), ainsi que dans les Principes de Nuremberg (Principe VI) et dans le projet de code de 1954 (art. 1, par. 11).[120]

It bears stressing, perhaps, that the relevance of the commission's commentary in this regard is not limited to murder as a crime against humanity, as specified in the 1996 Draft Code. As the commentary itself indicates, it also relates to murder as a crime against humanity, as specified in the Nürnberg Charter, the Control Council Law No. 10, the ICTR Statute, the ICTY Statute, the Nürnberg Principles, and the 1954 Draft Code. In other words, the ILC's commentary, as such, must be taken to have cleanly harmonized how murder has been understood as a crime against humanity in customary international law. It is perhaps instructive in this regard to note the commission's following commentary in regard to the understanding of crimes against humanity as provided for in Article 18 of the 1996 Draft Code:

The definition of crimes against humanity contained in article 18 is drawn from the Nürnberg Charter, as interpreted and applied by the Nürnberg Tribunal, taking into account subsequent developments in international law since Nürnberg.[121]

Of course, it would have been useful in this regard had the commission alluded to the fact that some of the documents mentioned in the commentary (specifically the Nürnberg Charter, the Control Council Law No. 10, the ICTR Statute, and the ICTY Statute) describe murder as *assassinat* in the French texts, suggesting premeditated homicide. On the other hand, the commission's failure to make such an allusion may underscore the ILC's expressed position that there is no doubt in their mind that, as a general

---

120 Nations Unies, *Rapport de la Commission du droit international sur les travaux de sa quarante-huitième session, 6 mai–26 juillet 1996*, Assemblée générale Documents officiels, Cinquante et unième session, Supplément no. 10, Doc. A/51/10 (1996) at 95.

121 *Report on Its Forty-Eighth Session, supra* note 114 at 47, para. 2 of commentary.

principle of law (if not of customary international law), murder is understood in the ordinary sense for the purposes of crimes against humanity. That is to say, it is to be understood as *le meurtre*, as indicated both in Article 18 of the French text of the 1996 Draft Code and in the French text of the commentary to this draft provision.

In July 1998, the International Conference of Plenipotentiaries, meeting in Rome, adopted the Statute of the International Criminal Court (ICC Statute). Article 5(1)(b) confers on the court jurisdiction over crimes against humanity. Article 7(1)(a) of the English text indicates murder as a crime against humanity, with the French text indicating *meurtre* — and not *assassinat*.[122] Given that the ICC Statute is the most multilateral and most widely negotiated of all the international codes of crimes since Nürnberg and before, the

---

[122] ICC Statute, *supra* note 68, Article 7(1) provides as follows: "For the purpose of this Statute, 'crime against humanity' means any of the following acts when committed as part of a widespread or systematic attack directed against any civilian population, with knowledge of the attack: (a) Murder; (b) Extermination; (c) Enslavement; (d) Deportation or forcible transfer of population; (e) Imprisonment or other severe deprivation of physical liberty in violation of fundamental rules of international law; (f) Torture; (g) Rape, sexual slavery, enforced prostitution, forced pregnancy, enforced sterilization, or any other form of sexual violence of comparable gravity; (h) Persecution against any identifiable group or collectivity on political, racial, national, ethnic, cultural, religious, gender as defined in paragraph 3, or other grounds that are universally recognized as impermissible under international law, in connection with any act referred to in this paragraph or any crime within the jurisdiction of the Court; (i) Enforced disappearance of persons; (j) The crime of apartheid; (k) Other inhumane acts of a similar character intentionally causing great suffering, or serious injury to body or to mental or physical health." And the French text provides as follows: "Aux fins du présent Statut, on entend par crime contre l'humanité l'un quelconque des actes ci-après lorsqu'il est commis dans le cadre d'une attaque généralisée ou systématique lancée contre toute population civile et en connaissance de cette attaque: (a) Meurtre; (b) Extermination; (c) Réduction en esclavage; (d) Déportation ou transfert forcé de population; (e) Emprisonnement ou autre forme de privation grave de liberté physique en violation des dispositions fondamentales du droit international; (f) Torture; (g) Viol, esclavage sexuel, prostitution forcée, grossesse forcée, stérilisation forcée ou toute autre forme de violence sexuelle de gravité compara.ble; (h) Persécution de tout groupe ou de toute collectivité identifiable pour des motifs d'ordre politique, racial, national, ethnique, culturel, religieux ou sexiste au sens du para.graphe 3, ou en fonction d'autres critères universellement reconnus comme inadmissibles en droit international, en corrélation avec tout acte visé dans le présent para.graphe ou tout crime relevant de la compétence de la Cour; (i) Disparitions forcées de personnes; (j) Crime d'apartheid; (k) Autres actes inhumains de caractère analogue causant intentionnellement de grandes souffrances ou des atteintes graves à l'intégrité physique ou à la santé physique ou mentale."

importance of this development must not be lost. In this connection, it is reasonably arguable that nations of the world, fully cognisant of the state of the law in 1998, opted to use *meurtre* in the French text of the ICC Statute instead of *assasinat*, thus signifying the current *opinio juris* on the matter. It is, perhaps, also interesting to note that clause 7(1)(k) suggests that the *mens rea* for each of these crimes against humanity is "intentionally causing great suffering, or serious injury to body or to mental or physical health." This level of *mens rea* is a further suggestion that premeditation is not the criterion for the fault element of murder as a crime against humanity.

The ICC Statute has been enabled into municipal legislation around the world. In countries such as Canada,[123] France,[124] and Belgium,[125] the French text refers to *meurtre* — and not *assasinat* —

[123] For instance, in the French text of section 4(3) of Crimes against Humanity and War Crimes Act of 2000 of Canada, 1985, R.S.C. 24, crimes against humanity are defined as follows: "[C]rime contre l'humanité meurtre, extermination, réduction en esclavage, déportation, emprisonnement, torture, violence sexuelle, persécution ou autre fait — acte ou omission — inhumain, d'une part, commis contre une population civile ou un groupe identifiable de personnes et, d'autre part, qui constitue, au moment et au lieu de la perpétration, un crime contre l'humanité selon le droit international coutumier ou le droit international conventionnel, ou en raison de son caractère criminel d'après les principes généraux de droit reconnus par l'ensemble des nations, qu'il constitue ou non une transgression du droit en vigueur à ce moment et dans ce lieu."

[124] See Décret n. 2002-925 du 6 juin 2002, portant publication de la convention portant statut de la Cour pénale internationale, adoptée à Rome le 17 juillet 1998.

[125] In Belgium, paragraph 2 of Loi du 16 juin 1993 relative à la répression des violations graves de droit international humanitaire (as amended by Loi du 10 février 1999) provides as follows: "Constitue un crime de droit international et est réprimé conformément aux dispositions de la présente loi, le crime contre l'humanité, tel que défini ci-après, qu'il soit commis en temps de paix ou en temps de guerre. Conformément au statut de la Cour pénale internationale, le crime contre l'humanité s'entend de l'un des actes ci-après commis dans le cadre d'une attaque généralisée ou systématique lancée contre une population civile et en connaissance de cette attaque: 1° meurtre; 2° extermination; 3° réduction en esclavage; 4° déportation ou transfert forcé de population; 5° emprisonnement ou autre forme de privation grave de liberté physique en violation des dispositions fondamentales du droit international; 6° torture; 7° viol, esclavage sexuel, prostitution forcée, grossesse forcée, stérilisation forcée et toute autre forme de violence sexuelle de gravité compara.ble; 8° persécution de tout groupe ou de toute collectivité identifiable pour des motifs d'ordre politique, racial, national, ethnique, culturel, religieux ou sexiste ou en fonction d'autres critères universellement reconnus comme inadmissibles en droit international, en corrélation avec tout acte visé dans le présent article."

as a crime against humanity. The Canadian law does, however, specially account for murder as a crime against humanity where intentional killing has formed the basis of the offence. In such cases, there is a *mandatory* penalty of life imprisonment.[126] In all other cases of crimes against humanity, the accused *may* be sentenced to life imprisonment.[127]

In regard to judicial decisions, we have seen earlier in this discussion that the preponderance of the decisions of the Trial Chambers of the ICTR and ICTY have settled on the broader understanding of murder in the context of crimes against humanity. Similarly, some eminent jurists with relevant expertise have indicated that no premeditated killing is required for murder as a crime against humanity under the ICTR and ICTY Statutes. For instance, Antonio Cassese, a former president of the ICTY, sees no such requirement.[128]

WHETHER MURDER AS CRIME AGAINST HUMANITY REQUIRES A HIGHER LEVEL OF *MENS REA* THAN GENOCIDE

One of the bases of the *Semanza* reasoning is the suggestion that murder as a crime against humanity has a higher level of *mens rea* than genocide in virtue of killing. The Trial Chamber expressed this view as follows:

> [B]oth the English and French versions of the Statute employ terms in Article 3(a) [murder as a crime against humanity] that denote a higher level of intention than is required for the *crimes* [sic] *in Article 2(2)(a)* [killing as an act of genocide]. By their ordinary meaning, the English term murder (crime against humanity) has a higher intent than killing (genocide), just as the French term *assassinat* (crime against humanity) requires a higher intention than *meurtre* (genocide). In Article 4(a) the term "murder" is paired with "*meurtre,*" again suggesting that on the basis of the French text, murder as a crime against humanity requires a higher mental element.[129]

It is somewhat curious to suggest that homicidal genocide has a

---

[126] See Crimes against Humanity and War Crimes Act of 2000, *supra* note 123 at section 4(2)(a).

[127] See *ibid.* at section 4(2)(b).

[128] For Cassese, murder as a crime against humanity means "intentional killing, whether or not premeditated." A. Cassese, *International Criminal Law* (Oxford: Oxford University Press, 2003) at 74.

[129] *Semanza, supra* note 42 at para. 338 [emphasis added].

lower *mens rea* than murder as a crime against humanity, simply because Article 2(2)(a) of the ICTR Statute,[130] which indicates "killing" as an act of genocide, was not expressed in terms of "murder." This view ignores the fact that Article 2(2)[131] sets out to describe the conducts therein enumerated as "acts" and not as *crimes*. It is when these *acts* are committed with the genocidal intent described in the general clause of Article 2(2) that we have the crime of genocide. Hence, genocide is one crime. It may be committed by way of any of the five acts listed under Article 2(2), including killing. As the general clause of Article 2(2) indicates, the intent required to convert any of these "acts" of genocide into the *crime* of genocide is the "intent to destroy, in whole or in part, a national, ethnic, racial or religious group, as such." This arrangement is perfectly consistent with the ordinary framework of criminal law in which a crime comprises an act and the proper mental element for it, according to the Latin maxim *actus non facit reum, nisi men sit rea* [the act alone does not make a crime, unless there also be a guilty mind].

For its part, Article 3 of the ICTR Statute[132] contains a list of various "crimes" against humanity. They are not just *acts*. Thus, murder, as expressed in Article 3(a), is not an "act," as is killing in Article 2(2)(a), whose *mens rea* is described in the general clause of the provision. It needs perhaps to be stressed that murder, as a crime against humanity, was imported into international law with its native *mens rea* in municipal law.[133] Murder and the other crimes will only become crimes against humanity when committed as part of a widespread or systematic attack against a civilian population.[134]

---

[130] ICTY Statute, *supra* note 1, Article 4(2)(a).

[131] *Ibid.*, Article 4(2).

[132] *Ibid.*, Article 5.

[133] It should perhaps be said that this requirement of discrimination indicated in the general clause of the provision, in order to convert a crime into a crime against humanity, is not a matter of *mens rea* for each of the crimes listed. In other words, it is not required that the accused must possess such a discriminatory *animus* against the victim when he committed the offence. It is only sufficient to show that the general widespread or systematic attack against the civilian population (as part of which the accused committed any of the listed crimes) was motivated by discrimination against the civilian population under attack. The only listed crime for which the discriminatory *animus* is specially required is persecution. See the judgment of the Appeals Chamber in *Prosecutor v. Akayesu (Judgment)* (1 June 2001) Case no. ICTR-96-4 (ICTR Appeals Chamber) at paras. 453–69 [*Akayesu* 2001]; see also *Tadić, supra* note 90 at paras. 281–305.

[134] See *Report of its Forty-Eighth Session, supra* note 114 at 94–95, paras. 3–5.

The question may then be asked why was the crime of genocide comprehensively framed in the statute by setting out both the *actus reus* and the *mens rea* of it, while not doing the same for each of the crimes listed as crimes against humanity. The answer is simple. It is perfectly understandable that great pains were taken to lay out the elements of the crime of genocide in terms of the *mens rea* plus *actus reus* construct, as the crime of genocide is of recent vintage, originally conceived as such in international law following the events of Second World War. In contrast, most of the "crimes" underlying the notion of crimes against humanity were crimes already known to municipal jurisdictions, but which were brought into the purview of international law when committed as part of a widespread or systematic attack against a civilian population.[135]

It is difficult then to see how it is that the "intent to destroy, in whole or in part, a national, ethnical, racial or religious group, as such," as the *mens rea* for genocidal killing, could be seen as of a lower level than any *mens rea* for murder — even under the premeditation theory. To put the matter differently, the acceptance of murder in the ordinary sense does not diminish the juridical quality of the notion of crimes against humanity nor does *assassinat* enhance it — if it is understood that this juridical quality is established at the level of the general clause requiring a widespread or systematic attack against a civilian population.

MURDER AS PERSECUTION OR OTHER INHUMANE ACT

If murder as a crime against humanity were to require premeditated homicide, it would still be possible to capture and punish the broader view of murder as a crime against humanity by prosecuting such varieties of murder under the rubric of persecution or other inhumane acts. The main problem with this approach though is that the net of proscription of murder as a crime against humanity will have been cast far short of the intended reach of interna-

---

135 Writing back in 1947, for instance, Descheemaeker observed as follows: "En effet, *tous les actes qui constituent les crimes contre l'humanité, ne sont que la transposition sur le plan international et avec un caractère d'amplitude et de généralité qui vient d'être souligné, de crimes de droit commun prévus et frappés par la législation pénale interne de tous les pays.* Il est exact que le droit pénal interne sanctionne des actes individuels ou groupant un nombre relativement peu élevé d'individus, alors que les crimes contre l'humanité ont eu pour victimes des populations entières." J. Descheemaeker, *Le tribunal militaire international des grand criminels de guerre* (1947) at 20–21 [emphasis in original text].

tional law, as far as persecution goes. This is because the Appeals Chambers of both the ICTY and the ICTR have held that persecution is the only crime against humanity for which discrimination on the grounds usually outlawed in international human rights law is an essential element.[136] Murder as a crime against humanity does not require such an element. In view of this reasoning, leaving murder (with less than premeditation) to be prosecuted under the rubric of persecution will still leave unpunished any murder committed as part of a widespread or systematic attack not based on discriminatory grounds. Granted that proceeding under the rubric of "other inhumane acts" may not be similarly ensnared, it seems, however, that it is neither necessary nor sufficient to proceed in this fashion since the foregoing review leads to the conclusion that the *Akayesu* analysis remains the better one on the subject of murder as a crime against humanity. Hence, there is no need to follow such contorted routes as "other inhumane acts" or persecution in order to prosecute murder.

CONCLUSION

In the final analysis, one thing is clear. The history of international statutory provisions on the subject of murder as an international crime has been sadly fraught with discrepancies. We have noted the discrepancies in the ICTR and ICTY Statutes in which the English texts provide for murder as a crime against humanity, while the French texts provide for *assassinat*. We have also seen the following discrepancies. While providing for *assassinat* as a crime against humanity in the ICTR Statute, the same French text provides for *meurtre* as a war crime; in the Nürnberg Charter, the French text provides for *assassinat* as a crime against humanity, while the French text of the Charter of the International Military Tribunal for the Far East provided for *meurtre* as a crime against humanity; and there is also the discrepancy between *assassinat* as a crime against humanity in the French text of the ICTR and ICTY Statutes and *meurtre* in the French text of the ICC Statute. Amid all of these discrepancies, one conclusion that appears unavoidable is best stated in the following quotation from *Oppenheim's International Law:* "The circumstances in which treaties are drafted are ... often such as to lead to lack of consistency in drafting and care must be taken in

---

[136] *Tadić, supra* note 90 at paras. 285 and 305. See also *Akayesu* 2001, *supra* note 133 at paras. 453–69.

attributing significance to variations in terminology: 'an interpreter is likely to find himself distorting passages if he imagines that their drafting is stamped with infallibility': *Pertulosa Claim*, I.L.R. 18 at 18 (1951), No. 129, p. 418."[137]

This bears out the opinion of the ICTR Trial Chamber I in *Akayesu* that *assassinat* in the French text of Article 5 of the statute, which imports a higher and narrower level of *mens rea* for murder, is the result of a "translation error." While it is certainly better to characterize the French text as an equally authentic version and not a "translation," it suffices to settle this controversy along the lines of the commentary of the ILC to the effect that murder in the sense of a crime against humanity means murder in the generally understood sense of the notion — it means *meurtre* in French.

Sommaire

Le meurtre en tant que crime contre l'humanité dans l'optique de tribunaux spéciaux: réconcilier les différences de sens selon la langue

Les statuts de la Cour pénale internationale pour le Rwanda et pour l'ex-Yougoslavie confèrent à ces tribunaux une compétence en matière de meurtres en tant que crimes contre l'humanité. Les juges de ces tribunaux diffèrent souvent d'opinion toutefois sur la question de la mens rea nécessaire pour justifier une déclaration de culpabilité. La controverse tient du fait que le texte français utilise le terme "assassinat" là où le texte anglais utilise le terme "murder." Or, l'assassinat s'entend seulement de la forme de meurtre prémédité. En conséquence, certains juges insistent que nul degré de mens rea moindre que la préméditation ne justifie une déclaration de culpabilité pour meurtre en tant que crime contre l'humanité en vertu des statuts TPIR et TPIY. L'article suggère que ni les exigences du droit pénal international ni la lecture contextuelle des statuts ne préconisent une interprétation aussi stricte de la notion de meurtre en tant que crime contre l'humanité, laquelle exclut une grande marge de mens rea qui, n'eût été l'utilisation du terme "assassinat" dans le texte français, fonderait nettement une déclaration de culpabilité.

---

[137] Jennings and Watts, *supra* note 70, parts 2–4 at 1273, note 12.

Summary

Murder as a Crime against Humanity at the Ad Hoc Tribunals: Reconciling Differing Languages

The statutes of the International Criminal Tribunals for Rwanda and for the Former Yugoslavia give these tribunals jurisdiction over murder as a crime against humanity. Yet the judges of these tribunals have often found themselves disagreeing as to the level of mens rea *required for conviction. The controversy results from the French text that employs the term "assassinat" in the place where the English text speaks of "murder." Assassinat is equivalent only to the premeditated kind of murder. This has led some of the judges to insist that no* mens rea *lower than premeditation is sufficient for conviction for murder as a crime against humanity under the statutes of the ICTR and the ICTY. It is suggested in this article that neither the requirements of international criminal law nor a contextual reading of the statutes truly favours such a strict view of murder as a crime against humanity, which effectively excludes a wide range of* mens rea, *which will, but for the use of the term "assassinat" in the French text, properly anchor a conviction for murder.*

Radiation Warfare:
A Review of the Legality of Depleted
Uranium Weaponry

KAREN HULME

Manufactured in the 1970s, depleted uranium ammunition was first deployed by British and American forces in the 1991 Gulf conflict, following the Iraqi invasion and occupation of Kuwait.[1] Since then, however, Iraq has attributed some disturbing medical consequences to the use of depleted uranium weaponry.[2] In particular, the findings detailed genetic mutations in infants born after the conflict. These scientific findings have been presented at the highest levels.[3] While many questioned the truth of the Iraqi findings, viewing them as mere propaganda of a defeated state, fear and suspicion still surrounded the use of depleted uranium weaponry during the 1999 Kosovo conflict.[4] So much so, that a number of participating states within the North Atlantic Treaty

---

Karen Hulme is in the Department of Law at the University of Essex, United Kingdom.

[1] Security Council Resolution 678, 29 November 1990, (1990) 29 I.L.M. 1565. Depleted uranium metal is also used in the armour of tanks, such as the American M1A1 Abrams main battle tank, which is protected by steel encased depleted uranium armour and is effective against chemical, biological, and nuclear warfare.

[2] *Some Facts Concerning the Use of Radioactive Weapons by the Coalition Forces and Their Effects on the Environment and the Population in Iraq,* Note Verbale dated 21 May 1996 from the Permanent Mission of Iraq to the United Nations Office at Geneva addressed to the Centre for Human Rights, Doc. E/CN.4/Sub.2/1996/32 (7 June 1996); *Post-War Environment in Iraq,* Note Verbale dated 27 July 1998 from the Permanent Mission of Iraq to the United Nations Office at Geneva addressed to the Secretariat of the Sub-Commission, Doc. E/CN.4/Sub.2/1998/ 32 (3 August 1998) [*Post-War Environment in Iraq*].

[3] *Ibid.*

[4] P. Brown, "Uranium Risk in War Zone," *The Guardian,* 13 April 1999; P. Brown, "UN to Tackle Deadly Legacy of War," *The Guardian,* 17 May 1999; M. Gorbachev, "Poison in the Air," *The Guardian,* 18 June 1999; and R. Norton-Taylor, "Doctor Blames West for Deformities," *The Guardian,* 30 July 1999.

Organization (NATO) questioned the potentially deadly effects of depleted uranium on the health of military personnel. France, Spain, Portugal, Belgium, the Netherlands, Turkey, and Finland all held official investigations into the effects of depleted uranium weapons, and the Italian prime minister, Amato Giuliano, requested that NATO carry out its own investigation.[5] Due principally to its chemically and radioactively toxic characteristics, depleted uranium was at that time viewed by many states as an extremely controversial weapon of war.

Was it then mere coincidence that so soon after the Kosovo conflict the British Royal Navy abandoned the use of depleted uranium, in preference of tungsten-tipped ammunition?[6] Similarly, in 2002, the UK Ministry of Defence also announced that in the future it would purchase tungsten alloy rounds (known as the "green" alternative) for its *Challenger* 2 tanks as an alternative to depleted uranium. Yet the United Kingdom made no secret of the fact that it still viewed depleted uranium as "the weapon of choice in combat."[7] Strange then, one might argue, that in the wake of the 2003 invasion of Iraq by UK and US forces the use of depleted uranium weaponry has been the subject of little adverse comment. How could the use of such a controversial weapon in 1999 go largely unnoticed in 2003? Does this lack of furore in 2003 necessarily lead to the conclusion that the "dictates of the public conscience"[8] have evolved in regard to the use of this previously controversial weapon of war?

---

[5] R. Norton-Taylor, "Italy Blames Army Deaths on US Shells," *The Guardian*, 4 January 2001, at 12; M. Evans, "France to Test Soldiers for Uranium Link," *The Times*, 5 January 2001; and R. Owen, "Italy Links Leukaemia Deaths to Nato Shells," *The Times*, 4 January 2001, at 17.

[6] "Royal Navy Phases out DU Ammo," 13 January 2001, BBC News Online, <http://news.bbc.co.uk/1/hi/uk/1115771.stm > (20 July 2001).

[7] See M. Smith, "Army Buys Safer Tank Ammunition," *Daily Telegraph*, 10 January 2002, at 12. According to the *Telegraph* report, the "Ministry of Defence denied that ... the decision was a tacit admission that DU [depleted uranium] might be harmful" and quoted a spokesman who said: "It is not going to replace the DU rounds. We're not going wholesale into tungsten at the expense of DU. It's an option. It's an alternative to DU."

[8] This is part of the eponymous Martens Clause included in the preamble of the 1907 Regulations Respecting the Laws and Customs of War on Land, annexed to the 1907 Convention (IV) Respecting the Laws and Customs of War on Land, 18 October 1907, (1910) U.K.T.S. 9, Cd.5030 (entered into force 26 January 1910) [1907 Hague Convention IV].

Every weapon will have some affect on health and the environment, either directly as part of the design of the weapon or indirectly in its incidental effects. Clearly, the level of harm produced
by each weapon will vary depending on the weapon's specific characteristics and design. What is certain, however, is that the laws of
armed conflict have evolved to place limits on the level of harm
deemed permissible and legal. For as long as there have been wars,
there have been limitations on the permissible methods and means
of waging those wars. The laws of armed conflict govern the specific situation of armed hostilities — both inter-state and intra-
state hostilities. Codified in the latter half of the nineteenth century
and the early twentieth century, the laws of war have also witnessed
many developments since the end of the Second World War. Before the World Wars, international law had already prohibited the
use of treacherous and cruel weapons, such as poisonous gas.[9] In a
major development in 1977, following the Vietnam conflict in particular, two protocols were enacted to supplement the four Geneva
Conventions of 1949[10] (in the form of Protocol Additional to the
Geneva Conventions of 12 August 1949, and Relating to the Protection of Victims of International Armed Conflicts (Geneva Protocol I) and Protocol Additional to the Geneva Conventions of 12
August 1949, and Relating to the Protection of Victims of Non-
International Armed Conflicts (Geneva Protocol II)).[11] It remains

---

[9] 1925 Geneva Protocol for the Prohibition of the Use in War of Asphyxiating,
Poisonous or Other Gases, and of Bacteriological Methods of Warfare, 17 June
1925, (1930) U.K.T.S. 24 (entered into force 8 February 1928) [Geneva Gas
Protocol].

[10] 1949 Geneva Convention for the Amelioration of the Condition of the Wounded
and Sick in Armed Forces in the Field of August 12, 1949, (1950) 75 U.N.T.S.
31–83 (entered into force 21 October 1950) [Geneva Convention I]; 1949
Geneva Convention for the Amelioration of the Condition of Wounded, Sick
and Shipwrecked Members of Armed Forces at Sea of August 12, 1949, (1950)
75 U.N.T.S. 85–133 (entered into force 21 October 1950) [Geneva Convention II]; 1949 Geneva Convention Relative to the Treatment of Prisoners of
War of August 12, 1949, (1950) 75 U.N.T.S. 135–285 (entered into force 21
October 1950) [Geneva Convention III]; and 1949 Geneva Convention Relative to the Protection of Civilian Persons in Time of War of August 12, 1949,
(1950) 75 U.N.T.S. 287–417 (entered into force 21 October 1950) [Geneva
Convention IV].

[11] Protocol Additional to the Geneva Conventions of 12 August 1949, and Relating to the Protection of Victims of International Armed Conflicts, 8 June 1977,
(1977) 16 I.L.M. 1391–441 (entered into force 7 December 1978) [Geneva
Protocol I]; and Protocol Additional to the Geneva Conventions of 12 August

the case that the situation of international armed conflict continues to be governed by Geneva Protocol I, and non-international armed conflict by Geneva Protocol II. Together with earlier Hague law,[12] the Geneva instruments clearly specify the most fundamental limitations applying to *all* weapons.[13] The Geneva Protocols have both a codification aspect by encompassing existing customary rules[14] as well as a progressive aspect by incorporating much needed new developments — particularly in relation to environmental protection during times of armed conflict.[15] It was during the negotiation of the protocols, however, that it became apparent that something more specific was required for a number of conventional weapons. Although the discussions of what this "something" should be emerged from the sessions fixed with the task of drafting the Geneva Protocols, it was later agreed by the participants that negotiations should be undertaken separately. Consequently, the International Committee of the Red Cross (ICRC) convened two further sessions of government experts — one in Lucerne in 1974 and the other in Lugano in 1976 — which were concerned with the regulation of certain conventional weapons. Finally, in 1980, the delegates were able to adopt a framework instrument in the form of the 1980 United Nations Convention on Prohibitions or Restrictions on the Use of Certain Conventional Weapons Which May Be Deemed to Be Excessively Injurious or to Have Indiscriminate Effects (Conventional Weapons Convention).[16]

1949, and Relating to the Protection of Victims of Non-International Armed Conflicts, 8 June 1977, (1977) 16 I.L.M. 1442–9 (entered into force 7 December 1978) [Geneva Protocol II].

12 1907 Hague Convention IV, *supra* note 8.

13 In drafting the Geneva Protocols, the International Committee of the Red Cross (ICRC) specifically omitted applicability of the instruments to nuclear weapons, which is also reflected in a number of statements made upon ratification. See the statements of the United Kingdom, Canada, France, Italy, and the United States (upon signature).

14 In 1995, the ICRC commenced a review of the provisions and principles of the two Geneva Protocols in order to establish which of these principles have evolved into customary international law. The study was completed and published in 2005. See Jean-Marie Henckaerts and Louise Doswald-Beck, *Customary International Humanitarian Law*, volume I: Rules and volume II: Practice (Parts 1 and 2) (Cambridge: Cambridge University Press, 2005).

15 Note Geneva Protocol I, *supra* note 11, Articles 35(3) and 55.

16 1980 United Nations Convention on Prohibitions or Restrictions on the Use of Certain Conventional Weapons Which May Be Deemed to Be Excessively

The scope of application of the Conventional Weapons Convention, as originally defined, referred only to conflicts of an international nature[17] and those detailed in Article 1 (4) of Geneva Protocol I;[18] commonly termed wars of national liberation.[19] Over the ensuing two decades, state parties continued to breathe life into the framework convention, ensuring its transition into a valuable living instrument. Two lines of development, in particular, have been of great benefit in ensuring the continuing viability and value of the Conventional Weapons Convention: (1) the willingness of state parties to adopt further protocols to the convention placing stringent limits on certain conventional weapons;[20] and (2) the general movement towards the extension of arms control and other principles of humanitarian law to internal armed conflicts. In regard to

---

Injurious or to Have Indiscriminate Effects, 10 April 1981, (1980) 19 I.L.M. 1523–36 (entered into force 2 December 1983) [Conventional Weapons Convention]. Three protocols were adopted at the same time as, and annexed to, the convention, see Protocol on Non-Detectable Fragments, 10 April 1981, (1980) 19 I.L.M. 1529 (entered into force 2 December 1983) [Protocol I], Protocol on Prohibitions or Restrictions on the Use of Mines, Booby-Traps and Other Devices, 10 April 1981, (1980) 19 I.L.M. 1529 (entered into force 2 December 1983) [Protocol II] and Protocol on Prohibitions or Restrictions on the Use of Incendiary Weapons, 10 April 1981, (1980) 19 I.L.M. 1534 (entered into force 2 December 1983) [Protocol III]. Others were added later, including the Protocol on Blinding Laser Weapons, 13 October 1995 (1996) 35 I.L.M. 1218 (entered into force 30 July 1998) [Protocol IV]; 1996 Amended Protocol II on Prohibitions or Restrictions on the Use of Mines, Booby-Traps and Other Devices, 3 May 1996, (1996) 35 I.L.M. 1206 (entered into force 3 December 1998) [Amended Protocol II on Mines]; and Protocol on Explosive Remnants of War, 28 November 2003, text available at <http://untreaty.un.org> (21 January 2003) [Protocol V on Explosive Remnants of War].

17 Conventional Weapons Convention, *supra* note 16, Article 1. More specifically, the provision mirrors the same scope as that of the Geneva Conventions at Common Article 2, which includes "all cases of partial or total occupation of the territory of a High Contracting Party." See the 1949 Geneva Conventions, *supra* note 10.

18 Geneva Protocol I, *supra* note 11.

19 In full. Article 1(4) states: "The situations referred to in the preceding paragraph include armed conflict in which peoples are fighting against colonial domination and alien occupation and against racist regimes in the exercise of their right to self-determination, as enshrined in the Charter of the United Nations and the Declaration on Principles of International Law concerning Friendly Relations and Co-operation among States in accordance with the Charter of the United Nations."

20 Details of these additional protocols are given in note 16.

the second point, and in line with similar developments in other forums including judgments of the International Criminal Tribunal for the Former Yugoslavia (ICTY),[21] states party to the Conventional Weapons Convention agreed, in 2001, to extend the application of this treaty to the situation of non-international armed conflict.[22] The consequence of the 2001 amendment was that, at least for these state parties, certain weapons' limitations are applicable regardless of the classification of the conflict as international or non-international.

Specific treaty limitations are not the end of the story, however. Humanitarian law is founded upon the basis of a number of fundamental principles, at the centre of which is the principle of humanity. Consequently, weapons must also conform to these fundamental humanitarian principles in order to remain lawful. Among these principles is (1) the prohibition of weapons causing unnecessary suffering to combatants; (2) the prohibition on indiscriminate warfare; and (3) the prohibition on disproportionate warfare. The origins of many of these principles can be traced back through the centuries, but they have found more recent codification in the Hague and Geneva laws.[23]

This article will analyze the current legality of the use of depleted uranium ammunition in armed conflict. Although depleted uranium ammunition is designed as a point weapon, fired with a level of accuracy at hard or armoured targets, it leaves a human and environmental legacy. The question is whether this legacy is in violation of the laws of armed conflict. Once the science and effects of

---

21 In a landmark judgment, the tribunal recognized that weapons prohibited, at customary law, as inhumane in international armed conflict must also be prohibited in situations of internal conflict. According to the tribunal, any other conclusion would be "preposterous." As a consequence, the prohibition on certain "inhumane" weapons is now absolute. *Prosecutor v. Dusko Tadić* (1996), Case no. IT-94-1 (International Criminal Tribunal for the Former Yugoslavia), (1996) 35 I.L.M. 32 at para. 119, available at <http://www.un.org/icty/judgement.htm> (3 September 2000).

22 1980 Conventional Weapons Convention, *supra* note 16, Amendment Article 1 (21 December 2001), available at <http://www.icrc.org> (1 July 2002). The amendment was brought into force on 18 May 2004 following the deposit of the twentieth instrument of ratification. As of December 2005, the 2001 amendment had forty-four ratifications, of the one hundred state parties to the 1980 convention.

23 The 1907 Hague Convention IV, *supra* note 8; the 1949 Geneva Conventions, *supra* note 10; and the 1977 Geneva Protocols, *supra* note 11.

depleted uranium ammunition have been demonstrated, the analysis will proceed to the question of legality. The analysis will not, however, be concerned with compliance with human rights instruments. If there is no specific treaty regarding the use of depleted uranium ammunition, the question will be raised of inclusion within existing treaty prohibitions of analogous weapons. If depleted uranium ammunition is not the subject of specific limitation, then the question of restriction by general (customary) principles arises. The relevant humanitarian law principles have now been codified into treaty form and are those that prohibit the use of weapons (1) that cause unnecessary suffering; (2) that are unable to distinguish between civilians and combatants; and (3) that cause disproportionality between civilian effects and military advantage. Consequently, if there are grounds for suggesting that depleted uranium ammunition violates any of these humanitarian law principles then this should be cause for states to negotiate a ban or to set limits on use. Finally, in addition to medical consequences, the effects of depleted uranium will also be encountered in the environment. While the laws of armed conflict have contained provisions limiting states' destruction of the environment in warfare since Geneva Protocol I, the analysis will seek to establish just how effective these regulations are with regard to depleted uranium ammunition.

DEVELOPMENT OF DEPLETED URANIUM AMMUNITION

Depleted uranium metal is a substance utilized by the armaments industry as a component in ammunition. Other common components of weapons are copper, steel, and lead. The primary military use of depleted uranium has been as a component in anti-armour ammunition, predominantly anti-tank ammunition. The development of depleted uranium weaponry can, therefore, be traced to the innovation of the tank in the First World War and to the continual improvements made both in its killing power and in the effectiveness of its armour.

Post-1945 tank ammunition used kinetic energy penetrators, incorporating a long thin rod of metal surrounded by a casing or "sabot." Fired from the tank guns, the explosive energy would be transferred to the thin metal rod — or penetrator — in the centre of the sabot. The penetrator would be launched on to its trajectory to the target, while the casing or sabot would separate and fall away soon after firing. Early kinetic energy penetrators were made from high carbon steel, and, later, improved performance capabilities were derived from tungsten carbide penetrators. In the

1950s, tungsten was the hardest, densest material readily available but was outperformed in the 1960s by thicker double- and triple-plated tank armour.[24] While more effective tungsten alloys were being developed, the fear was that they would not be able to defeat the thickest armour in development or at least feared to be in development. At the height of the Cold War when fears were at their peak, the Soviet Union began to experiment with depleted uranium instead of tungsten in its anti-tank penetrators. The United States quickly followed suit with successful tests by the navy and air force of smaller-calibre depleted uranium ammunition, such as the 20 millimetre (mm), 25 mm, and 30 mm rounds.[25]

Developments in these armaments continued, and, today, there is a multitude of applications for depleted uranium in ammunition used by land, sea, and air forces around the world. Key user states are the United States and the United Kingdom, although other states are known (or suspected) to have acquired depleted uranium ammunition. Unfortunately, due to the secretive nature of armaments contracts, it is difficult to establish a completely accurate list, but the main proliferation (including development) appears to be in Russia, China, France, Germany, Turkey, Israel, Jordan, Pakistan, Saudi Arabia, Bahrain, Egypt, Kuwait, Greece, Taiwan, Thailand, South Korea, and the United Arab Emirates.[26] By far the most common appears to be the "American" variants — those used by the American armed forces; the 120 mm and 105 mm tank ammunition, the 25 mm and 30 mm air force ammunition, and the 20 mm naval ammunition. The 20 mm ammunition is designed for naval applications using the PHALANX weapons system adopted by many states around the world, including the United Kingdom. The original tank ammunition for application by the United States was the 105 mm, but the necessity for inter-operability within and between

---

24 "Depleted Uranium," Global Security, available at <http://www.globalsecurity.org/military/systems/munitions/du.htm> (13 April 2004).

25 *Ibid.*

26 The US system allows for the sale of depleted uranium anti-tank ammunition to North Atlantic Treaty Organization (NATO) members and to major non-NATO allies, designated as Australia, Egypt, Israel, Japan, South Korea, Argentina, Jordan, Bahrain, Taiwan, New Zealand, Kuwait, Morocco, Pakistan, the Philippines, and Thailand and "any country the President determines that such a sale is in the U.S. national security to do so." See paras. 2378a and 2378b of Chapter 32, Subchapter III, Part I of the 1961 US Foreign Assistance Act, <http://www.law.cornell.edu/uscode/search/display.html?terms=2378a&url=/uscode/html/uscode22/usc_sec_22_00002378—a000-.html > (11 August 2006) as amended.

NATO forces has led to the adoption of the US 120 mm M829 series.

Unlike the use of lead or steel in weapons, depleted uranium has only been available in commercial quantities since the late 1950s. Depleted uranium is not a naturally occurring substance readily amenable for manufacturing. It is an isotope of uranium. Uranium itself is a naturally occurring element of the Earth's crust, composed of a number of different isotopes. The main isotope is uranium-238, which accounts for over 99 per cent of natural uranium. It is only due to the development of nuclear weapons and nuclear power industries — namely, their utilization of uranium — that depleted uranium has been "discovered." Depleted uranium is actually a by-product of the enrichment process of natural uranium for nuclear weapons and nuclear reactors. During the enrichment process of uranium, the more radioactive isotopes contained in uranium (U234 and U235) are removed for use in nuclear reactors and nuclear weapons, leaving a large amount of the less radioactive isotope (U238) as waste material. Therefore, the raw material for depleted uranium weapons is, in effect, radioactive waste from other peaceful and military nuclear programs. However, despite its name, "depleted" uranium remains 99.8 per cent U238. Depletion only refers to the U235 content, from 0.7 per cent content in natural uranium to 0.2–0.3 per cent in depleted uranium. As a consequence of the removal (or depletion) of the more radioactive isotopes, depleted uranium, according to the International Atomic Energy Agency (IAEA), is "about 40 per cent less radioactive than [natural] uranium."[27] This fact is not disputed, but, as a consequence of the enrichment process of uranium and the practice of reprocessing or "recycling" spent uranium fuel, many dangerous and highly radioactive substances (transuranics) are also present.[28] These trace elements in the depleted uranium include americium, neptunium, and — what is generally considered to be the most dangerous element known to man — plutonium.[29] Although dangerous and

---

27 "Depleted Uranium Information for Clinicians," Department of Defense Deployment Health Clinical Center, available at <http://www.pdhealth.mil/downloads/Clinicians_Guide_080604.pdf> (9 July 2005).

28 Trace elements of transuranics plutonium-239/240 and uranium-236 were detected in the United Nations Environment Programme's Kosovo field study. See *Depleted Uranium in Kosovo: Post Conflict Environmental Assessment* (Switzerland: UNEP, 2001) at 16.

29 A. Duraković, "Undiagnosed Illness and Radioactive Warfare" (2003) 44(5) Croatian Medical Journal 520 at 522.

radioactive, what is clear is that depleted uranium is not a nuclear weapon — it is not capable of an atomic chain reaction (because the fissile U235 is largely removed).

ADVANTAGES OF DEPLETED URANIUM WEAPONS

What is so special about depleted uranium penetrators can be listed as fourfold. The first advantage of depleted uranium in comparison with other metals is its greater density. Depleted uranium has a much greater density than other metals such as lead or steel commonly used in ammunition. Depleted uranium is almost twice as dense as lead, for example.[30] It is also 15 per cent denser than its closest competitor, tungsten.[31] In early trials in the 1970s, depleted uranium penetrators were found to outperform tungsten penetrators on the test ranges. A major aspect of this performance is a result of its greater density. For weapons systems, a greater density translates into a greater mass volume for volume of substance, and, as a consequence, depleted uranium penetrators were found to impact a target with greater force (a greater amount of stored kinetic energy) than the tungsten penetrators.

The second advantage of using depleted uranium in kinetic energy penetrators rather than other metals is due to its pyrophoric nature. Kinetic energy penetrators are dart-shaped, they have a long thin rod of metal down the centre with a wider-based sabot (casing or jacket), which can be tailored to fit the barrel width of the gun (usually approximately 120 mm). Due to its pyrophoric nature, when depleted uranium is used in kinetic energy penetrators the substance begins to burn in the air and thus the tip of the dart remains sharp in flight, even appearing to sharpen further. In addition, most metals will become blunt on impact with a hard target, appearing to mushroom, and so the kinetic energy transferred to the target is spread over a greater area as thermal energy.[32] Having this sharpening effect, depleted uranium penetrators are found to impact the target with greater pinpoint force. Ultimately, its pyrophoric capability adds to the weapon's penetrative power.

---

[30] It is actually 160 per cent more dense than lead, *ibid.* at 524.

[31] There are harder substances available but these have problems that are not found with depleted uranium, either they are not found in sufficient quantities or are difficult to work with. "The Two-Headed Serpent: Depleted Uranium," Military. com, available at <http://www.military.com/soldiertech/0,14632,Soldiertech_DU,,00.html> (19 August 2005).

[32] *Ibid.*

A third advantage of depleted uranium penetrators in comparison with those made from other materials is the degree of penetration. Due again to its pyrophoric nature, the high temperatures created on impact allow the depleted uranium tip to burn a hole straight through the thickest tank armour. In essence, the pressure released on impact causes the penetrator to melt, in turn causing the armour to liquefy and melt and allowing what is left of the penetrator to pass through the body of the tank. In one incident in Iraq, it was reported that one depleted uranium penetrator punched a hole straight through not one but two tanks lined up together.[33] This impact, in turn, gives the depleted uranium penetrators a fourth advantage over those made from other metals, an incendiary capacity. Once the tank armour has been pierced, any remaining depleted uranium metal and any other metal fragments of armour will enter the vehicle, with the result that it will spark electrical fires inside the vehicle and ignite any stored munitions or even the fuel tank.[34]

Leaving specific weapons advantages aside, depleted uranium as a substance has a further two advantages over other metals for use in the weapons industry. The first advantage is its relative inexpensiveness. Due to the growth of the nuclear power industry, depleted uranium is readily available in commercial quantities. In fact, since it constitutes radioactive waste, any application of depleted uranium is a welcome development for the governments of most nuclear states. The second advantage of depleted uranium over other metals is that it is relatively easy to use in manufacturing applications. Consequently, depleted uranium is cheaper and easier to work with than tungsten and many other metals.

The Weapons

Large-Calibre Anti-Tank Ammunition

The modern use of depleted uranium, therefore, has largely been within kinetic energy penetrators that are designed as armour-piercing rounds. The long rod design of the 105 mm and 120 mm anti-tank ammunition is generally issued to mechanized ground

---

33 "APFSDS Ammunition-Armoured Piercing Fin-Stabilised Discarding Sabot," Army-Technology.com, available at <http://www.army-technology.com/contractors/ammunition/apfsds.htm> (14 July 2005) ["APFSDS Army-Technology"].

34 "Depleted Uranium FAQs," Jane's Defense Weekly, 8 January 2001, available at <http://www.janes.com/defence/news/jdw/jdwo10108_1_n.shtml> (20 June 2001).

forces for tank-on-tank attacks. The ammunition can also be used against reinforced bunkers and other hard-armoured targets. The standard American version is the 120 mm M829A2 APFSDS-T. The acronym APFSDS-T stands for amour piercing fin-stabilized discarding sabot with tracer and simply refers to the design of the weapon as a long dart-like weapon. The French have acquired both 105 mm and 120 mm depleted uranium kinetic energy penetrators of the type OFL F2 APFSDS, and Russia has 115 mm 3UBM-13 APFSDS and 125 mm 3BM32 APFSDS.[35] The British version is the 120 mm kinetic energy penetrator of the type L26 (CHARM 1) APFSDS[36] and the newer version L27A1 (CHARM 3) APFSDS.

Used by British forces in *Operation Telic* during the recent Iraq conflict, the British *Challenger* 2 tank can fire kinetic energy penetrators at a rate of one every nine seconds. The 120 mm CHARM 1 penetrator is approximately 525 mm in length and has a total weight of 8.5 kilograms (kg).[37] American kinetic energy penetrators tend to be longer, with the more modern (the so-called next generation) M829A3 reportedly being some 892 mm in length and weighing 22.3 kg.[38] In regard to the amount of depleted uranium in each penetrator, the CHARM 1 and 3 penetrators have approximately 4.9 kg and the American M829A2 has approximately 5.35 kg.[39] And while the British forces expended less than 1,000 kg of depleted uranium anti-tank ammunition during the 1990–1 Gulf conflict, this amount reportedly doubled to 1,900 kg during the March 2003 invasion.[40] In the 1991 Gulf conflict, the US army re-

---

35 "DU Ammunition Types Taken into Service (Non-Exhaustive)," Jane's Defense Weekly, 11 January 2001, available at <http://www.janes.com/defence/news/jdw/jdw010111_2_n.shtm> (21 September 2001).

36 CHARM is an acronym for "Challenger armament," as designed and used by the British *Challenger* tanks.

37 "RO Defence 120 mm Tank Gun Ammunition," Jane's Defense Weekly, 8 January 2001, available at <http://www.janes.com/defence/news/jdw/jdw010108_4_n.shtml> (17 March 2002).

38 "120mm Tank Gun KE Ammunition," (2004) 5 Defense Update, available at <http://www.defense-update.com/products/digits/120ke.htm#M829A3> (2 May 2005).

39 V.S. Zajic, "Review of Radioactivity, Military Use, and Health Effects of Depleted Uranium," July 1999, available at <http://vzajic.tripod.com/3rdchapter.html> (12 May 2005).

40 The original weight was given in tonnes. See Ministry of Defence, *What's New*, available at <http://www.mod.uk/issues/depleted_uranium/index.htm> (20 September 2001).

portedly expended 9,552 rounds of anti-tank depleted uranium ammunition (both 120 mm and 105 mm).[41] Unfortunately, there has been no similar release of data by the American government with respect to the amount of depleted uranium anti-tank ammunition expended by US mechanized forces in *Operation Iraqi Freedom*. On an unofficial occasion, Michael Kilpatrick, deputy director of deployment health support in the Office of the Assistant Secretary of Defense for Health Affairs, put the figure at 21,800 kg.[42] This figure is said not to include use by the marine corps.

SMALL-CALIBRE AMMUNITION

In the mid-1970s, the US navy and air force tested the effectiveness of depleted uranium in smaller-caliber ammunition, in the range of 20 mm, 25 mm, and 30 mm. Developed in the 1990s, the 25 mm M919 APFSDS-T is a smaller version of the 120 mm kinetic energy penetrators outlined earlier. Often referred to as the super sabot kinetic energy dart, it is utilized by the American Bradley fighting vehicle and fires at a rate of 200 rounds per minute to defeat light-armoured vehicles.[43] Aside from the long-rod penetrator model, the other versions of small-calibre ammunition are more akin to the size of large bullets measuring approximately 95 mm in length. Used by the US marines, the 25 mm PGU-20 has a 150 gram (g) depleted uranium slug.[44] The US Marines reportedly fired some 67,436 of the 25 mm PGU-20 rounds during the 1991 Gulf conflict.[45] Accordingly, the amount of depleted uranium metal expended by the US marines during *Operation Desert Storm* was some 10,115 kg.

---

41 H. van der Keur, "Where and How Much Depleted Uranium Has Been Fired?" available at <http://www.laka.org/teksten/Vu/where-how-much-01/main.html> (8 May 2005).

42 "Statement by Dr. Kilpatrick," conference paper, 6 March 2004, available at <http://www.wise-uranium.org/dissgw.html#MITKILP> (3 September 2005). The amount was listed as twenty-four short tons.

43 "Global Security information on the M919 Cartridge 25mm, Armor Piercing, Fin Stabilized, Discarding Sabot, with Tracer (APFSDS-T)," available at <http://www.globalsecurity.org/military/systems/munitions/m919.htm> (1 June 2006).

44 "Global Security Information on the PGU-20–25mm Ammunition," available at <http://www.globalsecurity.org/military/systems/munitions/pgu-20.htm> (3 July 2005).

45 *Ibid.*

AIR FORCE APPLICATIONS

The 30 mm PGU-14/B API ammunition is utilized by the US air force on the A-10 *Thunderbolt II* aircraft.[46] The A-10 was designed in the early 1970s as a close air support aircraft and was equipped with a heavy eight-barrelled 30 mm cannon to penetrate the top of the heavily armoured enemy tanks of the Soviet Union.[47] The depleted uranium cone is encased in an aluminium jacket (60 mm long and 30 mm wide), which is discarded on impact with a hard target. Weighing in much lighter than tank rounds, the weight of the depleted uranium tip in a 30 mm round is approximately 300 g. A Gatling gun mounted onto the A-10 can fire the 30 mm ammunition up to speeds of 4,200 rounds per minute.[48] As a result, US aircraft fired approximately 10,000 rounds (3,350 kg) at twelve sites in Bosnia-Herzegovina in 1994–5,[49] and 31,000 rounds covering some 112 sites in Kosovo in 1999.[50] According to the best available figures for *Operation Iraqi Freedom* in 2003, the US air force expended approximately 93,442 kg of depleted uranium ammunition.[51]

NAVAL APPLICATIONS

The 20 mm MK149 and MK149–2 APDS depleted uranium ammunition has mostly had naval applications, in the PHALANX close-in weapons system (CIWS).[52] PHALANX is a missile defence system utilizing a 20 mm gun with a firing capacity of 4,500 rounds per minute. In recent years, both the US navy and the British royal navy have replaced depleted uranium rounds with tungsten rounds.[53]

---

46 "30 mm Cannon Ammunition," Global Security, available at <http://www.globalsecurity.org/military/systems/munitions/30mm.htm> (3 July 2005).

47 "Depleted Uranium," *supra* note 24.

48 "GAU-8 Avenger," FAS Military Analysis Network, available at <http://www.fas.org/man/dod-101/sys/ac/equip/gau-8.htm> (7 July 2005).

49 "Depleted Uranium," *supra* note 24.

50 See *Report of the World Health Organisation Depleted Uranium Mission to Kosovo* (Geneva: World Health Organization (WHO), 2001) [*WHO Mission to Kosovo*].

51 "Statement by Dr. Kilpatrick," *supra* note 42.

52 "PGU-20–25mm Ammunition," *supra* note 44.

53 For the UK decision to replace the depleted uranium rounds, see Ministry of Defence, *supra* note 40.

EFFECTS ON IMPACT

A direct hit with depleted uranium ammunition will leave a characteristic patch of black dust around the penetration hole of the vehicle. The black dust is evidence that the depleted uranium penetrator has aerosolized on impact, typically up to 70 per cent of the munition's weight. On impact with the target, temperatures up to 1,000 degrees Celsius are generated, which causes the uranium to aerosolize into fine particles of uranium oxide. While the penetrator can pass completely through a soft target, such as a non-armoured vehicle, it is designed to burn through the armour of a hard target leaving the black dust as proof of its successful deployment. As a consequence, the uranium oxide dust created on impact will contaminate the inside of the vehicle and can be dispersed into the air and onto the ground.[54] These are the major sources of concern for human health and the environment. Since the proportion of 30 mm rounds used in Kosovo that missed their intended hard target may have been as high as 90–5 per cent,[55] producing an estimated hit rate of only 5–10 per cent,[56] the question becomes what happened to the rest? According to official sources within the United States, the hit rate during testing was found to be slightly higher, at 26 per cent, but with only 4.2 per cent actually penetrating the target.[57] While those weapons impacting with their hard target will generally aerosolize on contact, those hitting a hard ground surface or bouncing off a hard or soft target will either be found intact on the surface (possibly still in their jackets) or will be split into large fragments. Off-target penetrators that impact in softer

---

[54] See *Depleted Uranium in Bosnia and Herzegovina: Post-Conflict Environmental Assessment* (Switzerland: UNEP, May 2003), at Appendix N on the Military Use of Depleted Uranium.

[55] "Opinion of the Group of Experts Established According to Article 31 of the Euratom Treaty: Depleted Uranium," 6 March 2001, European Commission, Directorate-General, Environment, Directorate C — Nuclear Protection and Civil Safety, Doc. ENV.C 4, Radiation Protection, available at <http://europa.eu.int/comm/environment/radprot/opinion.pdf> (8 March 2001) ["Opinion of the Group of Experts"].

[56] This figure was also suggested by UNEP following its field studies in Kosovo 2001, see *Depleted Uranium in Kosovo, supra* note 28 at 16.

[57] "Depleted Uranium Munitions," U.S. House of Representatives: Committee on Armed Services, Letter to Mr. Leonard A. Dietz, 13 May 1991, at 5, reprinted in D.A. Lopez, "Friendly Fire: The Link between Depleted Uranium Munitions and Human Health Risks," March 1995, available at <http://www.gulfwarvets.com/du8.html> (3 August 2004) ["Depleted Uranium Munitions"].

ground or sand will most likely not aerosolize but may become buried intact to depths of two metres, where they will corrode unless cleared.[58] Depleted uranium will, therefore, be deposited either (1) inside and on the surface of the hard target; (2) on the ground and other surfaces in the form of metal fragments and fine dust; (3) sub-surface intact; or (4) in the air in the form of uranium oxide.

POTENTIAL HEALTH AND ENVIRONMENTAL EFFECTS OF USING DEPLETED URANIUM AMMUNITION

Since the United States and the United Kingdom first used depleted uranium weaponry in the 1991 Gulf conflict, a growing body of medical and scientific opinion has raised alarm bells as to the potential health and environmental effects of these weapons. However, although the damaging effects of uranium have long been known, the effects of the weaker radioactive substance — depleted uranium — have become a deeply controversial subject — polarizing the scientific community, frequently with government sources of one opinion and independent scientists of another. It is in this regard that over the past few years the United Nations Environment Programme (UNEP)[59] has carried out a number of field assessments in conflict zones to establish the level, if any, of environmental contamination caused by the use of depleted uranium weapons.

UNEP studies were undertaken in Kosovo in November 2000[60] and in Serbia and Montenegro in November 2001,[61] following the United States's use of air-delivered 30 mm depleted uranium rounds during the NATO intervention in Kosovo in 1999. In addition, in 2002, UNEP undertook sampling of the effects of depleted uranium in the environment of Bosnia and Herzegovina following the use by the United States in 1994–5 in the Yugoslav conflict.[62] None of the UNEP assessments has undertaken human sampling to test for concentrations of depleted uranium in the organs of combat-

---

[58] *Depleted Uranium in Bosnia, supra* note 54 at 168–9.

[59] As the name suggests, UNEP is an organization of the United Nations and works to encourage care for the environment. It achieves this by a number of methods, including scientific assessments and advice on conservation strategies.

[60] *Depleted Uranium in Kosovo, supra* note 28.

[61] *Depleted Uranium in Serbia and Montenegro: Post Conflict Environmental Assessment in the Federal Republic of Yugoslavia* (Switzerland: UNEP, 2002).

[62] *Depleted Uranium in Bosnia, supra* note 54.

ants or civilians. Environmental sampling that did take place accounted for only 12 per cent of the sites targeted in Kosovo, with many thousands of depleted uranium munitions remaining unaccounted for.[63] And despite the risks of atmospheric dust particles, no air sampling was carried out in Kosovo. Furthermore, all three of these UNEP studies analyzed the effects of 30 mm depleted uranium rounds fired from aircraft. None have sampled the effects of the much larger tank-fired 120 mm depleted uranium shells. While the effects from these two types of depleted uranium munitions will arguably be the same, the volume of depleted uranium in the environment may be different, and, obviously, greater environmental and human harm may result from the use of the larger-calibre shells. These results, in turn, of course, must take into account the possibility that a greater volume of 30 mm depleted uranium rounds might be used than 120 mm shells. Studies in Kuwait in 2002, following use in the 1991 Gulf conflict some eleven years earlier, were undertaken jointly by UNEP and the IAEA.[64] This study, however, only focused on the radiological risks of depleted uranium, specifically excluding any assessment of harm by chemical toxicity. This assessment also failed to include sampling of humans. Its parameters were to assess and evaluate the possible radiological impact of depleted uranium residues at a number of sites in Kuwait as designated by the Kuwaiti government. However, these recent UNEP field assessments are merely the tip of the iceberg.[65] Two further studies have also been undertaken recently by the World Health Organization (WHO)[66] and the British branch of the Royal Society of Biology.[67] Both, however, are devoid of

---

[63] *Depleted Uranium in Kosovo, supra* note 28 at 10.

[64] *Radiological Conditions in Areas of Kuwait with Residues of Depleted Uranium*, Executive Summary (Vienna: International Atomic Energy Agency (IAEA), 2003).

[65] For a comprehensive account of health and environmental studies on depleted uranium, see D. Bishop, ed., "Compendium of Uranium and Depleted Uranium Research 1942-2004," available at <http://www.motherearth.org/du/compendium.pdf> (2 August 2005). It is important to note that the study was commissioned by the International Coalition to Ban Uranium Weapons and the International Depleted Uranium Study Team, which also has as its objective the banning of depleted uranium weaponry. The compendium is nonetheless extensive in the resources it contains.

[66] *WHO Mission to Kosovo, supra* note 50.

[67] "The Health Hazards of Depleted Uranium Munitions," Royal Society of Biology, May 2001, available at <http://www.royalsoc.ac.uk/document.asp?tip=o&id=1431> (15 July 2001) at 11.

sampling (human and soil/water) and provide only a review of published scientific literature. Additionally in Iraq, scientists have been studying the potential health and environmental effects from depleted uranium weaponry since its use in the first Gulf conflict. Since then, independent scientists from all over the world have published their research findings in peer-reviewed journals. Even scientists from government departments have published findings contrary to their official governmental position on the effects of depleted uranium. As a consequence, there is a vast and ever-expanding body of knowledge on the effects of depleted uranium on both humans and the environment.

The deep division that exists among scientists as to the actual effects of depleted uranium on human health and the environment does not generally concern the pathways for damage or the type of damage but, instead, lies in the potential severity of harm. There is no doubt that depleted uranium is both a chemically toxic and radioactive substance. However, controversy surrounds the view, held by the US government and others, that the dangers from both the chemotoxicity and radiotoxicity are very low. In fact, Ministry of Defence sources in the United Kingdom have described the radiological characteristic of depleted uranium as being "of little concern" since its radioactivity is possibly of a level even "too small to be detectable."[68] This issue of the radioactivity of depleted uranium and its consequent effects will be analyzed first since it is the most controversial aspect, with the issue of chemotoxicity to follow. An important point that is often missed in the literature and risk assessments is the possible synergistic effects of depleted uranium — the dual effects of its chemotoxicity and radiotoxicity on human cells and the wider environment.

RADIOTOXICITY OF DEPLETED URANIUM

There is no doubt that depleted uranium is a radioactive substance, but it is of weaker radioactive magnitude than natural

---

[68] "Testing for the Presence of Depleted Uranium in UK Veterans of the Gulf Conflict: The Current Position," United Kingdom Ministry of Defence, March 1999, available at <http://www.gulfwar.mod.uk> (7 July 2001). S. Fetter and F. Von Hippel, "After the Dust Settles" (1999) 55(6) Bulletin of Atomic Scientists 42, available at <http://www.thebulletin.org/issues/1999/nd99/nd99vonhippel. html> (7 February 2001). See also "Anti-Armour Ammunition with Depleted Uranium Penetrators," Memorandum with the Ministry of Defence, March 1979, at para. 3, available at <http://www.mod.uk/linked_files/anti-armour_ ammunition.pdf > (20 January 2001) ["Anti-Armour Ammunition"].

uranium or other uranium isotopes. In 2002, the IAEA carried out studies at eleven sites in Kuwait where depleted uranium ammunition had been fired during the 1991 Gulf conflict. Using the data collected, the IAEA came to the opinion that "potential annual radiation doses arising from exposure to depleted uranium residues are very low and of little radiological concern."[69] This conclusion varies significantly from that previously derived by the UK's own Atomic Energy Agency in 1991, when it warned of a "significant problem" of depleted uranium radioactivity.[70]

The position taken by the US (domestic) Nuclear Regulatory Commission (NRC) is that depleted uranium would be classifiable as a Class A low-level radioactive waste.[71] At least this would be so if it were not classed as a "source" material, thus avoiding the waste terminology and the waste regulations altogether. By treaty definition, a material that has a use will not be considered "waste."[72] Radioactive waste is specifically excluded from the general legal regime governing hazardous waste,[73] but it is included in the dumping regime established by the 1972 International Convention on the Prevention of Marine Pollution by the Dumping of Wastes and

---

[69] *Radiological Conditions in Areas of Kuwait, supra* note 64.

[70] See R. Norton-Taylor, "MP's Press Hoon on Uranium Risk," *The Guardian*, 15 January 2001, at 6.

[71] U.S. Nuclear Regulatory Commission, Office of Nuclear Material Safety and Safeguards, Division of Waste Management and Environmental Protection, *Environmental Impact Statement for the Proposed National Enrichment Facility in Lea County, New Mexico: Draft Report for Comment*, Doc. NUREG-1790 (September 2004), available at <http://www.nrc.gov/reading-rm/doc-collections/nuregs/staff/sr1790/> (2 October 2005) at 2–21.

[72] See Article 2(h) of the 1997 IAEA Joint Convention on the Safety of Spent Fuel Management and on the Safety of Radioactive Waste Management, 29 September 1997, (1997) 36 I.L.M. 6 at 1436 (entered into force 18 June 2001) [IAEA Joint Convention]. Both the United Kingdom and United States are state parties to this treaty. However, during the negotiation of the 1997 convention, states specifically kept off the agenda the issue of the safety of radioactive waste used for "military purposes." Consequently, Article 3(3) stipulates that "radioactive waste does not include waste within the military or defence programmes." Depleted uranium is also included within the IAEA statutory definition of "source materials," which is a material suitable for transformation into a special nuclear material, at Article XX, 1957 Statute of International Atomic Energy Agency, available at <http://www.iaea.or.at/About/statute_text.html> (10 October 2005).

[73] Article 1(3) of the 1989 Basel Convention on the Control of Transboundary Movements of Hazardous Wastes and Their Disposal, 22 March 1989, (1989) 28 I.L.M. 657 (entered into force 24 May 1992) [Basel Convention].

Other Matter (London Dumping Convention).[74] In 1993, both low and intermediate level radioactive wastes were elevated to Annex I of the London Dumping Convention — and the result is a complete prohibition on the dumping of any radioactive waste at sea.[75] Thus, there is no longer a distinction with respect to the dumping at sea of radioactive waste based on the level of radioactivity, since even low-level radioactive waste is included in the prohibition. As for the NRC classification of depleted uranium as low-level radioactive waste, this is open to dispute based on the radiological similarities between depleted uranium and transuranics, where transuranic waste is qualified in a higher class by the NRC.[76]

In addition, states have enacted domestic legislation governing the disposal of radioactive waste in their territory,[77] and the IAEA establishes radiation and waste safety standards, based on the recommendations of the International Commission on Radiological Protection (ICRP) and the United Nations Scientific Committee on the Effects of Atomic Radiation. The ICRP's work has included assessments of the risk of radioactive waste, and one aspect of this study is the setting of dose limits, which have become widely incorporated into domestic and international standard setting. Accordingly, the current ICRP recommendation for a total maximum permissible dose to members of the public from all human nuclear practices is no more than one millisievert (mSv) per year. This

---

74 1972 International Convention on the Prevention of Marine Pollution by the Dumping of Wastes and Other Matter, 29 December 1972, (1972) 1046 U.N.T.S. 120 (entered into force 30 August 1975) [London Dumping Convention]; and Resolution LDC 51(16), List of London Convention Resolutions, Office for the London Convention, International Maritime Organization, available at <http://www.londonconvention.org/documents/lc72/LIST_LC_Resolutions.doc> (13 August 2005).

75 For the sake of completeness, it was also decided in 1990 that the moratorium on sea disposal of radioactive waste includes the sub-seabed disposal of waste. See Resolution LDC 41(13), *supra* note 74.

76 A. Makhijani and B. Smith, "Costs and Risks of Management and Disposal of Depleted Uranium from the National Enrichment Facility Proposed to the Built in Lea County New Mexico by LES," Institute for Energy and Environmental Research, redacted version, 1 February 2005, available at <http://www.ieer.org/reports/du/LESrptfeb05.pdf> (2 September 2005) at 4–5. Transuranics is the name given to substances with an atomic number greater than 92 (uranium) and are largely man-made radioactive substances that can undergo nuclear fission.

77 See the 1993 Radioactive Substances Act applicable in the United Kingdom, 12 (1993) 1 Law Reports Statutes 467.

figure is used by the WHO[78] and others and has formed the basis of various UNEP field assessments in conflict zones (detailed earlier in this article). The UNEP field assessments used the one mSv limit as the threshold to determine whether radioactive measurements were "significant" if above one mSv or "insignificant" if below. However, recently, the risk model used by the ICRP has been criticized by the independent European Committee on Radiation Risk (ECRR).[79] The research of the ECRR has focused on the risks from low-dosage exposures and has concluded that the current ICRP risk model is flawed in several respects.[80] Consequently, the ECRR argues that the current annual dose for members of the public is far too high and recommends a limit of only 0.1 mSv per year.[81] Finally, this research also points to the fact that children and women are at greater risk from radiation than are men.

Consequently, it is widely agreed that the radiation dose from depleted uranium is much lower, approximately 40 per cent lower, than that of natural uranium. Yet many scientific studies appear to contest the view that the resultant risk to human health and the environment is "of little radiological concern."[82] There is even evidence of disagreement *within* the US administration regarding the level of risk from depleted uranium.[83]

CHEMOTOXICITY OF DEPLETED URANIUM

Since the US government views the radioactivity levels of depleted uranium to be extremely low, it has concluded that the chemical

---

[78] See WHO, *Depleted Uranium*, Fact Sheet no. 257, Revised January 2003, available at <http://www.who.int/mediacentre/factsheets/fs257/en/> (2 May 2004).

[79] This independent committee was formed in 1997 and is composed of scientists and risk specialists within Europe.

[80] C. Busby, R. Bertell, I. Schmitz-Feuerhake, M. Scott Cato, and A. Yablokov, eds., *ECRR 2003 Recommendations of the European Committee on Radiation Risk: The Health Effects of Ionising Radiation Exposure at Low Doses for Radiation Protection Purposes* (Brussels: Green Audit, 2003).

[81] *Ibid.*

[82] *Radiological Conditions in Areas of Kuwait, supra* note 64.

[83] US Department of Defense, "Exemption — Hazardous Materials — Transportation in Commerce of Munitions of Class 1 (Explosive) Hazard Containing Components Manufactured of Depleted Uranium," Doc. RSPA-2004-18576-276, 18 May 2005. The issue concerns a DOD HazMat exemption (DOT-E 9649) from marking requirements for depleted uranium weapons. The US Department of Transportation has revoked the exemption on the basis that unmarked radioactive hazards are a risk to fire crews should there be an accident and the appreciable levels of external radiation exposure to transport workers.

toxicity risk is of greater concern. Somewhat surprisingly, despite this conclusion there does not appear to be a wealth of scientific studies on the chemotoxicity of depleted uranium, and even fewer studies on the combined chemical and radiation effects on health.

The chemical toxicity of depleted uranium is similar to that of other heavy metals such as lead, cadmium, nickel, cobalt, copper, mercury, arsenic, and tungsten — some of which are also common components of munitions. Heavy metals are undoubtedly hazardous to human health and particularly hazardous to marine environments, soils, and plant life.[84] While *radiological* damage can be caused in the form of cancer, many heavy metals are also carcinogens. Lead exposure, for example, is known to be neurotoxic (damaging to nerves) and is linked with growth retardation and reduced intellectual functioning in humans and animals.[85] As a consequence of the recognition of the effects of lead poisoning in children, the safety limit of exposure has constantly been lowered since the 1960s.[86] Similarly, studies undertaken by the staff at the US Armed Forces Radiobiology Research Institute have confirmed that exposure to depleted uranium can cause neurological damage.[87] Chronic copper exposure, for example, can cause brain damage and psychiatric illness. Other symptoms of heavy metal chemical toxins include damage to the kidneys, brain damage, and reduction in fertility of men and women, impaired foetal development, and cardiovascular problems. Children are at greater risk than adults, potentially being exposed both during pregnancy and post-pregnancy to any contaminants.

PATHWAYS AND HUMAN HEALTH EFFECTS OF DEPLETED URANIUM

The human body is exposed to depleted uranium in two ways: externally and internally. The potential radiological and chemical

---

84 For example, mercury and cadmium are regulated under the 1976 EC Directive 76/464 Governing Pollution Caused by Certain Dangerous Substances into the Aquatic Environment of the Community, [1976] O.J. L.129/23 at List I of Annex I; and the 1998 Protocol on Heavy Metals to the 1979 Convention on Long Range Transboundary Air Pollution, 24 June 1998, (1979) 18 I.L.M. 1442, available at <http://www.unece.org/env/lrtap/hm_h1.htm> (10 June 2002) (entered into force 29 December 2003).

85 For more information, see Makhijiani and Smith, *supra* note 76 at 18–19.

86 *Ibid.*

87 See T.C. Pellmar, D.O. Keyser, C. Emery, and J.B. Hogan, "Electrophysiological Changes in Hippocampal Slices Isolated from Rats Embedded with Depleted Uranium Fragments" (1999) 20(5) Neurotoxicology 785 at 790.

risks from *external* exposure appear to be relatively low, described by the United Kingdom Ministry of Defence as being "relatively harmless."[88] In regard to its radiological aspect, this is because depleted uranium primarily emits alpha radiation particles, which are easily prevented from entering the body by the outer layer of skin or clothing. The lower level of beta particles emitted by depleted uranium should also be blocked by clothing and boots, while the gamma rays — although of stronger penetrative power — are present at very low levels. Prolonged skin contact, however, could result in exposures of radiological significance.[89] Such contact might occur, for example, where scavengers remove contaminated tank debris, most often as a trophy or for commerce.

The greatest health effects, therefore, result from the internalization of uranium oxide dust into the blood stream. This is equally applicable for both chemical and radiological toxicity. Internalization may occur in any of three ways: (1) the inhalation of uranium oxide dust through breathing; (2) the ingestion of depleted uranium-contaminated foodstuffs (including contaminated water); or (3) the embedment of depleted uranium shrapnel in a wound.[90] The black uranium oxide dust created when a depleted uranium weapon impacts with a target will consist of both soluble and insoluble particles. *Insoluble* uranium particles cannot be dissolved and so will not move around the body as easily as soluble particles, resulting in long-term deposits. Insoluble particles, therefore, will settle in the first organ that is encountered — which will be the lungs if inhaled, the stomach if ingested, and in tissue if embedded in a wound — and may cause localized radiation damage to the organ due to the presence of alpha radiation particles.[91] Consequently, via the inhalation pathway, a long retention time in the lungs could cause damage to the whole respiratory system, particularly to the

---

88 See "Clearance of Depleted Uranium (DU) from Range Areas," Royal Army Ordnance Corp Technical Ammunition Bulletin no. 21/2024, 14 January 1999, available at <http://www.mod.uk/linked_files/technical_ammunition_bulletin.pdf> (2 October 2005).

89 This was recognized by the IAEA. See *Radiological Conditions in Areas of Kuwait*, *supra* note 64.

90 For an in-depth study of these various pathways, see "Opinion of the Group of Experts," *supra* note 55.

91 "The Use and Hazards of Depleted Uranium Munitions," Doc. LAND/Med/5072, 4 March 1997, available at <http://www.mod.uk/linked_files/use_and_hazards_of_du.pdf> (20 January 2001).

lung tissue.[92] In support of this finding, Asaf Duraković of the Uranium Medical Research Centre in the United States, has confirmed the presence of elevated levels of depleted uranium in the respiratory system of veterans of the Gulf conflict after nine years of exposure.[93] From the lungs, the depleted uranium will be slowly absorbed into the blood stream to be distributed throughout the body, eventually settling in the bones, brain, liver, kidneys, heart, lymph nodes, testes, and spleen.[94]

Soluble uranium particles inhaled or ingested will rapidly be absorbed into the bloodstream.[95] Most of these soluble substances, however, should be excreted just as rapidly out of the body through normal digestion, which is estimated to occur within twenty-four hours of exposure.[96] There remains the danger, however, that inhalation or ingestion at critical levels may cause damage to the kidneys.[97] It is the organ deemed to be most at risk of damage, since it functions as the body's filter and is where such harmful chemical components will accumulate. The nephrotoxicity of uranium has been recognized since the nineteenth century and is frequently reported by official sources as being the only potentially harmful effect of depleted uranium. Despite such findings, though, British government scientists maintain that any such kidney damage that does manifest is likely to be reversible.[98] On the other hand, the WHO has recognized an increased risk of kidney damage "following *ingestion* of depleted uranium depend[ing] on the amount of

---

92 "Review of the Hazards of Depleted Uranium: The Aftermath of the Gulf War," draft paper, December 1993, at para. 37, available at <http://www.mod.uk/linked_files/aftermath_of_gulf_war_part1.pdf> (20 January 2001) ["Review of the Hazards"].

93 A. Duraković, P. Horan, L.A. Dietz, and I. Zimmerman, "Estimate of the Time Zero Lung Burden of Depleted Uranium in Persian Gulf War Veterans by the 24-hour Urinary Excretion and Exponential Decay Analysis" (2003) 168 Military Medicine 600.

94 Bishop, ed., *supra* note 65 at 11.

95 "Review of the Hazards," *supra* note 92.

96 "Persons Affected from Depleted Uranium Weapons," in "Radiation Exposure from Depleted Uranium Weapons," World Information Service on Energy: Uranium Project, available at <http://www.antenna.nl/wise/uranium/#MILDU> (3 October 2005).

97 "Review of the Hazards," *supra* note 92. Unlike much of this UK Ministry of Defence document, this was not denied by the subsequent paper entitled "The Use and Hazards of Depleted Uranium Munitions," *supra* note 91.

98 "Review of the Hazards," *supra* note 92.

soluble uranium compounds present" (in other words, the effects increase with higher solubility).[99]

In addition, there is a growing body of reputable evidence that shows that at the cellular and genetic level depleted uranium is carcinogenic, mutagenic, and terotogenic. This is due both to its chemotoxicity and radiotoxicity. Although such a finding was admitted in part in an internal US army document in 1993,[100] the US government has since backtracked and now denies any link between its depleted uranium weapons use and cancers, such as leukaemia.[101] However, there is a growing body of research that goes some way to prove otherwise. Research by the US Armed Forces Radiobiology Research Institute indicates that depleted uranium is toxic and therefore damaging to cells, genes, and the central nervous system. According to Dr. Alexandra Miller of the institute, her studies have shown the "first indication that uranium's radiological and chemical effects might potentially play both a tumour-initiating and a tumour-promoting role."[102] In her previous work in 1998, Miller demonstrated that internalized depleted uranium could result in "a significant enhancement of urinary mutagenicity" (or mutation of the urinary system).[103] The presence of depleted uranium has been detected in the urine of Gulf conflict veterans, in some cases, ten years after exposure.[104] Research indicates that even at low doses, depleted uranium may cause genetic damage,[105] induce cancers, and increase cell death.

99 [Emphasis added]. See *WHO Mission to Kosovo, supra* note 50 at 10.

100 This is according to an internal US army document, drawn up by the US army surgeon-general's office in 1993 and seen by *The Guardian* newspaper. See R. Norton-Taylor, "Cancer Risk Hard to Avoid in Battle," *The Guardian*, 13 January 2001, at 9.

101 R. Beeston and R. Owen, "Deaths Threaten Unity of NATO," *The Times*, 6 January 2001, at 14.

102 A.C. Miller, M. Stewart, K. Brooks, L. Shi, and N. Page, "Depleted Uranium-Catalyzed Oxidative DNA Damage: Absence of Significant Alpha Particle Decay" (2002) 91 J. Inorganic Biochemistry 246 at 251.

103 A.C. Miller et al., "Urinary and Serum Mutagenicity Studies with Rats Implanted with Depleted Uranium or Tantalum Pellets" (1998) 13(6) Mutagenesis 643 at 646–47.

104 See M.A. McDiarmid et al., "Health Effects of Depleted Uranium on Exposed Gulf War Veterans: A 10-Year Follow Up" (2004) 67 J. Toxicology and Environmental Health, 277 at Part A. For the Canadian assessments, for example, carried out in 2002, see E.A. Ough et al., "An Examination of Uranium Levels in Canadian Forces Personnel Who Served in the Gulf War and Kosovo" (2002) 82 Health Physics 527.

105 A.C. Miller, J. Xu, M. Stewart, P.G.S. Prasanna, and N. Page, "Potential Late Health Effects of Depleted Uranium and Tungsten Used in Armor-Piercing

At the organ level, exposure to depleted uranium dust will primarily affect the kidneys and lungs, as admitted by official sources. Yet internalized depleted uranium may also affect other organs, such as the spleen, brain, and reproductive organs. Damage in these areas can lead to psychological disorders, skeletal malformations, and reproductive problems. Uranium is known to concentrate in the male testes and has been detected in the sperm of soldiers returning from the Gulf conflict zone.[106] Finally, in rats and mice, exposure to uranium has been demonstrated to cause "decreased fertility, embryo/foetal toxicity including teratogenicity, and reduced growth of the offspring."[107] Extensive studies of the effects on human reproduction appear to be lacking, but it is known that depleted uranium particles can cross the placental barrier via the blood stream.[108] Studies in rats and mice have observed reproductive problems, skeletal abnormalities, developmental effects and malformations, and a decrease in foetal development.[109] On the other hand, similar studies in post-conflict Iraq, suggesting an increased incidence of birth defects, but this time in humans, have been denied by Western governments. According to Iraqi scientists, a genetic study carried out in southern Iraq found an increase in birth malformations, together with "deformed or missing eyes, ears, nose, tongue, and genital organs."[110] Some confirmation of these medical reports has apparently been given by independent

---

Munitions: Comparison of Neoplastic Transformation and Genotoxicity with the Known Carcinogen Nickel" (2002) 167 Military Medicine 120 at 121–22, Supplement 1.

106 M.A. McDiarmid et al., "Health Effects of Depleted Uranium on Exposed Gulf War Veteran," (2000) 82(2) Environmental Research 168. The research tested the semen of a sample of Baltimore soldiers returning from the first Gulf conflict.

107 J.L. Domingo, "Reproductive and Developmental Toxicity of Natural and Depleted Uranium: A Review" (2001) 15 Reproductive Toxicology 603 at 603.

108 D.E. McClain et al., "Biological Effects of Embedded Depleted Uranium (DU): Summary of Armed Forces Radiobiology Research Institute Research" (2001) 274 Science of the Total Environment 115.

109 See WHO, Department of Protection of the Human Environment, "Depleted Uranium: Sources, Exposure and Health Effects," Doc. WHO/SDE/PHE/01.1 (Geneva: WHO, April 2001) available at <http://www.who.int/ionizing_radiation/pub_meet/ir_pub/en/> (20 June 2002) and "Health Hazards of Depleted Uranium Munitions," Part II, Royal Society, March 2002, available at <http://www.royalsoc.ac.uk/displaypagedoc.asp?id=9825> (5 June 2002).

110 See Zajic, *supra* note 39, quoting "Guidelines for Safe Response to Handling, Storage, and Transportation Accidents Involving Army Tank Munitions and Armor Which Contain Depleted Uranium," Doc. TB 9-1300-278 (September

scientists,[111] and similar reports have been given of children born to Gulf veterans.[112]

The final pathway of harm is due to the internalization of depleted uranium fragments. In this respect, the experts' report to the European Commission recognized that "DU [depleted uranium] dissolves *continuously* from the tissue, and can still be measured in the urine after 7 years."[113] Depleted uranium shrapnel or the contamination of open wounds appears to be the most serious health concern for military personnel, particularly for those inside or near targeted vehicles. The US Baltimore study on veterans from the first Gulf conflict found that a number of veterans had multiple tiny depleted uranium fragments scattered in their muscles and soft tissue.[114] The report concluded, however, that "these fragments cannot be surgically removed without causing extensive damage to the surrounding tissues."[115] In rats implanted with various sizes of depleted uranium, studies have shown that the greater the size of the depleted uranium fragment the greater the risk of the rats developing malignant tumours in the soft tissue surrounding the contaminant.[116] This also appears to be a safe conclusion in regard to human exposure. As a consequence, exposure pathways that result in the long-term retention of depleted uranium appear to produce a greater risk of very severe health effects. It appears difficult or impossible to remove depleted uranium once it has been internalized in this way, and there is no cure for many of the resultant health effects.

1990), at Appendix F, available at <http://www.members.tripod.com/vzajic/9thchapter.html> (3 September 2004).

[111] See the working paper submitted by Y.K.J. Yeung Sik Yuen to the Sub-Commission on the Promotion and Protection of Human Rights, UN ESCOR, *Human Rights and Weapons of Mass Destruction, or with Indiscriminate Effect, or of a Nature to Cause Superfluous Injury or Unnecessary Suffering*, UN Doc. E/CN.4/Sub.2/2002/38 (27 June 2002) at paras. 144(c)(d).

[112] *Ibid.* at para. 144(g). See also J. McHugh, "Sick Guard Members Blame Depleted Uranium," *Army Times*, 9 April 2004.

[113] [Emphasis added]. See "Opinion of the Group of Experts," *supra* note 55.

[114] Department of Defence, *Environmental Exposure Report, Depleted Uranium in the Gulf (II)*, 13 December 2000, available at <http://www.deploymentlink.osd.mil/du_library/du_ii/index.htm#tabp> (10 August 2001).

[115] *Ibid.*

[116] See Flecther F. Hahn, Raymond A. Guilmette, and Mark D. Hoover, "Implanted Depleted Uranium Fragments Cause Soft Tissue Sarcomas in the Muscles of

A ten-year follow-up study on the US Baltimore veterans has confirmed the findings of the European Commission's experts, identifying ongoing uranium absorption from embedded depleted uranium fragments.[117] The US Baltimore study's base involves a group of thirty-nine Gulf War veterans (1990–1) who were victims of depleted uranium "friendly fire." As a consequence, many of the veterans sustained internalized depleted uranium — fragments of depleted uranium in the body. First, the participants were urine tested and ranked in order of uranium concentration — from high to low levels of retained urinary uranium levels. In their findings, Dr. Melissa McDiarmid et al. recorded the following health problems in those veterans with higher levels of retained depleted uranium in their urine: (1) chromosomal aberrations;[118] (2) some neurocognitive impairment;[119] and (3) some mutagenic effect.[120] The findings of Dr. McDiarmid et al. are also confirmed by studies in rats, mice, and other animals.

ENVIRONMENTAL EFFECTS OF DEPLETED URANIUM

Depleted uranium may also have environmental effects. Tests show that weathered depleted uranium penetrators will corrode to produce hydrated uranium oxide, which is highly soluble in water. And while corrosion rates were originally estimated to be some five hundred years for depleted uranium — a very slow rate, meaning that the leaching of depleted uranium into the soil would be slow and so hardly noticeable — evidence from Yugoslavia is that corrosion can occur within twenty years.[121] Therefore, water supplies and agricultural areas may quickly become contaminated. There are some, albeit unconfirmed, environmental findings of such a nature in Iraq. Iraqi scientists have reported, for example, that air, soil, and water samples collected in the southern provinces of Iraq in 1998 have evidenced abnormally high levels of radiation following the

---

Rats," Respiratory Research Institute, New Mexico, (2002) 110(1) Environmental Health Perspectives 51.

[117] See McDiarmid et al., *supra* note 104.

[118] *Ibid.* at 289.

[119] *Ibid.* at 287–88.

[120] *Ibid.* at 291.

[121] *Depleted Uranium in Serbia, supra* note 61 at 27.

use of depleted uranium in the 1991 Gulf conflict.[122] In 2000, Iraq reported that flora and fauna around Basra had radiation levels eighty-four times higher than those suggested by the WHO.[123] To some extent, the UNEP studies in the Balkan conflict zones substantiate the Iraqi findings with respect to the potential nature of environmental harm caused by depleted uranium. For instance, UNEP has suggested that heavy firing of depleted uranium in a concentrated area could "increase the potential source of uranium contamination of groundwater by a factor of 10 to 100."[124] The resulting uranium concentration might, therefore, exceed WHO health standards for drinking water[125] and have an adverse affect on flora and fauna. Although water sampling from Serbia, Montenegro, and Kosovo indicated no "significant" contamination of water by depleted uranium,[126] sampling undertaken in Bosnia Herzegovina — some eight years after use — did find some depleted uranium contamination of the water. As a consequence, UNEP has suggested that heavy firing, coupled with the burial of corroding penetrators, *may* cause contamination of drinking water.[127]

On the other hand, official sources — including the UK government,[128] the Swiss Department of Defense,[129] NATO,[130] and the

---

[122] Zajic, *supra* note 39.

[123] See the *Questions on the Violation of Human Rights and Fundamental Freedoms in Any Part of the World*, Iraq Note Verbale dated 3 Feburary 2000 to the United Nations High Commissioner for Human Rights, Doc. E/CN.4/2000/121 (16 February 2000) at 3.

[124] "United Nations Environment Programme Recommends Precautionary Action Regarding Depleted Uranium in Kosovo," UNEP News Release 01/36, available at <http://www.unep.org/Documents.Multilingual/Default.asp?Document ID=193&ArticleID=2789&l=en> (3 April 2001) ["UNEP Recommends Precautionary Action"].

[125] *Ibid.*

[126] *Depleted Uranium in Serbia, supra* note 61 at 33; and *Depleted Uranium in Kosovo, supra* note 28 at 34.

[127] *Ibid.*; and *Depleted Uranium in Serbia, supra* note 61 at 34.

[128] See Ad Hoc Committee on Depleted Uranium, Statement by the United Kingdom Minister for the Armed Forces on Depleted Uranium, 10 January 2001, available at <http://www.nato.int/du/docu/d010110a.htm> (10 September 2001).

[129] Ad Hoc Committee on Depleted Uranium, Actions Taken by Switzerland Concerning Depleted Uranium, 25 January 2001, available at <http://www.nato.int/ du/docu/d010125a.htm> (27 August 2001).

[130] Statement by the Secretary General on the Use of Depleted Uranium Munitions in the Balkans, Doc. NATO 10/01/01, available at <http://www.nato.int/docu/ pr/2001/p01-002e.htm> (4 March 2001).

European Union panel of experts[131] — have continually referenced scientific findings that suggest the impact on the environment and the health hazards related to depleted uranium are "negligible."[132] In support of this assessment, tests carried out in Scottish waters adjacent to a depleted uranium firing range apparently evidenced no alteration in the level of uranium from that which would be naturally present in the water.[133] Furthermore, studies undertaken at US proving grounds are produced in evidence as indicating no measurable effects on drinking water from depleted uranium weapons use.[134] These studies also allegedly prove that depleted uranium has not been detected in the groundwater supplies near to the testing grounds.[135]

In regard to soil contamination, the UNEP survey undertaken in Bosnia and Herzegovina in 2002 did find localized ground contamination around the site of impact with "widely variable concentrations: 0.01–100 g DU [depleted uranium]/kg of soil."[136] UNEP was still able to conclude, however, that "contamination of the ground surface and upper layer (0–5 [centimetres (cm)]) of the ground was very low."[137] A particularly important finding by UNEP concerned the dispersion rate of soil contamination over time. UNEP's findings indicated that in Bosnia and Herzegovina — in the five additional years since impact — the "detectable dispersion had increased from 10 to 40 cm, compared to the Kosovo findings (of 0–10 cm)."[138] Therefore, the depleted uranium had dispersed further into the environment, spreading the contaminants further into the soil and affecting a greater amount of plant life. Since it is the policy of the United Kingdom and the United States to remove contaminated soil (as radioactive waste) to a depth of 35 cm, remediation in itself, while arguably a necessity in some form, is

---

131 "No DU Weapons Risk, Say Experts," 6 March 2001, *Newsnight*, available at <http://news.bbc.co.uk/1/hi/world/europe/1205632.stm> (21 March 2001).

132 *Ibid.*

133 "DU Test Shell Firing Resumes," *BBC News Online*, 21 February 2001, reporting comments of Defence Minister Dr Lewis Mooney; and D. Shukman, "Scots Fear Ill Wind," *BBC News Online*, 20 February 2001.

134 See W.C. Hanson and F.R. Miera, "Further Studies of Long-Term Ecological Effects of Exposure to Uranium," Los Alamos Scientific Laboratory, University of California, July 1978.

135 *Ibid.*, Chapter 7.

136 *Depleted Uranium in Bosnia, supra* note 54 at 30.

137 *Ibid.*

138 *Ibid.* at 32.

also highly damaging to plant life.[139] Lichen and tree bark are good bio-indicators of the presence of depleted uranium, and, indeed, in the UNEP Serbia and Montenegro study, lichen samples did indicate the earlier presence of depleted uranium at three sites.[140] Similarly, bark samples in Kosovo indicated an earlier presence of depleted uranium atmospheric contamination and showed low levels of depleted uranium contamination in the trees.[141] Furthermore, soil samples taken from areas adjacent to destroyed tanks in Kosovo were found to be contaminated with depleted uranium more than a year and a half after deployment,[142] and "contamination points" — indicating "significant" contamination — were identified by UNEP in Kosovo, Serbia, and Montenegro.[143]

Most alarming is the conclusion reached by UNEP to explain the discrepancy between the volume of weapons reportedly used at particular sites and the number of spent depleted uranium penetrators recovered. While up to 70 per cent of a depleted uranium kinetic energy penetrator will aerosolize on contact with a hard target/surface, UNEP was unable to account for more than a handful of spent weapons at each site. As a result, thousands of penetrators remain unaccounted for. The more likely scenario, suggested by UNEP, is that the penetrators had missed the target and were buried in the ground. One consequence admitted by UNEP, therefore, is that "drinking water could possibly become contaminated in the future."[144] Therefore, these findings do indicate some cause for concern in regard to the potentially permanent soil and water contamination from depleted uranium weapons.

Official government sources indicate that most of the atmospheric depleted uranium particles should reach ground level within five minutes and 500 metres of impact,[145] while the UNEP Bosnia study

---

139 Hanson and Miera, *supra* note 134, Chapter 7.

140 *Depleted Uranium in Serbia, supra* note 61 at 30–31 and 140–51.

141 *Depleted Uranium in Kosovo, supra* note 28 at 75.

142 Ad Hoc Committee on Depleted Uranium, "Health Aspects of the Balkans-DU Crisis: The Italian Experience," 1 February 2001, available at <http://www.nato. int/du/docu/d010201a.htm> (6 March 2001).

143 *Depleted Uranium in Kosovo, supra* note 28 at 27; and *Depleted Uranium in Serbia, supra* note 61 at 24.

144 *Depleted Uranium in Kosovo, supra* note 28 at 50, 56, 65, and 90. At one site in Bellobrade/Belobrod, more than one thousand rounds were fired and not one depleted uranium penetrator was found (at 91).

145 "House of Lords: Lord Parry's 'Starred' Question on 8 December on Depleted Uranium Shells," Doc. C.585/1/3/HDRPS (1 December 1993) at para. 40,

puts the distance at only 200 metres of impact.[146] In its report, UNEP was unable to fully account for the continued presence of airborne depleted uranium contamination in Serbia and Montenegro. One possibility was the recent excavation of depleted uranium penetrators in these areas, which could therefore be a future and continual risk to the environment and to human health from depleted uranium ammunition.[147] Also in Bosnia Herzegovina, UNEP found concentrations of depleted uranium — albeit at very low levels — remaining in the air some eight years after use.[148]

EFFECTS SUMMARY

Based on the still uncertain risks from depleted uranium, bodies such as the WHO remain concerned about the use of depleted uranium weapons in conflict, and the European Parliament and others have gone so far as to call for a moratorium on the use of the ammunition until its effects have been conclusively assessed.[149] At this point in time, however, there still remains a wide divergence of scientific opinion on the true effects of such weapons on human health and the environment. What can be stated is that in regard to human health effects a greater number of studies — including studies by scientists working within the US administration (McDiarmid and Miller) — are linking depleted uranium contamination with potentially severe illnesses and genotoxic effects. With respect to the environmental effects, the UNEP Serbia and Montenegro study was able to conclude (1) low levels of widespread depleted uranium contamination; (2) the possibility of future groundwater contamination; and (3) the presence of airborne contamination only two years after the use of depleted uranium and despite a comprehensive decontamination exercise by the Yugoslav authorities, including the removal of two tonnes of rock, soil,

---

available at <http://www.mod.uk/linked_files/lord_parry_brief.pdf.> (20 January 2001) ["Lord Parry's 'Starred' Question"].

146 *Depleted Uranium in Bosnia, supra* note 54 at 30.

147 *Depleted Uranium in Serbia, supra* note 61 at 30.

148 *Depleted Uranium in Bosnia, supra* note 54 at 36.

149 For the European Parliament, see "Unexploded Ordnance and Depleted Uranium Ammunition," Verbatim Report of Proceedings, 12 February 2003, available at <http://www.europarl.eu.int/cre/cre?FILE=20030212r&LANGUE =EN&LEVEL=DOC&NUMINT=3-224&LEG=L5> (3 January 2004); see also K. Scott, "Moratorium Sought on DU Shell Testing," *The Guardian*, 21 February 2001.

and humus.[150] Indeed, more worrying is the finding of depleted uranium contamination at one site that was not on the NATO list of targeted areas, having implications for NATO's accuracy of targeting and mapping of weapons use. Furthermore, with the exception of the sampling of cow's milk in Kosovo,[151] no human sampling or health examinations and no activity measurement of food was carried out during any of the UNEP missions.

Although there still remains a degree of scientific uncertainty in regard to the effects of depleted uranium, this section has certainly demonstrated that there is at least some cause for concern for people and the environment within conflict zones. As a consequence, it is conceivable that any human and environmental damage caused by depleted uranium weapons will be both an *immediate* and a *long-term* consequence of use. Finally, since these weapons were used on the battlefield during the first Gulf conflict, over fifteen years ago, it is arguable that any health and environmental effects are, therefore, a foreseeable consequence of use. While the user states may not have known about the specific dangers and the extent of the risks in the interim period — arguably these are still in doubt today — they were alerted to the potential dangers of using depleted uranium weaponry. Having established the dangers that depleted uranium weapons present, the next section will seek to examine their legality under current provisions of the laws of armed conflict.

LEGAL PARAMETERS OF DEPLETED URANIUM AMMUNITION

The laws of armed conflict have evolved over the centuries to place limits on warfare. As the principle of state sovereignty suggests, states are free to do anything that is not prohibited by international law[152] and, so, are free to employ any arms that are not subject to prohibition in international law. However, limits on warfare are as old as war itself. Where early weapons prohibitions were based on chivalrous or honourable courtesies between combatants, later developments have been based on balancing military necessity with humanity concerns. In particular, with technological developments in weaponry also came pressure for limitation due to their often cruel and inhumane effects.

---

[150] *Depleted Uranium in Serbia, supra* note 61 at 9–10.

[151] *Depleted Uranium in Kosovo, supra* note 28 at 35. Here none of the cow's milk tested showed depleted uranium contamination.

[152] *Lotus Case (France v. Turkey)* (1927), P.C.I.J. (Ser. A) No. 10 at 239.

Today, the laws governing weapons limitations tend to take two forms, either qualitative limitations or quantitative limitations.[153] The most successful of these methods has been qualitative limits, such as those imposed on poisons and exploding bullets — the subject of specific treaty prohibition in the 1868 St. Petersburg Declaration Renouncing the Use, in Time of War, of Explosive Projectiles under 400 Grammes Weight (St. Petersburg Declaration).[154] Aside from such instruments creating prohibitions for specific weapons, states also began to draft more general rules in the form of military codes of conduct. The 1863 Lieber Code[155] represents one of the first attempts to establish such a code and to recognize and write down the rules already in existence. In this case, the code was written for the US army fighting the American Civil War, but was quickly followed in Europe.[156] The principles contained in these codes formed the basis of the Final Act of the 1899 International Peace Conference (Hague Convention (II) with Respect to the Laws and Customs of War on Land and its Annex: Regulations Concerning the Laws and Customs of War on Land Hague).[157] Such

---

153 D.F. Vaghts, "The Hague Peace Conferences: The Hague Conventions and Arms Control" (2000) 94 Am. J. Int'l L. 31.

154 1868 St. Petersburg Declaration Renouncing the Use, in Time of War, of Explosive Projectiles under 400 Grammes Weight, 11 December 1868, (1907) 1 Am. J. Int'l L. 95 at Supplement (entered into force 11 December 1868) [St. Petersburg Declaration]. See also D. Schindler and J. Toman, *The Laws of Armed Conflicts: A Collection of Conventions, Resolutions and Other Documents* (Leiden: Martinus Nijhoff, 2004) at 91. Invented by the Russian military, the bullet would explode and shatter on contact with a soft target.

155 1863 Lieber Code, reprinted in R. Shelly Hartigan, *Lieber's Code and the Law of War* (Chicago: Precedent Press, 1983).

156 1874 Project of an International Declaration Concerning the Laws and Customs of War, adopted by the Conference of Brussels, 27 August 1874, (1907) 1 Am. J. Int'l L. 1 at Supplement (not yet entered into force) [1874 Brussels Declaration]. The declaration was not ratified in binding form, but the Institute of International Law later adopted the text as the 1880 *Oxford Manual of the Laws and Customs of War: The Laws of War on Land* (No. 3), which was adopted by the Institute of International Law, Oxford, 9 September 1880; originally written in French, an English translation is available at <http://www.icrc.org/ihl.nsf> (3 April 2004) (No. 3). Both instruments would form the basis of a new convention in 1899.

157 1899 Hague Convention (II) with Respect to the Laws and Customs of War on Land and Its Annex: Regulations Concerning the Laws and Customs of War on Land, 29 July 1899, 26 Martens Nouveau Recueil (Ser. 2) 949 (entered into force 4 September 1900) [1899 Hague Convention II].

rule-making would be followed during the second Hague Conference,[158] which was convened in 1907 and again in Geneva in 1949[159]
and in 1977.[160]

In addition to the Final Act, states at the 1899 Hague Conference adopted a number of instruments — similar in sentiment to
those adopted in St. Petersburg in 1868 — imposing new qualitative prohibitions on certain weaponry. The first prohibited the use
of projectiles diffusing asphyxiating gases,[161] and the second prohibited the so-called "dum dum" bullet — a small-calibre bullet
configured to expand on impact with soft targets.[162] It is these early
limits, and the principle of weapons limitation that they enshrine,
that became the cornerstone of modern legal limits on weaponry
in warfare.

Possibly the most important of the principles codified in these
early documents is that governing the limitation of arms during
conflict, which is found in Article 12 of the Brussels Final Act of
1874[163] and Article 22 of the 1899 Hague Convention II.[164] Simply
phrased, the rule stipulates that war cannot be fought with any and
every means available, and it has been formally recognized as a
rule of customary international law since the International Military
Tribunal in The Hague declared it so in 1946.[165] Most recently, the
customary principle of limitation was stated in Article 35(1) of the
1977 Geneva Protocol I,[166] directing that "[i]n any armed conflict,

---

[158] 1907 Hague Convention IV, *supra* note 8.

[159] Geneva Conventions I–IV, *supra* note 10.

[160] Geneva Protocol I and Geneva Protocol II, *supra* note 11.

[161] Hague Declaration (IV, 2) Concerning Asphyxiating Gases, 29 July 1899, (1907)
1 Am. J. Int'l L. 157 at Supplement (entered into force 4 September 1900).

[162] Hague Declaration (IV, 3) Concerning Expanding Bullets, 29 July 1899, (1907)
U.K.T.S. 32, Cd. 3751 (entered into force 4 September 1900) [Hague Declaration IV]. The bullet was manufactured by the British in Calcutta to face a very
specific target — the toughened fighters of Afghanistan. See B.M. Carnahan,
"Unnecessary Suffering: The Red Cross and Tactical Laser Weapons" (1996)
18 Loy. L.A. Int'l & Comp. L.J. 705 at 718–21.

[163] 1874 Brussels Declaration, *supra* note 156.

[164] 1899 Hague Convention II, *supra* note 157. See also Article 22 of 1907 Hague
Convention IV, *supra* note 8.

[165] *1946 Judgment of the International Military Tribunal at Nuremberg*, Trial of the Major War Criminals before the International Military Tribunal, vol. XXII (Nuremberg: International Military Tribunal Secretariat, 1948) at 497.

[166] 1977 Geneva Protocol I, *supra* note 11.

the right of the Parties to the conflict to choose methods or means of warfare is not unlimited." As a result, the means used to wage war are not without limitation. As was seen in the Russian-sponsored prohibition of exploding bullets, the military self-interest[167] and notions of humane treatment — or humanity[168] — often coincide.

Consequently, a weapon may be subject to a specifically agreed prohibition or limitation. Following the early prohibitions created in St. Petersburg and during the 1899 Hague conferences, states met in Geneva in 1925 to prohibit the use of gas warfare[169] and following the Vietnam conflict to prohibit the use of environmental forces as weapons.[170] Finally in 1980, states meeting in Geneva adopted a framework treaty to place limits on certain existing and emerging conventional weapons.[171] The subject of the 1980 Conventional Weapons Convention would be those weapons that states deemed to be excessively injurious or to have indiscriminate effects. These two principles are now fundamental in humanitarian law and represent the second method by which a weapon may violate international humanitarian laws. The prohibition against weapons designed to cause unnecessary suffering (excessively injurious) developed as a consequence of the earlier specific treaty prohibitions, particularly the language of the St. Petersburg Declaration and the 1899 Hague Convention II. The principle of distinction (indiscriminate effects) has its roots in the long-established practice of non-combatant immunity and requires military forces to target their actions only at the enemy military, avoiding harm to the civilian population.[172] Both principles form part of customary

---

167 For a detailed analysis of military self-interest as it evolved from early Greek warfare to Napoleonic times and the twentieth century, see M. Howard, G.J. Andreopoulos, and M.R. Shulman, *The Laws of War: Constraints on Warfare in the Western World* (London: Yale University Press, 1994) at 13. Also worthy is J. Turner Johnson, *Just War Tradition and the Restraint of War* (Guildford: Princeton University Press, 1981) at 297.

168 See the philosophy of Hugo Grotius, in H. Bull, B. Kingsbury, and A. Roberts, *Hugo Grotius and International Relations* (Oxford: Clarendon Press, 1992); and the Martens Clause in the 1899 Hague Convention II, *supra* note 157.

169 1925 Geneva Gas Protocol, *supra* note 9.

170 1977 United Nations Convention on the Prohibition of Military or Any Other Hostile Use of Environmental Modification Techniques, 18 May 1977, (1977) 16 I.L.M. 88–94 (entered into force 5 October 1978) [Environmental Modification Convention].

171 1980 Conventional Weapons Convention, *supra* note 16.

172 W.L. LaCroix, *War and the International Ethics: Tradition and Today* (Lanham: University Press of America, 1988) at 69; and Johnson, *supra* note 167 at 133–9.

international law and, together with the principle of proportionality in force and effects,[173] place limits on the design and use of weapons and tactics in warfare.

In this part, therefore, the legality of the use of depleted uranium ammunition will be analyzed according to (1) any existing or analogous treaty prohibition or limitation specifically created for depleted uranium ammunition; (2) the customary prohibition on weapons causing unnecessary suffering; (3) the customary principle of distinction; (4) the treaty protections afforded the environment in times of armed conflict;[174] and (5) the principle of proportionality. The environmental provisions emerged as a consequence of the US tactics in Vietnam, the possibility of nuclear warfare, and a new found awareness of environmental damage. Given the potential for environmental harm that depleted uranium ammunition presents, the efficacy of the environmental protection provisions may be well tested.

TREATY-SPECIFIC PROHIBITION OR LIMITATION ON USE

Depleted Uranium

There has been no treaty enacted that specifically outlaws the use in armed conflict of depleted uranium weapons. There is, furthermore, no treaty limiting the use, specifically, of depleted uranium weapons.

Other Analogous Weapons

Due to the characteristics of depleted uranium weapons, it may be the case that these weapons are subject to prohibition, or at least limitation, under existing rules governing other weaponry. In the case of depleted uranium, the closest analogous weapons in terms of the health and environmental effects would be chemical or nuclear weapons. The question, therefore, is whether these

---

173 The principle of proportionality is a customary rule, first being incorporated in the 1863 Lieber Code, *supra* note 155, which stipulates that "[m]ilitary necessity admits of all direct destruction of life or limb of armed enemies, and of other persons whose destruction is *incidentally unavoidable* in the armed contests of war" [emphasis added]. The latest treaty provision is included in Article 51(5)(b) of Geneva Protocol I, *supra* note 11.

174 Articles 35(3) and 55 of Geneva Protocol I, *ibid.* For a similar statement regarding the assessment of legality for nuclear weapons, see the *Case Concerning the Legality of the Threat or Use of Nuclear Weapons*, 8 July 1996, (1996) 35 I.L.M. 809 at para. 105(2)(D) [*Nuclear Weapons*].

other specific weapon regimes also govern the legality of depleted uranium weapons.

Analogy with Nuclear Weapons

Depleted uranium is a radiologically and chemically toxic substance. Therefore, the closest analogous weapon may be nuclear weapons. However, what is a "nuclear weapon"? And even if depleted uranium falls within the nuclear regime, does this fact automatically lead to a ban? According to the United Nations General Assembly in its 1961 Declaration on the Prohibition of the Use of Nuclear and Thermo-Nuclear Weapons,[175] "[a]ny State using nuclear and thermo-nuclear weapons is to be considered as violating the Charter of the United Nations, as acting contrary to the laws of humanity and as committing a crime against mankind and civilization." Again in Resolution 2936 of 1972, the UN General Assembly "[s]olemnly declares, on behalf of the States members of the Organization, their renunciation of the use or threat of force in all its forms and manifestations in international relations, in accordance with the Charter of the United Nations, and the *permanent prohibition of the use of nuclear weapons.*"[176]

Despite efforts by the UN General Assembly, however, there is no global treaty that specifically prohibits the use of nuclear weapons. Such weapons are unlike chemical and biological weapons in this regard.[177] There are two major instruments in the field of nuclear

175 See General Assembly Resolution 1653 (XVI), 24 November 1961, at para. 1(d), reproduced in *Resolutions Adopted by the General Assembly during its Sixteenth Session*, Volume 1, 19 September 1961–23 February 1962, General Assembly Official Records: Sixteenth Session, Supplement no. 17 (A/5100) (New York: United Nations, 1962) at 4. The resolution was adopted by fifty-five votes to twenty, with twenty-six abstentions.

176 See General Assembly Resolution 2936 (XXVII), 29 November 1972, at para. 1, reproduced in *Resolutions Adopted by the General Assembly during its Twenty-seventh Session*, 19 September–19 December 1972, General Assembly Official Records: Twenty-Seventh Session, Supplement No. 30 (A/8730) (New York: United Nations, 1973) at 5. The resolution was adopted by seventy-three votes to four, with forty-six abstentions.

177 1993 Convention on the Prohibition of the Development, Production, Stockpiling and Use of Chemical Weapons and on Their Destruction, 13 January 1993, (1993) 32 I.L.M. 800 (entered into force 29 April 1997) [Chemical Weapons Convention]; and 1972 Convention on the Prohibition and Development, Production and Stockpiling of Bacteriological (Biological) and Toxin Weapons and Their Destruction, 10 April 1971, (1972) 11 I.L.M. 309 (entered into force 28 March 1975).

weapons, but they do not amount to an absolute ban on use. These two instruments instead focus on the production, or proliferation, and testing of nuclear weapons: the 1967 Treaty on the Non-Proliferation of Nuclear Weapons (Non-Proliferation Treaty)[178] and the 1996 Comprehensive Test Ban Treaty.[179] The aim of the Non-Proliferation Treaty is to ensure that the existing nuclear powers do not transfer nuclear weapons to other non-nuclear powers — the ultimate goal being absolute disarmament of nuclear weapons. However, the five original nuclear weapons states have extended their obligations under the treaty, each declaring the non-use of nuclear weapons against a non-nuclear state party to the Non-Proliferation Treaty, albeit with certain conditions. The statement by the United Kingdom reads as follows:

The United Kingdom will not use nuclear weapons against non-nuclear-weapon States parties to the Treaty on the Non-Proliferation of Nuclear Weapons except in the case of an invasion or any other attack on the United Kingdom, its dependent territories, its armed forces or other troops, its allies or on a State towards which it has a security commitment, carried out or sustained by such non-nuclear-weapon State in association or alliance with a nuclear-weapon State.[180]

The statement by China is slightly different, declaring an absolute ban on first use under any circumstances and undertaking not

---

[178] 1968 Treaty on the Non-Proliferation of Nuclear Weapons, 1 July 1968, 729 U.N.T.S. 161 (entered into force 5 March 1970). Despite the twenty-five-year clause in the original treaty, state parties met in 1995 and voted to extend the applicability of the treaty indefinitely.

[179] 1996 Comprehensive Test Ban Treaty, 24 September 1996, (1996) 35 I.L.M. 1443 (not yet entered into force). The treaty has some 135 ratifications in 2006, but will not enter into force until all of the states listed in Annex II to the treaty have ratified. The following states are missing from the list, the United States and China, and nuclear weapon states Pakistan, North Korea, and India, plus Colombia, Egypt, Indonesia, Iran, and Israel.

[180] Letter dated 21 April 1995 from the Head of the Delegation of the United Kingdom of Great Britain and Northern Ireland Addressed to the Secretary-General of the 1995 Review and Extension Conference of the Parties to the Treaty on the Non-Proliferation of Nuclear Weapons, New York, Doc. NPT/CONF.1995/24 (21 April 1995). The court in the *Nuclear Weapons* advisory opinion highlighted the fact that the nuclear weapons states had, in these declarations, reserved the right to use nuclear weapons in certain circumstances without objection by other states. Thus, the court concluded that there was no customary or treaty law prohibiting nuclear weapons. See *Nuclear Weapons*, *supra* note 174 at para. 62.

to use or threaten to use nuclear weapons against non-nuclear weapon states or nuclear weapon-free zones at any time or under any circumstances.[181] On the other hand, the 1996 Comprehensive Test Ban Treaty prohibits absolutely the testing of nuclear weapons, but it has yet to enter into force. Previous attempts have only produced a partial test ban in regard to explosions in the atmosphere, underwater, and in space and have failed to secure French and Chinese acceptance.[182] There is, however, no definition of "nuclear weapons" or "nuclear explosions" in either treaty.

In addition, there have been a number of treaties adopted at the regional level. Unlike any other weapon, the nuclear weapons regime attempts to limit ownership of these weapons to a handful of states — the so-called nuclear states, comprising the United States, the United Kingdom, France, China, and Russia. While a number of other states have acquired nuclear weapons in recent years, the global emphasis to date has been on the maintenance of the *status quo*. As a consequence, there are whole regions that do not possess nuclear weapons, many of which have adopted regional nuclear non-proliferation treaties. One such treaty is the Treaty for the Prohibition of Nuclear Weapons in Latin America and the Caribbean (Latin American Nuclear-Free Zone Treaty).[183] The Latin American Nuclear-Free Zone Treaty achieves two things: a definition of "nuclear weapons" and a prohibition on use. With respect to the second issue first, the treaty does include an obligation on state parties not to use or threaten the use of nuclear weapons against other state parties.[184] As a result, it is a mutual non-use pact. Due to the signature of the five nuclear states, however, it has evolved into a non-use treaty among the Latin American and five nuclear states

---

181 Letter dated 25 April 1995 from the Permanent Representative of the People's Republic of China to the United Nations and Deputy Head of the Chinese Delegation Addressed to the Secretary-General of the 1995 Review and Extension Conference of the Parties to the Treaty on the Non-Proliferation of Nuclear Weapons, New York, Doc. NPT/CONF.1995/26 (27 April 1995).

182 1963 Treaty Banning Nuclear Weapons Tests in the Atmosphere, in Outer Space and Under Water, 5 August 1963, (1963) 480 U.N.T.S. 43 (entered into force 10 October 1963) [Partial Test Ban Treaty].

183 Treaty for the Prohibition of Nuclear Weapons in Latin America and the Caribbean, 14 February 1967, (1967) 6 I.L.M. 521 (entered into force 22 April 1968) [Latin American Nuclear-Free Zone Treaty].

184 Additional Protocol II to the Treaty for the Prohibition of Nuclear Weapons in Latin America, in *ibid.*

inter se.[185] One caveat included by the United States concerns the situation where, in an armed attack by a contracting state, assistance is given to that state by a nuclear weapon state.[186] Similar obligations are also included within the other regional regimes governing the South Pacific, African, and southeast Asian regions and Mongolia.[187] As a consequence, much of the world is treaty-bound not to use nuclear weapons. However, it is certainly not a global treaty system and does not include the very many new (and suspected) nuclear weapon states, including Israel, Pakistan, India, South Africa, Iran, and North Korea.

According to the Latin American Nuclear-Free Zone Treaty, "nuclear weapon" means "any device which is capable of releasing nuclear energy in an uncontrolled manner and which has a group of characteristics that are appropriate for use for warlike purposes."[188] Nuclear energy is usually caused by nuclear fission or fusion. Yet, again, there is no definition and no indication of what an "uncontrolled" manner might include or exclude. However, it is of little immediate concern since depleted uranium weapons are certainly not capable of an atomic chain reaction and, hence, do not fall within the definition. Consequently, depleted uranium weapons are not generally considered to be nuclear weapons in any sense of this term and do not appear to fall within any of the disarmament treaties for nuclear weapons. Even if it were a nuclear weapon, its use could still be lawful since there is no specific treaty prohibiting it. As a consequence, and despite previous resolutions of the UN

185 The signatory states are Antigua and Barbuda, Argentina, Bahamas, Barbados, Belize, Bolivia, Brazil, Chile, Colombia, Costa Rica, Cuba, Dominica, Dominican Republic, Ecuador, El Salvador, Grenada, Guatemala, Guyana, Haiti, Honduras, Jamaica, Mexico, Nicaragua, Panama, Paraguay, Peru, St. Kitts and Nevis, St. Lucia, St. Vincent/Grenadines, Suriname, Trinidad and Tobago, Uruguay, and Venezuela.

186 See Proclamation by President Nixon on Ratification of Additional Protocol II to the Treaty for the Prohibition of Nuclear Weapons in Latin America, 11 June 1971, available at <http://www.state.gov/t/ac/trt/4796.htm> (12 September 2005) at para. I.

187 1985 South Pacific Nuclear Free Zone Treaty, 6 August 1985, (1988) 24 I.L.M. 142 (entered into force 11 December 1986) [South Pacific Nuclear-Free Zone Treaty]; 1996 African Nuclear Weapon-Free Zone Treaty, 11 September 1996, (1996) 35 I.L.M. 698 (not yet entered into force) (so far the treaty has only eighteen out of the twenty-eight ratifications needed) [African Nuclear Weapon-Free Zone Treaty]; and 1996 Treaty on Southeast Asia Nuclear Weapon-Free Zone, 15 December 1995, (1996) 35 I.L.M. 698 (entered into force 27 March 1997) [Southeast Asia Nuclear Weapon-Free Zone].

188 Latin American Nuclear-Free Zone Treaty, *supra* note 183, Article 5.

General Assembly, which have declared that "the use of nuclear weapons would be a violation of the Charter and a crime against humanity,"[189] the International Court of Justice (ICJ) in its 1996 advisory opinion was forced to conclude that the use of nuclear weapons would not always be unlawful.[190] By a majority of eleven votes to three, the court concluded that "[t]here is neither in customary nor conventional international law any comprehensive and universal prohibition of the threat or use of nuclear weapons as such."[191]

Although not involving a nuclear reaction, one aspect of nuclear weaponry, however, accompanies the use of depleted uranium — the release of radioactive material. In the 1963 Treaty Banning Nuclear Weapons Tests in the Atmosphere, in Outer Space and Under Water,[192] the preamble stipulates the desire of states to "put an end to the contamination of man's environment by radioactive substances." This mandate is again a feature of the nuclear-free zone treaties for the South Pacific, African, and southeast Asian regions,[193] which refer in their respective preambles to "keep the [region] free of environmental pollution by radioactive wastes and other radioactive matter." The use of depleted uranium weaponry, therefore, by state parties would appear to be in clear violation of the treaty objectives. On the other hand, there is no mention specifically of depleted uranium weapons, and the only reference to a prohibition on the use of weapons is in regard to nuclear weapons.

Analogy with Chemical Weapons and Poisons

So-called chemical weapons are similar to depleted uranium weaponry in that both types of weapons have chemically toxic effects. Chemical weapons have a lengthier battle history than nuclear

---

189 See UNGA Resolutions, 1653 (XVI), 24 November 1961, Doc. 33/71 B of 14 December 1978, Doc. 34/83 G of 11 December 1979, Doc. 35/152 D of 12 December 1980, Doc. 36/92 1 of 9 December 1981, Doc. 45/59 B of 4 December 1990, and Doc. 46/37 D of 6 December 1991.

190 *Nuclear Weapons*, Advisory Opinion, *supra* note 174. The conclusion reached by the court and its lack of application of legal norms in a logically coherent way have attracted considerable criticism. For example, see M.N. Schmitt, "The International Court of Justice and the Use of Nuclear Weapons" (1996/7) 7 USAFA J. Leg. Stud. 57.

191 *Ibid.* at para. 105(2)B.

192 Partial Test Ban Treaty, *supra* note 182.

193 South Pacific Nuclear-Free Zone Treaty, *supra* note 187; African Nuclear Weapon-Free Zone Treaty, *supra* note 187; and Southeast Asia Nuclear Weapon-Free Zone, *supra* note 187.

weapons (discussed earlier), and, as a consequence of their devastating effects, their use is absolutely banned. The road to prohibition of chemical weapons began with the recognition of the cruel effects of poison. Poisoning the enemy chief or leader historically was a valuable military strategy. Often, the elimination of the enemy's leader from the equation would result in their defeat. Yet poisons and similar tactics, such as polluting rivers with diseased animals (early forms of bio-warfare), were also often used in siege situations and against the civilian population to deny them clean water.[194] The prohibition on the use of poison arrows dates back centuries[195] and, in the modern era, was first codified in the 1863 Lieber Code at Principle 16, such that "military necessity ... does not admit of the use of poison in anyway."[196]

Although the earliest prohibitions concerned the use of poisonous weapons only, other harmful effects of such weapons were later recognized. For example, the 1899 First Hague Peace Conference[197] was concerned with both poisons and other asphyxiating or deleterious gases. Of the six instruments (three conventions and three declarations) adopted by the twenty-six delegations present, two of those texts included reference to the prohibition. The prohibition on poisons, viewed as forming part of customary international law at this point, was codified in Article 23(a) of the 1899 Hague Convention II.[198] As a slight extension of the poisons prohibition, the Declaration (2) Concerning Asphyxiating Gases of 1899[199] recognizes a prohibition on "*projectiles* the sole object of which is the diffusion of asphyxiating or deleterious gases."[200] Again, the treaty prohibition on poisons was reiterated in Article 23(a) of the 1907

---

194 Apparently the 1988 Yugoslavian military manual contains a provision allowing for the poisoning of drinking water and food if it is announced or marked. See Henkaerts and Doswald-Beck, *supra* note 14 at volume I, chapter 23, p. 253 and Volume II, Chapter 21, para. 52.

195 L.C. Green, "What One May Do in Combat: Then and Now," in A. Delissen and G. Tanja, eds., *Humanitarian Law of Armed Conflict: Challenges Ahead, Essays in Honour of Frits Kalshoven* (London: Martinus Nijhoff, 1991) at 269.

196 Lieber's Code and the Law of War, *supra* note 155. A similar provision was then included within the 1874 Brussels Declaration, *supra* note 156, which influenced the text of the 1899 Hague Convention II, *supra* note 157. Consequently, Article 13(a) prohibited the employment of poison or poisoned weapons.

197 1899 Hague Convention II, *supra* note 157. See also Vaghts, *supra* note 153.

198 1899 Hague Convention II, *supra* note 157.

199 1899 Declaration (IV, 2) Concerning Asphyxiating Gases, *supra* note 161.

200 [Emphasis added]. *Ibid.*

Convention (IV) Respecting the Laws and Customs of War on Land,[201] but a treaty prohibition on asphyxiating gases was not achieved until 1925.

Despite such provision, states nevertheless resorted to gas warfare during the First World War. For example, in one incident in Ypres, Belgium, five thousand French soldiers were killed by chlorine gas in a single afternoon.[202] Despite flagrant violation by states during the war, in the peace settlements that followed, states maintained the position that poisonous weapons were "illegal."[203] Finally, in 1925, a broader treaty was negotiated under the auspices of the League of Nations, namely the 1925 Geneva Gas Protocol,[204] which restated and expanded the prior customary and treaty prohibitions on poisonous gas warfare. Still in force, the 1925 Geneva Gas Protocol prohibits the use in international armed conflict of "asphyxiating, poisonous or other/similar gases and of all analogous liquids materials or devices."[205] State practice appears to suggest that the protocol forms part of customary international law. Albeit, due to reservations, it may be that the customary rule is one forbidding first use.[206] There is some suggestion that depleted uranium would fall within these prohibitions on the use of poisons or the broader category of "analogous materials." A similar suggestion defining nuclear weapons as "poison" was examined by the ICJ in its 1996 advisory opinion in the *Case Concerning the Legality of the Threat or Use of Nuclear Weapons*.[207] Interpreting the treaty text,

---

[201] Hague Convention IV, *supra* note 8. The convention is generally taken to be customary law. See 1946 *Judgment of the International Military Tribunal at Nuremberg, supra* note 165 at 497.

[202] J. Smolowe, "Return of the Silent Killer," *Time*, 22 August 1988, at 26.

[203] 1919 Treaty of Versailles, 28 June 1919, available at <http://history.acusd.edu/gen/text/versaillestreaty/vercontents.html> (10 June 2002), Article 171.

[204] Geneva Gas Protocol, *supra* note 9.

[205] *Ibid.* Here, both the English text is referred to — "other" — and the French text — "similaires." Both texts are authoritative. Many reservations were attached to the treaty to ensure that it applied only between states. See, for example, the reservation of Iraq.

[206] There are 139 state parties to the treaty in 2005, which has been widely adopted in the instruments of the Security Council and General Assembly. See, for example, General Assembly Resolution 3465 (XXX), Chemical and Bacteriological Weapons, 11 December 1975, 2437th Plenary Meeting, where the UN General Assembly "reaffirms the necessity of strict observance by all states of the principles and objectives of that Protocol."

[207] *Nuclear Weapons, supra* note 174.

the majority of the court decided that state practice did not support such an interpretation of the term "poisons."[208] Clearly, such earlier prohibitions were more concerned with the direct use of poisoned weapons or poison gas on the enemy than with the side effects of such weapons on health and the environment. In her statement to the court in the *Nuclear Weapons* case, the United Kingdom commented that treaty provisions prohibiting poison "were intended to apply to weapons whose primary effect was poisonous and not to those where poison was a secondary or incidental effect."[209] It would appear, therefore, to be extending the treaty text too far to suggest that depleted uranium ammunition — even if its effects could be described as being poisonous — would fall within the 1925 prohibition.

Finally, in 1993, the comprehensive Convention on the Prohibition of the Development, Production, Stockpiling and Use of Chemical Weapons and on Their Destruction (Chemical Weapons Convention)[210] was adopted and, with it, a definition of the concept of "chemical weapons." The 1993 Chemical Weapons Convention makes no distinction as to the level of conflict (international or internal) and contains an absolute prohibition on the use of chemical weapons "in all circumstances."[211] The phrase "all circumstances" imposes the treaty prohibition even against non-parties, whether in attack or defence — for example, where the enemy use chemical weapons — and in situations of internal armed conflict.[212] The convention is probably as comprehensive as it is possible to be. It includes an absolute prohibition on the development, production, and stockpiling of chemical weapons,[213] since if use is absolutely prohibited there is no need to own or develop such weapons. Furthermore, it includes a specific prohibition on any assistance, encouragement, or inducement of others in such prohibited

---

208 *Ibid.* at paras. 54–56. See also the dissenting opinion of Judge Koroma at 933.

209 *Advisory Proceedings on the Legality of the Threat or Use of Nuclear Weapons* (Question Posed by the General Assembly): Written Observations on the Request by the General Assembly for an Advisory Opinion Government of the United Kingdom, 16 June 1995, available at <http://www.icj-cij.org/icjwww/icases/iunan/iunanframe.htm> (10 September 2002) at para. 3.59–3.60 [*Advisory Proceeding on Nuclear Weapons*].

210 Chemical Weapons Convention, *supra* note 177.

211 *Ibid.*, Article I(1)).

212 *Ibid.*, Article I(1)(b).

213 *Ibid.*, Article I(1)(a).

activities[214] and a clear obligation on state parties of non-proliferation to non-state actors. Adherence to convention obligations is monitored by a comprehensive system of verification by on-site inspections.[215] Finally, as of 2005, the convention boasts some 169 state parties and so has secured widespread acceptance in the international community.[216]

As a consequence of the foregoing, if depleted uranium weapons were to fall within the 1993 Chemical Weapons Convention, not only their use but also their production, transfer, and stockpiling would be absolutely prohibited. The question, therefore, is whether the definition of chemical weapons is sufficiently wide enough to incorporate depleted uranium weaponry. According to Article II(1),

"Chemical Weapons" means the following, together or separately:

(a) Toxic chemicals and their precursors, *except where intended for purposes not prohibited under this Convention,* as long as the types and quantities are consistent with such purposes;

(b) Munitions and devices, *specifically designed* to cause death or other harm *through the toxic properties* of those toxic chemicals specified in subparagraph (a), which would be released as a result of the employment of such munitions and devices;

(c) Any equipment specifically designed for use directly in connection with the employment of munitions and devices specified in subparagraph (b) [emphasis added].

Consequently, a key component of the definition of chemical weapons is that of toxicity. A definition of toxicity ("toxic chemical") is provided by the convention:

Any chemical which *through its chemical action* on life processes can cause death, temporary incapacitation or permanent harm to humans or animals. This includes all such chemicals, regardless of their origin or of their method of production, and regardless of whether they are produced in facilities, in munitions or elsewhere."[217]

---

214 *Ibid.*, Article I(1)(d).

215 *Ibid.*, Article IX.

216 Not including the Holy See.

217 Chemical Weapons Convention, *supra* note 177, Article II(2) [emphasis added]. See also the Annex on Chemicals for the guidelines on including chemicals in the schedules.

The Annex on Chemicals to the convention includes within the schedules on toxic chemicals such infamous substances as sarin, soman, tabun, mustard gas, ricin, hydrogen cyanide, and phosgene. Further assistance is given by a set of guidelines for scheduling a substance. The guidelines refer to a number of criteria to be taken into account, which include that

- it has been developed, produced, stockpiled, or used as a chemical weapon as defined in Article II;
- it poses a significant risk to the object and purpose of this convention because it possesses such lethal or incapacitating toxicity as well as other properties that could enable it to be used as a chemical weapon;
- it has little or no use for purposes not prohibited under the convention; and
- it is not produced in large commercial quantities for purposes not prohibited under this convention.

It is clear that depleted uranium is not listed as a toxic chemical in the annex and, arguably, does not appear to fall within the criteria for listing. Some would disagree with this last assessment, however, and might suggest that the use of depleted uranium weaponry would fall within paragraph (2) due to its toxic properties. In light of all of the scientific research to date, this author does not believe that depleted uranium weapons could be brought within the phrase "such lethal or incapacitating toxicity" for paragraph (2).

While important, toxicity is clearly not the only component in the definition of "chemical weapons." The definition also requires a particular purpose or intent. While this is hinted at in paragraph (a) of the earlier-mentioned definition, it becomes much clearer in paragraph (b), which refers to a specific design to cause harm through the toxic properties of the chemical, in effect, utilizing that toxic property as the means of destruction. This language has been used previously by the UN General Assembly when, in 1966, it adopted several resolutions calling for adherence to the 1925 Geneva Gas Protocol.[218] Interpreting the obligations under the 1925 treaty, the

---

[218] See "Question of Chemical and Bacteriological Weapons," UN General Assembly Resolution 2603A (XXIV), 16 December 1969, 1836th Plenary Meeting, reprinted in *Resolutions Adopted by the General Assembly during its Twenty-Fourth Session*, 16 September — 17 December 1969. General Assembly Official Records: Twenty-fourth Session Supplement No. 30 (A/7630) (New York: United Nations, 1970); and the 1925 Geneva Gas Protocol, *supra* note 9.

UN General Assembly declared its prohibition to include "[a]ny chemical agents of warfare — chemical substances, whether gaseous, liquid or solid — which might be employed because of their *direct* toxic effects on man, animals or plants."[219] This was of course a pointed response to the American use of herbicides in the Vietnam conflict, but the reference indicates a *direct* link between the weapon's nature and effect. Such a connection was also recognized by the ICJ in the 1996 *Nuclear Weapons* case,[220] which noted that "the terms [poison, analogous materials] have been understood, in the practice of States, in their ordinary sense as covering weapons whose *prime, or even exclusive, effect* is to poison or asphyxiate."[221] Similarly, a leading commentary on the definition of the term "chemical weapons" also refers to the intention to use the toxicity of the chemical as the "*predominant* weapons effect."[222] And while the use of depleted uranium in anti-armour ammunition may cause these side effects, they are certainly not the primary reason for using this kind of weapon. As a consequence, the analogy between depleted uranium weapons and chemical weapons falls down on both grounds. Therefore, it does not appear to be the case that depleted uranium weaponry is regulated or prohibited by the chemical weapons regime.

LIMITATION BY OTHER RULES OR PRINCIPLES OF
HUMANITARIAN LAW

In the previous section, it was concluded that depleted uranium ammunition is not subject to a specific treaty prohibition on use. In this section, the legality of the use of depleted uranium ammunition will be assessed according to customary principles of humanitarian law, namely the prohibition on causing unnecessary suffering and the principle of distinction. Depleted uranium ammunition has the potential to create problems for human health and the environment both at the point of use as well as post-conflict and on both the civilian population and the military. Therefore, it may well be the case that existing principles of humanitarian law may place limits on the use of this ammunition.

---

219 [Emphasis added]. UN General Assembly Resolution 2603A, reprinted in *Resolutions Adopted by the General Assembly during its Twenty-Fourth Session, supra* note 218 at 16.

220 *Nuclear Weapons, supra* note 174.

221 [Emphasis added]. *Ibid.* at para. 55.

222 [Emphasis added]. See W. Krutzsch and R. Trapp, *A Commentary on the Chemical Weapons Convention* (London: Martinus Nijhoff, 1994) at 25.

Prohibition on Means of Warfare Causing Unnecessary Suffering

The principal aim of warfare is to *weaken* the military forces of the enemy.[223] It is inherently recognized, therefore, within the laws of armed conflict that combatants may harm, disable, and even kill enemy combatants, provided that this action is achieved by using lawful weapons and tactics of warfare. What is not permitted is the use of a weapon that causes suffering or injury superfluous to the requirements of military necessity.

The prohibition on weapons that cause unnecessary suffering evolved from early weapons prohibitions in the late 1800s as states realized that they could not legislate for all technical weapons developments in the future.[224] Ways would be found to circumvent the specific weight limitations on explosive bullets in the 1868 St. Petersburg Declaration[225] and the prohibited design characteristics of expanding bullets in the 1899 Hague Declaration (IV, 3) Concerning Expanding Bullets.[226] As a result of this recognition and Article 16 of the Lieber Code[227] excluding cruelty from the principle of military necessity, states included within the St. Petersburg Declaration the following prohibition on the "employment of arms which uselessly aggravate the sufferings of disabled men, or render their death inevitable."[228] The provision was later included in Article 23(a) of the 1899 Hague Convention II[229] and has consistently been included within treaty law governing armed conflict ever since. Today, the principle undoubtedly forms part of customary international law and is absolute in application.[230] Although not adopted in the final text of Geneva Protocol II, it was not because states found it objectionable.[231] The principle is included at

---

[223] 1868 St. Petersburg Declaration, *supra* note 154.

[224] Vaghts, *supra* note 153 at 35.

[225] 1868 St. Petersburg Declaration, *supra* note 154.

[226] 1899 Hague Declaration (IV), *supra* note 162.

[227] Lieber's Code and the Law of War, *supra* note 155.

[228] 1868 St. Petersburg Declaration, *supra* note 154.

[229] 1899 Hague Convention II, *supra* note 157. See also 1907 Hague Convention IV, *supra* note 8, Article 23(e).

[230] Henkaerts and Doswald-Beck, *supra* note 14 at volume I, chapter 20, pp. 237–44, and Volume II, Chapter 20, Section A, at paras. 1–126. There is no similar provision in Geneva Protocol II, *supra* note 11.

[231] Despite earlier inclusion, the draft article containing the provision (Draft Article 20(2)) was dropped as part of the package to adopt a simplified text. As

Article 35(2) of Geneva Protocol I, such that "[i]t is prohibited to
employ weapons, projectiles and material and methods of warfare
of a nature to cause superfluous injury or unnecessary suffering."[232]
The inclusion of both terms "unnecessary suffering" and "superfluous injury" in Geneva Protocol I is not intended to refer to two
different tests but is due to translation difficulties from earlier treaties.[233] Unlike late nineteenth-century treaties that focus on the cruel
effects of a particular weapon, more recent practice has been to place
the principle at the heart of the 1980 Conventional Weapons
Convention.[234]

The principle prohibits the causing of suffering or injury that is
unnecessary or superfluous to military needs. And so what is meant
by suffering that is unnecessary or superfluous? Clearly, a degree of
suffering and disablement among combatants is inherent in warfare, and so the principle is not a limit on the amount of injury that
one can cause an enemy combatant — it does not, therefore, prohibit extreme suffering or extensive injuries.[235] What the principle
does prohibit are weapons that cause injury *superfluous to military
needs*. What is deemed *superfluous*, however, is a difficult judgment
to make.

While there is no authoritative definition of the principle in treaty
law, state practice at least evidences a test. It appears to require a
balancing exercise that weighs the calculation of the anticipated
military advantages to be gained from using a particular weapon
against the expected suffering or injury to be caused by its use. In
other words, "the 'necessity' of the suffering must be judged in

---

recognized in the International Commission of the Red Cross (ICRC) study,
there was no objection to inclusion by states to situations of internal armed
conflict at that time, see Henkaerts and Doswald-Beck, *supra* note 14 at volume
I, chapter 20, p. 239.

[232] 1977 Geneva Protocol I, *supra* note 11. The principle can also be found in
Article 8(2)(b)(xx) of the 1998 Rome Statute of the International Criminal
Court, 17 July 1998, (1998) 37 I.L.M. 999 (entered into force 1 July 2002)
[Rome Statute].

[233] Two English translations ("superfluous injury" and "unnecessary sufferings")
were provided for the original French expression "maux superflus" found in
the 1874 Brussels Declaration, *supra* note 156. While the 1899 Hague Convention II, *supra* note 157, preferred the translation of "superfluous injury," the
1907 Hague Convention IV, *supra* note 8, text refers to "unnecessary suffering." To avoid doubt, English treaty texts routinely refer to both.

[234] 1980 Conventional Weapons Convention, *supra* note 16.

[235] Carnahan, *supra* note 162 at 712–13.

relation to the military utility of the weapon."[236] It is not simply, therefore, a question of the subjective suffering of the victim.[237] The application of the principle to the issue of poisoned arrows, for example, is relatively easy to undertake.[238] The arrow will usually be sufficient to disable enemy combatants. The poison, therefore, is superfluous and will only make death inevitable. The poison has no real military purpose other than to kill a combatant already rendered *hors de combat* by the arrow. Similar analyses can also be made for bullets that explode on contact with the human body[239] or those designed to flatten and expand on contact.[240] Such additional anti-personnel effects simply have little military utility once the bullet has contacted with the enemy and he is rendered *hors de combat*. In practice, therefore, international law only forbids the use of weapons that increase suffering without really increasing the military advantage. And, in reality, many such weapons have never been used on the battlefield,[241] including anti-personnel (anti-optic) blinding laser weapons and weapons with non-detectable fragments (such as glass or plastic), which are prohibited under the first and fourth protocols to the 1980 Conventional Weapons Convention respectively.[242] In such cases, legal restrictions were enacted before the weapons had reached the deployment stage, but there

---

[236] As expressed by the United States delegation to the 1974 Conference of Government Experts on Weapons Which May Cause Unnecessary Suffering or Have Indiscriminate Effects (1974 Lucerne Conference), in "Resort to War and Armed Force" (1974) Digest 1 at 707 ["Resort to War"].

[237] In trying to establish universal measuring tools for the principle, the ICRC has created criteria for "unnecessary suffering." Criteria recognized by the authors as breaching the principle include specific disease, specific abnormal physiological state, specific and permanent disability or specific disfigurement. The criteria are not binding however, and have been the subject of heavy criticism. See R.M. Coupland, "The SIrUS Project: Towards a Determination of Which Weapons Cause 'Superfluous Injury or Unnecessary Suffering'," in H. Durham and T.L.H. McCormack, eds., *The Changing Face of Conflict and the Efficacy of International Humanitarian Law* (London: Martinus Nijhoff, 1999), 99.

[238] See the early prohibition on poison and poisoned arrows in the Hindu Laws of Manu, c. 200 BC, in Green, *supra* note 195 at 269.

[239] 1868 St. Petersburg Declaration, *supra* note 154.

[240] 1899 Hague Declaration (IV, 3), *supra* note 162.

[241] Major D.M. Verchio, "Just Say NO! The SIrUS Project: Well-Intentioned, But Unnecessary and Superfluous" (2001) 51 Air Force L. Rev. 183.

[242] Protocol I to the CCW on Non-Detectable Fragments, *supra* note 16; and Protocol IV on Blinding Laser Weapons, *supra* note 16.

was certainly a market for weapons such as blinding lasers and expanding bullets, however small.[243]

Thus, what are the factors included in the balance? The first point to note is that the evaluation is not contingent upon the design of the weapon. Despite the inclusion in some earlier treaties of the notion of a weapon being "calculated to cause" superfluous injury,[244] the evaluation should be carried out not solely on the basis of such design (or objective) but rather on the basis of the weapon's ordinary use.[245] Referring to it as the guiding principle, the United Kingdom, in its 2004 *Manual of the Law of Armed Conflict*, states: "[T]he correct criterion is whether the use of a weapon is of a nature to cause injury or suffering greater than that required for its military purpose."[246] The military manual then continues with the statement that in calculating the "legality of use of a specific weapon, it is necessary to assess;

a. its effects in battle;
b. the military task it is required to perform; and
c. the proportionality between factors (a) and (b)."[247]

The first criticism to be made is that paragraph (a) only refers to the weapons effects in battle. To the untrained eye, this phraseology is not abundantly clear. It may be interpreted as a repetition of paragraph (b), which refers to the military use of the weapon. It is,

---

243 China developed the ZM-87 anti-optic laser in 1995 and began marketing the product abroad. Unlike other laser systems under development, the product appeared to be marketed with the emphasis on its potential for blinding the enemy. See J.H. McCall, "Blinded by the Light: International Law and the Legality of Anti-Optic Laser Weapons" (1997) 30 Cornell Int'l L.J. 1 at 9–11.

244 See 1874 Brussels Declaration, *supra* note 156, Article 13(e); and 1907 Hague Convention IV, *supra* note 8, Article 23(e).

245 For an account of a similar debate at the drafting sessions of the 1998 Rome Statute, *supra* note 232, establishing the International Criminal Court, see R.S. Clark, "Methods of Warfare That Cause Unnecessary Suffering or Are Inherently Indiscriminate: A Memorial Tribute to Howard Berman" (1998) 28 Cal. W. Int'l L.J. 379.

246 United Kingdom Ministry of Defence, *Manual of the Law of Armed Conflict* (Oxford: Oxford University Press, 2004) at 103, quoting M. Bothe, K.J. Partsch, and W.A. Solf, *New Rules for the Victims of Armed Conflicts: Commentary on the Two 1977 Additional Protocols to the Geneva Conventions of 1949* (The Hague: Martinus Nijhoff, 1982) at 196.

247 United Kingdom Ministry of Defence, *supra* note 246.

however, supposed to refer to the non-military — or medical — effects accruing to the combatant. Second, it is not at all clear why the provision relates to the weapon's "effects in battle" and not simply the weapon's "effects." To what do the effects in battle refer? Is this wording intended to limit consideration of the weapon's medical effects to those inflicted only at the time of the attack as opposed to those that might result years later, due, for example, to cancer from the irradiated tissue of a nuclear attack. The manual is not clear. What the UK military manual does seem to conclude is that "all that can be done, in very general terms, is to try and balance the military utility of weapons with the wounding and incidental effects that they have."[248] What this sentence does recognize is that the principle may be applied to anti-*matériel* weapons, but, in so doing, the manual does imply that it may be easier to apply it to anti-personnel weapons, as has been the case with all prohibitions to date.[249]

Greater assistance is provided by the following legal test, which was the subject of general agreement by delegates to the 1974 Lucerne conference on the Conventional Weapons Convention, "unnecessary suffering requires a compromise between the suffering or damage caused by the weapon and the weapon's anticipated military advantage."[250] Captain Paul Robblee, as he then was, wrote in 1976 that this essentially boils down to military necessity versus humanity.[251] In Captain Robblee's opinion, the anticipated military advantage has two factors: (1) the evaluation of the military use of the weapon; and (2) the military necessity for resort to that particular weapon for legitimate military purposes.[252] Clearly, a determination must be made for each weapon on an individual basis. Yet, as Captain Robblee explains, these are highly subjective criteria susceptible to highly varied interpretation. He continues by developing further subjective factors to be analyzed for criterion (1). Accordingly, writing in 1976, Captain Robblee lists as factors in evaluating a weapon's military use: (1) the weapon's effectiveness to destroy or neutralize enemy *matériel*; (2) the weapon's

---

[248] *Ibid.* at 102.

[249] *Ibid.*

[250] Reproduced in Captain P.A. Robblee, Jr., "The Legitimacy of Modern Conventional Weaponry" (1976) 71 Military L. Rev. 95 at 119.

[251] *Ibid.*

[252] *Ibid.*

effectiveness against particular targets; (3) the weapon's ability to interdict enemy lines of communication and to affect morale; (4) the weapon's cost; (5) the weapon's effectiveness in providing security for friendly troops; and (6) the availability of alternative weapons.[253] The final factor was also mentioned in the UK military manual so that comparisons must be made with "the effectiveness and effects of existing weapons that are required for the same purpose."[254] As a result of such balancing, Captain Robblee and others have suggested that only where the suffering inflicted clearly outweighs the military advantage will the principle come into play.[255] This requirement, of course, which is added to the very subjective nature of the military necessity factors, affords a hefty preference for the military use of a weapon.

Three of Captain Robblee's factors for evaluating a weapon's military use need to be highlighted further. These are factors (2), (4), and (6). Factor (2) gives weight to the weapon's effectiveness against particular targets and points, *inter alia*, to the "high military value" of weapons that can eliminate the threat of high priority targets, such as aircraft or tanks.[256] Factor (4) points to the cost of the weapon, but there is no elucidation as to whether this is purely a monetary assessment. If this factor does point purely to a monetary cost, then one would expect that the total cost of development, testing, and production should be included. Factor (6) points to the availability of alternative weapons and ensures that the effects of a particular weapon are not assessed in isolation but rather in conjunction with comparable weapons in use on the battlefield.[257] A final point may be made regarding Captain Robblee's factors. Although listed numerically in his article, there does not appear to be any indication made — or that is clear from practice — of a hierarchy among the factors. Each factor, therefore, appears to have only that weight accruing to it based on the particular nature of the weapon concerned.

One issue remains. This issue concerns the status of the determination of a weapon as causing unnecessary suffering or superfluous

---

253 *Ibid.* See also Carnahan, *supra* note 162 at 714.

254 This factor is also recognized by the United Kingdom. See United Kingdom Ministry of Defence, *supra* note 246 at 102.

255 Robblee, Jr., *supra* note 250 at 119; see also "Resort to War," *supra* note 236 at 708.

256 Carnahan, *supra* note 162 at 726.

257 H. Parks, "Joint Service Combat Shotgun Program" (1997) Army L. 16 at 19.

injury. States clearly have to make such a legal determination (1) in using weapons on the battlefield[258] and (2) before the acquisition or adoption of a new weapon.[259] In regard to the latter obligation, it was included within the 1977 Geneva Protocol I in Article 36 and clearly places the state at the heart of the determination.[260] The principle behind the obligation contained in Article 36 appears to have been based on the US Department of Defence's Instruction 5000.2,[261] which requires a comprehensive legal assessment by the Judge Advocate General's Offices of the army, navy, and air force. The issue, however, is whether the customary prohibition alone is sufficient to render a weapon illegal or whether the principle is simply one reason for states to negotiate a specific legal instrument prohibiting a weapon.[262] The UK military manual suggests that the "current practice is to combine the two approaches by regarding the 'unnecessary suffering' provision as a guiding principle upon which specific prohibitions or restrictions can be built."[263] This appears to be a good reflection of what has occurred to date — including the negotiation of the 1980 Conventional Weapons Convention and its five protocols — and has the advantage of promoting certainty in the law. Ultimately, this approach does leave the classification in states' hands, but non-governmental organizations and other interested parties can still perform a valuable campaigning and educational role in seeking the classification of certain weapons as breaching the principle.[264] On the other hand, the authors in the ICRC customary law study refer to states' submissions

---

258 Geneva Protocol I, *supra* note 11, Article 35(2).

259 *Ibid.*, Article 36.

260 Verchio, *supra* note 241 at 195 and 225.

261 This is the current version dated 12 May 2003. The original provision in 1977 was the Department of Defence Instruction 5500.15 (16 October 1974). Article 36 is not binding as treaty law on the United States.

262 Henkaerts and Doswald-Beck, *supra* note 14 at volume 1, chapter 20, pp. 242–43.

263 United Kingdom Ministry of Defence, *supra* note 246 at 103.

264 The ICRC has traditionally performed a very important role in overseeing the implementation of the laws of armed conflict on the battlefield and is often viewed as the guardian of Geneva law. In trying to establish a purely medical test for weapons that cause unnecessary suffering, however, the ICRC, and one of its authors, Robin Coupland, in particular, has faced fierce criticism from military figures. See Durham and McCormack, eds., *supra* note 237; and Verchio, *supra* note 241.

before the ICJ in the nuclear weapons advisory opinion.[265] Most states, according to the ICRC study, have "assessed the legality of the effects of nuclear weapons on the basis of the rule [prohibiting unnecessary suffering] itself."[266] This approach would appear to suggest that a specific treaty prohibition is not needed. And, yet, while the statements made by the United Kingdom, the United States, and others in those proceedings can be presented in this way, they actually appear to be discussing the customary and treaty law principle of unnecessary suffering in abstract and do not specifically state that a weapon can be prohibited without such a treaty.[267]

Application of the Principle to Depleted Uranium Weapons

The more effective the weapon is from the military point of view, the less likely that the suffering its use causes will be characterized as unnecessary.[268]

To restate the principle, the laws of armed conflict prohibit weapons and methods of warfare of a nature that cause suffering or injury that is unnecessary or superfluous to military needs. From the balancing test outlined earlier and the suggested factors listed by Captain Robblee, it is clear that military necessity is the dominant factor in the equation, resulting in a high threshold for injury to be classified as "unnecessary" or "superfluous."[269] Moving on to the compatibility of depleted uranium ammunition with this principle, there are three ways in which depleted uranium is used in weaponry: (1) 105–20 mm kinetic energy penetrators (anti-tank); (2) 25–30 mm bullets; or (3) 20 mm naval missile defence

---

[265] *Nuclear Weapons, supra* note 174.

[266] See Henkaerts and Doswald-Beck, *supra* note 14, at volume 1, chapter 20, p. 243. The oral pleadings and written statements of fourteen states are then listed in evidence, including those of the United Kingdom and the United States.

[267] *Ibid.* The Samoan statement (at Volume 2, Chapter 20, Section A, at para. 175) is interesting in that it declares its belief that the prohibition on the use or threat of use of nuclear weapons has already been achieved under international law and then goes on to quote a number of treaties, including the St. Petersburg *Declaration, supra* note 154, and the 1907 Hague Convention IV, *supra* note 8. In its statement, Samoa does not specifically mention the principle prohibiting unnecessary suffering, but it is implicit by its quoting of these particular treaties.

[268] *Advisory Proceeding on Nuclear Weapons, supra* note 209 at 50.

[269] Verchio, *supra* note 241 at 194.

systems.[270] The main military utility of such weapons is for their armour-piercing capabilities due, in particular, to the dense and pyrophoric nature of depleted uranium.

Analyzing the injury component of the equation first, the main injuries will be sustained by combatants inside targeted vehicles, including tanks, and any combatants targeted in the open.[271] Such combatants are likely to be injured in the following ways: (1) death by asphyxiation, explosion, or burning inside the tank or other vehicle; (2) burn injuries; (3) limb or organ damage by embedded shrapnel; (4) cardio-vascular damage as a result of exposure to uranium oxide dust created on impact and any re-suspended particles; and (5) potential carcinogenic, mutagenic, and terotogenic effects of internalization of depleted uranium. In essence, if the tank crew survive the attack, they are potentially also at the same risk of long-term medical problems due to the radiologically and chemically toxic properties of depleted uranium as combatants targeted in the open.[272]

In the case of combatants, internalization of depleted uranium particles may occur as a result of inhalation, embedded depleted uranium fragments, and depleted uranium contamination of open wounds. Each 120 mm depleted uranium kinetic energy penetrator can create three kilograms of uranium oxide dust. Wounds caused by depleted uranium fragments will need to be cleaned, but any contaminated particles or fragments that cannot be removed may cause irradiation of the local tissue.[273] Hundreds of soldiers returning from Iraq recently have complained of headaches, pain when swallowing, blurred vision, joint aches, and constant nausea,[274]

---

270 Depleted uranium may also have been used inside the nosecone of cruise missiles, but this has not been confirmed. Some Russian anti-tank cartridges also measure up to 125 mm.

271 Because of the lengthier periods of exposure, soldiers firing depleted uranium ammunition are expected to have a much higher dosage of depleted uranium contamination. Tests indicate that the gamma radiation these soldiers receive after 1,000 hours is equivalent to the average *annual* external dose from natural background radiation. See N.H. Harley, E.C. Foulkes, L.H. Hilborne, A. Hudson, and C.R. Anthony, "A Review of the Scientific Literature as It Pertains to Gulf War Illnesses," 1999, Depleted Uranium, RAND Corporation National Defense Research Institute, no. 7, Washington, DC, available at <http://www.gulflink.osd.mil/library/randrep/du/> (10 July 2005).

272 See earlier section regarding health effects.

273 See "Opinion of the Group of Experts," *supra* note 55 at 5.

274 McHugh, *supra* note 112.

which are common symptoms of exposure to radiation. Indeed, urine samples taken from Gulf conflict veterans were found to contain traces of depleted uranium some seven years after exposure.[275] Furthermore, the Royal Society of Biology in the United Kingdom has concluded that soldiers inside vehicles hit by a depleted uranium shell "may experience a doubling in the lifetime risk of developing leukaemia and other cancers."[276] Even former generals of the US army report that the levels of depleted uranium remaining in the system can be many times higher than they should be. According to Major General Ervin Rokke, the former head of the Pentagon's depleted uranium project, his internal levels of radiation are five thousand times higher than normal.[277] This level, he maintains, is the result of working in areas contaminated with depleted uranium. He also claims that at least thirty members of his depleted uranium clean up team have died prematurely due to exposure to depleted uranium.[278] Further evidence of the potential effect of depleted uranium is provided by the practice of the Dutch armed forces, to whom, during the 1999 Kosovo conflict, protective clothing was apparently issued, which was then disposed of as dangerously contaminated material.[279]

Therefore, in medical terms, the effects of using depleted uranium on the battlefield, as opposed to most other weaponry, include an increase in the risk of tissue and organ damage caused by the radiation and toxic chemicals in the weapon. Thus, it remains to be seen what are the advantages of using depleted uranium in the place of any other readily available substance and whether any such advantages would preserve its legality of use. Depleted uranium ammunition is designed as an anti-*matériel* weapon and appears to

---

[275] Dr. Rosalie Bertell, "Gulf War Veterans and Depleted Uranium," Depleted Uranium: A Post-War Disaster for Environment and Health, Part 3, Laka Foundation, May 1999, available at <http://www.laka.org/teksten/Vu/hap-99/3.html> (7 May 2001).

[276] "Depleted Uranium May Cause Higher Risk of Lung Cancer for Some Soldiers," Royal Society of Biology, 22 May 2001, available at <http://www.royalsoc.ac.uk/news.asp?id=2526> (2 July 2002).

[277] His levels in 1994 were reported as 2,000 times the norm, in Yeung Sik Yuen, *supra* note 111 at para. 155.

[278] *Ibid.*

[279] See the letter of 15 September 2000, entitled "Facts on Consequences of the Use of Depleted Uranium in the NATO Aggression against the Federal Republic of Yugoslavia in 1999," Doc. A/55/398-S/2000/883 (20 September 2000) at para. 8 ["Yugoslavia Letter 2000"].

entail three major military advantages in warfare: (1) armour-piercing capability; (2) effectiveness over distance; and (3) incendiary capacity. The review will commence with a more detailed look at the 120 mm cartridges, followed by the 25–30 mm and 20 mm rounds.

120 mm

These larger-calibre tank cartridges (approximately 120 mm) tend to be used in tank-on-tank engagements. Tank crews can carry only a limited number of munitions and tend to have rounds similar to the US high explosive anti-tank (HEAT), high explosive dual purpose (HEDP), or high explosive squash head (HESH) rounds, in addition to the depleted uranium kinetic energy penetrators. HEAT, HEDP, and HESH rounds are members of the high explosive family of weapons and operate by way of an explosive charge to blow up the tank.[280] Kinetic energy rounds, on the other hand, penetrate the tank, usually the side or front where the armour is the strongest, to disable the tank from the inside. Whereas the high explosive rounds are generally viewed as most effective against bunkers and buildings, the kinetic energy rounds are generally viewed as the most effective ammunition in *penetrating* tank armour.[281] Picatinny, the manufacturer of the US 120 mm cartridges (M829A1-A3), states that it became clear in the 1970s that tungsten carbide penetrators would not be effective against new and improved tank armour.[282] Probably a product of the Cold War, states tend to use either American- or Russian-made tanks. Certainly the Russian T-72 tanks were used on the Balkan battlefields of Bosnia and Kosovo, where US forces fired 30 mm depleted uranium rounds, and in Iraq, where UK and US forces fired 120 mm rounds, and since the 1980s these tanks incorporated improved composite armour.[283] This was the threat that the depleted uranium kinetic energy penetrator was designed to overcome. With further improvements in tank

280 For weapon specifications, see Global Security, available at <http://www.globalsecurity.org> (10 May 2005).

281 Cf., in a letter submitted to the secretary-general of the United Nations, Yugoslavia reported that for the 30,000–50,000 depleted uranium weapons dropped only twelve tanks had been destroyed. See the "Yugoslavia Letter 2000," *supra* note 279 at para. 8.

282 Picatinny Products, available at <http://www.pica.army.mil/PicatinnyPublic/products_services/products12.asp> (20 September 2005).

283 "Depleted Uranium FAQs," *supra* note 34.

armour — including explosive reactor armour (ERA) — possibly incorporated in the latest Russian T-90S model[284] — the United States has developed the M829A3 APFSDS-T to be effective against all threats. Accordingly, the M829A3 boasts greater penetrative capability, improved accuracy at greater range, and the capability to defeat advanced threat armour.[285]

So far it has been easy to state the military advantages to be gained by using depleted uranium kinetic energy penetrators. The main military advantage to be gained is the elimination of enemy tanks, and, like aircraft, tanks are a highly valuable target. So much so that "a high level of suffering such as wounding and death by molten metal fragments or asphyxiation, may legitimately be imposed on an entire tank crew in order to render the vehicle inoperative."[286] Similarly, the United States, in a statement to the ICJ regarding the nuclear weapons advisory opinion, wrote that the principle of unnecessary suffering "does not prohibit the use of anti-tank munitions which must penetrate armor by kinetic-energy or incendiary effects, even though this may well cause severe and painful burn injuries to the tank crew."[287] The ability to destroy an enemy tank at ranges over five kilometres[288] and even behind large sand hills[289] would provide a very high military advantage in any ground combat, particularly a desert ground war as occurred in Operations Desert Storm, Iraqi Freedom, and Telic. But what is to be made of factor (6) in Captain Robblee's list — the availability of alternative weapons. Depleted uranium is not the only metal suitable for use in armour-piercing kinetic energy penetrators. Other dense materials said to offer similar armour-piercing advantages to depleted

---

[284] "T-90s Main Battle Tank, Russia," Army-Technology, available at <http://www.army-technology.com/projects/t90/> (21 September 2005).

[285] "M829E3 120-mm APFSDS-T Cartridge," Global Security, available at <http://www.globalsecurity.org/military/library/budget/fy2001/dot-e/army/01m829e3.html> (21 September 2005).

[286] Carnahan, *supra* note 162 at 726. See also F. Kalshoven, "Conventional Weaponry: The Law from St. Petersburg to Lucerne and Beyond," in M.A. Meyer, ed., *Armed Conflict and the New Law* (London: British Institute of International and Comparative Law, 1989), 251 at 254–62.

[287] *Advisory Proceeding on Nuclear Weapons, supra* note 209 at 28–9.

[288] The actual range achieved in combat was 5.1 kilometres (km) apparently by a British *Challenger* 2 tank firing 120 mm APFSDS CHARM rounds. See "APFSDS Army-Technology," *supra* note 33.

[289] *Ibid.*

uranium include tantalum, hafnium, and tungsten.[290] While the first two materials are still only in the experimental stages, tungsten weaponry used in the earlier stages of kinetic energy cartridges may still provide a real alternative to depleted uranium.

Tungsten is often referred to as the "green" alternative to depleted uranium ammunition. It was apparently clear by the 1970s that depleted uranium would be "superior" to tungsten, as endorsed in a 1979 report by the UK Ministry of Defence on the basis of tests carried out in the United States.[291] Depleted uranium penetrators are generally reported by user states and manufacturers to have a 5 to 20 per cent better penetration effect than the alternative tungsten-alloyed rounds.[292] In regard to armour-piercing capability, the characteristics of depleted uranium on impact appear to offer a major tactical advantage over tungsten alloys. Significantly, while depleted uranium penetrators will "sharpen" on contact with the target, tungsten kinetic energy penetrators, like most other metals, will "mushroom." The consequence of this difference, according to the military, is a reduction in the range of effective deployment from the five to six and a half kilometres anticipated range for depleted uranium kinetic energy penetrators. So much so, that tank crews would need to close in further on the enemy before firing; placing them in greater danger. Not everyone agrees with these assessments, however. André Gsponer of the Independent Scientific Research Institute in Geneva suggests that depleted uranium weapons outperform tungsten penetrators by less than 10 per cent.[293] This view would appear to be bolstered by previously disclosed

---

290 D. Hambling, "Why Deadly Depleted Uranium Is the Tank Buster's Weapon of Choice," *The Guardian*, 18 May 2000. Tantalum is used in a new generation of anti-armour weaponry, the Sadarm (seek and destroy armour), which in missile form, appears to have a range of up to 100 km combined with infrared sensors to seek out their target. It can also come in a manually emplaced form (see discussion of the US M93 Hornet, "M93 Hornet," Global Security, available at <http://www.globalsecurity.org/military/systems/munitions/m93.htm> (22 September 2005). Still in the experimental stages of development, the environmental and human effects of tantalum, however, are not yet fully known, but it is highly toxic.

291 "Anti-Armour Ammunition," *supra* note 68 at para. 1.

292 The 20 per cent figure was quoted in P. Brown, "Cheap and Lethal Nuclear By-Product," *The Guardian*, 12 January 2001, at 8; and see "Depleted Uranium FAQs," *supra* note 34.

293 See A. Gsponer, "Depleted Uranium Weapons, The Whys and Wherefores," 2003, Independent Scientific Research Institute, Switzerland, available at <http://arxiv.org/PS_cache/physics/pdf/0301/0301059.pdf> (21 July 2004) at 10.

(1991) official documents within the United States, which report that during testing only 26 per cent of depleted uranium ammunition impacted with the target and only 4.2 per cent actually penetrated the target.[294] On the other hand, Gsponer does concede that once inside the target vehicle, tungsten penetrators would not have the same lethality as the uranium oxide dust produced by depleted uranium, which ignites in air. After all, penetration of the tank is the first stage of attack, the second is the destruction of the tank by the resultant fire. In this regard, Gsponer does recognize that even tungsten penetrators would have some interior effect — albeit less than depleted uranium penetrators, as the metal fragments might ignite the fuel tank or disable personnel.[295] Gsponer also suggests that an incendiary device could be added to these alternative weapons, thus reducing or eliminating this particular military advantage of depleted uranium ammunition. Gsponer also recognizes that depleted uranium kinetic energy penetrators, while having a greater depth of penetration, have a narrower penetration point than tungsten.[296] He suggests that the two aspects of (1) depth of penetration and (2) width of penetration may cancel each other out, resulting in little difference in practice between the effectiveness of the two weapons.[297]

Satisfied by tungsten rounds, a number of states have refused to purchase or develop depleted uranium ammunition. Instead, these states have continued to develop new versions of the tungsten rounds, improving the tungsten alloys in order to enhance performance.[298] The great majority of states, including Germany, Italy, China, Sweden, Spain, Australia, the Netherlands, and Israel all utilize newer tungsten anti-tank rounds,[299] which they view as good enough to defeat the armour of all existing tanks.[300] Speaking to the Australian Senate in 2003, the Australian defence minister was of the opinion that "DU is not the most desirable material to use where there are other alternatives."[301] The latest versions are the

[294] "Depleted Uranium Munitions," *supra* note 57 at 5.

[295] Gsponer, *supra* note 293 at 14.

[296] *Ibid.* at 13.

[297] *Ibid.*

[298] *Ibid.*

[299] "Depleted Uranium FAQs," *supra* note 34.

[300] For the German view, see Gsponer, *supra* note 293 at 4; and for the Australian government's view, see Official Hansard of the Commonwealth of Australia, Senate, No. 3, 2003, 20 March 2003, at 9873.

[301] Official Hansard of the Commonwealth of Australia, *supra* note 300 at 9873.

120 mm KEW-A1 and KEW-A2 APFSDS-T cartridges, a tungsten-based kinetic energy penetrator described by the manufacturer as providing "state-of-the-art" tungsten armor-piercing capabilities with the "ability to defeat currently fielded armor targets."[302] In all, the cartridge is said to provide "a high-performance alternative to other heavy metal projectiles ... [and] has demonstrated excellent dispersion and lethality."[303] The German, Swiss, and Dutch ground forces, on the other hand, prefer the DM-53 and DM-63 tungsten-based kinetic energy penetrators.[304] In 2002, in the midst of the controversy surrounding the use of depleted uranium in Kosovo, the UK Ministry of Defence also announced that it would purchase tungsten alloy rounds for its *Challenger 2* tanks as an alternative to depleted uranium.[305] The United Kingdom has consistently expressed its opinion, however, that depleted uranium is "the weapon of choice in combat," so much so that it was employed in Iraq.[306]

In assessing the legality of the 120 mm depleted uranium kinetic energy penetrators, the comparable weapons on the battlefield are the tungsten kinetic energy penetrators and the high explosive family of weapons. The high explosive cartridges appear to be used mostly against bunkers and buildings, and the kinetic energy penetrators appear to be the weapon of choice in anti-tank warfare — remembering that the destruction of a tank has a very high military value. It does appear that tungsten-alloyed 120 mm cartridges do have reduced capability over the depleted uranium 120 mm cartridges. Exactly how reduced a capability is still subject to debate. In addition, as a heavy metal, tungsten presents similar chemical toxicity problems as depleted uranium but not, of course, the same potential radiological risk.[307] Indeed, if the tank crew survives an

---

302 "120mm Advanced Tungsten Cartridge KEW-A1 APFSDS-T" and "120mm KEW-A2 APFSDS-T," Direct Tank Fire Ammunition, General Dynamics Ordnance and Tactical Systems, available at <http://www.gd-ots.com/sitepages/dirfire.html#KEW> (25 September 2005).

303 *Ibid.*

304 "120mm Tank Gun KE Ammunition" (2004) 5 Defense Update, available at <http://www.defense-update.com/products/digits/120ke.htm> (26 September 2005).

305 M. Smith, "Army Buys Safer Tank Ammunition," *Daily Telegraph*, 10 January 2002, at 12.

306 *Ibid.*

307 A. Miller et al., "Potential Late Health Effects of Depleted Uranium and Tungsten used in Armor-Piercing Munitions: Comparison of Neoplastic Transformation and Genotoxicity with the Known Carcinogen Nickel" (2002) 167(2

attack, the men would ordinarily be peppered with harmful metal shards and other debris. The added danger that tungsten or depleted uranium metals pose may be small in comparison with the burn injuries that tank crews face from weapons with undoubted legality. Finally, state practice in rejecting the use of depleted uranium ammunition, while valuable, is probably not sufficient, however, to qualify as evidence of opposition on the basis of illegality. Since the potential injury from depleted uranium may not be viewed as "manifestly disproportionate"[308] to the anticipated military advantage of its use, it may be the case that these weapons would not fall within the principle prohibiting unnecessary suffering or superfluous injury.[309] This balance may change in the future, particularly if the results of more studies find greater health consequences from depleted uranium.

25–30 mm

Although a number of states may possess the smaller-calibre (25 mm and 30 mm) depleted uranium cartridges, it appears that only the United States has actually employed these on the battlefield in Iraq, Bosnia, and Kosovo.[310] The smaller-calibre 30 mm cartridges are fired from aircraft, including helicopters, and have armour-piercing capabilities aimed particularly at the lighter top armour

---

Supplement) Military Medicine 120. Miller et al. work for the Applied Cellular Radiobiology Department in the Armed Forces Radiobiology Research Institute, Bethesda.

308 W. Hays Parks, "Memorandum for Office of the Project Manager, Tank and Medium Caliber Armament System, Picatinny Arsenal, NJ 07806-5000: Subject – Cartridge 25mm, Armour-Piercing, Fin-Stabilized Discarding Sabot with Tracer (APFSDS-T), M919, Legal Review," Doc. DAJA-IO (27-1a) (16 March 2001) at 2 [hard copy on file with author] ["Memorandum for Office of the Project Manager, M919"]. This is the US Judge Advocate General of the army's final legal review of the 25 mm M919 APFSDS-T.

309 This view is held by the United States and others, see W. Hays Parks, "Memorandum for Office of the Project Manager, Tank and Medium Caliber Armament Systems (SFAE-GCSS-TMA), Picatinny Arsenal, New Jersey 07806-5000: Subject – M829E3 Cartridge, 120mm Armour-Piercing, Fin-Stabilized Discarding Sabot with Tracer, Final Legal Review," Doc. DAJA-IO (27-1a) (4 October 2001) [hard copy on file with author]. This is the US Judge Advocate General of the army's final legal review of the M829E3 cartridge 120 mm armour-piercing fin-stabilized discarding sabot with tracer.

310 See "Depleted Uranium (DU)," United Kingdom Ministry of Defence, available at <http://www.mod.uk/DefenceInternet/AboutDefence/WhatWeDo/HealthandSafety/Depleted+Uranium/> (15 August 2006).

of tanks. An aircraft-mounted Gatling gun can fire such rounds at a top rate of 4,200 per minute,[311] making the ammunition effective against enemy tanks with heavy armour and lightly armoured vehicles and personnel. Although not designed as an anti-personnel weapon, it can be used as such by aircraft that tend to carry only a limited amount and variety of ammunition.[312] According to Lieutenant Colonel Burrus Carnahan of the US air force, as he then was, "there are other exceptions concerning the use of small-caliber incendiary or explosive bullets. Because a combat aircraft in flight cannot change its ammunition load, such aircrafts may use incendiary or explosive bullets when strafing enemy ground troops. Again, such munitions may cause greater suffering for the wounded, but such suffering is necessary in light of the realities of air warfare."[313] Consequently, combatants in the field would be injured in much the same way by depleted uranium rounds as other rounds employed. In regard to the 25 mm M919 APFSDS-T, for example, the United States deploys these smaller-calibre cartridges from its Bradley fighting vehicle against other light armour threats.[314] However, in comparison to the three hundred grams of depleted uranium in each 30 mm cartridge, the 25 mm has only eighty-five grams.

In relation to the 25 mm and 30 mm ammunition, André Gsponer suggests that since it is designed only to be effective against light armour threats, there is no difference between the performance of these smaller-calibre depleted uranium and tungsten rounds.[315] Some military sources, on the other hand, have suggested that there is a difference — involving a reduction in the range of effective deployment from three thousand metres for air-delivered depleted uranium bullets to only two thousand metres for tungsten.[316] In addition, Gsponer has suggested that the incendiary capacity of

---

311 "GAU-8," Military Analysis Network, available at <http://www.fas.org/man/dod-101/sys/ac/equip/gau-8.htm> (26 September 2005).

312 Carnahan, *supra* note 162 at 717.

313 *Ibid.* As Carnahan recognizes, however, this is not a universally held view. He quotes D. Hughes-Morgan, "Legal Criteria for the Prohibition or Restriction of Use of Categories of Conventional Weapons," in Meyer, ed., *supra* note 286 at 259.

314 "Memorandum for Office of the Project Manager, M919," *supra* note 308 at 3.

315 Gsponer, *supra* note 293 at 14.

316 Briefing by Mr. Mark Laity, NATO acting spokesman, Lt. Col. Scott Bethel, Dr. Michael Kilpatrick, and Col. Eric Daxon, 10 January 2001, available at <http://www.nato.int/docu/speech/2001/s010110b.htm> (3 February 2001).

the depleted uranium bullet could easily be recreated in the tungsten ammunition. Since both may defeat the same targets — lightly armoured and other vehicles — the only factor of relevance may be that of cost. Tungsten weaponry, however, is more expensive than weapons containing depleted uranium — apparently some ten times the cost of depleted uranium weapons.[317] This fact brings the cost of the weapon into the equation, which is factor (4) on Captain Robblee's list. Depleted uranium weaponry is also cheaper to manufacture. Since the melting point of tungsten is much higher, it is, therefore, much harder and more expensive to use. How realistic though is it to suggest that, assuming the military advantages of tungsten and depleted uranium were on a par, the cheaper financial cost of depleted uranium weaponry would swing the balance in favour of its legality? This point is particularly biting in the case of such wealthy states as the United Kingdom and the United States. On the other hand, on the injury side of the balance, the injury from depleted uranium may be less for the smaller-calibre rounds than for the 120 mm cartridges. While more direct hits of combatants may be witnessed and the risk of inhalation of uranium oxide dust greater, the smaller-calibre rounds contain less depleted uranium. Consequently, it would take approximately fifty-three of the 25 mm rounds and fifteen of the 30 mm rounds to account for the same level of depleted uranium in one 120 mm cartridge. Finally, therefore, as in the case of the 120 mm cartridges, while some states appear to prefer other weapons, there is not sufficient evidence of states rejecting the 25–30 mm depleted uranium weapons due to violation of the unnecessary suffering principle.

20 mm

This leaves only the 20 mm MK149–2 APDS cartridges for analysis. The 20 mm cartridge is designed for use in the PHALANX naval CIWS and contains seventy grams of depleted uranium per cartridge. Here, however, both the United States and the United

---

Although soldiers also reported that the range was so long that they were not always able to positively record a direct hit. See Health and Environmental Consequences of Depleted Uranium Use in the U.S. Army: Technical Report, US Army Environmental Policy Institute Report, June 1995, available at <http://www.fas.org/man/dod-101/sys/land/docs/techreport.html> (10 January 2001) at Chapter 4.1.

317 Scott Peterson, "Depleted Uranium Concerns Boost Non-Radioactive Bullet," *Christian Science Monitor*, 18 January 2001.

Kingdom have abandoned use of their 20 mm arsenal.[318] The US navy abandoned its use as far back as 1989, noting that the "tungsten penetrator provides improved ... effectiveness whilst eliminating safety problems associated with DU [depleted uranium]"[319] and reverted to the use of tungsten penetrators.[320] Similarly, in 2001, the United Kingdom announced the phasing out of its 20 mm depleted uranium rounds used by the Royal Navy's PHALANX missile defence system.[321] The main reason for the shift appears to be that there is simply no need for naval forces to have armour-penetrating capability in such defensive weapons systems.[322] Since inbound missiles are usually soft (non-armoured) targets, defensive missiles used to destroy them do not, therefore, need such capability. Again, tungsten is used in its place. Indeed, Gsponer suggests that tungsten rounds are better in this regard because they have a higher velocity.[323] As a consequence, the 20 mm depleted uranium rounds appear to have been phased out because there is no military advantage to be gained from these over and above what is afforded by tungsten rounds. While state practice does not indicate the abandonment of the depleted uranium rounds based on the principle of unnecessary suffering, it would at least point to a precedent for other larger-calibre applications should tungsten rounds be developed that are as efficient as those utilizing depleted uranium.

In conclusion, the extent of combatant injuries from depleted uranium rounds largely remains unknown or at least unconfirmed. While voluminous laboratory experiments have indicated potentially very serious health effects, such results have not been so evident in a human sampling of combatants. On the other hand, the

---

318 The 20 mm rounds remain in the arsenal of these states and may be owned by other states, therefore, the legality of the rounds needs to be assessed. According to one journalist, following its naval forces, the US air force announced in 2003 that in the future its anti-tank weaponry will not employ depleted uranium weaponry. See J. Fialka, "Weighing Claims about Depleted Uranium," *Wall Street Journal*, 2 January 2003, at A4. This does not appear to have been reported elsewhere, particularly by the US airforce.

319 R. Norton-Taylor, "Ministry with a Vested Interest," *The Guardian*, 16 January 2001, at 22.

320 Even the manufacturer has commented that it ceased production "amid safety fears," quoted from the "Royal Navy Phases out DU Ammo," *supra* note 6.

321 *Ibid.*

322 "Depleted Uranium," *supra* note 310.

323 Gsponer, *supra* note 293 at 15.

military advantage to be gained from depleted uranium ammunition appears to reduce with the size of the round. The 120 mm round appears to produce a great military advantage, which may, therefore, tip the balance. In the middle are the 25–30 mm rounds. These smaller-calibre rounds may produce only a slight military advantage over comparable tungsten rounds, but is it sufficient for their legality? The 20 mm naval rounds appear to produce no military advantage over comparable tungsten rounds and have already been abandoned by the United Kingdom and the United States.

Principle of Distinction or Discriminate Warfare

The prohibition on the targeting of non-combatants has been in existence for almost as long as warfare itself and is recognized by most cultures. The primary humanitarian consideration for civilians is due to their non-involvement in the war — the fact that they are "innocents." Military considerations would advocate saving valuable ammunition, in not attacking unarmed civilians, and in the avoidance of unnecessary retribution. After all, routine massacring of the local civilian population would only increase popular resistance to the conflict, swell the military ranks of the enemy, and, hence, strengthen the enemy's war effort. Accordingly, the 1868 St. Petersburg Declaration[324] stipulated that "[t]he only legitimate object which States should endeavour to accomplish during war is to weaken the *military forces* of the enemy."[325]

Today, non-combatant immunity is incorporated in the principle of discriminate warfare. The principle of discrimination or distinction was codified[326] in Article 48 of Geneva Protocol I,[327] which requires state parties to distinguish at all times between the civilian population/civilian objects and combatants/military objectives. Consequently, legitimate actions are those directed only against the latter. The terms "civilians and civilian population" are defined negatively as any person not belonging to one of those categories mentioned in Article 43 ("combatants").[328] In international armed

324 St. Petersburg Declaration, *supra* note 154.

325 *Ibid.* at para. 3 [emphasis added].

326 Henkaerts and Doswald-Beck, *supra* note 14 at volume I, chapter 3, p. 37, recognizes the customary status of the prohibition of indiscriminate attacks for both international and internal armed conflict. This is included as Rule 11.

327 Geneva Protocol I, *supra* note 11.

328 *Ibid.*, Article 50(1).

conflict, Article 43 of Geneva Protocol I, together with Article 4A(1)(2)(3) and (6) of Geneva Convention (III) Relative to the Treatment of Prisoners of War,[329] define those who are to be considered as combatants. In sum, the term "combatants" involves members of the armed forces and other militia fulfilling certain conditions. Similarly, civilian objects are defined negatively in Article 52(1) as "all objects which are *not* military objectives" [emphasis added]. Military objectives are defined as those objects that make an "effective" contribution to military action, are dependent upon the ambient circumstances, and offer a "definite" military advantage.[330] Clearly, attacks directed at persons and property that do not fulfil the criteria in these provisions are unlawful. Additional Protocol II contains essentially the same distinction between civilian and military persons and objects, albeit without reference to "combatant" status.[331] As a consequence, civilians in both internal and international armed conflicts are protected against direct conflict. They are not a military target and, hence, should not be attacked. Unfortunately, however, civilians will often be harmed indirectly in the bombing and destruction. The military are, however, under an obligation to keep the number of collateral casualties to a minimum.[332]

Unlike their inclusion of the prohibition on causing unnecessary suffering, states did include within Geneva Protocol I a definition of discrimination with regard to weapons use.[333] Accordingly, elucidation of the customary prohibition can be found in Article 51(4). Before moving on to discuss the definition, an important legal point must be made. Clearly, in qualifying as part of customary law, the principle of discrimination itself is universally binding. The definition, however, may represent only treaty law. With 166 states party

---

[329] Geneva Convention III, *supra* note 10.

[330] Geneva Protocol I, s*upra* note 11, Article 52(2).

[331] Geneva Protocol II, *supra* note 11, Article 4(1). See also Article 13 in Additional Protocol II, which directs in more basic terms only that civilians shall not be the object of attack. The concept can also be discerned from Common Article 3 of the 1949 Geneva Conventions, *supra* note 10. The principle has also been more recently included in treaty law applicable in internal armed conflicts, namely Article 3(8) of Amended Protocol II to the 1980 Conventional Weapons Convention, *supra* note 16.

[332] This is known as the rule of proportionality in attack and can be found at Article 51(5)(b) of Geneva Protocol I, *supra* note 11.

[333] The *first* definition, according to Bothe, Partsch, and Solf, *supra* note 246 at 305.

to Geneva Protocol I,[334] this point may be moot, but while the United States refuses to ratify the treaty it remains a valid one. This is particularly the case in regard to subparagraph (c), which merges other violations of the protocol into the prohibition.

Indiscriminate attacks, according to Article 51(4) are defined to include those employing a *means* (or method) of combat the effects of which cannot be limited to military objectives. More specifically, subparagraph (a) refers to *weapons* not directed at a specific military objective, subparagraph (b) to *weapons* that *cannot* be directed at a specific military objective, and subparagraph (c) to *weapons* with effects that cannot be limited as required by the protocol. An almost identical definition of "indiscriminate attacks" is included in both Protocol II and Amended Protocol II to the 1980 Conventional Weapons Convention.[335] In the case of these two protocols to the 1980 Conventional Weapons Convention, paragraph (c) refers to the principle of proportionality in attack. With respect to paragraph (c) in Article 51(4) of Geneva Protocol I, it is suggested that those provisions that afford protection to the natural environment (Articles 35(3) and 55) and to certain works or installations containing dangerous forces (Article 56[336]) might be viewed as limiting the effects of weapons, in addition to the principle of proportionality (Article 51(5)). This clearly relies on the basis that because of their effects certain weapons *cannot* be strictly limited in geographical or temporal dimensions to the military objective targeted, and so they will strike civilians and combatants — or only civilians in the post-conflict period — without distinction.[337] Further support is provided for the inclusion of environmental effects within Article 51(4)(c) by a joint United States and Jordanian memorandum of 1992. In the joint memorandum to the Sixth Committee of the UN General Assembly, entitled "International

---

[334] As of August 2006.

[335] See Protocol II of the 1980 Conventional Weapons Convention, *supra* note 16, Article 3(3)(c); and Amended Protocol II to the 1980 Convention Weapons Convention, *supra* note 16, Article 3(8)(c).

[336] A similar provision is included in Geneva Protocol II, *supra* note 11, at Article 15.

[337] In its recently completed study, of the customary law status of the provisions of humanitarian law including those contained in Geneva Protocols I and II, the ICRC concludes that this provision is indeed a norm of international law but only in so far as those limits imposed are "required by international humanitarian law" and not simply by Geneva Protocol I. The ICRC customary study includes at Rule 12 the provisions set forth in Article 51(4). See Henkaerts and Doswald-Beck, *supra* note 14, at volume I, chapter 3, p. 41.

Law Providing Protection to the Environment in Times of Armed Conflict," the states refer to the limits on weaponry — as basically laid out in Article 51(4) — as a war crime.[338] Therefore, for both subparagraphs (b) and (c), it is the actual weapon that cannot discriminate and not its manner of use (as in subparagraph (a)). Consequently, while subparagraphs (b) and (c) can be viewed as outlining a prohibition on inherently indiscriminate weaponry — or weapons that by nature are indiscriminate under international humanitarian law — subparagraph (a), on the other hand, is directed at a prohibition on using an otherwise discriminatory weapon in an indiscriminate way (notably in targeting civilians).

It follows that the use of a weapon that breaches the definition of an indiscriminate attack is illegal. Practically speaking, one could suggest, therefore, that weapons may violate the prohibition if they (1) are by nature (inherently) indiscriminate or else have unlimited effects in regard to the limits established by humanitarian law (Geneva Protocol I, Article 51(4)(b) and (c)) or (2) while being capable of discriminating are, however, used in an indiscriminate way for Article 51(4)(a). Again, as with the principle of unnecessary suffering, the question arises as to the status of any determination to this effect. It is suggested, as many states have done, that the determination of a weapon as having inherently indiscriminate effects is the task of the community of states in ratifying a treaty prohibition to that effect.

Application of the Principle to Depleted Uranium Weapons

Prohibited attacks under Article 51(4)(a) are those in which *weapons* were not directed at a specific military objective. This aspect of legality, therefore, applies the prohibition on directing attacks at the civilian population or civilian objects and involves a close analysis of actual military uses of a particular weapon on the battlefield. It is not always possible, however, to gain an absolutely accurate account of events. Therefore, the events documented in the following section must be read in light of this general qualification.

Depleted uranium kinetic energy penetrators are designed as anti-*matériel* weapons. As a consequence, even human military personnel should not be targeted with such weaponry, let alone civilians.

---

[338] See Jordan and United States, "International Law Providing Protection to the Environment in Times of Armed Conflict, annexed to Letter dated 28 September 1992 to the Chairman of the Sixth Committee of the UN General Assembly," UN Doc.A/C.6/47/3 (28 September 1992), para. 1(g).

Tank-fired 120 mm kinetic energy penetrators have a high degree of accuracy, due to the tank's very sophisticated range-finder, stabilization systems, and targeting equipment. Therefore, it appears to be the case that these could even be used in populated areas, for example, in a town, and would cause very few civilian casualties. Certainly, it appears that in Iraq the main use of depleted uranium kinetic energy penetrators by UK tank forces was in the desert, absent civilians. According to the report in the *Sandy Times* — the weekly newspaper published by and for the British armed forces — fourteen British *Challenger 2* tanks took on fourteen Iraqi T55 tanks and four companies of infantry in the plains south of Basra.[339] Despite thick fog, the *Challenger 2*'s picked off the Iraqi tanks from a distance of 1,500 metres.[340] According to the report, this range was sufficiently close for accurate targeting. There appears to be little indication, therefore, that the depleted uranium weaponry was used indiscriminately.

However, how far this supposedly high degree of accuracy corresponds to the 30 mm depleted uranium rounds is more debateable. These rounds are typically fired by the US air force from a Gatling gun. Certainly, available evidence indicates a much lower accuracy rating for these smaller-calibre depleted uranium rounds. Again, one can quote official sources within the United States, which report that during testing only 26 per cent of depleted uranium ammunition impacted with the target, and only 4.2 per cent actually penetrated the target.[341] Yet surely this level of accuracy is consistent with air-delivered ammunition in general, whether depleted uranium tipped or not. It is highly unlikely, therefore, that one could outlaw depleted uranium weaponry on this basis alone. Therefore, even if Coalition forces did use depleted uranium ammunition within populated areas, it is not suggested that they deliberately targeted civilians or used the depleted uranium weaponry in an indiscriminate manner. The main civilian threat is not, however, due to the lawful targeting of the weapon but, rather, to its potential side effects on human health and the environment — either as an immediate consequence of the use of depleted uranium weaponry or in the long term. This will be the subject of the following section.

---

339 See T. Shipman, "British Victory in Basra Tank Battle," *Sandy Times*, No. 29, 1 April 2003, at 6.

340 See R. Norton-Taylor and R. McCarthy, "Scots Guards Destroy Fourteen Iraqi Tanks in Confrontation," *The Guardian*, 28 March 2003, at 6.

341 "Depleted Uranium Munitions," *supra* note 57.

Inherently Indiscriminate or Unlimited Effects Weapons

The title of this section loosely corresponds to the provisions in Articles 51(4)(b) and (c) in regard to those weapons (respectively) that cannot be directed at a specific military objective and weapons with effects that cannot be limited as required by Geneva Protocol I or humanitarian law. It is suggested that the use of depleted uranium weapons, in general, contravenes the latter, notably as a result of its inherently indiscriminate or unlimited effects. Some support for this terminology and classification of depleted uranium weapons is provided by state practice. While as many as twenty states may possess depleted uranium weapons, including the United States, the United Kingdom, Israel, Japan, France, China, Russia, Germany, Pakistan, Iran, and Turkey, there are indications among other states that depleted uranium weapons are viewed as, at the very least, inherently indiscriminate weapons. Furthermore, a reasonable number of states have classified depleted uranium rounds as weapons of mass destruction (WMD).

The United Nations Sub-Commission on the Promotion and Protection of Human Rights has stated that in its opinion depleted uranium weapons fall within the prohibitions on indiscriminate warfare and/or weapons of mass destruction.[342] This classification appears to have been largely prompted by Iraqi *notes verbale* and the "evidence" contained therein. Annually during the 1990s, the Permanent Mission of Iraq sent a *note verbale* to the United Nations concerning the effects of depleted uranium and proposed a number of draft resolutions in which it described depleted uranium rounds as a weapon of mass destruction.[343] Following discussion in the UN General Assembly of the 2001 Iraqi proposal, the assembly recorded a vote in favour of this wording by forty-nine states to forty-five, with thirty-nine state abstentions.[344] Many states among those voting against the resolution and abstaining did so due to the classification of depleted uranium as a weapon of mass destruction. Clearly,

---

[342] United Nations Commission on Human Rights, Sub-Commission on Prevention of Discrimination and Protection of Minorities, "International Peace and Security as an Essential Condition for the Enjoyment of Human Rights, Above All, the Right to Life," Res. 1996/16, 1996, UNCHR OR, 34th Mtg, UN Doc. E/CN.4/Sub.2/1996/L.11/Add.3 (29 August 1996). The sub-commission also includes within this designation nuclear weapons, chemical weapons, fuel-air bombs, napalm, biological weaponry, and cluster bombs.

[343] *Post-War Environment in Iraq, supra* note 2.

[344] General Assembly Official Records, First Committee, 56th session, Doc. A/C.1/56/PV.23 (5 November 2001).

however, some forty-nine states were of the belief that depleted uranium weaponry was not only inherently indiscriminate but also qualified as a weapon of mass destruction. A similar proposal drafted in 2002 was on this occasion defeated by fifty-nine votes against to thirty-five in favour, with fifty-six states abstaining and forty-one not voting.[345] From these two resolutions, it becomes clear that the majority of Arab states,[346] together with some from South America, Asia, and Africa, including India, Cuba, Indonesia, and Nigeria, voted in favour of the proposals, while those against included the majority of European states plus the United States, Australia, Canada, Israel, Kuwait, and New Zealand. Of the states opposing the proposal — that depleted uranium weapons are weapons of mass destruction, it is interesting to note that Canada and Australia, among others, have stopped using depleted uranium weaponry, although they do not admit that these weapons are outlawed. Furthermore, the European Parliament,[347] the ICRC, Germany, Italy, Portugal, Pakistan, and France have all previously called for a moratorium on the use of depleted uranium weapons. It is interesting to note that Russia, China, and Pakistan — which are all owners of depleted uranium weaponry — abstained in the votes. Of the forty-nine states in favour of the proposal in 2001, thirteen shifted position in 2002 to abstain. Furthermore, rather bizarrely, while Yugoslavia branded depleted uranium weapons as inhumane and their use as a crime against humanity in its 2000 letter to the United Nations secretary-general,[348] and cited their use as contrary to international law by NATO during the Kosovo conflict,[349] it chose to

345 General Assembly Official Records, First Committee, 57th session, Doc. A/C.1/57/PV.21 (25 October 2002).

346 Iraq reported to the UN General Assembly meeting of 2002 that recently the Standing Committee on Human Rights of the League of Arab States had adopted a decision entitled "Human Rights and Weapons of Mass Destruction, Including Depleted Uranium." See General Assembly Official Records, First Committee, 57th session, Doc. A/C.1/57/PV.16 (18 October 2002).

347 Both in 2002 and 2003, see "Unexploded Ordnance and Depleted Uranium Ammunition," *supra* note 149; and "No DU Weapons Risk, Say Experts," *Newsnight*, 6 March 2001.

348 "Facts on Consequences of the Use of Depleted Uranium in the NATO Aggression Against the Federal Republic of Yugoslavia," letter dated 15 September 2000 from the chargé d'affaires of the Permanent Mission of Yugoslavia to the United Nations Addressed to the Secretary-General, Doc. A/55/398-S/2000/883 (20 September 2000).

349 In its case before the International Court of Justice (ICJ), Yugoslavia attempted to argue that the NATO bombing of 1999 breached numerous international

abstain in the UN General Assembly vote in 2001 and to vote against the proposal in 2002.

Although this evidences the *opinio* of a reasonable number of states, it may be insufficient to brand these particular weapons as weapons of mass destruction. There remain a large number of states that do not subscribe to this point of view. From the evidence, however, it is suggested that though many of the abstention states were not willing to view depleted uranium weapons as fulfilling the requirements of weapons of mass destruction, they were willing to view them as breaching the provisions on discrimination.

Like any other bullet or missile, depleted uranium ammunition in all of its forms *is* capable of being targeted with a relative degree of accuracy. At first sight, therefore, depleted uranium poses no breach of the principle of distinction. However, on second glance, it is the potentially devastating toxicological and radiological effects of depleted uranium in the environment that is cause for concern. This section will now focus upon an examination of whether the effects of depleted uranium weapons cannot be limited as required by Geneva Protocol I and humanitarian law in regard to (1) provisions affording protection to the environment and (2) the principle of proportionality.

Articles 35(3) and 55 of Geneva Protocol I

These two provisions were included in the 1977 Geneva Protocol I as a development of international law.[350] Consequently, they were

---

legal obligations, particularly citing the use of depleted uranium weapons and international law designed to protect the environment, prohibit use of certain weapons, and protect against the physical destruction of a national group (genocide). See *Legality of the Use of Force, (Yugoslavia v. Belgium), (Yugoslavia v. Canada), (Yugoslavia v. France), (Yugoslavia v. Germany), (Yugoslavia v. Italy), (Yugoslavia v. Netherlands), (Yugoslavia v. Portugal), (Yugoslavia v. United Kingdom), (Yugoslavia v. Spain), (Yugoslavia v. United States of America)*, 1999, nos. 104–14, (1999) 38 I.L.M. 950, available at <http://www.icj-cij.org/icjwww/idecisions.htm> (19 December 2004). The cases against the United States and Spain were dismissed earlier due to lack of jurisdiction. In December 2004, the remaining cases were unanimously dismissed due to lack of jurisdiction. See the judgment of 15 December 2004. See also J. Burton, "Depleted Morality: Yugoslavia v. Ten NATO Members and Depleted Uranium" (2000) 19 Wis. Int'l L.J. 17.

350 Germany considered the provisions an "important *new* contribution to the protection of the natural environment in times of international armed conflict" and joined in the consensus on this basis. See "Official Records of the Diplomatic Conference on the Reaffirmation and Development of International

not considered to represent customary obligations at the time of
adoption but may have since gained sufficient supporting practice
to have crystallized into customary norms.[351] The need to introduce measures of direct environmental protection has resulted from
the global outrage resulting from the US attacks on the environment in the Vietnam conflict. Such tactics included large-scale crop
destruction and deforestation by means of incendiary weapons
(namely napalm), chemical weapons in the form of herbicides, and
mechanized land-clearing systems.[352] These environmentally destructive tactics provided the inspiration needed for the inclusion
of environmental protections within Geneva Protocol I. The major
influence in drafting the provisions was the global consensus to
prohibit, or at least to limit, such damaging tactics in future conflicts. There is, however, no equivalent provision within Geneva
Protocol II with respect to the protection of the environment during non-international armed conflicts.[353]

Articles 35(3) and 55 specifically prohibit environmental damage in armed conflict, albeit only above a specified threshold of
harm. While they include the same terminology of environmental
harm, they set two very different thresholds. Article 55(1) appears

---

Humanitarian Law Applicable in Armed Conflicts," Geneva, 1974–7, Doc.
CDDH/SR.39 (25 May 1977), O.R. vol. 6, at 115 [emphasis added] ["International Humanitarian Law Applicable in Armed Conflicts"]. Similarly, other states
considered the purpose of the provisions to be "to fill a gap in international
humanitarian law." See N. van Huong, Democratic Republic of Viet-Nam, Official Records of the Diplomatic Conference, Doc. CDDH/III/SR.26 (27 February 1975), vol.14, at 238, para. 15; and, as a consequence, the Third (drafting)
Committee concluded that it was "the *first occasion* on which an attempt has
been made to provide in express terms for the protection of the environment
in time of war." See Report to Committee III on the Work of the Working Group
Submitted by the Rapporteur, Official Records of the Diplomatic Conference,
Doc. CDDH/III/275 3 February–18 April 1975, vol. XV at 358 [emphasis
added].

351 Henkaerts and Doswald-Beck, *supra* note 14 at volume I, chapter 14, p. 147,
recognizes the customary status of the very basic notion that methods and means
of warfare must be employed with due regard to the protection and preservation of the environment. This is included as Rule 44.

352 See generally A.H. Westing, *Ecological Consequences of the Second Indochina War*
(Stockholm: Almqvist and Wiskell International, 1976).

353 Although similar provisions to those in Geneva Protocol I were envisaged for
inclusion within Geneva Protocol II, these were included within the "Pakistan
proposal" to reduce the protocol with the aim of ensuring that acceptance of
the final text was as broad as possible. See Bothe, Partsch, and Solf, *supra* note
246 at 606.

to present the highest threshold of environmental damage and stipulates that

[c]are shall be taken in warfare to protect the natural environment against widespread, long-term and severe damage. This protection includes a prohibition of the use of methods or means of warfare, which are intended or may be expected to cause such damage to the natural environment and thereby to prejudice the health or survival of the population.

The first sentence of Article 55(1) contains a general, positive obligation of environmental protection, which is articulated in stronger terms in the second sentence by way of a specific prohibition. It is the second sentence, therefore, that is of greater relevance to the present analysis. The prohibition appears only to apply where environmental damage would have the potential to cause consequent harm to humans.[354] Article 35(3), on the other hand, relates to weapons and stipulates that

[i]t is prohibited to employ methods or means of warfare which are intended, or may be expected, to cause widespread, long-term and severe damage to the natural environment.[355]

Where the prohibition contained in Article 35(3) differs from that contained in Article 55(1), it is in the absence of the requirement for consequent human injury.[356] In this regard, Article 35(3) concerns the protection of the natural environment *per se* and entails a lower threshold of harm than Article 55(1). The similarity between the two prohibitions cannot be denied, therefore, and the key to understanding and differentiating between the two provisions is in

354 For an in-depth analysis, see K. Hulme, *War Torn Environment: Interpreting the Legal Threshold* (Leiden: Martinus Nijhoff, 2005).

355 At Rule 45, the ICRC in its customary law study proposes that the principle established in Article 35(3) is a norm of customary international law, applicable in both international and internal armed conflict. See Henkaerts and Doswald-Beck, *supra* note 14 at volume I, chapter 14, p. 151. The ICRC also suggests that the United States may be a persistent objector to this rule. For the concept of persistent objector, see *Anglo-Norwegian Fisheries Case (UK v. Norway)*, (1951) I.C.J. Rep. 139, and *Asylum Case (Colombia v. Peru)*, (1950) I.C.J. Rep. 266.

356 Some delegates at the negotiating conference saw no need for two separate provisions. Note the opinion of Mr. Eaton, the UK delegate, in "International Humanitarian Law Applicable in Armed Conflicts," *supra* note 350 at vol. 14 at para. 46.

their positioning within Geneva Protocol I. Article 55 is included within Part IV (on civilian populations), Chapter III on Civilian Objects, and appears to reflect and emphasize the principle of distinction as it relates to the environment. This context is provided by its surrounding provisions, namely Articles 52(1) and 48, which codify the principle that military forces must distinguish between civilian persons and objects and military persons and objectives. The military must direct its conflict only to the latter. Article 35(3), on the other hand, finds inclusion within Part III (on Methods and Means of Warfare, Combatant and Prisoner of War Status), Section I on Methods or Means of Warfare, and extends the prohibition of "unnecessary suffering" contained in Article 35(2)[357] to the natural environment.[358]

For both Articles 55(1) and 35(3), it is only the use of those means and methods *intended* or *expected* to have the stated environmental result that is prohibited. Clearly, therefore, state parties must address the possibility of environmental damage resulting from their actions. It would not be sufficient for a state to simply deny that it had the intention or purpose to cause the environmental damage if the damage would have been a foreseeable consequence of its actions. Similarly, *neither* prohibition would apply if the threshold of "widespread, long-term and severe damage to the natural environment" were not foreseeably breached. The language remains unclear, however, in regard to the effects of a particular weapon. In line with other provisions, it is suggested that the weapon's effects are judged on the basis of the "attack considered as a whole and not from isolated or particular parts of that attack."[359]

It is clear from the language of the two provisions that the threshold that is indicated — namely, that of "widespread, long-term and severe" environmental damage — is intended to be an absolute maximum level of harm. Consequently, violation of the prohibition would occur where a state intended or expected such a high level of environmental damage to result from its actions. No definition of the three terms (widespread, long term, and severe) was included

---

[357] Geneva Protocol I, *supra* note 11, Article 35(2), states the basic and customary prohibition on the infliction of unnecessary suffering and superfluous injury.

[358] This distinction was drawn in committee discussions. See "Biotope," Report to the Chairman of the Group Official Records of the Diplomatic Conference, Doc. CDDH/III/GT/35 (11 March 1975) at para. 11.

[359] In relation to the aspects of military advantage, many delegates made reference to this definition, for the comments by Australia and New Zealand, see Henkaerts and Doswald-Beck, *supra* note 14 at volume II, chapter 4, section C, para. 161.

within Geneva Protocol I, but some indications were given at the committee stage and on ratification of what they did *not* mean.[360] According to delegates, the terms were not to be given the same meaning as those recently defined for the 1977 United Nations Convention on the Prohibition of Military or Any Other Hostile Use of Environmental Modification Techniques (Environmental Modification Convention).[361] The 1977 Environmental Modification Convention prohibits the modification of the environment as a weapon of war, namely, for military or hostile purposes. Accordingly, Article I of the convention stipulates that "[e]ach State Party to this Convention undertakes not to engage in military or any other hostile use of environmental modification techniques having widespread, long-lasting or severe effects as the means of destruction, damage or injury to any other State Party." Included within a set of understandings written contemporaneously,[362] the three terms have been defined as follows: "Widespread" means "an area of several hundred square kilometres,"[363] "long-lasting" means "several months or more, or approximately a season,"[364] and "severe" means "severe or significant disruption or harm to human life, natural or economic resources, or other assets." The main difference between the two thresholds is that one is cumulative (Geneva Protocol I) and the other disjunctive (Environmental Modification Convention). This factor immediately raises the threshold for environmental "harm" under Geneva Protocol I before any analysis of terminology is addressed. Other statements given during the committee stages indicate that the time scale of harm for Geneva Protocol I was that of "decades, twenty or thirty years as being a minimum."[365] With the inclusion of the notion of long-term harm, the environmental provisions clearly contain a temporal dimension to the anticipated harm. In other words, the military must assess the potential environmental harm arising from a particular

---

360 "International Humanitarian Law Applicable in Armed Conflicts," Comments by the German delegate, Plenary Meeting, Doc. CDDH/SR.39 (25 May 1977), at vol. 6, 113, annex.

361 Environmental Modification Convention, *supra* note 170.

362 See generally P. Fauteux, "The Gulf War, The ENMOD Convention and the Review Conference" (1992) 18 UNIDIR Newsletter 6.

363 To give some indication of scale, Greater London is 1,620 square kilometres.

364 "Several" for the scale of harm generally indicates more than two but is not a precise quantity.

365 "International Humanitarian Law Applicable in Armed Conflicts," *supra* note 350 at para. 27.

military operation both (1) as an immediate consequence and (2) as a future consequence.

Despite the general understanding that the Environmental Modification Convention standard was not to be adopted, the United States appears to have done just that. In the 1995 *Operational Law Handbook of the United States*, the definition suggested for "widespread" is akin to the Environmental Modification Convention's scale of "hundreds of kilometres."[366] This phrasing is interesting from a number of perspectives — first and foremost, since the United States has not ratified Geneva Protocol I and, hence, indicates state *opinio iuris* of the standard for a possible customary rule.[367]

In regard to "severe" harm, the *travaux préparatoires* indicate the "severity or prejudicial effect of the damage *to the civilian population.*"[368] Clearly the element of "severe" refers to the *intensity* of the resulting environmental damage, but, in this remark, the delegates have referenced the human population as forming an essential component of this intensity.[369] If this is the case then, similarly to earlier definitions of "pollution,"[370] the environment is not "severely" damaged unless humans, or some human utility, are prejudiced. If this is the definition of "severe" environmental damage, the protection provided by Article 35(3) is not afforded the environment

---

366 See International and Operational Law Department, U.S. Army, *Operational Law Handbook* (1995), reproduced in part in M.N. Schmitt, "Green War: An Assessment of the Environmental Law of International Armed Conflict" (1997) 22 Yale J. Int'l L. 1 at 71.

367 Other states have also adopted the terminology of the provision in their military manuals, domestic legislation, and other statements, including Belgium, the United Kingdom, Azerbaijan, and Kenya, at a date before becoming a party to the treaty. In its report to the ICRC on its practice, the non-party Israel also refers to the threshold of harm established in Geneva Protocol I. See Henkaerts and Doswald-Beck, *supra* note 14 at volume II, chapter 14, section C. paras. 166, 175, 184, 191, and 241.

368 [Emphasis added]. "International Humanitarian Law Applicable in Armed Conflicts," *supra* note 350 at para. 27.

369 The committee's reference here to the "civilian" population is too narrow. See Y. Sandoz, C. Swinarski, and B. Zimmermann, eds., *International Committee of the Red Cross Commentary on the Additional Protocols of 8 June, 1977, to the Geneva Conventions of 12 August, 1949: In Collaboration with Jean Pictet* (Geneva: Martinus Nijhoff, 1987) at 663–64.

370 For example, air pollution is defined as "deleterious effects as to *endanger human health*, harm living resources and ecosystems and material property and impair or interfere with amenities and other legitimate uses of the environment," see Article 1(a) of the 1979 Convention on Long-Range Transboundary

per se as appeared to be the purpose behind the inclusion of two separate provisions in Geneva Protocol I. The US army handbook bolsters this interpretation, when it explains the concept of "severe" in terms of the reference in Article 55 to the "health or survival of the population."[371] However, it is possible that while states did intend the additional human element for Article 55(1), they did not intend it for Article 35(3), wherein "severe environmental damage" would include changes in the ecosystem of the *type* that would induce human effects it was *not* intended to be a requirement for breach of the provision that those human effects actually be induced. This might, for instance, include the causing of mutagenic effects in animal species that could harm humans if they were actually present in the environment. Finally, the "population" that is referred to might be that of today or future generations,[372] thus both short-term and long-term health and survival is contemplated. Likewise, the inclusion of the words "health or survival" was viewed as adding a further element to both human and environmental protection.[373] Consequently, actions are also prohibited that would cause, should the population survive, such serious health problems as to pass from one generation to another. The delegates spoke on this point of such health problems as congenital defects.[374]

Since what is at issue is the environmental effects of the depleted uranium metal used in the weapons, the effects of individual types of depleted uranium weaponry (120 mm tank rounds, 25 mm

---

Air Pollution, 13 November 1979, (1979) 18 I.L.M. 1442 (entered into force 16 March 1983) [emphasis added]. Arguably, this is still the most common approach to environmental protection taken today.

371 The United States has not ratified the Geneva Protocols. However, it includes reference to the provision in its army handbook. See International and Operational Law Department, US Army, *Operational Law Handbook* (1995), reproduced in part in Schmitt, *supra* note 366 at 71.

372 Note the environmental law principle of inter-generational equity. Principle 3 of the 1992 Rio Declaration on Environment and Development, 13 June 1992, (1992) 31 I.L.M. 874 (1992) [Rio Declaration], accordingly directs that the right to development is to be fulfilled "so as to equitably meet developmental and environmental needs of present and future generations." The notion has also been recognized in Article 3(1) of the 1992 United Nations Framework Convention on Climate Change, (1992) 31 I.L.M. 849 (opened for signature 9 May 1992, in force 24 March 1994) [UNFCCC].

373 Report of Committee III, Second Session, in "International Humanitarian Law Applicable in Armed Conflicts," *supra* note 350 at para. 82.

374 Sandoz, Swinarski, and Zimmermann, eds., *supra* note 369 at 663.

rounds, and 20 mm naval rounds) need not form part of the analysis. It must be recognized, however, that tank rounds contain a larger volume of depleted uranium metal and produce a greater volume of aerosolized uranium oxide on impact. Consequently, the use of tank rounds may more easily violate the threshold of environmental harm than the smaller-calibre rounds. Using the interpretations suggested earlier as a basis for the analysis, therefore, "widespread" effects of depleted uranium rounds could be caused by (1) the migration of depleted uranium oxide particles outside the area of impact; (2) the penetration of the water table; (3) the contamination of soil; and (4) genetic and terotogenic effects in species (including humans) affecting future generations that migrate out of the impact area. Contamination of the three environmental pathways (1–3) may all lead to human (combatant and civilian) victims. From the published evidence, however, the potential extent of such contamination is still disputed.

It might be suggested that the most serious concerns for water contamination are in regard to groundwater and drinking water. While NATO admitted the use of depleted uranium ammunition at 112 sites in Kosovo, firing some 31,000 rounds, the UNEP Kosovo study suggests that there is no evidence, to date, of depleted uranium having penetrated the Kosovan water table.[375] The UNEP Bosnian study has also concluded that contamination of the groundwater can only be expected in the "worst geochemical conditions,"[376] but it failed to define these further. Much is dependent upon the soil and sub-surface rock types and the depth of the groundwater table, but the UNEP Bosnia report does indicate that this may be a cause for concern, particularly at the sites of corroding depleted uranium penetrators.[377] This same report also found some evidence of contamination of drinking water with depleted uranium at one site.[378] Although the report concludes that the "concentration was low and insignificant from a radiological and chemical toxicological point of view," it also recognizes that it "was indicative of possible future water contamination over time."[379] Accordingly, UNEP suggests that this finding justifies the need for continued

---

[375] *Depleted Uranium in Kosovo, supra* note 28 at 34.

[376] *Depleted Uranium in Bosnia, supra* note 54 at 186.

[377] *Ibid.* at 186–7 and 31.

[378] This involved a tank repair facility. *Ibid.* at 36 and 71.

[379] *Ibid.* at 36.

checking in the future.[380] In all, nineteen water samples were taken from eleven selected sites, including springs, streams, wells, reservoirs, rivers, and public taps. From these nineteen samples, the uranium concentration was found to be within the "normal range" for drinking water,[381] which is the threshold of "significant" contamination chosen by the UNEP experts. The range of uranium concentrations found in the water samples is given as 0.02–2.7 micrograms per litre. This appears to be well within the various state guidelines given in Appendix O of the UNEP report, of 30 micrograms per litre for the United States, 100 micrograms per litre for the European Union, and 10 micrograms per litre for Canada.[382] However, it is above the current WHO standard of just 2 micrograms per litre. The report, however, suggests that the WHO is considering revising this standard upwards to 9 micrograms per litre.[383]

With respect to the airborne pathway of depleted uranium contamination, both Greece and Bulgaria reported that higher than normal levels of radiation had been detected following the 1999 Kosovo conflict.[384] According to the Yugoslavian letter to the UN secretary-general in 1999, levels in Greece were apparently twenty-five times higher than normal, while in Bulgaria they were eight times higher.[385] Official US government sources, however, indicate that most depleted uranium particles should reach ground level within five minutes and 500 metres of impact.[386] The UNEP Bosnia study puts the distance at only 200 metres of impact.[387] While these numbers appear to suggest that there may not be widespread migration of airborne contaminants, there remains the possibility of the re-suspension of uranium oxide dust and the problem of multiple small pockets of depleted uranium contaminated land. Re-suspension of uranium oxide dust during excavation, farming, or house building, for example, may certainly be a future problem.[388]

[380] *Ibid.*

[381] *Ibid.* at 35.

[382] *Ibid.* at 186 and 280.

[383] *Ibid.* at 186.

[384] See the "Facts on Consequences of the Use of Depleted Uranium," *supra* note 348 at para. 8.

[385] *Ibid.*

[386] "Lord Parry's 'Starred' Question," *supra* note 145 at para. 40.

[387] *Depleted Uranium in Bosnia, supra* note 54 at 30.

[388] *Depleted Uranium in Serbia, supra* note 61 at 30.

The UNEP study in Bosnia Herzegovina took some twenty-four samples from six sites, two of which showed clear indications of depleted uranium in the air.[389] Furthermore, the two samples had higher than "normal" concentrations. This result, the report suggests, was due to the re-suspension of depleted uranium dust by either wind conditions or human activities.[390] Consequently, UNEP was able to comment that, "with conservative assumptions, inhalation might lead to significant doses (defined to exceed 1 mSv)."[391] These are the first substantial indications, therefore, that depleted uranium weaponry has long-term contaminants and the potential for long-term pollution.

Furthermore, during its Kosovo field assessment, UNEP found traces of airborne contamination and soil contamination of depleted uranium near to the targeted sites more than a year and a half after deployment[392] and seven years and twelve years in Bosnia and Kuwait respectively. Although localized, the concentration of depleted uranium at impact points was described to be "very high."[393] Furthermore, the dispersion of depleted uranium in the soil was measured at a depth of 40 cm, which is an increase from the 10 cm depth measured in Kosovo.[394] This appears to show that in the five additional years since the use of depleted uranium weaponry in Bosnia the contaminants had travelled deeper into the ground. Most alarming is the discrepancy between the volume of weapons reportedly used at a particular site and the number of spent depleted uranium penetrators recovered. While up to 70 per cent of depleted uranium penetrators will aerosolize on contact with a hard target/ surface, UNEP was unable to account for more than a handful of spent weapons at each site. The more likely scenario, suggested by UNEP, was that the penetrators had missed the target and were buried in the ground.

The UNEP studies, therefore, appear to evidence high localized contamination, with long-term potential, but only a small risk of migration. Since Article 55(1) specifically mentions the effects on

---

389 *Ibid.* at 36.

390 *Ibid.*

391 *Depleted Uranium in Bosnia, supra* note 54 at 34. Note that the European Committee on Radiation Risk (ECRR) has recently criticized this "safe" level of 1 mSv and has suggested a preferred level of 0.1 mSv per year. Busby et al., eds., *supra* note 80.

392 "UNEP Recommends Precautionary Action," *supra* note 124.

393 *Depleted Uranium in Bosnia, supra* note 54 at 30.

394 *Ibid.* at 32.

civilians, and people form part of the environment in any event, the more pertinent issue concerns the health effects in humans. None of the UNEP assessments, however, included human sampling to test for concentrations of depleted uranium in the organs of combatants or civilians. And yet there is a growing body of independent scientific evidence that links depleted uranium with genetic mutations and other long-term and incurable illnesses. Studies undertaken by staff at the US Armed Forces Radiobiology Research Institute have confirmed that embedded depleted uranium can cause neurological damage,[395] in addition to damage to cells, genes, and the central nervous system.[396] The UK government admits that depleted uranium causes kidney damage and possible malfunction but suggests that such damage is "likely" to be reversible.[397] In regard to embedded depleted uranium fragments, the Baltimore study has confirmed the findings of the European Commission's experts, of ongoing uranium absorption from embedded depleted uranium fragments.[398] Among the health effects recorded in those studied are (1) chromosomal aberrations;[399] (2) some neurocognitive impairment;[400] and (3) some mutagenic effects.[401] These effects are confirmed by studies in rats and other animals as well as by "decreased fertility, embryo/foetal toxicity including teratogenicity, reduced growth of the offspring,"[402] skeletal abnormalities, and developmental malfunctions.[403] These findings are no doubt strongly suggestive of both "severe" and "long-term" harm.

---

[395] See T.C. Pellmar, D.O. Keyser, C. Emery, and J.B. Hogan, "Electrophysiological Changes in Hippocampal Slices Isolated from Rats Embedded with Depleted Uranium Fragments" (1999) 20(5) Neurotoxicology 785 at 790.

[396] A.C. Miller, M. Stewart, K. Brooks, L. Shi, and N. Page, "Depleted Uranium-Catalyzed Oxidative DNA Damage: Absence of Significant Alpha Particle Decay" (2002) 91 J. Inorganic Biochemistry 246 at 251.

[397] "Review of the Hazards," *supra* note 92.

[398] See McDiarmid et al., *supra* note 104.

[399] *Ibid.* at 289.

[400] *Ibid.* at 287–88.

[401] *Ibid.* at 291.

[402] J.L. Domingo, "Reproductive and Developmental Toxicity of Natural and Depleted Uranium: A Review" (2001) 15 Reproductive Toxicology 603 at 603.

[403] See WHO, Department of Protection of the Human Environment, *Depleted Uranium: Sources, Exposure and Health Effects*, Doc. WHO/SDE/PHE/01.1 (Geneva: WHO, April 2001), available at <http://www.who.int/ionizing_radiation/pub_meet/ir_pubs/en/> (3 July 2001)); and "Health Hazards of Depleted Uranium Munitions," *supra* note 109.

Does the evidence suggest that the use of depleted uranium weaponry inevitably breaches Article 35(3) or 55(1)? If the answer is yes, then depleted uranium weapons also violate Article 51(4) of Geneva Protocol I, with the result that they are inherently indiscriminate or unlimited effects weapons. All weapons are composed of chemicals dangerous to humans and the environment. Clearly, therefore, all weapons will cause some — however minute — level of chemical contamination in the environment. Yet this contamination is not what the environmental provisions were designed to prohibit. The threshold of harm incorporated within Articles 35(3) and 55(1) was set at a high level in order to balance the needs of the military in using effective weaponry with the needs of the environment and humans of ensuring their continued health and viability. Early concerns of the potential harm of depleted uranium metal have now been supplemented by a growing body of scientific evidence of actual harm in humans. This evidence, however, may only show a violation of the forbidden threshold of harm in the case of embedded depleted uranium fragments. The UNEP studies appear to confirm the long-term presence of depleted uranium in some water, soil, and air samples but indicate little evidence of the adverse consequences of such findings. Since the embedment of depleted uranium would tend to occur only as a result of direct fire, it is suggested that other principles of humanitarian law may be more relevant, such as the principles of (1) unnecessary suffering; (2) indiscriminatory use of a particular weapon at the point of use; and (3) proportionality. Since the first two of these principles have already been examined, the article will now turn to the principle of proportionality.

Principle of Proportionality

Certainly since the conflict in Vietnam, which introduced the world to the notion of environmental warfare, the principle of proportionality has encompassed the expected or foreseeable effects on both civilians and the environment.[404] From the perspective of depleted uranium weapons, such effects include environmental contamination and the long-term threat to environmental viability and, for civilians, the risk of internalization and carcinogenic or genetic problems. How does the rule of proportionality apply so as to minimize or prevent such harm?

---

[404] See generally Schmitt, *supra* note 366.

The customary law principle of proportionality derives from the principle of discrimination (or distinction) between military and non-military persons and objects. While the concept of discrimination dictates that only military persons and objectives should be targeted in an attack, the principle of proportionality recognizes that sometimes lawful targeting will involve harm to civilians and their property. For example, civilians working within, or within the vicinity of, military installations may be harmed during a lawful attack on that objective. While the principle certainly recognizes that some civilian harm in warfare may be lawful, it also establishes the limits of potential harm. In this way, the principle establishes the compromise between the two competing concepts of military necessity and humanity. In sum, the principle of proportionality serves to reduce the amount of incidental damage caused in wartime to non-military objects, which would result from an attack. The principle may have received its first recognition as a limit on lawful warfare in the 1863 Lieber Code — Article 15 of which stipulates that "[m]ilitary necessity admits of all direct destruction of life or limb of armed enemies, and of other persons whose destruction is *incidentally unavoidable* in the armed contests of war."[405]

While the Lieber article is a good first indication of the principle, it raises many more questions than it answers. For example, what is meant by "incidentally unavoidable destruction"? When is destruction "incidental" and to what must it be incidental to? How far is a party obliged to go to avoid incidental civilian "destruction"? Is he obliged to take extra risks that might endanger his own forces in order to avoid such incidental civilian harm? Is there any limit on the volume of civilian "destruction" — in other words, the number of persons that might be incidentally killed or harmed? Some of these issues of course would have been resolved largely due to the nature of warfare at that time. Certainly before the Second World War, civilians tended to be absent from the battlefields, usually fleeing upon the approach of the enemy, and so many issues of discrimination and proportionality failed to arise.[406] Furthermore, so-called collateral damage to civilians and civilian property only really became an issue after the advent of air warfare and large-tonnage bombs. And so many of these questions remained until the drafting of the Geneva Protocols in 1977, and, to some extent, many still remain unanswered today.

---

[405] Lieber's Code and the Law of War, *supra* note 155 [emphasis added].

[406] W. Hays Parks, "Air War and the Law of War" (1990) 32 A.F.L. Rev. 1.

The customary principle of proportionality was codified in Article 51(5)(b) of Geneva Protocol I as

[a]n attack which may be expected to cause incidental loss of civilian life, injury to civilians, damage to civilian objects, or a combination thereof, which would be *excessive* in relation to the *concrete and direct* military advantage *anticipated*.[407]

Consequently, collateral damage, in the legal sense, is only that damage which is incidental to the attack of a military objective and, in any case, must not be excessive when compared to the military advantage that it is anticipated will be gained from the attack.[408] In this way, the likely harm to civilian persons and objects forms part of the military calculation for a particular attack. The definition clearly requires a balancing exercise. Obviously, if a target is a military objective it may be attacked. Only if there are also present at the scene of the attack, persons or objects that are not military objectives does the principle of proportionality arise. The military must then make a decision, based on all of the information available to it at the time,[409] whether the military advantage that it anticipates to be gained from the attack outweighs the incidental damage likely to be inflicted on civilian objects in the vicinity. Proportionality is thus a judgment that must be made at the time of attack, and, while it does not guarantee absolute protection to civilians and civilian objects, it does provide a method of balancing the values at stake, albeit not a very helpful one. Dieter Fleck outlines the need for incidental civilian harm that is "commensurate" with the anticipated military advantage, but he continues by pointing

---

[407] Geneva Protocol I, *supra* note 11 [emphasis added]. See Bothe, Partsch, and Solf, *supra* note 246 at 309, where Article 51(5)(b) is viewed as a "concrete codification of the principle of proportionality." The United States view that the original ICRC provision regarding proportionality was a codification of existing international law, in W.J. Fenrick, "The Rule of Proportionality and Protocol I in Conventional Warfare" 98 (1982) Mil. L. Rev. 91 at 104. See also Article 57(2)(a)(iii) and (b) of Geneva Protocol I; and Henkaerts and Doswald-Beck, *supra* note 14 at volume I, chapter 4, p. 46, where the ICRC concludes that state practice establishes the rule of proportionality (Rule 14) as a customary norm applicable in international and non-international armed conflict.

[408] An indiscriminate attack launched with the knowledge of disproportionate effects is also classified as a grave breach of the Geneva Conventions by Article 85(3)(b) of Geneva Protocol I, *supra* note 11.

[409] See the statements made on ratification by Algeria, Australia, Austria, Belgium, Canada, Egypt, Germany, Ireland, Italy, the Netherlands, New Zealand, Spain,

out that this approach creates "serious difficulties in practice."[410] Michael Schmitt emphasizes that "optimally, balancing tests compare like values," whereas he posits how one should "objectively calculate the relative weight of an aircraft, tank, ship, or vantage point in terms of human casualties?"[411] While some indicate that the decision is one for the "reasonable military commander,"[412] others recognize the inherent subjectivity of the exercise for military decision-makers.[413] Furthermore, it is suggested that the value of human life may not even be the uniform factor that one might have thought it to be. Schmitt suggests that more developed states may allocate greater value to human life than lesser-developed states — the latter he describes as having a more fatalistic populace.[414] This would appear to complicate further the concept of "excessive" civilian harm, which William J. Fenrick defines to mean at a minimum as "severe."[415] Furthermore, in the case of collateral environmental damage, many would seem to suggest that the level of military advantage required is much less than if civilians were endangered.[416] From this viewpoint, the current evidence on environmental harm from depleted uranium weapons may lack the level of severity demanded to outweigh even the most lowly anticipated military advantages.

From the provision in Article 51(5)(b), the particular military advantage anticipated must be both a "concrete" and "direct" result of the attack. In this way, the proportionality equation serves to narrow down the range of lawful attacks derived from the definition of "military objectives." The definition of "military objectives" already

---

and the United Kingdom, restated in the ICRC customary study, Henkaerts and Doswald-Beck, *supra* note 14 at volume II, chapter 4, paras. 193–205.

410 D. Fleck, ed., *The Handbook of Humanitarian Law in Armed Conflicts* (Oxford: Oxford University Press, 1995) at para. 456.

411 M. Schmitt, "The Principle of Discrimination in Twenty-First Century Warfare" 2 (1999) Yale H.R. & Dev.L.J. 143 at 151. See also W. Fenrick, "The Rule of Proportionality and Protocol I in Conventional Warfare" 98 (1982) Mil. L. Rev. 91 at 95.

412 International Criminal Tribunal for the Former Yugoslavia (ICTY), "Final Report to the Prosecutor by the Committee Established to Review the NATO Bombing Campaign against the Federal Republic of Yugoslavia," 8 June 2000, (2000) 39 I.L.M. 1257 at para. 50.

413 Schmitt, *supra* note 411 at 157.

414 *Ibid.* at 158.

415 Fenrick, *supra* note 411 at 111.

416 ICTY, *supra* note 412 at para. 22.

reduces the number of targets to those offering a "definite" advantage, but, in order to comply with the rule of proportionality, the military advantage must also be a "concrete" result of the attack. While no definition is given of these two terms and the rapporteur was unable to draw any significance from the chosen words,[417] in the context that they are used, "definite" may refer to a specific advantage, the limits of which can be exactly discerned in advance, while "concrete" may refer to advantages that are realistic or tangible. "Direct" will clearly rule out any military advantages that are not sufficiently linked to the particular target(s) to be attacked or results of the attack taken as a whole.[418] The terms "concrete" and "direct," therefore, place further limits on the ability to launch an attack where incidental civilian harm will occur. The additional requirement is that the military advantage anticipated *outweighs* the damage likely to be inflicted, incidentally and unavoidably, on civilian objects in the vicinity. The value that can be assigned to the military advantage is also a fluid factor and is often dependent upon such factors as the stage in the conflict that an objective is attacked and any disparity in military strength of the parties.[419] This latter point also affects the notion of "unavoidable" harm. As Schmitt recognizes, a subjective assessment should be made of the type and level of harm that is unavoidable based upon a state's own military and technological capabilities. In essence, he suggests that "different states will be subject to different standards based upon their capabilities."[420] Beyond this suggestion though, he again raises even more questions regarding whether a state would be required to use precision-guided munitions if they are in its possession, whether the state is allowed to hold such weapons in reserve, and to what extent its capacity to acquire more stocks of such weapons should affect their rate of deployment.[421]

---

417 Sandoz, Swinarski, and Zimmermann, eds., *supra* note 369 at 326 and 637; and Bothe, Partsch, and Solf, *supra* note 246 at 365.

418 Fleck refers to the "wider military campaign of which the attack forms part." Fleck, ed., *supra* note 410 at para. 456, which is based on statements made by a number of states during the diplomatic conference. In their instruments of ratification, Belgium, Canada, France, Germany, Italy, the Netherlands, Spain, and the United Kingdom refer to the "military advantage that can be expected from the attack as a whole and not only of isolated or specific parts of the attack." See Henkaerts and Doswald-Beck, *supra* note 14 at volume II, chapter 4, para. 161.

419 Schmitt, *supra* note 411 at 157.

420 *Ibid.* at 170.

421 *Ibid.*

Finally, what is not clear from the provision — and what would appear vital to the issue of the proportionality of depleted uranium weapons attacks — is the scope of the necessary "expectation" or foreseeable effects. In essence, the question is whether the military commander must base his expectations of collateral damage on the moment or on the immediate aftermath of the attack, or, indeed, if possible, if he must include future harm if that is reasonably foreseeable. Clearly, the anticipated military advantage is based in terms of a future benefit — possibly having both immediate and longer-term gains.[422] And yet the issue of basing the expected harm beyond the immediate aftermath of the attack is controversial. The question appears by many to be left open — a Pandora's Box, the contents of which few would wish to be unleashed.[423] In the context of unexploded cluster weapons, Christopher Greenwood argues that only the immediate effects of such weapons should be included within the military calculation of proportionality.[424] He does in fact extend the time frame to include the risks from unexploded sub-munitions in the "hours immediately after the attack" but no further. The basis of Greenwood's opinion is a list of factors that may affect the return of civilians to the affected area, such as "when and whether civilians will be permitted to return to an area, what steps the party controlling that area will have taken to clear unexploded ordnance, what priority that party gives to the protection of civilians and so forth."[425] As a consequence, Greenwood suggests that the attacking state would be incapable of making this assessment at the time of the attack, as envisaged by states parties to Geneva Protocol I.[426] On the other hand, the ICRC's response was for the inclusion of all "foreseeable short and long

---

[422] Fenrick, for example, addresses the issue of the scale on which the military advantage is to be weighed — both temporally and geographically. He suggests that these are unclear. See Fenrick, *supra* note 411 at 126.

[423] "What is the standard of measurement in time or space?" This question was among those raised but left unanswered in the report of the ICTY, *supra* note 412 at para. 49.

[424] C. Greenwood, "Legal Issues Regarding Explosive Remnants of War," Group of Government Experts of States Parties to the Convention on Prohibitions or Restrictions on the Use of Certain Conventional Weapons Which May Be Deemed to Be Excessively Injurious or to Have Indiscriminate Effects, Doc. CCW/GGE/I/WP.10 (23 May 2002) at 8.

[425] *Ibid.*

[426] The United Kingdom, among others, included such a declaration with its instrument of ratification of Geneva Protocol I, see the United Kingdom Ministry of Defence, *supra* note 246 at 87.

term effects."[427] While these comments were made in the context of the collateral effects of unexploded cluster weapons, there is no reason for them to be confined to that specific weapon type. The factors to which Greenwood refers could easily be transposed to an analysis of depleted uranium weaponry, leading to the question, *inter alia*, concerning how quickly the affected state could be decontaminated.

The essential point of contention, therefore, is whether the concept of proportionality includes any reference to time. There is clearly a spatial element to the proportionality principle in regard to the collateral harm caused in the vicinity of the attack at the point of use. Temporal proportionality, however, would be concerned with the harm to civilians beyond the point of use and into the future. For example, such effects would include the potentially long-term effects in the environment, such as contamination of the groundwater and agricultural soils, and the resulting human health effects. Additional support is provided for this interpretation by Michael Bothe, Karl Josef Partsch, and Waldemar A. Solf in their official commentary to Geneva Protocol I, which makes reference to unmarked minefields as offending against Article 51(4)(b) and (c) due to being blind as to time.[428] The ICRC in its recent study on customary humanitarian law also refers to the element of time when providing an interpretation of Article 51(4)(c) of Geneva Protocol I.[429] This provision, it will be recalled, incorporates the rule of proportionality as a limit on the use of weapons that would cause indiscriminate effects. Practice regarding paragraph (c), according to the ICRC, "points to weapons whose effects are uncontrollable in *time* and space and are likely to strike military objectives and civilians or civilian objects without distinction."[430] In the section of the report dedicated to state practice, the ICRC makes reference to Article 14 of the 1956 ICRC New Delhi Draft Rules for

---

[427] ICRC, "Existing Principles and Rules of International Humanitarian Law Applicable to Munitions that may become Explosive Remnants of War," Group of Government Experts of States Parties to the Convention on Prohibitions or Restrictions on the Use of Certain Conventional Weapons Which May Be Deemed to Be Excessively Injurious or to Have Indiscriminate Effects, Doc. CCW/GGE/XI/WG.1/WP.7 (28 July 2005) at 4.

[428] Bothe, Partsch, and Solf, *supra* note 246 at 308.

[429] Henkaerts and Doswald-Beck, *supra* note 14 at volume I, chapter 3, p. 43.

[430] *Ibid.* at 43 [emphasis added].

the Limitation of the Dangers Incurred by the Civilian Population in Time of War,[431] which states that,

[w]ithout prejudice to the present or future prohibition of certain specific weapons, the use is prohibited of weapons whose harmful effects — resulting in particular from the dissemination of incendiary, chemical bacteriological, radioactive or other agents — could spread to an unforeseen degree or escape, either in space or *time*, from the control of those who employ them, thus endangering the civilian population.[432]

In addition, the practice of the ICRC, in disseminating the rules of humanitarian law, teaches that "belligerent Parties and their armed forces shall abstain from using weapons whose harmful effects go beyond the control, in *time* or place, of those employing them."[433] Finally, some support for the contention that Article 51(4)(c) includes effects in time is given by the United States. In its 1976 US air force pamphlet,[434] the United States establishes an interpretation of disproportionate effects as being caused by those weapons that entail uncontrollable effects, such as biological weapons. Accordingly, the pamphlet states that

[u]ncontrollable refers to effects which escape in *time* or space from the control of the user as to necessarily create risks to civilian persons or objects excessive in relation to the military advantage anticipated.[435]

Although the requirements of the principle are not precise, there are clearly suggestions that an evolving principle of proportionality

---

431 The draft rules were a result of ICRC efforts on texts designed to "protect civilian populations efficiently from the dangers of atomic, chemical and bacteriological warfare." The draft rules were submitted to governments but made little progress, although many of the draft rules were later adopted in the 1977 Geneva Protocols. "1956 ICRC New Delhi Draft Rules for the Limitation of the Dangers incurred by the Civilian Population in Time of War," available at <http://www.icrc.org/ihl.nsf/WebList?ReadForm&id=420&t=art> (10 October 2005).

432 *Ibid.* [emphasis added].

433 F. de Mulinen, *Handbook on the Law of War for Armed Forces* (Geneva: ICRC, 1987) at 199, para. 912(c), reprinted in Henkaerts and Doswald-Beck, *supra* note 14 at volume II, chapter 3, section B, para. 279 [emphasis added].

434 US, Air Force Pamphlet (1976), para. 6-3(c), reprinted in Henkaerts and Doswald-Beck, *supra* note 14, at volume II, chapter 3, section B, para. 258.

435 *Ibid.* [emphasis added]. See also the dissenting opinion of Judge Higgins in *Nuclear Weapons, supra* note 174 at para. 18.

should take into account anticipated future harm (beyond the immediate aftermath of an attack) if those effects are clearly within the realms of (reasonable) foreseeability. There is also evidence from state practice that this approach has met with some degree of acceptance. It may therefore be the case that the element of proportionality in time is evolving or emerging into a customary notion. If this were the case, then it is suggested that when it comes to specific weapons and their long-term collateral effects, these would fulfil the necessary requirements of foreseeability in order to form part of the proportionality equation. The fact that this should be so is inherent in the legal requirement for thorough testing of weapons before acquisition or deployment, as established in Article 36 of Geneva Protocol I.[436] However, this is a major stumbling block for depleted uranium weaponry, in that thirteen years of deployment has not yet resulted in complete agreement as to the weapon's effects.

It is suggested, therefore, that there are two scenarios by which to consider the proportionality of using depleted uranium weapons in an attack: (1) the longer-term human health and environmental harm due to the presence of depleted uranium in the environment and (2) direct civilian injury at the point of use of depleted uranium rounds, particularly by the embedding of depleted uranium fragments in the body. Current scientific evidence suggests that the level of foreseeable future harm in the first scenario is not that high and one might suggest that as a consequence it would be difficult to prove the disproportionality of any attack that had even a low- to middle-range advantage. At this point, the evidence does not appear to support the requirement for a complete prohibition on the use of depleted uranium weapons on the basis that their very use in any attack would be disproportionate.

The second scenario involves a more specific injury and so a more specific attack scenario. The point has already been made that due to the greater degree of accuracy achieved by tank fire, it may be the case that the 120 mm tank rounds may safely and lawfully be used in the presence of civilians. There may, of course, be the additional risk of ricochet of depleted uranium rounds off the tank itself or off the ground in the event of a miss. The probability of civilians receiving embedded fragments of depleted uranium is increased — and therefore the risk of developing cancers and other genetic defects would also be greater — if those civilians are in the vicinity

---

436 Geneva Protocol I, *supra* note 11.

of an attack with smaller-calibre (30 mm) rounds. These rounds are generally fired from Gatling guns mounted onto aircraft, which achieve a substantially lower degree of accuracy — possibly as little as 4–10 per cent.[437] In aerial attacks of this nature, where civilians and military objectives are in relatively close proximity, it may be argued that the foreseeable level of collateral harm — specifically due to the effects of embedded fragments — is clearly high.[438] This is so whether the weapon contains depleted uranium or not. In the case of depleted uranium weapons, however, the risks of injury appear to be greater due to the potentially long-term carcinogenic and genetic effects that do not generally accompany other bullet materials. In other words, with any bullet the victim can be killed or maimed, but not all leave a cancerous legacy in the living. Consequently, if the foreseeable level of collateral harm is high, it is suggested that the military would need to demonstrate an anticipated advantage of (at least) correspondingly high magnitude.[439] In order to risk such direct harm to a large number of civilians nearby — of being hit with a depleted uranium bullet or fragment — aerial attacks would need to produce a weighty military advantage. Of course, this is not to suggest that it is never proportionate to use depleted uranium weapons in the vicinity of civilians but, rather, that when it is to be carried out the corresponding military advantage that is anticipated must be very high in order for the attack to remain legal.

DEPLETED URANIUM WEAPONS: OPTIONS FOR THE FUTURE

What scientific studies to date suggest is that there are very real health and environmental concerns surrounding the military use of depleted uranium weapons. What the laws of armed conflict suggest is that their use may in certain scenarios be testing the limits of legality. Yet if there is little prospect of possessor states agreeing to a complete prohibition on the use of some or all types of depleted uranium weapons, then more realistic limitations may remain possible. Consequently, the final point for consideration is whether

---

[437] "Depleted Uranium Munitions," *supra* note 57 at 5.

[438] Clearly barrage fire directed at an area of mixed military and civilian persons and objects would breach Article 51 (4) (a) of Geneva Protocol I, *supra* note 11, as recognized by Fleck, ed., *supra* note 410 at para. 455.

[439] See Bothe, Partsch, and Solf, *supra* note 246 at 310, where the authors suggest that since the two sides of the equation cannot easily be quantified, only an *obvious* imbalance will be considered "disproportionate" or "excessive."

there are *any* realistic options to limit the future use of depleted uranium weapons.

The laws of armed conflict and the laws governing environmental protection both recognize the concept of precaution. In the context of environmental law, the precautionary principle has been recognized in a number of international treaties and soft law instruments and requires that where activities may potentially cause serious or irreversible damage, states should not delay preventive measures until the effects are scientifically proven.[440] In other words, states should not wait for the stage of full scientific certainty to be reached in regard to the effects of hazardous activities before putting in place measures to alleviate or prevent such harm.[441] The laws of armed conflict also recognize the necessity for precaution, in the context of an attack. Article 57(2)(a)(ii) of Geneva Protocol I[442] requires that states

take all feasible precautions in the choice of *means* and methods of attack with a view to avoiding, and in any event to minimising, incidental loss of civilian life, injury to civilians and damage to civilian objects [emphasis added].

Bearing in mind the continued state of divergence surrounding scientific evidence on the effects of depleted uranium, it would appear reasonable to suggest that depleted uranium weapons should not, therefore, be used in an attack where more than a minimal number of civilians are present. Precedent already exists for the specific prohibition of certain weapons within populated areas. The international community has prohibited the use in all circumstances of air-delivered incendiary weapons against military objectives located within a concentration of civilians.[443] In the case of non-air-delivered incendiary weapons treaty law limits their use to circumstances where (1) the military objective is clearly separated from the civilian

---

440 For example, see Principle 15 of the 1992 Rio Declaration, *supra* note 372; Article 3(3) and the preamble to the 1992 UNFCCC, *supra* note 372; and Article 2(2)(a) of the 1992 Paris Convention for the Protection of the Marine Environment of the North-East Atlantic, 22 September 1992, (1993) 32 I.L.M. 1068 (entered into force 25 March 1998).

441 Hulme, *supra* note 354 at Chapter 4.

442 Geneva Protocol I, *supra* note 11.

443 See Protocol III to the 1980 Conventional Weapons Convention, *supra* note 16, Article 2(2).

population; and (2) all feasible precautions have been taken to minimize incidental harm to civilians.[444] Clearly, the danger inherent in the use of incendiary weapons is a special one in that the user risks causing fires, which could quickly spread to engulf civilian areas. While this danger is not present with the use of depleted uranium weapons, it is suggested that it would provide a valuable first step to limiting their civilian effects. Extending this notion one stage further, it is suggested that a minimum safe distance be allocated for the use of depleted uranium weapons in the vicinity of civilians. Similar to the issues arising from the use of area weapons, such as cluster bombs,[445] it would be reasonable to suggest that in the case of depleted uranium weapons a "safe" distance be calculated between deployment and civilian presence. The United States ground forces in Iraq, for example, strove to keep cluster weapon strikes to a distance of at least five hundred metres (sometimes reduced to three hundred metres) away from civilian targets.[446] Therefore, it may be a reasonable measure for such states to also adopt for depleted uranium weapons, due to the potentially deadly effects of such weapons on the civilian population.

As a final note, it is hoped that states will work towards a moratorium on the use of depleted uranium weapons until agreement is reached on their true health and environmental effects. Even the most cursory respect for the precautionary principle would demand some hesitation in using such weapons in the first place, and, consequently, where used, some effort should be made in cleaning up the affected areas. On this last point, there is certainly some evidence from Iraq that the coalition forces are removing the top soil from contaminated areas (particularly those within the vicinity of coalition military bases) and removing or decontaminating vehicles struck by depleted uranium weapons.[447] At present, treaty obligations of post-conflict clean up are few and far between.[448] The

---

[444] *Ibid.*, Article 2(3).

[445] K. Hulme, "Of Questionable Legality: The Military Use of Cluster Bombs in Iraq, 2003" (2004) 42 Can. Y.B. Int'l L. 143

[446] Human Rights Watch, *Off Target: The Conduct of the War and Civilian Casualties in Iraq* (New York: Human Rights Watch, 2003) at 94.

[447] "Depleted Uranium and the Environment," United Kingdom Ministry of Defence, available at <http://www.mod.uk/DefenceInternet/AboutDefence/WhatWeDo/HealthandSafety/Depleted+Uranium/DepletedUraniumAndTheEnvironment.htm> (15 August 2006).

[448] Amended Protocol II on Mines to the 1980 Conventional Weapons Convention, *supra* note 16, Articles 10 and 11; see also Articles 5 and 6 of the 1997

burden of clean up is said to lie where it falls — in the target state.[449] New developments, however, have recently emphasized financial obligations where actual removal is impossible, but these obligations have yet to gain a significant number of state parties.[450] State attitudes towards clean up do appear to be changing, and a number of states have been keen to recognize the need for environmental restoration, notably the United Kingdom.[451]

CONCLUSIONS

The question of the legality of the use of depleted uranium weapons is complex. The major stumbling block is the question mark over the long-term human health and environmental consequences of depleted uranium. Although UNEP has carried out samplings in post-conflict Kosovo, Bosnia and Herzegovina, and Serbia and Montenegro, this data cannot be used to assess the longer-term consequences of depleted uranium in the environment and, in particular, the corrosion effects of depleted uranium in soils and its transfer into underground aquifers. It may be a further twenty years before the true long-term effects of using depleted uranium weaponry in war can be fully assessed. In light of the continuing doubts surrounding the health and environmental effects of depleted uranium, therefore, this author suggests the implementation of a cautionary approach. In effect, since other weaponry are relatively, if not fully, as effective as depleted uranium weaponry, it is suggested that these alternative weapons be used exclusively. Where states are not willing to adopt alternative materials, such as tung-

---

Ottawa Convention on the Prohibition of the Use, Stockpiling, Production and Transfer of Anti-Personnel Mines and on Their Destruction, 3 December 1997, (1997) 36 I.L.M. 1507 (entered into force 1 March 1999).

[449] Hulme, *supra* note 354 at Case 6, pp. 274–75.

[450] Protocol V on Explosive Remnants of War, *supra* note 16. In August 2006, the protocol had only twenty-three state parties — a list that does not include the United Kingdom, the United States, France, Russia, or China.

[451] "Depleted Uranium and the Environment," *supra* note 447. Serbia has also recently announced that it is carrying out clean up of depeted uranium remnants following the 1999 use by NATO in Kosovo. According to local news reports, "nuclear experts and clean-up teams removed 3,468 cubic meters of contaminated soil from the Borovac site, 280 kilometers south of Belgrade, where 44 depleted uranium shells exploded." See "Serbia Cleans Up Depleted Uranian From 1999 NATO Bombing," Serbianna.com, 12 December 2005, available at <http://www.serbianna.com/news/2005/02239.html> (14 December 2004).

sten, then it is suggested that the use of depleted uranium weapons within the vicinity of civilians be limited. Such practical limits might include a minimum safe distance between the use of depleted uranium weapons and the known presence of civilians. Furthermore, it is imperative that states and other organizations continually monitor the effects of depleted uranium on human health and the environment, particularly with a view to mounting speedy clean up operations to reduce their potential adverse effects.

Sommaire

La conduite de la guerre radioactive: étude de la légalité des armements à uranium appauvri

L'utilisation des munitions en uranium appauvri, que plusieurs critiquent comme étant la nouvelle "arme de destruction massive" et que d'autres louent comme étant l'"arme de combat de choix" dans la conduite de la guerre, soulève bien des questions juridiques. Les études scientifiques démontrent que l'uranium appauvri, cette arme de pointe conçue pour pénétrer un objectif blindé, présente des caractéristiques chimiques et radioactives toxiques. Toute arme de guerre, bien sûr, a des effets quelconques sur la santé humaine et sur l'environnement. Par contre, les lois sur les conflits armés ont évolué et cherchent à limiter le dommage en définissant ce qui est permis et légal. Cette "arme de choix," par conséquent, est-elle contraire aux lois internationales régissant les conflits armés?

Bien que les médias aient traité du sujet avec frénésie immédiatement après l'incident de 1999 au Kosovo, l'utilisation des munitions en uranium appauvri en Iraq en 2003 a reçu une attention médiatique bien mitigée. Comment l'utilisation d'une arme si controversée en 1999 peut-elle passer presque inaperçue quatre ans plus tard? Faut-il nécessairement en déduire que les préceptes de la conscience publique concernant l'utilisation de cette arme de guerre jadis controversée ont changé? Cet article cherche à analyser la légalité de l'utilisation des munitions en uranium appauvri; il pose la question clé: les lois existantes sur les conflits armés répondent-elles adéquatement aux préoccupations actuelles en matière de la protection des personnes et de l'environnement, quelle que soit leur nature?

Summary

Radiation Warfare: A Review of the Legality of Depleted
Uranium Weaponry

*Criticized by many as the new "weapon of mass destruction," lauded by
some as the "weapon of choice in combat," the use of depleted uranium
ammunition in warfare raises many legal questions. Designed as a point
weapon to penetrate armoured targets, scientific studies prove that depleted
uranium has both chemically and radioactively toxic characteristics. Clearly,
every weapon of war will have some affect on human health and the environment, but the laws of armed conflict have evolved to place limits on the
level of harm viewed as permissible and legal. Does this "weapon of choice,"
therefore, breach the international laws of armed conflict?*

*Although the subject of media frenzy in the immediate aftermath of the
1999 Kosovo conflict, the use of depleted uranium ammunition in Iraq
2003 raised little media attention. How could the use of such a controversial weapon in 1999 go largely unnoticed just four years later? Does this
lack of global condemnation necessarily lead to the conclusion that the "dictates of the public conscience" have evolved in regard to the use of this previously controversial weapon of war? This article seeks to analyze the legality
of the use of depleted uranium ammunition — the main question being
whether the existing laws of armed conflict are already sufficient to address
any human and environmental concerns.*

Determining the Existence of Countervailable Subsidies in the Context of the Canada–United States Softwood Lumber Dispute: 1982–2005

IAIN SANDFORD

INTRODUCTION

Tensions between the United States and Canada over Canadian exports of softwood lumber are long-standing. The more recent history of trade remedy actions by the United States with respect to Canadian softwood lumber began in 1982 when the Coalition for Fair Canadian Lumber Imports[1] (CFLI), representing interests from the competing US industry, first petitioned the US Department of Commerce (USDOC) for countervailing duty relief from alleged Canadian subsidies in the forestry sector. The dispute has remained a perennial feature of Canada–United States trade relations since then, and it is the source of considerable passion on both sides.

This article reviews the history of softwood lumber countervailing duty determinations between 1982 and the time of writing in December 2005. In the second and third sections, the article chronicles the main events that have occurred in this period. As part of this exercise, certain key legal determinations are reviewed. The article does not provide a comprehensive review of all of the legal issues or separate legal proceedings that have arisen but, instead,

Iain Sandford, BA, LL.B. (Victoria University of Wellington), LL.M. (University of Ottawa), of the Bars of New Zealand and the Australian Capital Territory. The author is deputy director of the International Trade Group of Minter Ellison in Canberra but, at the time of writing, was a legal officer in the WTO Appellate Body Secretariat. The author wishes in particular to thank Valerie Hughes for her encouragement on this article as well as the other friends and colleagues who offered useful comments as the piece evolved including Werner Zdouc, Victoria Donaldson, Arun Venkataraman, and Scott Gallacher. Errors and omissions remain the responsibility of the author.

1 In subsequent phases of the softwood lumber dispute, the Coalition for Fair Canadian Lumber Imports became, simply, the Coalition for Fair Lumber Imports (CFLI).

concentrates on certain themes that have recurred during the various episodes of the dispute and on issues that shed light upon some
of the more interesting jurisprudential questions that arise out of
the case study. Having completed this review, the article turns in
the fourth section to distil some lessons from this somewhat unique
trade dispute. These observations are separated into two groups.
First, the note comments on the light shed by the lengthy history of
countervailing duty actions involving softwood lumber from Canada upon the nature of subsidies disciplines in international trade.
In particular, the article comments upon the evolution of the "specificity" test and upon the manner in which the amount of
subsidization may be measured. Second, the article considers what
the softwood lumber dispute reveals about the relationship between
different judicial actors at the international level — in this case,
the relationship between dispute settlement organs established
under the General Agreement on Tariffs and Trade (GATT)[2] or
within the World Trade Organization (WTO), on the one hand,
and panels under Chapters 19 of the Canada–United States Free
Trade Agreement (CUSFTA)[3] or the North American Free Trade
Agreement (NAFTA),[4] on the other. The article closes with some
reflections on the limits of international dispute settlement tools
in highly contentious and politicized cases.

HISTORICAL REVIEW

This section considers the so-called *Lumber I* to *Lumber III* episodes. For each phase, the analysis comments on the overall result
of the proceeding, then turns to consider two key recurring issues
in the analysis of the alleged stumpage[5] subsidy: specificity and the
existence and amount of the subsidy. The focus on these two issues
provides background for a similar analysis with respect to the ongoing *Lumber IV* episode in the third section of this article as well as
for some conclusions in the fourth section.

---

[2] General Agreement on Tariffs and Trade, 30 October 1947, 55 U.N.T.S. 187
[GATT].

[3] Canada–United States Free Trade Agreement, 22 December 1987 and 2 January 1988, Can. T.S. 1989 No. 3 [CUSFTA].

[4] North American Free Trade Agreement, 2 December 1992, Can. T.S. 1994 No. 2.

[5] The term "stumpage" refers to the set of legal arrangements whereby timber
harvesters access timber growing on Canadian crown lands. For further discussion of the respective Canadian and US views as to the legal character of stumpage,
see discussion later in this article.

LUMBER I (1982–3)

The USDOC initiated a countervailing duty investigation on certain softwood lumber from Canada on 27 October 1982, following a petition from the CFLI.[6] This investigation and related developments are known as the "*Lumber I*" episode. At the conclusion of its investigation, the USDOC issued a final negative countervailing duty determination.[7] Although some nineteen Canadian programs were found to confer subsidies, the cumulative level of these subsidies was deemed to be *de minimis* and thus not countervailable. Most importantly, the USDOC rejected the claims of the CFLI that federal and provincial stumpage programs represented countervailable subsidies. In 1982, as essentially remains the case today, US countervailing duty law allowed programs to be countervailed if they met certain criteria. These included that a subsidy had to be found to exist and that any subsidy had to be provided to a specific enterprise, industry, or group. Under US countervailing law in force at the time of *Lumber I*, a subsidy could take a variety of forms. In *Lumber I*, the CFLI alleged that stumpage programs provided subsidies through "the assumption of a cost of production" by Canadian governments. At length, in its negative determination, the USDOC rejected the industry's claims with respect to both specificity and subsidization.

Specificity

Although the USDOC gave little by way of general interpretation of the meaning of the specificity requirement, it nevertheless reached the view that stumpage programs were not specific. Rather, stumpage was available generally in Canada and could be accessed on similar terms regardless of the identity of the recipient. According to the USDOC,

the only limitations as to the types of industries that use stumpage reflect the inherent characteristics of this natural resource and the current level of technology. As technological advances have increased the potential users of standing timber, stumpage has been made available to the new users. Any current limitations on use are not due to the activities of the Canadian governments.[8]

6 *Initiation of Countervailing Duty Investigations: Certain Softwood Lumber Products from Canada*, 47 Fed. Reg., 49878 (1982) [*Lumber I*].

7 *Final Negative Countervailing Duty Determination: Certain Softwood Products from Canada*, 48 Fed. Reg., 24159 (1983) [*Lumber I*, Final Determination].

8 *Ibid.* at 24167.

Furthermore, the department found that several groups of industries — lumber and wood products; veneer, plywood, and building boards; pulp and paper; furniture; as well as others — made use of stumpage.[9] The USDOC concluded that there was nothing, therefore, to indicate that access to the programs was limited to a specific group, as required by the governing US law.

Existence of a Subsidy (Assumption of Costs of Production)

Moreover, the USDOC found that, even if the stumpage programs could be said to be specific, they nevertheless would not confer a subsidy. In particular, the programs did not "assume a cost of production" as the petitioners alleged, because the programs did not relieve the recipients of any pre-existing statutory or contractual obligations.[10] The USDOC further indicated that, even if it read the word "assume" more broadly to encompass any lowering of overall costs of production, there was no indication that stumpage programs had effectively reduced any of the costs associated with lumber production. The issues considered in this regard raise interesting contrasts with the approach taken in subsequent proceedings. In reaching its conclusion on this issue, the USDOC considered two possible approaches to calculate whether costs had been lowered.[11] The first possible approach involved the setting of a benchmark against which to compare the Canadian stumpage prices. The petitioners had argued that US prices were an appropriate benchmark. Such a cross-border analysis was, however, rejected by the USDOC as "arbitrary and capricious" in view of a number of material differences between stumpage in Canada and the United States.[12] Moreover, although it gave no detail in its analysis, the USDOC noted that the results of such analysis, after adjustment for the differences between conditions in Canada and the United States, revealed no differential between the benchmark and actual Canadian prices. A second possible approach, which was considered briefly by the USDOC, was the construction of a "true market value" for stumpage. The USDOC considered that a reasonable approach to the construction of such a

9 *Ibid.*

10 *Ibid.* at 24168.

11 Neither of the approaches appears to have been expressly contemplated by the governing US law but, rather, appear to have been based on the USDOC's interpretation of the statutory language regarding "assum[ption of] a cost of production."

12 *Lumber I*, Final Determination, *supra* note 7 at 24168.

value would be a "residual value" analysis, under which sums would be deducted from the ultimate consumer price for the costs and profit of everything involved in the manufacture of the product, so as to arrive at a reasonable price for the basic input.[13]

The USDOC also observed that it was, in fact, inappropriate to make claims under the heading of assumption of costs of production. In the view of the USDOC, stumpage programs fell more appropriately under another provision of the governing statute — that dealing with the "provision of a good at preferential rates." In the view of the USDOC, "stumpage programs clearly involve the provision of a good (raw timber)."[14]

LUMBER II AND THE 1986 MEMORANDUM OF UNDERSTANDING

On 5 June 1986, the USDOC initiated a new countervailing duty investigation in regard to softwood lumber from Canada, thus beginning the *Lumber II* episode.[15] On 16 October 1986, the department issued a preliminary affirmative determination of subsidization at a rate of 15 per cent.[16] This determination was based, essentially,

13 The USDOC noted that this was the method through which British Columbia determined its price for stumpage. With British Columbia accounting for some 67 per cent of lumber exports, the USDOC felt that it could not be said that Canadian stumpage prices did not reflect a true market value. *Lumber I*, Final Determination, *supra* note 7 at 24168.

14 *Ibid.* After noting that the "preferential" standard "normally means only more favourable to some within a jurisdiction than to others within that jurisdiction," the department made no finding with respect to the applicability of the provision dealing with providing goods at preferential rates.

15 *Initiation of Countervailing Investigation: Certain Softwood Lumber Products from Canada,* 51 Fed. Reg., 21205 (1986) [*Lumber II*]. Canada challenged the initiation of the countervailing duty investigation by the United States in the GATT under the dispute settlement provisions of the Tokyo Round Agreement on the Application of Articles VI, XVI and XXIII of the GATT, 12 April 1979, 31 U.S.T., 4919 [SCM Code]. Canada's central claim was that there had been no material changes in the situation since the negative countervailing duty determination in 1982. In the absence of such changes, there was not sufficient evidence to initiate an investigation consistent with Article 2(1) of the SCM Code. The panel established to consider this matter did not issue its report until 25 May 1987, a date subsequent to the resolution of the dispute. The brief report, *United States – Initiation of a Countervailing Duty Investigation into Softwood Lumber Products from Canada (Complaint by Canada)* (1987), unadopted, 34th Supp. B.I.S.D. (1988) at 194 [*US – Softwood Lumber I*], simply records the conclusion of a mutually satisfactory settlement and briefly outlines its terms.

16 *Preliminary Affirmative Countervailing Duty Determination: Certain Softwood Lumber Products from Canada,* 51 Fed. Reg., 37453 (1986) [*Lumber II*, Preliminary Determination].

on a reversal of the previous determination that stumpage programs were not countervailable. In doing so, the USDOC revisited, and reversed, its finding that stumpage programs in British Columbia, Alberta, Québec, and Ontario were not specific. It also found that the stumpage programs in these four provinces represented the provision of goods at preferential rates. With the US International Trade Commission (USITC) having determined, on 16 July 1986, that there was a reasonable indication that a US industry was materially injured by imports from Canada,[17] provisional countervailing measures were imposed on Canadian imports.

Specificity

With respect to specificity, the USDOC found that a re-examination of its earlier finding that stumpage was not specific was warranted, first, in light of new evidence presented by the petitioners suggesting that stumpage programs were limited by certain government policies and, second, because of its own revision of the approach applied to determining specificity.[18] Accordingly, the USDOC set aside the "inherent characteristics" approach upon which it had relied in *Lumber I* and, instead, considered other factors, developed in the interim period, to analyze the specificity question. One such factor was the degree to which governments exercised discretion in granting stumpage rights and whether, in exercising this discretion, governments effectively limited access to a program. The USDOC found that provincial governments exercised considerable discretion in allocating stumpage rights. Moreover, it accepted, for the purposes of its preliminary determination, the petitioner's argument that the exercise of this discretion had led to stumpage being targeted towards particular industries. In addition, the USDOC called into question certain factual findings upon which it had relied in *Lumber I*, in particular, those regarding the range of industries using stumpage. Based on these considerations, the USDOC preliminarily found that stumpage was specific.[19]

Existence of a Subsidy (Provision of Goods at Preferential Rates)

The petitioners in the *Lumber II* proceeding, clearly taking into account the views expressed by the USDOC on this point in *Lumber*

17 *Softwood Lumber from Canada: Results of Import Investigation*, 51 Fed. Reg., 25752 (1986).

18 *Lumber II*, Preliminary Determination, *supra* note 16 at 37455.

19 *Ibid.* at 37456.

I, asserted that stumpage represented the provision of goods by governments. Accepting this assertion, the USDOC considered whether the timber furnished by stumpage arrangements was provided at "preferential rates" — the test for the existence of a subsidy that continued to be applied under US law at that time. Thus, as it had tentatively done in *Lumber I*, the USDOC explored options for determining an appropriate benchmark against which to compare actual stumpage prices, to assess whether they were preferential.[20]

Referring to a "preferentiality appendix," which was published in the context of an earlier investigation unrelated to lumber, the USDOC identified four alternative means through which to consider whether goods were provided at preferential rates: (1) prices charged by the government for a similar or related good; (2) prices charged within the jurisdiction by other sellers for an identical good; (3) the government's cost of producing the good; and (4) external prices.[21] Taking into account the facts before it, the USDOC rejected as inappropriate the first two of these alternatives. It chose, instead, to consider the third: whether the price charged for stumpage was less than the government's cost of production. The key element in this cost of production analysis was determining the cost to be attributed to the intrinsic value of the trees to be cut pursuant to stumpage rights. The USDOC estimated this imputed value by reference to surrogate values taken from data on actual transactions.

Different surrogate values were calculated for each of the four affected provinces. For British Columbia and Alberta, the price chosen was drawn from competitive bid prices from auctions of standing timber within the provinces themselves. For Québec and Ontario, private sale prices from New Brunswick were used. Using these surrogates, the USDOC calculated the amount by which costs associated with conferring stumpage exceeded stumpage revenues per cubic metre, then divided this amount by the total value of lumber sales in the four relevant provinces to reach its preliminary country-wide subsidy rate of 14.542 per cent.[22]

---

20 As had been the case in *Lumber I, supra* note 6, the USDOC's discretion in interpreting the basic statutory requirement was unfettered by further statutory or regulatory elaboration.

21 *Carbon Black from Mexico: Preliminary Results of Countervailing Duty Administrative Review*, 51 Fed. Reg., 13269 (1986), cited in *Lumber II*, Preliminary Determination, *supra* note 16 at 37457.

22 *Ibid.* at 37458. The overall preliminary rate of 15 per cent included this figure plus the sum of other federal and provincial programs found to provide subsidies.

Memorandum of Understanding (MOU)

In the context of the ongoing *Lumber II* countervailing duty investigation, Canada and the United States entered into negotiations to seek a mutually satisfactory resolution of their differences. As a result of these negotiations, a MOU was concluded between the two governments on 30 December 1986. Under the terms of the MOU, the United States terminated the countervailing duty investigation, released bonds, and refunded deposits paid in accordance with the preliminary determination. Canada, in return, undertook to collect an export charge of 15 per cent *ad valorem* on exports to the United States of softwood lumber products. The MOU allowed Canada to reduce or eliminate this charge, where provinces instituted "replacement measures," including increasing the price of stumpage.

LUMBER III (1991–4)

The 1986 MOU provided only a temporary solution to the ongoing softwood lumber dispute. By 1991, British Columbia and Québec had put in place replacement measures, and the export charge had been reduced for both provinces accordingly. Following an analysis that indicated that stumpage revenue exceeded stumpage costs in all affected provinces, Canada elected to terminate the MOU on 4 October 1991. On the same day, the United States, acting under the procedures contemplated by Sections 301–10 of the Trade Act of 1974,[23] imposed an interim trade remedy in the form of increased duties on certain softwood lumber from Canada, pending the outcome of a renewed countervailing duty investigation.[24] This action initiated the "*Lumber III*" episode. On 31 October 1991, the USDOC self-initiated a new countervailing duty investigation.[25]

---

[23] Trade Act of 1974, Pub. L. No. 93-618.

[24] *Initiation of Section 302 Investigation and Request for Public Comment on Determinations Involving Expeditious Action: Canadian Exports of Softwood Lumber*, 56 Fed. Reg., 50739 (1991) [*Lumber III*].

[25] *Self-Initiation of Countervailing Duty Investigation: Certain Softwood Lumber Products from Canada*, 56 Fed. Reg., 56055 (1991). The United States's interim measures and the initiation of the countervailing duty investigation were challenged under the dispute settlement mechanism of the GATT's SCM Code, *supra* note 15. The panel in *United States – Measures Affecting Imports of Softwood Lumber from Canada (Complaint by Canada)* (1993), 40th Supp. B.I.S.D. (1994), adopted 27 October 1993 [*US – Softwood Lumber II*], ruled that the imposition of interim

In its final affirmative countervailing duty determination, the USDOC found that subsidies were being provided at a country-wide rate of 6.51 per cent *ad valorem*.[26] This rate included a country-wide subsidy rate of 2.91 per cent, drawn from weight-averaging the benefits attributable to the stumpage programs of British Columbia, Québec, Ontario, and Alberta, as well as a further country-wide subsidy of 3.6 per cent resulting from benefits attributed to log export restraints in British Columbia.[27] In establishing that stumpage programs were countervailable, the USDOC affirmed the preliminary findings that it had made in *Lumber II* that stumpage was both specific and provided goods at preferential rates. Its reasoning, however, was somewhat different. In parallel to the USDOC's analysis, the USITC found that imports of Canadian softwood lumber caused material injury to the domestic industry in the United States.[28]

---

measures by the United States was inconsistent with its GATT obligations. In the view of the panel, the measures represented provisional measures applied *before* a countervailable subsidy had preliminarily been found to exist. As such, the measures were inconsistent with Article 5.1 of the SCM Code. The panel rejected, however, Canada's separate claim regarding the initiation of the countervailing duty investigation.

26 *Final Affirmative Countervailing Duty Determination: Certain Softwood Lumber Products from Canada*, 57 Fed. Reg., 22570 (1992) [*Lumber III*, Final Determination].

27 This article does not undertake a detailed analysis of the log export restraint issue. Nonetheless, for the sake of completeness, it is useful to incorporate the following points. The USDOC's *Lumber III* determination found, in essence, that, by limiting the quantity of logs that might be exported from the province, British Columbia increased the supply of such goods within its jurisdiction and thus pushed down the price that lumber manufacturers needed to pay to obtain these inputs. This was found to be both a subsidy and specific to certain enterprises. These findings were challenged, and ultimately overturned in the context of Canada's challenge under Chapter 19 of the CUSFTA, *supra* note 3 discussed later in this article in regard to its other dimensions. Subsequently, the United States's treatment generally of export restraints in countervailing duty investigations was also the subject of a separate challenge by Canada in the WTO. See *United States – Measures Treating Export Restraints as Subsidies* (*Complaint by Canada*), Panel Report, WTO Doc. WT/DS194/R and Corr. 2 (2001).

28 As with the export restraints issue, the scope of this review is such that the US International Trade Commission's (USITC) *Lumber III* injury findings, as well as CUSFTA Chapter 19 review thereof, are not examined in detail in this article. For present purposes, it is sufficient to note that the initial USITC determination was remanded by the Chapter 19 panel for want of support in substantial evidence. This was also the case with respect to the USITC's first and second determinations on remand. The *Lumber III* episode was ultimately settled before any third remand determination was issued by the USITC.

Specificity

In the period between *Lumber II* and *Lumber III*, the United States had amended the statutory rules relating to specificity. The amendments clarified that programs could be found to be specific in law or in fact. In light of these statutory amendments, the USDOC had issued "proposed regulations," which, *inter alia*, provided that the USDOC "will consider" four factors in assessing whether particular programs were *de facto* specific.[29] These factors were: (1) the extent to which a government acts to limit the availability of a program; (2) the number of enterprises, industries, or groups thereof that actually use a program; (3) whether there are dominant users of the program or whether certain enterprises, industries, or groups thereof receive disproportionately large benefits under the program; and (4) the extent to which a government exercises discretion in conferring benefits under a program. Beyond providing that the USDOC "will consider" these four factors, the proposed regulations gave no guidance on whether the USDOC could base its conclusion on any one of the factors or whether it was obliged to address them all.

In *Lumber III*, the USDOC used these factors as a basis for assessing whether provincial stumpage programs were specific. After dismissing arguments made by the Canadian parties to the effect that it needed to consider the "inherent characteristics" of timber, as it did in *Lumber I*, the USDOC found that the limited number of users of stumpage required a finding of specificity.[30] In the USDOC's view, the benefits of stumpage were limited to a single group, composed of the solid wood product and pulp and paper industries.[31]

Canada sought review of this finding, along with others, by a binational panel established under Chapter 19 of the CUSFTA. In its ruling, the CUSFTA panel found that the USDOC had failed to apply correctly US law relating to the *de facto* specificity standard. The panel found that the USDOC had acted improperly by considering only one of the four factors listed in the proposed

---

[29] These proposed regulations appear never to have entered into force. They were nevertheless applied by the USDOC, on something of a provisional basis, for the purposes of the *Lumber III* investigation.

[30] *Lumber III*, Final Determination, *supra* note 26 at 22583.

[31] *Ibid.* The USDOC did not, in its findings, *address* the other criteria, although it claimed to have "considered" them. Thus, unlike in *Lumber II*, the USDOC did not expressly address the degree to which governments exercised discretion in the allocation of stumpage rights.

regulations.[32] The CUSFTA panel remanded this issue to the USDOC. On remand, the USDOC addressed and weighed each of the four factors set out in its proposed regulations. It nevertheless maintained its conclusion that stumpage was specific, again, based largely on the weight of the "limited number of users" factor. The majority of the panel reviewing the remand determination, however, was unconvinced by the USDOC's revised analysis. The panel felt that the USDOC's reconsideration of the "number of users" criterion was flawed. According to the panel, the USDOC's reasoning amounted to little more than an assertion that the number of stumpage users "was small."[33] Further, a finding by the USDOC that the beneficiaries of stumpage programs were generally drawn from the "primary timber-processing industry" was circular, in that it defined the potential beneficiaries of stumpage largely by reference to the group of enterprises that actually used it.[34] The panel found that the USDOC's consideration of the second factor — dominant use — was inadequate for similar reasons. On this basis, the panel ruled that the USDOC had again been "unable to provide a rational legal basis for a finding that stumpage programs are specific."[35] It remanded the issue a second time, directing that the USDOC find that stumpage programs were not specific.[36] The USDOC ultimately complied with this direction and revoked the countervailing duties.

Existence of a Subsidy (Provision of Goods at Preferential Rates)

Having initially decided that stumpage was specific, the USDOC turned in its final determination to consider whether the trees

---

32 *Re Certain Softwood Lumber from Canada*, Chapter 19 Panel, Doc. USA-92-1904-01 (1993) at 43–4 [*Re Softwood Lumber*, CUSFTA Panel Report].

33 *Re Certain Softwood Lumber from Canada*, Chapter 19 Panel, Decision on Remand USA-92-1904-02 (1993) at 26 [*Re Softwood Lumber*, CUSFTA Report on Remand].

34 *Ibid.* at 40.

35 *Ibid.* at 50–51.

36 The panel's decision in this regard was challenged under the extraordinary challenge procedure of Chapter 19 of the CUSFTA. By a majority of two to one, the Extraordinary Challenge Committee found no reason to disturb the panel's findings and affirmed the panel's decision. See *Re Softwood Lumber from Canada*, Extraordinary Challenge Committee, Doc. ECC-94-1904-01USA (1994) [*Re Softwood Lumber*, Extraordinary Challenge Committee]. Subsequently, the CFLI initiated a constitutional challenge in respect of the CUSFTA Chapter 19 procedures. This challenge, however, was withdrawn around the time that the Softwood Lumber Agreement, discussed later in this article, was concluded.

provided, pursuant to stumpage programs, were provided at
"preferential rates" — the relevant test for subsidization, which
continued to be applied under US law at that time. According to
the USDOC's proposed regulations, a good was provided at preferential rates if the price charged by a government was less than a
certain benchmark price. The proposed regulations set out four
alternatives for determining the benchmark: (1) the price charged
by the government to other buyers, adjusted for any cost differences; (2) the price charged by other sellers within the same political jurisdiction for the same good; (3) the government's cost of
producing the good; and (4) the price paid for the identical good
outside of the political jurisdiction in question.[37]

The USDOC used two of these alternatives to construct benchmarks against which to measure whether provincial stumpage programs provided goods at preferential rates. For Ontario, Alberta,
and British Columbia, the USDOC used the first alternative and
considered prices otherwise charged by the provincial governments
for the same good. Thus, the USDOC considered the prices resulting from competitively bid auctions within each province to determine preferentiality for these provinces.[38] In Québec, the USDOC
used the second alternative — prices charged by private sellers —
as the benchmark against which to measure the government price.[39]
In choosing these benchmarks, the USDOC rejected the argument
of the US industry that it should use benchmarks from the United
States. The USDOC indicated that, "in the absence of clear and
persuasive evidence that comparisons made within the same jurisdiction would somehow yield skewed results," it would "not stray
from its methodological preference" to measure subsidies by reference to the jurisdiction under investigation.[40]

In its reasoning under this rubric, the USDOC also considered
arguments by the respondents that stumpage — a system for the
allocation of rights to harvest a natural resource — could, by its
nature, never provide subsidies. The USDOC initially found that
the governing statute did not allow consideration of such a "market

---

[37] These four alternatives are materially the same as the four alternatives put
forward by the USDOC in the context of the *Lumber II* investigation, see *supra*
note 16.

[38] *Lumber III*, Final Determination, *supra* note 26 at 22586–87.

[39] *Ibid.*

[40] *Ibid.*

distortion" analysis.[41] On review, however, the CUSFTA panel disagreed and remanded this issue with a direction to the USDOC to consider whether stumpage resulted in a market distortion, taking into account certain economic arguments put forward by the respondents.[42] On remand, the USDOC did so but maintained its rejection of the Canadian contentions. Based on its own economic modelling, the USDOC found that stumpage *did* have the potential to distort the softwood lumber market.[43] In essence, the USDOC argued that fewer trees would be harvested if an increase in stumpage fees increased the marginal costs for stumpage users. The majority of the CUSFTA panel on remand, however, felt that the USDOC had failed to address properly the issues remanded to it and had failed to demonstrate market distortion.[44] Since market distortion was a fundamental criterion for countervailability, the panel remanded the issue a second time, directing the USDOC to find that stumpage programs do not distort normal competitive markets and are therefore not countervailable. The USDOC ultimately complied with the panel's direction.[45]

1996 UNITED STATES – CANADA SOFTWOOD LUMBER AGREEMENT [SOFTWOOD LUMBER AGREEMENT][46]

Following the 1991–4 episode, Canada, the United States, and their respective industries established a consultative process, with a view to establishing a more resilient resolution to their dispute. As a result of this process, Canada and the United States signed on 29 May 1996 the Softwood Lumber Agreement. Pursuant to this agreement, the United States undertook to refrain from initiating any action under its trade remedy laws[47] for the duration of the agreement.

---

41 *Ibid.* at 22587.

42 *Re Softwood Lumber,* CUSFTA Panel Report, *supra* note 32 at 44–59.

43 See *Re Softwood Lumber,* CUSFTA Report on Remand, *supra* note 33 at 60.

44 *Ibid.* at 50–65.

45 The USDOC's decision on revocation followed affirmation of the panel's decision by an Extraordinary Challenge Committee. See *Re Softwood Lumber,* Extraordinary Challenge Committee, *supra* note 36.

46 United States – Canada Softwood Lumber Agreement, 29 May 1996, Can. T.S. 1996 No. 16.

47 Including the countervailing duty and anti-dumping provisions of Title VII of the Tariff Act of 1930, Pub. L. No. 103-465 [Tariff Act], as well as the actions provided for under sections 201–4 and 301–5 of the Trade Act of 1974, *supra* note 23.

In return, Canada undertook to control exports to the United States of softwood products originating in British Columbia, Alberta, Ontario, and Québec. Such control was to be put in place by a system of compulsory export permits and graduated export fees. Subject to certain adjustments and allowances, for exports of up to 14.7 billion board feet, no fee would be charged. For exports above this level, but less than 15.35 billion board feet, a US $50 fee per thousand board feet would be charged. For exports exceeding 15.35 billion board feet, a US $100 fee per thousand board feet would be charged. The agreement was to remain in force for five years but was extendable upon agreement by the parties. There was, however, no agreement to extend the agreement beyond the five-year period. Accordingly, it expired on 31 March 2001.

ONGOING PROCEEDINGS: *LUMBER IV* (2001–)

Having considered in the earlier section the previous episodes of the softwood lumber dispute, this article now turns to review the ongoing *Lumber IV* countervailing duty action. Developments reviewed in this section are current to 31 December 2005. The current episode of the dispute (including both the countervailing duty action as well as other actions, discussed later in this article) remains unresolved at the time of writing, and litigation continues before the WTO, under NAFTA Chapters 19 and 11, as well as in the US domestic courts. Consistent with the overall approach of this article, the following analysis focuses on the determination of countervailable subsidies. Some effort is made, nonetheless, to locate this analysis within the broader framework of the overall *Lumber IV* dispute.

BACKGROUND

On 2 April 2001, immediately following the expiry of the Softwood Lumber Agreement, the CFLI, and others representing US industry interests, again petitioned for relief from imports of Canadian lumber, this time alleging both countervailable subsidies and dumping. The subsidy allegations covered a number of programs, again, most importantly, provincial stumpage programs and British Columbia's log export restraints. Countervailing duty and anti-dumping investigations were initiated by the USDOC on 23 April 2001.

In the period between *Lumber III* and the new investigation, several important changes had been made to US law governing countervailing duty investigations. As a result of the Uruguay Round

Agreements Act (URAA),[48] new concepts were introduced into the definition of a subsidy in the law governing US countervailing duty proceedings, the Tariff Act of 1930 (Tariff Act).[49] Consistent with the WTO Agreement on Subsidies and Countervailing Measures (SCM Agreement),[50] the old tests for the existence of a subsidy were refined to focus on the existence of a "financial contribution" by a government (which could include the provision by a government of goods and services, other than general infrastructure), as well as a "benefit" to the recipient of the financial contribution. These amendments reflected Articles 1 and 14 of the SCM Agreement. Moreover, the US Congress acted to over-rule the finding of the *Lumber III* CUSFTA panel, which held that an analysis of "market distortion," or the price and volume effects of a subsidy, was a prerequisite to a finding of subsidization. The amended countervailing duty law made explicit that such an analysis was not required. In addition, the new legislation set out the same four factors for assessing *de facto* specificity as were provided in the USDOC's earlier proposed regulations. Implementing regulations[51] clarified that the factors were to be considered sequentially, with an affirmative finding in regard to any one factor sufficient to support a finding of specificity.[52] In addition to implementing elements of Article 2 of the SCM Agreement, the changes to the legislative framework also had the effect of overturning a further aspect of the decision of the *Lumber III* CUSFTA panel.[53]

On 2 April 2002, the USDOC issued a final affirmative countervailing duty determination.[54] Also on 2 April 2002, the

48 Uruguay Round Agreements Act, Pub. L. No. 103-465, 108 Stat. 4804.

49 Tariff Act, *supra* note 47.

50 Agreement on Subsidies and Countervailing Measures, Annex 1A of the Marrakesh Agreement Establishing the World Trade Organization, 15 April 1994, (1994) 33 I.L.M. 15 [SCM Agreement].

51 Antidumping and Countervailing Duties, 19 C.F.R. §351 (1994).

52 *Ibid.*

53 A comprehensive examination of the degree to which the softwood lumber dispute has been responsible for shaping elements of WTO subsidies rules is not undertaken in this article. The evolution of Article 2 of the SCM Agreement, *supra* note 50, may nevertheless be an excellent illustration of the dynamic relationship between WTO rules and the pressures created by domestic experience with trade regulation, such as the United States's experience with softwood lumber issues.

54 The final country-wide subsidy rate found was 19.34 per cent, based mainly on the sum of benefits attributable to stumpage transactions in British Columbia,

USDOC issued a final dumping determination.[55] On 16 May 2002, the USITC determined that imports of Canadian softwood lumber threatened material injury to the US domestic industry.[56] On 22 May 2002, the USDOC issued countervailing and anti-dumping duty orders with respect to softwood lumber from Canada.[57] Canada challenged the USDOC's final countervailing duty determination (as well as the parallel threat of injury and dumping determinations) in both the WTO[58] and under Chapter 19 of NAFTA. Selected

---

Alberta, Ontario, Québec, Saskatchewan, and Manitoba. *Notice of Final Affirmative Countervailing Duty Determination and Final Negative Critical Circumstances Determination: Certain Softwood Lumber Products from Canada*, 67 Fed. Reg., 15545 (2002) [*Lumber IV*, CVD Determination]. The majority of the department's reasoning for the *Lumber IV*, CVD Determination was provided in an unpublished "decision memorandum" [*Lumber IV*, Decision Memorandum]. The USDOC excluded exports from the Maritime provinces in the *Lumber IV*, CVD Determination. The rate was subsequently revised to 18.79 per cent following correction of "ministerial" errors. Unlike in its *Lumber III* investigation, the USDOC did not examine the claims pertaining to log export restraints in British Columbia.

55 Anti-dumping duty rates ranged from 2.18 per cent to 12.44 per cent. Six individual company-specific rates were determined for the six Canadian respondents, and an "all others" rate of 8.43 per cent was applied to other Canadian exporters.

56 Adopting what appears to be a fairly novel approach, in reaching its threat determination, the USITC *cumulated* the allegedly injurious effects of both the dumped and subsidized imports of softwood lumber and completed a single injury inquiry.

57 *Notice of Amended Final Determination of Sales at Less Than Face Value and Antidumping Duty Order: Certain Softwood Lumber Products from Canada*, 67 Fed. Reg., 36068 (anti-dumping) and 36070 (CVD) (2002).

58 Canada had previously challenged the USDOC's preliminary subsidy determination (and critical circumstances determination) at the WTO. The WTO panel report, *United States – Preliminary Determination with Respect to Softwood Lumber from Canada (Complaint by Canada)*, Panel Report, WTO Doc. WT/DS236/R (2002) [*US – Softwood Lumber III*, Panel Report], which was not appealed, confirmed the consistency of the USDOC's preliminary determination with the SCM Agreement, *supra* note 50, in some respects. In particular, the panel found at paras. 7.28–7.30 that the USDOC's determination that the provision of stumpage represented provision of a good, and therefore a financial contribution, by the provincial government to be consistent with the SCM Agreement. The panel, however, found other elements of the USDOC's preliminary countervailing duty determination to be contrary to the United States's WTO obligations. In particular, the panel found the USDOC's analysis of benefit to be flawed on account of its use of cross-border benchmarks for measuring the adequacy of Canadian stumpage prices (*ibid.* at paras. 7.46 and 7.57.) In addition, the panel found that aspects of the USDOC's preliminary critical circumstances determination were not consistent with the SCM Agreement (*ibid.* at para. 7.103).

elements of the USDOC's countervailing duty determination, and the various challenges to it, are reviewed in the next sections.

FINAL COUNTERVAILING DUTY DETERMINATION

Financial Contribution (Provision of Goods)

Under US law, a financial contribution may be made through a government "providing goods or services, other than general infrastructure."[59] This provision reflects closely the text of Article 1.1(a)(1)(iii) of the SCM Agreement. In *Lumber IV*, the USDOC determined that Canadian governments provided goods through stumpage arrangements. Thus, while the Canadian parties argued that stumpage did not provide goods but, instead, merely conferred, through a system of licences and tenures, a "right of access to exploit an *in situ* natural resource," the USDOC found that the "sole purpose of tenures is to provide lumber producers with timber" and that "[r]egardless of the form of the transaction between the Provincial governments and those who harvest the timber, in substance it is a sale of timber."[60]

In its analysis of this issue, the NAFTA Chapter 19 panel established to review the USDOC's countervailing duty determination[61] found no error with the USDOC's overall approach and its rejection of the Canadian arguments.[62] The USDOC's finding of a financial contribution was also upheld by the WTO's *Lumber IV* panel and the Appellate Body in *United States – Final Countervailing Duty Determination with Respect to Softwood Lumber from Canada (US – Softwood)*.[63] Both the panel and the Appellate Body agreed that

---

[59] Tariff Act, *supra* note 47 at § 771(5)(D)(iii).

[60] *Lumber IV*, Decision Memorandum, *supra* note 54 at 29–30.

[61] Separate Chapter 19 panels were established to review the USDOC's dumping determination and the USITC's threat of injury determination. More recently, Chapter 19 proceedings have been initiated in respect to certain administrative reviews of the softwood lumber measures.

[62] *Re Certain Softwood Lumber Products from Canada: Final Affirmative Countervailing Duty Determination,*Chapter 19 Panel, Doc. USA-CDA-2002-1904-03 (2003) at 20 [*Re Softwood Lumber,* NAFTA CVD Panel Report]. (In this article, consideration of subsequent remand determinations by the same NAFTA panel are referred to hereinafter as *Re Softwood Lumber,* NAFTA CVD Panel Report, Report on First Remand; *Re Softwood Lumber,* NAFTA CVD Panel Report, Report on Second Remand, and so on).

[63] *United States – Final Countervailing Duty Determination with Respect to Softwood Lumber from Canada (Complaint by Canada),* Appellate Body Report, WTO Doc. WT/DS257/AB/R (2003) at para. 167 [*US – Softwood Lumber IV,* Appellate Body

"goods" were "provided" through provincial stumpage programs and, therefore, that such programs represented a financial contribution within the meaning of Article 1.1(a)(1)(iii) of the SCM Agreement. According to the Appellate Body, the meaning of the term "goods," in the particular context in which it appeared, was broad and could encompass property, such as standing timber, that was not tradable in its existing state or that fell within a category of "real" (as opposed to "personal") property within Canada's legal system. Standing timber (a good) was "provided" through stumpage contracts because they put standing timber at the disposal of timber harvesters.[64]

Benefit (Adequacy of Remuneration)

A benefit may be conferred, according to section 771(5)(E)(iv) of the Tariff Act, where a government provides a good "for less than adequate remuneration." The statute directs that the adequacy of remuneration is to be determined "in relation to prevailing market conditions for the good ... in the country which is subject to the investigation."[65] This statutory language mirrors the requirements set forth in Article 14(d) of the SCM Agreement.

To further implement the terms of the statutory regime, the USDOC's regulations specify three alternative methods that the USDOC "normally" will use to determine the adequacy of government prices for goods or services in different situations: first, "in general," the USDOC is to measure adequacy by comparing the government price to a market-determined price for the good resulting from actual transactions in the country in question;[66] second, where such actual market-determined prices are unavailable, the USDOC is to compare the government price to world market prices, where it is reasonable to conclude that such a price would be available to purchasers in the country in question;[67] and, third,

---

Report). The Appellate Body report dealt with an appeal from the panel in *United States – Final Countervailing Duty Determination with Respect to Softwood Lumber from Canada (Complaint by Canada)*, Panel Report, WTO Doc. WT/DS257/R (2003) [*US – Softwood Lumber IV*, Panel Report).

[64] *US – Softwood Lumber IV*, Appellate Body Report, *supra* note 63 at para. 75.

[65] Tariff Act, *supra* note 47 at § 771(5)(E).

[66] Antidumping and Countervailing Duties, *supra* note 51, at para. 351.511(2)(i).

[67] *Ibid.* at para. 351.511(2)(ii).

if neither of these potential benchmarks is available, the USDOC is directed to assess whether the government price is consistent with market principles.[68]

Consistent with this legal framework, in *Lumber IV*, the USDOC first considered whether market prices from actual transactions within Canada might provide suitable benchmarks against which to compare provincial stumpage prices. The USDOC, however, rejected the appropriateness of such prices, based on a determination that private prices in Canada were significantly influenced by the predominant role of Canadian governments in the market place.[69] The USDOC thus concluded that there were "no useable market-determined prices between Canadian buyers and sellers."[70] Accordingly, the USDOC turned to the second possible source of benchmarks determined by its regulations — world market prices available to purchasers in Canada. The USDOC found that certain stumpage prices charged in these regions of the United States that bordered Canada represented world market prices available to Canadian timber mills.[71] The USDOC constructed a benchmark for each province, based on prices from neighbouring states in the United States, adjusted for certain distinguishing factors. These benchmarks were then compared with the stumpage programs in each province. This comparison revealed that prices in each province were less than the adjusted US benchmark price, thus indicating that the goods concerned were being provided for less than adequate remuneration, thereby providing a benefit.[72]

---

68 *Ibid.* at para. 351.511(2)(iii).

69 *Lumber IV,* Decision Memorandum, *supra* note 54 at 37. The rejection of internal Canadian prices as a benchmark makes the *Lumber IV* analysis markedly different from that adopted in *Lumber III* (see discussion earlier in this article). This difference in approach provides an illustration of one difference between the old "preferential" test for measuring the existence of a subsidy and the modern "adequacy of remuneration" test.

70 *Ibid.* The USDOC further rejected using sale prices from actual transactions in the Maritime provinces or from imports, citing insufficient information.

71 *Lumber IV,* Decision Memorandum, *supra* note 54 at 40–5. In so finding, the USDOC rejected a number of arguments by the respondents, in particular, those focusing on the inherent differences between stands of timber in Canada and the United States. The USDOC felt that adjustments to the US prices could address these considerations. These arguments echoed arguments that had been accepted by the USDOC in *Lumber II,* see *supra* note 15.

72 See assessment for each of the six provinces in the *Lumber IV,* Decision Memorandum, *supra* note 54 at 54–144.

The NAFTA panel accepted the USDOC's conclusion that market prices in Canada were distorted by Canadian government intervention and were not, therefore, available as first-tier benchmarks. The panel ruled, however, that the USDOC had made a fundamental error in deeming US prices to be "world market prices," which could be compared with prices in Canada.[73] The inherent differences between stands of timber in Canada and the United States — and even within Canada and the United States — meant that there was, in reality, *no world market price* for stumpage. This was underscored by the inability of the USDOC to even find a single US price for stumpage.[74]

Having overturned the USDOC's benefit analysis, the NAFTA panel remanded this issue to the USDOC for reconsideration, effectively dictating that the USDOC should look to analyze whether Canadian provincial stumpage programs generated prices that were "consistent with market principles." The USDOC issued its remand determination on 21 April 2004.[75] In this remand determination, the USDOC reaffirmed its finding of the existence of a benefit at a revised rate.[76] The USDOC's general approach in its first remand determination was affirmed by the NAFTA panel.[77] The NAFTA panel, however, found fault with a number of other technical aspects of the USDOC's first remand determination and remanded a second time. These aspects were addressed by the USDOC in a second remand determination and resulted in a further substantial reduction of the countervailing duty rate.[78] In reviewing this

---

[73] *Re Softwood Lumber,* NAFTA CVD Panel Report, *supra* note 62 at 20 ff.

[74] The findings of the NAFTA panel in this regard are notably similar to the view expressed by the USDOC itself during the course of the *Lumber I* proceedings. See note 12 in this article.

[75] *Remand Determination,* available at <http://ia.ita.doc.gov/remands/index.html> (15 December 2005) (*Lumber IV,* CVD Remand Determination). (Subsequent remand determinations by the USDOC in respect of this matter are hereinafter referred to in this article as *Lumber IV,* CVD Second Remand Determination; *Lumber IV,* CVD Third Remand Determination; and so on. They are available at the same online location).

[76] 13.23 per cent *ad valorem* (*Lumber IV,* Remand Determination, *supra* note 75 at 47). The USDOC's revised methodology was reminiscent of the "residual value" analysis discussed in *Lumber I, supra* note 6.

[77] *Re Softwood Lumber,* NAFTA CVD Panel, Report on First Remand (7 June 2004), *supra* note 62 at 7 ff.

[78] 7.82 per cent *ad valorem* for the period 1 April 2000 to 31 March 2001. See *Lumber IV,* CVD Second Remand Determination (30 July 2004), *supra* note 75 at 26.

second remand determination, the NAFTA panel found further substantial errors in the revised determination and remanded a third time.[79] The USDOC's third remand determination resulted in a further reduction of the countervailing duty rate for the period 1 April 2000 to 31 March 2001 to 1.88 per cent *ad valorem*.[80] The NAFTA panel's review of the third remand determination identified and remanded further technical errors.[81] The USDOC's fourth remand determination resulted in another reduction of the rate to 1.21 per cent *ad valorem*.[82] This was again remanded by the NAFTA panel.[83] According to Canadian government sources available at the time of writing, the USDOC's fifth remand determination issued on 22 November 2005 resulted in a finding of a *de minimis* level of subsidy.[84]

The USDOC's initial benefit determination (that is, the determination issued prior to initiation of a challenge under Chapter 19 of NAFTA) was the subject of an inconclusive result in the context of Canada's WTO challenge. Although the *US – Softwood Lumber IV* panel found that the USDOC had improperly determined the existence of a benefit through referring to prices other than those prevailing within the Canadian market,[85] the Appellate Body reversed this finding but found that there were insufficient facts available for it to complete the analysis and substitute its own conclusion regarding the consistency or otherwise of the USDOC's underlying

---

[79] *Re Softwood Lumber,* NAFTA CVD Panel, Report on Second Remand (1 December 2004), *supra* note 62 at 25–6.

[80] *Lumber IV,* CVD Third Remand Determination (24 January 2004), *supra* note 75 at 28–9.

[81] *Re Softwood Lumber,* NAFTA CVD Panel, Report on Third Remand (23 May 2005), *supra* note 62 at 26.

[82] *Lumber IV,* CVD Fourth Remand Determination (7 July 2005), *supra* note 75 at 36.

[83] *Re Softwood Lumber,* NAFTA CVD Panel, Report on Fourth Remand (5 October 2005), *supra* note 62 at 10.

[84] Specifically, 0.80 per cent *ad valorem.* See Canadian government press release "U.S. Finally Determines Canadian Lumber Not Subsidized: One Step towards Resolution," <http://wo1.international.gc.ca/MinPub/Publication.asp? Language=E&publication_id=383463> (15 December 2005). A finding of *de minimis* subsidy in an initial investigation requires termination of the investigation. The position with respect to the NAFTA review on this issue is complicated, however, by developments resulting from the parallel WTO review of this same issue. See discussion later in this article.

[85] *US – Softwood Lumber IV,* Panel Report, *supra* note 63 at para. 7.65.

determination with the requirements of the SCM Agreement.[86] In its analysis, the Appellate Body rejected the panel's approach requiring an investigating authority to use as a benchmark *private prices* in the country of provision, whenever they exist. Instead, the Appellate Body reasoned that the SCM Agreement allowed an investigating authority to use different benchmarks, in the event that it could properly determine that the private market was distorted as a result of the predominant role of the government in the market place and provided that any benchmark chosen related or referred to, or was connected with, prevailing market conditions in the country of provision.[87] Nevertheless, in the absence of any evidence on the record pertaining to the issues raised by this revised test, the Appellate Body did not go on to determine whether the benefit determination underlying the actual dispute was consistent with these requirements. The issue was, therefore, left open.

Specificity

Under the governing US statute, a finding of specificity may result from a determination that the subsidy in question is an export subsidy, is limited in law to a specific enterprise or industry or group of enterprises or industries, or is specific "as a matter of fact."[88] The relevant provision dictates that the USDOC should find a subsidy to be specific where (1) the actual recipients of the subsidy, whether considered on an enterprise or industry basis, are limited in number; (2) an enterprise or industry is a predominant user of the subsidy; (3) an enterprise or industry receives a disproportionately large amount of the subsidy; or (4) the manner in which the authority providing the subsidy has exercised discretion in the decision to grant the subsidy indicates that an enterprise or industry is favoured over others.[89] Regulations further implementing these provisions emphasize that the USDOC is to consider these alternatives in sequential order. Moreover, in the event that a single factor warrants a finding of specificity, then the USDOC is not required to complete the analysis of other factors.[90]

---

[86] *US – Softwood Lumber IV*, Appellate Body Report, *supra* note 63 at paras. 119–22.

[87] *Ibid.*, at para. 103.

[88] Tariff Act, *supra* note 47 at § 771(5A).

[89] These considerations parallel those set out in Article 2.1(c) of the SCM Agreement, *supra* note 50.

[90] Antidumping and Countervailing Duties, *supra* note 51 at para. 351.502(a).

In its *Lumber IV* investigation, the USDOC found that the recipients of the program were limited to sawmills and pulp and paper mills, thus rendering the program *de facto* specific under the first tier of the statutory test.[91] For the USDOC, the "vast majority" of Canadian enterprises did not receive stumpage benefits. Before the NAFTA panel, the Canadian parties took issue with this finding on several grounds. In particular, the Canadian parties argued that the USDOC's specificity finding failed to take account of ultimate findings in the earlier *Lumber I* and *Lumber III* proceedings, which held that stumpage did not confer specific subsidies. The NAFTA panel, however, rejected these contentions. In the panel's view, the precedents identified by the respondents arose under different legal frameworks, in which the specificity requirement was framed in different terms. The present legislation made it clear that the USDOC was entitled to find *de facto* specificity where it found the number of industries using a program to have been limited in practice. The USDOC had done just that. The panel accordingly indicated that it could find no error in the USDOC's approach.

A similar conclusion was reached by the WTO *US – Softwood Lumber IV* panel, whose finding in this regard was not appealed. The WTO panel did not accept Canada's argument that, for a subsidy to be specific under Article 2.1 (c) of the SCM Agreement, the granting authority must have somehow *deliberately* limited access to the subsidy program to particular enterprises. In so finding, the panel expressly rejected an argument based on the "inherent characteristics" of timber, finding that there was no textual basis "for Canada's argument that if the inherent characteristics of the good provided limit the possible use of the subsidy to a certain industry, the subsidy will not be specific unless access to this subsidy is limited to a sub-set of this industry."[92] For the panel, the "wood products industries" constituted, at most, a limited group of industries and, accordingly, fell within the definition of *de facto* specificity reflected in Article 2.1 (c) of the SCM Agreement.[93]

Pass-Through of Indirect Subsidies

Despite claims made by the respondents during the investigation, the USDOC did not consider the degree to which subsidies

91 *Lumber IV*, Decision Memorandum, *supra* note 54 at 52.

92 *US – Softwood Lumber IV*, Panel Report, *supra* note 63 at para. 7.116.

93 *Ibid.* at para. 7.121.

granted through provision of standing timber to loggers were passed through the production chain to lumber mills and further-processors of basic lumber outputs. The Canadian respondents appear to have raised the need for a pass-through analysis in two circumstances: submitting, first, that an analysis would be necessary in the event that logs were harvested, either by sawmill owners or by independent entities, and then sold to other sawmills in arm's-length transactions; and, second, that such an analysis would also be required where sawmills, through arm's-length transactions, sold softwood lumber to independent producers of remanufactured items falling within the scope of the investigation.[94] The respondents' arguments rested on the contention that any subsidy paid through stumpage attached, directly, only to logs or timber and could not necessarily be attributed to products further down the production chain in a countervailing duty investigation.

The USDOC disagreed with the respondents' contentions. It found that the subsidy was provided to lumber producers and that the provision of timber through stumpage was merely "the vehicle" for the subsidy to softwood lumber.[95] This obviated the need for any pass-through analysis where a mill processed subsidized logs. The same reasoning applied with regard to remanufactured products. According to the USDOC, both dimension lumber and remanufactured goods were within the scope of the investigation, which covered "softwood lumber" generally. Both of these categories of softwood lumber were produced by stumpage holders, meaning that both categories of product benefited from the stumpage subsidy.[96]

The NAFTA panel dismissed Canadian claims to the contrary and upheld the USDOC's approach to the pass-through issue. In the

---

[94] *Lumber IV,* Decision Memorandum, *supra* note 54 at 18–19. Canadian respondents in the earlier *Lumber III* episode had argued that the USDOC was required to complete an investigation into the existence of "upstream subsidies" in these same two situations and the USDOC had taken a similar approach in declining to make an assessment of upstream subsidies.

[95] *Ibid.* at 18–19.

[96] *Ibid.* Although the USDOC acknowledged that there might be cases in which subject merchandise was produced by remanufacturers who did not benefit from stumpage, it suggested that this should not affect its overall calculation of the country-wide rate of subsidization. Rather, it reasoned that it was simply a question of how the overall subsidy was divided amongst recipients, and, as such, a matter to be dealt with through the calculation of a company-specific rate (as opposed to affecting the country-wide rate).

panel's view, the only situation in which a pass-through analysis would be necessary is where a tenure holder is completely independent of producers of softwood lumber. It noted that there was a factual disagreement regarding the prevalence of independent operators in each of the provinces implicated in the investigation. In light of the deferential standard of review governing its consideration of the matter, the NAFTA panel found that the USDOC's conclusions were sufficiently based in the evidentiary record.[97]

The approach taken at the WTO to the two separate pass-through issues raised in the proceedings differed, at both the panel and appellate stages, from that taken by the NAFTA panel. The WTO *US – Softwood Lumber IV* panel differed from the NAFTA panel on its conclusions regarding both sales by independent loggers and sales by lumber remanufacturers. It ruled that "[i]f it is not demonstrated that there has been such a pass-through of subsidies from the subsidy recipient to the producer or exporter of the product, then it cannot be said that subsidization in respect of that product," in the sense of the applicable rules of the SCM Agreement and GATT 1994.[98] It thus went on to find that a pass-through analysis was, in principle, required whenever the recipient of a subsidy was different from the producer or exporter of the product subject to the countervailing duty investigation.

The Appellate Body upheld the panel's underlying interpretation that a pass-through analysis is required where a subsidy is conferred on an input product but countervailing duties are imposed on processed goods, where the producers of the input and finished products, respectively, operate at arm's length. It observed, however, that WTO members are entitled to conduct countervailing duty investigations on an *aggregate* basis, without being required to investigate individually each product or exporter falling within the scope of the investigation.[99] Based on this interpretation, the Appellate Body reversed the panel's finding that the USDOC had acted inconsistently with the provisions of GATT 1994 and the SCM Agreement by failing to conduct a pass-through analysis with respect to arm's-length sales of primary lumber by sawmills to unrelated lumber remanufacturers. As the NAFTA panel implicitly seemed to accept, the Appellate Body reasoned that both primary and

---

97 *Re Softwood Lumber,* NAFTA CVD Panel Report, *supra* note 62 at 58–65.

98 *US – Softwood Lumber IV,* Panel Report, *supra* note 63 at para. 7.91.

99 *US – Softwood Lumber IV,* Appellate Body Report, *supra* note 63 at para. 152.

remanufactured lumber fell within the "softwood lumber" category that was subject to the USDOC's aggregate investigation.[100]

Nevertheless, the Appellate Body upheld the panel's finding that an analysis was required to determine whether subsidies received by sawmill-owning harvesters of logs passed through to the production of lumber, where the logs are purchased in arm's-length transactions by unrelated sawmills.[101] This was because logs, as distinct from the lumber made from them, were not products subject to the aggregate investigation. Rather, logs are simply inputs into the production of subject merchandise. Accordingly, subsidies paid to harvesters of logs could not be assumed to have passed through arm's-length sales to lumber manufacturers. Instead, such pass-through of subsidies needed to be determined on the facts of the case.[102]

Following the adoption of the panel and the Appellate Body reports in *US – Softwood Lumber IV,* the US trade representative instructed the USDOC to carry out a review of the original final countervailing duty determination[103] under section 129 of the URAA (Countervailing Duties Section 129 Determination). After completing "pass-through" analyses, in accordance with its reading of the relevant WTO reports, the USDOC calculated a revised countervailing duty rate for the initial period of investigation.[104] The results of this Countervailing Duties Section 129 Determination were implemented by publication in the US Federal Register on 16 December 2004,[105] meaning that this was the rate at which bonds and deposits were collected "on or after" that date (and not before), in accordance with the terms of section 129.

This revised deposit rate was, however, soon replaced by the results of the first administrative review of the countervailing duties

---

[100] *Ibid.* at para. 163.

[101] The Appellate Body's ruling related only to cases of sales of logs by a *sawmill owning* harvester to another sawmill. The panel's pass-through finding with respect to sales of logs from independent harvesters was not appealed by the United States. *Ibid.* at para. 127.

[102] *Ibid.* at para. 157.

[103] That is, the *Lumber IV,* CVD Determination, *supra* note 54, as reviewed by the WTO, and not as revised following remands within the framework of review under NAFTA Chapter 19.

[104] The initial period of investigation was 1 April 2000 to 31 March 2001. The revised rate was 18.62 per cent *ad valorem.*

[105] *Amendment to Antidumping and Countervailing Duty Orders on Certain Softwood Lumber Products from Canada,* 69 Fed. Reg., 75305 (2004).

(first assessment review), which was issued on 20 December 2004.[106] Consistent with the United States's retrospective system of duty assessment, the first assessment review provided for the retrospective final assessment of the definitive countervailing duties levied on imports of softwood lumber from Canada liquidated[107] during the period between 22 May 2002 and 31 March 2003. The review also fixed the cash deposit rate for entries as of 20 December 2004.[108] The downward adjustment of the subsidy found to exist in the Countervailing Duties Section 129 Determination, and the absence of any adjustment in the first assessment review for situations in which a subsidy did not pass through led to further litigation in the WTO. In *United States – Final Countervailing Duty Determination with Respect to Certain Softwood Lumber from Canada – Recourse to Article 21.5 of the DSU by Canada (US – Softwood – Article 21.5)*,[109] the panel found that the failure to make any adjustment in the first assessment review rendered this review inconsistent with US WTO obligations. The panel found that the pass-through analysis in the Countervailing Duties Section 129 Determination also failed to implement the WTO's findings in the original *US – Softwood Lumber IV* proceedings. On 5 December 2005, the Appellate Body rejected an appeal by the United States regarding the jurisdiction of the panel to consider the first assessment review. The cash deposit rate was revised again on 6 December 2005 as a result of the second assessment review and remains at 8.7 per cent *ad valorem* at the time of writing.[110]

---

106 *Notice of Implementation under Section 129 of the Uruguay Round Agreements Act; Countervailing Measures Concerning Certain Softwood Lumber from Canada*, 69 Fed. Reg., 75917 (2004).

107 At the time of writing, liquidation, for the most part, remains suspended pending the outcome of the parallel proceedings under Chapter 19 of the NAFTA, discussed earlier in this article.

108 The rate of duty determined in the first assessment review was 17.18 per cent *ad valorem*. This was corrected for ministerial errors on 24 February 2005, resulting in a rate of 16.37 percent *ad valorem. Notice of Amended Final Results of Duty Administrative Review: Certain Softwood Lumber from Canada*, 70 Fed. Reg., 9046 (2005).

109 *United States – Final Countervailing Duty Determination with Respect to Certain Softwood Lumber from Canada – Recourse to Article 21.5 of the DSU by Canada*, Panel Report, WTO Doc. WT/DS257/RW (2005) [*US – Softwood – Article 21.5*].

110 The cash deposit rates cited here relate only to the countervailing duty element of the applicable duties. Further cash deposits are collected in respect of imports subjected to anti-dumping duties.

CONCLUSIONS

The thrust of this article so far has been to chronicle certain notable events during the history of softwood lumber countervailing duty proceedings since 1982. It is intended that this general narrative in itself will fill a gap in the available literature. Beyond this, however, the above review also sheds light upon issues of more general interest to practitioners and followers of international law. Accordingly, by way of conclusion, the following section comments upon what the softwood lumber dispute reveals about the nature of disciplines on subsidies in international trade and also about the relationship between different international dispute settlement organs.

DISCIPLINES ON SUBSIDIES IN INTERNATIONAL TRADE

One of the most striking features of the history of softwood lumber countervailing duty investigations is that the answers to recurring questions have not always been the same. One immediately apparent example of this evolution is the approach to specificity. In each phase of the softwood lumber dispute, the USDOC has been confronted with the apparent truism that the main consumers of the raw timber made available under stumpage arrangements tended to be the timber-consuming industries. In *Lumber I*, the fact that the "inherent characteristics" of timber (and not some *de jure* criterion within the stumpage programs themselves) limited the number of industries exploiting the resource was sufficient for a finding of no specificity. In *Lumber IV*, the opposite was true. The finding — in terms of the US statutory rule that mirrors the WTO requirements — that there was, in fact, a "limited number of users" was an almost inescapable consequence of the inherent characteristics of the good in question.

The *raison d'être* of disciplines on subsidies (including the availability of countervailing duties) is to manage the distortions to competitiveness and trade that such measures can cause. The apparent utility of a specificity test in this context is in removing from analysis, *a priori*, certain subsidies that may be deemed to have no trade distorting potential. The evolution of the approach to specificity taken over the history of the softwood lumber dispute — ranging from something approaching a strict *de jure* test to a very broad *de facto* one — illustrates the difficulty of setting a threshold of specificity at a level that serves as an appropriate filter.[111]

---

[111] Perhaps for this reason, further disciplines on applying countervailing measures to widely available subsidies (both under United States law and under the SCM

Current specificity rules (both in terms of US law and the multilateral rules of the SCM Agreement) appear now to lean heavily towards inclusiveness. For the NAFTA panel in *Lumber IV,* twenty-three separate classes of industries, identified by Canada as benefiting from stumpage, could still be considered as leaving the number of subsidy recipients "limited" in terms of the specificity test.[112] Similarly, the WTO *US – Softwood Lumber IV* panel felt that these same twenty-three industries could still be considered a limited "group of industries" for purposes of Article 2 of the SCM Agreement.[113] Recent developments in the softwood lumber dispute thus suggest that only the most widely available subsidies — subsidies available both in law and, in fact, to a largely *un*-limited group of potential recipients — will be treated as non-specific.

A second recurring issue raised in the context of the history of the softwood lumber dispute relates to the "pricing" of timber made available under harvesting rights. Like the situation with specificity, the determinations by the USDOC (and reviewing panels) on the question of whether or not stumpage was priced so as to provide a subsidy have been both negative and affirmative. Similarly, the tests applied in each phase have evolved in response to pressures from both internal and external developments. In particular, the manner in which US countervailing duty law assessed whether goods provided under stumpage programs delivered subsidy benefits changed with the conclusion of the Uruguay Round and the implementation of its results. Thus, the earlier "preferential pricing" standard was replaced with an "adequacy of remuneration" test. Under both tests, the USDOC has used comparisons between actual timber prices and some benchmark. Yet the difference between these standards appears to have broadened the range of

---

Agreement, *supra* note 50) have been imposed through other elements of the subsidy equation. For example, certain widely available government measures, the provision of "general infrastructure," is excluded from the part of the definition of "financial contribution" that was relevant to the softwood lumber dispute. Likewise, the principle recounted by both the NAFTA CVD panel and the WTO Appellate Body that the subsidy numerator in a countervailing duty rate determination must "match" and be spread over a denominator incorporating sales of all subsidized products will tend to dilute a thinly spread subsidy, making countervailability less likely, or, at least, reducing substantially any rate of subsidization found.

112 *Re Softwood Lumber,* NAFTA CVD Panel Report, *supra* note 62 at 39.

113 *US – Softwood Lumber IV,* Panel Report, *supra* note 63 at para. 7.121 and footnote 188 to para. 7.121. The panel's findings on specificity were not appealed.

comparators potentially available. In particular, whereas the USDOC opined in *Lumber I* that using cross-border prices would be "arbitrary and capricious," the department actually used adjusted cross-border prices as the comparator for assessing adequacy of remuneration in *Lumber IV*. And, although the USDOC's use of US prices in this case was rejected by both the NAFTA panel and the WTO, the *possibility* of using external prices was ultimately affirmed in both fora.

In the case of the NAFTA proceeding, it was never suggested that the statutory language making "world market prices" available for the purposes of comparing government prices with the adequacy of remuneration standard was equivocal. Indeed, the panel recognized that the authority to use world market prices was explicit. Rather, the rejection of external prices by the NAFTA panel in *Lumber IV* was based purely on its finding that there was no relevant "world market" for standing timber. The WTO Appellate Body reached its conclusion from a different direction. The Appellate Body reversed a finding of the *US – Softwood Lumber IV* panel, which held that an investigating authority was obliged to use as the comparator private prices in the country of provision, wherever they existed. Instead, the Appellate Body ruled that an investigating authority could, pursuant to the relevant rules of the SCM Agreement, use other than private prices in the country of provision, subject to important provisos concerning, in particular, the effect of governmental intervention in the marketplace upon private prices.[114] The rulings on this issue will be important in the context of future countervailing duty proceedings where goods subject to investigation are produced from the exploitation of natural resources, particularly in countries where access to natural resources is controlled by the state.

RELATIONSHIP BETWEEN DIFFERENT INTERNATIONAL DISPUTE SETTLEMENT REGIMES

A second set of insights that may be gleaned from the more recent history of the softwood lumber dispute relates to the relationship between different international dispute settlement regimes. The proliferation of international courts and tribunals is a *cause célèbre* among international law commentators. One key issue in this discussion pertains to what happens when different international tribunals seized of the same subject matter reach different views as

[114] *US – Softwood Lumber IV*, Appellate Body Report, *supra* note 63 at para. 167(b).

to the substance of a claim. The approach to the pass-through issue in *Lumber IV,* and, in particular, the divergent approaches taken by the NAFTA panel and the WTO panel and the Appellate Body provide an interesting illustration of the problems that this can cause.

On a formal level, the divergent approaches taken by the NAFTA panel and the WTO organs do not involve the same claims. Indeed, the NAFTA panel was not mandated to interpret US international obligations. Rather, under Chapter 19 of NAFTA, it operated like a domestic tribunal and decided the matter before it on the basis of US municipal law. Only the WTO dealt with US international obligations. Nevertheless, at a more practical level, the overlap between the competing jurisdictions in this case is clear, because the measures at issue (the USDOC determination) were the same, and the two legal frameworks (US trade law and WTO law) reflected essentially the same legal obligations. Moreover, Chapter 19 panels are not ordinary US courts but, rather, are supranational in nature.

The respective approaches taken by the NAFTA panel and the WTO were, at least in one respect, substantially different. It will be recalled that the pass-through issue arose in two situations, and the USDOC drew a distinction between the position regarding sales of logs by harvesters and mills, on the one hand, and sales of primary lumber to lumber remanufacturers, on the other. With regard to the level of subsidy countervailable in *remanufactured lumber,* the approach taken was harmonious among all of the ultimate arbiters on this point.[115] The USDOC's view was that both remanufactured and primary lumber were within the scope of the investigation and, therefore, that neither was upstream to the other. The NAFTA panel in *Lumber IV* accepted the USDOC position. Ultimately, so too did the WTO Appellate Body.

In the case of pass-through from *logs,* however, the USDOC found that the absence of evidence substantiating the existence of arm's-length transactions meant that it was not inappropriate to *assume* that subsidies passed from log harvesters to the mills they supplied.[116] The NAFTA panel upheld this approach, as it applied to sales of logs by both independent harvesters and unrelated sawmills. The WTO panel and the Appellate Body, by contrast, said that the existence of arm's-length sales of a product *outside of the scope of the*

115 The WTO Appellate Body reversed a finding by the panel regarding remanufactured lumber that differed from that adopted by the NAFTA panel. See *US – Softwood Lumber IV,* Appellate Body Report, *supra* note 63 at para. 163.

116 This was essentially the same approach that had been adopted to this issue in the earlier *Lumber III, supra* note 26, episode of the dispute.

investigation (that is, logs, as opposed to softwood lumber) *required* a pass-through analysis, if subsidies on the input were to be attributed to the finished product. On this basis, the USDOC's *assumption* of pass-through was not appropriate — pass-through needed to be demonstrated on the facts of the case.

The gap between these two sets of decisions may seem case-specific and technical. This issue has, nonetheless, been influential on how subsequent stages of the dispute have played out. The revision of the original countervailing duty determination following the WTO decision in order to remedy the lack of pass-through analysis resulted in a new countervailing duty determination in the form of the Countervailing Duties Section 129 Determination. Arguably — and it is a contentious point — the Countervailing Duties Section 129 Determination has superseded the determination that has been the subject of five remands within the framework of NAFTA Chapter 19, which have now resulted in a finding of a *de minimis* — that is, non-countervailable — level of subsidy. It thus seems that multi-track international litigation strategies have their risks. Although they open up the possibility of winning in one court, where you have lost in another, they also raise the possibility that implementation of one decision will lead to complications in securing a result in parallel proceedings.

This point seems to be underscored by developments in regard to proceedings continuing with respect to the *threat of injury* determination by the USITC, which followed the USDOC's original findings of subsidization and dumping. In this case, the United States maintains that a determination under section 129 of the URAA, in regard to the threat analysis, now forms the basis for the imposition of duties. Thus, countervailing duties continue to be applied, notwithstanding a different NAFTA Chapter 19 panel's affirmation of a remand determination by the USITC finding that there was no injury or threat in the initial period of investigation.[117] This complicated conflict within the US domestic law system implementing different trade agreements will play out in the US Court of International Trade during the course of 2006.

Yet if the recent history of the softwood lumber dispute highlights one of the problems that can arise with the proliferation of international and supranational courts and tribunals, the broader

---

[117] The decisions of this NAFTA Chapter 19 panel have been upheld by an extraordinary challenge committee. See *Re Certain Softwood Lumber Products from Canada*, Extraordinary Challenge Committee, Doc. ECC-2004-1904-01USA (2005).

context of the dispute may also illustrate one of the ways out of the
difficulties caused. Indeed, further softwood lumber proceedings
— those dealing with the USDOC's *dumping* determination in regard to softwood lumber from Canada — the problem of divergent
outcomes has been resolved through the use of existing tools for
managing the relationship between different legal frameworks.

In its dumping determination, the USDOC had used a "zeroing"
methodology for the calculation of the margin of dumping. The
NAFTA panel initially ruled that the use of such a methodology fell
within the USDOC's discretion under the governing statutory
framework — such methodology was neither proscribed nor required.[118] This finding by the panel was, however, revised during
the course of subsequent remand proceedings, in order to take
account of the intervening decision on zeroing by the WTO Appellate Body in *United States – Final Dumping Determination on Softwood
Lumber from Canada*.[119] The United States implemented this WTO
decision by means of a further determination under section 129 of
the URAA (Dumping Section 129 Determination), this time revising the initial final dumping determination. Based on these developments, the NAFTA dumping panel revisited and changed its
decision on zeroing.[120] The panel reasoned that the WTO rulings
demonstrated that zeroing was inconsistent with an international
obligation of the United States, a conclusion that the US government had acknowledged through its implementation of the Dumping Section 129 Determination. On this basis, and applying the
so-called *Charming Betsy* doctrine — which requires interpretation
of US statutes consistently with US international obligations, subject to provisos — the NAFTA panel ruled that the USDOC was
obliged to use its discretion not to adopt a zeroing methodology in
the present investigation. The decision represents an innovative

118 *Re Certain Softwood Lumber from Canada: Final Affirmative Antidumping
Determination*, Chapter 19 Panel, Doc. USA-CDA-2002-1904-02 (2003) at 61
[*Re Softwood Lumber*, NAFTA Dumping Panel Report]. (In this article, consideration of subsequent remand determinations by the same NAFTA panel are
referred to hereinafter as *Re Softwood Lumber*, NAFTA Dumping Panel, Report
on First Remand; *Re Softwood Lumber*, NAFTA CVD Panel, Report on Second
Remand, and so on).

119 *United States – Final Dumping Determination on Softwood Lumber from Canada*
(*Complaint by Canada*), Appellate Body Report, WTO Doc. WT/DS264/AB/R
(2004) [*US – Softwood Lumber V*, Appellate Body Report].

120 *Re Softwood Lumber*, NAFTA Dumping Panel, Report on Second Remand (9 June
2004), *supra* note 118 at 43.

use of the *Charming Betsy* doctrine and, arguably, also of "comity" between international tribunals.[121]

With respect to subsidies rules and the relationship between international tribunals, the softwood lumber dispute continues to be a crucible in which new international law developments are being forged. For this reason alone — and even leaving aside the considerable volume and value of trade affected — this aspect of Canada–United States relations deserves continued attention from international lawyers everywhere. Indeed, the recent history of litigation in regard to softwood lumber provides a rich and rapidly developing case study on many more legal fronts — one that, at the time of writing, is continuing to evolve in the WTO, under NAFTA Chapter 19, through proceedings under NAFTA Chapter 11, and in the US courts, with both substantive challenges from the parties and a constitutional challenge to the NAFTA Chapter 19 system as a whole.

However, although these developments are of great academic interest, they also highlight a cause for introspection by international lawyers. This is because none of the available international dispute settlement tools have, so far at least, been able to secure a resolution of the overall *Lumber IV* dispute. This observation is underscored when one considers the longer history of softwood lumber countervailing duty proceedings — one cannot help but be struck by the complete absence of an enduring solution to the differences between the relevant US and Canadian interests. Against this background, perhaps, the clearest lesson from the history of the softwood lumber dispute is that there remain severe limits to

---

[121] A similar approach was taken by another NAFTA Chapter 19 panel in the 2001 proceedings involving Mexico's anti-dumping measures in respect of high fructose corn syrup from the United States. In this case, which was governed by Mexican law, the panel applied a principle of "comity" between international tribunals and declined to itself review claims in regard to which the WTO panel in *Mexico – Anti-Dumping Investigation of High Fructose Corn Syrup (HFCS) from the United States* (referred to by the NAFTA panel as the SG-WTO case) had made findings. The report of the NAFTA panel recalls that the panel

issued an Order in which it … recognized that the SG-WTO had completed its review of the Final Determination and consequently, its review is limited, in what it considers legally justified to the points not considered by the SG-WTO applying the Principle of Comity.

See *Re Review of the Final Determination of the Antidumping Investigation on Imports of High Fructose Corn Syrup Originating from the United States of America*, Chapter 19 Panel, Doc. MEX-USA-98-1904-01 (2001) at para. 188.

what can be achieved through international trade dispute settlement in highly politicized cases.

Sommaire

Détermination de l'existence de droits compensatoires dans le contexte du différend canado-américain sur le bois d'œuvre: 1982–2005

Cet article dresse l'historique de la détermination des droits compensatoires en matière du bois d'œuvre entre 1982 et 2005. L'analyse est subdivisée en deux grandes parties. D'abord, l'article fait un compte rendu analytique de certaines déterminations clés sur le sujet au fil de l'histoire. En particulier, l'article examine quelques thèmes récurrents et quelques points utiles pour élucider certaines questions jurisprudentielles intéressantes qui se dégagent de cette étude de cas. Deuxièmement, au terme de ce survol, l'article présente les leçons qu'on peut tirer de l'expérience à ce jour. Il cherche à dégager, plus particulièrement, ce que cette longue histoire des différends liés au bois d'œuvre révèle, d'une part, sur la nature des disciplines visant les subventions en commerce international et, d'autre part, sur les rapports entre les différents acteurs juridiques en cause sur la scène internationale. L'article termine par des réflexions sur les limites des mécanismes internationaux de règlement de différends dans le secteur du bois d'œuvre dans des dossiers hautement contestés et politisés.

Summary

Determining the Existence of Countervailable Subsidies in the Context of the Canada–United States Softwood Lumber Dispute: 1982–2005

This article examines the history of countervailing duty determinations with respect to softwood lumber between 1982 and 2005. The piece is divided into two main areas of analysis. First, the article chronicles and reviews certain key determinations made throughout the history of softwood lumber countervailing duty proceedings. It examines, in particular, certain recurring themes as well as issues that shed light on some of the interesting jurisprudential questions that arise out of the case study. Second, having completed this review, the note turns to distill some lessons from the experience to date. These lessons focus on the light shed by the lengthy history of the softwood lumber dispute upon the nature of subsidies disciplines in international trade. They also focus on what the softwood lumber dispute reveals about the relationship between different judicial actors at the international level. The article closes with some reflections on the limits of international dispute settlement tools in highly contentious and politicized cases.

Transboundary Environmental Disputes along the Canada–US Frontier: Revisiting the Efficacy of Applying the Rules of State Responsibility

KEVIN R. GRAY

INTRODUCTION

A fundamental tenet underscoring the development of international environmental law in the last century is the "no harm" principle reflecting a state's responsibility to prevent environmental damage outside its territory as a result of activity taking place within the territory. Although the antecedents of state responsibility rest in general public international law,[1] stemming from the *sic utere* principle,[2] it takes on its own unique character in international environmental law. The whole ethos of multilateral or bilateral co-operation on environmental matters depends upon a recognition to cease or prevent transboundary environmental degradation. The collective duty to prevent environmental harm is operationalized through multilateral efforts to forge common solutions in international treaties. Such instruments are designed to address environmental problems shared by countries or affecting the global

Kevin R. Gray is currently counsel with the Trade Law Bureau at the Canadian Department of Foreign Affairs and International Trade. The views expressed in this article are entirely those of the author and in no way represent the positions of the Department of Foreign Affairs and International Trade or the government of Canada. The author is grateful to the helpful comments and suggestions from Jutta Brunnée, Marcia Valiante, Peter Fawcett, Philippe Sands, and Dean Sherratt.

1 See M. Shaw, *International Law*, 5th edition (Cambridge: Cambridge University Press, 2003); and I. Brownlie, *System of the Law of Nations: State Responsibility*, Part I (Oxford: Oxford University Press, 1983).

2 *Sic utere tuo ut alenum non laedas* can be translated to "one should use his own property in such a manner as not to injure that of another." *Black's Law Dictionary*, 6th edition (1990) at 380. Justice Sutherland in *Village of Euclid v. Amber Security and Reality Co.*, (1926) 272 U.S. 365 at 386, noted that this "maxim lies at the foundation of so much of the common law of nuisances)."

commons. The obligations are owed both to states as well as to, *erga omnes,* the international community as a whole.[3]

The scope of state responsibility for transboundary environmental harm is put to the test in instances of actual, or gravely potential, transboundary environmental harm. Instances of such harm occur regularly and, in most cases, without consequence. These occurrences undermine the universality of the state responsibility as an absolute precept. However, the degree of the potential or actual environmental harm can trigger a response by the injured state, thus, putting into effect the laws of state responsibility serving as the theoretical basis for restitution or compensation. The mode of delivering such a remedy still remains, at least initially, with the injured state.

The United States and Canada share a long contiguous border extending over 8,900 kilometres. Considering the extensive shared boundary that contains over 150 lakes and rivers lying along or flowing across the boundary, transboundary environmental harm is an inevitable consequence for two Organisation for Economic Co-operation and Development countries with advanced economies. In anticipation of a likelihood of such problems, there are a number of treaties and other international instruments that govern situations of transboundary environmental harm between the two states. In some cases, the spirit of cooperation is codified to the extent of effectively pre-empting any state-to-state litigation or private sector initiated suits.[4]

An effective body governing the US-Canada transboundary environmental relationship is the International Joint Commission (IJC). The IJC operates not only to resolve disputes but also to facilitate cooperation on research and scientific matters. It functions on a quasi-judicial basis and is authorized to issue non-binding reports containing conclusions and recommendations, bolstered by historical practice of both states referring disputes to the IJC with decisions made by consensus.[5]

---

[3] See *Barcelona Traction,* [1970] I.C.J. Rep. 3.

[4] Agreement between the Government of the United States of America and the Government of Canada on Air Quality (1991) 30 I.L.M. 676 [Air Quality Agreement]. See also E.K. Moller, "Comment: The United States-Canadian Acid Rain Crisis: Proposal for an International Agreement" (1989) 36 U.C.L.A. L. Rev. 1207 at 1212.

[5] Article IX states that the reports by the Commission are "not regarded as decisions of the questions or matters so submitted either in the facts or the law, and

The IJC was set up under the 1909 Treaty between the United States and Great Britain Relating to Boundary Waters between the United States and Canada (Boundary Waters Treaty), representing a significant event in addressing transboundary environmental issues considering that the predominant concerns, for both the United States and Canada, prior to its foundation were economic and commercial matters.[6] The Boundary Waters Treaty purports to address a number of instances where there are competing interests (for example, wastes, hydropower, and water removal) that are generally governed by principles of equality. Article VI(2) creates a specific obligation not to pollute waters flowing into the other country to the injury of health or property of the other.

The level of binational cooperation not only takes place between the two sovereign nations of Canada and the United States but also between the provinces and states that share the national frontier. There is an amicable history of entering into agreements to address transboundary environmental issues among the sub-federal government authorities along with their federal government counterparts, appreciating the existing transboundary environmental problems.[7]

Despite this historical relationship, the amicable experience of cooperation between Canada and the United States has seen some attempts to address transboundary environmental harm through the unilateral application of the injured states' laws. Where states assert their own jurisdiction, parallel to international mechanisms designed to achieve fair and equitable results in the face of a dispute, it undermines the collective weal of states to resolve disputes through bilateral means agreed upon in advance. This also leads to the patchwork application of the rules of state responsibility. Some

---

shall in no way have the character of an arbitral award." Under Article X, binding "decisions" can be made only if both parties consent. In the history of the International Joint Commission (IJC), there have been only two instances where no consensus was reached, and, resultantly, separate reports were issued by each government.

6 Treaty between the United States and Great Britain Relating to Boundary Waters between the United States and Canada, 36 Stat. 2448; T.S. 548 [Boundary Waters Treaty]. At the time, Canada and the United States were involved in a dispute over the diversion and use of the St. Mary and Milk Rivers in the prairies that cross the Saskatchewan-Montana border. This dispute, much like previous transboundary water cases, was addressed by ad hoc tribunals who resorted mainly to private common law riparian rights in their rulings.

7 See Great Lakes Water Quality Agreement, 22 November 1978, 30 U.S.T. 1383.

states may use the actual, or threatened, impacts allegedly caused by the injured state as a basis to mount a claim against a foreign entity or enterprise located outside its territory. The United States has been one of the few states in the international community that has not refrained from exercising their legal jurisdiction on the basis of the "effects" of the impugned activity on their territory. In choosing a judicial remedy that is domestic rather than international, entities in other states can be legally responsible in the United States for their activities that impact American territory.

Current US–Canada relations feature a number of transboundary environmental disputes both terrestrial and maritime. Such disputes call into question a state's sovereignty and, reversibly, its responsibility to develop its natural resources and undergo economic activity, when it impacts the environment of the neighbouring state. For instance, current plans to conduct oil drilling in the Arctic National Wildlife Refuge in Alaska have raised concerns in Canada because of its threat to the calving ground of the caribou population that straddles the border. North Dakota's decision to divert water from Devils Lake that potentially results in the introduction of invasive species into Canadian waterways has also challenged the general premise of state responsibility to ensure that activities do not cause adverse effects outside areas of national jurisdiction. *Pakootas v. Teck Cominco Metals Ltd.*[8] where a Canadian company's discharges into an international waterway have been linked to environmental damage south of the border, have led to the extension of US jurisdictional reach to activities in Canada and Canadian companies. As these examples are contemporary, they provide an ample opportunity to review the application of the principles of state responsibility for transboundary environmental damages and its usefulness in mediating disputes.

The first part of this article will examine the evolution of state responsibility in international environmental law. The *Trail Smelter* dispute between Canada and the United States represents the watershed ruling where domestic and international rules regarding the territorial obligation of a state to prevent damage from being incurred outside its territory were applied to an environmental dispute.[9] This lends some circularity to the discussion in the context of the *Teck Cominco* case involving similar facts and the same ecosystem

---

[8] *Pakootas v. Teck Cominco Metals Ltd.* (2004), 35 E.L.R. 20083, U.S. Dist. Ct, No. CV-04-256-AAM [*Teck Cominco*].

[9] See *Trail Smelter Arbitration (United States v. Canada),* (1935) R.I.A.A. 3 at 1965, reprinted in (1939) 35 Am. J. Int'l L. 182 and 684 [*Trail Smelter*].

in order to evaluate how the rules have evolved. The following section examines the facts and legal history surrounding the *Teck Cominco* case, highlighting how the exercise of unilateral jurisdiction has undermined the application of the rules of state responsibility and the rich history of binational cooperation between the two countries. The article then addresses the use of domestic laws to address cases of transboundary harm in light of the US District Court's decision. Two more examples, Devils Lake and the proposed oil drilling in the Arctic National Wildlife Refuge are subsequently presented, illustrating failures to account for transboundary effects and truly put the rules of state responsibility into operation.

Through this analysis, the nature of the rules of state responsibility in relation to transboundary environmental disputes evidently reveal the difficulty in applying a loosely defined set of principles to practical situations where vested interests beyond what are held by states are at play. The question whether this weakens international comity respecting the state's right to exercise its jurisdiction over the environment within its own territory as well as the communitarian shared responsibility towards the environment inherent in international environmental law is addressed.

STATE RESPONSIBILITY IN THE ENVIRONMENTAL CONTEXT

It is "well established in general international law that a state that bears responsibility for an internationally wrongful act is under an obligation to make full reparation for the injury caused by that act."[10] Responsibility arises despite any culpable contact or absence of care by the state, operating under an objective standard based on the breach of the obligation itself.[11] The responsibility could be triggered by the failure of the state to exercise due diligence,[12] a variable standard that can be based on the polluting state's level of

---

10 *Chorzów Factory Case (Indemnity)*, Jurisdiction, (1927), P.C.I.J. (Ser. A), No. 8/9, 21 at para. 259; *Case Concerning the Gabčíkovo-Nagymaros Project (Hungary v. Slovakia)*, Judgment, [1997] I.C.J. Rep. 92 at para. 152 (25 September) [*Gabčíkovo-Nagymaros*]; and *Avena and Other Mexican Nationals (Mexico v. United States of America)*, Judgment, [2004] I.C.J. Rep. 128 at para. 119.

11 I. Brownlie, *State Responsibility* (Oxford: Oxford University Press, 1983).

12 See Article 194 of the UN Convention on the Law of the Sea (1982) 21 I.L.M. 1261 [LOSC], which requires states to control pollution of the marine environment from any source, using as its purpose the best practicable means at their disposal and in accordance with their capabilities. See also *US Third Restatement of Foreign Relations Law of the United States* (Philadelphia, PA: American Law Institute, 1987) [*US Third Restatement*].

economic development.[13] The exercise of due diligence may render the state conduct lawful, but it may not excuse the state's responsibility to compensate or make reparations.

DRAFT INTERNATIONAL LAW COMMISSION (ILC) ARTICLES ON STATE RESPONSIBILITY

Article 2 of the Draft International Law Commission Articles on State Responsibility (ILC Draft Articles)[14] denotes that an internationally wrongful act of the state occurs when the conduct consists of an action or omission attributable to the state under international law. Traditionally, the conduct of individuals is not attributable to the state unless the individuals are organs of government or others who act under the direction, instigation, or control of those organs and are therefore agents of the state.[15] The application of the ILC Draft Articles is generally restricted to organs of the state, other entities empowered to exercise elements of government authority, or persons acting in fact on behalf of the state.[16]

However, there are instances where state responsibility can result from acts not committed by organs or entities of the state. Article 8

---

[13] P.N. Okowa, *State Responsibility for Transboundary Air Pollution in International Law* (Oxford: Oxford University Press, 2000)) at 82. Many transboundary pollution environmental treaties allow for varying requirements that contextualize the duty to prevent based on developmental concerns. For example, see Article 2 of the Convention on Long-Range Transboundary Air Pollution, (1979) I.L.M. 1442 [LRTAP Convention].

[14] Draft Articles on Responsibility of States for Internationally Wrongful Acts, in *Report of the International Law Commission on the Work of Its Fifty-third Session*, UN GAOR, 56th Sess., Supp. No. 10, UN Doc. A/56/10 (2001), reprinted in J. Crawford, *The International Law Commission's Articles on State Responsibility: Introduction, Text and Commentaries* (Cambridge: Cambridge University Press, 2002) [ILC Draft Articles]. The ILC Draft Articles were approved by the United Nations General Assembly in 2001 but were never presented to the UN in a form for state signature or ratification. As a result, some of the articles can be viewed as a consolidation of customary international law or a secondary source of public international law reflecting the views of the "most highly qualified publicists" pursuant to Article 38(d) of the Statute of the International Court of Justice (1945) U.S.T.D. 993.

[15] See Brownlie, *supra* note 11 at 132.

[16] ILC Draft Articles, *supra* note 14, Articles 7–9. Under Article 9, acts of a person or persons are considered to be an act of the state where it is acting on behalf of the state and the person was exercising elements of the governmental authority in the absence of the official authorities and in circumstances that justified the exercise of those elements of authority.

lays out rules of responsibility for the conduct when carried under the instructions of a state organ or under its direction. Article 11 concerns conduct not attributable to the state but, nonetheless, is adopted by the state, expressly or by conduct, as its own conduct.

Article 8 would attribute conduct to the state if the "State controlled the specific operation and the conduct complained of was an integral part of that operation."[17] Although the degree of control is not necessarily a high threshold in international law, it is unlikely that it encompasses activities of private actors that are permitted, and receive authorization, to operate under the state's law.[18] Even activities of state enterprise would not be attributed to the state unless they are exercising elements of governmental authority.[19]

Article 11 is seemingly the only rule applicable to a situation where the state has permitted the wrongful activity causing transboundary pollution. Being a catch-all provision, the internationally wrongful activity is attributable to the state where it is adopted by the state expressly or by its conduct. This can flow from actual knowledge by the state[20] of the wrongful act or where the state would have "effective control" over the entity committing the wrongful act.[21] What could lead to a finding of responsibility would be the failure to regulate economic activity occurring within the territory.[22] The

---

17 See Crawford, *supra* note 14 at 110.

18 See *Prosecutor v. Tadić*, (1999) 38 I.L.M. 1518 at para 117.

19 Crawford, *supra* note 14 at 112. The ILC Draft Articles on private actors has confirmed the customary international law status of these articles covering when state responsibility flows from the actions of private actors. See *Maffezini v. Spain*, ICSID Case no. ARB/97/07, (2002) 5 U.C.S.U.D. Reo., 396; (2003) 124 I.L.R. 9 (decision on jurisdiction of 25 January 2000); and *Salini v. Morocco*, ICSID Case no. ARB/00/0, (2004) 6 I.C.S.I.D. Rep. 400, (2003) 42 I.L.M. 609 (decision on jurisdiction of 23 July 2001).

20 *Corfu Channel (United Kingdom v. Albania)*, Merits, [1949] I.C.J. Rep. 4 [*Corfu Channel*]. In this case, the court acknowledged "every State's obligation not to allow knowingly its territory to be used for acts contrary to the rights of other States."

21 See *Military and Paramilitary Activities in and against Nicaragua (Nicaragua v. United States of America)*, Merits, Judgment, [1986] I.C.J. Rep.14 [*Nicaragua*]. The test for control is not subject to a high threshold as noted in *Prosecutor v. Tadić*, (1999) 38 I.L.M. 1518 at 1541.

22 Under the *US Third Restatement*, *supra* note 12 at sections 402 and 403, activity to be considered within a state's jurisdiction occurs if the state exercises jurisdiction to prescribe law with respect to the activity.

failure to regulate such activity cannot be excused on the basis of conformity with applicable domestic law within that state. Responsibility can be found even where the sub-federal level of government is directly charged with regulating the private entity.[23] When the state is aware of the international breach resulting from this failure, its responsibility can flow from that knowledge.[24] However, awareness may be difficult to prove and, therefore, inferences need to be drawn especially in light of the problems proving the state's knowledge of the delict.[25]

Under Article 11, however, awareness of the wrongful act must be coupled with the state's adoption of the conduct as its own. What is at issue is the level of knowledge about the impugned conduct of that individual and, ultimately, what is done in light of having such knowledge. Where the state has authorized the wrongful act, its responsibility would be present. In the *Case Concerning United States Diplomatic and Consular Staff in Iran,* [26] although a violation of international law was found on the basis of the failure to protect the embassy, the court did not attribute the initial activity to the state. However, the court found that the policy announced by the Iranian leader of maintaining the occupation of the embassy and the detention of its inmates as hostages, which was adopted and endorsed by the state on numerous occasions, "translated" the continuing occupation into acts of the state.[27]

A state's mere authorization of a company's creation in its territory would not be sufficient to show attribution under the rules of state responsibility.[28] Even a state's acknowledgment of the factual existence of the conduct or its verbal approval would not be considered conduct attributable to the state unless the state "identifies the conduct in question and makes it its own."[29]

---

[23] See *ibid.,* Article 4. See also *Youmans* claim (1926) R.I.A.A. 4 at 110; and *Mallén* claim (1927) R.I.I.A. 4 at 173.

[24] See *Corfu Channel, supra* note 20.

[25] *Ibid.* at 18.

[26] *Case Concerning United States Diplomatic and Consular Staff in Iran,* [1980] I.C.J. Rep. 3. Iran's failure to take necessary steps to protect the US embassy from seizure or regain control over it constituted a violation of the Vienna Convention on Consular Relations, (1969) 596 U.N.T.S. 261.

[27] *Ibid.* at para. 74.

[28] See *Schering Corporation v. Islamic Republic of Iran,* (1984) 5 Iran-U.S.C.T.R. 361.

[29] See Crawford, *supra* note 14 at 123.

CUSTOMARY INTERNATIONAL LAW

Outside these rules, customary international law or particular treaties, acting as *lex specialis,* could dictate if state responsibility exists.[30] State responsibility for transboundary environmental harm is generally accepted as representing customary international law.[31] Its codification as a fundamental principle is seen in a number of international instruments. Principle 21 of the Stockholm Declaration on the Human Environment,[32] echoed in Principle 2 of the Rio Declaration on Environment and Development,[33] as well as other international instruments, provides its strongest endorsement.[34] In these cases, the state's responsibility is invoked as a result of the abuse of the state's right to exploit its natural resources.

The customary international law basis of state responsibility for transboundary environmental harm has been accepted by jurists and academics. Some have even claimed that the principle can be considered a legal duty owed to all states *erga omnes.*[35] The International Court of Justice's (ICJ) advisory opinion regarding the legality of nuclear weapons[36] represented the first time the ICJ extended

---

[30] ILC Draft Articles, *supra* note 14, Article 55.

[31] M. Jabbari-Gharabagh, "Type of State Responsibility for Environmental Matters in International Law (1999) 33(1) R.J.T. 63 at 79. See also *Lac Lanoux Arbitration (France v. Spain)* (1957) 24 I.L.R. 100 (Arbitral Tribunal) [*Lac Lanoux*].

[32] Stockholm Declaration on the Human Environment, 16 June 1972, (1972) 11 I.L.M. 1420 [Stockholm Declaration]. In total, 112 states supported the adoption of Principle 21, with no states voting against it. The principle was subsequently confirmed by the United Nations General Assembly in UNGA Res. 2996 (XXVII) (1972); and Article 30 of the Charter of Economic Rights and Duties of States, UNGA Res. 3281 (XXVII) (1974).

[33] See Rio Declaration on Environment and Development, 13 June 1992, (1992) 31 I.L.M. 874 [Rio Declaration]. Principle 21 is repeated in Article 3 of the Convention on Biological Diversity, (1992) 31 I.L.M. 822, as well as the preamble of the United Nations Framework Convention on Climate Change, (1992) 31 I.L.M. 849 [UNFCCC]. These documents refer to a "responsibility to ensure that activities with their jurisdiction or control do not cause damage to the environment."

[34] See the LRTAP Convention, *supra* note 13 at 219; Vienna Convention for the Protection of the Ozone Layer, (1990) 19 U.K.T.S. Cm 977 [Vienna Convention]; and Kuwait Regional Convention for Co-operation in the Protection of the Marine Environment, (1978) 17 I.L.M. 511. LOSC, *supra* note 12.

[35] J.I. Charney "Third State Remedies in International Law" (1989) 10 Mich. J. Int'l L. 57 at 149.

[36] *Legality of the Threat or Use of Nuclear Weapons,* [1996] I.C.J. Rep. 226 [*Nuclear Weapons*].

the general international law of state responsibility in an environmental context, implicitly confirming that Principle 21 represents
customary international law.[37] The court ruled that "the existence
of the general obligation of States to ensure that activities within
their jurisdiction and control respect the environment of other states
or of areas beyond national control is now a part of the corpus of
international law relating to the environment."[38] Recognition by
states of the principle is evident in international dispute settlement
proceedings[39] as well as in state practice where activity has been
stopped or altered as a result of the potential transboundary environmental harm.

However, the threshold for state responsibility from transboundary
environmental harm rests on whether such harm is "significant."
As a result, the obligation is based upon the level of harm rather
than on the act causing the harm. The wrong does not have any
autonomous international legal consequences. Since the degree
of harm serves as a condition precedent, the applicability of state
responsibility for transboundary damage cannot be delineated in a
tangible or predictable way. The combination of state practice, international tribunal rulings, and the writings of jurists perhaps provide the clearest insight into what type of harm is "significant,"
warranting the invocation of state responsibility rules. An uneasy
comparison of environmental harm, based on different factual circumstances among a myriad of other variables, becomes necessary.

In the *Legality of the Threat or Use of Nuclear Weapons* case, the ICJ
heard arguments that the law of transfrontier industrial pollution
is subject to a *de minimis* rule that ultimately establishes a threshold

---

[37] P. Sands, *Principles of International Environmental Law*, 2nd edition (Cambridge:
Cambridge University Press, 2003) at 241. Judge Weeramantry, in his dissenting
opinion, noted that Principle 21 does in fact mirror the general obligation and,
therefore, is itself a principle of customary law. In *Gabčíkovo-Nagymaros, supra*
note 10, Judge Weeramantry added, in a separate opinion, that the general protection of the environment beyond national jurisdiction can be seen as an obligation *erga omnes*.

[38] *Nuclear Weapons, supra* note 36 at para. 29.

[39] Both Hungary and Slovakia referred to Principle 21 as the starting point for
assessing their state obligations in the environmental field. See Okowa, *supra*
note 13 at 70. Okowa adds (at 69) that the principle, including the principles
found in the *Trail Smelter* dispute, has been relied upon by Canada in relation to
air pollution disputes with the United States

for claims.[40] A state is not under a duty to prevent all harm but only harm that is appreciable, significant, or substantial. The degree of harm or injury becomes integrated into the calculus to determine whether a violation of state responsibility has occurred. The gravity of the violation of state responsibility not to cause transboundary harm can affect the scope of the obligations of cessation and reparation.[41]

The initial threshold standard was expressed in the *Trail Smelter* dispute where the tribunal concluded that the injury must be of "serious consequence" and that it must be established by clear and convincing evidence.[42] The words "significant," "serious," or "substantial" appear to be the standards codified in relevant multilateral environmental agreements (MEAs).[43] Such a threshold can be problematic due to its vagueness as an evidentiary standard. Moreover, the term may not appreciate the context of environmental harm where proof can only be ascertained over a considerable length of time and may not be immediately detectable. The actual violation of the no harm rule may not be immediately known until well after the damage has occurred.

In addition to the varying requirement to prevent transboundary environmental harm based on the scale of such harm, the residual obligation of restitution that represents the second component of state responsibility would be difficult to comply with. For any breach, there is a duty to reverse the harm or damage, as well as a possible obligation to provide payment of compensation. In most cases involving environmental damage, where such damage is irreversible, compensation is simply not possible. In lieu of this, other remedies

---

40 This argument was raised by Australia, although the court, in the end, did not rule on this part since the dispute was ruled, by the majority, to be moot as a result of the French undertaking not to continue nuclear testing. However, several dissenting judges held that the Australian position on this point was well founded in law. See Okowa *supra* note 13 at 71.

41 See ILC Draft Articles, *supra* note 14 at 176.

42 *Trail Smelter, supra* note 9.

43 See LRTAP Convention, *supra* note 13, Article 5; Vienna Convention, *supra* note 34, Article 1 (2); LOSC, *supra* note 12, Article 206; Convention on the Protection and Use of Transboundary Watercourses and International Lakes, (1992), 31 I.L.M. 1312, Article 1 (2); and Convention on the Transboundary Effects of Industrial Accidents, (1992) 31 I.L.M. 1330, Article 1 (d). See also the preamble to the 1991 Air Quality Agreement between the United States and Canada, Can. T.S. 1991 No. 3.

that require careful design are needed. Compensation or positive obligations to clean up an existing problem necessitate legal precision that a general customary international legal principle such as state responsibility is ill-equipped to provide.[44]

Identifying a fixed rule, based on a threshold of significance, is problematic due to the immeasurable number of instances where transfrontier environmental pollution can occur. The continuous number of violations, coupled with the lack of precision in identifying the threshold, can partly explain the limited number of state claims based on law of state responsibility for transboundary environmental harm.[45] Some avow that state responsibility for transboundary environmental damage is still *de lege ferenda* lacking any comprehensive confirmation in the practice of states and *opinio juris.*[46] Outside the treaty context, it is argued that the principle of state responsibility may be more indicative of "declaratory law" rather than customary international law since the principle has little normative force.[47] The regular flow of sources of pollution across national frontiers is apparently more the norm than the exception, with only a limited number of treaties prescribing the rules of responsibility.[48] As a result, the customary international legal status of state responsibility to prevent transboundary environmental harm is uncertain in the absence of the requisite *opinio juris.*

The counter-argument would posit that it is theoretically unsound to conclude that violations of a rule or principle invalidate the existence of such rules and principles. For transboundary environmental pollution, states retain the view that transfrontier environmental pollution is impermissible in international law notwithstanding the challenges in ensuring complete adherence to the obligation. As

---

44 Damages can be awarded for reimbursing the injured state for expenses reasonably incurred in preventing or remedying the pollution. See commentaries of ILC Draft Articles, *supra* note 14 at 251. Specific heads of environmental damage were outlined by the United Nations Compensation Commission, which assessed Iraqi liability for damages, including environmental damages, as a result of its unlawful invasion of Kuwait. See UN Security Council Res. 687 (1991) at para. 16.

45 Okowa, *supra* note 13 at 77.

46 See O. Schachter, *International Law in Theory and Practice* (Dordrecht/Boston: Martinus Nijhoff, 1991) at 365.

47 D. Bodansky, "Customary (and Not So Customary) International Environmental Law" (1995) 3 Ind. J. Global Legal Stud. 110–19.

48 *Ibid.* See also O. Schachter, "The Emergence of International Environmental Law" (1990) 44 J. Int'l Affairs 457.

Phoebe Okowa notes, the numerous cases of transboundary harm should "in principle be treated as breaches of the rule rather than the affirmation of a contrary principle."[49]

INTERNATIONAL ENVIRONMENTAL AGREEMENTS

International environmental instruments cover transboundary harm including the rules governing notice of harm and duties to compensate for loss. There are treaties that regulate particular substances or emissions[50] or more general treaties that address incidents of transboundary environmental harm.[51] The UN Convention on the Law of the Sea (LOSC) stipulates that states are under an obligation to ensure that activities under their jurisdiction or control are not conducted to cause damage by pollution to other states and that pollution arising from such activities does not extend beyond the areas where the state exercises its sovereign rights.[52] Under Article 235, states are under a general obligation to ensure that prompt and adequate compensation is paid to persons suffering damage caused by pollution.

However, most of these MEAs concerning transboundary environmental harm contain the norms and standards for pollution prevention rather than regulating issues of responsibility when such pollution, and damage, follow from non-compliance with such norms and standards.[53] Codification of the rules of state responsibility, establishing an obligation to make full reparation for injuries caused by an internationally wrongful act (that is, treaty violation), is not present. International agreements rarely embrace

---

49 Okowa, *supra* note 13 at 76, adds that the International Court of Justice (ICJ) in the *Nicaragua* case, *supra* note 21 at 186, did not require absolute uniformity for a rule of customary law as long as there is sufficient evidence to suggest that divergent practices are indications of a breach rather than an affirmation of a new emergent norm.

50 See LRTAP Convention, *supra* note 13. See also Protocol Concerning the Control of Emissions of Nitrogen Oxides or Their Transboundary Fluxes, (1988) 28 I.L.M. 214; Protocol on the Control of Emissions of Volatile Organic Compounds and Their Transbondary Fluxes, (1992) 31 I.L.M. 568; and Agreement between the Government of the United States of America and the Government of Canada on Air Quality, (1991) 30 I.L.M. 676.

51 Convention on Assistance in the Case of Nuclear Accident or Radiological Emergency, (1986) 25 I.L.M. 1370; and International Convention on Oil Pollution Preparedness Response and Cooperation, (1991) 30 I.L.M. 733.

52 LOSC, *supra* note 12, Article 194(2).

53 Okowa, *supra* note 13.

requirements for compensation or impose any direct liability, reflecting the complexity and controversy surrounding the framing of such rules.[54] Without such detail, states are held to the soft law principles of international comity and global responsibility to conserve and protect the environment.[55]

Where such treaties are implemented, customary international law and other instances of state practice are invoked to inform how the treaties ought to be applied.[56] For instance, Canada argued that the Soviet Union was liable to Canada for the falling of debris from the Cosmos 954 satellite into Canada's air space and the deposit on Canadian territory of hazardous radioactive debris.[57] The violation of Canada's sovereignty, and the claims for damages, was based on the 1972 Convention on International Liability for Damage Caused by Space Objects,[58] although Canada argued that the claims were also supported by the applicable principles of general international law with specific reference to how fair compensation was to be paid.

54 Article 8 of the LRTAP Convention, *supra* note 13, contains a footnote stipulating a commitment for parties to exchange information on the extent of that can be attributed to long-range transboundary air pollution. The footnote adds that the LRTAP Convention does not contain a rule on state liability as to damage. See also Sands, *supra* note 37 at 899.

55 Principle 7 of the Rio Declaration, *supra* note 33. Principle 13 calls on states to "cooperate, in an expeditious and more determined manner to develop further international law regarding liability and compensation for adverse effects of environmental damage caused by activities within their jurisdiction or control to areas beyond their jurisdiction." Principle 22 of the Stockholm Declaration, *supra* note 32, contains the same provision implying the lack of development in creating multilateral regimes, between 1972 and 1992, governing the consequences of a breach of state responsibility for transboundary environmental damage. See also the resolutions of the Institut de Droit International (IDI), the 1987 Resolution on Transboundary Air Pollution and the 1997 Resolution on Responsibility and Liability under International Law for Environmental Damage, (1998) 37 I.L.M. 1473.

56 See *Gabčíkovo-Nagymaros, supra* note 10. In this case, the court referred to the legal developments in the field of environmental law to interpret the state's commitments under a treaty governing the construction of a dam on the Danube.

57 See A. Cohen, "Cosmos 954 and the International Law of Satellite Accidents" (1984) 10 Yale J. Int'l L. 78.

58 Convention on International Liability for Damage Caused by Space Objects (1972) 961 U.N.T.S. at 187. The treaty provides for various forms of responsibility including absolute liability (Article II), as well as liability based on fault (Article VI). The treaty provides for absolute liability to pay compensation for damage and harm to the environment caused by the space object on the surface of the earth or to aircraft in flight.

States are reluctant to consent to the allocation of state responsibility due to the likely economic consequences.[59] In some instances, state practice has revealed a willingness to pay compensation for damages although this is offered without any admission of international responsibility.[60] Compounding this is the lack of clarity in applying the rules of state responsibility to environmental harm where a number of causes can be linked to the harm rendering it difficult to identify a singular source. Most of the treaties that operationalize Principle 21 of the Stockholm Declaration as well as Principle 2 of the Rio Declaration, such as the UN Framework Convention on Climate Change, the Montreal Protocol on Substances That Deplete the Ozone Layer,[61] or even the LOSC, lack specific rules regarding responsibility due partly to the difficulty in tracing specific damages to particular conduct.

Liability regimes in international treaties that address transboundary environmental damage can combine rules governing both civil and state liability. The MEA can require that liability be imposed directly on the private actor that caused the environmental harm, although liability for such harm may be exempted by local rules regulating the pollution source.[62] Rules regarding liability are currently being drawn up under the Basel Convention on the Control of Transboundary Movement of Hazardous Wastes and Their Disposal[63] as well as under the Cartagena Protocol on Biosafety.[64] Despite these examples, it is uncertain whether state liability and state responsibility are interchangeable. The ILC Draft Articles separate the two, holding that state responsibility is the obligation to make restitution for damage caused by international legal violations,

---

[59] See A. Cassese, *International Law* (Oxford: Oxford University Press, 2001) at 389.

[60] See the Cosmos 915 Satellite Incident explained, Cohen, *supra* note 57. See also the *Fukuryu Maru* incident involving damages and economic losses to Japanese fishermen resulting from US nuclear tests.

[61] UN Framework Convention on Climate Change, 37 I.L.M. 32 (1998); and Montreal Protocol on Substances That Deplete the Ozone Layer, (1987) 26 I.L.M. 154.

[62] The Convention on Civil Liability for Damage Resulting from Activities Dangerous to the Environment, (1993) 32 I.L.M. 1228, provides that an operator of a dangerous activity is not liable for damage caused by pollution at tolerable levels under local relevant circumstances (see Article 8(d)).

[63] Basel Convention on the Control of Transboundary Movement of Hazardous Wastes and Their Disposal, (1989) 28 I.L.M. 657.

[64] Cartagena Protocol on Biosafety, (2000) 39 I.L.M. 1027 [Cartagena Protocol].

while liability is an obligation to compensate for harm caused where no violation of law exists.[65] Liability is normally on a "strict liability" basis where no fault is required in order to award damages or compensation. The application of strict liability for environmental damage perhaps emerged in the common law in the case of *Rylands v. Fletcher*,[66] where the defendants were found liable without proof of fault for harm caused when water escaped from a reservoir of their land and caused damage to another property. This was so despite the lawfulness of building the reservoir.

Strict liability principles were applied in both the *Trail Smelter* case and the *Corfu Channel (United Kingdom v. Albania)* case, with the liability in the former without fault stemming from the inherently dangerous nature of the smelter operations.[67] It has been suggested that this is the standard for transboundary environmental harm or damages.[68] Some have argued, however, that strict liability cannot be found in customary international law and therefore is only applicable where an international agreement provides for it.[69] A duty of a state to compensate or make reparations is not necessarily equivalent to a rule of strict liability.[70]

Civil liability can be established either under domestic law or international legal rules.[71] As a result of such liability for private actors, states can incur liability caused by the actions of private entities

---

[65] Some have claimed that this distinction is less important than examining the nature and significance of the harm as well as the reasonableness of the state's actions. See D. Hunter, J. Salzman, and D. Zaelke, *International Environmental Law and Policy* (New York: Foundation Press, 1998) at 354.

[66] *Rylands v. Fletcher*, (1868) L.R. 3 H.L. 330.

[67] *Corfu Channel, supra* note 20. See W. Jenks, "Ultra-hazardous Liabilities" (1966) 117 Rec. des Cours 122.

[68] See ILC Draft Articles, *supra* note 14. The OECD Environment Committee noted that there is a "custom based rule of due diligence imposed on all states in order that activities carried out within their jurisdiction do not cause damage to the environment of other states, which includes establishing and applying an effective system of environmental law and regulation, and principles of consultation and notification." See report by the Environment Committee, *Responsibility and Liability of States in Relation to Transfrontier Pollution*, 14 November 1974, Doc. C (74)224 (1974) at 4.

[69] See J. Barron, "After Chernobyl: Liability for Nuclear Accidents under International Law" (1987) 25 Colum. J. Transnational L. 647 at 660.

[70] See D. Margraw, "The Transboundary Harm: The International Law Commission's Study of International Liability" (1986) 80 Am. J. Int'l L. 305 at 313.

[71] In these situations, civil liability can result irrespective of the existence of any breach of international law by a state.

and individuals under their jurisdiction. Some international treaties provide for regimes where subsidiary liability of the state flows from private actions. For instance, Article 8(3) of the Convention on the Conservation of Antarctic Marine Living Resources (CCAMLR) stipulates that a sponsoring state has subsidiary liability in conjunction with that of the operator if the damage would not have occurred or continued if such a state had carried out its obligations under the convention.[72] However, the state cannot be held jointly liable for the environmental damages under the CCAMLR. The state would only be obliged to ensure compliance with its own obligations but could not be held liable to make reparations.[73]

Despite the absence of provisions governing breaches of state responsibility in the transboundary environmental damage context, some recent MEAs contain mechanisms for transboundary environmental impact assessment (EIAs) so that information regarding the harm is known to the parties in advance of a particular project.[74] EIAs can be seen as an indicator for states in determining whether due diligence in preventing transboundary pollution was exercised.[75] The frequency of the obligation in both international instruments and international organizations and, retroactively, in state practice suggests that the procedural obligation to assess transboundary environmental impacts may be venturing closely to customary international law status. A recent dispute between Argentina and Uruguay has engaged the latter's duty to notify and

72 Convention on the Conservation of Antarctic Marine Living Resources, (1980) 19 I.L.M. 84. Under Article 8(10)), the state must allow for recourse in its national courts for the adjudication of liability claims against the sponsored operator.

73 L. Belotsky "State Responsibility and Liability for Damage to the Environment," in A. Gambaro and A.M. Rabello, eds., "Towards a New European *Jus Commune*: Essays on European, Italian and Israeli Law in Occasion of 50 years of the E.U. and of the State of Israel (Jerusalem: Hebrew University Press, 1999), 237 at 253.

74 See Convention on Environmental Impact Assessment in a Transboundary Context, (1991) 30 I.L.M. 802; and Convention on Access to Information, Public Participation and Decision-Making and Access to Justice in Environmental Matters, (1998) 39 I.L.M. 517. See also K.R. Gray, "The Internationalization of Environmental Impact Assessment: Potential for a Multilateral Environmental Agreement" (2000) 11(1) Colo. J. Int'l Envtl. L. & Pol'y 101.

75 In the *Gabčíkovo-Nagymaros* dispute, *supra* note 10, Hungary argued that the obligation to ensure that activities on their territory did not cause significant transboundary harm implied a subsidiary duty to conduct an environmental impact assessment (EIA). This point was not opposed by the Slovak Republic.

consult the former about a pulp and paper mill that potentially could result in toxic air and liquid emissions and the release of malodorous vapours allegedly causing harm to the River Uruguay ecosystem.[76]

Another hindrance to the fulsome codification of state responsibility in MEAs is the approach of such instruments to ensuring compliance. Most of these rules and regimes do not comport with the traditional and legalistic state responsibility remedial tools such as reparations or countermeasures, opting for more cooperative forms of ensuring compliance.[77] The rules of state responsibility, including the ability to exact countermeasures and demand compensation, may not work well in MEAs that contain detailed compliance mechanisms guided by an overriding perspective that non-compliance is often seen as a result of financial, technical, and administrative capacity deficits rather than a deliberate flouting of intentional law.[78] Furthering this division is the "bilateral" paradigm set in state responsibility, structured as rights and remedies in the face of harm done by one state against another.[79]

The bilateral types of environmental damages, representing the "classical" type of transfrontier pollution, still represent the arena where the rules of state responsibility are formed, albeit under the backdrop of multilateral frameworks.[80] Disputes between bordering nations have been the main contributors to the development of the

---

[76] *Pulp Mills on the River Uruguay (Argentina v. Uruguay)*, Case 2006/17 [*Pulp Mills*]. The duty to notify and consult is based on obligations under the 1975 Statute of the River Uruguay, which was agreed to by both parties. See <http://www.icj-cij.org/icjwww/idocket/iau/iauframe.htm>.

[77] See G. Handl, "Compliance Control Mechanisms and International Environmental Obligations" (1997) 5 Tul. J. Int'l & Comp. L. 29; M. Koskenniemi, "Breach of Treaty or Non-Compliance? Reflections on the Enforcement of the Montreal Protocol" (1992) 3 Y.B. Int'l Envtl. L. 123.

[78] See Handl, *supra* note 77. Some critics argue that where such mechanisms are weak or simply unenforceable, there is a stronger justification for using coercive measures such as countermeasures to ensure compliance (at 94). See J. Peel, "New State Responsibility Rules and Compliance with Multilateral Environmental Obligations: Some Case Studies of How the New Rules Might Apply in the International Environmental Context" (2001) 10(1) R.E.C.I.E.L. 82.

[79] See Peel, *supra* note 78. On the general contrast between bilateralism and communitarianism in international law, see B. Simma, "From Bilateralism to Community Interest in International Law" (1993-VI) Rec. des Cours 221.

[80] See A. Kiss, "Present Limits to the Environment of State Responsibility for Environmental Damage," in F. Francioni and T. Scovazzi, eds., *International Responsibility for Environmental Harm* (London: Graham and Trotman, 1991), 3 at 13.

law regarding state responsibility for transboundary environmental harm. The *Gabčíkovo-Nagymaros* case brought to the forefront the principle concerning the suspension of dam construction, partially for the purpose of environmental protection. This case can be seen as wholly significant for clarifying the law of state responsibility and the duty to prevent transboundary environmental harm since a state was attempting to claim injunctive relief in the face of potential transboundary environmental harm.[81] However, the *Trail Smelter* arbitration ruling represents the most direct invocation of state responsibility in a bilateral environmental dispute.

TRAIL SMELTER ARBITRATION

It is telling that a preponderance of the discourse on international environmental law starts with the seminal ruling in the *Trail Smelter* arbitration. This landmark ruling provides the template for customary international environmental law and sets the groundwork for international cooperation reflected in a multitude of environmental agreements. The ruling broke new ground in applying the concept of state responsibility to transboundary environmental disputes by establishing a causal link between the injury and the government act (in this case, an omission or failure to regulate economic production) and confirming that this was wrongful in international law.[82] The ruling also included an order to refrain from causing further damage and, therefore, crystallized a preventive remedy, including obligations aimed to cease further damage, into international environmental law. Ironically, the dicta of the ruling reflected more what existed in US law rather than in public international law at the time. The tribunal ruled that international

---

[81] It has been argued that injunctive relief is perhaps the most effective way to operationalize the duty to prevent transboundary environmental harm and corresponding state responsibility due to the inherent difficulties in quantifying environmental damages, problems in linking causation to injury as well as difficulty of linking compensation to irreparable harm. See *Amoco Production Co. v. Village of Campbell*, (1988) 480 U.S. 531, 107 S. Ct. 1396. In *Gabčíkovo-Nagymaros* dispute, *supra* note 10, Hungary was ruled to be entitled to compensation for damages sustained as a result of the diversion of the Danube but there was no specific mention on whether reparation was available for purely environmental damages (para. 151).

[82] F.O. Vicuña, "State Responsibility, Liability, and Remedial Measures under International Law: New Criteria for Environmental Protection," in E.B. Weiss, ed., *Environmental Change and International Law: New Challenges and Directions* (Tokyo: UNU Press, 1992).

law corresponded to existing principles in American law as developed in US Supreme Court decisions relating to air and water.[83]

In addition to the pronouncements regarding state responsibility and the awarding of compensation, the *Trail Smelter* ruling can also be applauded as establishing a duty of cooperation on transboundary matters and, correspondingly, obligations to prevent transboundary environmental damage. It also set the stage for designing control mechanisms to avoid such damage, which remain a prominent feature in bilateral treaties on transboundary water management.[84] The tribunal established a regime to control emissions including mandatory technical improvements to the smelter and created an institutional mechanism (ad hoc commission) consisting of three scientists with the power to adopt binding decisions. The utilization of scientific advisory bodies, which is now commonplace in many MEAs, can hark back to the decision to create one in the aftermath of the *Trail Smelter* ruling.[85]

The ruling involved the operations of the Trail smelter, located eleven miles north of the US–Canada border, which produced emissions of sulphur dioxide. There had been a smelter in Trail since 1896, not long after gold was discovered in the nearby hills. Being one of the largest and best equipped smelting plants in North America at the time, the height of its stacks allowed for increases in daily smelting of zinc and lead ores and large amounts of sulphur dioxide emissions.[86] In 1906, the Consolidated Mining and Smelting Company of Canada Limited acquired the smelter.[87]

Apple growers in Washington State, alleging physical injuries and proprietary damage from the air pollution crossing the border, lobbied the US government to sue the Canadian government for the

---

[83] *Ibid.* at para. 147

[84] See Great Lakes Water Quality Agreement, *supra* note 7, as amended by the protocol signed 18 November 1987. Another notable regime is under the La Paz Agreement between the United States and Mexico on Cooperation for the Protection and Improvement of the Environment in the Border Area, (1993) 32 I.L.M. 289, as well as the 1992 Integrated Environmental Border Plan for the Mexican-US Border Area, Washington, DC (February 1992).

[85] See Vicuñna, *supra* note 82.

[86] Between 1916 and 1940, the Trail Smelter emitted between 100 and 700 tonnes of sulphur dioxide per day. See G. Hess, "Trail Smelter, the Columbia River, and the Extraterritorial Application of CERCLA" (2005) 18(1) Geo. Int'l Envtl. L. Rev. 1 at 1.

[87] The company was officially renamed Cominco Limited. In 1996, it merged with Teck Limited, and, in 2001, the company become Teck Cominco Metals Limited, which is the current owner of the smelter.

pollution as neither Washington State nor the British Columbia (BC) government had the jurisdiction to entertain such a claim. Previously, some land owners in Canada were successful in getting redress against the owners of the smelter.[88] The common law rule known as the local action rule required that complaints relating to public property be brought in the territory where the harmed property is located. However, Washington State's rules of civil procedure did not allow the court to exercise jurisdiction over an out-of-state facility. Moreover, the court could not exercise personal jurisdiction over a corporate defendant outside the state since the defendant did not have physical assets in the state.[89]

The United States proposed to refer the legal questions to the IJC. Following a compromissary agreement between the two parties where Canada assumed responsibility for the damages, the IJC issued a report that found that the Trail smelter had caused serious harm and assessed the damages.[90] It was viewed as satisfactory by the Canadian government but rejected by the United States. The report recommended that Canada pay $350,000 to cover claims for damages to private persons, while Consolidated Mining agreed to certain pollution reduction devices. Canada was also ordered to take remedial measures to reduce sulphur dioxide fumes and adopt remedial measures to further reduce emissions. Both parties signed and ratified a *compromis* convention that established an arbitral tribunal to settle claims for the damage.[91]

[88] Consolidated was able to settle half of these claims while the remaining half was resolved under arbitration in British Columbia. In addition to the compensation, Consolidated was able to purchase smoke easements from the affected property owners. By comparison, US farmers had filed claims in US courts against a smelter on the US side of the border but were unsuccessful with the exception of one farmer who sold a smoke easement. Consolidated was unable to purchase smoke easements from Washington farmers since Washington law prohibited foreign ownership of lands in the state. See M.J. Robinson-Dorn, "The Trail Smelter: Is What's Past Prologue? EPA Blazes a New Trail for CERCLA" (2005) 14 N.Y.U. Envtl. L. J. 233 at 246–47.

[89] The US Supreme Court, in *International Shoe Co. v. Washington*, (1945) 326 U.S. 310, allowed for the exercise of personal jurisdiction where the foreign defendant had minimum contacts with the state. This, in fact, has also allowed Canadian plaintiffs to launch proceedings in US courts for damages from US-based facilities. See *Michie et al., v. Great Lakes Steel Division, Nation Steel Corp.*, 495 F. 2d213 (6th Cir. 1947), 419 U.S. 994 (1974).

[90] *Trail Smelter, supra* note 9.

[91] See 1935 Convention for Settlement of Difficulties Arising from Operation of Smelter at Trail, British Columbia, 15 April 1935, U.N.T.S. 74. Included in this agreement was the authorization given to the arbitrator to set emissions levels.

Subsequent negotiations led to the submission of the dispute to the three-member tribunal.

The panel addressed the question of whether US or international law should apply to the facts of the dispute. Instead of directly deciding this question, the tribunal held that US law in its regulation of sovereign rights of the states of the union in the matter of air pollution was in conformity with the general rules of international law. In the absence of any international decisions regarding transboundary environmental air pollution, the panel referred to the *ratio decidendi* in several cases before the US courts.[92] Accordingly, the tribunal ruled that under the principles of international law and US law, "no state has the right to use or permit the use of its territory in such a manner as to cause injury by fumes in or to the territory of another or the properties or persons there when the case is of serious consequence and the injury is established by clear and convincing evidence."[93]

Canada was held to be responsible in international law for the conduct of the Trail smelter. Compensation was awarded to the United States for damages to land and property (crops and trees) caused by the sulphur dioxide emissions.[94] Compensation was based on the reduction of the value of the affected land.[95] In the final decision of the arbitration in 1941, the tribunal also ordered the smelter to refrain from causing any further damage in the state of Washington or be faced with further claims for compensation and required to introduce a detailed pollution control regime at the Trail smelter.

The *Trail Smelter* case reflects the origins of the customary law on transboundary pollution, buttressed by considerable subsequent state practice guided by the *ratio* in the case.[96] Building on the ruling, the general law of state responsibility has developed in international cases where it has been determined that states cannot allow their territory to be used for acts contrary to the rights of other

[92] Under Article IV of the Boundary Water Treaty, *supra* note 7, which established the IJC, both national and international law can apply.

[93] *Trail Smelter, supra* note 9 at 1965.

[94] The arbitration awarded US $78,000 in compensation.

[95] *Trail Smelter, supra* note 9 at 1907. The United States later refunded some of that money after the tribunal ruled there was not enough evidence to prove damages to livestock or businesses.

[96] See Sands, *supra* note 37 at 242, referring to the International Law Association, *Report of the Committee on Legal Aspects of the Environment*, 60th Conference Report, (1984) at 163.

states.[97] State practice can also be gleamed from the non-litigious instances where states have endeavoured to cooperate in situations of cross-border environmental harm.

PUTTING THE RULES OF STATE RESPONSIBILITY TO THE TEST— *TECK COMINCO*

The case provides a timely opportunity to see the effectiveness of bilateral cooperation on transboundary environmental matters, supported by the customary international legal principle of state responsibility to prevent transboundary harm, can function. The use of domestic court litigation relying on extraterritorial jurisdiction as witnessed in *Teck Cominco* uncovers limitations of rules of state responsibility to resolve current transboundary environmental damage disputes.[98]

The Trail smelter is currently owned and operated by the Canadian company Teck Cominco Metals. It is presently the world's largest fully-integrated zinc and lead smelting and refining complex with production capacities of approximately 300,000 tonnes per year of zinc and 120,000 tonnes per year of lead. It is also a significant producer of silver, gold, indium, germanium, bismuth, and copper products, including copper sulphate and copper arsenate, as well as a large volume of sulphur products, including ammonium sulphate fertilizer, sulphuric acid, liquid sulphur dioxide, and elemental sulphur.[99] The majority of the zinc concentrates treated at the Trail smelter come from the Red Dog Mine in Alaska with the remainder coming from other mines in the United States and Canada. Lead concentrates are purchased from mines in the United States and South America.[100]

---

97 See *Corfu Channel, supra* note 20. See also *Lac Lanoux, supra* note 31, where the tribunal ruled that the upstream state cannot ignore the downstream state's interests and must respect them with such rights being considered when diverting an international river. In *obiter dicta,* the panel also ruled that where the proposed work would damage Spanish interests through chemical or thermal pollution, France would incur responsibility (at 101 and 123).

98 Interestingly, Article II of the Boundary Waters Treaty, *supra* note 6, allows for an "injured" party to seek relief in either state's courts if the injury took place in the other country. However, this article is applicable to water diversions but not to pollution.

99 A. Crook, *Trail Smelter* (Environmental Mining Council of British Columbia, 2003), <http://www.miningwatch.org/emcbc/Publications/briefing_papers/trail.htm>.

100 *Ibid.*

Since the 1970s, the company has invested significantly in improving its smelting operations, resulting in a more efficient operation and lower water and air emissions. Despite these advancements, there is still a historical record of pollution from the Trail smelter, which has left nearby soil and groundwater contaminated and has rendered deleterious impacts on fish and wildlife in the Columbia River watershed on both sides of the border.[101] Considerable concentrations of cadmium, copper, lead, and zinc have been recorded in aquatic organisms on both sides of the border. Fish tissue, in the Columbia River watershed, is reported to contain relatively high levels of lead, mercury, and dioxins and furan, exceeding levels recommended for the protection of human health and wildlife.[102] There are also public health consequences. The levels of heavy metals are alleged to be particularly high in children, potentially affecting their IQs, physical growth, and neurological development. Compounding these problems are several occurrences of toxic discharges, hazardous substances spills, and reported incidents of non-compliance with the BC permit requirements for air and water quality standards.

According to the US Environmental Protection Agency (EPA), the smelter has left a legacy of massive contamination. An EPA study chronicled a century of pollution from the Trail smelter. It concluded that the smelter dumped the equivalent of one full dump truck of slag — a black, sand-like substance including silica, iron, and calcium, which is a by-product of the smelting process, every hour for sixty years.[103] It also contended that slag contained toxic chemical and physical elements harmful to human and aquatic life.[104] In addition to the metals from the slag, it cited numerous

101 It should be noted that in the roughly 100 years of pollution of the Columbia River flowing into Lake Roosevelt, there were several other smelting operations operating on the US side, but these are no longer in operation.

102 This has been disputed by Teck Cominco who argue that recent water quality tests by BC Environment, Lands and Water show water quality levels in the Columbia River exceed Canadian government standards, whereas fish tissue for mercury are at levels in accordance with Canadian standards. See "Teck Cominco Responds to Misleading Reports on Trail Smelter," <http://www.teckcominco.com/news/04-archive/04-18-tc.htm>.

103 Much of the slag now coats the bottom of Lake Roosevelt, a 150 kilometre-long reservoir created when the Grand Coolie Dam was built on the Columbia River in the 1940s.

104 The EPA also claims that the Trail smelter also produces a variety of sulphur products and agricultural fertilizers, which represent a potential source of mercury.

other toxic spills and discharges of acids and chemicals, including mercury and arsenic. A study by the US Geological Survey confirmed that the source of the contamination that included lead, cadmium, and other heavy metals, in Washington's Lake Roosevelt was the Trail smelter.[105]

In December 2003, the EPA issued an administrative order requiring Teck Cominco to investigate the contamination and explore clean-up options.[106] The order required Teck Cominco to conduct and pay for an analysis to assess the nature and extent of the pollution or risk facing a fine of up to US $27,500 per day. This was issued after the company refused to sign an administrative order on consent (AOC), committing Teck Cominco to a remedial investigation/feasibility study (RI/FS) to collect data on the conditions at Lake Roosevelt, the potential risk to human health and the environment, and the cost of treating the pollution. The EPA conducted an assessment of contamination in Lake Roosevelt and determined that the upper Columbia River site was eligible to be listed under the Comprehensive Environmental Response, Compensation, and Liability Act (CERCLA)[107] as one of the nation's most hazardous waste sites. The order required the company to carry out a RI/FS of the contamination in the upper Columbia River from the US–Canada border south to the Grand Coulee Dam.

Prior to the issuance of the order, Teck Cominco American Incorporated (TCAI), a separate, US-based, corporate affiliate of the parent corporation Teck Cominco, voluntarily offered to enter into discussions with the EPA to identify a process to access, and, if necessary, address, the potential risks from the alleged metal contamination at the site. TCAI offered to enter into a legally binding commitment, enforceable in the United States, to fund the investigation at an estimated cost of US $13 million, and to finance the appropriate clean-up at Lake Roosevelt related to Teck Cominco's operation. In addition to determining that the clean-up offer was

---

105 *Vertical Distribution of Trace-Element Concentrations and Occurrence of Metallurgical Slag Particles in Accumulated Bed Sediments of Lake Roosevelt, Washington,* (2002), <http://water.usgs.gov/pubs/sir/2004/5090/>. Canadian scientists had discovered that copper and zinc can leach from the slag into the river. In 1995, Teck Cominco decided to stop dumping the slag.

106 US Environmental Protection Agency (EPA) Region 10, *Unilateral Administrative Order for Remedial Investigation/Feasibility Study,* Docket No. CERCLA-10-2004 (11 December 2003).

107 Comprehensive Environmental Response, Compensation, and Liability Act, 42 U.S.C. at paras. 9601 [CERCLA].

insufficient, the EPA refused to consider this offer unless TCAI was willing to subject itself to the CERCLA process and, ultimately, to submit to US jurisdiction under this statute. Without an agreement, the EPA issued the order authorizing the agency to draw other funds to conduct the studies and then subsequently to seek redress from the Canadian company.[108]

Teck Cominco refused to comply with this order while the Canadian government issued a diplomatic note,[109] registering its concern over the US actions attempting to apply US environmental law to a Canadian-based facility.[110] Bilateral negotiations commenced to develop a process, means, or mechanism, allowing Teck Cominco to carry out its work without placing the company under the jurisdiction of the US courts and the EPA. These were not successful, and, as a result, permission was not granted allowing EPA scientists to conduct sediment sampling along Canadian rivers in conjunction with its investigation.[111] Ultimately, the United States refused Canada's request to rescind the order.

Parallel with the assessments and activity undertaken by government agencies in British Columbia, the US authorities had also begun to assess the environmental quality in the Columbia River. The EPA and US Geological Service had begun Superfund investigations of the extent of contamination in the Columbia River system from the lower reach of Lake Roosevelt up to the Canadian

---

[108] 11 December 2003. At the same time, Teck Cominco still offered to have its US-based corporate affiliate investigate the risks and fund the appropriate clean-up.

[109] *Embassy of Canada to US Department of State,* Diplomatic Note (8 January 2004). See <http://www.teckcominco.com/articles/roosevelt/motion-attach-c-040102.pdf>.

[110] The British Columbia government is also concerned since the company operates under a permit issued by its regulatory authority, which had specifically allowed for slag releases into the waterways. Other stakeholders weighed in on the court's ruling on this point. For instance, the US Chamber of Commerce expressed concern that extraterritorial application of CERCLA would "have significant negative consequences for many U.S. businesses, particularly those operating in areas close to our nation's borders" and that it may engender retaliation from foreign governments. See *Letter Brief in Support of Petition for Permission to Appeal under 28 U.S.C. § 1292(b).* The Chamber of Commerce submitted an *amicus curiae* letter to the court on 7 January 2005.

[111] Canada was partially concerned that the study would not distinguish between historical discharges and the more current discharges. See G. George, "Over the Line-Transboundary Application of CERCLA" (2004) 34 Eur. L. Rev. 10275 at 10275.

border.[112] The largest source of pollution identified was from the Trail smelter.

The EPA never sought to enforce its order. However, two members of the nearby Confederated Tribes of the Colville Reservation Native American community, whose tribal lands are adjacent to Lake Roosevelt, brought a suit, pursuant to the "citizen suit" provisions of CERCLA.[113] The order sought to require Teck Cominco to conduct a remedial investigation/feasibility study into the impact of hazardous waste and sludge dumped by the smelter into the upper Columbia River.

The US federal judge ruled that discharges of waste from the smelter that entered the Columbia River and Lake Roosevelt in Washington State were subject to the US Superfund law, holding that CERCLA has "effects based jurisdiction."[114] Teck Cominco's motion to dismiss the lawsuit was denied, although leave to appeal was granted in the order to dismiss.[115]

The decision has set new precedent in US law, representing the first time that CERCLA has been applied to cleaning up waste located in the United States but originating from outside American territory. Although not directly extending the territorial reach of the statutory definition of "environment" subject to CERCLA, the court based its rulings on what is known as the "effects" doctrine. The court stated that "because the fundamental purpose of *CERCLA* is to ensure the integrity of the domestic environment, Congress intended to proscribe conduct associated with the degradation of the environment, regardless of the location of the agents responsible for said conduct."[116] It was added that a finding of no "extraterritorial application of CERCLA in this case would require reliance on a legal fiction that the 'releases' of hazardous substances into

---

112 Superfund is a US federal government program established to clean up uncontrolled hazardous waste sites that pose a current or future threat to human health or the environment. The EPA identifies the hazardous waste sites, tests the site's conditions, formulates clean-up plans, and ultimately cleans up the sites.

113 The Colville Nation, whose reservation borders the river, operates a casino and other businesses offering boat rentals, gasoline, and food. Subsequently, the state of Washington joined the citizen's suit.

114 8 November 2004. *Teck Cominco, supra* note 8.

115 In certifying the case, the judge noted that the case involves a "controlling question of law" with substantial grounds for disagreement with the ruling.

116 *Ibid.* at 53.

the Upper Columbia River Site and Lake Roosevelt are wholly separable from the discharge of those substances into the Columbia River at the Trail Smelter."[117]

The court added that a presumption against extraterritorial application of US laws does not apply in this case. According to US foreign relations law, the principle of extraterritoriality provides that US laws apply only to conduct occurring within or *having effects* within the territory of the United States. The site to which the order applied was entirely within US territory. As a result, the extraterritorial application of CERCLA was not precluded in this case particularly because the presumption against it is inapplicable where a failure to extend a statute to a foreign setting will result in adverse effects within the United States. Essentially, the court ruled that it is not a question of regulating the operations of the smelter but only of addressing the pollution resulting from its operations.[118] Canadian law would not be superseded nor would there be a conflict between US and Canadian laws, but the limitations in Canadian law in its ability to provide a remedy for damages outside its territory supported the need for the CERCLA order.[119]

Alternatively known as the objective territorial principle, the effects doctrine is invoked where the activities carried out in one state have or are likely to have injurious effects in another state. US practice has historically limited the effects to those that have had an impact in the American economy. Its use as a basis for exercising jurisdiction has not been accepted by most states in the international community. It has been endorsed by the Permanent Court of International Justice in the *Lotus (France v. Turkey)* case,[120] although the judgment has been the source of controversy among

---

[117] *Ibid.*

[118] Nevertheless, the court did not find any conclusive language in the statute or in its legislative history indicating that a foreign corporation cannot be held liable as an owner or operator as defined in CERCLA's section 9607 provisions for response costs and damages.

[119] *Ibid.* at 20. The court, at 32, added that "Canada's own laws and regulations will not compel the Canadian facility to clean up the mess in the United States which it has created." However, a wider view of whether there is a conflict arises from the fact that Canadian authorities parallel the operation of the smelter and emit the pollutants that the US retroactively alleges is contrary to US law by way of the remediation order. See T. Crossman, "Extraterritorial Reach of U.S. Environmental Laws: the Teck Cominco Decision," paper presented at Canadian Bar Association Conference, Second Annual Environmental, Energy and Resources Summit Canada-U.S. Cross-Border Issues, April 2006.

[120] *Lotus (France v. Turkey)*, 1927 P.C.I.J. (Ser. A) No. 9 (7 September 1927) [*Lotus*].

international legal scholars.[121] Otherwise, there is little international precedent accepting it as a proper basis for jurisdiction.[122]

The United States is one of the few states that allow for the application of the effects doctrine.[123] There is widespread authority in US law to prescribe rules for conduct on its territory, conduct of its nationals anywhere, as well as conduct affecting its territory.[124] However, the effects doctrine is rarely applied in areas of civil jurisdiction and is mainly used in cases regarding securities violations, anti-trust law, or other areas of economic regulation.[125]

The presumption against extraterritorial application of US law has been upheld in environmental cases.[126] Under CERCLA, there is seemingly legislative intent to regulate only domestic activities. The environment, under CERCLA, is defined as being limited to the land, water, and air within or under the jurisdiction of the United

---

[121] See I. Brownlie, *Principles of Public International Law*, 6th edition (Oxford: Oxford University Press, 2003) at 239; G. Fitzmaurice, "The General Principles of International Law Considered from the Standpoint of the Rule of Law" (1957) 92 Hague Recueil 2 at 56; and E. Lauterpacht, *International Law: Collected Papers* (London: Cambridge University Press, 1970). The court ruled that the Turkish authorities had wide discretion to extend its criminal law jurisdiction beyond its territory partly due to the absence of rules prohibiting this. Article 11(1) of the Convention on the High Seas, 29 April 1958, 450 U.N.T.S. 11; and Article 97(1) of the LOSC, *supra* note 12, have explicitly overturned this finding, allowing a state to exercise penal or disciplinary proceedings over its nationals.

[122] In one case decided by the European Court of Justice, a Netherlands plaintiff was successful in obtaining damages for pollution originating upstream from a source in France although this was a decision to accept the enforcement of a existing judgment in tort law. See *Handelswerkerig G.J. Bier B.V. v. Mines de Potasse D'Alsace S.A*, Case No. 21/76, [1976] E.C.R. 1735).

[123] See *United States v. Aluminium Co. of America*, 148 F. 2nd 416 (2nd Cir. 1945). Although laws for injury and damages from environmental harm have been applied extraterritorially in European courts in the 1970s, these actions were only initiated by private actors rather than by state authorities enforcing their domestic law against foreign entities. See J. Brunnée, "The United States and International Environmental Law: Living with the Elephant" (2004) 15 Eur. J. Int'l L. 617 at 633.

[124] See *US Third Restatement, supra* note 12 at sections 402 and 403, which states that under US statutory law (both federal and state levels) US law applies only to "conduct occurring within, or having effect within, the territory of the United States."

[125] *Ibid.* at 124. In these cases, private remedies are sought by the victims.

[126] See *ARC Ecology v. U.S. Department of the Air Force*, 294 F. Supp 2d 1152, 1156 (N.D. Cal. 2003) (appeal pending), where the courts dismissed an attempt to require remedial investigation of former US military bases in the Philippines.

States, although this may not preclude any environmental damages that are sustained to land, water, and air in US territory.[127] Irrespective of the effects on the "environment," the geographical scope of the legislation is limited, reflecting the congressional intent when drafting CERCLA.[128] However, upon further examination, the court noted that CERCLA expresses clear intent to remedy domestic conditions in the United States, irrespective of the source of the pollution.[129]

Similarly, the application of CERCLA could be seen as being restricted to US entities. However, the court was not convinced that the language or legislative history of CERCLA is conclusive that a foreign corporation cannot be held liable as an owner and/or operator, particularly where the conduct of such owner or operator causes adverse effects within the United States.[130] The term owner and operator under CERCLA is broad enough to include both on- and off-shore facilities, but these are still defined to be limited to facilities that are subject to the jurisdiction of the United States.[131] Off-shore facilities would include facilities located on or under any waters that are subject to the jurisdiction of the United States, while an on-shore facility is defined as any facility located on or under any land or non-navigable waters within the United States.[132] What is considered to be subject to the jurisdiction of the United States is seen by virtue of citizenship, vessel documentation or numbering, or pursuant to a treaty.[133] Nevertheless, the court queried whether "on-shore facility" and "off-shore facility" exhaust what can be a "facility" under CERCLA.[134] The term facility includes a site or area where the hazardous substance has been located, which, in this case, was US territory.[135]

127 CERCLA, *supra* note 107 at para. 101(8).

128 During the drafting of CERCLA, the State Department had provided limited geographical scope to the definition in order to prevent the use of any authority to assert jurisdiction over foreign vessels and foreign nationals "in a manner inconsistent with general principles of international law and specific U.S. treaty obligations." Comments of Senator Cannon, 126 Congressional Record 26056 (18 September 1980).

129 *Teck Cominco, supra* note 8 at 28.

130 *Ibid.* at 37–38.

131 CERCLA, *supra* note 107 at para. 9601(20)(A)(ii).

132 *Ibid.* at 9601(17)(18).

133 *Ibid.* at 9601(19).

134 *Teck Cominco, supra* note 8 at 39.

135 CERCLA, *supra* note 107 at para. 9601(9)(B).

Irrespective of any territorial limitation on what is a "facility," the court expressed concern that an "absurd" result would follow where such a limitation would undermine the statutory purpose of an order to remediate "domestic conditions" in the United States.[136] From this, the effects from the Trail smelter "manifested itself at a facility, being the Upper Columbia River Site within the territorial boundaries of the United States."[137] The legal reasoning of this case, heavily based on a need to apply the "effects" doctrine in order to avoid a jurisdictional vacuum where the polluter would not be responsible, appears to influence a reading of CERCLA that foreign owners and operators are subject to CERCLA not by statutory definition but by consequence, where their activities damaged the environment in the United States.

The extraterritorial application of CERCLA also results in an inequitable situation for a foreign-based company or individual. Teck Cominco would be disadvantaged by not being able to seek remedies or other exceptions that US-based polluters could benefit from. Compensation or assistance from federal grants or funding programs is not available to foreign-based companies. Furthermore, US facilities, which may be similarly situated and the source of the same pollutant, may be excluded from liability and can avoid or mitigate costs if they can show that they are in compliance with regulatory permits issued by American federal and state governmental authorities.[138] Facilities in Canada or Mexico, which may operate under more stringent permit specifications, would not be able to justify their actions on the basis of compliance with the regulatory standards in their own jurisdiction.[139]

Another disadvantage for foreign companies or individuals is the inability to avoid official sanctions through informal consultations. Pre-emptive action, in advance of any formal action by the EPA or the launching of a civil suit, would also not be an option since the foreign entity would lack standing under US jurisdiction.[140] By

---

[136] *Teck Comnico, supra* note 8 at 40.

[137] *Ibid.*

[138] CERCLA, *supra* note 107 at para. 9607(j). However, the use of this exemption is circumscribed by the qualifications that the releases must be expressly permitted, not exceed the limitations established in the permits. See *United States v. Iron Mountain Mines,* 912 F. Supp. 1528 (1992), which denied the defence when the terms of the permit were breached by the respondent.

[139] It should be noted that in British Columbia, no "permit compliance" defence is available to avoid liability. See Robinson-Dorn, *supra* note 88 at 312.

[140] See George, *supra* note 111 at 10278.

challenging the EPA order, Teck Cominco would be subjecting itself to US environmental regulatory jurisdiction. Under CERCLA,
where a party wishes to challenge an administrative order, it must
either comply with the order or face penalties and potentially punitive damages. The order cannot be challenged until the EPA seeks
enforcement of the order in a federal court. If successful, the polluter can apply to the Superfund for reimbursement if it is a domestic party,[141] but, if not, its ability to seek reimbursement is subject
to the limitations placed upon foreign claimants.[142]

The court, in this case, was not sympathetic to the potential ineq-
uities to Teck Cominco as a result of being a foreign-based defendant. It was held that there would be no infringement of fair play or
a substantial injustice by exercising personal jurisdiction due to
the proximity of the defendant to the US border.[143] Furthermore,
enforcing the order would not "create any conflicts with Canadian
sovereignty."[144] The court did note that US-based companies whose
operations were authorized under federal law could use such authorization as a defence to an action for response costs and damages.[145] However, this is offset by the potential liability under other
US environment legislation that is not applicable to a Canadian
company.[146]

EXTRATERRITORIAL APPLICATION OF ENVIRONMENTAL LAW TO
ENFORCE STATE RESPONSIBILITY RULES—A FAILURE TO
EFFECTIVELY IMPLEMENT THE RULES ON STATE RESPONSIBILITY?

Neither the Canadian nor BC governments have attempted to
enjoin Teck Cominco from discharging deleterious material into
an international waterway.[147] Regulatory attempts to manage the
discharge of such material would not necessarily preclude any

---

[141] See CERCLA, *supra* note 107 at para. 106(b)(2).

[142] *Ibid.* at section 111.

[143] *Teck Cominco, supra* note 8 at 12.

[144] *Ibid.*

[145] *Ibid.* at 44. A federally permitted release would still not be a defence to a clean-
up order.

[146] *Ibid.* at 45. Liability under the Clean Air Act, *infra* note 209 and the Clean
Water Act, *infra* note 208, were mentioned.

[147] Regulation of the Teck Cominco smelter is subject primarily to provincial jurisdiction in Canada. The government of Canada has exercised jurisdiction under the Fisheries Act (1996), requiring the smelter to cease discharges of slag
that have impacts on fish habitat.

responsibility to ensure that the material flows across the frontier, although good faith efforts could be seen as mitigating the degree of responsibility. There would be a general obligation for Canada to prevent transboundary environmental effects. The question that arises is whether, by virtue of this failure, the injured state can resort to extraterritorial application of its legislation to remediate the damages.

The fact that the US authorities are resorting to the application of domestic laws to foreign-based sources of the pollution implies the limited effect of the rules of state responsibility for transboundary environmental harm. This can counteract attempts to fully put into effect the polluter pays principle, irrespective of questions of jurisdiction and sovereignty.[148] Any international regime with more precise rules would most likely not tolerate the exercise of such legal jurisdiction since it undermines the spirit of comity and cooperation instilled in international relations. Since the rules of state responsibility do not account for differences of opinions between two states as to the proper way to address a violation, it is possible that a state, frustrated by the lack of progress towards resolution or aggravated by the extent of the pollution, may advance their use of domestic environmental legislation to provide the appropriate remedy.

What is dubious about the court's decision in *Teck Cominco* is that US courts were willing to allow the enforcement of the order in the face of extensive jurisprudence revealing a conservative attitude towards extraterritorial application of environmental statutes.[149] The general rule of thumb is that there must be a clear legislative intent that the law is to be applied extraterritorially before the court will read in the extraterritorial application of the law.[150] Under US law, the courts have maintained a presumption against extraterritorial

---

148 N. Craik, "Trail Smelter Redux: Transboundary Pollution and Extraterritorial Jurisdiction" (2004) 14 J. Envtl. L. & Prac. 139 at 141.

149 *Teck Cominco, supra* note 8. See C. Kormos et al., "US Participation in International Environmental Law and Policy" (2001) 13 Geo. Int'l Envtl. L. Rev. 661; and S.M. Murphy, "Extraterritorial Application of NEPA" (2003) 97 Am. J. Int'l L. 962.

150 See *Smith v. United States*, (1993) 507 U. & S. 197. According to the ratio in *Smith*, there must be clear evidence in the statute to demonstrate that it is to be applied extraterritorially. See also *Equal Employment Opportunity Commission v. Arabian American Oil Company*, (1991) 499 U.S. 244, where the court ruled that for an intention of the law's application beyond national borders, "affirmative evidence clear manifested" is needed. For an extensive discussion of the US jurisprudence regarding the extraterritorial application of US laws, see W.S.

application stemming back to the *Foley/Aramco* doctrine.[151] This has become a rule of statutory construction, and US law therefore applies only within the territorial limits of the United States unless a contrary intent or "clear statement" is expressed in the statute or in relevant legislative history.[152] This is consistent with a canon of statutory construction in the United States where acts of Congress will not be given an interpretation that would violate international law (the *Charming Betsy* doctrine).[153]

However, US jurisprudence has periodically moved away from this presumption based on the "effects doctrine," which is justified mainly in cases of anti-trust activity occurring abroad that has an effect on economic interests in the United States.[154] The presumption was

---

Dodge, "Understanding the Presumption against Extraterritoriality" (1998) 16 Berkeley J. Int'l L. 85. See also the recent Supreme Court pronouncement in *F. Hoffman-La Roche Ltd. v. Empagran S.A.*, 124 S. Ct. 2359, 2366 (2004) [*Hoffman*], where the court cautioned against applying US law extraterritorially in order to avoid interference with the sovereign authority of other nations and therefore clear and affirmative indication to do must be indicated in the statute.

151 This doctrine was first applied in *Foley Bros., Inc. v. Filardo*, where the court ruled that US labour laws requiring an eight-hour work day, and overtime afterwards did not apply for work performed in Iraq. The doctrine was confirmed in *EEOC v. Arabian American Oil Co.*, 499 U.S. 244 (1991) [*Aramco*], where the court held that Title VII of the Civil Rights Act (1964) does not apply to employment practices of US employers who employ US citizens abroad.

152 See *Aramco, supra* note 151 at 258. The presumption against extraterritoriality can be sourced back to *American Banana v. United Fruit Co.*, 213 U.S. 347 (1909), involving a case where the defendant was alleged to hold a monopoly over trade in bananas and, therefore, was in violation of US law. The Supreme Court dismissed the claim holding that "the general and almost universal rule is that the character of an act as lawful or unlawful must be determined wholly by the law of the county where the act is done."

153 See *Murray v. Schooner Charming Betsy*, 6 U.S. (2 Cranch) 64, 118 (1804), where the court ruled that "an act of Congress ought never to be construed to violate the law of nations, if any other possible construction remains."

154 See *United States v. Aluminum Co. of America*, 148 F. 2d 416 (2d Cir. 1945). See also *Hartford Fire Ins. Co. v. California*, 113 S. Ct. 2891 (1993). The Federal Trade Improvement Antitrust Act (FTAIA) of 1982, provides that US anti-trust law only applies to foreign conduct if such conduct has (1) a "direct, substantial, and reasonably foreseeable effect" on the US market; and (2) "such effect gives rise to a claim under the provisions of" the Sherman Act. See also *Laker Airways Ltd. v. Sabena, Belgian World Airlines*, 731 F.2d 909 (D.C. Cir. 1984). However, see *Hoffman, supra* note 150, where the Supreme Court restricted the applicability of US anti-trust laws with regard to injuries suffered abroad independently from effects on the US market.

held not to apply in *Pakootas* where the failure to apply a statute can result in adverse effects in the United States.[155] In this case, the interpretation of CERCLA provisions regarding terms such as "facility," "releases," and "environment" implied a legislative intent to broaden the ambit of CERCLA orders to cover entities operating entirely outside the territorial United States. The court's reasoning lifted the presumption against extraterritoriality despite the absence of any explicit intent of the legislation to do so as required under the US jurisprudence.

States extending their jurisdictional reach to apply their own legislation and regulations is also problematic as it subverts the general rule to exhaust local remedies. Domestic proceedings in the state where the environmental harm is sourced, such as seeking compensation, are bypassed altogether. The availability of these actions would be premised, however, on the ability of foreign claimants to bring cases for transboundary environmental harm even where the polluter is in compliance with domestic regulatory requirements.

Some jurisprudence has allowed for extraterritorial application of US environmental laws, although, in these cases, the source of the pollution was still from an American entity.[156] Where there is a possible infringement of another nation's sovereignty, which implies second guessing the conservation or environmental decision-making of other nations, US courts will generally refrain from exercising extraterritorial jurisdiction.[157] There is a presumption

---

155 For this point, the court referred to the decision in *Environmental Defense Fund v. Massey*, 300 U.S. App. D.C. 65, 986 F.2d 528 (D.C. Cir. 1993). In this case, the District Court held that there was no issue of extraterritorial application to National Environmental Policy Act (NEPA) (requirement to undertake an environmental impact assessment), *infra* note 182, actions in Antarctica since Antarctica is part of the global commons where no state has sovereignty and, as a result, there is no scope for conflict between US laws and laws of other nations.

156 In *National Resources Defense Council v. Dep't of the Navy*, No. 01-07781, 2002 W.L. 32095131 (C.D. Cal. 17 September 2002), the court ruled that the federal Environmental Protection Agency (EPA) can be applied to the US Navy's Littoral Warfare Advanced Development program, which used sonar and therefore had an impact on, due to the sonar pulses traveling at low frequencies that travel hundreds of miles, a number of ocean species including marine mammals. The court was careful to make the distinction however that the EPA requirements were merely procedural and had no substantive effects outside the United States. The court refused to infringe other nations' sovereignty or implicate important foreign policy concerns (at 10).

157 In *Born Free USA v. Norton*, No. 03-1497, 2003 U.S. Dis. (8 August 2003), the plaintiffs attempted to stop the import of eleven elephants from Swaziland,

against extraterritorial application designed to avoid any conflicts with the laws of other nations and to ensure that Congress and the Executive Branch have the appropriate freedom of action in the sensitive area of foreign relations.[158]

The absence of any conflict between US and Canadian laws was factored in to the determination that the presumption against extraterritoriality would not apply in *Pakootas*. This decision was buttressed by the *ratio decidendi* in *Environmental Defence Fund v. Massey*, where the court ruled that where there is no potential for a conflict of laws, the presumption is seen to have less force since the potential is a "purpose behind the presumption."[159] In *Pakootas*, the court determined that exercising jurisdiction requiring Teck Cominco to clean up the environmental damage is not aimed to supercede Canadian environmental regulation since such regulation can only apply to what happens inside Canada. Since those laws could not apply extraterritorially and such US environmental regulatory legislation could not govern the activities of Teck Cominco inside Canada, this would leave a legal vacuum where no remedies would be available to rectify the damage. Moreover, since CERCLA does not establish standards but focuses almost exclusively on remediation, it cannot be argued that any US standards are being imposed on another sovereign nation. This informed the court in *Pakootas* when distinguishing between the regulation

---

arguing that the US Fish and Wildlife Service was required to conduct an environmental impact review as required by NEPA. The court expressed reluctance to conduct an environmental analysis that would result in challenging the validity of Swaziland's decision to permit the exports. For the ban of extraterritorial application of the Endangered Species Act, see *Lujan v. Defenders of Wildlife*, 504 U.S. 555, 222 E.L.R. 20913 (1992). In the decision in *Center for Biological Diversity v. National Science Foundation*, No. 02-5065, 2002 W.L. 31548073 (N.D. Cal. 30 October 2002), the court ruled that the research conducted by the National Science Foundation in the Gulf of California, which had potential effects on Mexico's exclusive economic zone (EEZ), did not impinge on Mexican sovereignty since most of the research took place outside the Mexican territorial waters and the decision-making process for organizing and planning the project was secured in the United States. The United States, in its domestic law, does not recognize that the EEZ of other nations are considered part of its territorial waters and therefore they are considered to be part of the high seas or global commons.

158 *Subafl.L.M.s, Ltd. v. MGM-Pathe Communications Col,* 24 F. 3d 1088, 1095-6 (9th cir. 1994).

159 *Environmental Defence Fund v. Massey,* 986 F. 2d 528 (DDC 29 January 1993) at 533.

of the emissions, which would purely be for the Canadian authorities, and cleaning up the damages resulting from such emissions. The overall context of bilateral relations between Canada and the United States is not assessed in the court's reasoning. As highlighted in earlier parts of this article, the two countries have historically resolved transboundary water disputes peacefully without the intervention of either country's domestic courts. The hallmark of this success is rooted partly in the frequent resort to diplomatic and institutional methods. This is arguably historical precedent of which the court should have taken judicial notice, particularly when one of the countries had filed an *amicus curiae* brief proposing recourse to state-to-state dispute settlement mechanisms such as under the IJC.[160] In the interests of international comity, which US courts have recognized,[161] more attention to how extraterritorial application of domestic environmental laws upset bilateral relations steeped in a spirit of cooperation would have been warranted.

Furthermore, the court's reasoning appears to gloss over the situation where there are in fact differing regulatory regimes and standards in the two countries. What might be permitted in Canada may not be allowed in the United States. As a result, the potential for conflict in light of these differences is ultimately triggered where one state imposes its remedial legislation against the other. By implication, the application of remedial legislation upon previous actions permitted by other states, calls into question the appropriateness of the standard in the polluter's state. The application of the rules on state responsibility do not address matters of conflicts and regulatory diversity, leaving it an open question on what mechanisms are needed to ensure that the rules are adhered to. States may aim to fully implement the polluter pays principle and combat relatively lax environmental standards (and a "race to the bottom"), which were perhaps deliberately set by a neighbouring state, and therefore overlook questions of improper application of domestic law to foreign entities or activities.[162]

160 Canada included in its *amicus* brief offers to negotiate a settlement with the United States or a reference to the IJC pursuant to Article IX of the Boundary Waters Treaty, *supra* note 6.

161 See *Societé Nationale Industrielle Aeropsatiale* v. *United States District Court*, 482 U.S. 522, (1987); and *Hilton v. Guyot*, 159 U.S. 113 (1895).

162 There is an excellent discussion of this tension between extraterritorial application and the need to combat limitations for plaintiffs to sue for transboundary environmental damage in the International Law Association (ILA), *Transnational*

Sensitivity to the extraterritorial application of environmental laws dates back to the era when the principles of international environmental law were being first clarified. The arbitral tribunal in the *Bering Sea Fur Seals Fisheries Arbitration (Great Britain v. United States)* denied a request by the United States to apply its legislation to protect fur seals in areas beyond the then three-mile limit of the territorial sea and the right to interfere in the internal affairs of other states for a resource shared as the "common property of mankind."[163] Almost a century later, the US ban[164] on the importation of yellow-fin tuna caught by Mexican vessels that were caught in Mexico's exclusive economic zone (EEZ) and on the high seas, absent purse seine nets prescribed by US EPA standards, was not upheld because of the extra-jurisdictional application of these standards. The measure was held to be inconsistent with the General Agreement on Tariffs and Trade (GATT) as it was not justified under the GATT environment-related exceptions.[165]

The issue of extra-jurisdictional application was revisited in *US – Import Prohibition of Certain Shrimp and Shrimp Products,* which involved a US law requiring shrimp importers to demonstrate no turtle by-catch in their haulings, where the WTO Appellate Body did not preclude the application of US laws to a global resource that was threatened with extinction from being a justifiable trade restrictive measure.[166] However, the sufficient nexus between the migratory populations of turtles located in both Asian waters and US territory, thus warranting a legitimate US interest in their conservation, rendered the extraterritorial/extra-jurisdictional point moot.

The general principle in international law against extraterritorial application of national law was addressed by the Permanent Court

Enforcement of Environmental Law Committee Report from the Berlin Conference (2004). See also P. Beaumont, "Private International Law of the Environment" (1995) Judicial L. Rev. 35.

163 *Bering Sea Fur Seals Fisheries Arbitration (Great Britain v. United States),* (1893) Moore's Int'l Arb. 755.

164 *United States – Restrictions on Imports of Tuna,* GATT Doc. DS21/R (unadopted) (3 September 1991).

165 General Agreement on Tariffs and Trade, (1947) 55 U.N.T.S. 194.

166 *US – Import Prohibition of Certain Shrimp and Shrimp Products,* Report of the Appellate Body, 12 October 1998, (1999) 38 I.L.M. 118; and *US – Import Prohibition of Certain Shrimp and Shrimp Products;* Recourse to Article 21.5 of the DSU by Malaysia, Doc. WT/DS58/AB/RW (22 October 2001).

of International Justice in the *Lotus* case.[167] In the same decision, it was noted that there is no general prohibition against applying domestic laws and jurisdiction to persons, property, and acts outside their territory. Subsequent jurisprudence at the ICJ has not, however, endorsed the application of domestic laws outside the territory of the state. It was raised in *Fisheries Jurisdiction (Spain v. Canada)*,[168] involving the extraterritorial application of Canadian fisheries legislation to outside its EEZ, but the ICJ inevitably did not rule on this when rejecting jurisdiction, on other grounds, to hear the matter.

This principle of non-extraterritorial application is manifest in the area of international environmental law despite the commonplace occurrence of transboundary environmental effects from pollution. Consequently, there are a number of treaties that function by mandating cooperation, rather than unilateral action, between states in incidences of transboundary environmental damage. The employment of unilateral actions to deal with environmental challenges outside the jurisdiction of the importing country is strongly discouraged. A multilateral solution, or at least an international consensus-driven result, is the preferred approach.[169] Principle 13 of the Rio Declaration calls on states to "cooperate in an expeditious and more determined manner to develop further international law regarding liability and compensation for adverse effects of environmental damage caused by activities within their jurisdiction or control to areas beyond their jurisdiction."[170] Multilateral regimes that establish cooperative decision mechanisms are integral to achieving outcomes, otherwise the temptation for asserting domestic environmental jurisdiction would be great in an area where there are few international environmental disputes solved by arbitration, let alone international courts in general. This may reflect the reluctance of states to entrust an independent arbiter to

---

[167] In this case, Turkish criminal law was applied to a French national on a French ship although the effects were felt in Turkey. See *Lotus, supra* note 120 at 19–20. Turkish jurisdiction applied to the acts of a French officer in French territory (that is, a ship) and was held not to conflict with international law because the "effects" of his action were felt in Turkish territory (that is, a Turkish ship).

[168] *Fisheries Jurisdiction (Spain v. Canada)*, [1998] I.C.J. Rep. 432.

[169] Rio Declaration, *supra* note 33, Principle 12.

[170] See also Principle 18, *ibid.*, which declares that "States shall immediately notify other States of any natural disasters or other emergencies that are likely to produce sudden harmful effects on the environment of those States."

determine sensitive issues regarding land stewardship and transboundary environmental responsibility.[171]

The use of US domestic law to inform the principle of state responsibility was evident in the *Trail Smelter* case. Since that time, the ability to use American regulatory and legislative approaches to influence the regulatory behaviour of other states, as an example of the use of soft power, has become increasingly attractive for US law-makers.[172] In the context of environmental regulation, the need for transposing domestic standards can be motivated by a number of factors. Extraterritorial application of domestic environmental law can have various motivations, including ones that are both altruistic and self-serving.[173] Such motivations can include a predilection to regulate corporations in states where environmental legislation is perceptively weak or ineffective; the need to ensure that companies do not seek jurisdictions with weak environmental regimes to gain an economic advantage; or concerted efforts to protect domestic industries that compete against foreign producers who benefit from weaker enforcement.[174] In many cases, the ineffectiveness of the international regime to address such phenomena can motivate states to take unilateral action.

The need to mitigate any unchecked exercise of environmental jurisdiction is rooted in international comity. In the United States, in order to invoke the obligations underlying state responsibility with respect to the environment, there must be some violation of the internationally accepted rules and standards.[175] If not, the extraterritorial application of domestic environmental law would not infringe upon the sovereign ability of states to regulate economic activity absent any significant injuries incurred outside its borders, which is the case in the *Teck Cominco* dispute. The general concern with extraterritorial application is that it infringes upon the principle of non-intervention and the sovereignty of other nations to

---

171 See D. Hunter, J. Salzman, and D. Zaelke, *International Environmental Law and Policy* (New York: Foundation Press, 1998).

172 See generally J. Nye, *Paradox of American Power: Why the World's Only Superpower Can't Go It Alone* (New York: Oxford University Press, 2002).

173 See S. Spracker and E. Naftalin, "Applying Procedural Requirements of U.S. Environmental Laws to Foreign Ventures: A Growing Challenge to Business" (1991) 25 Int'l Lawyer 1043 at 1051–52.

174 *Ibid.*

175 See *US Third Restatement, supra* note 12, where states are under an obligation to ensure activities within their jurisdiction or control conform to generally

regulate activity within their borders, based on their own environmental policies, development needs, economic priorities, and regulatory standards. State sovereignty over natural resources is enshrined in international law.[176] Extraterritorial application indirectly questions the standards of other states in regard to environmental protection and presupposes the determination of its path towards sustainable development. It could be seen as a masked attempt by states to alter the regulatory behaviour of other states.[177]

Although there may be cases where a failure to prevent significant transboundary environmental harm can be tantamount to a violation of international law, the subsidiary question is whether international law sanctions, in response, unilateral extraterritorial measures. Absent any international mechanisms to coordinate a response to such harm, instances of transboundary pollution causing imminent harm, necessitating the unilateral exercise of a state's jurisdiction, could lead other countries to apply their legislation for arguably more remote cases of transboundary pollution such as mercury contamination or greenhouse gas emissions where the attribution of the environmental problem to one particular state is difficult.[178] Efforts to move the international agenda forward by

---

accepted international rules and standards to prevent, reduce, and control environmental injury outside their areas of national jurisdiction.

[176] See UN General Assembly (UNGA) Res. 1803(XVII) (14 December 1962); Declaration on the Establishment of New International Economic Order, UNGA Res. 3201 (1 May 1974); and Charter of Economic Rights and Duties of States, UNGA Res. 3281 (XXIX) (12 December 1974). The principle's status as customary international law was confirmed by the ICJ in *Case Concerning Armed Activities on the Territory of the Congo (Democratic Republic of the Congo v. Uganda)*, (2006) 45 I.L.M. 271.

[177] See the discussion in the *Tuna-Dolphin* disputes by the GATT panels, where the blatant extra-jurisidictionality of the US measures was noted. The *Shrimp-Turtle* decision by the WTO Appellate Body revisited the general rule against using trade measures to apply domestic environmental regulations by permitting the use of a US trade prohibition against states that do not effectively prevent turtle by-catch in their shrimp-fishing haulings. However, this is arguably not a bold assertion of US domestic law since the species protected by the measure (sea turtles) is a global/transboundary resource and its conservation is covered under a number of MEAs.

[178] Specific types of trasnboundary environmental harm running across national boundaries are only the tip of the iceberg in the area of state responsibility for transboundary harm. See J.R. Goldfarb, "Extraterritorial Compliance with NEPA amid the Current Wave of Environmental Harm (1991) 18 Envtl. Affairs 543. More evidence is emerging that there are tangible effects of transoceanic pollution with respect to persistent organic pollutants and even mercury. See R.

individual state action has considerable merit, but international comity demands a cooperative approach, at least in the first instance.[179]

An example of where the application of environmental laws is sanctioned extraterritorially by law is the Marine Mammals Protection Act.[180] This statute permits the United States to prohibit persons and vessels from taking marine mammals on the high seas and even fish imports with by-catches that endanger certain marine mammals such as dolphins. Under the Fishermen's Protective Act (Pelly Amendment),[181] the importation of fish products can be prohibited from a country certified to be conducting fishing operations in a manner, or under circumstances, that diminishes the effectiveness of an international fishery conservation program. Although empowered to do so, the United States has rarely resorted to such action, as it is perhaps mindful of the potential backlash that could come from the international community.

In recent years, the EPA has expressed interest in examining how CERCLA and the National Environmental Policy Act (NEPA)[182] can be applied to address the sources of cross-boundary pollution.[183] The EPA has issued subpoenas to US companies operating in Mexico demanding information on the use and release of chemicals into the New River that flows to the United States.[184] However, the extraterritorial application of US legislation is not uniform, particularly where the provisions under those statutes could be

---

Renner, *Asia Pumps Out More Mercury Than Previously Thought,* Environmental Science and Technology, Science News, 5 January 2005.

[179] A liability and redress regime is currently being negotiated under the Stockholm Convention on Persistent Organic Pollutants, (2001) 40 I.L.M. 532, although one pinnacle issue of disagreement among states is how to attribute liability to particular states, and even activities within those states.

[180] Marine Mammals Protection Act, 16 U.S.C. 1361–407, P.L. 92–522.

[181] Fishermen's Protective Act (Pelly Amendment), 22 U.S.C. at paras. 1971–79.

[182] National Environmental Policy Act, Pub. L. 91–190, 42 U.S.C. 4321–47, 1 January 1970, as amended by Pub. L. 94-52, 3 July 1975, Pub. L. 94-83, 9 August 1975, and Pub. L. 97-258, para. 4(b), 13 September 1982.

[183] See George, *supra* note 111 at 10275. To support the EPA's interest in applying its regulations outside the territorial United States, George notes a report from the Environmental Law Institute supported from legal counsel in the EPA. See Environmental Law Institute, *U.S. plus Mexico Transboundary Environmental Enforcement: Legal Strategies for Preventing the Use of the Border as a Shield against Liability* (2002).

[184] Hunter, Salzman, and Zaelke, *supra* note 171 at 1417.

applied to prevent environmental damage occurring outside the United States. The utility of the rules of state responsibility to provide resounding authority for demands to stop or modify activities causing transboundary effects becomes the focal point of discussion. Its role as a proactive principle rather than being invoked in response to transboundary environmental harm is amplified and tests the genuine efficacy of the rules of state responsibility. The following section will examine a few recent cases where transboundary environmental damage has been predicted as a result of potentially harmful activities, but where US authorities have refrained from adhering to the rules of state responsibility to prevent transboundary environmental harm through the application of its own domestic environmental laws.

EMERGING ISSUES IN TRANSBOUNDARY HARM BETWEEN THE UNITED STATES AND CANADA

As discussed in this article, incidents of transboundary harm and environmental disputes have characterized the relations between Canada and the United States. Underscoring the relationship, however, is a mutual concern to resolve disputes amicably. The transparency of both countries' policy-making process also allows each of them to intervene when transboundary impacts are possible. Where this is known, government and non-governmental actors have participated actively in the other state's domestic processes in order to communicate concern about potential transboundary harm. The assessment of such activities in each jurisdiction benefits from the appreciation of cross-border environmental concerns.

DEVILS LAKE: A DOUBLE STANDARD IN TRANSBOUNDARY ENVIRONMENTAL HARM

A dispute that has challenged the amicable nature of the Canada–US relationship involves two projects in North Dakota. The US and North Dakota position regarding the transboundary environmental impacts reveals some inconsistency with the arguments that hold that Teck Cominco and, ultimately, Canada, are accountable for the pollution of the Columbia River waterways. The apparent variance highlights the difficulty in retaining a coherent position on the management of transboundary rivers and shared natural resources for states due to the uniqueness of the facts and the context, including the political dimensions, of the disagreement.

Devils Lake is a small, closed sub-basin within the Hudson Bay drainage basin, although it is not connected to it (no water flows out). High water levels have recently caused damage to the town of Devils Lake.[185] The North Dakota government decided to divert waters from the lake to the Red River, which flows across the national frontier, into Manitoba waterways and lakes and eventually into the Hudson's Bay. A proposed US $28 million outlet would drain about 100 cubic feet of water per second from Devils Lake to ease chronic flooding. The diversion, pursuant to the 2000 amendments to the Dakota Water Resources Act (DWRA),[186] would divert water from the Missouri/Mississippi basin into the Hudson Bay basin via the Sheyenne and Red rivers. This would effectively undo a compromise reached between Canada and the United States as reflected in the Garrison Diversion Reformulation Act of 1986.[187] This legislation outlined a process for seeking US domestic consensus on, and approval of, Garrison-related projects. It also provided for consultations between the United States and Canada on water projects that might affect the other states' waters. The DWRA, unlike its predecessor, no longer contains a requirement for consultations with Canada.

The US Congress has twice allocated funds for the diversion. The funding was based on conditions set by Congress: that construction be economically justified and be in compliance with NEPA; that the secretary of state, after consultation with the IJC, provide assurances that the "requirements and intent" of the Boundary Waters Treaty will not be violated; and that no funds would be used to permit a diversion of water from the Missouri River basin into Devils Lake (that is, there would be no inlet).

The Garrison Dam on the Missouri River was originally completed in the mid-1950s (creating a huge reservoir known as Lake Sakakawea/Lake Audubon). Since then, there have been a variety of proposed irrigation projects and water distribution proposals for municipal, rural, and industrial uses. In 1975, Canada and the

185 This was a relatively new phenomenon for the period between 1993–9. No overflows had been recorded for the preceding 200 years.

186 Dakota Water Resources Act, H.R. 2918, s. 623 [DWRA].

187 Garrison Diversion Reformulation Act, 1986. The DWRA revives some of the original Garrison diversion project features and introduces new ones, which involve inter-basin diversions of water into Canada. By transferring significant federal oversight to the state of North Dakota in the DWRA, it also substantially weakens the US government's ability to meet its commitments to Canada under the Boundary Waters Treaty as outlined in the 1986 act.

United States referred the matter of the transboundary implications of the Garrison diversion to the IJC. Two years later, the IJC recommended against any diversion construction that could affect waters flowing into Canada, unless Canada and the United States agree that the risk to Canadian waters is either eliminated or no longer of concern.[188] In a prescient passage in the report, the commission stated that "international boundaries may separate countries, but such political arrangements should not divide ecosystems."[189] In addition, the IJC expressed concerns over the negative environmental impacts that could occur, for example, from the transfer of non-native species between basins and the introduction of invasive species, fish disease, and pathogens. In the spirit of precautionary thinking, the commission noted that remedial measures to control invasive species are often futile and the realization of full impacts of such invasion can take many years.[190] As a result, it was recommended that the project should not proceed until the parties agree that methods have been proven that eliminate the risk of biota transfer or until the transfer is agreed to be no longer a matter of concern.[191]

In the early 1980s, a congressional commission on the diversion studied the issue and came up with recommendations. The US Congress subsequently enacted the Garrison Unit Reformulation Act.[192] Concurrently, the United States and Canada established the Garrison US/Canada Consultative Group to continue the dialogue regarding the project. The group set up a joint technical committee in 1993 and, under it, an engineering-biology task group to review the Garrison project. They ruled that the most acceptable way to fully overcome the transfer of non-native biota into the Hudson Bay basin was to treat the water to acceptable drinking water standards prior to its transport into the Hudson Bay drainage. The

---

188 IJC, Canada, and the United States, *Transboundary Implications of the Garrison Diversion Unit* (1977) [*Garrison* report]. Under Article IX of the Boundary Waters Treaty, *supra* note 6, reports of the commission "are not be regarded as decisions of the question or matters so submitted either on the facts or the law, and shall in no way have the character of an arbitral award." Reports pursuant to Article IX stand in contrast to "decisions" under Article X, which can address the facts and circumstances of particular questions and referred matters, and can include conclusions and recommendations.

189 *Garrison* report, *supra* note 188 at 97.

190 *Ibid.* at 102.

191 Recommendation No. 2.

192 Garrison Unit Reformulation Act, Pub. L. No. 99-194.

findings predated the discovery of cryptosporidium found in municipal water supplies in Detroit, which could not be treated by chloramination. This resulted in a change of the Canadian position since reliance on chloramination was no longer considered reasonable,[193] and, therefore, the Garrison project would be built using an outdated standard without the ability to be upgraded when additional scientific information emerged.

In June 1999, the US Army Corps of Engineers recommended that an outlet was not the necessary or appropriate solution. Despite this recommendation, the plans to construct an outlet were scheduled to begin in early 2001. The US federal government indicated that there would be a review of the diversion under NEPA, and Canada would be consulted. At the same time, the governor of North Dakota announced that the state government would build its own outlet, without any US federal involvement.[194]

Both the Canadian and Manitoba provincial governments expressed opposition to the project because of the irreversible and catastrophic economic and environmental damage that could occur from inter-basin diversions of water.[195] Any partial diversion might lead to transfers of water, carrying foreign fish diseases and biota from the Missouri River basin to the Hudson Bay basin.[196] Such inter-basin transfers have the potential to seriously damage Canadian waters and Manitoba's lucrative fishery[197] as well as drinking

---

[193] It was also submitted that it was not effective against other pathogens.

[194] The state contends that in the absence of that federal interest, the state is relieved of any obligation under NEPA to carry out an environmental impact statement (EIS).

[195] Other US states such as Minnesota and Missouri shared these concerns.

[196] The diversion will also pump water from a part of the lake where there are higher concentrations of salts and other potential pollutants.

[197] The Manitoba government claims the fishing industry brings in $150 million of revenue a year and employs 3,500 fishermen. Threats to the downstream (US) sport fishing industry, along with the associated economic infrastructure, due to the damage to the fish habitat in Canada, was a determining factor in a report completed by the IJC recommending against the proposed coal mine in Canada on a tributary to the nearby Flathead River. See *Impacts of a Proposed Coal Mine in the Flathead River Basin* (1988) [*Flathead* report]. The report, at 11, recommended that the mine proposal not receive regulatory approval unless and until the potential transboundary impacts had been determined with reasonable certainty and constituted an acceptable risk to both governments. Ultimately, the project never went forward. There are currently plans to auction off rights to drill for methane on nearly 100,000 acres near the Flathead and Elk rivers, which will produce large amounts of waste water. The Flathead basin

water quality, ultimately violating the Boundary Waters Treaty.[198] In particular, there are foreign alien invasive species that could contaminate Canadian waterways such as the Red River and Lake Winnipeg[199] and, ultimately, Hudson's Bay. As the impacts of new species into Canadian waters are presently unknown, Canada argued that the precautionary principle should be invoked.[200]

Invasive species can lead to habitat destruction and threaten the existence of endangered species. In North America, significant, and irreversible, environmental impacts, as well as considerable financial costs, have been incurred as a result of foreign biota and invasive species such as zebra mussels, which have spread throughout the Great Lakes and have reached the Missouri River. Sea lamprey have also spread throughout the Great Lakes and have devastated the fishery.[201] The mixing of waters could introduce new life forms such as striped bass and many microscopic species into Lake Winnipeg, where they will not have natural predators. There is also concern about the possible infusion of salt, mercury, arsenic, boron, nitrogen, phosphate, and mercury, since Devils Lake is fed solely by runoff from surrounding farmland.[202]

Global concern for the control and prevention of alien invasive species has emerged in a number of international fora,[203] including the Convention on Biological Diversity,[204] as well as at the International Maritime Organization, which has recently passed

---

is home to abundant wildlife, including the largest concentration of grizzly bears in southern Canada. Cabin Creek crosses into the United States and forms the western boundary of the joint Waterton Lakes/Glacier National Parks before emptying into Flathead Lake.

[198] Article IV of the treaty requires that waters shall not be polluted on either side to the injury or health or property on the other side.

[199] Lake Winnipeg is considered to be one of the largest freshwater lakes in the world.

[200] See Government of Canada, *Downstream Effects of the Devils Lake Outlet*, <http://www.dfait-maeci.gc.ca/can-am/washington/pdf/fact-biota.pdf>.

[201] Another invasive species, Eurasian watermilfoil, is now found in thirty-seven states and three provinces.

[202] See C. Krauss, "Water Everywhere: But Is It Good for the Fish," *New York Times* (6 June 2004). See also M. Byers, "The Devils Diversion," *Globe and Mail* (31 January 2005).

[203] According to the World Conservation Union, the global economic costs of damage from invasive alien species are estimated at US $137 billion per year.

[204] The Convention on Biological Diversity, (1992), 31 I.L.M. 822, calls upon its parties to prevent the introduction, control, or eradication of alien species that

the Ballast Water Management Convention.[205] Despite these developments at the multilateral level, there remains a major regulatory
gap due to the lack of international standards related to invasive
animal species that do not qualify as pests under the International
Plant Protection Convention.[206] Measures to control the spread of
alien invasive species are subject to the WTO Agreement on Sanitary and Phytosanitary Measures, which encourages members to
conform to standards, guidelines, or recommendations identified
by international standard-setting bodies.[207]

A central issue in this dispute relates to process. The decision to
divert the waters was not the result of any consultation with the
affected nations. This oversight represents a deviation from general procedural requirements in US law that allow for the participation of foreign states in the domestic planning process or the
presentation of claims. Under both the Clean Water Act[208] and the
Clean Air Act,[209] foreign states can participate, on conditions of
reciprocity, in hearings for the revision for a state implementation
plan in order to eliminate adverse consequences for the particular
foreign state.

The dispute spawned a host of legal proceedings in the US
courts. North Dakota environmentalists and the National Wildlife

---

threaten ecosystems, habitats, or species. Other MEAs such as the Cartagena
Protocol, *supra* note 64; Convention on International Trade in Endangered
Species of Wild Fauna and Flora, (1973) 993 U.N.T.S. 243; Convention on the
Conservation of Migratory Species of Wild Animals, (1980), 19 I.L.M. 15; and
the Convention on Wetlands of International Importance Especially as Water-
fowl Habitat, (1971) 996 U.N.T.S. 245, have also addressed the issue.

205 2004 Ballast Water Management Convention, <http://globallast.imo.org/
index.asp?page=mepc.htm&menu=true>.

206 International Plant Protection Convention, 6 December 1951, <http://www.fao.
org/legal/treaties/004t-e.htm>. The Office International des International des
Epizooties manages risks associated with animal diseases but does not include
species that may be invasive alien species. See "Experts Identify Regulatory Gaps
for Invasive Alien Species" (2005) 5(10) Bridges Trade Biores.

207 The WTO Agreement on Sanitary and Phytosanitary Measures, Article 3.2, states
that WTO members would benefit from a presumption of consistency with the
agreement when the measures conform to such standards, guidelines or recommendations. Members are also free to provide a higher level of protection
under their measures although the burden of proof reverts to them to justify
that the measure is consistent with the SPS Agreement. See Articles 3(3).

208 Clean Water Act, 33 U.S.C. § 1251–1387.

209 Clean Air Act 42 U.S.C. § 7622.

Federation joined the Manitoba government in trying to stop the diversion. The North Dakota Department of Health National Pollutant Discharge Elimination System's (NPDES) permit, which was issued in 2003 pursuant to the delegated authority under the US Clean Water Act, was appealed. The permit sets guidelines for the outlet so that a restricted amount of water may be pumped from May through November only, and it must stop when the lake declines to 1,445 feet above sea level. The state of Minnesota, the governments of Canada and Manitoba, and the citizens of North Dakota petitioned the department to reconsider its decision. The North Dakota Supreme Court rejected the claim, holding that the Health Department followed North Dakota law and did not act unreasonably in issuing a permit for the project.

Another application before the court, which was initiated by the Spirit Lake Nation and several US states as well as the Manitoba government, has called for a full environmental impact statement (EIS) on any temporary or permanent outlet project proposal. Other groups as well as the state of Missouri opposed the project because of the exceedingly high financial and environmental costs, which far outweigh the flood control benefits.[210] The proposed project was not forwarded for an environmental review regarding diversion, along with the proposed sand filtration as a mitigating measure that the Army Corps reported would trap hazardous minerals and life forms.

In another proceeding, the US District Court for the District of Columbia ruled that the issue of biota transfer associated with the North West Area Water Supply project (NAWS), a bulk water distribution system for the purpose of providing drinking water, required serious consideration and that it had not been given a hard look by the US Department of Interior.[211] The NAWS project was a component of the Garrison Diversion Unit, which was first authorized by the US Congress in 1965. A decision was made not to complete a full EIS after a finding of no significant impact. The project was designed to transfer water from the Missouri River basin into the Hudson Bay basin in order to provide water to numerous small communities in North Dakota. The NAWS project would be the

---

210 Natural Wildlife Federation, "Powell Gives Devils Lake Project Green Light," 2003, <http://www.nwf.org/enviroaction/index.cfm?articleid=281&issueid=31>.

211 *Government of the Province of Manitoba v. Gale A. Norton, Secretary, United States Department of the Interior, et al.*, Civil Action No. 02-cv-02057 (RMC) (3 February 2005).

first diversion project for inter-basin water transfer. The Manitoba provincial government applied for an order compelling the Department of the Interior to do a comprehensive environmental analysis of the project pursuant to NEPA. In support of the application, the Canadian government submitted an *amicus curiae* brief to the court, arguing that customary international law (no harm principle and duty to cooperation) mandated a thorough evaluation of the project and, hence, the preparation of a complete EIS. IJC rulings were cited as defining the standards of Canada–US relations and informing the application of NEPA.

The court found the Bureau of Reclamation's initial environmental assessment and finding of no significant impact to be unlawful,[212] as the proposed Minot water treatment plant on the Hudson's Bay basin side was not fully reviewed to address consequences of leakage from the pipelines.[213] The court remanded the defendants to complete a "more searching EA that considers an integrated analysis of the possibility of leakage and the potential consequences of the failure to fully treat the Missouri River water at its source given the agency's awareness of treatment-resistant biota."[214] As a result, the Bureau of Reclamation was required to evaluate the consequences to the Hudson Bay drainage basin of even a small amount of water lost from the present design as compared to placing the full drinking water treatment facility on the Missouri River side of the continental divide.

The Canadian and Manitoban governments petitioned the US government to halt construction of the Devils Lake outlet until it could be reviewed by the IJC.[215] The US government never accepted the request. By failing to adhere to an environmental assessment under IJC auspices, there might be a potential violation of the Boundary Waters Treaty because of its impact on transboundary waters. In August 2005, the governments of Canada, United States,

---

212 The court determined that the finding was arbitrary, capricious, and an abuse of discretion.

213 There was no evaluation of the consequences of the failure compared to the complete treatment at source for a plant on the Missouri basin side.

214 See *ibid.* at 38.

215 Some alternatives to an actual reference of the matter to the IJC were also suggested including having the IJC oversee the implementation of any agreement that the United States and Canada agree to or overseeing the installation of any environmental protection such as sand filters. P. Samyn, "Devils Lake Dispute: Canada Appears to Give Up Hope for IJC Review: Washington Talks Look for New Solution," *Winnipeg Free Press* (21 June 2005).

Manitoba, Minnesota, and North Dakota reached an agreement where an advanced filter would be constructed at the Devils Lake outlet to prevent the flow of unwanted species, salt, and the runoff of farm chemicals (for example, sulphate and phosphorous) into Lake Sheyenne and, ultimately, into the Red River watershed. There would also be a temporary filter put in place while the advance filter was being completed.[216] As part of the agreement, the IJC's Red River Board would develop and oversee a downstream water-monitoring program and basin-wide early detecting and management plan for invasive species. An assessment of any risks from the transfer of Devils Lake water to Manitoba waterways would be required with a requirement for additional measures where the assessment determines that there are, in fact, risks. The agreement is non-binding, however,[217] and, therefore, does not prevent North Dakota from future water diversions from the Missouri River basin.[218]

ARCTIC NATIONAL WILDLIFE REFUGE: ASSESSING POTENTIAL
WILDLIFE IMPACTS

There are plans to expand oil drilling in the Arctic National Wildlife Refuge.[219] The 1980 Alaska National Interests Lands Conservation Act[220] called for the conservation of fish and wildlife

216 The agreement stipulates that North Dakota would install a temporary crude rock-and-gravel filter at the start of the outlet's new drainage system. Some have criticized this initiative as limited since it would not prevent water from pouring over the top of the filter when it fills up. See G. Galloway, "Critics Call Devils Lake Deal 'A Joke': Invasive Species Still a Threat, Activists Warn," *Globe and Mail* (8 August 2005). The temporary gravel filter has been proven to be ineffective as parts of it washed away when the outlet was tested under a full flow of water.

217 More accurately, the understanding between all the parties was never transformed into a legal document. See M. Robson, "Pact to Safeguard Manitoba's Water Was Never Signed," *Toronto Star* (20 April 2006).

218 See J. Ibbitson, "Canada Must Swallow Its Devils Lake Mistakes," *Globe and Mail* (11 August 2005).

219 The current US plan developed by the presidential administration would open part of the refuge to oil drilling. The area is claimed to hold between 10 to 16 million barrels of crude oil and would satisfy future energy needs of the United States. The plan would open 1.5 million acres on Alaska's north coast for exploration, although only 2,000 acres could be under development at any given time.

220 National Interests Lands Conservation Act, 16 U.S.C. § 410.

populations and habitats in their natural diversity, thus creating the refuge, which ranks as one of the largest wildlife refuges in the United States. Containing one of the largest complete ecosystems on the planet, including an array of Arctic and sub-Arctic habitats as well as being rich in flora and fauna, its fragility renders it highly sensitive to any development. The biological heart of the Arctic refuge is a narrow 1.5 million acre coastal plain, the so-called "1,002 lands," which extends from the foothills of the Brooks Range some 15–20 miles back from the edge of the Arctic Ocean. This is the area planned for the proposed drilling. This ecosystem consists of the 130,000-strong porcupine caribou herd, which migrates almost 400 miles each year from the Yukon to the Alaskan coastal plain to calve and graze on the rich vegetation in preparation for the winter. The narrow coastal plain is the principal calving area for the caribou herd, with an average of 40,000 calves born there annually.

The Canadian government claims that the United States is under a duty to provide permanent protection for wildlife populations that straddle the frontier. Canada has met this obligation by banning development in areas frequented by the porcupine caribou herd and by providing permanent wilderness status through the establishment of the Ivvavik and Vuntut National Parks in northern Yukon. Canada also recognizes the environmental and socio-economic concerns of the Gwich'in First Nations people in Alaska and Canada who have relied on the porcupine caribou herd for their traditional livelihood and health. A request was made to the United States to provide similar protected status so that all of the herd's calving grounds would benefit from wilderness protection.

In 1987, Canada and the United States signed an Agreement on the Conservation of the Porcupine Caribou Herd.[221] The agreement requires the parties to take appropriate action to conserve the herd and its habitat.[222] Article 5 obliges the parties to consult to consider appropriate action in the event of any significant damage to the herd or its habitat for which there is a responsibility under international law. Activities that have a potential impact on the conservation of the herd (including a significant disruption of its migration) or its habitat are subject to an impact assessment and review. There is an additional obligation to consult with the other

[221] Agreement on the Conservation of the Porcupine Caribou Herd, <http://www.taiga.net/pcmb/documents/international_conservation_agreement.pdf>.

[222] *Ibid.*, Article 3(a).

state where there is likely to be significant long-term adverse impacts on the herd or its habitat.[223]

Conclusions

The cases of the Arctic National Wildlife Reserve and Devils Lake reinforce how the rules of state responsibility, despite their rhetorical merit, are limited in pre-empting transboundary disputes. Independent of its codification in the ILC Draft Articles, the rules, as exemplified in the *Trail Smelter* dispute,[224] operate under the tension between the theoretical advancement of international law and the empirical difficulties of implementation. Although similar disputes have been resolved peacefully in the past,[225] certain extraneous factors along with political considerations can contribute to enervating the rules as a deterrent for state action. Historical experience has also demonstrated the difficulties when applying the rules retroactively after the damage has occurred. This can lead to extra-jurisdictional efforts by states to apply environmental laws and regulations as evidenced in the *Teck Cominco* dispute. As a legal principle, respect for the obligation to prevent, or at least to mitigate, transboundary environmental damage continues to be challenged particularly along the US–Canada frontier, where transboundary environmental disputes are expected to escalate in number.[226]

Coupled with higher degrees of economic development, population growth, and bilateral trade, climatic factors, such as drought and flooding have placed greater stress on the transboundary watercourses shared by both states. Water resources management in

---

[223] *Ibid.,* Articles 3(c) and (d).

[224] Some critics have noted the marginal relevance that the ruling has in resolving transboundary environmental disputes. See P.H. Sand, *Transnational Environmental Law: Lessons in Global Change* (Dordrecht: Kluwer Law International, 1999) at 87; and P.W. Birnie and A.E. Boyle, *International Law and the Environment*, 2nd edition (Oxford: Oxford University Press, 2003).

[225] In the *Gut Dam* dispute between Canada and the United States, (1969) 8 I.L.M. 118, Canada agreed to compensate US citizens for damage caused to their property because of a rise in the level of a lake in US territory partly attributable to a dam constructed by Canada across the St. Lawrence River. The dam was built with the consent of the United States but in accordance with a treaty that required compensation for losses attributable to the dam. Canada was required to pay compensation irrespective of any questions of fault or negligence.

[226] See A.L. Parrish, "Trail Smelter Déjà vu: Extraterritoriality, International Environmental Law, and the Search for Solutions to Canadian-U.S. Transboundary Water Pollution Disputes" (2005) Boston U. L. Rev. 85.

an era of scarcity, in addition to the natural resources development that impacts such watercourses, will characterize future relations between Canada and the United States, which share an exponential number of waterways, lakes, oceans as well as groundwater sources.

Examples of current disputes that may, in the near future, define the transboundary environmental relationship between Canada and the United States include plans for a reconstruction of a causeway built over Missisquoi Bay on Lake Champlain, which would allow a free flow of pollution out of the northern portion of the lake to dissipate.[227] The state of Vermont has agreed to rip out part of the causeway but not all of it, arguing that an endangered species, the spiny turtle, has adopted the causeway as a basking spot. On Lake Memphrémagog, which is also shared by the province of Québec and the state of Vermont, Canadians are concerned that a planned enlargement of a waste disposal site near the Vermont town of Coventry will leak into the Black River and then into the nearby lake frequented by many Québec summer residents.

With drought a growing concern on the Great Plains, Montana has argued that it is not receiving its fair share of water, as allotted pursuant to the Boundary Water Treaty,[228] from the St. Mary and Milk rivers, which flow through it and Alberta. The International St. Mary-Milk Rivers Administrative Measures Task Force recently released a report,[229] examining ways to improve current administrative measures (from a IJC 1921 Order[230] used in apportioning the flows of such waterways. The report made recommendations to improve the water flow. In British Columbia, Canadian environmentalists and Native American groups have initiated legal action to prevent a mining company and the British Columbia government from reopening a mine on the Taku River, which allegedly

---

[227] The IJC has issued a final report: *Transboundary Impacts of the Missisquoi Bay Causeway and the Missisquoi Bay Bridge Project,* 31 March 2005. The report concluded that the current state of water quality in the bay from phosphorous levels "presents an unacceptable situation that is adversely affecting health and property in both countries and constitutes a threat to the health of Lake Champlain." It was recommended that the causeway be removed.

[228] Boundary Water Treaty, *supra* note 6, Article VI.

[229] April 2006.

[230] International Joint Commission, Order in the Matter of the Measurement and Apportionment of the Waters of the St. Mary and Milk Rivers and Their Tributaries in the State of Montana and the Provinces of Alberta and Saskatchewan, October 1921.

could pollute a watershed that is rich in wild salmon that runs into Alaska.[231] The proposed gold and copper mine, where toxic metal tailings are slated to be buried along a stream that joins the Taku is also being challenged by the Taku River Tlingit First Nations tribe, which opposes the tailings disposal plan and the construction of a 100-mile access route to the mine across its land holdings. Within the same proximity, Alaskan commercial fishermen and Canadian native people are concerned about a proposal to reopen the Tulsequah Chief mining complex by a Vancouver company across the border from Juneau. They are concerned that mining waste could impact fisheries and that access roads will disturb wild lands. British Columbia has refused to submit the contested developments to any binational review mechanism.

The issue of transboundary environmental harm and the possible application of the rules of state responsibility have crept into non-environmental resource management dispute settlement fora that are unaccustomed to entertaining such claims. For instance, an International Center for Settlement of Investment Disputes (ICSID) tribunal will be hearing a case where US investors, who hold water rights, will be challenging Mexico's diversion of waters for the purpose of irrigating Mexican agricultural lands.[232] It is alleged that the diversion violates the US investors' rights under the North American Free Trade Agreement (NAFTA).[233] Another trade-related fora, the North American Commission on Environmental Cooperation (CEC), an institution created under a side agreement to NAFTA,[234] has received a complaint from various American and Canadian non-governmental organizations, alleging that both Canada and the United States have failed to uphold international environmental law by allowing for the diversion of water from Devils Lake. The petitioners also argue that both states have failed to effectively enforce their environmental laws, which, in this case, would be the Boundary Waters Treaty. Violations of the treaty are cited,

---

231 See T. Wilkinson, "US Clashes with Canada over Pollution at the Border," *Christian Science Monitor* (6 August 2004).

232 *Bayview Irrigation District and Others v. United Mexican States*, 1 July 2005, ICSID Case no. ARB(AF)/05/1).

233 North American Free Trade Agreement, (1993) 32 I.L.M. 289 [NAFTA].

234 North American Agreement on Environmental Cooperation, (1993) 32 I.L.M. 1480 [NAAEC]. Article 5 of the NAAEC establishes an obligation on all state parties to "effectively enforce its environmental laws."

including the obligation to attempt to make a joint reference to the IJC.[235]

Some argue that state responsibility is perhaps not suitably designed to address environmental protection issues between states due to its "enforcement-oriented approach."[236] State responsibility for transboundary environmental harm may also be an outdated modality to prevent such harm since pollution does not necessarily move in a linear fashion over a particular boundary. Pollution can be disaggregated so as to impact an ecosystem shared by a number of states. The whole "ecosystem" approach to shared watercourses is starting to be reflected in the decisions by certain IJC commissions.[237] As a result, if environmental pollution travels more cyclically, the application of the rules of state responsibility premised on a pinpoint violation caused by an individuated factual scenario is more difficult to apply.

The transboundary application (or lack thereof) of domestic law, either to remediate existing environmental damage or to assure that transboundary effects are accounted for, is seemingly asserted as being consistent with the customary international law of state responsibility. Where a state refuses to adhere to its obligations to prevent such damage, the application is justified in the absence of any treaty prohibitions against such application. In *Teck Cominco*, it entails the extraterritorial application of environmental legislation to address a harm that should have been avoided, while, in Devils Lake, it involves a failure to apply domestic legislation including requirements for environmental assessment in order to pre-empt any transboundary harm. *Teck Cominco* represents the residual response by a state to what can be seen as the ineffectiveness of international rules to prevent transboundary environmental pollution. With Devils Lake, the rules of state responsibility are intertwined in a complicated web of federal and transfrontier politics, which weakens the rules in the face of perceived crisis situations. However, the notoriety of these disputes does not discount the practice of state

---

[235] Boundary Waters Treaty, *supra* note 6, Article X. The brief also cites an obligation on either party to make a unilateral reference to the IJC under Article IX. *Submission to the Commission for Environmental Cooperation*, 24 March 2006, <http://www.sierralegal.org/reports/devilslake_cec_submission_mar06.pdf>.

[236] See J. Brunnée, *American Society of International Law 100th Anniversary Conference Proceedings* (2006).

[237] In the *Flathead* report, *supra* note 197 at 9, the source of the environmental pollution to US fisheries was not attributed to its exposure to the polluting itself but to the initial damage to the fish habitat inside Canadian territory.

responsibility that has imbued transfrontier relations between Canada and the United States. With every dispute, there are new challenges testing the bounds of where, and to what extent, the rules can be applied and ultimately enforced. Overall, respect for state responsibility will be the recurrent theme, providing the architecture to peacefully resolve natural resource conflicts that are expected to continue apace in the twenty-first century.

As transboundary environmental disputes are not expected to wane in number or importance, one can expect reinvigorated efforts, or at least legal advocacy to this effect, to give meaningful application to the rules of state responsibility. Alternatively, and perhaps in response to the rules of state responsibility and the need to find diplomatic solutions based on transboundary cooperative institutional mechanisms and respect for territorial sovereignty, one may observe similar attempts to apply domestic environmental law extraterritorially for incidents of transboundary environmental pollution. One compromise might be an approach that allows the courts of the pollution source state to entertain private cross-boundary claims and, therefore, provide a vehicle to enforce obligations under the rules of state responsibility. A parallel opportunity exists for claims of water diversion under the Canadian implementing legislation of the Boundary Waters Treaty,[238] which allows US plaintiffs to bring actions in Canada where the plaintiff has suffered injury that has taken place in the United States from a Canadian source.[239] This would put into effect the "place of damage rule," which can ultimately address the imbalances of environmental enforcement and provide access to justice for victims of unwarranted environmental harm.[240] Applying this approach to incidents of transboundary pollution would circumvent the jurisdictional question while giving effect to the rules of state responsibility in domestic courts.

Ultimately, newer understanding of how the rules of state responsibility apply to transboundary environmental disputes may emerge in international law jurisprudence. One opportunity could arise in the ICJ, which currently has a transboundary waterway dispute on its docket concerning the construction of pulp mills in Uruguay that allegedly impact the Rio Plata, which abuts Argentina.[241] In

---

238 International Boundary Waters Treaty Act, R.S., c I-20, s. 1.

239 Such claims are limited to claims of interference with the transboundary river rather than pollution pursuant to Article II of the treaty.

240 See ILA, *supra* note 162.

241 See *Pulp Mills, supra* note 76.

addition to alleged violations of a bilateral treaty between Uruguay and Argentina, the claim invokes violations of international law requiring obligations to take necessary measures to preserve the environment and prevent pollution, an obligation to undertake an environmental impact study, and an obligation to cooperate regarding the prevention of pollution and the protection of biodiversity and fisheries.[242] One can hope that this potentially seminal ruling by an authoritative source of international law creates an invaluable opportunity for the advancement of the law of state responsibility and, therefore, the solidification of the legal architecture underpinning transboundary environmental issues.

EPILOGUE

In June 2006, the EPA and Teck Cominco announced they had reached an agreement. The company would pay for an investigation into the reservoir's contamination and fund the clean-up process. The EPA agreed to drop the order, ending the company's concerns over the attempt to apply US laws extraterritorially. This article was completed on the eve of this agreement and therefore does not address the terms of the agreement. In addition, on 3 July 2006, the US Court of Appeals dismissed the *Teck Cominco* appeal of the application challenging the jurisdiction to apply the CERCLA order.[243] The court did not address the extraterritoriality question since the suit was seen as involving exclusively the domestic application of CERCLA. According to the ruling, the release of the hazardous substances took place within the United States (that is, the leaching of hazardous substances from the slag at the site).[244]

Sommaire

Différends environnementaux transfrontières dans la zone limitrophe canada–américaine: les règles de la responsabilité des États demeurent-elles efficaces?

[242] The pleadings are available at <http://www.icj-cij.org/icjwww/idocket/iau/iauframe.htm>.

[243] *Pakootas v. Teck Cominco Metals, Ltd.*, No. 05-35153, D.C. No. CV-04-00256-AAM, (U.S. Court of Appeals-Ninth Circuit).

[244] This was distinguished from the discharge of the waste from the smelter into the Columbia River in Canada and the discharge or escape of the slag from Canada when the Columbia River enters the United States.

Les différends récents opposant le Canada et les États-Unis invitent à réflé-chir à l'efficacité des règles sur la responsabilité des États relativement aux dommages environnementaux transfrontières. Issue du principe de la "res-ponsabilité sans faute," l'obligation de prévenir les dommages transfrontières fait partie intégrale du droit international de l'environnement. L'obligation est énoncée dans un bon nombre de traités internationaux qui reflètent la pratique étatique. Elle constitue aussi un des fondements de la coopération internationale en matière des questions environnementales transfrontières et mondiales. Cet article examine l'application des règles sur la responsabi-lité des États relativement aux dommages environnementaux transfrontières par deux États qui partagent des frontières contiguës sur une longue dis-tance et une tradition de rapports amicaux. L'étude de ces différends récents démontre les limites de plus en plus flagrantes de ces règles. Leur portée s'atténue étant donné les démarches entreprises afin d'outrepasser les règles et l'exercice de compétences extraterritoriales. Ces phénomènes font ressortir en outre la difficulté à appliquer des principes flous du droit international dans des situations concrètes où les intérêts en jeu dépassent les seuls intérêts des États en cause.

Summary

Transboundary Environmental Disputes along the Canada–US Frontier: Revisiting the Efficacy of Applying the Rules of State Responsibility

The efficacy of the rules of state responsibility for transboundary environ-mental harm can be questioned in light of recent disputes between Canada and the United States. Stemming from the "no-harm" principle, the obliga-tion to prevent transboundary damage represents an integral part of inter-national environmental law. It is reflected in a wide body of international treaties, mirroring state practice. It also forms the basis for international cooperation on transboundary and global environmental issues. This arti-cle examines how the rules of state responsibility regarding transboundary environmental damage are applied by two states that share a long contigu-ous border and a legacy of amicable relations. Upon examination, the limits of such rules are increasingly becoming evident in light of some recent dis-putes. Attempts to overlook the rules of state responsibility, paralleled with the exercise of extraterritorial jurisdiction, have undermined the status of the rules of state responsibility. Moreover, these phenomena highlight the difficulty of applying loosely defined international legal principles to practi-cal situations where vested interests beyond those of the states involved are at play.

Notes and Comments /
Notes et commentaires

—

A Canadian Perspective on the Continued Non-Ratification of the Convention on the Law of the Sea by the United States

INTRODUCTION

The road for the United States towards ratification[1] of the 1982 United Nations Convention of the Law of the Sea (LOS Convention)[2] has been long and winding. An initial promoter of, and active participant in, the third United Nations Conference on the Law of the Sea (UNCLOS III), the US government (Reagan administration), during the very last stages of the negotiations, announced that it would not support the convention[3] and, during the mid-1980s, worked to undermine it. The principal stumbling block for the United States was the deep seabed mining regime of the LOS Convention (Part XI), which the United States saw as being deeply flawed and unworkable.[4] The US view that Part XI was

---

An earlier version of this comment was presented at the International Workshop on the United States and the United Nations Convention on the Law of the Sea, which was held 2 December 2005 in Taipei, sponsored by the Institute of European and American Studies, Academia Sinica, Taipei.

1 As a technical matter, the issue is one of accession rather than ratification since the United States is not a signatory of the 1982 United Nations Convention on the Law of the Sea, 1833 U.N.T.S. 397 [LOS Convention]. Nevertheless, throughout this comment, ratification and accession will be used interchangeably.

2 LOS Convention, *supra* note 1.

3 For a detailed study, see J.B. Morell, *The Law of the Sea: An Historical Analysis of the 1982 Treaty and Its Rejection by the United States* (London: McFarland and Company, 1992).

4 For a detailed study of the US concerns regarding the deep seabed mining regime of the LOS Convention, see M.G. Schmidt, *Common Heritage or Common Burden? The United States Position on the Development of a Regime for Deep Sea-Bed Mining in the Law of the Sea Convention* (Oxford: Clarendon Press, 1989). See more concisely, Morell, *supra* note 3 at 96–189.

problematic came to be shared by most industrialized states, such that through the 1980s and the early 1990s industrialized states opted to delay becoming parties to the LOS Convention.

As the magic number of sixty state parties for entry into force of the LOS Convention crept into view, the secretary-general of the United Nations convened meetings to try and find a means to accommodate the concerns of the states respecting Part XI. This accommodation was accomplished with the 1994 Agreement Relating to the Implementation of Part XI of the United Nations Convention on the Law of the Sea.[5] Within months, most industrialized states became party to the LOS Convention, and the Clinton administration signalled the United States's contentment with the convention and sent the LOS Convention to the US Senate for advice and consent.[6]

The LOS Convention languished in the Senate until 2003 when it finally became the subject of consideration by the Senate Foreign Relations Committee, as well as a number of other Senate committees.[7] In February 2004, the Senate Foreign Relations Committee voted unanimously to recommend US accession to the LOS Convention and reported this decision to the full Senate for consideration.[8] Attached to the advice and consent resolution before the Senate were twenty-four "declarations and understandings" proposed to be attached by the United States to its instrument of accession.[9]

---

[5] Agreement Relating to the Implementation of Part XI of the United Nations Convention on the Law of the Sea, (1994), 33 I.L.M. 1309.

[6] "Message from the President of the United States Transmitting United Nations Convention on the Law of the Sea," with Annexes, Montego Bay, 10 December 1982 (the convention); and the Agreement Relating to the Implementation of Part XI of the United Nations Convention on the Law of the Sea of 10 December 1982, (1994), 39 U.S.T., 103d Congress, 2d Session IV (adopted at New York, 28 July 1994 (the agreement) and signed by the United States, subject to ratification, on 29 July 1994).

[7] See generally J.A. Duff, "A Note on the United States and the Law of the Sea: Looking Back and Moving Forward" (2004) 35 Ocean Development & Int'l L. 195.

[8] Senate Executive Report 108–10, *Part VII – Text of Resolution of Advice and Consent to Ratification*, 2004, S. Cong. Rec. S2712-S2716 (11 March 2004) at 16–21. See also Duff, *supra* note 7 at 214–19.

[9] Senate Executive Report 108–10, *supra* note 8. See also Duff, *supra* note 7 at 206–7 and 214–19. LOS Convention, *supra* note 1, Article 310 allows states when signing, ratifying, or acceding to the convention to make statements or declarations "provided that such declarations or statements do not purport to exclude

Many of these "declarations and understandings" provide an insight into how the United States views or interprets provisions of the LOS Convention.[10] However, the US Senate did not make a decision on US accession to the LOS Convention prior to the expiration of the 108th Congress at the end of 2004.[11] The consequence of this inaction is that before the US Senate can now consider the LOS Convention the Senate Foreign Relations Committee must reconsider the accession issue and make a new recommendation to the full US Senate. In short, the Senate process regarding the LOS Convention has to start again from the beginning.[12] Despite support for accession to the LOS Convention from the Bush administration, which was expressed at the beginning of the 109th Congress,[13] the Senate Foreign Relations Committee did not have the LOS Convention on its agenda, and until it reconsiders the convention there is no possibility of US accession to the LOS Convention.

The Canadian perspective on this long and winding road of the United States's ratification of the LOS Convention involves an equal measure of (1) frustration/disappointment; (2) appreciation/understanding; and (3) ambivalence. Colouring Canada's perspective is its own twenty-one year trek towards ratification, which only ended in late 2003. Canada's two-decade delay in ratifying the LOS Convention ensures its avoidance of using over-heated rhetoric to describe the continuing failure of the United States to become a party to the "constitution of the oceans." This unwillingness to scold the United States not only is a reaction to Canada's own delayed ratification but also is reinforced by the reality that Canada was

---

or modify the legal effect of the provisions of this Convention in their application to that State."

10 For a review of certain of the US Senate "Declarations and Undertakings," see Y.-H. Song, "Declarations and Statements with Respect to the 1982 UNCLOS: Potential Legal Disputes between the United States and China after U.S. Accession to the Convention" (2005) 36 Ocean Development & Int'l L. 261.

11 J.A. Duff, "UNCLOS and the United States," part of "From the Desk of the Editor-in-Chief" (2005) 36 Ocean Development & Int'l L. 317.

12 Duff, *supra* note 11 at 317–18.

13 During the January 2005 Senate Confirmation Hearings, Secretary of State Condoleeza Rice indicated that the president would like to see the LOS Convention "passed as soon as possible." See <www.lugar.senate.gov/sfrc/rice_endorsement.html> (20 January 2006); and noted in Duff, *supra* note 11 at 318. Rice also urged the Senate Foreign Relations to revisit the convention and report favourably on accession. See <www.lugar.senate.gov/sfrc/rice_qfa.html> (20 January 2006); and noted in Duff, *supra* note 11 at 318.

one of the big "winners" from the LOS Convention[14] and that for a number of years Canada was an advocate for states to ratify the convention. Nevertheless, Canada (and, in 2004, Denmark) became a party to the LOS Convention, leaving the United States as the only industrialized state outside the convention.

FRUSTRATION/DISAPPOINTMENT

In the early 1980s, Canada was frustrated with the hostility of the United States to the LOS Convention. The origin of the frustration was the 1982 decision by the Reagan administration not to support the LOS Convention. Canada had invested heavily in the negotiation of the LOS Convention, had been on the opposite side from the United States on many issues[15] and on the same side on other issues, and generally perceived the convention as being very much in its interests.[16] As one commentator has well summarized,

[i]n sharp contrast to the Reagan administration's attempt to achieve security *from* international regulation, Canada's large stake in the Law of the Sea lay precisely in achieving security *via* the reinforcement of international authority.[17]

Beyond the specifics of the LOS Convention, there was also the perception of the United States rejecting multilateralism and "one of the greatest accomplishments of the United Nations."[18]

While the US decision not to support the convention was unrelated to any specific US–Canadian matter, the decision was characterized by one commentator as a "direct menace to Canada."[19] Although the wording on the 1982 official record of the statement

---

14 For an overview of Canada and the LOS Convention, see R. Hage, "Canada and the Law of the Sea" (1984) 8 Marine Policy 2; and T.L. McDorman, "Will Canada Ratify the Law of the Sea Convention?" (1988) 25 San Diego L. Rev. 535.

15 D.M. Johnston, *Canada and the New International Law of the Sea* (Toronto: University of Toronto Press, 1985) at 74, notes: "Canada and U.S. negotiators clashed frequently, and sometimes bitterly, over some ... issues."

16 See Hage, *supra* note 14; and A.J. MacEachen, Foreign Minister of Canada, "Statement by Canada," 6 December 1982, in UNCLOS III, *Official Records*, vol. 17 (New York: United Nations, 1984) at 14–16.

17 S. Clarkson, *Canada and the Reagan Challenge: Crisis and Adjustment, 1981-1985* (Toronto: James Lorimer and Company, 1985) at 216 [emphasis in original].

18 MacEachen, *supra* note 16 at 16.

19 Clarkson, *supra* note 17 at 216.

by then foreign minister of Canada Allan J. MacEachen is carefully measured,[20] the Canadian newspaper headlines noted that the speech urged the United States to reverse its position of non-support of the LOS Convention.[21]

The US rejection of the LOS Convention was seen in Canada as being tied to the bilateral ocean issues of the day. There is a long multi-century history of marine living resources and maritime boundary disputes between the United States and, first, the United Kingdom, then, the United Kingdom on behalf of Canada, and, finally, Canada,[22] which has also involved peaceful resolution of bilateral disputes through numerous bilateral agreements and adjudication.[23] The early 1980s was a period when there existed a number of intense bilateral ocean issues: renegotiation of the out-dated 1930 Pacific salmon treaty;[24] the failed 1979 East Coast

20 MacEachen, *supra* note 16.

21 "Canada Calls for American Reversal at Law of the Sea," *Halifax Mail-Star*, 7 December 1982, at 2; and "Sign Sea Pact, MacEachen Urges U.S.," *Globe and Mail*, 7 December 1982, at 17. See also J.A. Beesley, "International Political Context of the LOS Negotiations," in L. Juda, ed., *The United States without the Law of the Sea Treaty: Opportunities and Costs* (Wakefield, RI: Times Press, 1983), 11. The author was the former ambassador of Canada to UNCLOS.

22 The evolution of Canada as an independent state is complicated. Prior to 1867, there were a collection of British colonies under the United Kingdom. In 1867, a number of these colonies combined to form Canada, but the United Kingdom retained the authority to conduct foreign affairs on behalf of Canada. Precisely when, between 1919 and 1931, Canada "disconnected" from the United Kingdom is uncertain, but, by 1931, it was a legal certainty that Canada was an independent state on the world stage.

23 For example, the 1846 Treaty Establishing the Boundary in the Territory on the Northwest Coast of America Lying Westward of the Rocky Mountains (Oregon Treaty), reprinted in C. Parry, ed., *Consolidated Treaty Series*, vol. 100 (Dobbs Ferry, NY: Oceana Publications, 1969), 39, created the maritime boundary between Vancouver Island and the state of Washington. A disagreement about the interpretation of one part of the Oregon Treaty regarding the maritime boundary was resolved through an arbitration with the Emperor of Germany siding with the United States. See the 1872 *Award of the Emperor of Germany under the XXXIVth Article of the Treaty of May 8, 1871 Giving the Islands of San Juan to the United States*, reprinted in J.H. Haswell, ed., *United States Treaties and Conventions, 1776-1889* (Washington, DC: US Government Printing Office, 1889), 494.

24 Commencing in 1971, Canada and the United States began negotiation of a replacement treaty for the 1930 Convention for the Protection, Preservation and Extension of the Sockeye Salmon Fishery in the Fraser River System, 8 U.S.T. 1058. An agreement was reached in 1982, but, due to opposition from Alaska, the agreement was never considered by the US Senate. See M. Shepard and

fisheries agreement,[25] which was tied to the Gulf of Maine maritime boundary dispute;[26] and the movement of oil by tankers into the United States through Canadian waters.[27]

Canada's frustration with, and even hostility towards, the US rejection of the LOS Convention dissipated quickly however. First, the two high profile bilateral disputes were calmed. In 1985, Canada and the United States completed the Treaty Concerning Pacific Salmon, with annexes (I to IV) and a memorandum of understanding.[28] And, in 1984, the International Court of Justice muted the Gulf of Maine fishing dispute by establishing a maritime boundary between Canada and the United States in the area.[29] Second, it became clear that the central concern of the United States with the LOS Convention, the alleged unworkability of the deep seabed mining regime (Part XI), was also of concern to other industrialized states including Canada. Germany and the United Kingdom, while not rejecting the LOS Convention, had declined to sign the convention primarily because of concerns over deep seabed mining. Many industrial states that did sign the LOS Convention "made it clear ... that their ratification ... would be subject

---

A.W. Argue, *The 1985 Pacific Salmon Treaty: Sharing Conservation Burdens and Benefits* (Vancouver: UBC Press, 2005) at 53–76; and T.C. Jensen, "The United States-Canada Pacific Salmon Interception Treaty: An Historical and Legal Overview" (1986) 16 Envtl. L. 363 at 380–96, in particular at 395, where Canada was described as being "literally outraged" by the Senate actions on the 1982 Pacific salmon agreement.

25 See D.L. VanderZwaag, *The Fish Feud: The U.S. and Canadian Boundary Dispute* (Lexington, MA: Lexington Books, 1983) at 1–35 and 89–112. Like the 1982 Pacific salmon agreement, the 1979 east coast fisheries agreement was withdrawn from the consideration of the US Senate because of opposition from certain US fishing interests.

26 See generally D.M. Johnston, *The Theory and History of Ocean Boundary-Making* (Montreal: McGill-Queen's University Press, 1988) at 178–81.

27 The west coast issue involved tanker traffic through the Strait of Juan de Fuca between Vancouver Island and Washington State. On the east coast, the issue involved a possible oil refinery in northern Maine and passage through Canada's Head Harbour Passage. See J.E. Carroll, *Environmental Diplomacy: An Examination and a Prospective of Canada-U.S. Transboundary Environmental Relations* (Ann Arbour: University of Michigan Press, 1983) at 62–79.

28 Treaty Concerning Pacific Salmon, 99 Stat. 7, Can. T.S. 1985 No. 7 [Pacific Salmon Treaty]. See generally Shepard and Argue, *supra* note 24.

29 *Gulf of Maine Case (Canada and the United States)*, [1984] I.C.J. Rep. 246 [*Gulf of Maine*].

to improvements to the Part XI regime."[30] In the mid-1980s, while being careful not to directly undermine or act inconsistently with the UNCLOS deep seabed mining regime, several industrialized states entered into a series of controversial agreements regarding deep seabed mining, which were indicative of their concerns with the UNCLOS regime.[31] Canada participated in the last of the three agreements because of the involvement of Inco and Noranda in deep seabed mining corporate consortia.[32] Canada's engagement in the negotiation of the deep seabed mining regime at UNCLOS III was "unique,"[33] as was its position regarding deep seabed mining in the post-UNCLOS period:

Canada's position at the Preparatory Commission[34] and in relation to sea-bed mining in general is unique and often difficult. Like other industrialized states, Canada recognizes that only a regime that takes account of changes in economic circumstances will produce an economically viable system that will benefit the international community. At the same time, as a major land-producer, Canada does not want a system that would unduly disrupt the market. Finally, as a signatory with reservations and a

30 P. Kirsch and D. Fraser, "The Law of the Sea Preparatory Commission after Six Years: Review and Prospects" (1988) 26 Can. Y.B. Int'l L. 119 at 122.

31 The 1982 Agreement Concerning Interim Arrangements Relating to Polymetallic Nodules of the Deep Sea Bed, (1982) 21 I.L.M. 950 (France, Germany, the United Kingdom, and the United States); the 1984 Provisional Understanding Regarding Deep Seabed Matters, (1984), 23 I.L.M. 1365 (Belgium, France, Germany, Italy, Japan, the Netherlands, the United Kingdom, and the United States); and the 1987 Agreement on the Resolution of Practical Problems with Respect to Deep Seabed Mining Areas, including an Exchange of Notes between the United States and Other States on This Matter, (1987), 26 I.L.M. 1502 (Canada, Belgium, Italy, Netherlands, and the Soviet Union). See generally R.R. Churchill and A.V. Lowe, *The Law of the Sea*, 3rd edition (Manchester: Manchester University Press, 1999) at 232–34.

32 See "Memorandum from Foreign Affairs," 6 August 1987, excerpted in part in (1988) 26 Can. Y.B. Int'l L. 320.

33 See E. Riddell-Dixon, *Canada and the International Seabed* (Montreal: McGill-Queen's University Press, 1989) at 3–4 and more generally on Canada's role in the negotiation of the deep seabed regime of the LOS Convention. See also Johnston, *supra* note 15 at 13–17; and Hage, *supra* note 14 at 9–12. Hage comments: "In perhaps no other part of the law of the sea negotiations was the Canadian position as controversial and misunderstood as it was with regard to seabed mining" (at 9).

34 The Preparatory Commission was created by Resolution I of UNCLOS to prepare the technical rules for the Part XI deep seabed mining regime. See generally Kirsch and Fraser, *supra* note 30.

major beneficiary of the positive development the convention has made in international law, Canada does not want to endanger the integrity of the Convention.[35]

As one author notes, Canada considered the LOS Convention's deep seabed mining regime "unacceptable" in its original form and, like most other industrialized states, adopted a wait-and-see attitude regarding change.[36] The consequence of this position was that Canada was in no hurry to become a party to the LOS Convention. Finally, Canada was comforted by the fact that the emanations from the United States led Canada to believe that the United States had found much of the LOS Convention, with the exception of those provisions relating to deep seabed mining (Part XI), either part of customary international law or evidence of customary international law.[37]

Following the "fix" of Part XI of the LOS Convention through the 1994 agreement, most industrialized states became a party to the "revised" LOS Convention, and the Clinton administration signalled US contentment by endorsing the LOS Convention and sending it to the US Senate. Canada was in no position to be frustrated with the United States since, despite having undertaken a review of its position on ratification in the mid-1990s, Canada remained undecided.

While the initial cause of Canada's delay in ratification of the LOS Convention had been removed, a new high-profile issue had emerged in the 1990s to hinder Canada's ratification of the convention. This issue concerned alleged uncontrolled foreign fishing outside the 200-nautical-mile zone along Canada's east coast, which was made politically acute in Canada by the 1992 moratorium on northern cod harvesting in Canada's Atlantic coast waters.[38] Ratification of the LOS Convention was not politically possible without a "fix" of this issue. The perceived "fix" came with the conclusion of the 1995 Agreement for the Implementation of the

---

35 "Memorandum from Foreign Affairs," 7 November 1989, excerpted in part in (1990) 28 Can. Y.B. Int'l L. 486. For a more detailed articulation of many of these same points, see Kirsch and Fraser, *supra* note 30 at 149–50.

36 Riddell-Dixon, *supra* note 33 at 180.

37 See the exchange between J.A. Beesley and B. Hoyle, deputy director, Office of Ocean Law and Policy, U.S. State Department, in Juda, *supra* note 21 at 139–43.

38 See G.D. Taylor, "The Collapse of the Northern Cod Fishery: A Historical Perspective" (1995) 18 Dalhousie L.J. 13; and A.T. Charles, "The Atlantic Canadian Groundfishery: Roots of a Collapse" (1995) 18 Dalhousie L.J. 65.

Provisions of the United Nations Convention on the Law of the Sea Relating to the Conservation and Management of Straddling Fish Stocks and Highly Migratory Fish Stocks (Fish Stocks Agreement),[39] in the negotiation of which Canada had invested heavily.[40] When it became clear that the European Union and its member states, which were the major players of concern to Canada respecting fishing activities outside the Atlantic 200-nautical-mile zone, were to become party to the Fish Stocks Agreement, Canada proceeded with ratification of the LOS Convention.[41]

Canada's "delayed" ratification and the evolution of events took the passion out of Canada's initial frustration with the US position on the LOS Convention. What remained, given Canada's new status as a party to the convention, was a disappointment that the United States had not yet joined what Canada, and other states, saw as an important foundational treaty of the international legal and political system. Canada had a commitment to multilateralism and to the United Nations, in particular,[42] as well as to the development of international legal structures. *Canada's International Policy Statement* of 2005 trumpets Canada's support for multilateralism:

[Canada must] ... reiterate the case for multilateral institutions in contemporary global society. A key plank in ... [this] ... case derives from Canadian values: a rule-based and more predictable international system produces better results than one that is dominated by independent and uncoordinated action.[43]

---

39 Agreement for the Implementation of the Provisions of the United Nations Convention on the Law of the Sea Relating to the Conservation and Management of Straddling Fish Stocks and Highly Migratory Fish Stocks, (1995) 34 I.L.M. 1542 [Fish Stocks Agreement].

40 See P. Fauteux, "The Canadian Legal Initiative on High Seas Fishing" (1993) Y.B. Int'l Envtl. L. 51; and R. Rayfuse et al. "Australia and Canada in Regional Fisheries Organizations: Implementing the United Nations Fish Stocks Agreement" (2003) 6 Dalhousie L.J. 47.

41 T.L. McDorman, "Canada Ratifies the 1982 United Nations Convention on the Law of the Sea: At Last" (2004) 35 Ocean Development & Int'l L. 103 at 104.

42 Regarding Canada and the United Nations, see J. Welsh, *Home in the World: Canada's Global Vision for the Twenty-First Century* (Toronto: Harper Collins, 2004) at 208–15; and P. Heinbecker, "The UN in the Twenty-First Century," in D. Carment, F. Osler Hampson; and N. Hillmer, eds., *Setting Priorities Straight: Canada among Nations 2004* (Montreal: McGill-Queen's University Press, 2005) at 255–58.

43 Canada, *Canada's International Policy Statement: A Role of Pride and Influence in the World – Overview* (Ottawa: Government of Canada, 2005) at 27.

More directly, Canada saw itself as a builder of international institutions and a supporter of international rules both as a means for attaining peace and security at the multilateral level and as a means of interacting with the United States.

While the US position on the LOS Convention can be isolated from other multilateral issues and while there is a difference between the stance of the US presidency and the Senate, there is a perceived connection between the LOS Convention and the US decisions not to support multilateral treaties[44] that are strongly endorsed by Canada, such as the Convention on the Prohibition of the Use, Stockpiling, Production and Transfer of Anti-Personnel Mines and on Their Destruction[45] and the Rome Statute on the International Criminal Court.[46] In addition, there is non-American support for the Kyoto Protocol,[47] the Convention on Biological Diversity (CBD),[48] the Comprehensive Nuclear Test Ban Treaty,[49] and the

[44] The linkage among all of the treaties noted below is made in J.F. Murphy, *The United States and the Rule of Law in International Affairs* (Cambridge: Cambridge University Press, 2004) at 367.

[45] Convention on the Prohibition of the Use, Stockpiling, Production and Transfer of Anti-Personnel Mines and on Their Destruction, (1997), 36 I.L.M. 1507 [Landmines Convention]. The United States has not joined the Landmines Convention "because its terms would have required us to give up a needed military capability." See "New United States Policy on Landmines: Reducing Humanitarian Risk and Saving Lives of United States Soldiers," 27 February 2004, <www.state.gov/t/pm/rls/fs/30044.htm> (20 January 2006). See also Murphy, *supra* note 44 at 218–19.

[46] Rome Statute on the International Criminal Court, (1998) 37 I.L.M. 999. Regarding the United States and the International Criminal Court (ICC), see <www.state.gov/t/pm/rls/fs/2002/23426.htm> (20 January 2006). See Murphy, *supra* note 44 at 317–18, where he notes: "It is clear ... that a major reason for the US opposition is its concern that its military personnel and government officials will be subject to politically motivated prosecutions." There has also been strong opposition to the ICC expressed by the US Congress.

[47] Kyoto Protocol to the United Nations Framework Convention on Climate Change, (1998) 37 I.L.M. 22. In an unusual resolution, the US Senate in 1997 by a vote of ninety-five to zero indicated its opposition to the Kyoto Protocol prior to its finalization. Nevertheless, the United States signed the Kyoto Protocol in 1998. The Kyoto Protocol has not been sent to the Senate for consideration. See Murphy, *supra* note 44 at 338–41.

[48] Convention on Biological Diversity, 1760 U.N.T.S. 79 [CBD]. The United States is a signatory to the convention. The US presidency sent the convention to the US Senate. The Senate has taken no action regarding the CBD since 1994. See also Murphy, *supra* note 44 at 341–44.

[49] Comprehensive Nuclear Test Ban Treaty, (1996) 35 I.L.M. 1439. The United States signed the treaty, but, by a vote of fifty-one to forty-eight, the US Senate rejected the treaty. See Murphy, *supra* note 44 at 208–9.

perceived shunning of the United Nations in regard to Iraq.[50] While the United States has the international legal right to accept or not to accept these conventions, the policy choices can be seen as being part of a pattern that is at odds with Canada's support for multilateralism.

APPRECIATION/UNDERSTANDING

As already noted, Canada's trek to ratification of the LOS Convention took twenty-one years for a treaty that was perceived as being a major accomplishment of Canadian diplomacy. In the face of this delay, it is not surprising that Canada has a degree of appreciation for the problems and difficulties that have arisen within the United States with respect to ratification of the LOS Convention, particularly since the initial US position was ideologically opposed to the convention.

As is well known, the US domestic process in regard to treaty ratification requires the advice and consent of the US Senate. Canada is as aware as any state of the peculiarities of the internal politics that play themselves out in US Senate discussions and decisions on treaties.[51] On paper, there is no equivalent process in Canada — in fact, there is no mandated process at all. Under Canadian constitutional law and practice, the executive (the cabinet of the federal government in Ottawa) has the exclusive decision-making authority over ratification of an international treaty.[52] There is no legal requirement for approval from, or discussion within, the House of Commons or for approval from, or discussion with, the provinces, territories, or the Canadian citizenry.[53] It is, however, the Canadian practice not to ratify an international treaty that requires legislative implementation until the necessary legislation is enacted. As a consequence, indirectly, the ratification of international treaties is usually brought before the House of Commons. This formal practice was followed in the case of the LOS Convention. As it was determined that Canada would be in compliance with its obligations under the LOS Convention without the need of new

50 Canada elected not to participate with the United States and United Kingdom respecting Iraq. See generally Welsh, *supra* note 42 at 38–47.

51 See discussion in notes 24–25 and 47–49 in this article.

52 G. Van Ert, *Using International Law in Canadian Courts* (The Hague: Kluwer Law International, 2002) at 66–74.

53 See "Canada Ratification Practice, April 2002 Memorandum from the Legal Bureau," reprinted in (2002) 40 Can. Y.B. Int'l L. 490.

legislation or legislative changes, it was merely a brief statement made by the prime minister informing the House of Commons that Canada would be ratifying the LOS Convention:

I am pleased to inform ... the House that this afternoon the Minister of Foreign Affairs will sign Canada's instrument of ratification for the UN convention on the law of the sea. The instrument will be deposited with the secretary general of the United Nation soon after.

This is great news for all Canadians. By ratifying, Canada gains a voice in an international institution set up by the convention and will be able to advance our commitment to improving the conservation of fisheries on the high seas.[54]

Despite the ultimate authority of the Canadian federal government's cabinet on treaty ratification decisions, discussions with the provinces, territories, and relevant groups and individuals are undertaken, and, of course, there are inter-departmental consultations within the federal government. While less public than debates within the United States, discussions on treaty ratification often follow a somewhat similar course within Canada, the major difference being that the Canadian federal cabinet ultimately can impose its will in a manner that the US presidency cannot.

In 2003, both Canada and the United States commenced a re-evaluation of their non-party status of the LOS Convention. In the case of the United States, this was done primarily by the Senate Foreign Relations Committee. Within Canada, the Department of Foreign Affairs commenced a process of consultation and inter-departmental discussions. Both processes found that the proponents of ratification were essentially in the "same place" regarding the LOS Convention, despite the very different histories the two countries had with the convention. The "same place" was that, while Canada and the United States calculated their interest in the LOS Convention differently, the interests of both states were seen as having been largely attained irrespective of the ratification of the LOS Convention through developments in customary international law and state practice. Most visibly, the entitlement to exclusive national jurisdiction over resources within 200-nautical-mile exclusive economic zones (EEZs) had long been acquired and exercised by both Canada and the United States.[55] Both states exercised

---

[54] Canada, House of Commons, *Debates*, 6 November 2003 at 1455.

[55] Both Canada and the United States established 200-nautical-mile fishing zones in 1977. In the United States, this was done through the Fishery Conservation

exclusive authority over the mineral resources in the continental shelf beyond 200 nautical miles (where the physical shelf allowed for it)[56] and based their actions on customary international law.[57] However, the LOS Convention provides a framework for the attainment of certainty respecting the location of the outer limit of a state's shelf beyond 200 nautical miles.[58] Canada saw this certainty as an important benefit in becoming a party to the LOS Convention.[59] For Canada, a major issue was the support in the LOS Convention for Canadian laws allowing for special measures to be applied to vessels navigating in Canada's Arctic (Article 234),[60] although there did not appear to be any opposition to Canada's authority in this regard. For the United States, a major interest was

---

and Management Act (renamed the Magnuson Fishery Conservation and Management Act), 90 Stat. 331, L. 94-265. Canada established a 200-nautical-mile fishing zone on the east and west coast on 1 January 1977 through the Fishing Zones of Canada (Zones 4 and 5) Order, (1978) 18 Consolidated Regulations of Canada, Ch. 1548. For the Arctic, the 200-nautical-mile fishing zone came on 1 March 1977. Fishing Zones of Canada (Zone 6) Order, (1978) 18 Consolidated Regulations of Canada, Ch. 1549.

56 In 1945, the United States through the Truman Proclamation on the "Policy of the United States with Respect to the Natural Resources of the Subsoil and Sea Bed of the Continental Shelf" made known its claim regarding the continental shelf. This was followed in 1953 with the Outer Continental Shelf Lands Act, 67 Stat. 462, L. 83-212. See A.L. Hollick, *U.S. Foreign Policy and the Law of the Sea* (Princeton: Princeton University Press, 1981) at 19–22, 28–61, and 114–17. Canada made no sweeping continental shelf claim, although it did issue oil and gas permits in the 1960s for large tracts of offshore areas. See B.G. Buzan and D.W. Middlemiss, "Canadian Foreign Policy and the Exploitation of the Seabed," in B. Johnson and M.W. Zacher, eds., *Canadian Foreign Policy and the Law of the Sea* (Vancouver: UBC Press, 1977), 3 at 6 and 9. Only in 1970 did Canada legislate a definition of its continental shelf in section 3 of the Oil and Gas Production and Conservation Act, R.S.C. 1970 (1st. Supp.), c. O-4.

57 See *North Sea Continental Shelf Cases*, [1969] I.C.J. Rep. 3 at 23; and LOS Convention, *supra* note 1, Articles 76(1) and 77(1)-(3). See also T.L. McDorman, "The Role of the Commission on the Limits of the Continental Shelf: A Technical Body in a Political World" (2002) 17 Int'l J. Marine and Coastal L. 301 at 305.

58 LOS Convention, *supra* note 1, Article 76 and see discussion in notes 72–74. See generally United Nations, Division of Ocean Affairs and the Law of the Sea, Office of Legal Affairs, *The Law of the Sea: Definition of the Continental Shelf* (New York: United Nations, 1993) at 49; J. Cook and C.M. Carleton, eds., *Continental Shelf Limits: The Scientific and Legal Interface* (New York: Oxford University Press, 2000) at 363; and V. Prescott and C. Schofield, *The Maritime Political Boundaries of the World*, 2nd edition (Leiden: Martinus Nijhoff, 2005) at 183–214.

59 McDorman, *supra* note 41 at 106–7.

60 *Ibid* at 108.

freedom of navigation and, in particular, the transit right regime
with respect to international straits in the convention.[61] Both of these
interests were seen as having been satisfied by subsequent state practice pursuant to the LOS Convention, although it remains doubtful
whether the relevant provisions on transit passage in international
straits in the LOS Convention are part of customary international
law.[62] The acquisition of the most obvious benefits of the convention and the passage of time undermined any urgency for ratification and left promoters of ratification with only a few readily
identifiable tangible benefits that would flow from ratification.[63]

In announcing Canada's decision to ratify the LOS Convention
in 2003, the prime minister referred to it as "great news for all
Canadians" and that by ratifying "Canada gains a voice in international institution[s] set up by the convention."[64] Three institutions
are created by the LOS Convention:[65] the International Tribunal
for the Law of the Sea (ITLOS);[66] the Commission on the Limits
of the Continental Shelf (CLCS);[67] and the International Seabed

[61] G.V. Galdorisi and K.R. Vienna, *Beyond the Law of the Sea: New Directions for U.S.
Oceans Policy* (London: Praeger, 1997) at 27, refer to preserving navigation and
overflight freedoms against the creeping jurisdiction of coastal States as "the
paramount concern" of the United States at the beginning of the negotiations
of the LOS Convention. Note also Murphy, *supra* note 44 at 229–33.

[62] Churchill and Lowe, *supra* note 31 at 110-13, where they state: "[A] general
right of transit passage may not yet have become established in customary international law," although they allow that in particular international straits "a customary law right akin to transit passage does exist."

[63] Murphy, *supra* note 44 at 241 notes:

Perhaps the most salient argument made by those opposing ratification is that the United
States already enjoys the benefits the Convention would provide while avoiding the burdens being a party would entail. Specifically, the opponents argue, the United States already benefits from the navigational and overflight provisions of the Convention because
they have become part of the corpus of customary international law ... Similarly, the opponents contend, the United States currently benefits fully from the Convention's provisions
on coastal state's control over natural resources, since the declarations on its territorial sea,
contiguous zone, exclusive economic zone and continental shelf have gone unchallenged.

[64] See Canada, House of Commons, *supra* note 54.

[65] See generally D.R. Rothwell, "Building on the Strengths and Addressing the
Challenges: The Role of Law of the Sea Institutions" (2004) 35 Ocean Development & Int'l L. 131.

[66] LOS Convention, *supra* note 1, Annex VI on "Statute of the International Tribunal for the Law of the Sea."

[67] *Ibid.*, Annex II on "Commission on the Limits of the Continental Shelf."

Authority (ISA).[68] While participation in these institutions is more advantageous for national interests than non-participation, it is difficult to make the case for Canada or the United States that involvement in two of these three institutions is critical, with involvement in the third being more debatable. All three institutions have been functioning since shortly after the entry into force of the LOS Convention in 1994 without a noticeable impact on Canada or the United States. Regarding the ISA, little deep seabed mining activity is anticipated for decades and when such activity arises the existing work of the ISA is most likely to need to be revisited.[69] In regard to ITLOS, it is a dispute settlement body of fifteen elected judges for which, since it deals with a small number of cases,[70] it is difficult to assess if Canadian or American absence or presence would make a difference.[71] It is the CLCS, which deals with the application of the criteria in Article 76 of the LOS Convention for the determination by a state of its outer limit of the continental shelf where the physical shelf extends beyond 200 nautical miles, in which participation by Canada and the United States is arguably important.[72] As noted, both Canada and the United States have an interest since both states have physical continental shelves that extend beyond 200 nautical miles. However, the CLCS's role is only in relation to the determination of the outer limit of the continental shelf and does not affect in a direct way the exercise by Canada and the United States of exclusive jurisdiction over hydrocarbon resources in the shelf area beyond 200 nautical miles, which is based on customary international law.[73] Moreover, the CLCS's role respecting the outer limit is not as a court since the commission is without authority to dictate to a

---

[68] *Ibid.*, Articles 156–85 and also Annex IV on "Statute of the Enterprise."

[69] For a recent review of the history and operation of the International Seabed Authority (ISA), see C.L. Antrim, "Mineral Resources of Stateless Space: Lessons from the Deep Seabed" (2005) 59(1) J. Int'l Aff. 55.

[70] See the ITLOS website at <www.itlos.org> (20 January 2006). See also T.L. McDorman, "An Overview of International Fisheries Disputes and the International Tribunal for the Law of the Sea (ITLOS)" (2002) 40 Can. Y.B. Int'l L. 119.

[71] More generally on Canada and the US interests in the dispute settlement regime in the LOS Convention, see notes 109–12 in this article.

[72] See the material set out in note 58.

[73] See *North Sea Continental Shelf Cases, supra* note 57 and LOS Convention, *supra* note 1, Articles 76(1) and 77(1)-(3).

state the delineation of its continental shelf outer limit.[74] Nevertheless, the commission is part of the process that the LOS Convention provides for ascertaining with certainty the outer limit of a coastal state's shelf beyond 200 nautical miles. It is to be noted that the CLCS has decided to disregard a recent communication from the United States respecting technical issues raised by a state's information submitted to the commission because of the US status as a non-party to the LOS Convention.[75]

While not an institution directly contemplated by the LOS Convention, the state parties to the LOS Convention (SPLOS) have met annually since the entry into force of the convention.[76] The SPLOS has been slow to deal with matters that are not administrative (such as election of judges for ITLOS and of members for the CLCS), but some discussions have taken place over whether the annual meeting should be used for raising and discussing substantive matters.[77] If this suggestion gains wide acceptance, non-party status may inhibit the United States's engagement in key discussions among LOS Convention state parties.

While some other treaties, for example, the Fish Stocks Agreement,[78] mandate the convening of a review conference of state parties at a set time and can limit a state's participation in the review if it is a non-party, the LOS Convention does not mandate the convening of a review conference of state parties at a set time. The exception is in regard to the operation of Part XI on deep seabed mining, where a review conference is to be held fifteen years after commercial production under Part XI commences.[79] The LOS Convention does provide that, ten years after entry into force, state

---

[74] McDorman, *supra* note 57 at 305–24.

[75] See "Statement of the Chairman of the Commission on the Limits of the Continental Shelf on the Progress of Work of the Commission," Doc. CLCS/42 (14 September 2004) at para. 17. See also the letter from the United States to the Commission of 25 October 2004. Both of these documents are available at <www.un.org/Depts/los/clcs_new/clcs_home.htm> (20 January 2006).

[76] See the website of the United Nations, Division of Ocean Affairs and Law of the Sea, respecting the state parties of the LOS Convention at <www.un.org/Depts/los/meeting_states_parties/meeting_states_parties.htm> (20 January 2006).

[77] T. Treves, "The General Assembly and the Meeting of States Parties in the Implementation of the LOS Convention," in A.G. Oude Elferink, ed., *Stability and Change in the Law of the Sea: The Role of the LOS Convention* (Leiden: Martinus Nijhoff, 2005), 55 at 55–58, 62–65, and 68–74.

[78] Fish Stocks Agreement, *supra* note 39.

[79] LOS Convention, *supra* note 1, Article 155.

parties may propose amendments to the convention and request the convening of a conference of the parties to consider the proposed amendment.[80] There does not appear to be any appetite at present by any state to trigger this process.[81]

In addition to the inertia that arises because the ocean interests of Canada and the United States have not been adversely affected by non-membership in the LOS Convention, there being few readily identifiable substantive benefits to be gained from ratification and that, for the most part, participation in the LOS Convention institutions does not appear to be an imperative, there has been (and, in the case of the United States, continues to be) significant direct opposition to, or concerns about, the LOS Convention within both Canada and the United States. This opposition or concern was in regard to very different matters in each state. In the United States, the opposition to, or concern about, ratification of the LOS Convention was based on ideology; the history of the US opposition to the convention; and fears regarding internationalization.[82] In Canada, the opposition to, or concern about, ratification of the LOS Convention revolved primarily around fisheries and money, both of which directly engaged the province of Newfoundland and Labrador. The fisheries issue was that of continuing concern about foreign fishing beyond Canada's 200-nautical-mile zone adjacent to Newfoundland and Labrador[83] and the view that the LOS Convention did not adequately address the matter and/or might be an impediment on Canadian actions to deal with the problem.[84] The money issue concerned Article 82 of the LOS Convention and the sharing of revenues with developing states from hydrocarbon development on a state's continental shelf beyond 200 nautical miles, which, in Canada's case, is most likely to occur in the future adjacent to Newfoundland and Labrador.[85]

---

[80] *Ibid.*, Article 312.

[81] See generally D. Freestone and A.G. Oude Elferink, "Flexibility and Innovation in the Law of the Sea – Will the LOS Convention Amendment Procedures Ever Be Used?" in Oude Elferink, *supra* note 77 at 169–221.

[82] Duff, *supra* note 7 at 205–6. The detail of this opposition will not be discussed here. See, however, Doug Bandow, "Don't Resurrect the Law of the Sea Treaty," *Policy Analysis*, no. 552, 13 October 2005.

[83] See notes 38–40 and notes 98–103 in this article.

[84] McDorman, *supra* note 41 at 110.

[85] *Ibid.* at 106–8. Given the legal/political nature of Article 82 on revenue-sharing, it is asserted that this provision only creates an obligation on state parties to the LOS Convention and not on non-state parties. One should not under-estimate,

Canada's history regarding the ratification of the LOS Convention leads to a degree of appreciation of the United States's situation regarding ratification. Internal politics and concerns are difficult to overcome for a convention where there are few readily tangible benefits to be reaped by ratification. For Canada, the case in favour of the LOS Convention was based ultimately on certainty, foreign policy, and closure with the decision to ratify "seen as a necessary consequence and duty of being a responsible international citizen."[86] This situation may eventually also prevail in the United States.

AMBIVALENCE

The acceptance of large parts of the LOS Convention as customary international law and in practice, as noted earlier, contributes to a Canadian perspective of ambivalence regarding the United States and ratification of the LOS Convention. As the principal elements of the LOS Convention are in place, US non-membership is not seen as a significant concern for Canada since, on almost all ocean matters between the two states, they have been applying the contents of the LOS Convention. This situation is particularly true in the case of today's highest profile issue — maritime security. In the 2005 *Canadian International Policy Statement on Defence*, it is noted that "[i]t is clearly in our sovereign interest to continue doing our part in defending the continent with the United States."[87] In

---

however, the political importance of the revenue-sharing obligation. In 1980, Canada expressed concerns that the revenue-sharing formula (specifically the rate) "could make it uneconomic for Canada to explore and exploit its continental margin." "Statement of the Delegation of Canada," 2 April 1980, in UNCLOS III, *Official Records*, vol. 13 (New York: United Nations, 1982) at 102.

The internal Canadian issue is whether the responsibility for the revenues, should production outside 200 nautical miles take place (most likely adjacent to Newfoundland and Labrador), would be with the federal government or with the province of Newfoundland and Labrador. This issue arises since, although the Supreme Court of Canada has determined that the federal government has exclusive constitutional authority over the adjacent shelf area (*Re: the Continental Shelf Offshore Newfoundland*, [1984] 1 S.C.R. 86), through a 1985 Canada-Newfoundland Agreement (referred to as the Atlantic Accord) there is a complex joint and cooperative management and benefit-sharing structure for the hydrocarbon resources in the continental shelf adjacent to Newfoundland and Labrador.

86 McDorman, *supra* note 41 at 111.

87 Canada, *Canada's International Policy Statement: A Role of Pride and Influence in the World – Defence* (Ottawa: Government of Canada, 2005) at 21.

conjunction with the expanded responsibility of the US Navy and
Coast Guard to "protect" the sea approaches to the United States,
Canada has announced an enhancement of resources and a rede-
sign of internal command structures to deal with the sea approaches
to Canada.[88] Cooperation between the Canadian-American navies
and coast guard is accepted as being critical.[89] Beyond border waters, Canada is a participant in the Proliferation Security Initiative
(PSI), which was promoted by the United States in 2003 as a means
to curtail the international movement of weapons of mass destruction, their delivery systems, and related materials between "states
and non-state actors of proliferation concern."[90] Thus, Canada and
the United States are working together and have a similar understanding of the relevance and application of the LOS Convention,
which is unaffected by party status.

Canadian ambivalence to the United States and ratification of
the LOS Convention is further reinforced by the nature of the ocean
"issues" between Canada and the United States, none of which would
be directly affected by US ratification of the LOS Convention. The
present is a unique time in Canada-US relations as the bilateral
agenda is devoid of high profile ocean-related disputes. While most
Canada-US maritime boundaries remain unresolved,[91] since the

88 See Canada, *Securing an Open Society: Canada's National Security Policy* (Ottawa:
Government of Canada, 2004) at 37–9. See generally J.J. Sokolsky, "Guarding
the Continental Coasts: United States Maritime Homeland Security and Canada" (2005) 6(1) Institute for Research on Policy Matters 67.

89 *Securing an Open Society, supra* note 88 at 39:

Canada and the United States will work more closely to protect and defend our coasts and
our territorial waters. Given that we share responsibility for our contiguous waters, we will
work with the United States to pursue enhanced marine security cooperation, including
encouraging mutually high and compatible rules, standards and operations, among other
measures.

90 See the US Department of State website respecting the Proliferation Security
Initiative at <www.state.gov/t/np/c10390/htm> (20 January 2006); and the Canadian Department of Foreign Affairs website at <www.dfait-maeci.gc.ca/arms/
psioverview-en.asp> (20 January 2006). See generally M. Byers, "Policing the
High Seas: The Proliferation Security Initiative" (2004) 98 Am. J. Int'l L. 526.

91 Canada and the United States have overlapping offshore claims in the Beaufort
Sea (Alaska-Yukon); in and seaward of the Dixon Entrance (Alaska and British
Columbia); seaward of the Juan de Fuca Strait (Washington State and British
Columbia); and in two areas on the east coast, one around the disputed island
of Machais-Seal Island and the other seaward of the so-called Hague line (*Gulf of
Maine, supra* note 29). For an excellent overview, see D.H. Gray, "Canada's Unre-
solved Maritime Boundaries" (1994) 48 Geomatica 131.

1984 International Court of Justice's *Gulf of Maine Case (Canada and the United States)* established the ocean boundary in this region,[92] maritime boundaries have not been a significant irritant. The most recent high-profile Canada-US fisheries dispute was in the 1990s concerning Pacific salmon and the renegotiation of the expired allocation arrangements under the 1985 Pacific Salmon Treaty. The two states reached an agreement in 1999,[93] and the issue has largely disappeared, although it can be expected to reappear as the 1999 agreement expires in 2009. The long-running Canadian-American disagreement over whether the Northwest Passage is, or is not, a "strait used for international navigation"[94] has been largely dormant since the 1988 Canada–United States "agreement to disagree."[95] However, concerns over a possible increase in vessel traffic in the Canadian North as a result of global warming trends have placed this issue back on the radar.[96] Moreover, one of the US Senate's proposed "declarations and understandings" to be appended to an American instrument of accession to the LOS Convention notes the US position that "the term 'used for international navigation' includes all straits capable of being used for international

---

[92] *Gulf of Maine, supra* note 29.

[93] The 1999 agreement concerns salmon management and harvesting and replaces the expired Annex IV under the 1985 Pacific Salmon Treaty, *supra* note 28. Regarding the 1999 Annex IV, see the website of the Pacific Salmon Commission at <www.psc.org> (20 January 2006). See generally T.L. McDorman, "The 1999 Canada-United States Pacific Salmon Agreement: Resolved and Unresolved Issues" (2000) 15 J. Envtl. L. & Litigation 1.

[94] See generally E.B. Elliot-Meisel, *Arctic Diplomacy: Canada and the United States in the Northwest Passage* (New York: Peter Lang, 1998); F. Griffiths, ed., *Politics of the Northwest Passage* (Montreal: McGill-Queen's University Press, 1987); and D. Pharand, *Northwest Passage: Arctic Straits* (Dordrecht: Martinus Nijhoff, 1984).

[95] Agreement on Arctic Cooperation, 11 January 1988, (1989) 28 I.L.M. 141. Paragraph 3 provides: "The Government of the United States pledges that all navigation by US icebreakers within waters claimed by Canada to be internal will be undertaken with the consent of the Government of Canada." This is followed by Paragraph 4, which reads in part: "Nothing in this agreement of cooperation ... nor any practice thereunder affects the respective positions of the Governments of the United States and Canada on the Law of the Sea in this or other maritime areas."

[96] See F. Griffiths, "The Shipping News: Canada's Arctic Sovereignty Not on Thinning Ice" (2003) 58 Int'l J. 258; R. Huebert, "The Shipping News Part II: How Canada's Arctic Sovereignty Is on Thinning Ice" (2003) 58 Int'l J. 295; and F. Griffiths, "Pathetic Fallacy: That Canada's Arctic Sovereignty Is on Thinning Ice" (2004) 11 Can. Foreign Pol'y 1.

navigation,"[97] which is counter to the Canadian position that a geographic strait has to have been used for international navigation in order for it to become an international strait. The dispute regarding the international legal status of the Northwest Passage and the re-negotiation of an agreement for Pacific salmon, while debated by referencing interpretations of the LOS Convention, are not matters to which the convention provides a definitive answer, such that being or not being a party would be decisive.

Canada's highest profile ocean matter continues to be fish stocks that straddle Canada's 200-nautical-mile zone adjacent to Newfoundland and Labrador.[98] This issue has been a major focus of Canadian attention for decades[99] and one that has led Canada to the unprecedented action of seizing a Spanish fishing trawler on the high seas in March 1995.[100] It is the European Union and fishing "flag of convenience" states that are the primary targets of Canadian concern, not the United States, and the United States, like Canada, is a party to the relevant regional treaty (the Convention on Future Multilateral Cooperation in the Northwest Atlantic[101]) and multilateral treaty (Fish Stocks Agreement[102]). Unilateral assertions of exclusive authority over straddling fish stocks beyond 200 nautical miles that are mooted within Canada,[103] if undertaken, are, however,

97 US Senate, "Declarations and Undertakings," in Senate Executive Report 108-10, *supra* note 8 at section 3(3)(D).

98 This is clearly articulated in *Canada's International Policy Statement – Overview*, *supra* note 43 at 19.

99 See notes 38–41 and 83–84 in this article.

100 For a colorful recitation of the seizing of the Spanish vessel *Estai*, see M. Harris, *Lament for an Ocean* (Toronto: McClelland and Stewart, 1998) at 1–38. A more scholarly and insightful discussion is provided by P.M. Saunders, "Jurisdiction and Principle in the Implementation of the Law of the Sea: The Case of Straddling Stocks," in C. Carmody, Y. Iwasawa, and S. Rhodes, eds., *Trilateral Perspectives on International Legal Issues: Conflict and Coherence* (Washington, DC: American Society of International Law, 2003) at 382–93.

101 Convention on Future Multilateral Cooperation in the Northwest Atlantic (1978) is available on the website of the Northwest Atlantic Fisheries Organization at <www.nafo.org> (20 January 2006).

102 Fish Stocks Agreement, *supra* note 39.

103 Recent discussions within Canada refer to "custodial management" as a manner of dealing with fishing activities and resources beyond Canada's 200-nautical-mile zone on the east coast. The June 2005 report of the Advisory Panel on Straddling Stocks, "Breaking New Ground: An Action Plan for Rebuilding The Grand Banks Fisheries," noted that while custodial management "has widespread support in Newfoundland and Labrador, and in other parts of Canada, it is not a well-defined nor understood notion. Its interpretation varies with its various

highly likely to result in a strong counter response by the United States, but this is unrelated to LOS Convention party status. More generally, many of the current ocean "issues" at the multi-lateral level do not directly engage the LOS Convention. Matters relating to vessels and navigation are dealt with in the International Maritime Organization, and such matters include those related to terrorism at sea[104] and vessel-source pollution.[105] Fisheries matters are being discussed in various fora including the Food and Agriculture Organization with respect to the important matter of illegal, unreported, and unregulated fishing activity[106] and the numerous regional fisheries management organizations.[107] Marine biodiversity

---

proponents, including federal and provincial representatives, a variety of public and private institutions, industry participants, and members of the public" (at 60–61). The report notes that:

> [a]ny form of a custodial management regime, as propose to date, involves Canada exercising the same types of management rights on the adjacent high seas as it exercises in its EEZ. The idea that Canada would enforce these decisions outside its own 200 mile EEZ is particularly difficult to envisage, given the jealously guarded principle of flag state enforcement. In any case, the international community and international law do not accept any of these types of expanded coastal state rights.
>
> Short of unilateral action (which would be hotly disputed), the adoption of a custodial management approach to straddling stocks is not possible unless advances in international law either reduce the extent of the high seas or remove flag state authority over a country's vessels when they are fishing in the regulatory area of an RFMO. Neither of these changes is in the immediate offing (at 70–1).

104 In October 2005, the International Maritime Organization (IMO) adopted a protocol to the Convention for the Suppression of Unlawful Acts against the Safety of Maritime Navigation, which will update this 1988 treaty by broadening the list of offences made unlawful to include offences such as transporting weapons or equipment that could be used for weapons of mass destruction and introducing provisions on boarding where there are reasonable grounds to suspect a vessel is engaged in the commission of an offence under the convention. See "Revised Treaties to Address Unlawful Acts at Sea Adopted at Conference," from the news section of the IMO website at <www.imo.org> (20 January 2006).

105 Respecting the work of IMO in this area, see generally P. Boisson, *Safety at Sea: Policies, Regulations and International Law* (Paris: Bureau Veritas, 1999) at 536. See also the marine pollution section of the IMO website, *supra* note 104.

106 See International Plan of Action to Deter, Prevent and Eliminate Illegal, Unreported and Unregulated Fishing, adopted by the Food and Agriculture Organization (FAO) in 2001, <www.fao.org/DOCREP/005/Y3274E/y3274e04.htm> (20 January 2006). More generally, see W. Edeson, "The International Plan of Action on Illegal, Unreported and Unregulated Fishing: The Legal Context of a Non-Legally Binding Instrument" (2001) 16 Int'l J. Marine & Coastal L. 603.

107 See generally A.K. Sydnes, "Regional Fishery Organizations: How and Why Organization Diversity Matters" (2001) 32 Ocean Development & Int'l L. 349.

and marine bio-resources are being discussed within the framework of the CBD.[108] LOS Convention party status is not seen by Canada or other states as a primary concern regarding these fora and issues.

It might be suggested that the compulsory dispute settlement procedures within the LOS Convention may be useful for Canada *vis-à-vis* the United States and that this should alter Canada's ambivalent perspective on US ratification. However, while Canada and the United States have used adjudicative dispute settlement for ocean matters,[109] this action is rare not only between Canada and the United States but also internationally since states are reluctant to use formal adjudicative processes to resolve disputes. The United States is growing increasingly allergic to compulsory adjudicative dispute settlement,[110] and this anathema includes concerns about the dispute settlement regime in the LOS Convention.[111] Moreover, Canada has in the past artfully avoided the possible use of adjudicative dispute settlement on ocean matters.[112] Thus, while the compulsory dispute settlement provisions of the LOS Convention may provide an avenue for resolution for Canada and the United States should the United States ratify the LOS Convention,

---

[108] CBD, *supra* note 48. See the marine and coastal diversity section of the website for the CBD at <www.biodiv.org> (20 January 2006).

[109] Most recently in the 1984 *Gulf of Maine* case, *supra* note 29, before the International Court of Justice.

[110] Murphy, *supra* note 44 at 350–51.

[111] *Ibid.* at 242.

[112] While Canada accepts the compulsory adjudicative jurisdiction of the International Court of Justice (ICJ) under Article 36(2) of the Statute of the International Court of Justice, Canada amended its declaration of acceptance in 1970 to exclude disputes regarding Canada's then-novel Arctic legislation. This "exception" was subsequently removed in 1985.

In 1994, Canada again altered its declaration of acceptance to exclude enforcement of national laws relating to certain foreign fishing activities adjacent to Canada's east coast 200-nautical-mile zone. Following the Canadian arrest of the Spanish trawler *Estai*, the ICJ determined that as a result of the Canadian exclusion in its declaration that the court did not have jurisdiction to hear the merits of the dispute brought by Spain. *Fisheries Jurisdiction Case (Spain v. Canada)*, Jurisdiction, [1998] I.C.J. Rep. 432.

There is a much more limited opportunity to avoid the compulsory dispute settlement provisions of the LOS Convention. The subject matter that is or can be excluded from compulsory dispute settlement is set out in Articles 297 and 298. Canada has made use of the opportunity to exclude permitted subject matter from the compulsory dispute settlement regime of the LOS Convention. Note McDorman, *supra* note 41 at 106.

the procedures are highly likely to be neglected by both states. Canadian ambivalence to the United States and ratification of the LOS Convention was graphically displayed during the internal Canadian ratification process where the posture of the United States towards the convention, for or against, was not a factor.[113]

CONCLUSION

The LOS Convention has survived and prospered without US ratification and in the face of Canada's long-delayed ratification. Canada's decision to ratify was made without regard to the US posture on the convention, and this *ambivalence* was fuelled by the current calmness of Canada-US bilateral ocean issues and the fact that the national and global focus on maritime issues is not directly related to the LOS Convention. Canada's long-delayed ratification creates a degree of *appreciation* of the difficulties within the United States for those making the case for ratification where, in the face of no immediate challenges to Canada and US ocean interests, few easily tangible benefits can be directly attributed to ratification. However, international institutions and international law, particularly constitutional treaties, benefit from having the United States as a party. Thus, despite Canada's ambivalence to, and appreciation of, the United States's situation regarding the LOS Convention, there is also significant *disappointment* that the United States (in particular, the US Senate) has not yet reached the conclusion that ratification of the LOS Convention is important not only for the United States itself in reaffirming its participation as a responsible international citizen but also for the global community as a whole.

TED L. MCDORMAN
Faculty of Law, University of Victoria

---

[113] McDorman, *supra* note 41 at 108–9 and see also McDorman, *supra* note 14 at 570–74.

Sommaire

Les États-Unis et la ratification de la Convention sur le droit de la mer: un regard sur la perspective canadienne

Pendant vingt ans ni le Canada ni les États-Unis n'étaient partie à la Convention du droit de la mer des Nations Unies de 1982. En 2003, le Canada a finalement ratifié cette convention; de tous les États industrialisés, seuls les États-Unis ne sont pas parties à la "constitution des océans." Le point de vue canadien sur le fait que les États-Unis ne soient pas partie à la convention se résume à un mélange de frustration et de déception, d'appréciation et de compréhension, enfin d'ambivalence.

Summary

A Canadian Perspective on the Continued Non-Ratification of the Convention on the Law of the Sea by the United States

For twenty years, both Canada and the United States were non-parties to the 1982 UN Convention on the Law of the Sea (LOS Convention). In 2003, Canada finally ratified the LOS Convention, leaving the United States as the only industrialized state that was not a party to the "constitution of the oceans." Canada's perspective on the US non-party status involves an equal measure of frustration/disappointment, appreciation/understanding, and ambivalence.

Is a New State Responsible for Obligations Arising from Internationally Wrongful Acts Committed before Its Independence in the Context of Secession?

INTRODUCTION

This comment addresses an aspect of one of the most controversial issues in the field of state succession:[1] whether there is a succession of states to obligations arising from an internationally wrongful act committed by the predecessor state against a third state *before* the "date of succession."[2] There is no straightforward answer to this question, which is rarely addressed in doctrine by scholars.[3]

This article is a summary of part of the author's doctoral dissertation, "State Succession to Rights and Obligations Arising from the Commission of Internationally Wrongful Acts in International Law," which was completed in February 2006 at the Graduate Institute for International Studies, Geneva, under the supervision of Marcelo G. Kohen. It will be published as *State Succession to International Responsibility* (The Hague: Brill Publishing, 2007). This article reflects facts that are current as of December 2005.

[1] State succession is defined as "the replacement of one State by another in the responsibility for the international relations of territory." Article 2(1)b) of the Vienna Convention on Succession of States in Respect of Treaties, UN Doc. ST/LEG/SER.E/10 (22 August 1978), 17 I.L.M. 1488 (entered into force on 6 November 1996) [Vienna Convention].

[2] *Ibid.*, Article 2(1)(e), which defines the "date of the succession of States" as "the date upon which the successor State replaced the predecessor State in the responsibility for the international relations of the territory to which the succession of States relates."

[3] This question has been the object of a few comprehensive studies in doctrine: B. Stern, "Responsabilité internationale et succession d'Etats," in L. Boisson de Chazournes and V. Gowlland-Debbas, eds., *The International Legal System in Quest of Equity and Universality: Liber amicorum Georges Abi-Saab* (The Hague: Martinus Nijhoff, 2001), 327; Sir C.J.B. Hurst, "State Succession in Matters of Tort" (1924) 5 Br. Y.B. Int'l L. 163; J.P. Monnier, "La succession d'Etats en matière de responsabilité internationale" (1962) 8 A.F.D.I. 65; W. Czaplinski, "State Succession and State Responsibility" (1990) 28 Can. Y.B. Int'l L. 339; M.J. Volkovitsch, "Righting Wrongs: Toward a New Theory of State Succession to Responsibility

The International Law Commission (ILC) special rapporteur, James Crawford, has indeed stated that "[i]n the context of State succession, it is unclear whether a new State succeeds to any State responsibility of the predecessor State with respect to its territory."[4] The aim of this comment is *not* to provide a comprehensive analysis of this complex and controversial question.[5] It only addresses the issue in the context of *secession* — that is, when a *new state* (the successor state) emerges from the break-up of an already existing state, which nevertheless continues its existence after the loss of part of its territory.[6] Cases of secession should be distinguished from

---

for International Delicts" (1992) 92(8) Colum. L. Rev. 2162; M. Peterschmitt, "La succession d'Etats et la responsabilité internationale pour fait illicite" (LL.M dissertation, Graduate Institute for International Studies, Geneva, 2001, unpublished); and H.M. Atlam, "Succession d'Etats et continuité en matière de responsabilité internationale" (doctoral dissertation, Université de droit, d'économie et des sciences d'Aix-Marseille, France, 1986, unpublished).

4   "Commentaries to the Draft Articles on Responsibility of States for Internationally Wrongful Acts Adopted by the International Law Commission at Its Fifty-Third Session (2001)," November 2001, *Report of the ILC on the Work of Its Fifty-Third Session*, Official Records of the General Assembly, 56th Session, Supplement No. 10, Doc. A/56/10 (2001), ch. IV.E.2, at 119, para. 3.

5   The author has conducted such analysis. P. Dumberry, "State Succession to Rights and Obligations Arising from the Commission of Internationally Wrongful Acts in International Law" (doctoral dissertation, Graduate Institute for International Studies, Geneva, 2006). See also P. Dumberry, *State Succession to International Responsibility* (The Hague: Brill Publishing, 2007).

6   There is some controversy as to the proper terminology that should be used to make reference to this phenomenon and whether the term "separation" should not be used instead. The term "separation" is used in both the Vienna Convention, *supra* note 1 at Article 34, and the Vienna Convention on Succession of States in Respect of State Properties, Archives and Debts, 8 April 1983, UN Doc. A/CONF.117/14, 22 I.L.M. 298 at Article 17. This is also the case of the Draft Articles on Nationality of Natural Persons in Relation to the Succession of States, adopted by the International Law Commission (ILC) on second reading in 1999, ILC Report, UN Doc. A/54/10 (1999), ch. IV at paras. 44 and 45, in *Yearbook of the International Law Commission 1997*, vol. 2 at 13. In doctrine, the two terms are sometimes used as distinct concepts describing different situations. Thus, for some writers, the term "secession" should be used to describe instances where the removal of one part of the territory is made without the consent of the predecessor state, while cases of "separation" should refer instead to instances where such removal is *accepted* by the predecessor state. These writers make such distinction: M.G. Kohen, "Le problème des frontières en cas de dissolution et de séparation d'Etats: quelles alternatives ?" in O. Corten, B. Delcourt, P. Klein, and N. Levrat, eds., *Démembrement d'Etats et délimitations territoriales: L'uti possidetis en question(s)* (Brussels: Bruylant, 1999), 368; M.G. Kohen, "Introduction," in M.G. Kohen, ed., *Secession: International Law Perspectives* (Cambridge: Cambridge

the creation of *newly independent states* in the context of decolonization.[7] In the context of secession, the question addressed in this comment is who from the continuing state or the new state (the "secessionist" successor state) should be held responsible for the obligation to repair towards the injured third state *after* the date of succession.[8] There are basically two possible answers to this question: the obligation remains that of the continuing state or the obligation is transferred to the new state. To the best of the author's knowledge, this question has not been comprehensively addressed in doctrine.[9]

This comment will first critically examine the arguments advanced by scholars for whom the successor state does not take over the obligations arising from internationally wrongful acts committed by the predecessor state before the date of succession. We will offer a less dogmatic approach to the issue whereby the solution to the question whether or not the successor state takes over such

---

University Press, 2006) at 2–3; J. Crawford, *The Creation of States in International Law* (Oxford: Clarendon Press, 1979) at 247; and J. Crawford, "State Practice and International Law in Relation to Secession" (1998) Br. Y.B. Int'l L. 85. Similarly, D.P. O'Connell, *State Succession in Municipal Law and International Law*, vol. 2 (Cambridge: Cambridge University Press, 1967) at 88, speaks of "revolutionary secession" and "evolutionary secession." Other writers use the term "separation" in the context of "unitary" state, while "secession" is used for cases involving "federal" states. For instance, see J. Brossard and D. Turp, *L'accession à la souveraineté et le cas du Québec*, 2nd edition (Montreal: Presse de l'Université de Montréal, 1995) at 94; and D. Turp, *Le droit de choisir: Essais sur le droit du Québec à disposer de lui-même / The Right to Choose: Essays on Québec's Right of Self-Determination* (Montreal: Editions Thémis, 2001) at 22.

7   Cases of newly independent states are similar to secession insofar as they both involve the creation of a new state while the predecessor state continues to exist. However, cases of newly independent states arise in the context of decolonization where the territory of a colony is not considered as part of the territory of the colonial state administering it (Declaration of Principles of International Law Concerning Friendly Relations and Co-Operation among States in Accordance with the Charter of the United Nations, adopted by General Assembly Res. 2625 (XXV) (24 October 1970). In this sense, a newly independent state is a new state, which, however, cannot be said to have "seceded" from the colonial power to the extent that its territory was never formally part of it. The most recent example of a newly independent state is East Timor in 2002.

8   This comment will not address the other question of the right for the successor state to claim reparation as a consequence of internationally wrongful acts committed by a third state against the predecessor state before the date of succession. This question is fully examined by Dumberry, *supra* note 5 at 357–480.

9   This question is examined in detail by the author Dumberry, *supra* note 5 at 175–202.

obligations essentially depends on *different factors and circumstances* as well as the *types* of succession of states involved. This comment will then examine state practice and case law in the context of secession, which shows that the continuing state usually continues its previous responsibility for internationally wrongful acts committed before the date of succession, notwithstanding the transformation affecting its territory. A more controversial issue, which is never addressed in doctrine, is whether this principle of non-succession should *always* apply in the context of secession and whether there should not be some circumstances that would instead call for the new state (the successor state) to be responsible for internationally wrongful acts committed before the date of succession. This comment is an attempt to systematically establish under which specific circumstances secessionist states take over the obligation to repair towards injured third states.

Traditional Doctrine of Non-Succession

This section briefly summarizes the position adopted in doctrine in the *general context* of state succession (not limited to the specific context of secession). In almost all general textbooks, scholars support the general rule of non-succession, whereby the successor state is not bound by obligations arising from internationally wrongful acts committed by the predecessor state before the date of succession.[10] The doctrine of non-succession usually refers to two old international arbitral awards: the 1923 *R.E. Brown Case (United States v. Great Britain)* (in the context of the annexation of the Boer Republic of South Africa by Great Britain in 1902),[11] and the 1925 *F.H. Redward and Others Case (Great Britain v. United States)* (also known as the *Hawaiian Claims* case) (in the context of the annexation of Hawaii by the United States in 1898).[12] Two arguments are usually submitted in favour of the rule of non-succession.

The first argument is that, as a state is not responsible for acts committed by other states, only the state that has actually committed an internationally wrongful act should be held responsible for

---

[10] For a long list of scholars who have adopted this position, see *ibid.* at 58–60.

[11] *R.E. Brown Case (United States v. Great Britain)*, Award of 23 November 1923, 6 R.I.A.A. at 129 (British-United States Claims Commission).

[12] *F.H. Redward and Others Case (Great Britain v. United States)*, Award of 10 November 1925, 6 R.I.A.A. 157 (British-United States Claims Commission) [*Hawaiian Claims*].

it.[13] Should the predecessor state cease to exist (such as in case of a dissolution of state), the legal liability for internationally wrongful acts is extinguished at the same time.[14] This argument is self-evident and sound, but it is nonetheless beside the point.[15] The question here is *not* whether the successor state should be "responsible" for internationally wrongful acts that it has not *itself* committed. Such "responsibility" no doubt remains with the predecessor state. What matters is whether the *international obligations resulting from an internationally wrongful act* committed by the predecessor state can, in some circumstances, be "transferred" to the successor state.[16]

The second argument usually submitted to support the rule of non-succession relates to the "personal character" of an internationally wrongful act, which would not enable its transfer from one state to another — *action personalis moritur cum persona*.[17] These writers draw a parallel with the concept of succession under Roman law whereby liability for an action *ex delicto* does not pass to the heirs.[18] There are at least two reasons to reject this theory.

13 Monnier, *supra* note 3 at 89; A. Cavaglieri, "Effets juridiques des changements de souveraineté territoriale" (1931-I) Annuaire I.D.I. 190; N. Quoc Dinh, P. Daillier, and A. Pellet, *Droit international public*, 6th edition (Paris: Librairie Générale de Droit et de Jurisprudence, 1999) at 550; P.-M. Dupuy, *Droit international public*, 4th edition (Paris: Dalloz, 1998) at 54; C. Rousseau, *Droit international public*, vol. III (Paris: Sirey, 1977) at 505; and C. de Visscher, *Théories et réalités en droit international public* (Paris: Editions Pedone, 1953) at 210.

14 This solution was adopted by the tribunal in the *Hawaiian Claims* case, *supra* note 12 at 158: "[T]he legal unit which did the wrong no longer exists, and legal liability for the wrong has been extinguished with it."

15 According to the ILC Special Rapporteur James Crawford (*First Report on State Responsibility (Addendum no. 4)*, 26 May 1998, UN Doc. A/CN.4/490/Add.4 (1998), at para. 110), Article 1 of the ILC's Articles on Responsibility of States for Internationally Wrongful Acts ("Every internationally wrongful act of a State entails the international responsibility of that State") "affirms the basic principle that each State is responsible for its own wrongful conduct."

16 The question is (rightly) identified as such by, *inter alia*, J. Verhoeven, *Droit international public* (Brussels: Larcier, 2000) at 189; and Stern, *supra* note 3 at 338.

17 This theory is supported by these writers: M. Huber, *Die Staatensuccession: völkerrechtliche und staatsrechtliche Praxis im XIX. Jahrhundert* (Leipzig: Duncker and Humblot, 1898) at 65 and 95; M. Udina, "La succession des Etats quant aux obligations internationales autres que les dettes publiques" (1933-II) 44 Rec. des Cours 767; A. Cavaglieri, "Règles générales du droit de la paix" (1929-I) 26 Rec. des Cours 374; P. Malanczuk, *Akehurst's Modern Introduction to International Law*, 7th edition (London: Routledge, 1997) at 169; and I. Brownlie, *Principles of Public International Law*, 6th edition (Oxford: Clarendon Press, 2003) at 632.

18 J.B. Moyle, *The Institutes of Justinian Translated into English*, 3rd edition (Oxford: Clarendon Press, 1913), at Book IV, Title 12. A good example is the work of

First, the analogy it draws between private law and international law is misleading since the consequence of the extinction of an individual and a state are simply not comparable.[19] Thus, if the death of an individual is a *sine qua non* prerequisite to the application of the rule of succession under private law, the same cannot be transposed automatically in the field of succession of states.[20] For example, a state does not necessarily lose its international legal personality as a result of a change in its territory.[21] Indeed, in the context of secession, cession, and transfer of territory, such territorial losses do not affect the predecessor state's identity (and do not result in its "death").[22] Even if one were to accept the analogy with private law, it remains that modern private law rules of succession no longer follow the principle of Roman law of non-succession of the heirs for "personal" delictual acts of the *cujus*.[23]

The second reason for rejecting the theory of the personal character of the internationally wrongful act is that it is based on the outdated concept of *culpa* ("*faute*"), which has long been recognized in doctrine[24] as well as by the work of the ILC, as not a necessary condition to determine a state's liability under contemporary

---

H. Lauterpacht, *Private Law Sources and Analogies of International Law* (London: Longmans, 1927) at 131–32 and 283.

[19] B. Stern, "La succession d'Etats" (1996) 262 Rec. des Cours 37; and Volkovitsch, *supra* note 3 at 2196.

[20] A. Gruber, *Le droit international de la succession d'Etats* (Paris: Publications de la faculté de droit de l'Université René Descartes (Paris V), Editions Bruylant, 1986) at 30 and 35.

[21] W. Schoenborn, "La nature juridique du territoire" (1929-V) 30 Rec. des Cours 119; and L. Delbez, "Du territoire dans ses rapports avec l'Etat" (1932) R.G.D.I.P. at 719.

[22] Stern, *supra* note 19 at 38; E. Suy, "Réflexions sur la distinction entre la souveraineté et la compétence territoriale," in R. Marcic, H. Mosler, E. Suy, and K. Zemanek, *Internationale Festschrift für Alfred Verdross* (Munich: Wilhem Fink Verlag, 1971) at 494.

[23] This is stated by the French-Greek arbitral tribunal in the *Lighthouse Arbitration* case (*Sentence arbitrale en date des 24/27 juillet 1956 rendue par le Tribunal d'arbitrage constitué en vertu du Compromis signé à Paris le 15 juillet 1932 entre la France et la Grèce*), Award of 24/27 July 1956, 12 R.I.A.A. 155 at 199 [*Lighthouse Arbitration* case]. See also Volkovitsch, *supra* note 3 at 2196. This is, indeed, the situation prevailing under English law. R.W.M. Dias and B.S. Markesinis, *Tort Law* (Oxford: Clarendon Press, 1984) at 416.

[24] I. Brownlie, *State Responsibility*, Part I (Oxford: Clarendon Press, 1983) at 39; and Dupuy, *supra* note 13 at 437.

international law.[25] For those writers who maintain that a *faute* needs to be proven for a state to engage its international responsibility,[26] an internationally wrongful act has conceivably a "personal character." It has been rightly observed by Brigitte Stern that when international responsibility is conceived as an *objective* concept rather then a *personal internationally wrongful act involving culpa or intention,* the transferability of the obligation to repair to the successor state becomes possible.[27]

AN ALTERNATIVE APPROACH TO THE ISSUE

For the most part of the twentieth century, very few authors have challenged the doctrine of non-succession to obligations arising from the commission of internationally wrongful acts.[28] The 1956 award of the arbitral tribunal in the *Lighthouse Arbitration* case appears to be a milestone in this respect.[29] It clearly rejects the position of non-succession traditionally taken by the doctrine as "not well found."[30] Contemporary scholars are much more critical of the traditional doctrine of non-succession.[31]

These criticisms are sound. Indeed, no general solution may resolve all questions of state succession to international responsibility.[32] A general theory, such as the one advanced by the traditional doctrine of non-succession, is bound to be inconsistent with the much more complex reality of the issue.[33] As a matter of fact,

---

25 *First Report on State Responsibility (Addendum no. 4),* James Crawford, Special Rapporteur, 26 May 1998, UN Doc. A/CN.4/490/Add.4 (1998) at para. 122.

26 Udina, *supra* note 17 at 767.

27 Stern, *supra* note 3 at 335.

28 Mention should be made of the following writers who have criticized this doctrine: E.H. Feilchenfeld, *Public Debts and State Succession* (New York: Macmillan, 1931) at 689 and 728; C. Cheney Hyde, *International Law Chiefly as Interpreted and Applied by the United States,* vol. I, 2nd edition (Boston: Little, Brown and Company, 1945) at 437–38; and J.H.W. Verzijl, *International Law in Historical Perspective,* vol. 7 (Leiden: A.W. Sijthoff, 1974) at 219–20.

29 *Lighthouse Arbitration* case, *supra* note 23, dealing with Claim no. 4.

30 *Ibid.* at 198.

31 Mention should be made here of the work of Volkovitsch, *supra* note 3 at 2198 and 2172–73; Stern, *supra* note 3 at 336, 338, and 355; and Peterschmitt, *supra* note 3 at 72–73.

32 This is the conclusion reached by the tribunal in the *Lighthouse Arbitration* case, *supra* note 23 at 197.

33 See also O'Connell, *supra* note 6, vol. 1 at 486; and Atlam, *supra* note 3 at 15 and 235–36.

analysis has shown that modern state practice and case law of the 1990s clearly support the principle of succession to obligations arising from the commission of internationally wrongful acts.[34]

The solution to the question whether or not the successor state takes over the obligations arising from internationally wrongful acts committed by the predecessor state before the date of succession depends, on the one hand, on the different factors and circumstances involved.[35] Thus, specific problems of state succession to international responsibility will indeed require specific solutions.[36] On the other hand, the answer also depends on the type of succession of states involved.[37] In other words, a solution that may very well be appropriate in the context of the dissolution or unification of states may not be adapted to another type of state succession, such as secession. This is so for the simple reason that, in the former case, the predecessor state ceases to exist at the date of succession, while, in the latter situation, it continues its existence as an independent state. In practical terms, the application of the doctrine of non-succession in the context of the dissolution of a state results in an internationally wrongful act remaining unpunished since the injured state victim of such an act is left (after the date of succession) with no debtor against whom to file a claim for reparation. In the context of secession, the doctrine of non-succession calls for the continuing state to *always* remain responsible for the act, while the new successor state can *never* take over such responsibility after it becomes an independent state. It is this last assumption that the present text is challenging.

---

[34] In fact, the present author (Dumberry, *supra* note 5 at 495 et seq) did not find a single case of recent state practice where the successor state refused to be held responsible for pre-succession obligations. This is discussed in P. Oumberry, "The Controversial Issue of State Succession to International Responsibility Revisited in Light of Recent State Practice" (2006) 49 German Y.B. Int'l L. (forthcoming).

[35] This is also the conclusion reached by D.P. O'Connell, "Recent Problems of State Succession in Relation to New States" (1970-II) 130 Rec. des Cours 164.

[36] The present author (Dumberry, *supra* note 5 at 244–344) has identified several specific circumstances under which state practice and international and municipal case law (as well as doctrine) support the application of the principle of succession or, on the contrary, that of non-succession. Some of these circumstances will be examined later in this comment in the context of secession.

[37] The present author (Dumberry, *supra* note 5 at 82–246) has conducted a comprehensive analysis of state practice based on the different types of succession of states (that is, secession, the creation of "newly independent states," dissolution of states, unification and integration of states, and cession and transfer of territory).

ANALYSIS OF STATE PRACTICE: THE CONTINUING STATE REMAINS
RESPONSIBLE FOR INTERNATIONALLY WRONGFUL ACTS COMMITTED
BEFORE THE DATE OF SUCCESSION

State practice and case law in the context of secession confirms
(with only one significant exception that will be examined later in
this comment) the principle that after the date of succession the
continuing state should continue its previous responsibility for internationally wrongful acts committed before the date of succession, notwithstanding the transformation affecting its territory. This
practice is in line with the prevailing view in doctrine in the context of secession.[38]

POSITION TAKEN BY AUSTRIA AND THE ALLIES IN THE CONTEXT OF
THE BREAK-UP OF THE AUSTRIA–HUNGARY DUAL MONARCHY

The break up of the Austria–Hungary Dual Monarchy after the
First World War was considered by Austria to be a case of the dissolution of a state with itself being a new state.[39] This claim of
non-continuity with the Dual Monarchy was endorsed by the Austrian Constitutional Court in several cases, where it was held that
Austria should not be responsible for the obligations of Austria-
Hungary.[40] On the contrary, the "allied and associated powers" (the

---

[38] Stern, *supra* note 3 at 335–36 ("En vertu des principes très clairs gouvernant
l'imputation de l'acte illicite à un Etat ... on peut affirmer que l'Etat continuateur
continue bien entendu à être responsable des actes qu'il a commis, même s'il
subit certaines transformations"). See also Czaplinski, *supra* note 3 at 357; W.L.
Gould, *An Introduction to International Law* (New York: Harpers and Brothers,
1957) at 428; Monnier, *supra* note 3 at 67; K. Marek, *Identity and Continuity of
States in Public International Law* (Geneva: Librairie Droz, 1968) at 11; Volkovitsch,
supra note 3 at 2200; Atlam, *supra* note 3 at 258; Peterschmitt, *supra* note 3 at
54; Ch. Rousseau, "Jurisprudence française en matière de droit international
public" (1976) 80 R.G.D.I.P. 969; Sir R. Jenning and Sir A. Watts, *Oppenheim's
International Law*, vol. I, 9th edition (London: Longman, 1996) at 224; and H.
Kelsen, "Théorie générale du droit international public. Problèmes choisis"
(1932-IV) 42 Rec. des Cours 327 at 333–34.

[39] The majority of the scholars are of the opinion that the case of Austria–Hungary
is one of state dissolution. An overview of the legal arguments advanced by both
sides in doctrine is found in O. Lehner, "The Identity of Austria 1918/19 as a
Problem of State Succession" (1992) 44 Österreichische Zeitschrift für
öffentliches Recht und Völkerrecht 63 at 81.

[40] *Military Pensions (Austria) Case*, 7 May 1919, Case no. 126, (1919) 1 Sammlung
der Erkenntniss des österreichischen Verfassungsgerichtshofes, no. 9 at 17 (1919–
22) Ann. Dig. I.L.C. 66 (Austrian Constitutional Court); and *Austrian Empire*

British Empire, France, Italy, Japan, the United States, and so on) held that this was not a case of state dissolution but, rather, a secession of Poland, Czechoslovakia, and Yugoslavia, with both Austria and Hungary being considered as the continuing states of the Dual Monarchy. The allies held that post-war Austria and Hungary were *identical* with the former dual monarchy.[41] The allies insisted on both states being considered as the continuing states of the Dual Monarchy in order to make sure that they would be held responsible for the internationally wrongful acts committed by the latter during the war.[42] This is clear in the St. Germain Peace Treaty (entered into by the European powers and Austria),[43] and in the separate peace treaties entered into in 1921 by the United States with Austria[44] and with Hungary.[45] A commission set up under a 1924 treaty[46] entered into by the United States with Hungary and Austria specifically stated that the other secessionist states (that is, Poland, Czechoslovakia, and Yugoslavia) should bear *no responsibility* for internationally wrongful acts committed during the war.[47]

(Succession) Case, 11 March 1919, Case no. 18, in *ibid.*, no. 2 at 5 (1919–22)Ann. Dig. I.L.C. 67 (Austrian Constitutional Court). See also another case decided by the Austrian Constitutional Court on 20 October 1919, Case no. 253–54, in *ibid.*, no. 18–19 at 36–37 (1919–22) Ann. Dig. I.L.C. 67.

[41] Marek, *supra* note 38 at 220 et seq.

[42] Verzijl, *supra* note 28 at 126.

[43] Treaty of Peace between the Allied and Associated Powers and Austria, including Protocol, Declaration and Special Declaration, St. Germain-en-Laye, 10 September 1919, U.K.T.S. 1919 No. 11 (Cmd. 400) (entered into force on 16 July 1920), at Article 177.

[44] Treaty between the United States and Austria, signed on August 24, 1921, to Establish Securely Friendly Relations between the two Nations (1922 Suppl.), 16 A.J.I.L. 13–16.

[45] Treaty Establishing Friendly Relations between the United States of America and Hungary, Budapest, 29 August 1921, U.S.T.S. No. 660; (1922 Suppl.) 16 A.J.I.L. 13–16.

[46] Agreement of 26 November 1924, 48 L.N.T.S. 70; 6 R.I.A.A. 199.

[47] Administrative Decision no. 1, 25 May 1927, 7 R.I.A.A. 203 at 210 (Tripartite Claims Commission). The commission set up under this treaty decided that compensation for damage suffered by American nationals during the war would be borne by Austria in the percentage of 63.6 per cent and by Hungary for 36.4 per cent.

POLISH AND GERMAN COURT CASES IN THE CONTEXT
OF THE SECESSION OF POLAND

After Poland became an independent state in 1918, few cases
decided by courts of the new state of Poland dealt with issues of
state succession to obligations arising from the commission of internationally wrongful acts. These cases support the principle that
the continuing state remains responsible for the commission of its
own internationally wrongful acts on the territory that has since
then seceded. For instance, in the case of *Dzierzbicki v. District Electric Association of Czestochowa*, the Supreme Court of Poland dealt
with a claim arising from an accident caused by the Russian railway authorities in a territory that was at the time still part of the
Russian Empire.[48] The court concluded that the new state of Poland should not bear any responsibility for the internationally
wrongful acts committed by the predecessor state (Russia) against
a polish national:

In accordance with the views of the contemporary science of international
law, the new State is not the legal successor of the previous State from
which it took over part of the territory, and is responsible for the charges
and debts only in so far as it has expressly assumed them. There is no
reason for not applying this principle to the obligations of the partitioning power arising from the responsibility for damage and losses caused in
the course of running railways.[49]

In several other cases, the Supreme Court of Poland also held that
the Polish State Treasury was not bound to pay damages on account of accidents involving state railways that, at the time of the
incident, belonged to Austria–Hungary. It held that Austria was
not a new state and that it was the "continuator" of the Dual Monarchy's previous responsibility. This principle has been applied in

---

48 *Dzierzbicki v. District Electric Association of Czestochowa*, 21 December 1933, (1934)
O.S.P. no. 288, (1933–34) Ann. Dig. I.L.C. 89 (Supreme Court of Poland,
First Division) [*Dzierzbicki*]. A sum was awarded by a Russian court in Warsaw in
April 1914.

49 *Ibid.* The court also stated: "[T]he Polish State is entirely free of obligations
which were incumbent upon any of the partitioning powers with the exception
of such obligations as the Polish State had itself assumed." The court noted that
under the Peace Treaty of Riga entered into between Russia and Poland the new
Polish state did not accept responsibility for such obligations.

Niemiec and Niemiec v. Bialobrodziec and Polish State Treasury[50] and in *Olpinski v. Polish Treasury (Railway Division).*[51]

Finally, the principle was also applied by a German Court in the context of a delict that took place in 1913 in a territory that was then part of Germany and later became part of Poland.[52] The German *Reichsgericht* found that Poland was not responsible for the sum awarded by a German court for internationally wrongful acts committed by Prussia when the territory was still part of Germany.[53]

---

[50] *Niemiec and Niemiec v. Bialobrodziec and Polish State Treasury,* 20 February 1923, (1923–24) 2 Ann. Dig. I.L.C. 64 (Supreme Court of Poland, Third Division) [*Niemiec and Niemiec*]. In this case, an incident took place in 1917 in a territory then part of Austria–Hungary where the plaintiffs' building was destroyed by a fire, which had allegedly been caused by sparks from the engine of a passing train belonging to the Austrian state railways.

[51] *Olpinski v. Polish Treasury (Railway Division),* 16 April 1921, 1 O.S.P. no. 15, (1919–22) Ann. Dig. I.L.C. 63 (Supreme Court of Poland, Third Division) [*Olpinski*]. In this case, an individual had suffered damage in August 1918 caused by the conductor of a train in a territory that was still under Austria–Hungary rule. After the independence of Poland, the plaintiff sued the Polish Treasury on the ground that the Polish state took over Austria–Hungary's state railways on its territory. The Court of First Instance and the Court of Appeal rendered judgments in favour of the plaintiff based, *inter alia,* on the principle of legal continuity according to which the new state takes over obligations localized in territories that it acquired. The two lower courts also rendered their decisions based on the ground that a new state cannot take over assets without taking over liabilities. The Supreme Court of Poland rejected the claim and decided that the plaintiff would have to file suit against the Austrian railway authorities since this state continued to exist after 1918.

[52] *Baron A. v. Prussian Treasury,* 19 December 1923, 107 E.R.Z. 382 (1923–24) Ann. Dig. I.L.C. 60 (Germany, Reichsgericht in Civil Matters) [*Baron*]. This case involved an action introduced in 1913 by the legal predecessor of the plaintiff, the owner of some landed property, against the Prussian state for damage caused to him in consequence of some irrigation works undertaken by Prussia. The case was decided in favour of the plaintiff by the District Court of Danzig (May 1913) and by the Court of Marienwerder (Prussia, June 1920).

[53] Prussia contended that, *inter alia,* as the land in question was now situated in Poland, the latter should be held responsible for the amount claimed by the plaintiff and that German courts could not assume jurisdiction in an action that was in fact against a foreign state. The German court indicated that in accordance with Article 256 of the Treaty of Versailles, Paris, signed on 28 June 1919, entered into force on 10 January 1920, U.K.T.S. 1919, No. 8 (Cmd. 223), Poland acquired all the property of Germany and of the German states in the ceded territories. However, it also added that Poland, in the absence of a special agreement, was not responsible for the payment of the sum claimed by the plaintiff.

POSITION ADOPTED BY THE GERMAN DEMOCRATIC REPUBLIC
AFTER THE SECOND WORLD WAR

After the Second World War, the Federal Republic of Germany was considered the legal "continuator" of the German Reich. The official position of the German Democratic Republic (GDR) concerning its legal status is confused, as it was modified several times.[54] Its final position was adopted in 1956. The GDR was of the view that there were two different *new* states in Germany and that both states were *successor states* to the German Reich, which had disappeared.[55] The GDR therefore believed that this was a case of a dissolution of state. The prevailing view in doctrine, however, was that in 1949 the GDR was a new state that had, in effect, "seceded" from the German Reich.[56]

The official position taken by the authorities of the GDR was that it was a new state "ideologically" totally different from the German

[54] This official position, as well as the relevant case law and doctrine, is discussed in B. Guerin, *L'évolution du statut juridique de l'Allemagne de 1945 au traité fondamental* (Düsseldorf: Droste, 1978) at 97–105. During a first period (1949–51), the GDR considered itself as *identical* with the German Reich. At the time, the GDR viewed itself as representing Germany as a whole. This position was radically changed by a decision of the District Court of Appeal (Oberlandesgericht) of Schwerin of 18 June 1951, (1951) N.J., 468 et seq., and by another one of the GDR's Oberlandesgericht of 31 October 1951, (1952) N.J., 222 et seq., where it was held that the German Reich had disappeared as a result of the war by *debellatio*. According to this new position, the GDR was a different state and, most importantly, it was *not a successor state*. This position prevailed until 1956.

[55] Guerin, *supra* note 54 at 109 et seq., provides many examples illustrating this new position of the GDR.

[56] S. Oeter, "German Unification and State Succession" (1991) 51(2) Zeitschrift für ausländisches öffentliches Recht und Völkerrecht 350–51, explains that the dominant interpretation in doctrine is that the GDR had in fact seceded, but that such secession was "provisional" and not "final" since no final settlement on the status of Germany had been reached. He quotes the following writers supporting this view: G. Ress, "Germany, Legal Status after World War II," in R. Bernhardt, ed., *Encyclopaedia of Public International Law*, vol. 10 (North Holland: Max Planck Institute, 1984), 199; J.A. Frowein, "Die Rechtslage Deutschlands und der Status Berlins," in E. Benda, W. Maihofer, and H.-J. Vogel, eds., *Handbuch des Verfassungsrechts der Bundesrepublik Deutschland* (Berlin: Walter de Gruyter, 1983), 48; and G. Ress, "Grundlagen und Entwicklung der innerdeutschen Beziehungen," in J. Isensee and P. Kirchhof, eds., *Handbuch des Staatsrechts*, vol. 1 (Heidelberg: Müller, 1987), 492. This is also the position of K. Heilbronner, "Legal Aspects of the Unification of the Two German States" (1991) 2 Eur. J. Int'l L. 21, indicating that "the process of German division and secession of the G.D.R. remained provisional until a final settlement on Germany as a whole could be achieved with the Four Powers."

Reich and that, consequently, it could not be held responsible for obligations arising from internationally wrongful acts committed by Nazi Germany.[57] One illustration is the position adopted by the GDR with respect to the claims of Libya for damages arising from the presence of remnants of the Second World War on its territory. The GDR refused to cooperate with Libya on the ground that it could not be held accountable for the acts committed by the Third Reich.[58] We will now examine two examples of state practice that may be interpreted as exceptions to the official position taken by the GDR.

The Union of Soviet Socialist Republics (USSR) and Poland requested war reparation from the GDR for damage resulting from internationally wrongful acts committed during the Second World War by the predecessor state (the German Reich). In accordance with the Tripartite Agreement by the United States, the United Kingdom, and Soviet Russia (Potsdam Agreement), Germany was to pay war reparation to the USSR in the form of direct taking and seizure of industrial equipments situated in the German territories occupied by the Soviet Red Army (and in other parts of Eastern Europe).[59] A treaty between Poland and the USSR subsequently dealt with the allocation between the two states of compensation resulting from war reparation paid by Germany.[60] This reparation regime was essentially enforced during the period of Soviet occupation (1945–9). It continued for a few years after the official creation of the GDR in 1949. Therefore, after 1949, the reparation regime established under the Potsdam Agreement was imposed upon the GDR. In a declaration made on 22 August 1953, the USSR declared that it no longer requested the payment of any war reparations by

[57] This question is discussed in B.-W. Eichhorn, *Reparation als völkerrechtliche Deliktshaftung: Rechtliche und praktische Probleme unter besonderer Berücksichtigung Deutschlands (1918–1990)* (Baden Baden: Nomos Verlagsgesellschaft mbH and Co. KG, 1992).

[58] This point is discussed in A. Dawi, "Les problèmes juridiques internationaux posés par les restes matériels des guerres, notamment en Libye" (doctoral dissertation, Université d'Orléans, France, 1994, unpublished) at 105.

[59] Section IV of the Tripartite Agreement by the United States, the United Kingdom and Soviet Russia, 2 August 1945, 68 U.N.T.S. 190 [Potsdam Agreement].

[60] Agreement between the USSR and the Provisional Government of National Unity of Poland Concerning the Reparation of Damage caused by the German Occupation, Moscow, 16 August 1945 (1943–45) 145 British and Foreign State Papers 1168–70.

the GDR.[61] This is an illustration of a new state taking over responsibility for internationally wrongful acts committed before the date of independence. This example is, however, not entirely significant as its outcome was dictated by an agreement between the victorious powers after the Second World War and the defeat of Germany, which was not a party to the Potsdam Agreement. This is also ultimately an example driven by Cold War *realpolitik* rather than by the application of any legal principles, since the GDR, being part of the Socialist Bloc, was certainly not in a position to refute any Soviet claims for compensation.

Notwithstanding its official position of non-succession, the GDR recognized in February 1990 the responsibility of "all Germans" for past crimes committed by the Third Reich against the Jewish people before and during the Second World War.[62] This change of policy was made after the fall of Erich Honecker as general secretary of the Socialist Unity party and as head of the government (October 1989) and after the fall of the Berlin Wall (November 1989). A few months later (in April 1990), the GDR reiterated its acceptance of responsibility for these crimes and pledged to pay DM 6.2 million in compensation in the following years.[63] This

---

61 Protocol Concerning the Discontinuance of German Reparations Payments and Other Measures to Alleviate the Financial and Economic Obligations of the German Democratic Republic Arising in Consequence of the War, 22 August 1953, 221 U.N.T.S. 129. In May 1950, the USSR had already decided to reduce the total amount in reparation due by the GDR, having seized property in an amount of US $3.6 billion. On 23 August 1953, Poland also renounced to reparation payments from the GDR. Declaration of the Polish People's Republic (1953) 9 Zbior Documentow, no. 9 at 1830 (quoted in (no date) 49 Bundesverfassungsgericht 169).

62 The declaration was attached to a letter dated 1 February 1990 signed by the GDR's Prime Minister Modrow and addressed to the president of the World Jewish Congress, Edgard Bronfman. At that time, the question of the amount of reparation was still not settled. The history of the negotiations and the content of the declaration are discussed in G. Winrow, "East Germany, Israel and the Reparations Issue" (1990) 20(1) Soviet Jewish Affairs 37 et seq. These facts are also exposed in J. Charpentier, "Pratique française du droit international" (1990) 35 A.F.D.I. 986; Ch. Rousseau, "Chronique des faits internationaux" (1990) R.G.D.I.P. 764–65; G. Schuster, "Volkerrechtliche Praxis der Bundesrepublik Deutschland im Jahre 1990" (1992) 52 Zeitschrift für ausländisches öffentliches Recht und Völkerrecht 1026; and P. D'Argent, *Les réparations de guerre en droit international public* (Brussels: Bruylant, 2002) at 217.

63 This declaration was made before the GDR's Parliament (Volkskammer) by its newly elected prime minister, Lothar de Maizière.

marked a radical change from the previous attitude adopted by the GDR, which had always rejected any international responsibility for the atrocities committed by the Third Reich against the Jewish people.[64] However, due to the integration of the GDR in the Federal Republic of Germany a few months later (3 October 1990),[65] no compensation was actually paid by the GDR. This example, therefore, is not significant as, ultimately, no reparation was ever made.

STATE PRACTICE IN THE CONTEXT OF THE BREAK UP OF THE USSR

Upon the break up of the USSR in 1991, it was agreed between the former republics that Russia would be considered as the "continuator" of the international legal personality of the USSR in international organizations and, in particular, at the United Nations Security Council.[66] This decision was largely accepted by other states in the international community.[67] The doctrine has, however, been

---

[64] The GDR never responded to a demand made by the government of Israel in March 1951, requesting compensation in the amount of US $500 million. A little known fact is that in November 1976, the GDR offered to a Jewish organization (named "Claims Conference") the amount of US $1 million in reparation to former German nationals of Jewish origin now living in the United States. The Claims Conference rejected the proposal. It requested instead in 1979 the payment of some US $100 million in compensation. The GDR refused to pay compensation. See Winrow, *supra* note 62 at 32–33.

[65] Treaty on the Establishment of German Unity, 31 August 1990, (1991) 30 I.L.M. 457.

[66] Declaration of Alma Ata, 21 December 1991, UN Doc. A/46/60, (1992) 31 I.L.M. 147. See also the Decision by the Council of Heads of State of the Commonwealth of Independent States, 21 December 1991, (1992) 31 I.L.M. 151, and "Letter of Russia's President Mr Elstin to the U.N. Secretary General," 24 December 1991, (1992) 31 I.L.M. 138. On this question, see Y. Z. Blum, "Russia Takes over the Soviet Union's Seat at the United Nations" (1993) 3(2) Eur. J. Int'l L. 354.

[67] See, for instance, the position of the European Union examined by P. Jan Kuyper, "The Community and State Succession in Respect to Treaties," in D. Curtin and T. Heukels, eds., *Institutional Dynamics of European Integration, Essays in Honour of Henry G. Schermers*, vol. 2 (Dordrecht: Martinus Nijhoff, 1994), 633. On the position of the United States government, see E.D. Williamson and J.E. Osborn, "A U.S. Perspective on Treaty Succession and Related Issues in the Wake of the Break-up of the U.S.S.R. and Yugoslavia" (1992–33) 33 Va. J. Int'l L. 264; L. Love, "International Agreement Obligations after the Soviet Union's Break-up: Current United States Practice and Its Consistency with International Law" (1993) 26(2) Vanderbilt J. Transnatl. L. 373. The practice of states is analyzed in K.G. Bühler, "State Succession, Identity/Continuity and Membership in the United Nations," in P.M. Eisemann and M. Koskenniemi, dir., *La succession d'Etats: la*

divided on the question whether Russia should indeed be considered as the continuing state of the USSR.[68] The question whether the break up of the USSR should be regarded as a case of the dissolution of a state or as a series of secessions is also controversial.[69] It has been suggested in doctrine that because Russia is the "continuator" of the USSR, it results that all of the other former republics have seceded from the union.[70] The affirmation that Russia is a "continuator" of the USSR is clearly based on a legal fiction.[71] Thus, the USSR did cease to exist as a result of both the Declaration of Alma Ata and the Agreement Establishing the Commonwealth of Independent States (Minsk Agreement).[72] Logically, Russia could not continue the existence of a

---

codification à l'épreuve des faits / State Succession: Codification Tested against the Facts (The Hague: Martinus Nijhoff, 2000), 258.

[68] The position supporting the "continuity" is adopted by, *inter alia*, these writers: R. Mullerson, "Law and Politics in Succession of States: International Law on Succession of States," in G. Burdeau and B. Stern, eds., *Dissolution, continuation et succession en Europe de l'Est* (Paris: Cedin-Paris I, 1994), 19; M. Bothe and C. Schmidt, "Sur quelques questions de succession posées par la dissolution de l'URSS et celle de la Yougoslavie" (1992) 96 R.G.D.I.P. 824; and M. Koskenniemi and M. Letho, "La succession d'États dans l'ex-URSS, en ce qui concerne particulièrement les relations avec la Finlande" (1992) 38 A.F.D.I. 189–90. Other writers support the other view that Russia is not the continuing state, but a new state. R. Rich, "Recognition of States: The Collapse of Yugoslavia and the Soviet Union" (1993) 4(1) Eur. J. Int'l L. 45; Blum, *supra* note 66 at 357–59; and H. Tichy, "Two Recent Cases of State Succession: An Austrian Perspective" (1992) 44 Österreichische Zeitschrift für öffentliches Recht und Völkerrecht 130. On this question, see Bühler, *supra* note 67 at 256; and T. Langstöm, "The Dissolution of the Soviet Union in the Light of the 1978 Vienna Convention on Succession of States in Respect to Treaties," in Eisemann and Koskenniemi, *supra* note 67, 723.

[69] The only non-controversial point is that the three Baltic states are regarded not as new states (and not as successor states of the USSR) but as identical to the three Baltic states that existed before their 1940 illegal annexation by the USSR.

[70] Mullerson, *supra* note 68 at 19; W. Czaplinski, "La continuité, l'identité et la succession d'États — évaluation de cas récents" (1993) 26 R.B.D.I. 388; M. Koskenniemi, "Report of the Director of Studies of the English-Speaking Section of the Centre," in Eisemann and Koskenniemi, *supra* note 67 at 71 and 119 et seq.; and P. Pazartzis, *La succession d'États aux traités multilatéraux à la lumière des mutations territoriales récentes* (Paris: Editions Pedone, 2002) at 55–56.

[71] Of the same view, P.M. Eisemann, "Rapport du Directeur de la section de langue française du Centre," in Eisemann and Koskenniemi, *supra* note 67 at 40.

[72] Declaration of Alma Ata, *supra* note 66. The preamble of the Agreement Establishing the Commonwealth of Independent States, 13 December 1991, UN Doc.

state, which had ceased to exist — there is no "resurrection" of states in international law.[73] From a logical point of view, the break up of the USSR should be regarded as a case of state dissolution rather than as a series of secessions by the former republics.[74] However, since all states concerned (including Russia itself) view Russia as the continuing state of the USSR, for *practical reasons*, the following two examples of state practice will be analyzed with the assumption that the break up of the USSR resulted from a series of secessions by the former republics (except for the Baltic states). These two examples illustrate the principle according to which, whenever a state does not cease to exist as a result of territorial transformations, it should remain responsible for internationally wrongful acts that it committed in the past.

Pillage of Works of Art and Cultural Property in Germany during and after the Second World War

During the Second World War, German troops seized numerous works of art in the USSR. The victory of the Red Army in 1945 was also followed by the pillage of works of art and cultural property in Germany.[75] Some of these works of art were returned to the GDR in the 1950s and 1960s.[76] Before the break up of the USSR, two

---

A/46/771 (1992) 31 I.L.M. 138 [Minsk Agreement] clearly states that the USSR "as a subject of international law and geopolitical reality no longer exists." The Alma Ata Declaration, *supra* note 66 at 147, also mentions that "with the establishment of the C.I.S., the U.S.S.R. ceases to exist."

[73] Marek, *supra* note 38 at 6: "[T]here is no legal resurrection in international law. Once a State has become extinct, it cannot resume a continued existence."

[74] On this point, P. Dumberry and D. Turp, "La succession d'États en matière de traités et le cas de la sécession: du principe de la table rase à l'émergence d'une présomption de continuité des traités" (2003–2) R.B.D.I. 377 at 401.

[75] It is thus estimated that more than 2.5 million works of art were transferred from Germany to the Soviet Union at the time.

[76] Protocol signed on 8 September 1958 between the GDR and the USSR (the final protocol is dated 29 July 1960). This example is discussed in M. Boguslavsky, "Legal Aspects of the Russian Position in Regard to the Return of Cultural Property," in E. Simpson, ed., *The Spoils of War. World War II and Its Aftermath: The Loss, Reappearance, and Recovery of Cultural Property* (New York: Harry N. Abrams, 1997), 189. It is estimated that some 1.9 million cultural objects belonging to German owners were returned by the USSR to the GDR. P. Kuhn, "Comment on the Soviet Returns of Cultural Treasures Moved Because of the War to the GDR," *Spoils of War*, Newsletter no. 2, 1996.

treaties were entered into on 9 November 1990 between the USSR and the Federal Republic of Germany.[77] After the break up of the Soviet Union, a cultural agreement was entered into in 1992 between Germany and Russia, where the parties committed to the restitution of cultural property that had been "lost" or "unlawfully brought into the territory" of Russia.[78] This agreement thus contains the commitment by Russia (as the "continuator" of the USSR) to provide reparation to Germany (in the form of the restitution of German cultural property) as a result of internationally wrongful acts committed by the USSR (that is, the cultural property "unlawfully brought" into its territory).[79] It should be noted that negotiations between the two states to organize the restitution of cultural property have so far remained unfruitful.[80]

[77] Treaty between the Federal Republic of Germany and the Union of Socialist Republics on Good-Neighbourliness Partnership and Cooperation, 9 November 1990, (1991) 30 I.L.M. 505; (1991) R.G.D.I.P. 214; and Treaty on the Development of Comprehensive Cooperation in the Field of Trade, Industry, Science and Technology, 9 November 1990, (1991) 2 B.G.Bl. 700.

[78] Abkommen Zwischen der Regierung der Bundesrepublik Deutschland und der der Regierung der Russischen Föderation über kulturelle Zusammenarbeit, 16 December 1992, (1993) 2 B.G.Bl. 1256, at Article 15 [Abkommen Zwischen].

[79] The legal issues on the question of the restitution of cultural property between Russia and Germany are discussed in W. Fiedler, "Legal Issues Bearing on the Restitution of German Cultural Property in Russia," in Simpson, *supra* note 76 at 175–80; A. Hiller, "The German-Russian Negotiation over the Content of the Russian Repositories," in Simpson, *supra* note 76; A. Gattini, "Restitution by Russia of Works of Art Removed from German Territory at the End of the Second World War" (1996) 7(1) Eur. J. Int'l L. 66–88; and S. Wilske, "International Law and the Spoils of War: To the Victor the Right of Spoils?: The Claims for Repatriation of Art Removed from Germany by the Soviet Army During or as a Result of World War II" (1998) 3 U.C.L.A. J. Int'l L. & Foreign Aff. 223.

[80] A dispute arose between the two states concerning the interpretation to be given to Article 15 of the Abkommen Zwischen, *supra* note 78. In 1997, a Russian law was passed stating that all cultural properties brought to Russia as a result of the Second World War were now properties of the Russian Federation and that, consequently, no restitution (with very few exceptions) would be made to Germany. Federal Law on Cultural Values Removed to the USSR as Result of World War II and Located in the Territory of the Russian Federation, 5 February 1997, in *Spoils of War*, Newsletter no. 4 (1997) at 10–19. The law is discussed in detail in P. D'Argent, "La loi russe sur les biens culturels transférées: Beutekunst, agression, réparations et contre-mesures" (1998) A.F.D.I. 114–43. The constitutionality of the law was upheld by the Russian Constitutional Court in its decision of 20 July 1999. See A. Blankenagel, "Eyes Wide Shut: Displaced Cultural Objects in Russian Law and Adjudication" (1999) 8(4) E. Eur. Const. Rev. 75.

Measures of Expropriation of French Bonds after the 1917 Revolution

Private and public pre-revolutionary Russian bonds issued in France were nationalized as a result of the Russian Revolution of 1917. Since that time, the USSR has always refused to compensate the hundreds of thousands of private owners of bonds on the ground that the revolutionary Soviet government was not bound by the debts contracted by the previous Tsarist government. A final settlement of reciprocal financial and property demands was signed by the Federation of Russia and France on 27 May 1997.[81] The agreement provided for Russia to pay France US $400 million in exchange for both signatories giving up financial and property claims (which arose before May 1945) on their own behalf or on behalf of their national corporations and individuals. Even if the measures of expropriation taken by the Soviet authorities against French properties, rights, and assets without any compensation in return were undoubtedly internationally wrongful acts,[82] the settlement reached between the parties is, however, clearly *ex gratia* in the sense that Russia does not recognize any legal responsibility for the acts committed after the 1917 revolution. In this agreement, the Federation of Russia is therefore viewed as the continuing state of the Soviet Union, which was itself the "continuator" of the Russian state existing between 1917 and 1922 (that is, before the USSR was officially created in 1922).

CLAIMS ARISING IN THE CONTEXT OF THE SECESSION
OF BELGIUM IN 1830

Problems of state succession arose in the context of the struggle for independence of the Belgian provinces, which finally ended with their secession from the Kingdom of the Netherlands in

81 Accord du 27 mai 1997 entre le Gouvernement de la République française et le Gouvernement de la Fédération de Russie sur le règlement définitif des créances réciproques financières et réelles apparues antérieurement au 9 mai 1945, in (1997) R.G.D.I.P. 1091. The agreement and the memorandum of 26 November 1996 for mutual understanding were approved by the French National Assembly on 19 December 1997 (Bill No. 97–1160, J.O.R.F., 15 May 1998). The historical background and a comprehensive analysis of the agreement can be found in S. Szurek, "Epilogue d'un contentieux historique. L'accord sur le règlement des créances réciproque entre la France et la Russie" (1998) 44 A.F.D.I. 144; and P. Juillard and B. Stern, eds., *Les emprunts russes et le règlement du contentieux financier franco-russe* (Paris: Cedin Cahiers internationaux n° 16, 2002).

82 On this question, see P. Shahrjerdi, "L'indemnisation à raison des mesures soviétiques de nationalisation ou d'expropriation à l'encontre de biens français,"

November 1830. During the armed revolt, the city of Antwerp (situated in the Belgian provinces) was bombarded in October 1830 by the Dutch forces. During the bombardment, a public warehouse was destroyed in which were stored the goods of several foreigners. Some years later, Austria, Brazil, France, Great Britain, Prussia, and the United States submitted claims for compensation for the damage suffered by their nationals.[83]

Great Britain took the view that the Kingdom of the Netherlands (the predecessor and continuing state) "was not liable for the disasters occasioned by the bombardment" of October 1830.[84] Apparently, Austria, Brazil, France, and Prussia also adopted the same position.[85] There is also some indication in the diplomatic correspondence of the time that France, Great Britain, Prussia, and the United States made a joint application to Belgium (the successor state) requesting compensation for the damage "solely [based] upon the ground that the obligation to indemnify for such losses rested upon the country within which the injury was inflicted."[86]

More information is available with respect to the claims filed by the United States against *both* Belgium and the Kingdom of the Netherlands in the hope that they would come up with a satisfactory and voluntary arrangement as to the proportion of responsibility that each one would bear for the damage suffered by US nationals as a result of the bombardment of October 1830.[87] Accordingly, the United States submitted its claim against the

---

in Juillard and Stern, eds., *supra* note 81 at 89–120. This is also the position of P.M. Eisemann, "Emprunts russes et problèmes de succession d'Etats," in Juillard and Stern, *supra* note 81 at 53–78.

[83] J. Bassett Moore, *Digest of International Law*, vol. 6 (Washington: Government Printing Office, 1906) at 942.

[84] This is apparently what the Attorney General of England concluded following a request made by the British Minister of Foreign Affairs. This information is found in a letter of US Secretary of State Mr. Marcy to French Minister Count Sartiges concerning the claims of French subjects as a result of the US bombardment of Greytown in 1854 (letter dated 26 February 1857), 6 Ms. Notes to French Leg. 301; S. Ex. Doc. 9, 35 Cong. 1 sess. 3, reprinted in Moore, *ibid.* at 929.

[85] This is the conclusion reached by US Secretary of State, Mr. Marcy, in a correspondence dated 26 February 1857, *ibid.*

[86] *Ibid.*

[87] "Message of US President Jackson of 5 December 1836," 3 Messages and Papers of the Presidents at 237, reprinted in Moore, *supra* note 83 at 947 et seq. The issue is also mentioned in this internal US diplomatic communication. "Letter of U.S. Secretary of State Mr Forsyth to Mr Davezac, U.S. Chargé d'Affaires to the Netherlands" (10 September 1836), 14 MS. Inst. Netherlands, 24, reprinted

Kingdom of the Netherlands as the actual perpetrator of the act. Apparently, the Dutch government excused its bombardment of the city on the ground of a breach by the Belgian insurgents of a suspension of hostilities that had been agreed upon for the protection of the city.[88] It is not clear from the information available whether or not the Kingdom of the Netherlands ended up paying any compensation to the United States.

The position adopted by the United States towards Belgium, however, is clear. It requested a prompt and speedy settlement of the dispute:

Policy as well as justice prescribes to Belgium the course she ought to pursue, and the forbearance of the United States in pressing these claims, notwithstanding their urgency and the sufferings of our citizens interested, furnishes a powerful reason for their speedy settlement by the Belgian Government, and imposes additional obligation upon the President [of the United States] who greatly regrets the circumstances which have heretofore occasioned such unexpected delay, to adopt the most prompt and efficient measures for their satisfactory adjustment. It is the [United States] President's wish therefore that you should ascertain whether any measures have been taken by Belgium towards the accomplishment of an object deemed by him of the greatest consequence in the preservation and promotion of those feelings of amity which subsist between the two nations, and to urge upon that government such speedy action on the subject as the equity of the claims, and the length of time which has elapsed since the injuries were sustained clearly demand.[89]

---

in Moore, *supra* note 83 at 943. This is the relevant quote taken from the letter: "Had the contest, in the course of which this bombardment took place, terminated favourably to the Netherlands, no doubt is entertained that United States would have had a just claim upon the Government of that country to the indemnification of [United States] citizens for the loss which they had sustained. The fact that the conflict had a different termination can not impair the right of this [United States] Government or its citizens to indemnification; but from which of the countries, or in what proportion from both, the satisfaction is to come it would have been most gratifying to the President [of the United States] to have had determined by themselves. He has accordingly for a long time forborne, notwithstanding the importunity of the sufferers, to urge their claims which appeared to him so just, in the hope that some mutual and voluntary arrangement for their liquidation would have been made ere this between the Governments of Belgium and the Netherlands."

88 *Ibid.* at 947.

89 "Letter of U.S. Secretary of State Mr. Forsyth to Mr. Marcy, U.S. Chargé d'affaires to Belgium" (12 June 1837), 1 MS. Inst. Belgium, 24, reprinted in *ibid.* at 945.

For the United States, there was no doubt as to the responsibility of the new state of Belgium for the internationally wrongful act committed by the Netherlands against the Belgian city. One of the legal grounds invoked by the United States for Belgium to be held responsible for the action concerned the territorial link between the internationally wrongful act and the tortfeaser, as illustrated by this other internal diplomatic correspondence:

> The governments of the respective merchants whose property was destroyed by the bombardment claimed indemnity for these losses from the Kingdom of Belgium. The ground of the claims was, that the injury was inflicted on a territory which, at the time the reclamation was made, had become a part of Belgium; but Belgium attempted to evade it by alleging that the Dutch government received the property, had it in possession, and destroyed it; and from Holland, and not Belgium, indemnity must be sought.[90]

Another legal argument invoked by the United States was that Belgium should be held responsible based on the well-recognized principle of international law according to which a new government is responsible for the acts committed by the previous government.[91] The position adopted by the United States seems to be based on a fundamental mischaracterization of the events of

---

[90] This assessment of the position taken by the United States concerning the Antwerp bombardment is made in *ibid.* at 929–30.

[91] "Letter of U.S. Secretary of State Mr. Webster to Mr. Marcy, U.S. Chargé d'Affaires to Belgium" (26 February 1842), 1 MS. Inst. Belgium, 34, reprinted in Moore, *supra* note 83 at 945–47: "There is no doubt that the duty or obligation of indemnity, whatever it is, for the losses at Antwerp, falls upon Belgium. The Belgians, as a civilized people, must be considered at all times under some form of civil government, and however often they may see fit to change this form, these changes cannot affect their just responsibility to any foreign state, its citizens or subjects. Succeeding governments necessarily take upon themselves, so far at least as foreign nations are concerned, the obligations of the governments which preceded them, whether those obligations were created by treaty or by the general principles of national law. It is on this ground that the restored governments of Europe have made indemnities to foreign states for excesses committed on the property of citizens or subjects of these states by the revolutionary governments ... The Belgians saw fit to change their government which, so far as foreign nations are concerned, they had a right to do. But in doing this they shook off no national responsibility. The moment the authority of the King of the Netherlands ceased over the Belgians, that moment every one of his obligations towards foreign nations, so far as that part of his Kingdom was concerned, devolved on the new government that succeeded him."

November 1830. These events should not be analyzed as mere *change of government* but, rather, as the emergence of a *new state*.

In any event, Belgium initially denied its responsibility on the obvious ground that the acts were committed by the Dutch forces and that, therefore, only the Dutch government should be responsible for them.[92] Belgium apparently subsequently changed its initial position and finally agreed to pay compensation to the owners of the merchandise that had been destroyed during the incident.[93]

J.H.W. Verzijl described this example as a "clear case of asserted responsibility of a territorial successor to injuries inflicted by its predecessor."[94] This example is indeed one where the successor state took over the obligations arising from internationally wrongful acts committed by the predecessor state. It is the only clear example of state practice in the context of secession where the continuing state did not remain responsible for internationally wrongful acts that it committed before the date of succession.

The outcome of this case is very surprising. It is also contrary to another principle applicable in the context of state succession. In cases where the insurgents are successful at establishing a new state, the latter should (in principle) not be held accountable for internationally wrongful acts committed by the predecessor state against third states in its efforts to block the rebels' struggle for independence.[95] The surprising fact that the new successor state was forced to pay compensation for acts for which it had simply nothing to do, and of which it was in fact the victim, may be based on *political* reasons. Thus, at the time of its independence, Belgium was probably not in a position to refuse to provide reparation to the much more powerful claimant states. In other words, the solution adopted in this case can hardly be considered as the foundation of any *general* principle in favour of succession in the context where the predecessor state continues its existence.

---

92 Moore, *supra* note 83 at 947. Belgium also pleaded that the injuries suffered were due to an unavoidable incident of war.

93 This is, for instance, the conclusion reached by Verzijl, *supra* note 28 at 226–27.

94 *Ibid.*

95 The principle of non-transfer of obligations is explicitly affirmed in the work of the ILC. *Report of the International Law Commission on the Work of its Twenty-Seventh Session*, 5 May to 25 July 1975, Draft Articles on State Responsibility, UN Doc. A/10010/Rev.1 (1975), in *Yearbook of the International Law Commission 1975*, vol. 2, 47 at 101, para. 6. This principle is discussed in Dumberry, *supra* note 5 at 297–307.

TREATY BETWEEN THE UNITED STATES AND PANAMA IN THE
CONTEXT OF THE SECESSION OF PANAMA IN 1903

In 1903, Panama seceded from Colombia. Many years before (in 1855), a fire broke out in the city of Colon, situated in the Department of Panama, which was then part of the territory of Colombia.[96] The fire caused damage to American nationals. After Panama's secession, the United States submitted a claim against the new state for the acts committed on its territory while it was still part of Colombia. Panama refused to be held responsible. On 28 July 1926, the United States and Panama signed a treaty concerning reciprocal claims which arose *after* 1903.[97] The treaty also envisaged future arbitration proceedings with respect to the consequences of the 1855 fire in the city of Colon.[98] The two questions that Panama and the United States agreed should be put to a future arbitral tribunal, upon a new convention being entered into, clearly dealt with the issue of state succession to international responsibility.[99]

No subsequent convention was entered into by Panama and the United States on this issue, and no arbitration ever took place. This example of state practice is therefore less significant, as it remains theoretical. It is nevertheless interesting to note that both

[96] The facts are explained in: Feilchenfeld, *supra* note 28 at 351–52; and Verzijl, *supra* note 28 at 222.

[97] Claims Convention between the United States and Panama, 28 July 1926, 138 L.N.T.S. 120–26; 6 R.I.A.A. 301 (ratified on 3 October 1931) [Claims Convention]. Extracts of the text are reproduced in Feilchenfeld, *supra* note 28 at 351–52. Under the treaty, both parties agreed to submit to an arbitral tribunal all claims of their nationals against the other state arising out of events that took place *after* Panama became an independent state in 1903. However, claims for compensation for damage caused in connexion with the construction of the Panama Canal were excluded as they were to be dealt with by the Joint Land Commission under the Panama Canal Convention of 18 November 1903.

[98] Claims Convention, *supra* note 97, Article I at para. 2, reads as follows: "Panama agrees in principle to the arbitration of such claims under a Convention to which the Republic of Colombia shall be invited to become a party and which shall provide for the creation or selection of an arbitral tribunal."

[99] These questions read as follows: "First, whether the Republic of Colombia incurred any liability for losses sustained by American citizens on account of the fire that took place in the city of Colon on the 31th of March 1885; and, second, in case there should be determined in the arbitration that there is an original liability on the part of Colombia, *to what extent, if any, the Republic of Panama has succeeded Colombia in such liability on account of her separation from Colombia on November 3, 1903*" [emphasis added].

the injured state (the United States) and the new successor state (Panama), had, at least theoretically, recognized that the successor state could be held liable for the internationally wrongful act committed by the predecessor state (Colombia) before the date of succession.[100]

SPECIFIC CIRCUMSTANCES UNDER WHICH THE SECESSIONIST STATE SHOULD TAKE OVER THE OBLIGATION TO REPAIR

The analysis of state practice has shown that in principle (with only one significant exception) the continuing state should remain responsible for the consequences of its own internationally wrongful acts committed before the date of succession. This proposition is not controversial. The question nevertheless remains as to whether this principle of non-succession should *always* apply in the context of secession. In other words, it remains open whether there are not some circumstances under which it should instead be for the secessionist state to be accountable for internationally wrongful acts committed before the date of succession. This point is rarely addressed in doctrine.[101]

It is submitted that in the following circumstances (which will now be examined in detail) the secessionist state should take over obligations arising from internationally wrongful acts committed before the date of succession:

- the successor state has freely accepted (after the date of succession) to take over the obligations arising from the commission of the internationally wrongful act;
- the internationally wrongful act is committed by an insurrectional movement during an armed struggle that eventually lead to secession;
- the internationally wrongful act is committed by an autonomous government (while still part of the predecessor state) with which the successor state has an "organic and structural continuity";
- the successor state has unjustly enriched itself as a result of an internationally wrongful act committed before the date of succession; and

---

100 Thus, Panama "agreed in principle to the arbitration of such claims" and for the establishment of an Arbitral tribunal to decide "to what extent, if any" it had succeeded to the original liability of the predecessor state. (Claims Convention, *supra* note 97, Article I).

101 Stern, *supra* note 3 at 335–36, makes reference to the issue.

• the acts committed by the predecessor state were *specifically linked* to what is now the successor state's territory (violation of territorial regimes).[102]

The new state should take over the obligations arising from internationally wrongful acts committed before the date of succession whenever it has freely accepted (after the date of succession) to take over such obligations. There is unanimity in doctrine on this point.[103] In the *Case Concerning the Gabčíkovo-Nagymaros Project (Hungary v. Slovakia)*, in the context of the dissolution of Czechoslovakia, the *compromis* between Hungary and Slovakia to submit a dispute to the International Court of Justice (ICJ) had recognized the Slovak Republic as the "sole successor state in respect of rights and obligations relating to the Gabčíkovo-Nagymaros Project."[104] The ICJ did not question whether the Slovak Republic could freely decide to be held solely liable for the internationally wrongful act committed by the predecessor state — it simply accepted this position as a fact.[105] Similarly, in the context of the independence of Namibia (which is an example of a newly independent state), the sitting judge of the Namibian High Court interpreted Article 140(3) of the Namibian Constitution and stated that "in the present case the new State chose to accept liability, subject to its right to repudiate,

---

102 The present author has examined (Dumberry, *supra* note 5 at 247–336) in detail these different specific circumstances under which the principle of succession should apply in the general context of the issue of state succession to international responsibility (not limited to cases of secession).

103 Udina, *supra* note 17 at 768; Stern, *supra* note 3 at 350; H. Lauterpacht, *Oppenheim's International Law*, vol. 1 (London: Longmans Green and Company, 1955) at 162; Jenning and Watts, *supra* note 38 at 218; J. O'Brien, *International Law* (London: Cavendish, 2001) at 605; Dupuy, *supra* note 13 at 54; Brownlie, *supra* note 17 at 632 (arguing that the successor state's acceptance of succession to obligations arising from the commission of internationally wrongful acts creates "an estoppel in various particular respects"); W. Schönborn, *Staatensuccession, Handbuch des Völkerrechts*, vol. 2, Part. 5 (Stuttgard, 1913) at 49; Monnier, *supra* note 3 at 67 and 90; Volkovitsch, *supra* note 3 at 2199–200; N. Ronzitti, *La successione internazionale tra stati* (Milan: Dott. A. Giuffrè, 1970) at 221; J. Dugard, *International Law: A South African Perspective*, 2nd edition (Kenwyn: Juta, 2000) at 232–33; H. Booysen, "Succession to Delictual Liability: A Namibian Precedent" (1991) 24 Comp. and Int'l L.J. S. Afr. 207; and T.S.N. Sastry, *State Succession in Indian Context* (New Delhi: Dominant, 2004) at 209.

104 *Case Concerning the Gabčíkovo-Nagymaros Project (Hungary v. Slovakia)*, [1997] I.C.J. Rep. 3 [*Gabčíkovo-Nagymaros*].

105 *Ibid.* at para. 151.

and is therefore liable."[106] He added: "I know of no principle whereby international law can step in and undo such an acceptance by a State."[107]

The new state should be held responsible for obligations arising from internationally wrongful acts committed by rebels or insurgents against third states during their struggles to achieve secession.[108] The general principle is stated in Article 10(2) of the ILC Articles on State Responsibility,[109] and it is largely supported in doctrine[110] as well as by (limited) state practice.[111] This is so because there is a "structural" continuity between the insurrectional movement and the organization of the new state as they both have

---

106 *Mwandinghi v. Minister of Defence, Namibia,* 14 December 1990, 1991 (1) S.A. 851 (Nm) at 864, 91 I.L.R. 343 at 355 (Namibia, High Court). See also *Minister of Defence, Namibia v. Mwandinghi,* 25 October 1991, 1992 (2) S.A. 355 (NmS), 91 I.L.R. 358 (Namibia, Supreme Court).

107 *Ibid.* at 354–55.

108 This question is examined in detail in Dumberry, *supra* note 5 at 268–96. See also Patrick Dumberry, "New State Responsibility for Internationally Wrongful Acts by an Insurrectional Movement" (2006) 17(3) Eur. J. Int'l L. 605.

109 Titles and Texts of the Draft Articles on Responsibility of States for Internationally Wrongful Acts Adopted by the Drafting Committee on Second Reading, 26 July 2001, UN Doc. A/CN.4/L.602/Rev.1 (2001) [2001 ILC Articles on State Responsibility].

110 Stern, *supra* note 3 at 344; Atlam, *supra* note 3 at 422; L. Zegveld, *Accountability of Armed Opposition Groups in International Law* (Cambridge: Cambridge University Press, 2002) at 155–56; G. Balladore Pallieri, *Diritto internazionale pubblico,* 8th edition (Milan: Giuffrè, 1962) at 173; Udina, *supra* note 17 at 768–69; G. Arangio-Ruiz, *L'Etat dans le sens du droit des gens et la notion du droit international* (Bologna: Cooperatura libraria universitaria, 1975) at 45; G.A. Christenson, "The Doctrine of Attribution in State Responsibility," in R.B. Lillich, ed., *International Law of State Responsibility of Injuries to Aliens* (Charlottesville: University Press Virginia, 1983) at 334; Moore, *supra* note 83, vol. I at 44; J. Quigley, "State Responsibility for Ethnic Cleansing" (1999) 32 U.C. Davis L. Rev. 357; Czaplinski, *supra* note 3 at 353; and Volkovitsch, *supra* note 3 at 2199. See also Article 18(1) of Harvard's Draft Convention on the International Responsibility of States for Injuries to Aliens, 15 April 1961, (1961) 55 Am. J. Int'l L. at 576; and Article XIII (b) of the Harvard Draft of 1929 (1929 Supp.) 23 Am. J. Int'l L. 131–239.

111 In the context of the independence of Algeria (a newly independent state), French municipal courts have consistently held that the new state of Algeria should (in principle) provide compensation to French nationals victims of internationally wrongful acts committed by the insurgents of the Front de libération nationale (FLN) in their war efforts to achieve independence. These examples of state practice are analyzed in detail in Dumberry, *supra* note 5 at 268 et seq.: and Dumberry, *supra* note 108.

essentially the *same* legal entity: "[F]rom being only an embryo State, the insurrectional movement has become a State proper, without any break in the continuity between the two."[112] The principle has also been specifically endorsed by the ILC in the context of secession.[113] In the *Socony Vaccum Oil Company* case,[114] the United States's International Claims Commission made reference in the form of an *obiter dictum* to the successful secession of the United States from the British Crown in 1776 and indicated that in such a case the new state was responsible for the acts of the rebels committed during the revolution.[115] Similarly, in the context of the (unsuccessful) struggle of the Confederate Army for secession of the southern states from the United States during the American Civil War (1861–5), the Law Officers of the British Crown gave a legal opinion during the war (on 16 February 1863). The opinion stated that if the rebels were to succeed in their secession efforts, the new state should be held responsible for its acts committed before independence.[116] It should be noted, however, that this devolution of

---

[112] *Report of the International Law Commission on the Work of its Twenty-Seventh Session, supra* note 95 at 101, para. 6. The same explanation is found in "Commentaries to the Draft Articles on Responsibility of States for Internationally Wrongful Acts," *supra* note 4 at 114, para. 6. See also in *Fourth Report on State Responsibility of the Special Rapporteur,* Mr. Roberto Ago, 24th session of the I.L.C., 1972, UN Doc. A/CN.4/264 and Add.1, in I.L.C. Report, Doc. A/8710/Rev.1 (A/27/10) (1972), ch. IV(B), paras. 72–73, in *Yearbook of the International Law Commission 1972,* vol. 2, 71 at 131, paras. 159 and 194.

[113] "Commentaries to the Draft Articles on Responsibility of States for Internationally Wrongful Acts," *supra* note 4 at 114, para. 6.

[114] *Socony Vaccum Oil Company Case (Settlements of Claims)* (1949–55) at 77, (1954) I.L.R. 55 (US International Claims Commission).

[115] *Ibid.*: "Such was the case of the State government under the old [United States] confederation on their separation from the British Crown. *Having made good their declaration of independence, everything they did from that date was as valid as if their independence has been at once acknowledged. Confiscations, therefore, of enemy property made by them were sustained as if made by an independent nation.* But if they had failed in securing their independence and the authority of the [British] King had been reestablished in this country, no one would contend that their acts against him, or his loyal subjects, could have been upheld as resting upon any legal foundation" [emphasis added].

[116] Legal Opinion of the Law Officers of the British Crown (16 February 1863), in L. McNair, *International Law Opinions,* vol. 2 (Cambridge: Cambridge University Press, 1956) at 257: "In the event of the war having ceased, and the authority of the Confederate State being de *jure* as well as de facto established, it will be competent to Her Majesty's Government to urge the payment of a compensation for the losses inflicted on Her Majesty's subjects by the Confederate

responsibility is solely based on the mechanisms of state responsibility and not on any rules of state succession.[117] Similarly, the secessionist state should be held responsible for obligations arising from internationally wrongful acts committed before its independence insofar as the acts were committed by an autonomous government (or by any other political entity clearly identifiable) with which the new state has an organic and structural continuity.[118] There is some support in doctrine for such a general proposition.[119] This principle was applied by one international tribunal,[120] as well as by a municipal court [121] in the context of a cession of territory.[122] Doctrine favours the application of this

Authorities during the War." This example is reported in *Report of the International Law Commission on the Work of its Twenty-Seventh Session, supra* note 109 at 103, para. 12.

[117] *Report of the International Law Commission on the Work of its Twenty-Seventh Session, supra* note 95 at 101, para. 8.

[118] Even if Article 10(2) of the 2001 ILC Articles on State Responsibility, *supra* note 109, in the specific context of acts committed by insurrectional movements in their armed struggle for independence does not deal with issues of state succession, it is submitted that the principle it establishes should be used, by analogy, in the different context where independence is achieved as a result of a democratic process instead of an armed struggle. In other words, the principle set out in Article 10(2) of the ILC Articles should apply in the context of succession of states to international responsibility.

[119] Peterschmitt, *supra* note 3 at 62–63. See also M. Waelbroeck, "Arrêt no. 8160 du Conseil d'Etat Belge, note d'observations" (1961–61) R.J.D.A. 36; and Udina, *supra* note 17 at 769.

[120] In its evaluation of Claim no. 4, the French-Greek arbitral tribunal in the 1956 *Lighthouse Arbitration* case, *supra* note 23 at 196–200, decided that Greece (the successor state) should be responsible for its own acts of omission committed after the date of succession (1913) as well as for those committed by the *de facto* autonomous government of Crete before that date at the time when the Island was (at least formally) under Ottoman sovereignty .

[121] In the *Samos (Liability for Torts) Case*, 1924, no. 27, 35 Thémis 294 (1923–24) Ann. Dig. I.L.C. 70 (Court of the Aegean Islands, Greece), a Greek court decided that it was for the successor state (Greece) to be held responsible for the damage caused by local customs officials of the Island of Samos at the time when it was still (at least formally) under Ottoman rule.

[122] Cases of cession of territory are different from cases of secession. A case of cession or transfer of territory arises when the events affecting the territorial integrity of the predecessor state (which continues to exist) result in the enlargement of the territory of an existing state. In such a case, there is no new state created. A classic example of a cession of territory is that of Alsace-Lorraine from Germany to France in 1919.

principle in the context of newly independent states where a colony has had certain autonomy before independence.[123] There is no reason why the principle of succession should not be adopted in the context of secession.

To the extent that a new state has *unjustly enriched* itself as a result of an internationally wrongful act committed before the date of succession, it should provide reparation to the injured third state after the date of succession.[124] There is support in doctrine for such a solution,[125] even by some scholars who generally reject the possibility of succession to international responsibility.[126] In certain situations, both the continuing state and the successor state may have enriched themselves. In such cases, they should then both be held accountable to the injured third state in proportion to their actual benefits/advantage arising from the commission of the internationally wrongful act.

It has been suggested in doctrine that in cases where the continuing state loses a great portion of its initial territory following the creation of a new state, there should be a transfer of the obligation to repair to the new state.[127] This last argument is not entirely

---

[123] Czaplinski, *supra* note 3 at 356–57; and Verzijl, *supra* note 28 at 219–20.

[124] This question is addressed in Dumberry, *supra* note 5 at 307–22.

[125] Volkovitsch, *supra* note 3 at 2210–11; Peterschmitt, *supra* note 3 at 55–61; Eisemann, *supra* note 82 at 62; and P. Drakidis, "Succession d'Etats et enrichissements sans cause des biens publics du Dodécanèse" (1971) 24 R.H.D.I. 109.

[126] See the following writers: Udina, *supra* note 17 at 769–70; O. Schachter, "State Succession: The Once and Future Law" (1993) 33(2) Va. J. Int'l L. 256; I.A. Shearer, *Starke's International Law*, 11th edition (Sydney: Butterworths, 1994) at 303; A. Verdross, *Völkerrecht*, 4th edition (Vienna: Springer Verlag, 1959) at 198; A. Verdross and B. Simma, *Universelles Völkerrecht, Theorie und Praxis* (Berlin: Dunker and Humblot, 1984) at 633–34; Waelbroeck, *supra* note 119 at 35; L. Berat, "Genocide: The Namibian Case Against Germany" (1993) Pace Int'l L.Rev. 193; and Ronzitti, *supra* note 103 at 220–21. See also *Restatement (Third), Foreign Relations Law of the United States*, vol. 1 (St. Paul: American Law Institute, 1987) at 105, para. 209(g) and also reporters' notes no. 7 (at 107).

[127] For Hyde, *supra* note 28 at 437, there has been "little or no concern" on the question whether a "considerable diminution of territory ... might serve greatly to impair the ability of [the continuing state] to make adequate redress for wrongs chargeable to it" and that this should therefore "be regarded as a limitation upon [the continuing state] to make a valid cession." This is also the opinion of Peterschmitt, *supra* note 3 at 64: "[l]orsque l'Etat prédécesseur a perdu une très grande partie de son territoire, il peut, dans certains cas, paraître injuste que l'Etat continuateur porte tout seul l'obligation de réparer."

convincing. As a matter of principle, the size of the territory that secedes should not, in itself, determine which of the states — the "continuator" or the new state — should be held responsible for obligations arising from internationally wrongful acts committed before the date of succession. Similarly, the new state should not be automatically responsible for obligations arising from an internationally wrongful act committed by the predecessor state solely based on the fact that such an act took place prior to its independence on what is now its territory.[128] In other words, the fact that such an act took place on the territory of the new state before its independence should not, in itself, be a ground for finding this state responsible for the act. However, the successor state should be responsible for obligations arising from internationally wrongful acts committed by the predecessor state that are specifically linked to what is now its territory, such as violations of territorial regimes obligations.[129] This solution is in line with the well-recognized principle that for considerations of stability in international relations successor states are bound to respect pre-existing international frontiers, international boundary treaties, and any "objective" situation created by a treaty regarding a territory.[130] To the extent that a successor state inherits territorial regime obligations from the predecessor state, it is only logical that it should also take over the consequences of the violation of such obligations committed by the predecessor state prior to the date of succession

CONCLUSION

The analysis of state practice and case law in the context of secession shows the existence of a general principle: the continuing state

---

[128] This question is examined in Dumberry, *supra* note 5 at 336–41.

[129] This question is examined in *ibid.*

[130] *Frontier Dispute Case (Burkina Faso v. Mali)*, [1986] I.C.J. Rep. 554; *Case Concerning the Determination of the Maritime Boundary between Guinea and Guinea-Bissau*, Award of 14 February 1985, 19 R.I.A.A. 149 at para. 40. On this point, see M. del Carmen Marquez Carrasco, "Régimes de frontières et autres régimes territoriaux face à la succession d'États," in Eisemann and Koskenniemi, *supra* note 67 at 493–577; Pazartzis, *supra* note 70 at 164–69; Stern, *supra* note 19 at 255–62. The rule that the successor state cannot denounce an "objective" situation created by a treaty is provided for in Article 12 of the Vienna Convention, *supra* note 1. In the *Gabčíkovo-Nagymaros* case, *supra* note 104 at para. 123, the International Court of Justice considered that "Article 12 reflects a rule of customary international law."

remains responsible for its own internationally wrongful acts committed before the date of succession notwithstanding the transformation affecting its territory. The principle is well established by several decisions of municipal courts of the new successor state[131] as well as by one court decision of the continuing state.[132] There are several examples of state practice supporting this principle. One such example is in the context of the break up of the USSR. In one treaty entered into with Germany in 1992, the Federation of Russia (as the continuing state) continued its responsibility for internationally wrongful acts committed by the USSR during and after the Second World War, namely for the pillage of works of art and cultural property in Germany. In another treaty signed with France in 1997, the Federation of Russia continued its responsibility for measures of expropriation of bonds issued in France, which were taken by newly Soviet Russia after the 1917 revolution. This principle is also supported by the official position taken by the authorities of the GDR, which held that it was not responsible for obligations arising from internationally wrongful acts committed by the Third Reich before and during the Second World War.[133] The position taken by the "allied and associated powers" in the context of the break up of the Austria–Hungary dual monarchy (in 1918) also supports the principle of non-succession. From this review of the state practice, it seems that in only one significant instance was the principle of succession to the obligations arising from internationally wrongful acts applied — claims in the context of the secession of Belgium (1830).[134]

The aim of this comment was to go beyond the mere examination of state practice and to enquire whether there should not be exceptions to the well-established general principle, according to which the continuing state continues its own responsibility after

---

[131] For instance, in three cases decided by the Supreme Court of Poland, *Dzierzbicki, supra* notes 48, *Niemiec and Niemiec, supra* note 50, and *Olpinski, supra* note 51.

[132] *Baron, supra* note 52.

[133] As examined earlier, there exist two less significant examples where the opposite principle of succession was adopted: the war reparation paid by the GDR to the USSR and the offer of compensation made to Jewish groups in the context of internationally wrongful acts committed by the German Reich.

[134] As explained earlier, political considerations may explain the outcome. There is another less significant example where the principle of succession was (at least theoretically) referred to, namely the 1926 treaty between the United States and Panama in the context of the secession of Panama in 1903. Claims Convention, *supra* note 97.

the date of succession. This comment argues that there are indeed several circumstances under which the secessionist state should take over obligations arising from internationally wrongful acts committed before the date of succession. One (quite obvious) scenario is when the successor state has freely accepted (after the date of succession) to take over such obligations.

Ultimately, the question of who from the continuing state or the new state should be responsible for obligations arising from internationally wrongful acts committed before the date of succession should be answered taking into account the principles of equity and justice. Thus, the outcome of any allocation of liability between the continuing state and the new state in the context of secession should be fair and equitable, not only from their own perspectives but also from the point of view of the injured third state.[135] Thus, fairness and equity requires, on the one hand, that an internationally wrongful act does not remain unpunished and that the injured state victim of such an act is not left (after the date of succession) without any debtor against whom it can file a claim for reparation. Fairness also necessitates, on the other hand, that a state should not be held responsible for obligations arising from wrongful acts with which it has nothing to do and for which it has received no benefit/advantage.

There are indeed circumstances where fairness and equity call for the principle of succession to apply. This is certainly the case whenever the internationally wrongful acts were in fact committed by rebels or an autonomous government that succeeded in establishing a new state. In this case, it would, no doubt, be unjust for the continuing state to be held liable for these acts with which it has simply nothing to do. This is all the more so considering that the consequence of such wrongful acts ultimately has led to the dismembering of the continuing state's territorial integrity and the loss of part of its territory. It is further submitted that the application of the traditional doctrine of non-succession to cases of secession when unjust enrichment occurred would certainly also result in unfair consequences. Thus, it would no doubt be unjust for the continuing state to be held liable for the commission of internationally wrongful acts for which it did not receive any benefit/advantage. In other words, the continuing state should not pay reparation to the injured third state, while it is the successor state that

---

135 This question is examined in Dumberry, *supra* note 5 at 323–28.

has enriched itself as a result of the commission of the acts. Finally, it is submitted that the present outline of allocation of responsibility for pre-secession internationally wrongful acts between the continuing state and the new state is not only based on fairness but also necessary in contemporary international law as it addresses the important concern of the international community for predictability, order, and stability of international legal relations between states.[136]

PATRICK DUMBERRY
Of the law firm Ogilvy Renault, Montreal

Sommaire

Un nouvel État est-il responsable des obligations découlant de ses actes internationalement illicites posés dans un contexte de sécession avant d'obtenir son indépendance?

Le présent article traite de la question de la succession d'États en matière de responsabilité internationale dans le contexte particulier de la sécession. La pratique des États et la jurisprudence montrent que l'État continuateur demeure le plus souvent lié par sa propre responsabilité internationale pour les actes internationalement illicites qu'il a commis avant la date de la succession d'États. Une question plus controversée est celle de savoir si le principe de non-succession devrait toujours s'appliquer et s'il n'y a pas des circonstances dans lesquelles l'État successeur sécessionniste devrait être tenu responsable pour les actes internationalement illicites commis avant la date de succession. La question n'est jamais traitée dans la doctrine. Le présent article soutient qu'il y a, en effet, cinq circonstances différentes dans lesquelles le nouvel État sécessionniste devrait prendre en charge les obligations découlant des actes internationalement illicites commis avant son indépendance.

---

[136] Mullerson, *supra* note 68 at 44.

Summary

Is a New State Responsible for Obligations Arising from Internationally Wrongful Acts Committed before Its Independence in the Context of Secession?

This comment addresses the question of the succession of states to obligations arising from the commission of internationally wrongful acts in the specific context of secession. It examines state practice and case law, which shows that the continuator state usually continues its own previous responsibility for internationally wrongful acts committed before the date of succession, notwithstanding the transformation affecting its territory. A more controversial issue is whether this principle of non-succession should always apply in the context of secession and whether there should not be some circumstances where the secessionist state should be responsible for internationally wrongful acts committed before the date of succession. This question is never addressed in doctrine. This article argues that there are, indeed, at least five different circumstances under which the new state should take over obligations arising from internationally wrongful acts committed before the date of succession.

Chronique de Droit international économique en 2004 / Digest of International Economic Law in 2004

I Commerce

préparé par
RICHARD OUELLET

I Introduction

En 2004, le Ministère du Commerce international du Canada, distinct de celui des Affaires étrangères depuis décembre 2003,[1] avait plusieurs raisons d'afficher un certain optimisme quant à l'état du commerce international canadien. Les négociations multilatérales dans le contexte du Cycle de Doha ont porté fruit en juillet et permis d'aboutir à un cadre de négociations encourageant qui tranchait avec les piètres résultats de la Conférence de Cancun de 2003. Des missions commerciales au Brésil et en Amérique centrale ont été couronnées de succès et une entente cadre a été signée avec l'Union européenne pour le renforcement du commerce et de l'investissement.[2] Les choses ont aussi évolué plutôt à l'avantage du Canada dans les conflits commerciaux l'impliquant. Parmi les

---

Richard Ouellet, Professeur à la Faculté de droit et à l'Institut québécois des hautes études internationales de l'Université Laval et membre du Centre d'études interaméricaines (CEI). L'auteur tient à remercier le CEI pour son appui financier et Mme Nadine Martin pour sa collaboration dans la préparation de cette chronique.

[1] Il faut savoir que c'est par décision du Premier Ministre Paul Martin que les Ministères des Affaires étrangères et du Commerce international ont été séparés le 12 décembre 2003. Un an plus tard, un projet de loi qui avait notamment pour but de formaliser juridiquement cette séparation a été déposé au Parlement. Ce projet de loi n'est jamais devenu loi et le 6 février 2006, lors de l'assermentation du nouveau Premier Ministre Stephen Harper, celui-ci annonçait la réunification des deux ministères.

[2] Canada, Communiqué de presse du 7 décembre 2004, disponible à: <http://wo1. international.gc.ca/minpub/Publication.asp?publication_id=381867& Language=F> (date d'accès: le 5 mai 2006).

objectifs de la politique commerciale du Canada pour l'année 2004, on retrouvait en tête de liste le règlement du conflit avec les États-Unis au sujet du bois d'œuvre résineux:[3] trois décisions plutôt favorables des instances de l'Organisation mondiale du commerce (OMC) et cinq dans le cadre de groupes spéciaux de l'*Accord de libre-échange nord-américain* (ALENA) ont pu donner de l'espoir malgré la réticence des autorités américaines à mettre en œuvre les recommandations et conclusions favorables au Canada.

Au surplus, deux rapports économiques pouvaient aussi donner confiance en l'avenir. En début février furent publiés les résultats d'une étude portant sur les coûts des entreprises à l'échelle internationale. Le Canada fut classé comme le plus concurrentiel des pays du Groupe des Sept (G-7) au chapitre des coûts. Le climat d'investissement des plus attrayants et la main-d'œuvre hautement qualifiée comptaient parmi d'autres facteurs qui, jugeait-on, contribueraient à attirer encore plus d'entreprises à venir s'installer au pays.[4]

Un mois plus tard, le Ministre du Commerce international, M. Jim Peterson, rendait public *Le point sur le commerce en 2004: Cinquième rapport annuel sur l'état du commerce au Canada*, soulignant que le Canada continuerait d'offrir un cadre très favorable pour faire des affaires et que les exportations canadiennes en matière de haute technologie et autres services commerciaux avaient progressé.[5]

II   LE COMMERCE CANADIEN AUX PLANS BILATÉRAL ET RÉGIONAL

En 2004, l'*Accord de libre-échange nord-américain* fêtait ses dix ans. Lors de la dixième Réunion ministérielle annuelle de la Commission du libre-échange de l'ALENA à San Antonio, au Texas, les

---

[3] Canada, Document d'information à la suite du Communiqué de presse du 23 avril 2004, disponible à: <http://wo1.international.gc.ca/minpub/Publication.asp?publication_id=381069&Language=F> (date d'accès: le 5 mai 2006).

[4] Il s'agissait d'un rapport commandé par le Ministère à la firme KPMG. Canada, Communiqué de presse du 18 février 2004, disponible à: <http://wo1.international.gc.ca/minpub/Publication.asp?publication_id=380776&Language=F> (date d'accès: le 5 mai 2006). On peut consulter l'étude intégrale à <http://www.choixconcurrentiels.com> et les résultats canadiens détaillés à <http://www.investiraucanada.gc.ca> (date d'accès: le 5 mai 2006).

[5] La version en ligne du rapport est disponible à: <http://www.dfait-maeci.gc.ca/eet/trade/state-of-trade-fr.asp> (date d'accès: le 5 mai 2006).

Ministres en ont profité pour célébrer les avantages qu'avait procurés l'accord, mais ont également discuté de moyens de l'améliorer. Entre autres, ils ont convenu d'une série de mesures, dont la mise en place d'un ensemble de règles d'origine libéralisées visant un large éventail de produits alimentaires, de consommation et industriels.[6]

Après dix ans d'application de l'ALÉNA, à l'heure des bilans, on constate aujourd'hui que plus de 86 % de toutes les marchandises exportées par le Canada sont destinées à ses partenaires mexicain et américain. De plus, près de 2,3 millions d'emplois ont été créés au Canada depuis 1994, ce qui représente une augmentation de 17,5 % par rapport aux niveaux d'emploi avant l'ALÉNA.[7]

Depuis la signature de l'ALÉNA, les relations entre le Canada et le Mexique ont évolué en un étroit partenariat économique, politique et social. Les échanges commerciaux entre les deux pays ont presque triplé et dépassent maintenant les 15 milliards de dollars canadiens. Le progrès économique considérable qu'a fait le Mexique a attiré l'attention des gens d'affaires de partout au Canada.

À la fin de l'année 2004, le programme de précontrôle Canada-États-Unis, qui permet entre autres de réduire les délais d'attente pour les secteurs canadiens qui exportent des marchandises et des services vers les États-Unis, offrait ses services à l'aéroport de Halifax, en plus des sept autres où le programme est déjà en vigueur: Vancouver, Calgary, Edmonton, Winnipeg, Toronto, Ottawa et Montréal.[8]

A   LES NÉGOCIATIONS COMMERCIALES AUX PLANS BILATÉRAL ET RÉGIONAL

1   Le projet de la ZLEA

En ce qui concerne la Zone de libre-échange des Amériques (ZLEA), 2004 a été une année plutôt tranquille puisqu'il n'y a pas eu de Réunion ministérielle pendant cette année. Par ailleurs, à

---

6 Canada, Communiqué de presse du 16 juillet 2004, disponible à: <http://wo1. international.gc.ca/minpub/Publication.asp?publication_id=381336& Language=F> (date d'accès: le 5 mai 2006).

7 Commerce international Canada, Vue d'ensemble de l'ALÉNA, disponible à: <http://dfait-maeci.gc.ca/nafta-alena/over-fr.asp> (date d'accès: le 5 mai 2006).

8 Pour plus de renseignements sur le Plan d'action pour la création d'une frontière sûre et intelligente, voir <http://www.dfait-maeci.gc.ca/can-am/main/ border/default-fr.asp> (date d'accès: le 5 mai 2006).

l'occasion de la réunion tenue en novembre entre le Premier Ministre Paul Martin et le Président Luiz Inácio Lula da Silva du Brésil, ces derniers en ont profité pour indiquer dans une déclaration conjointe que le dialogue Canada-Mercosur sur le commerce et l'investissement se ferait dans le contexte de la création d'une future Zone de libre-échange des Amériques.[9] Malgré l'incertitude qui plane sur la future ZLEA, deux choses sont malheureusement certaines: les négociations, qui devaient s'achever au plus tard en janvier 2005, sont loin d'être terminées, et l'Accord n'entrera certainement pas en vigueur en décembre 2005, date limite qui était fixée à l'échéancier. Les Amériques ne semblent pas être prêtes pour faire un si grand pas pour l'instant.

2   *Les autres développements aux plans bilatéral et régional*

Les représentants du Canada et du Groupe des quatre de l'Amérique Centrale (Salvador, Guatemala, Honduras et Nicaragua) se sont réunis en février pour la dixième série de négociations officielles en vue d'un accord de libre-échange. Malgré le fait que des progrès considérables aient été faits, il reste un grand nombre de questions en suspens, dont l'accès aux marchés pour les textiles et les vêtements qui bénéficient de subventions à l'exportation, et l'accès aux marchés des produits agricoles.[10]

Moins d'un mois plus tard, une mission commerciale a eu lieu au Guatemala, au Salvador, au Costa Rica et au Panama, dirigée par le ministre d'État (Marchés nouveaux et émergents), accompagné de représentants d'entreprises dans des secteurs comme l'agroalimentaire et les boissons, la construction et les produits de construction ainsi que les services et les technologies de l'environnement. Les exportations canadiennes dans la région ont connu une hausse vertigineuse pendant les années 1990, et le commerce bilatéral de marchandises a atteint plus de 968 millions de dollars.[11]

---

[9] Commerce international Canada, ZLEA–Négociations en cours, texte disponible à: <http://dfait-maeci.gc.ca/tna-nac/FTAA/mercosur-fr.asp> (date d'accès: le 5 mai 2006).

[10] Commerce international Canada, Initiatives régionales et bilatérales, texte disponible à: <http://dfait-maeci.gc.ca/tna-nac/ca4-fr.asp> (date d'accès: le 5 mai 2006).

[11] Canada, Communiqué de presse du 5 mars 2004, disponible à: <http://w01. international.gc.ca/minpub/Publication.asp?publication_id=380855& Language=F> (date d'accès: le 5 mai 2006).

En ce qui a trait à l'*Accord de libre-échange entre le Canada et le Costa Rica,* entré en vigueur en novembre 2002, les échanges entre les deux pays ont augmenté de 11 % dès la première année.[12]

En septembre, la visite du Ministre des Affaires étrangères et du Commerce de la Corée du Sud a été l'occasion d'échanger des idées sur la libéralisation du commerce. Les échanges en biens, en services et en savoir avec le Canada ne cessent de croître: la Corée du Sud est le huitième partenaire commercial en importance du Canada, et le troisième en Asie.[13] En novembre, l'ouverture de pourparlers exploratoires entre les deux pays sur la possibilité d'un accord de libre-échange a été annoncée.[14]

Une mission commerciale au Brésil a été pilotée en novembre par le Ministre du Commerce international, afin d'accroître le commerce et l'investissement canadiens dans ce pays dont le marché affiche la croissance la plus rapide du monde. Le commerce canado-brésilien atteint près de 3 milliards de dollars par an et le Brésil est actuellement le quinzième partenaire commercial du Canada en importance.[15]

En novembre également s'est tenue la cinquième Réunion de la Commission du libre-échange Canada-Chili, à Santiago. Les deux pays connaissent des relations commerciales florissantes grâce à cet accord: les échanges bilatéraux ont dépassé 1,2 milliard de dollars, soit une hausse de 68 % par rapport à 1997, l'année de l'entrée en vigueur de l'accord.[16]

Une étude sur les partenariats entre le Canada et l'Inde en sciences et technologie, rendue publique en novembre, fait ressortir la

[12] Pour plus de renseignements sur l'*Accord de libre-échange entre le Canada et le Costa Rica,* consulter en ligne l'adresse suivante: <http://dfait-maeci.gc.ca/tna-nac/costa_rica-fr.asp> (date d'accès: le 5 mai 2006).

[13] Canada, Communiqué de presse du 27 septembre 2004, disponible à: <http://wo1.international.gc.ca/minpub/Publication.asp?publication_id=381559&Language=F> (date d'accès: le 5 mai 2006).

[14] Commerce international Canada, Initiatives régionales et bilatérales, disponible à: <http://dfait-maeci.gc.ca/tna-nac/RB/korea-fr.asp> (date d'accès: le 5 mai 2006).

[15] Canada, Communiqué de presse du 13 octobre 2004, disponible à: <http://wo1.international.gc.ca/minpub/Publication.asp?publication_id=381632&Language=F>; et Communiqué de presse du 25 novembre 2004, disponible à: <http://wo1.international.gc.ca/minpub/Publication.asp?publication_id=381817&Language=F> (date d'accès: le 5 mai 2006).

[16] Pour plus de renseignements sur les cinq ans de l'ALECC, consulter <http://dfait-maeci.gc.ca/tna-nac/ccftabrochure-fr.asp> (date d'accès: le 5 mai 2006).

complémentarité qui existe entre les deux pays dans de nombreux domaines d'expertise. La coopération canado-indienne en recherche et développement connaît une croissance constante depuis 1990, et l'étude recommande un renforcement de la présence canadienne en Inde en matière de sciences et technologie.

Toujours dans le but de faciliter les échanges commerciaux, mais cette fois avec l'Union européenne (UE), le Canada et la Commission européenne ont adopté un cadre de coopération réglementaire visant à réduire les obstacles bilatéraux au commerce, comme par exemple les écarts en matière d'étiquetage. L'Union européenne est le deuxième partenaire commercial du Canada après les États-Unis: 10 % des importations canadiennes proviennent de l'UE et 6 % des exportations s'y dirigent. C'est cependant l'investissement qui est la composante la plus importante des relations économiques entre l'UE et le Canada, et ce cadre sera un élément clé pour la conclusion d'un accord bilatéral de renforcement du commerce et de l'investissement.[17]

B   LES DIFFÉRENDS LIÉS À L'ALÉNA

En 2004, huit décisions ont été rendues sous le chapitre 19 de l'ALÉNA relatif au dumping et aux droits compensateurs. Cinq de ces décisions étaient relatives au conflit du bois d'œuvre. Les trois autres portaient sur le commerce de l'acier et du magnésium.

1   Le bois d'œuvre[18]

Les recours entrepris dans le dossier du bois d'œuvre peuvent être portés devant le Département du commerce des États-Unis (DOC), l'International Trade Commission (ITC) et même d'autres instances américaines, en plus des groupes spéciaux binationaux et comités pour contestation extraordinaire de l'ALÉNA. Ces recours

---

[17] Canada, Communiqué de presse du 21 décembre 2004, disponible à: <http://wo1.international.gc.ca/minpub/Publication.asp?publication_id=381918&Language=F>; et Délégation de la Commission européenne au Canada, Communiqué de presse du 21 décembre 2004, disponible à: <http://www.delcan.cec.eu.int/fr/press_and_information/press_releases/2004/04PR038.shtml> (date d'accès: le 5 mai 2006).

[18] Sur le dossier du bois d'œuvre en général, consulter <http://www.boisdoeuvre.gc.ca>. Pour un accès rapide aux décisions, consulter le site du Ministère du Commerce international <http://www.dfait-maeci.gc.ca/eicb/softwood/nafta_challenges-fr.asp> (date d'accès: le 14 mai 2006).

peuvent porter sur des enquêtes en dumping ou en droits compensateurs qui portent sur des périodes différentes et qui en sont à des phases différentes. Ces recours ont été particulièrement divers et nombreux en 2004. Pour offrir une explication intelligible de ces recours qui puisse tenir à l'intérieur du format de cette chronique, nous nous limiterons ici à présenter les décisions des groupes et comités dont l'existence est prévue dans l'ALÉNA. Nous tenterons à chaque fois d'offrir l'explication et la mise en contexte la plus claire et la plus courte possible. Quelques rares ajouts débordant des strictes décisions permettront, nous l'espérons, de mieux comprendre le déroulement du conflit.

Le 5 mars 2004, un Groupe spécial renvoyait pour la deuxième fois au DOC sa décision rendue le 22 mai 2002 portant sur le dumping pour la période du 1er avril 2000 au 31 mars 2001. Le Groupe spécial donnait au DOC la directive de revoir les calculs pour les compagnies Tembec Inc., West Fraser et Slocan.[19]

Le 19 avril, un autre groupe spécial renvoyait une décision de l'ITC du 15 décembre 2003. Le Groupe spécial a jugé que plusieurs constats de l'ITC à l'effet que la branche américaine de production de bois d'œuvre résineux était menacée de dommage important n'étaient pas étayés par une preuve substantielle.[20] Le Groupe a donc fourni des directives afin qu'une décision étayée par une preuve suffisante soit rendue. Il a dû revenir à la charge le 31 août puisque l'ITC, dans sa deuxième décision, a refusé de tenir compte des directives du Groupe spécial. Dans des termes durs, le Groupe spécial donne dix jours à l'ITC pour rendre une nouvelle décision conforme à la décision du Groupe spécial.[21]

Le 7 juin, un groupe spécial examinait pour la deuxième fois une décision du DOC à l'effet que les droits de coupe concédés

---

[19] Examen par un Groupe spécial binational constitué en vertu de l'article 1904 de l'*Accord de libre-échange nord-américain*, Certains produits de bois d'œuvre résineux en provenance du Canada, Décision définitive positive de dumping (5 mars 2004), USA-CDA-2002-1904-02 (Groupe spéc. art. 1904).

[20] Examen par un Groupe spécial binational constitué en vertu de l'article 1904 de l'*Accord de libre-échange nord-américain*, Certains produits de bois d'œuvre résineux en provenance du Canada, Décision définitive positive de dommage important (19 avril 2004), USA-CDA-2002-1904-07 (Groupe spéc. art. 1904).

[21] Examen par un Groupe spécial binational constitué en vertu de l'article 1904 de l'*Accord de libre-échange nord-américain*, Certains produits de bois d'œuvre résineux en provenance du Canada, Décision définitive positive de dommage important (31 août 2004), USA-CDA-2002-1904-07 (Groupe spéc. art. 1904).

par certaines provinces canadiennes constituent des subventions aux producteurs de bois d'œuvre résineux. La première fois, le Groupe spécial avait jugé que ces droits de coupe pouvaient être des subventions mais avait renvoyé la décision du DOC parce que celui-ci n'avait pas correctement déterminé l'avantage découlant de ce subventionnement. Cette fois, le Groupe spécial a demandé au DOC de refaire les calculs quant aux prix de référence applicables dans plusieurs provinces canadiennes.[22] Ces calculs ont été refaits et une nouvelle décision du DOC fut rendue le 30 juillet 2004. Les Parties canadiennes ont soulevé des questions sur ces nouveaux calculs. Le Groupe spécial a donc dû se pencher sur ces nouveaux calculs. Estimant que plusieurs questions soulevées par les Canadiens étaient sans réponse, le Groupe spécial a ordonné au DOC de modifier ses calculs.[23]

Cette saga où, du point de vue canadien, il est parfois permis de douter de la bonne volonté des autorités américaines, a cours aussi devant l'OMC. Elle se poursuivra en 2005.

2   *Les autres dossiers reliés au chapitre 19 de l'ALÉNA*

Trois autres affaires liées au dumping ont donné lieu à des décisions en 2004. Un comité pour contestation extraordinaire a rejeté une plainte américaine logée en vertu de l'article 1904.13.[24] Deux groupes spéciaux binationaux ont renvoyé des décisions devant l'ITC, pour défaut de preuve substantielle dans un cas,[25] pour

---

[22] Examen par un Groupe spécial binational constitué en vertu de l'article 1904 de l'*Accord de libre-échange nord-américain*, Certains produits de bois d'œuvre résineux en provenance du Canada, Décision définitive positive en matière de droits compensateurs (7 juin 2004), USA-CDA-2002-1904-03 (Groupe spéc. art. 1904).

[23] Examen par un Groupe spécial binational constitué en vertu de l'article 1904 de l'*Accord de libre-échange nord-américain*, Certains produits de bois d'œuvre résineux en provenance du Canada, Décision définitive positive en matière de droits compensateurs (1 décembre 2004), USA-CDA-2002-1904-03 (Groupe spéc. art. 1904).

[24] Contestation extraordinaire en vertu de l'article 1904 de l'*Accord de libre-échange nord-américain*, Magnésium pur en provenance du Canada, Décision et ordonnance du comité pour contestation extraordinaire (5 octobre 2004), ECC-2003-1904-01USA (Groupe spéc. art. 1904).

[25] Examen par un Groupe spécial binational constitué en vertu de l'article 1904 de l'*Accord de libre-échange nord-américain*, Certains produits d'acier plat au carbone traités contre la corrosion importés du Canada, Réexamen complet (19 octobre 2004), USA-CDA-00-1904-11 (Groupe spéc. art. 1904).

n'avoir pas collecté la preuve disponible et avoir mal jugé d'une présomption dans l'autre cas.[26]

III Le commerce canadien et l'OMC

A Les négociations commerciales multilatérales

1 *Le programme de Doha*

Malgré le fait qu'il n'y ait pas eu de Conférence ministérielle en 2004, la tenue d'intenses négociations a permis d'espérer pendant cette année que le Cycle de Doha ne cesse de faire du surplace comme dans les deux années précédentes. Après les conclusions très décevantes de la Conférence ministérielle de Cancún, les résultats obtenus à Genève en juillet ont été qualifiés d'avancée "véritablement historique."[27] Conscients des progrès qui devaient être accomplis, les 147 membres de l'OMC se sont réunis jour et nuit fin juillet pour aboutir à un cadre de négociations qui permettra peut-être de relancer le Cycle de Doha.

Ce Programme de travail comprend un cadre de négociations en matière d'agriculture qui engage les Membres de l'OMC à éliminer les subventions agricoles à l'exportation, ouvre la voie vers un accès amélioré aux marchés pour tous les produits agricoles et réduit considérablement le niveau de l'appui national exercé par les pays qui offrent le plus de subventions, appui qui a un effet de distorsion sur le commerce. Toujours en matière agricole, le Programme de travail s'attaque à la question du commerce du coton et prévoit la tenue de consultations à ce sujet. Le programme comprend un cadre de négociations pour l'accès aux marchés pour les produits non agricoles. Quant aux questions liées au développement, le programme engage les Membres à accorder une grande attention à certains enjeux particulièrement importants pour le commerce des pays en voie de développement tels le traitement spécial et différencié, l'assistance technique et les problèmes de

---

26 Examen par un Groupe spécial binational constitué en vertu de l'article 1904 de l'*Accord de libre-échange nord-américain,* Fils machine en acier au carbone et certains fils machine en acier alliés au Canada: Décision définitive de dommage (12 août 2004), USA-CDA-2002-1904-09 (Groupe spéc. art. 1904).

27 Déclaration du Directeur général, M. Supachai Panitchpakdi, le 2 août 2004, OMC, *Programme de Doha pour le développement,* disponible à: <http://www.wto.org/french/news_f/news04_f/dda_package_sum_31july04_f.htm> (date d'accès: le 14 mai 2006).

mise en œuvre. Plusieurs autres questions et thèmes sont moins avancés et abordés plus brièvement dans ce programme. En ce qui concerne les services, par exemple, des offres révisées devraient être présentées pour mai 2005.[28] Bien que l'on soit encore bien loin de l'aboutissement du Cycle de Doha, ce Programme de travail a redonné espoir aux Membres de l'OMC qui souhaitent que les résultats de ce cycle de négociations permettent aux pays en voie de développement de profiter davantage de la libéralisation des échanges.

2   *L'action canadienne au sein de l'OMC*

L'un des objectifs de la politique commerciale du Canada en 2004 était de faire progresser les négociations à l'OMC tout en défendant le droit des Canadiens à maintenir des régimes de commercialisation ordonnée, telles la gestion de l'offre et la Commission canadienne du blé. L'agriculture est un secteur essentiel pour le Canada au cœur de ces négociations et, au stade où en étaient les négociations en 2004, le Canada avait pu obtenir et préserver presque tout ce qu'il souhaitait dans ce cadre. Avec l'aide de plusieurs intervenants du secteur de l'agriculture, l'équipe canadienne a réussi à faire apporter d'importantes modifications au cadre de travail lors des négociations à Genève, en juillet.

S'agissant des représentants canadiens à Genève, il convient de souligner que S.E. Donald Stephenson a succédé en mai 2004 à S.E. Sergio Marchi à titre de Représentant permanent et Ambassadeur du Canada auprès des Nations Unies et auprès de l'OMC à Genève.[29] Entré à la fonction publique fédérale en 1981, M. Stephenson, qui est parfaitement biligue, a occupé d'importants postes de direction dans plusieurs ministères dont ceux des Communications, de la Consommation et des sociétés, d'Industrie Canada, du Patrimoine canadien et des Affaires étrangères et du Commerce international. Juste avant sa nomination, M. Stephenson

---

28   OMC Conseil général, *Programme de travail de Doha*, Déc. du 1er août 2004, OMC doc. WT/L/579 (2 août 2004), disponible à: <http://www.wto.org/french/tratop_f/dda_f/draft_text_gc_dg_31july04_f.htm> (date d'accès: le 14 mai 2006). Voir l'annexe A pour les modalités concernant l'agriculture, l'annexe B pour l'accès aux marchés pour les produits non agricoles, l'annexe C pour les services et l'annexe D pour la facilitation des échanges.

29   Canada, Ministère des Affaires étrangères du Canada, "Nominations diplomatiques," *Communiqué* no° 73 (21 mai 2004).

était secrétaire Adjoint du Cabinet, Politique de développement économique et régional, au Bureau du Conseil privé.

B   LES DIFFÉRENDS DEVANT L'OMC IMPLIQUANT LE CANADA

I   *États-Unis – Loi de 2000 sur la compensation pour continuation du dumping et maintien de la subvention (CDSOA)*

On se rappelle que la CDSOA, mieux connue sous le nom d'Amendement Byrd, avait pour objet de permettre non seulement aux entreprises étasuniennes qui appuient les requêtes visant l'ouverture d'enquêtes sur les droits antidumping et compensatoires contre les importations étrangères d'obtenir que soient imposés des droits supplémentaires à la frontière, mais aussi d'obtenir que ces droits leur soient versés directement par le Trésor des États-Unis.

Dès la mi-janvier, le Canada et sept autres Membres de l'OMC (le Brésil, le Chili, la Corée du Sud, l'Inde, le Japon, le Mexique et l'Union européenne) présentaient des recours en vue d'obtenir l'autorisation de suspendre certaines de leurs obligations à l'égard des États-Unis.[30] Ces recours étaient entrepris du fait que les États-Unis avaient fait défaut de rendre la CDSOA compatible avec les rapports adoptés par l'Organe de règlement des différends (ORD) à l'intérieur du délai raisonnable établi par un arbitre désigné par le Directeur général de l'OMC.[31] Dans les jours qui suivirent, les États-Unis demandèrent que le niveau des suspensions demandées soit tranché par arbitrage, conformément à l'article 22:6 du Mémorandum d'accord sur le règlement des différends.[32]

La décision de l'arbitre fut rendue le 31 août.[33] Les huit membres plaignants se sont vus autorisés par les instances d'arbitrage de l'OMC, à prendre des mesures de rétorsion de plus de 150

---

30   On trouve le recours du Canada à *États-Unis – Loi de 2000 sur la compensation pour continuation du dumping et maintien de la subvention*, Recours du Canada à l'article 22:2 du Mémorandum d'accord sur le règlement des différends, OMC doc. WT/ DS234/25 (16 janvier 2004).

31   Ce délai avait été établi par l'arbitre comme expirant le 27 décembre 2003.

32   *États-Unis – Loi de 2000 sur la compensation pour continuation du dumping et maintien de la subvention*, Demande d'arbitrage présentée par les États-Unis au titre de l'article 22:6 du Mémorandum d'accord sur le règlement des différends, OMC doc. WT/DS234/28 (26 janvier 2004).

33   On trouve la decision touchant le Canada à *États-Unis – Loi de 2000 sur la compensation pour continuation du dumping et maintien de la subvention (Plainte initiale du Canada)*, Recours des États-Unis à l'arbitrage au titre de l'article 22:6 du Mémorandum d'accord sur le règlement des différends, Décision de l'arbitre, OMC doc. WT/DS234/ARB/CAN (31 août 2004).

millions de dollars américains à l'encontre des États-Unis, qui ne se conformaient toujours pas à la décision de janvier 2003, laquelle déclarait illégal le désormais célèbre Amendement.[34] Le Canada fut autorisé à suspendre ses concessions et donc à imposer des mesures de rétorsion qui équivalent à 72 % des droits payés en trop aux douanes américaines en une année. Les producteurs américains ont reçu chaque année de deux à cinq millions de dollars américains au titre des droits compensateurs et antidumping perçus sur des biens importés du Canada.[35] En novembre, le Canada et six autres Membres plaignants ont présenté la demande finale d'autorisation en vue d'instituer des mesures de rétorsion, étape obligatoire préalable à l'application de telles mesures dans le cadre de l'OMC.[36] La suspension des concessions ou d'autres obligations au titre de l'article 22:7 du Mémorandum d'accord a été accordée par l'ORD à sa réunion du 17 décembre 2004. Il revenait donc au gouvernement canadien de déterminer quels produits américains entrant au Canada seraient visés par les mesures de rétorsion. Des consultations publiques à ce sujet ont d'ailleurs été tenues par le Ministère du Commerce international du Canada entre le 23 novembre et le 22 décembre.[37] C'est un peu plus tard, en 2005, que l'on connaîtra en détails les modalités d'application de ces mesures de rétorsion.

2   *Communautés européennes – Mesures affectant l'approbation et la commercialisation des produits biotechnologiques*

Peu de progrès sensibles dans cette affaire très importante débutée en 2003. Le Groupe spécial a été constitué en mars et celui-ci a

---

[34] Délégation de la Commission européenne au Canada, Communiqué de presse du 13 août 2004, disponible à: <http://www.delcan.cec.eu.int/fr/press_and_information/press_releases/2004/04PR021.shtml> (date d'accès: le 14 mai 2006).

[35] Gouvernement du Canada, Communiqué de presse du 31 août 2004, disponible à: <http://wo1.international.gc.ca/minpub/Publication.asp?publication_id=381466&Language=F> (date d'accès: le 14 mai 2006).

[36] *États-Unis – Loi de 2000 sur la compensation pour continuation du dumping et maintien de la subvention*, Recours du Canada à l'article 22:7 du Mémorandum d'accord sur le règlement des différends, OMC doc. WT/DS234/31 (11 novembre 2004).

[37] Gouvernement du Canada, Communiqué de presse no° 134 du Ministère du commerce international, *Amendement Byrd: Le Gouvernement du Canada sollicite l'avis des Canadiens sur l'application d'éventuelles mesures de rétorsion commerciales contre les États-Unis*, le 23 novembre 2004.

plusieurs fois demandé, au cours de l'année 2004, des délais plus longs que ceux prévus au Mémorandum d'accord sur le règlement des différends pour accomplir les différentes étapes de son mandat. Les rebondissements sont à venir plus tard.

3   Le blé canadien

Dans l'affaire des *Mesures concernant les exportations de blé et le traitement des grains importés,* le Groupe spécial chargé d'étudier les questions de fond soumises par les États-Unis rendait ses rapports en avril.[38] Selon le Groupe spécial, les pratiques de la Commission canadienne du blé sont conformes aux obligations commerciales internationales du Canada, notamment à l'article XVII du GATT. Le Groupe spécial a également statué que certaines politiques du secteur canadien des céréales (plafond de recettes des chemins de fer, ségrégation du grain et exigence d'autorisation de l'entrée) étaient incompatibles avec la règle de l'octroi du traitement national consignée à l'article III du GATT. Les États-Unis ont annoncé, le 3 juin, qu'ils en appelaient de cette décision et demandaient que soient examinées les conclusions relatives à la compatibilité des actions de la Commission canadienne du blé avec l'article XVII du GATT.[39] Le 30 août, l'Organe d'appel confirmait quasiment en tous points le rapport du Groupe spécial et rappelait que les pratiques de la Commission canadienne du blé sont conformes aux obligations commerciales internationales du Canada.[40] Le 27 septembre, l'Organe de règlement des différends a adopté le Rapport de l'Organe d'appel et le Rapport du Groupe spécial tel que – légèrement modifié par l'Organe d'appel.[41] Le 17 novembre, les représentants du Canada et des États-Unis auprès de l'OMC indiquaient qu'ils en étaient venus à un accord quant au délai de mise

---

[38] *Canada – Mesures concernant les exportations de blé et le traitement des grains importés,* Rapports du Groupe spécial, OMC doc. WT/DS276/R (6 avril 2004).

[39] *Canada – Mesures concernant les exportations de blé et le traitement des grains importés,* Notification d'un appel des États-Unis présentée conformément au paragraphe 4 de l'article 16 du Mémorandum d'accord sur les règles et procédures régissant le règlement des différends, OMC doc. WT/DS276/15 (3 juin 2004).

[40] *Canada – Mesures concernant les exportations de blé et le traitement des grains importés,* Rapport de l'Organe d'appel, OMC doc. WT/DS276/AB/R (30 août 2004).

[41] *Canada – Mesures concernant les exportations de blé et le traitement des grains importés,* Rapport de l'Organe d'appel et Rapport du Groupe spécial – Dispositions prises par l'Organe de règlement des dfférends, OMC doc. WT/DS276/18 (30 septembre 2004).

en œuvre de la décision rendue dans cette affaire. Aux termes de cet accord, la mise en œuvre des recommandations et décisions doit être achevée pour le 1ᵉʳ août 2005.[42] Il sera intéressant de voir si les Parties pourront respecter ce délai.

Une autre affaire affectant le commerce international du blé canadien s'est ouverte en 2004. Le Canada a demandé l'ouverture de consultations puis l'établissement d'un groupe spécial pour entendre l'affaire *États-Unis – Détermination de la Commission du commerce international concernant le blé de force roux de printemps en provenance du Canada*. Le Canada estime que les autorités américaines, à la suite d'enquêtes antidumping et en matière de droits compensateurs, ont rendu des ordonnances qui ne sont pas conformes aux obligations incombant aux États-Unis aux termes de l'*Accord antidumping* et de l'*Accord sur les subventions et mesures compensatoires* (l'Accord SMC). Le Canada reproche notamment aux États-Unis de ne pas avoir correctement examiné un certain nombre d'éléments de preuve et d'avoir mal examiné certains critères avant d'appliquer des droits antidumping et compensateurs sur le blé de force roux de printemps provenant du Canada.[43] L'affaire n'a pas évolué davantage en 2004.

4   *La saga du bois d'œuvre résineux*

Les trois affaires en cours portées par le Canada devant les instances de l'OMC relativement au conflit du bois d'œuvre ont progressé de façon significative en 2004. À ces trois affaires, s'est ajoutée une quatrième relative aux droits compensateurs. Le déroulement de ces dossiers révèle de plus en plus clairement que les États-Unis n'ont en fait aucune intention d'appliquer les recommandations des instances de l'OMC et de l'ALÉNA et tiennent mordicus à forcer le Canada à négocier de nouveaux termes d'échange du bois d'œuvre qui ne seront pas ceux qui ont cours en 2004 et qui devraient s'appliquer entre les deux pays!

Dans l'affaire *États-Unis – Détermination finale en matière de droits compensateurs concernant certains bois d'œuvre résineux en provenance du*

---

[42] *Canada – Mesures concernant les exportations de blé et le traitement des grains importés*, Accord au titre de l'article 21:3 (b) du Mémorandum d'accord sur le règlement des différends, OMC doc. WT/DS276/19 (17 novembre 2004).

[43] *États-Unis – Détermination de la Commission du commerce international concernant le blé de force roux de printemps en provenance du Canada*, Demande d'établissement d'un groupe spécial présentée par le Canada, OMC doc. WT/DS310/2 (11 juin 2004).

Canada,[44] le Rapport de l'Organe d'appel, distribué en janvier, confirme la constatation du Groupe spécial comme quoi les droits de récolte accordés par les pouvoirs publics provinciaux canadiens en ce qui concerne le bois sur pied constituaient la fourniture de biens visée à l'article 1.1 de l'Accord SMC. L'Organe d'appel infirme l'interprétation de l'article 14 (d) de l'Accord SMC donnée par le Groupe spécial et la constatation du Groupe spécial selon laquelle les États-Unis avaient déterminé à mauvais escient l'existence et le montant de l'"avantage" résultant de la contribution financière fournie. L'Organe d'appel a ensuite constaté qu'il ne pouvait pas compléter l'analyse juridique de la question, faute de constatations factuelles et de faits non contestés. Enfin, l'Organe d'appel a confirmé que les États-Unis avaient agi d'une manière incompatible avec les dispositions de l'Accord SMC et du GATT de 1994 en n'analysant pas si les subventions étaient transmises, au moyen de ventes de grumes, par les exploitants possédant des scieries à des producteurs de bois d'œuvre non apparentés. Ce Rapport fut adopté par l'Organe de règlement des différends (ORD). En avril, les États-Unis et le Canada notifiaient au secrétariat de l'OMC un accord selon lequel les recommandations adoptées par l'ORD dans cette affaire devraient être mises en œuvre au plus tard le 17 décembre 2004.[45] Le 30 décembre, dans une communication où il ne dissimulait pas son agacement, le Canada indiquait que les États-Unis n'avaient pas respecté le délai de mise en œuvre convenu et demandait l'autorisation de suspendre, à l'égard des États-Unis, l'application de ses concessions et obligations jusqu'à hauteur de 200 millions de dollars canadiens par année.[46]

Le Groupe spécial formé en 2003 dans l'affaire *États-Unis – Détermination finale de l'existence d'un dumping concernant certains bois d'œuvre résineux en provenance du Canada* a rendu son Rapport en

---

44 *États-Unis – Détermination finale en matière de droits compensateurs concernant certains bois d'œuvre résineux en provenance du Canada*, Rapport de l'Organe d'appel, OMC doc. WT/DS257/AB/R (19 janvier 2004).

45 *États-Unis – Détermination finale en matière de droits compensateurs concernant certains bois d'œuvre résineux en provenance du Canada*, Accord au titre de l'article 21:3 (b) du Mémorandum d'accord sur le règlement des différends, OMC doc. WT/DS257/13 (30 avril 2004).

46 *États-Unis – Détermination finale en matière de droits compensateurs concernant certains bois d'œuvre résineux en provenance du Canada*, Recours du Canada à l'article 22:2 du Mémorandum d'accord sur le règlement des différends, OMC doc. WT/DS257/16 (4 janvier 2005).

avril 2004.[47] Il a constaté que, dans sa détermination finale de l'existence d'un dumping, le Département du commerce des États-Unis ne s'était pas conformé aux prescriptions de l'article 2.4.2 de l'*Accord antidumping* parce qu'il n'avait pas pris en compte toutes les transactions à l'exportation en appliquant la méthode de la "réduction à zéro" pour le calcul de la marge de dumping. Le Groupe spécial a estimé que les autres prétentions du Canada n'étaient pas fondées. Les États-Unis ont fait appel. Dans son Rapport distribué en août, l'Organe d'appel a notamment confirmé que la pratique de la réduction à zéro utilisée par les États-Unis dans les calculs de marges de dumping était incompatible avec l'*Accord antidumping*.[48] Après de longs pourparlers qui ont permis d'éviter un autre arbitrage, le Canada et les États-Unis ont convenu que ces derniers auraient jusqu'au 15 avril 2005 pour publier une nouvelle détermination en dumping respectueuse des règles de l'OMC.

Dans l'autre affaire démarrée en 2003, *États-Unis – Enquête de la Commission du commerce international dans l'affaire concernant les bois d'œuvre résineux en provenance du Canada,* le Rapport du Groupe spécial fut distribué en mars.[49] Le Groupe spécial a constaté que, dans sa détermination finale concluant à l'existence d'une menace de dommage, l'International Trade Commission des États-Unis ne s'était pas conformée aux prescriptions des articles 3.5 et 3.7 de l'*Accord antidumping,* ni de l'article 15.5 et 15.7 de l'Accord SMC, en constatant qu'il y avait probablement un accroissement substantiel et imminent des importations et un lien de causalité entre les importations et une menace de dommage pour la branche de production nationale. Le Groupe spécial a constaté que les mesures antidumping et compensatoires imposées par les États-Unis étaient incompatibles avec les obligations des États-Unis au titre de ces dispositions.[50] Encore ici, de longues négociations à propos du délai de mise en œuvre de la décision ont finalement abouti le 1er

47 *États-Unis – Détermination finale de l'existence d'un dumping concernant certains bois d'œuvre résineux en provenance du Canada,* Rapport du Groupe spécial, OMC doc. WT/DS264/R (13 avril 2004).

48 *États-Unis – Détermination finale de l'existence d'un dumping concernant certains bois d'œuvre résineux en provenance du Canada,* Rapport de l'Organe d'appel, OMC doc. WT/DS264/AB/R (11 août 2004).

49 *États-Unis – Enquête de la Commission du commerce international dans l'affaire concernant les bois d'œuvre résineux en provenance du Canada,* Rapport du Groupe spécial, OMC doc. WTDS277/R (22 mars 2004).

50 Plus spécifiquement, le Groupe spécial a estimé que "en égard à la totalité des facteurs considérés et au raisonnement de l'USITC dans sa détermination, nous

octobre, les Parties convenant de se conformer à la décision pour le 26 janvier 2005.

Aux affaires conclues ou pendantes devant l'OMC relativement au conflit canado-américain du bois d'œuvre, s'est ajoutée en 2004 l'affaire *États-Unis – Réexamen du droit compensateur concernant le bois d'œuvre résineux en provenance du Canada*. En avril, le Canada a demandé l'ouverture de consultations à propos du fait que, malgré des engagements en ce sens, le DOC n'avait pas achevé des réexamens accélérés de l'ordonnance en matière de droits compensateurs pour plusieurs exportateurs canadiens de bois d'œuvre qui avaient demandé un tel réexamen. Ces exportateurs canadiens sont pénalisés du fait qu'en l'absence d'examen particulier de leur cas, ils sont assujettis au taux de droit compensateur applicable à l'ensemble du Canada tel qu'établi dans le cadre d'un examen administratif global. Le Canada prétend que les États-Unis agissent ainsi d'une manière incompatible avec les articles 10, 19.1, 19.3, 19.4, 21.1, 21.2, 21.4, et 32.1 de l'Accord SMC et l'article VI:3 du GATT de 1994. Aucun groupe spécial n'a encore été chargé de cette affaire.

Il sera intéressant de voir si les positions américaine et canadienne dans la saga du bois d'œuvre pourront se rapprocher en 2005. Ce fut de toute façon loin d'être le cas en 2004, les gains canadiens devant l'ORD étant mal accueillis et appliqués avec beaucoup de résistance par les autorités américaines.

5   La réactivation de l'affaire du bœuf aux hormones

En novembre 2004, l'Union européenne déposait des demandes d'ouverture de consultations avec le Canada et avec les États-Unis relativement au maintien de la suspension d'obligations dans le différend *CE – Hormones*.[51] On se rappellera que dans cette

---

ne pouvons pas conclure que la constatation selon laquelle il y aurait probablement une augmentation substantielle et imminente des importations est une constatation qui aurait pu être établie par une autorité chargée de l'enquête objective et impartiale. En conséquence, nous constatons que la détermination de l'USITC n'est pas compatible avec les obligations énoncées aux articles 3.7 et 15.7." *Ibid.*, par. 7.96. Voir aussi le par. 8.1 (a) dans les recommandations.

51 *Canada – Maintien de la suspension d'obligations dans le différend CE – Hormones*, Demande de consultations présentée par les Communautés européennes, OMC doc. WT/DS321/1 (10 novembre 2004); *États-Unis – Maintien de la suspension d'obligations dans le différend CE – Hormones*, Demande de consultations présentée par les Communautés européennes, OMC doc. WT/DS320/1 (10 novembre 2004).

première guerre commerciale de l'ère OMC à avoir opposé l'Amérique du Nord et l'Europe, le Canada et les États-Unis avaient été autorisés à suspendre des obligations à l'égard des Communautés européennes (CE) parce que ces dernières avaient refusé de mettre en œuvre le rapport adopté par l'Organe de règlement des différends. Pour le Canada, cette suspension permettait un rehaussement des droits de douanes appliqués sur les produits importés des CE jusqu'à hauteur de 11,3 millions de dollars annuellement. En déposant leur nouvelle demande de consultations, les CE se sont dites d'avis que le Canada et les États-Unis ne devraient pas pouvoir maintenir sur les produits européens des droits d'importation plus élevés que les taux consolidés, étant donné que les CE ont éliminé les mesures qui avaient été constatées incompatibles avec les règles de l'OMC dans l'affaire *CE – Hormones*. Les Communautés européennes prétendent que les seules interdictions et conditions d'importation qu'elles continuent d'appliquer sont fondées sur des évaluations de risques conformes aux accords de l'OMC.[52] Le Canada, comme les États-Unis, conteste cette prétention des CE. À la fin de l'année 2004, aucun groupe spécial n'avait encore été chargé de cette affaire.

IV   Conclusion

L'année commerciale 2004 fut bonne pour le développement du commerce canadien. Confiance et espoir sont permis dans les négociations multilatérales et quant aux relations bilatérales qu'entretient et développe le Canada. L'attitude des autorités commerciales américaines est toutefois inquiétante. Notre principal partenaire commercial s'est plusieurs fois montré très réticent à appliquer les décisions des groupes spéciaux tant de l'ALÉNA que de l'OMC. Il faut souhaiter que le ton restera cordial entre les autorités politiques chargées du commerce entre le Canada et les États-Unis.

---

[52] *Canada – Maintien de la suspension d'obligations dans le différend CE – Hormones,* Demande de consultations présentée par les Communautés européennes, OMC doc. WT/DS321/1 (10 novembre 2004) à la p. 2.

II Le Canada et le système financier international en 2004

préparé par
BERNARD COLAS

D epuis la perpétration des attentats terroristes du 11 septembre 2001 aux États-Unis, la communauté internationale consacre une grande part de ses travaux à la lutte contre le terrorisme et le blanchiment d'argent. L'année 2004 n'y fait pas exception. En effet, une fois encore, la lutte contre le terrorisme a retenu l'attention de la communauté internationale qui dans le même temps a également œuvré au renforcement de la transparence en matière d'informations financières ainsi qu'à l'aide aux États frappés par le tsunami en décembre 2003. Ces travaux ont été menés de concert par le Groupe des Vingt (I), les institutions financières internationales (II) et les organismes de contrôle des établissements financiers (III), le Groupe d'action financière (IV) et le Joint Forum (V) au sein desquels le Canada joue un rôle de premier plan.

I LE GROUPE DES VINGT

À l'occasion de sa réunion annuelle tenue à Berlin les 20 et 21 novembre 2004, le Groupe des Vingt (G-20) a salué le contexte macroéconomique favorable dans l'économie mondiale caractérisé par une forte croissance et de faibles taux d'intérêts. Toutefois, le G-20 a souligné l'augmentation des facteurs de risque en raison de la volatilité du prix du pétrole, des déséquilibres externes persistant et des préoccupations liées au contexte géopolitique. Par conséquent, le G-20 a insisté sur l'importance de développer des

Bernard Colas, Avocat associé de l'étude Gottlieb & Pearson (Montréal), Docteur en droit, et Vice-Président, Commission du droit du Canada. L'auteur remercie Xavier Mageau, LL.M., de la même étude pour son importante contribution à la préparation de cet article ainsi que Evenelle Durand.

capacités d'adaptation et d'assurer la viabilité de l'économie mondiale.[1]

Le G-20 a confirmé la poursuite de la mise en œuvre du Consensus de Monterrey et des Objectifs du millénaire pour le développement (OMD). Dans le contexte de changement démographique, le G-20 a mené une évaluation des effets sur les politiques économiques, encourageant la poursuite de réformes structurelles.[2]

Le G-20 a également souligné l'importance d'une architecture financière internationale stable soutenant l'application de politiques viables et la prise de risques prudents. Il a réitéré son engagement dans la lutte contre les abus du système financier international et la prévention des risques.[3] À cette occasion, le G-20 a adopté un certain nombre de principes communs applicables aux politiques nationales qui auraient pour effet de stimuler une croissance économique soutenue.[4]

Parallèlement, le G-20 a adopté un certain nombre de mesures pour mettre en place l'Accord sur la croissance soutenue.[5] À cet égard, le Canada s'est engagé à se concentrer sur le relèvement de son niveau de vie grâce à la croissance de la productivité et à maintenir une politique d'équilibre budgétaire. Cet objectif du Canada devrait notamment être atteint en procédant à un examen des dépenses permettant de réaffecter certaines ressources à de nouvelles priorités. Les membres du G-20 réévalueront ces mesures et les engagements pris au cours de la prochaine rencontre du G-20, qui se tiendra à Beijing en 2005.

Enfin, le G-20 a adopté une déclaration sur la transparence et l'échange d'informations à des fins fiscales encourageant les États à appliquer le Modèle de Convention sur l'échange de renseignements en matière fiscale publié par l'Organisation de coopération et de développement économiques (OCDE) en 2002.[6]

---

1 *Berlin Communiqué, G-20 Finance Ministers' and Central Bank Governors' Meeting dated 20–21 November 2004,* par. 2 [ci-après *Communiqué du G-20*].

2 *Ibid.,* par. 7.

3 *Ibid.,* par. 10.

4 *G-20 Accord for Sustained Growth, Stability, Competition and Empowerment: Mobilising Economic Forces for Satisfactory Long-Term Growth,* 21 November 2004.

5 *G-20 Reform Agenda, Agreed Actions to Implement the G-20 Accord for Sustained Growth,* 21 November 2004.

6 *G-20 Statement on Transparency and Exchange of Information for Taxes Purposes,* 21 November 2004.

II   LES INSTITUTIONS INTERNATIONALES

A   FONDS MONÉTAIRE INTERNATIONAL (FMI)

En 2004, l'ensemble des quotes-parts des 184 Membres s'établissait à 212,8 milliards de DTS. Le FMI a conclu des accords de prêt d'une valeur de 58,7 milliards de DTS avec quarante-sept pays membres et a fourni une aide d'urgence aux pays membres s'élevant à 306 millions de DTS. A la fin de l'année 2004, la capacité d'engagement prospectif du FMI s'élevait à 72 milliards de DTS.[7]

Depuis quelques années, le FMI a engagé un processus de réformes visant à accroître son efficacité dans la promotion de la stabilité financière. Ces réformes sont vigoureusement soutenues par le Canada. Le Canada milite toujours au sein du FMI en faveur du renforcement de la gouvernance et de l'accroissement de la responsabilisation du FMI et de ses membres.[8]

Concernant la surveillance et la prévention des crises, le Comité monétaire et financier international (CMFI) du Conseil des gouverneurs du FMI a, en 2004, plaidé en faveur de l'intensification des efforts visant à accroître le ciblage, la qualité, l'effet, l'incidence et l'efficacité globale de la surveillance.

Lors de son examen biennal de la mise en œuvre de la surveillance, le FMI a mis l'accent sur la façon d'accroître son efficacité au sein des pays membres. Pour atteindre cet objectif, le Canada a soutenu la création d'un mécanisme intensifié de surveillance dirigé par les pays eux-mêmes alors que le personnel du FMI a plutôt proposé de mettre en place un mécanisme permettant d'assurer un signalement et une surveillance assidus des politiques des pays.

Le Canada appuie les mesures prises ces dernières années par le FMI en faveur de l'accroissement de la transparence du FMI. À cet égard, la politique de présomption de publication des rapports sur les consultations est entrée en vigueur en juillet 2004, remplaçant le mécanisme de la publication volontaire.

Concernant le renforcement du secteur financier international, le FMI a examiné le programme pilote en matière d'évaluation de lutte contre le blanchiment d'argent et le financement des activités terroristes. À ce jour, plus de quarante centres financiers extra-

---

[7] *Rapports sur les opérations effectuées en vertu de la Loi sur les accords de Bretton Woods et des accords connexes 2004* aux pp. 24 et suivantes [ci-après *Bretton Woods 2004*].

[8] *Ibid.* à la p. 9.

territoriaux ont déjà fait l'objet d'une évaluation. Le FMI a approuvé une proposition tendant à faire de ces évaluations une activité permanente de surveillance. Le FMI a également approuvé les recommandations révisées du Groupe d'action financière (GAFI) à titre de nouvelles normes des Rapports sur l'observation des normes et des codes (RONC) aux termes desquelles quarante évaluations devraient être menées chaque année et réparties entre le FMI, la Banque mondiale, le GAFI et d'autres organismes.[9]

Suite à l'adoption de la nouvelle approche en matière de soutien des pays pauvres,[10] le Rapport du Bureau d'évaluation indépendant (BEI) en a souligné les résultats positifs tout en constatant que la mise en œuvre n'a pas permis d'atteindre tous les objectifs.

Le Conseil d'administration a souligné la contribution essentielle de l'assistance technique du FMI auprès des pays pauvres et des pays se relevant d'un conflit. En octobre 2004, le FMI a inauguré à Beyrouth le Centre d'assistance technique du Moyen Orient (METAC). Le FMI continue de fournir une aide spécialisée en Afghanistan et en Irak visant à rétablir les infrastructures économiques et financières des deux pays.

Dans le cadre de la mise en œuvre des Objectifs du millénaire pour le développement des Nations-Unies, le FMI s'est engagé à aider les pays membres à faible revenu à progresser. Le CMFI a réitéré en septembre 2004 l'importance du rôle du FMI visant à appuyer les efforts de ces pays et à assurer la stabilité macroéconomique et la croissance nécessaires.[11] Suite au tsunami survenu en Asie, le FMI a fourni une assistance technique afin d'évaluer l'impact macroéconomique et les besoins budgétaires et de balance des paiements découlant de la catastrophe et a notamment offert une aide financière aux pays touchés par cette catastrophe.

Le Comité monétaire et financier a réaffirmé le rôle du FMI dans la libéralisation multilatérale du commerce et dans la conclusion des négociations menées dans le cadre du Cycle de Doha. Le FMI a instauré le mécanisme d'intégration du commerce (MIC) conçu comme un instrument pour améliorer la prévisibilité des ressources disponibles aux termes des facilités existantes. Le MIC vise notamment à permettre aux pays membres de combler les déficits de la

---

9 *Ibid.* à la p. 17.

10 Cette approche a été adoptée en 1999 par le FMI et la Banque mondiale afin de renforcer la prise en charge par les pays et mettre davantage l'accent sur la pauvreté.

11 *Bretton Woods 2004, supra* note 7 à la p. 18.

balance des paiements découlant de la libéralisation multilatérale du commerce.[12]

B BANQUE MONDIALE

Au cours de l'année 2004, la Banque mondiale s'est engagée à accorder des prêts et des crédits totalisant 20,1 milliards de dollars américains à quatre-vingt-onze pays en développement ou en transition.[13] Afin d'accroître l'efficacité de ses activités en faveur du développement, la Banque mondiale a notamment continué d'accorder une grande importance aux services autres que les prêts, tels que le conseil, l'analyse et la formation.

En vue d'atteindre les Objectifs du millénaire pour le développement, la Banque mondiale poursuit l'adaptation de son système de surveillance et d'évaluation des projets. Elle a développé et mis en œuvre en 2004 le programme de renforcement des capacités statistiques afin d'aider les pays en développement à améliorer les systèmes statistiques, la capacité institutionnelle et la planification. À ce chapitre, la Banque mondiale et les Nations-Unies collaborent étroitement afin d'élaborer un cadre visant à surveiller et à évaluer la mise en œuvre des politiques nécessaires à l'atteinte des Objectifs du millénaire et en vue de produire chaque année le *Global Monitoring Report*. Ce Rapport a été publié pour la première fois en 2004 pour communiquer les conclusions de la Banque mondiale aux décideurs et acteurs du développement international. Au cours du même exercice, la Banque mondiale a également entrepris un examen de son Cadre de développement intégré au terme duquel elle a souligné l'importance d'instaurer des mécanismes de disciplines budgétaires.

Dans le cadre d'une réorganisation complète de ses politiques opérationnelles, la Banque mondiale a remplacé les prêts d'ajustement par le nouveau cadre de prêts de politiques de développement. Ce faisant, la Banque mondiale a aboli le niveau théorique de 25 % représenté par les prêts d'ajustement par rapport à l'ensemble des prêts consentis par la Banque. Ces nouveaux prêts servent à appuyer les réformes dans l'ensemble des secteurs ainsi que les efforts de restructuration. Ces prêts ont représenté 31 % des prêts consentis par la Banque mondiale en 2004.[14]

---

[12] *Ibid.* à la p. 22.

[13] *Ibid.* à la p. 33.

[14] *Ibid.* à la p. 39.

En 2004, les engagements de la Banque mondiale en faveur de l'éducation ont atteint 1,7 milliards de dollars américains.[15] En vue d'appuyer l'initiative *Éducation pour tous,* la Banque mondiale poursuit son programme d'aide accéléré aux pays qui se sont dotés d'une stratégie efficace en faveur de l'éducation. Ce programme pourrait profiter à vingt-cinq nouveaux pays à condition que ces derniers se dotent de plans solides en vue d'accroître leurs investissements dans le secteur de l'éducation. Le Canada a réitéré son engagement à l'égard de la Tanzanie, du Mozambique et du Honduras dans le cadre de cette initiative. Dans le cadre des discussions sur l'éducation, la Banque mondiale a abordé la question de l'égalité des sexes.

Sur le plan du développement du secteur privé, le Canada appuie les démarches de la Banque mondiale en vue de créer un milieu propice à l'investissement et des cadres de saines réglementations. Pendant l'exercice 2004, la Banque internationale pour la reconstruction et le développement (BIRD) et l'Association internationale de développement (IDA) ont accordé des prêts totalisant 4 176,6 millions de dollars américains à l'appui du développement du secteur financier et du secteur privé. En 2004, la Banque mondiale a publié le Rapport *Doing Business 2005,* qui cette année fournit des indicateurs servant à déterminer et à encourager les réformes nécessaires à l'élimination des obstacles à la croissance. En 2004, la Banque mondiale et la Société financière internationale ont lancé une nouvelle initiative de soutien des entreprises novatrices suscitant des possibilités économiques durables pour les gens très pauvres et marginalisés.

Parmi les priorités de la Banque mondiale et du Canada figurent la saine gouvernance et la lutte contre la corruption. Depuis plusieurs années, la saine gouvernance et la lutte contre la corruption font partie intégrante des programmes de prêts d'ajustement et d'investissement de la Banque mondiale. En 2004, la Banque mondiale a adopté de nouvelles orientations stratégiques, un plan d'activités ainsi qu'une nouvelle stratégie de communications extérieures concernant les enquêtes et les sanctions. La Banque mondiale continue de rayer les entreprises et particuliers de la liste des Parties autorisées à conclure des marchés financés par la Banque mondiale. Deux-cent soixante-sept sociétés et particuliers ne peuvent plus profiter des marchés adjugés dans le cadre de projet de financement de la Banque mondiale et dix lettres de réprimande

---

[15] *Ibid.* à la p. 48.

ont été adressées en 2004. Les administrateurs de la Banque mondiale ont également approuvé, cette année, la création d'un fonds fiduciaire spécial pour les pays à faible revenu, en vue de financer les projets pilotes visant à améliorer la gouvernance au sein des institutions.

Afin d'accroître la transparence et la responsabilisation, la Banque mondiale a, en 2004, notamment accepté la publication des résultats des pays dans le cadre de l'exercice annuel d'évaluation des politiques et des institutions nationales de l'IDA portant des indicateurs sociaux, économiques et de gouvernance. Le comité indépendant chargé d'examiner les plaintes de l'extérieur concernant les projets soutenus par la Banque mondiale a reçu, au cours de l'année, six nouvelles demandes d'inspection. Celles-ci portent sur des projets soutenus par la Banque mondiale aux Philippines, au Cameroun, au Mexique, en Colombie et en Inde.[16]

Concernant l'allègement de la dette, la Banque mondiale poursuit l'*Initiative en faveur des pays pauvres les plus endettés* (PPTE) et envisage de l'étendre à quarante-deux pays. En 2004, vingt-sept pays en profitaient. Quinze d'entre eux ont franchi toutes les étapes de l'Initiative et ont bénéficié d'un allègement irrévocable de leur dette.[17] Le fardeau de la dette de ces pays devrait diminuer des deux tiers. La Banque mondiale et le FMI ont décidé de prolonger de deux ans la disposition de temporisation applicable à l'Initiative en faveur des PPTE de manière à ce que les pays n'ayant pas entamé le processus disposent de temps supplémentaire pour mettre en place les réformes exigées.

III Organismes de contrôle des établissements financiers

A comité de bâle sur le contrôle bancaire

En juin 2004, le Comité de Bâle a enfin publié les dispositions révisées portant sur la détermination des exigences réglementaires en matière de fonds propres des banques appliquées par plus d'une centaine de pays (Bâle II).[18]

---

[16] *Ibid.* à la p. 65.

[17] Le Bénin, la Bolivie, le Burkina Faso, l'Ethiopie, le Ghana, le Guyana, Madagascar, le Mali, la Mauritanie, le Mozambique, le Nicaragua, le Niger, l'Ouganda, le Sénégal et la Tanzanie.

[18] *Rapport de gestion de la Commission fédérale des banques* 2004 à la p. 99 [ci-après *Commission fédérale*].

Les méthodes simples pourront être appliquées dès la fin 2006. En revanche, les méthodes internes complexes particulières à certains établissements pour la couverture des risques de crédit et des risques opérationnels ne seront disponibles qu'à compter de la fin 2007. Jusqu'à la promulgation définitive de l'accord, la réglementation sera approfondie au niveau de la méthode de notation interne des crédits afin de suivre l'évolution du marché et les progrès dans le domaine de la gestion des risques. Les exigences de fonds propres devraient être majorées de 6 % jusqu'à l'entrée en vigueur du nouveau texte.

Le Comité a publié plusieurs documents consacrés à la gestion de risques et mis à jour les principes relatifs à la gestion et à la surveillance du risque de taux d'intérêt.[19] Désormais, le risque de taux n'est plus soumis aux exigences minimales de fonds propres du premier pilier[20] mais les établissements s'écartant de la norme devront être appréhendés dans le cadre de la procédure de surveillance du deuxième pilier. Le Comité a repris les principes relatifs à la surveillance globale et à la limitation des risques juridiques et de réputation des groupes bancaires établis par le Groupe de travail commun avec les autorités de surveillance des places financières *offshore.*

Le Comité recommande une coordination plus étroite entre les autorités nationales de surveillance lorsqu'un groupe bancaire exerce son activité à l'échelle internationale et envisage d'appliquer ses méthodes internes sur une base consolidée et sur une base individuelle au niveau de toutes ses filiales.

Le Working Group on Cross Border Banking, groupe composé du Comité et du groupement des autorités de surveillance des places financières *offshore* a poursuivi ses travaux dans le domaine de la surveillance et de la limitation des risques juridiques et de réputation.

L'Accounting Task Force (ATF), sous-groupe du Comité de Bâle, a poursuivi ses efforts, en vain, auprès de l'International Accounting Standards Boards en vue de faire accepter les normes comptables internationales.

---

[19] *Ibid.* à la p. 98.

[20] L'accord de Bâle prend appui sur trois piliers, à savoir le ratio minimal de fonds propres, le processus de surveillance prudentielle et les exigences en matière de communication financière.

B   ORGANISATION INTERNATIONALE DES COMMISSIONS
    DE VALEURS (OICV)

La vingt-neuvième Conférence annuelle de l'OICV a eu lieu en mai à Amman en Jordanie. À cette occasion, l'organisation compte désormais 174 adhérents. Les discussions ont porté sur la réglementation dans les domaines des fonds de placement, de l'établissement et de la révision des comptes, des mécanismes de formation des prix en bourse et des bouleversements en cours dans les structures boursières.[21] En fin octobre 2004, a eu lieu une autre conférence de l'OICV, organisée à New York par la Securities and Exchange Commission, sur la réglementation et la surveillance des marchés mondiaux des valeurs mobilières et le rétablissement de la confiance dans les marchés mondiaux.

Suite aux récents scandales financiers, l'OICV a travaillé en étroite collaboration avec les agences de notation en vue d'élaborer de grands principes qui leurs sont applicables. Ces principes reposent sur quatre thèmes principaux: la qualité et l'intégrité du processus de notation, les modalités de diffusion des notations, la prévention des conflits d'intérêts et le traitement de l'information non publiques par les agences. L'OICV a décidé en 2004 d'aller plus loin en publiant le 23 décembre 2004 un code de conduite intitulé "Eléments fondamentaux du code de bonne conduite des agences de notation."[22] Ce code, une fois adopté, sera intégré dans les réglementations propres des agences de notation.

L'analyse des divers mécanismes de rachat et les différentes réglementations en vigueur dans les États membres a pris fin en 2004. Le Rapport final préconise l'adoption de mesures portant sur les droits des actionnaires, les mécanismes de contrôle permettant d'éviter les délits d'initiés, des règles visant à garantir un négoce intègre et l'octroi de compétences supplémentaires aux autorités de surveillance.

Au cours de l'exercice 2004, le sous-comité sur l'information financière a eu pour mission d'élaborer un schéma de prospectus valable pour l'émission et/ou la cotation de titres de dettes simples (*plain vanilla*) par des émetteurs *corporate*. Parallèlement, les Groupes de travail du Comité technique se sont penchés sur deux thèmes: le rachat d'actions et la transparence du marché des

---

[21] *Commission fédérale, supra* note 18 à la p. 107.

[22] *Rapport annuel 2004 de l'Autorité des Marchés Financiers* à la p. 48.

obligations émises par des entités privées. Le premier rapport adopté analyse les principales questions soulevées pour le régulateur par les rachats d'action à l'égard du traitement équitable des investisseurs, de l'intégrité du marché et de la transparence. Dans un second temps, après avoir constaté que le marché obligataire est dans de nombreux pays un marché de gré à gré non réglementé et peu transparent, le deuxième rapport formule des recommandations et des mises en garde aux régulateurs nationaux tout en encourageant les régulateurs à acquérir une meilleure connaissance de leur marché obligataire *corporate.*[23]

Enfin, le Comité technique a lancé un projet visant à élever les standards en matière de coopération internationale entre les régulateurs des marchés. D'autres problématiques ont été confiées à des Comités permanents sur le *market timing* et la gouvernance dans les fonds de placement.

Au cours de l'année 2004, l'OICV a engagé plusieurs activités de lutte contre le blanchiment. Certains de ses membres ont adhéré au Protocole d'Accord portant sur la coopération et l'échange d'informations sur les questions opérationnelles.[24] Lors de la réunion du Comité du président, l'OICV a adopté les Principes en matière d'identification et de propriété effective dans le secteur des valeurs mobilières.

IV   Le Groupe d'action financière (GAFI)

Au cours de la session 2003–4, de nouveaux progrès significatifs ont été constatés dans la lutte contre le blanchiment d'argent et le financement du terrorisme. Certains changements apportés au fonctionnement du GAFI devrait permettre d'accroître l'efficacité de l'institution.[25]

Durant l'année 2004, le GAFI a poursuivi l'examen de son futur mandat. Le nouveau mandat a été approuvé par la Réunion ministérielle qui eut lieu à Paris le 14 mai 2004 en marge de la Réunion du Conseil de l'OCDE. Au terme de ce mandat, les principales missions dévolues au GAFI seront la définition des normes internationales de lutte contre le blanchiment de capitaux et le financement du terrorisme, l'adoption de mesures à cet égard, le renforcement de la coopération avec le FMI et la Banque mondiale,

---

23 *Commission fédérale, supra* note 18 aux pp. 107–8.

24 Ce Protocole a été adopté lors de la Conférence annuelle de l'OICV en mai 2002.

25 *Rapport annuel du GAFI 2003–2004,* point 9.

la surveillance de la mise en œuvre des recommandations révisées du GAFI par les membres de manière efficace et exhaustive, l'accueil de nouveaux membres, le renforcement de la coopération entre le GAFI et les organismes régionaux type GAFI et les pays non-membres, l'intensification de l'étude des techniques et des tendances du blanchiment de capitaux et du financement du terrorisme. Ce mandat du GAFI a été renouvelé pour une période de huit ans.[26]

En parallèle, le GAFI mène une réforme interne de son organisation. Un groupe *ad hoc* constitué à cet effet a remis son Rapport en juillet 2004. Celui-ci préconise des changements dans les procédures, en particulier en ce qui concerne la structure des réunions plénières, la préparation de documents et l'organisation des groupes de travail.

Suite à l'adoption des huit Recommandations spéciales relatives à la lutte contre le financement du terrorisme, plusieurs directives ont été adoptées pour faciliter leur mise en œuvre. En 2004, le GAFI a publié une Note interprétative relative à la Recommandation spéciale II sur l'incrimination du financement du terrorisme et du blanchiment de capitaux commis dans le cadre des activités terroristes.[27]

Le 24 février 2004, le GAFI a organisé une session spéciale consacrée à l'examen des risques liés aux systèmes alternatifs de remise de fonds, aux passeurs de fonds, aux organismes à but non lucratif et aux liens entre le trafic de stupéfiants et le financement du terrorisme. Au terme de celle-ci, les participants ont manifesté leur volonté de mettre en place des instruments plus adaptés et plus sophistiqués de collecte et d'échange d'informations sur le financement du terrorisme.

Depuis 2003, le GAFI travaille conjointement avec d'autres organismes pour lancer des activités d'ouverture destinées à améliorer la fourniture d'assistance technique par la communauté internationale. Dans ce cadre, le GAFI a poursuivi ses évaluations des besoins techniques des pays en ce qui a trait à la lutte contre le terrorisme.

Dans le cadre du contrôle de la mise en œuvre des recommandations et des normes par les Membres, le GAFI poursuit les cycles d'évaluations mutuelles. À ce titre, le GAFI a élaboré et mis en place la nouvelle méthodologie commune d'évaluation des mesures

---

[26] *Ibid.*, point 17.

[27] *Ibid.*, point 24.

prises par les pays pour lutter contre le blanchiment de capitaux et contre le financement du terrorisme. Cette méthodologie a été adoptée par le FMI et la Banque mondiale en février 2004. Un troisième cycle d'évaluations mutuelles a été lancé à la fin de l'année 2004. Compte tenu de leur progrès, l'Ukraine, l'Egypte et le Guatemala ont été retiré de la liste des pays et territoires non coopératifs.[28] Le GAFI a souligné l'évolution positive de certains territoires tels que Nauru, tout en les maintenant sur la liste des territoires non-coopératifs en raison d'importantes lacunes.

En 2004, le GAFI a poursuivi sa collaboration avec les organisations internationales, notamment avec le FMI et la Banque Mondiale, ainsi que sa politique d'élargissement. Des négociations sont actuellement en cours avec la Chine. Parallèlement, des efforts ont été faits pour favoriser le développement de la coopération avec des organismes régionaux de types GAFI. Au cours de la période 2003–4, plusieurs initiatives ont vu le jour pour créer des organismes régionaux de ce type au Moyen Orient, en Afrique du Nord ainsi qu'en Eurasie.

La procédure de l'exercice sur les typologies du GAFI a fait l'objet d'un réexamen en 2003 afin d'assurer la collecte d'informations pour suivre les méthodes et les tendances du blanchiment et du financement du terrorisme. À cette fin, le GAFI a créé un nouveau groupe de travail en février 2004.

V   LE JOINT FORUM

Créé en 1996, le Joint Forum est un organisme de concertation sur les thèmes prudentiels transectoriels en vue de l'élaboration de normes de contrôle des conglomérats financiers.

En 2004, l'instance s'est intéressée au transfert du risque de crédit entre les secteurs des banques, du négoce de valeurs mobilières et des assurances. Le Rapport qui en résulte s'attache aux répercussions des activités de transfert du risque de crédit sur la stabilité du système financier, aux tendances et aux développements sur le marché ainsi qu'à l'ampleur et aux sources du transfert de risque.[29] Ce rapport se contente simplement d'énoncer un certain nombre de recommandations à l'attention des autorités nationales de surveillance sans les imposer.

---

[28]   *Ibid.*, points 33 et suivants.

[29]   *Commission fédérale, supra* note 18 à la p. 113.

Ainsi, en 2004, l'intensification de la lutte contre le blanchiment de capitaux et contre le financement du terrorisme demeure la priorité des acteurs du système financier international. Au cours de cette même année, le renforcement de la transparence et de la surveillance en matière financière ont également retenu l'attention du FMI, de la Banque mondiale, du Comité de Bâle et de l'OICV.

III Investissement

préparé par

CHARLES-EMMANUEL CÔTÉ

I Introduction

L e droit international de l'investissement a continué d'afficher un grand dynamisme au cours de l'année 2004, tant au chapitre de la juridisation des relations internationales qu'à celui des recours internationaux exercés par des investisseurs étrangers et présentant un intérêt pour le Canada.

En dépit de l'abandon par l'Organisation mondiale du commerce (OMC) des négociations multilatérales relatives à l'investissement étranger direct, le dynamisme des négociations bilatérales s'est maintenu, comme en a fait foi la publication par le Canada et les États-Unis de leurs nouveaux traités-types sur l'investissement. Le Centre international pour le règlement des différends relatifs aux investissements (CIRDI) entend suivre la cadence et s'est attaché à réfléchir à l'amélioration possible de ses règles de procédures, avec la publication d'un document sur le sujet.

L'année 2004 a aussi marqué le dixième anniversaire de l'*Accord de libre-échange nord-américain*[1] (ALENA) et de son chapitre 11 sur l'investissement. La popularité du mécanisme de règlement des différends de ce chapitre auprès des investisseurs étrangers ne s'est pas démentie, même si aucune sentence importante n'a été rendue dans une affaire intéressant le Canada, à l'exception d'une

---

Charles-Emmanuel Côté, Professeur à la Faculté de droit de l'Université Laval, Docteur en droit de l'Université McGill, Avocat au Barreau du Québec et ancien conseiller en politiques institutionnelles et constitutionnelles au Secrétariat aux Affaires intergouvernementales canadiennes du Ministère du Conseil exécutif du Québec.

1 *Accord de libre-échange nord-américain entre le gouvernement du Canada, le gouvernement des États-Unis et le gouvernement du Mexique*, 17 décembre 1992, R.T. Can. (1994) n° 2, 32 I.L.M. 289 (entrée en vigueur: le 1er janvier 1994).

dernière décision rendue dans l'affaire *Loewen* entre des investisseurs canadiens et les États-Unis. Le Canada s'est toutefois fait signifier deux nouvelles notifications d'intention de soumettre une
plainte à l'arbitrage par des investisseurs américains, selon les informations rendues publiques, tandis que deux nouvelles plaintes
ont été formellement déposées par des investisseurs canadiens contre les États-Unis. Cette année a aussi vu une première plainte être
soumise à l'arbitrage international par un investisseur canadien,
sur la base d'un traité bilatéral sur l'investissement.

II   Juridisation des relations internationales en matière
     d'investissement étranger direct

A   abandon par l'omc des négociations sur
     l'investissement étranger direct

En ce qui concerne le droit international de l'investissement, l'année 2004 a d'abord été marquée par l'abandon par l'OMC des
négociations visant l'adoption de règles multilatérales sur l'investissement étranger direct. L'idée d'explorer la possibilité de négocier de telles règles dans l'enceinte de l'OMC avait d'abord été
inscrite dans sa première déclaration ministérielle, en 1996, lors
de la Conférence de Singapour.[2] Elle fut surtout promue par la
Communauté européenne, avec trois autres thèmes dits "de Singapour," soit la politique de la concurrence, la facilitation du commerce et la transparence des marchés publics. L'échec des
négociations de l'*Accord multilatéral sur l'investissement,*[3] en 1998, dans
l'enceinte de l'Organisation de coopération et de développement
économiques (OCDE) a fait de l'OMC l'unique forum où l'adoption de règles multilatérales générales sur l'investissement étranger direct devenait envisageable à court ou moyen terme. Bien
qu'elles aient été officiellement inscrites au programme de négociations multilatérales du Cycle de Doha, en 2001, le Conseil général de l'OMC a finalement décidé, le 1er août 2004, d'abandonner
les négociations sur l'investissement étranger direct.[4] L'opposition

---

2 OMC, Conférence ministérielle, *Déclaration ministérielle de Singapour* (adoptée le
  13 décembre 1996), OMC doc. WT/MIN(96)/DEC, §20.

3 OCDE, *Accord multilatéral sur l'investissement,* projet daté du 24 avril 1998, en
  ligne: OCDE <http://www1.oecd.org/daf/mai/pdf/ng/ng987r1f.pdf> (date
  d'accès: 3 novembre 2004).

4 OMC, Conférence ministérielle, *Déclaration ministérielle* (adoptée le 14 novembre
  2001), OMC doc. WT/MIN(01)/DEC/1, §§ 20–22; *Programme de travail de Doha,*
  OMC Conseil général, Déc. du 1er août 2004, OMC doc. WT/L/579, § 1(g).

de nombreux pays en voie de développement, soutenus par des organisations non gouvernementales (ONG) du Nord, dans une alliance qui ressemble à celle qui contribua à empêcher la conclusion de l'*Accord multilatéral sur l'investissement*, semble avoir conduit à cet abandon. La tiédeur des États-Unis et leur préférence pour poursuivre la création de règles internationales sur l'investissement étranger direct par la voie bilatérale expliqueraient également cet abandon des négociations multilatérales.

Il faudra évaluer l'impact de cette décision sur l'évolution des négociations pour l'adoption de règles multilatérales concernant l'investissement étranger direct dans le secteur énergétique, à la phase pré-investissement. Les négociations visant l'adoption d'un traité complémentaire au *Traité sur la Charte de l'énergie*[5] et applicable à cette phase, laquelle correspond au stade précédant la réalisation de l'investissement, avaient été suspendues en 2002, afin de ne pas interférer avec les négociations qui étaient en cours à l'OMC dans le cadre du Cycle de Doha.[6] On se souviendra que le retrait de la phase pré-investissement du champ d'application des règles juridiquement contraignantes du *Traité sur la Charte de l'énergie*, proposé par la Commission européenne, avait permis la conclusion du traité, mais avait amené le Canada et surtout les États-Unis à quitter les négociations. L'arrêt des négociations à l'OMC marquera-t-il la reprise des travaux à la Conférence de la Charte de l'énergie sur ce traité complémentaire, ou marquera-t-il plutôt la fin de toutes négociations multilatérales sur l'investissement étranger direct pour un long moment? En attendant de pouvoir répondre à cette question, il semble bien que c'est au plan bilatéral que l'attention devra se tourner au cours des prochaines années, pour connaître l'évolution du droit international de l'investissement.

B   PUBLICATION PAR LE CANADA DE SON NOUVEAU TRAITÉ-TYPE
      SUR L'INVESTISSEMENT ÉTRANGER DIRECT

Le gouvernement du Canada a rendu public, en 2004, son nouveau traité-type sur l'investissement étranger direct, destiné à servir

---

[5] *Traité sur la Charte de l'énergie*, 17 décembre 1994, 33 I.L.M. 382 (entrée en vigueur: le 16 avril 1998; modifié le 24 avril 1998).

[6] Secrétariat de la Charte de l'énergie, *Overview of Investment Provisions Contained in the Energy Charter Treaty*, en ligne: Secrétariat de la Charte de l'énergie <http://www.encharter.org/index.jsp?psk=03&ptp=tDetail.jsp&pci=127&pti=23> (date d'accès: le 29 mai 2006).

de base à la négociation de ses traités bilatéraux sur l'investissement, aussi appelés "Accords sur la promotion et la protection des
investissements étrangers" (APIE) dans le jargon fédéral.[7] Celui-ci
fait fond sur l'expérience acquise avec la mise en œuvre du chapitre 11 de l'ALÉNA et de son mécanisme de règlement des différends reconnaissant le droit de l'investisseur étranger d'invoquer
la responsabilité de l'État hôte auprès d'un tribunal arbitral international. Il tente de remédier à plusieurs problèmes survenus dans
l'opération de ce mécanisme au cours des dix dernières années à
l'instar du nouveau traité-type américain sur l'investissement, également rendu public en 2004.[8] À certains égards, le traité-type canadien fait cependant preuve de plus d'audace que le traité-type
américain dans les solutions qu'il propose, particulièrement au
chapitre des exceptions aux règles matérielles du traité.

Le traité-type canadien reprend pour l'essentiel la structure du
chapitre 11 de l'ALÉNA, en la réaménageant légèrement et en y
ajoutant une nouvelle section sur le règlement des différends
interétatiques. La section A pose les définitions nécessaires à la
bonne intelligence du traité; la section B prévoit les règles matérielles applicables aux investissements étrangers directs; la section
C met en place le mécanisme de règlement des différends entre
investisseur étranger et État hôte; la section D fait de même en ce
qui concerne les différends interétatiques; la section E contient
quelques dispositions finales. Les quatre annexes au traité-type sont
censées contenir les réserves et certaines exceptions que les parties
inscriront au traité, d'une manière semblable à l'ALÉNA. Sur le
fond, le traité-type suit de très près le modèle du chapitre 11 de
l'ALÉNA, aussi les commentaires qui suivent se concentreront-ils
sur les éléments nouveaux qu'il entend introduire dans la pratique
conventionnelle du Canada.

Le préambule du traité-type se conclut avec une affirmation nouvelle, voulant que les parties reconnaissent que la promotion et la

---

7 Canada, *Accord entre le Canada et [Pays] pour la promotion et la protection des investissements,* en ligne: Commerce international Canada <http://www.dfait-maeci.gc.
ca/tna-nac/documents/2004-FIPA-model-fr.pdf> (date d'accès: le 3 juin 2006)
[ci-après *APIE-type*].

8 États-Unis, Office of the United States Trade Representative, *Treaty between the
Government of the United States of America and the Government of [Country] concerning
the Encouragement and Reciprocal Protection of Investment,* en ligne: Office of the
United States Trade Representative <http://www.ustr.gov/assets/Trade_Sectors/
Investment/Model_BIT/asset_upload_file847_6897.pdf> (date d'accès: le 3 juin
2006) [ci-après *US Model BIT*].

protection des investissements sont propres à favoriser "la promotion du développement durable." Si le lien logique entre investissement étranger direct et développement économique peut sembler évident, celui entre ce type d'investissement et le développement durable l'est moins. Le développement durable ne devrait-il pas plutôt résulter de l'application de politiques intégrées de développement de la part des gouvernements, ainsi que de la responsabilisation des entreprises privées? Il est vrai que plusieurs nouvelles exceptions introduites par le traité poursuivent un objectif de développement durable, mais celles-ci visent à justifier des entraves à la promotion et la protection des investissements étrangers, qui seraient pourtant censés promouvoir le développement durable.

La définition juridique de la norme minimale de traitement des investissements que les parties devront appliquer est resserrée pour ne viser que la norme minimale de traitement des étrangers du droit international coutumier.[9] Il est explicitement prévu que les expressions "traitement juste et équitable" et "protection et sécurité intégrale" des investissements ne sont pas censées aller au-delà de la coutume internationale. Le traité-type précise également que la violation d'une autre de ses dispositions ou d'un autre traité ne démontre pas qu'il y a eu une violation de la norme minimale de traitement. L'origine de ce resserrement de la définition se trouve dans la controverse qui a eu lieu à ce sujet avec le chapitre 11 de l'ALÉNA. Une jurisprudence arbitrale commençait à se constituer sur la question de l'interprétation de la norme minimale de traitement, voulant qu'elle aille plus loin que la coutume internationale, et que la violation d'une autre norme conventionnelle internationale suffise à établir sa violation, ce qui a amené un juge national à annuler partiellement une sentence arbitrale en contrôle judiciaire, et a conduit la Commission du libre-échange à adopter des notes d'interprétation pour corriger cette jurisprudence arbitrale émergente.[10] Ces événements n'ont pas été sans

---

[9] *APIE-type, supra* note 7, art. 5.

[10] Voir Commission du libre-échange de l'ALÉNA, *Notes d'interprétation de certaines dispositions du chapitre 11*, Washington, 31 juillet 2001, en ligne: Commerce international Canada <http://www.dfait-maeci.gc.ca/tna-nac/NAFTA-Interpr-fr.asp> (date d'accès: le 16 septembre 2004); *Mexique c. Metalclad Corporation*, [2001] B.C.S.C. 664, 5 I.C.S.I.D. Rep. 238, § 65 (Canada, C.S. C.-B.); *Pope & Talbot Inc. c. Canada (Deuxième sentence sur le fond)* (2001), § 111 (CNUDCI), (Arbitres: Lord Devaird, B.J. Greenberg, M.J. Belman), en ligne: Commerce international Canada <http://www.dfait-maeci.gc.ca/tna-nac/documents/Award_Merits-e.pdf> (date d'accès: 12 octobre 2004); *S.D. Myers Inc. c. Canada*

troubler le fonctionnement du mécanisme de règlement des différends du chapitre 11 pour un temps, ce qui rend bienvenues ces
nouvelles dispositions du traité-type.

La principale nouveauté introduite par le traité-type canadien
est qu'il prévoit de nombreuses exceptions pour justifier des entraves à la promotion et la protection des investissements étrangers
directs. De telles exceptions ne sont pas prévues dans le chapitre
11 de l'ALÉNA, et la question de l'applicabilité des exceptions générales de l'ALÉNA à ce chapitre n'a pas été clairement tranchée.[11]
Une première série d'exceptions particulières sont prévues, visant
notamment la norme du traitement national à l'égard des activités
ou des services faisant partie d'un régime de retraite public ou d'un
régime de sécurité sociale.[12] Les exceptions générales nouvellement
prévues par le traité-type sont inspirées du célèbre article XX de
l'*Accord général sur les tarifs douaniers et le commerce*,[13] et reprennent sa
structure, comportant une disposition introductive — le "chapeau"
— qui vise à s'assurer que les exceptions ne sont pas utilisées à des
fins protectionnistes, suivie des exceptions proprement dites. Ces
dernières visent la protection de la santé et de la vie des personnes
et des animaux et la préservation des végétaux, l'exécution des lois
et règlements compatibles avec les dispositions du traité-type, ainsi
que la conservation des ressources naturelles épuisables, biologiques ou non biologiques.[14] D'autres exceptions générales sont également prévues par le traité-type, mais ne comportent pas de

---

(*Première sentence sur le fond*) (2000), §§ 266–267 (CNUDCI), (Arbitres: B.P.
Schwartz, E.C. Chiasson, J.M. Hunter), en ligne: Commerce international Canada <http://www.dfait-maeci.gc.ca/tna-nac/documents/myersvcanadapartial
award_final_13-11-00.pdf> (date d'accès: le 13 octobre 2004); *Metalclad Corporation c. Mexique* (2000), 5 I.C.S.I.D. Rep. 212, 40 I.L.M. 36, 16 I.C.S.I.D. Rev.
168, 129 J.D.I. 233, § 76 (Mécanisme supplémentaire du CIRDI), (Arbitres: E.
Lauterpacht, B.R. Civiletti, J.L. Siqueiros), en ligne: CIRDI <http://www.
worldbank.org/icsid/cases/mm-award-e.pdf> (date d'accès: le 12 octobre 2004).
Voir aussi Commission du libre-échange Canada-Chili, *Notes d'interprétation de
certaines dispositions du chapitre G*, Quito, 31 octobre 2002, en ligne: Commerce
international Canada <http://www.dfait-maeci.gc.ca/tna-nac/ccftacommission-
fr.asp> (date d'accès: 25 octobre 2004).

[11] Voir notamment *S.D. Myers Inc. c. Canada (Première sentence sur le fond)*, *ibid.* §§
294 et 298.

[12] *APIE-type*, *supra* note 7, art. 9.

[13] *Accord général sur les tarifs douaniers et le commerce*, 30 octobre 1947, 55 R.T.N.U.
187, R.T. Can. 1947 n° 27, 4 I.B.D.D. (1969) 1.

[14] *APIE-type*, *supra* note 7, art. 10(1).

disposition introductive, ce qui semble signifier qu'elles pourraient
être utilisées à des fins protectionnistes; elles visent notamment les
mesures prudentielles dans le secteur financier, la sécurité de l'État,
ainsi que, chose importante au regard du développement de normes internationales relatives à la promotion et la protection de la
diversité culturelle, les industries culturelles.[15]

Les effets juridiques de ces nouvelles exceptions dans le domaine
de l'investissement étranger direct restent à vérifier, mais l'on peut
déjà observer que les États-Unis n'ont pas suivi cette voie dans leur
propre nouveau traité-type sur l'investissement, ce qui laisse présa-
ger une certaine division des gouvernements sur la question. S'agit-
il d'une solution facile à des problèmes difficiles? Les exceptions
générales relatives à la protection de la santé et de l'environnement visent vraisemblablement à remédier au *"regulatory chill"* dont
les gouvernements souffriraient dans ces domaines en raison du
chapitre 11 de l'ALÉNA. Mais une interprétation plus fine du concept de "mesure concernant un investissement" — concept opéra-
toire de tout traité sur l'investissement, circonscrivant son champ
d'application — qui ferait en sorte qu'une mesure d'application
générale touchant à un investissement étranger n'est pas une mesure concernant un investissement, comme a commencé à le faire
le tribunal arbitral dans l'affaire *Methanex*,[16] ne permettrait-elle pas
d'atteindre les mêmes objectifs? Le jeu entre ces exceptions et la
norme minimale de traitement des étrangers de la coutume internationale pourrait aussi conduire à des situations délicates: une
mesure étatique violant cette norme pourrait être justifiée par une
exception, mais être néanmoins fondée en droit international coutumier, ce qui pourrait de toute façon permettre à l'État de nationalité de l'investisseur étranger de faire une réclamation
internationale en se fondant sur la théorie de la protection diplo-
matique. Le résultat net de ces exceptions, à l'égard du renvoi à la
coutume internationale, serait donc de réduire le domaine cou-
vert par le droit privé d'invoquer la responsabilité de l'État créé
par le traité basé sur le traité-type.

Le concept d'expropriation est aussi clarifié par le traité-type,
qui précise, d'une part, que l'expropriation indirecte et l'expropriation au moyen de mesures équivalant à une nationalisation ou

---

[15] *Ibid.*, art. 10 (2), (4) et (6).

[16] *Methanex Corporation c. États-Unis (Sentence sur la compétence)* (2002), § 147
(CNUDCI), (Arbitres: V.V. Veeder, W. Rowley, W. Christopher), en ligne: US
Department of State <http://www.state.gov/documents/organization/12613.
pdf> (date d'accès: le 30 septembre 2004).

à une expropriation sont une seule et même chose.[17] Le caractère équivoque du chapitre 11 de l'ALÉNA à cet égard a notamment été souligné par un tribunal arbitral, dans l'affaire *Feldman*.[18] D'autre part, une annexe interprétative vise aussi à éliminer le *"regulatory chill,"* en précisant que "ne constituent pas une expropriation indirecte les mesures non discriminatoires d'une Partie qui sont conçues et appliquées dans un but légitime de protection du bien public, par exemple à des fins de santé, de sécurité et d'environnement."[19] On peut s'interroger sur la logique interne du traité-type à cet égard, lui qui prévoit de toute façon des exceptions générales lorsqu'une mesure poursuit ces fins. À trop vouloir corriger ce problème prétendument posé par le chapitre 11 de l'ALÉNA, le traité-type canadien semble tirer dans plusieurs directions à la fois et le résultat net de cette situation est que la sécurité juridique des investissements étrangers pourrait s'en trouver réduite. À nouveau, l'interprétation plus fine du concept de "mesure concernant un investissement," amorcée dans l'affaire *Methanex,* aurait peut-être pu conduire au même résultat, comme l'aurait pu celle du concept d'expropriation indirecte, faite par le tribunal arbitral dans l'affaire *Feldman,* suivant laquelle l'État ne saurait être rendu responsable de tous les aléas de la vie économique d'une entreprise, résultant de l'action gouvernementale normale.[20]

Parmi les autres nouveautés introduites par le traité-type canadien, une disposition vise à assurer un traitement non discriminatoire aux investisseurs quant aux mesures relatives aux pertes subies suite à un conflit armé, une guerre civile ou une catastrophe naturelle.[21] Enfin, les mesures fiscales reçoivent un traitement particulier, et une nouvelle obligation de transparence est prévue, sans toutefois être très contraignante pour les parties contractantes.[22] Il faut rappeler que la question de l'existence d'une obligation de transparence dans la norme minimale de traitement prévue par le chapitre 11 de l'ALÉNA avait été au cœur de la controverse qui a

---

17 *APIE-type, supra* note 7, art. 13(1).

18 *Feldman c. Mexique (Sentence sur le fond)* (2002), 18 I.C.S.I.D. Rev. 488, 42 I.L.M. 625, § 100 (Mécanisme supplémentaire du CIRDI), (Arbitres: J. Covarrubias Bravo, D.A. Gantz, K.D. Kerameus), en ligne: CIRDI <http://www.worldbank.org/icsid/cases/feldman_mexico-award-en.PDF> (date d'accès: le 4 octobre 2004).

19 *APIE-type, supra* note 7, annexe B.13(1).

20 *Feldman c. Mexique (Sentence sur le fond), supra* note 18, §§ 103–5.

21 *APIE-type, supra* note 7, art. 12.

22 *Ibid.,* art. 16 et 19.

conduit un juge canadien à annuler partiellement une sentence arbitrale dans l'affaire *Metalclad.*[23]

En ce qui concerne le mécanisme de règlement des différends entre investisseur étranger et État hôte, il faut signaler plusieurs nouveautés introduites par le traité-type, lesquelles constituent souvent des codifications de la pratique développée sous le chapitre 11 de l'ALÉNA. La principale innovation est sans doute la création d'une phase de consultation obligatoire, insérée entre la notification de l'intention de déposer une plainte à l'arbitrage et le dépôt formel de cette plainte.[24] Des formulaires obligatoires de renonciation aux autres recours et de consentement à l'arbitrage sont également prévus, ce qui devrait permettre d'éviter le rejet d'une plainte pour vice de consentement et de renonciation, comme ce fut le cas sous le régime du chapitre 11 de l'ALÉNA dans l'affaire *Waste Management.*[25] Par contre, aucun formulaire de notification de l'intention de soumettre une plainte à l'arbitrage n'est prévu, alors que la Commission du libre-échange en a adopté un, qui est facultatif, pour le chapitre 11.[26] La pratique voulant que les objections préliminaires relatives à la compétence ou à l'admissibilité de la plainte soient tranchées avant que le tribunal arbitral ne se penche sur le fond de l'affaire est codifiée.[27] Les avancées importantes réalisées sous le régime du chapitre 11 de l'ALÉNA au plan de l'accès de la société civile au processus sont également codifiées dans le traité-type: l'accès du public aux audiences et aux documents est prévu en principe, de même que l'est la possibilité de soumettre un mémoire au tribunal arbitral à titre d'*amicus curiae*, pour laquelle un formulaire obligatoire est aussi prévu.[28]

---

23 *Metalclad Corporation c. Mexique, supra* note 10, § 76; *Mexique c. Metalclad Corporation, supra* note 10, § 69.

24 *APIE-type, supra* note 7, art. 25.

25 *Ibid.* art. 26 et annexe C.26; *Waste Management Inc. c. Mexique (Sentence sur la compétence)* (2000), 40 I.L.M. 56, 15 I.C.S.I.D. Rev. 211, § 31 (Mécanisme supplémentaire du CIRDI), (Arbitres: K. Highet, E. Siqueiros T., B.M. Cremades), en ligne: CIRDI <http://www.worldbank.org/icsid/cases/waste_award.pdf> (date d'accès: le 29 septembre 2004).

26 Voir Commission du libre-échange de l'ALÉNA, *Formulaire de notification de l'intention de soumettre une plainte à l'arbitrage*, Montréal, 7 octobre 2003, en ligne: Commerce international Canada <http://www.dfait-maeci.gc.ca/nafta-alena/NoticeIntent-fr.pdf> (date d'accès: le 16 septembre 2004).

27 *APIE-type, supra* note 7, art. 37.

28 *Ibid.*, art. 38, 39 et annexe C.39. Voir Commission du libre-échange de l'ALÉNA, *Déclaration de la Commission du libre-échange sur la participation d'une tierce partie,*

Au moins deux problèmes demeurent cependant concernant la transparence du processus, ayant trait à la manière dont le gouvernement du Canada gère l'opération de ces mécanismes de règlement des différends. Il s'agit, d'une part, de la question de la publication obligatoire et systématique des notifications d'intention de soumettre une plainte à l'arbitrage reçues par le gouvernement. À l'heure actuelle, cette publication n'est pas obligatoire et les sources gouvernementales et privées divergent parfois quant aux notifications d'intention signifiées aux gouvernements. De manière générale, les sources privées, souvent alimentées par les procureurs agissant au nom des investisseurs étrangers, recensent davantage de notifications que les gouvernements. Ces divergences, volontaires ou non, peuvent contribuer à entretenir un certain flou autour du processus. La publication d'une notification peut aussi avoir un effet non négligeable sur les négociations entre les parties et sur le sort du différend. C'est pourquoi il semble souhaitable que ces notifications d'intention fassent l'objet d'une publication systématique, en vue d'accroître la transparence et la légitimité du processus, mais aussi pour empêcher que cette publication ne soit utilisée à d'autres fins que la publicité du processus. Il s'agit, d'autre part, de la question de la traduction en français des documents, ainsi que de l'utilisation du français par le gouvernement du Canada dans les procédures entreprises sous l'égide de ces mécanismes d'arbitrage entre investisseur étranger et État hôte. Bien que l'usage de l'anglais soit généralisé dans ces procédures, le gouvernement du Mexique rend généralement publiques des versions espagnoles des documents de procédure et des sentences arbitrales. Les arbitrages entrepris sous l'égide du chapitre 11 de l'ALÉNA impliquant le Mexique utilisent également l'espagnol, en plus de l'anglais, tandis que ceux impliquant le Canada n'utilisent jamais le français, et le gouvernement du Canada n'a jamais traduit un seul document en français, alors qu'il s'agit pourtant de litiges de droit international public intéressant l'action gouvernementale canadienne. Bien entendu, ces lacunes importantes devraient être réglées au plan interne et non dans un traité-type.

Il faut finalement noter que l'idée de créer une juridiction d'appel n'est pas du tout abordée par le traité-type canadien, contrairement au traité-type américain, qui envisage explicitement cette

---

Montréal, 7 octobre 2003, en ligne: Commerce international Canada <http://www.dfait-maeci.gc.ca/nafta-alena/Nondisputing-fr.pdf> (date d'accès: le 20 octobre 2004).

possibilité.[29] On peut regretter que le gouvernement du Canada n'ait pour le moment pas envisagé d'explorer cette voie, qui pourrait s'avérer le complément indispensable de la reconnaissance du droit des investisseurs étrangers d'invoquer la responsabilité de l'État hôte. L'éventuelle ratification par le Canada de la *Convention pour le règlement des différends relatifs aux investissements entre États et ressortissants d'autres États*[30] (*Convention CIRDI*) pourrait cependant remettre cette idée à l'avant-plan, car les investisseurs étrangers privilégieront sûrement cette voie procédurale si elle devait être mise à leur disposition, puisqu'elle leur permettrait d'échapper totalement au contrôle judiciaire des juridictions internes canadiennes, ce qui pourrait rendre nécessaire la mise en place d'une forme de juridiction d'appel au plan international.

Le traité-type canadien crée finalement un mécanisme interétatique de règlement des différends, qui peut notamment être utilisé en cas de refus par une partie contractante d'exécuter une sentence arbitrale rendue au profit d'un investisseur étranger.[31] Un tel mécanisme n'est pas prévu par le chapitre 11 de l'ALÉNA, puisque celui-ci renvoie au mécanisme général de règlement des différends du chapitre 20, qui s'applique à l'ensemble du traité à l'exception du chapitre 19, concernant l'imposition de droits *antidumping* et compensateurs. Contrairement au mécanisme du chapitre 20 de l'ALÉNA, le mécanisme interétatique créé par le traité-type semble permettre aux parties contractantes d'obtenir une indemnisation financière si une violation de ses règles matérielles est constatée par le groupe spécial arbitral; mais le traité-type ne pèche pas par excès de clarté à cet égard. La question de l'articulation juridique entre un recours privé et un recours étatique fondés sur le traité-type n'est pas du tout abordée, ce qui est certainement une lacune importante, mais il est vrai que cette question est généralement négligée dans les traités bilatéraux sur l'investissement.[32] Les difficultés que

29 *US Model BIT, supra* note 8, annexe D.

30 *Convention pour le règlement des différends relatifs aux investissements entre États et ressortissants d'autres États*, 18 mars 1965, 575 R.T.N.U. 160.

31 *APIE-type, supra* note 7, art. 48.

32 Voir A. Broches, "The Convention on the Settlement of Investment Disputes between States and Nationals of Other States" (1972) 136 Rec. cours 331, réédité dans A. Broches, *Selected Essays: World Bank, ICSID, and Other Subjects of Public and Private International Law*, Dordrecht, Martinus Nijhoff, 1995, 188 aux pp. 218–19.

pourraient poser l'exercice parallèle de tels recours ne devraient pourtant pas être sous-estimées.

L'impact du nouveau traité-type canadien sur l'investissement reste à voir. Il sera intéressant d'observer si le gouvernement du Canada réussira à convaincre d'autres gouvernements de l'utiliser, mais aussi de voir si le traité-type canadien réussira à offrir un modèle concurrent du traité-type américain, particulièrement au chapitre des exceptions aux règles matérielles. Le Canada et les États-Unis étant parmi les États les plus expérimentés avec de tels recours des investisseurs étrangers à l'arbitrage international, la manière dont ils ont adapté leurs nouveaux traités-types devrait vraisemblablement intéresser d'autres États désireux de conclure des traités bilatéraux sur l'investissement. Le traité-type canadien n'a pas encore servi de base à l'adoption d'un traité bilatéral par le Canada, mais des négociations sont en cours avec l'Inde, la Chine et le Pérou. L'histoire du chapitre 11 de l'ALÉNA enseigne que le Canada ne doit pas avoir comme prémisse qu'il est uniquement un exportateur de capitaux et que les traités bilatéraux sur l'investissement visent seulement à protéger les investissements canadiens à l'étranger; des pays de la taille de l'Inde ou de la Chine, par exemple, pourraient devenir des exportateurs de capitaux au Canada, ce qui placerait ce dernier dans la position de l'État hôte. Le traité-type canadien démontre que le gouvernement du Canada a bien retenu cette leçon et est prêt, cette fois, à faire face à cette nouvelle réalité.

C   PUBLICATION D'UN DOCUMENT DE RÉFLEXION PAR LE CIRDI

Face au dynamisme des négociations bilatérales sur l'investissement et à l'évolution rapide de la pratique des mécanismes de règlement des différends entre investisseur étranger et État hôte prévus par des traités sur l'investissement, comme celui du chapitre 11 de l'ALÉNA, le CIRDI n'entend pas être en reste, aussi tient-il à s'adapter afin de demeurer un forum incontournable pour le règlement de ce type de différends. En 2004, le CIRDI a donc publié un document de réflexion sur les améliorations possibles qui pourraient être apportées à son cadre pour l'arbitrage des différends entre investisseur et État.[33] Vu les contraintes entourant la

---

[33] CIRDI, *Possible Improvements of the Framework for ICSID Arbitration* (Document de réflexion du Secrétariat du CIRDI), Washington (DC), CIRDI, 2004.

modification de la *Convention CIRDI*, ces améliorations seraient plutôt apportées au moyen de l'adoption de nouveaux règlements par le Conseil administratif du CIRDI.

Différentes questions qui pourraient faire l'objet d'améliorations sont abordées. La création d'une procédure accélérée est envisagée pour permettre au tribunal arbitral de recommander des mesures conservatoires propres à sauvegarder les droits des parties, de même que pour lui permettre de se prononcer sur le caractère manifestement non fondé d'une plainte. En ce qui concerne l'ouverture du processus à la société civile, la publication plus rapide des sentences arbitrales est aussi envisagée, ainsi que la reconnaissance du droit des tribunaux arbitraux de recevoir des mémoires d'*amicus curiae* et l'amélioration de la publicité des audiences. L'amélioration des règles sur la divulgation des conflits d'intérêts par les arbitres est aussi discutée dans le document de réflexion du CIRDI, en raison de l'accroissement considérable du nombre d'affaires au cours des dernières années. L'introduction d'une procédure optionnelle de médiation, moins formelle que la procédure de conciliation qui existe actuellement, est également examinée, tout comme la possibilité de renforcer les activités de formation à destination des fonctionnaires provenant des pays en voie de développement.

Finalement, la pièce de résistance du document de réflexion du CIRDI est la question de la création d'une juridiction d'appel pour les sentences arbitrales, qui viserait à améliorer la cohérence de la jurisprudence arbitrale. L'avantage de mettre en place une procédure d'appel au CIRDI serait de prévenir la création de multiples juridictions d'appel dans les traités bilatéraux sur l'investissement; une telle multiplication pourrait autrement devenir problématique et déjouer l'objectif même poursuivi par la création d'une juridiction d'appel. La réflexion du CIRDI à ce sujet semble être sérieuse, puisque son document y consacre une annexe unique de huit pages, alors que le document principal compte seize pages. Cette question pourrait devenir un des principaux sujet de discussion au cours des prochaines années en droit international de l'investissement; elle sera sûrement fertile en études doctrinales, portant par exemple sur sa compatibilité avec la conception classique de l'arbitrage, ou encore sur son impact sur les phénomènes de la multiplication des juridictions internationales et de la possible fragmentation du droit international.

III Différends internationaux relatifs à l'investissement intéressant le Canada

A Décision sur la demande de décision supplémentaire présentée dans l'affaire LOEWEN

L'affaire *Loewen* a connu son point final en 2004, lorsque le tribunal arbitral a rendu sa décision sur la demande de décision supplémentaire présentée par les États-Unis, afin qu'il précise la base juridique sur laquelle il a rejeté la plainte personnelle de l'investisseur canadien, M. Raymond Loewen. Il faut rappeler que cette affaire tire son origine de la plainte déposée par cet investisseur et son entreprise canadienne Loewen Group contre les États-Unis, en vertu du chapitre 11 de l'ALÉNA, suite au jugement des tribunaux du Mississippi ayant condamné l'entreprise à verser 500 millions de dollars américains en dommages, dont 400 millions à titre de dommages punitifs, dans le cadre d'un litige commercial qui l'opposait à son concurrent américain. L'entreprise canadienne, œuvrant dans le secteur des services funéraires, n'a pu exercer son droit d'appel devant la Cour suprême du Mississippi, car il lui a été impossible de verser la caution requise de 625 millions de dollars américains. Pour éviter l'exécution forcée du jugement, Loewen Group a finalement décidé de régler le litige à l'amiable pour un montant de 175 millions de dollars américains. Les investisseurs canadiens réclamaient 725 millions de dollars américains en dommages dans leur recours entrepris en vertu du chapitre 11.

Cette affaire est importante dans le développement de la jurisprudence arbitrale concernant le chapitre 11 de l'ALÉNA, puisqu'elle a permis de préciser la portée de ses règles matérielles à l'égard des jugements et décisions judiciaires. Le tribunal arbitral a d'abord jugé qu'il était compétent pour connaître de la plainte, parce qu'un jugement est une "mesure" au sens de l'ALÉNA, et que si tous les actes posés par la branche judiciaire de l'État hôte ne sont pas des "mesures adoptées ou maintenues," au sens du chapitre 11, les décisions judiciaires ayant valeur de précédent le sont.[34]

---

[34] *Loewen Group Inc. et Loewen c. États-Unis (Sentence sur la compétence)* (2001), 129 J.D.I. 217, §§ 40–41, 52 (Mécanisme supplémentaire du CIRDI), (Arbitres: A. Mason, L.Y. Fortier et A.J. Mikva), en ligne: US Department of State <http://www.state.gov/documents/organization/3921.pdf> (date d'accès: le 6 octobre 2004).

La question de savoir si tous les recours internes doivent être épuisés pour qu'un jugement devienne une "mesure adoptée ou maintenue" a été tranchée dans la sentence sur le fond. Le tribunal arbitral a interprété l'article 1121, concernant la renonciation à ses recours internes par l'investisseur étranger, comme n'ayant pas écarté la règle de l'épuisement des recours internes lorsque la mesure visée par une plainte est une décision judiciaire.[35] Même s'il a été d'avis que les agissements des tribunaux internes américains constituaient un déni de justice au sens de la coutume internationale et de l'article 1105 de l'ALÉNA, le tribunal arbitral a jugé que M. Loewen n'avait pas épuisé ses recours internes.[36] La plainte a finalement été rejetée pour défaut de compétence, en raison du changement de nationalité que l'entreprise canadienne a subi pendant les procédures d'arbitrage, étant devenue une société américaine et manquant ainsi à l'exigence de continuité de nationalité jusqu'au règlement du différend.[37]

C'est alors que les États-Unis ont demandé au tribunal arbitral de préciser son raisonnement juridique concernant les motifs du rejet de la plainte personnelle de Raymond Loewen. Dans une décision rendue le 13 septembre 2004, le tribunal arbitral a confirmé que celle-ci a été rejetée sur le fond, en raison de son omission d'avoir épuisé ses recours internes, et non par défaut de compétence.[38] Le tribunal a rejeté l'argument des États-Unis voulant que cette sentence manque de clarté, ainsi que celui de M. Loewen qui avançait que la question n'avait pas été tranchée dans la sentence et que le passage sur l'omission d'avoir épuisé ses recours internes n'était qu'un *obiter dictum*. Le tribunal a donc refusé de rendre une décision supplémentaire, mettant un terme à cette affaire qui fera date en droit international de l'investissement.

---

[35] *Loewen Group Inc. et Loewen c. États-Unis (Sentence sur le fond)* (2003), 42 I.L.M. 811, § 164 (Mécanisme supplémentaire du CIRDI), (Arbitres: A. Mason, M. Mustill et A.J. Mikva), en ligne: US Department of State <http://www.state.gov/documents/organization/22094.pdf> (date d'accès: le 6 octobre 2004).

[36] *Ibid.*, §§ 137, 217 et 225.

[37] *Ibid.*, §§ 223–225.

[38] *Loewen Group Inc. et Loewen c. États-Unis (Décision sur la requête des États-Unis pour une décision supplémentaire)* (2004), 44 I.L.M. 836, §§ 20–21 (Mécanisme supplémentaire du CIRDI), (Arbitres: A. Mason, M. Mustill et A.J. Mikva), en ligne: US Department of State <http://www.state.gov/documents/organization/36260.pdf> (date d'accès: le 6 juin 2006).

B   NOTIFICATIONS D'INTENTION DE SOUMETTRE UNE PLAINTE À
    L'ARBITRAGE SIGNIFIÉES AU CANADA

Le 26 février 2004, un investisseur américain, M. Albert Connolly,
a signifié au gouvernement du Canada son intention de soumettre
une plainte à l'arbitrage en vertu du chapitre 11 de l'ALÉNA.[39]
Connolly entendrait porter plainte contre le Canada en raison du
refus de la part du gouvernement de l'Ontario de lui avoir accordé
un crédit auquel il aurait eu droit en vertu de la législation
ontarienne, concernant la production d'une évaluation profession-
nelle relative à un terrain de prospection minière sur lequel il détenait un claim. L'investisseur allègue notamment que ces
agissements constitueraient une expropriation contraire à l'ALÉNA,
et réclame la restitution de son claim ou, subsidiairement, le verse-
ment de dommages-intérêts d'un montant indéterminé. L'investisseur n'a pas soumis sa plainte à l'arbitrage en 2004.

Une deuxième notification d'intention de soumettre une plainte
à l'arbitrage en vertu du chapitre 11 de l'ALÉNA a été signifiée au
gouvernement du Canada, le 15 juin 2004, par trois investisseurs
américains, Contractual Obligations Productions LLP, Charles
Robert Underwood et Carl Paolino.[40] Ceux-ci entendraient porter
plainte contre le Canada en raison du refus du Bureau de certification des produits audiovisuels canadiens (BCPAC) de leur avoir
accordé une subvention pour le développement d'une émission
de télévision, au motif qu'ils n'étaient pas citoyens canadiens. Les
investisseurs allèguent que le programme canadien de subvention
pour la production audiovisuelle et la décision des autorités canadiennes violent plusieurs dispositions de l'ALÉNA, dont la norme
du traitement national, la norme minimale de traitement, les
normes relatives aux prescriptions de résultats, ainsi que la norme
relative à l'expropriation, et ils réclament des dommages-intérêts
d'un montant indéterminé. La plainte n'a pas été soumise à l'arbitrage en 2004. Si elle devait aller plus loin, cette affaire pourrait

---

39 *Connolly c. Canada,* "Notification de l'intention de soumettre une plainte à
   l'arbitrage par Albert Connolly" (26 février 2004), en ligne: Commerce international Canada <http://www.dfait-maeci.gc.ca/tna-nac/documents/
   Brownfields.pdf> (date d'accès: le 4 juin 2006).

40 *Contractual Obligations Productions LLP, Underwood et Paolino c. Canada,* "Notification de l'intention de soumettre une plainte à l'arbitrage par Contractual Obligations LLP, Charles Robert Underwood et Carl Paolino" (15 juin 2004), en
   ligne: Commerce international Canada <http://www.dfait-maeci.gc.ca/tna-nac/
   documents/NoticeofIntent15June2004.pdf> (date d'accès: le 4 juin 2006).

illustrer un autre aspect de l'impact des traités de libre-échange sur l'intégrité des politiques culturelles nationales, après l'affaire *Project Blue Sky c. Australian Broadcasting Authority,*[41] qui avait trait à la libéralisation du commerce des services de télédiffusion entre l'Australie et la Nouvelle-Zélande.[42]

C   PLAINTES SOUMISES À L'ARBITRAGE PAR DES INVESTISSEURS
    CANADIENS

Une entreprise canadienne de fabrication et d'exportation de produits du tabac, Grand River Enterprises Six Nations, ainsi que trois autres investisseurs canadiens, ont soumis une plainte à l'arbitrage contre les États-Unis en vertu du chapitre 11 de l'ALÉNA.[43] Ils allèguent que le règlement global intervenu entre quarante-six États américains et les quatre plus grands producteurs de tabac américains, qui a permis le retrait des poursuites intentées contre ceux-ci par ces États, les toucherait d'une manière qui serait contraire à plusieurs dispositions de l'ALÉNA, dont l'article concernant l'expropriation. Les investisseurs canadiens réclament 340 millions de dollars américains en dommages.

La deuxième affaire ayant fait l'objet d'une plainte de la part d'un investisseur canadien, en vertu du chapitre 11 de l'ALÉNA, met en cause la querelle du bois d'œuvre entre le Canada et les États-Unis. Une entreprise forestière canadienne, Terminal Forest Products, allègue que l'imposition de droits *antidumping* et compensateurs par le gouvernement américain contre les importations de bois d'œuvre résineux en provenance du Canada l'a touchée d'une manière qui violerait plusieurs dispositions de l'ALÉNA, dont la norme du traitement national, la norme minimale de traitement ainsi que celle relative à l'expropriation.[44] L'investisseur canadien réclame 90 millions de dollars américains en dommages. Il faut

---

[41] *Project Blue Sky c. Australian Broadcasting Authority* [1998] H.C.A. 28; 194 C.L.R. 355; 153 A.L.R. 490 (Australie, H.C.).

[42] Voir C.-E. Côté, "L'invocabilité des traités de libre-échange en droit interne: nouveau regard sur l'arrêt *Project Blue Sky v. Australian Broadcasting Authority* de la Haute Cour d'Australie" (2003) 41 A.C.D.I. 387.

[43] *Grand River Enterprises Six Nations Ltd. et al. c. États-Unis,* "Plainte soumise à l'arbitrage par Grand River Enterprises Six Nations Ltd. *et al.*" (10 mars 2004) (CNUDCI), en ligne: US Department of State <http://www.state.gov/documents/organization/30961.pdf> (date d'accès: le 4 juin 2006).

[44] *Terminal Forest Products Ltd. c. États-Unis,* "Plainte soumise à l'arbitrage par Terminal Forest Products Ltd." (30 mars 2004) (CNUDCI), en ligne: US Department

rappeler que des plaintes semblables ont été soumises au cours des dernières années par deux autres investisseurs canadiens, Canfor et Tembec, mettant toujours en cause la querelle du bois d'œuvre entre le Canada et les États-Unis.[45]

Finalement, l'année 2004 a aussi vu ce qui semble être la première plainte soumise à l'arbitrage par un investisseur canadien en vertu d'un traité bilatéral sur l'investissement. Une entreprise minière canadienne, Vannessa Ventures, a soumis une plainte à l'arbitrage contre le Venezuela, sur la base du traité bilatéral conclu entre le Canada et ce pays en 1998, en raison des agissements du gouvernement vénézuelien, qui auraient eu pour effet de la déposséder de ses droits contractuels sur le développement d'un gisement aurifère, en violation des dispositions du traité.[46] L'investisseur canadien réclamerait la restitution de ses droits et 50 millions de dollars américains en dommages ou, subsidiairement, plus d'un milliard de dollars américains en dommages.

IV CONCLUSION

En somme, ces développements survenus au cours de l'année 2004 illustrent que le Canada demeure très actif dans le domaine du droit international de l'investissement, que ce soit au plan de son élaboration ou à celui de son application. Deux questions d'intérêt seront à surveiller particulièrement au cours des prochaines années, soit celle de l'utilisation du nouveau traité-type canadien sur l'investissement, ainsi que celle de l'éventuelle adhésion du Canada à la *Convention CIRDI.*

---

of State <http://www.state.gov/documents/organization/31360.pdf> (date d'accès: le 4 juin 2006).

[45] *Tembec Inc. c. États-Unis,* "Plainte soumise à l'arbitrage par Tembec Inc." (3 décembre 2003) (CNUDCI), en ligne: US Department of State <http://www.state.gov/documents/organization/27805.pdf> (date d'accès: le 19 octobre 2004); *Canfor Corporation c. États-Unis,* "Plainte soumise à l'arbitrage par Canfor Corporation" (9 juillet 2002) (CNUDCI), en ligne: US Department of State <http://www.state.gov/documents/organization/13203.pdf> (date d'accès: le 19 octobre 2004).

[46] Voir Groupe CNW, Communiqué, "Vannessa Commences International Arbitration Process" (9 juillet 2004), en ligne: Groupe CNW <http://www.newswire.ca/fr/releases/archive/July2004/09/c2104.html> (date d'accès: le 9 juin 2006), cité dans A. Newcombe, "Canada's New Model Foreign Investment Protection Agreement" (2004) Bull. C.C.D.I., vol. 30, n° 14, n. 1, en ligne: Conseil canadien de droit international <http://www.ccil-ccdi.ca/index.php?option=com_content&task=view&id=89&Itemid=76> (date d'accès: le 9 juin 2006).

Canadian Practice in International Law / Pratique canadienne en matière de droit international

At the Department of Foreign Affairs and International Trade in 2004–5 / Au ministère des Affaires étrangères en 2004–5

compiled by / préparé par
ALAN KESSEL

DIPLOMATIC AND CONSULAR PROTECTION

In June 2005, the Legal Bureau wrote:

Diplomatic and consular protection of nationals by their state of nationality while they are abroad is an aspect of foreign policy. International law, both customary and treaty based, recognizes that states have the right to protect their nationals who are wronged abroad in their person or their property, but international law clearly imposes no duty upon a state to protect its nationals abroad (*Oppenheim*, 9th edition, Volume 1, page 910, heading 410) (see below for quote). Rather it leaves the matter to the discretion of the state.

While international law does not create any such duty on a state, states by their domestic law may imposes such a duty upon themselves. This is clearly the case in a number of states. But even in situations where there is a constitutional right to diplomatic protection under domestic law, the

---

Alan Kessel, Legal Adviser, Department of Foreign Affairs and International Trade, Ottawa. The extracts from official correspondence contained in this survey have been made available by courtesy of the Department of Foreign Affairs and International Trade. Some of the correspondence from which extracts are given was provided for the general guidance of the enquirer in relation to specific facts that are often not described in full in the extracts within this compilation. The statements of law and practice should not necessarily be regarded as definitive.

courts of such states have found that there must necessarily be a very wide discretion granted to the government in how it chooses to respond in any particular case. This reflects the complex and sensitive nature of foreign policy. Thus in Germany, where a constitutional right to diplomatic protection has been found to exist, the courts have said (*Rudolph Hess Case*, 90 I.L.R. 386) that the government must enjoy "wide discretion in deciding whether and in what manner to grant discretion in each case." Both the UK Court of Appeal, in *Abbassi and Another v. Secretary of State for Foreign and Commonwealth Affairs* in 2002, and the South African Constitutional Court, in *Kuanda and Other v. the President of the RSA* in 2004, have found a domestic legal duty to provide diplomatic protection abroad, based on the doctrine of reasonable expectations. But the courts in both countries have noted that they must give particular weight to the government's special responsibility and expertise in the field of foreign affairs. The duty found has been a duty to consider the case and the need for protection, within a wide discretion on the part of the government as to whether, when and how to provide protection.

INTERNATIONAL ECONOMIC LAW

NAFTA: Chapter 1102 and "Like Circumstances"

In a submission to a North America Free Trade Agreement (NAFTA) tribunal dated 22 June 2005, the government of Canada wrote:

The words of Article 1102 are clear. The phrase "treatment no less favorable than that it accords, in like circumstances" calls for a contextual analysis to determine whether the treatments in question were less favourable for the Claimant than for a domestic investor. In other words, the Tribunal must look at the totality of the circumstances in which treatment is accorded in order to determine whether those circumstances are "like."

The Claimant suggests that it need only demonstrate that two investments are in the same business or economic sector. The fact that two businesses are in the same business sector may be the beginning of an examination of the circumstances of the particular treatments. However, it cannot be made the sole or determining factor — the mere fact that two businesses are in the same economic sector may not demonstrate that their circumstances are "like" in respect of the treatment at issue. Article 1102 is concerned with the question of whether treatment was accorded "in like circumstances," not whether it was accorded to "like investors."

Article 1102 calls on the Tribunal to examine all of the factors surrounding the treatment, including the nature of the two businesses, whether they share any characteristics beyond being in the same business sector, the purposes the businesses serve within the community, and the policy context in which the treatments were accorded.

This interpretation is well-supported by the ordinary meaning of the terms used by the Parties. According to the *New Shorter Oxford English Dictionary*, the term "circumstance" includes "that which stands around or surrounds; surroundings" or "the material, logical or other environmental conditions of an act or event." The *Webster's Dictionary* definition of "circumstance" includes "a condition, fact, or event accompanying, conditioning, or determining another." The *Funk and Wagnals Standard Handbook of Synonyms, Antonyms and Prepositions* explains that a circumstance is "something existing or occurring in connection with or relation to some other fact or event, modifying or throwing light upon the principal matter without affecting its principal character."

Canada's interpretation also finds favour in the decisions of previous Tribunals. In *S.D. Myers v. Canada*, the Tribunal stated that the phrase "like circumstances" is open to a wide variety of interpretations in the abstract and in the context of a particular dispute. Citing the OECD Declaration on International and Multinational Enterprises, the Tribunal found: "OECD practice suggests that an evaluation of 'like situations' in the investment context should take into account policy objectives in determining whether enterprises are in like circumstances."

The Tribunal concluded "like circumstances" must take into account general principles emerging from the NAFTA's context, including "its concern with the environment." The assessment must also "take into account circumstances that would justify governmental regulations" that treat investors differently.

In *Pope & Talbot v. Canada*, the Tribunal also looked to public policy considerations in determining whether treatment was accorded "in like circumstances." It called business or economic sectors the "first step" of the test. In applying its test to the facts, the Tribunal explicitly found an absence of "likeness" based on public policy considerations.

In the *Loewen* case, the Tribunal found that two operators of funeral homes were not accorded treatment in like circumstances. It concluded that their "circumstances as litigants were very different," and refused to engage in any comparison between them.

In *GAMI Investments Inc. v. Mexico*, the Tribunal was faced with domestic and foreign investments, each of which operated five sugar mills. Each was operating at a loss, each was in debt to its cane growers, and each secured its debt with its sugar inventories. Nevertheless, the Tribunal concluded:

> The Arbitral Tribunal has not been persuaded that GAMI's circumstances were demonstrably so "like" those of non-expropriated mill owners that

it was wrong to treat GAMI differently. Mexico determined that nearly half of the mills in the country should be expropriated in the public interest. The reason was not that they were prosperous and the Government was greedy. To the contrary: Mexico perceived that mills operating in conditions of effective insolvency needed public participation in the interest of the national economy in a broad sense. The Government may have been misguided. That is a matter of policy and politics. The Government may have been clumsy in its analysis of the relevant criteria for the cutoff line between candidates and non-candidates for expropriation. Its understanding of corporate finance may have been deficient. But ineffectiveness is not discrimination.

The Tribunal must therefore take into consideration other elements such as the activities and operations of the respective investors or investments, as well as the public policy considerations that these activities raise. Which specific circumstances may be relevant in any particular case will depend on the treatment at issue — for example, a facility's proximity to a sensitive ecosystem may be relevant in a case dealing with effluent controls, but may not be in a case dealing with restrictions on gambling.

The context of Article 1102 and the object and purpose of the NAFTA also demonstrate that "like circumstances" cannot mean "like investors." Such an interpretation could only be derived from WTO cases dealing with the issues of "like products," "like services" or "like service providers" arising from GATT Articles I and III and GATS Article XVII.

These cases can provide only limited contextual assistance in interpreting Article 1102, because the textual differences between them are manifest, and they operate in very different contexts.

The Parties did not use the terms "like products," "like service providers" or even "like investors." The text of Article 1102 may be easily contrasted with GATT Article III. In paragraph 4, that article reads, "... shall be accorded treatment no less favourable than that accorded to like products of national origin." Article 1102 reads, "... shall accord to investors of another Party treatment no less favorable than that it accords, in like circumstances, to its own investors."

Similarly, GATT Article III, in paragraphs 1 and 4 applies to measures affecting the "internal sale, offering for sale, purchase, transportation, distribution or use of products." Article 1102 applies to treatment accorded with respect to the "establishment, acquisition, expansion, management, conduct, operation, and sale or other disposition of investments."

The Claimant itself cites an excellent statement of the contextual differences that flow from the different scope of the two articles. Citing the United Nations Conference on Trade and Development, the Claimant stressed:

The scope of national treatment in the investment field goes well beyond its use in trade agreements. In particular, the reference to "products" in article III of the GATT is inadequate for investment agreements in that it restricts national treatment to trade in goods. The activities of foreign investors in their host countries encompass a wide array of operations, including international trade in products, trade in components, know-how and technology, local production and distribution, the raising of finance capital and the provision of services, not to mention the range of transactions involved in the creation and administration of a business enterprise. Hence, wider categories of economic transactions may be subjected to national treatment disciplines under investment agreements than under trade agreements.

In other words, UNCTAD states that the context, object and purpose of Article 1102 are unlike that of GATT Article III, and, by extension, GATS Article XVII. Indeed, UNCTAD said precisely that with respect to GATT Article III only two paragraphs earlier in the same document:

> because the distinction made in the field of trade in goods between border measures and internal measures has no meaningful equivalent in the field of investment, national treatment clauses in IIAs [international investment agreements] differ in scope and purpose from the national treatment principle of GATT article III.

The distinction between the contexts of GATT Article III and Article 1102 has particular significance for the interpretation of the phrase "in like circumstances." Article 1102 applies to "a wide array of operations" not covered by WTO provisions. Given this fact, in assessing whether the treatment accorded to investors engaged in those operations was accorded "in like circumstances," the Tribunal cannot limit itself to a consideration of the products or services they offer.

The position would become even more untenable when considering a complaint concerning treatment accorded to investments. "Investments" as defined in Article 1139 includes land, stocks, loans and a variety of other items that do not offer products and may not compete in any marketplace. A "like circumstances" test limited to "business sector" would be simply inapplicable in such cases.

Canada accepts that Article 1102, GATT Article III and GATS Article XVII share a broad purpose of preventing nationality-based discrimination. However, this purpose itself demonstrates the importance of the "in like circumstances" determination. It serves Article 1102's purpose by establishing a nexus between the treatment at issue and the investor's foreign nationality.

There may be a number of valid reasons for a government to distinguish between investors or investments operating in the same business sector. For example, a government may wish to offer privileges to small businesses, or to businesses operating in economically depressed areas. A proper application of the "in like circumstances" test ensures that there can be no finding of a violation of Article 1102 merely because a small domestic business receives such a privilege and a large foreign-owned business does not.

Canada is not arguing that establishing a violation of Article 1102 requires a demonstration of discriminatory intent. Moreover, the Tribunal need not consider the question, because the Claimant cannot establish a discriminatory intent or effect to any of Canada's measures.

Virtually all previous Tribunals have found no violation of Article 1102 unless they were convinced a Party had discriminated on the basis of nationality.

The ADF Tribunal refused to make a finding of a de facto violation of Article 1102 in the absence of evidence of discrimination on the basis of nationality. It set out the sort of evidence it expected to see:

> Evidence of discrimination, however, is required. For instance, it appears to the Tribunal that specific evidence concerning the comparative economics of the situation would be relevant, including: whether the cost of fabrication was significantly lower in Canada; whether fabrication capacity was unavailable at that time in the United States and whether transportation costs to Canada were sufficiently low to make up the differential. We note the U.S. did submit evidence of available capacity and Mr. Paschini referred to massive increases in costs due to fabrication in the U.S. This scant evidence is, however, not sufficient to show what the relevant competitive situation of Canadian fabricators and U.S. fabricators was in general, nor was it evidence of the comparative costs of steel fabrication in the U.S. and Canadian facilities, in particular.

The *Myers* Tribunal considered nationality-based discrimination to be a relevant factor in finding a violation of Article 1102. In *Pope & Talbot*, the Tribunal found an absence of "like circumstances" based at least in part on the absence of discriminatory intent. The Tribunal in *Loewen* concluded that Article 1102 is directed only at "nationality-based discrimination" and proscribes only "demonstrable and significant indications of bias and prejudice on the basis of nationality…" In *GAMI*, the Tribunal based its decision in part on the absence of a discriminatory measure.

In sum, the question of whether treatment was accorded "in like circumstances" establishes the basis for comparing the treatment accorded to the foreign and domestic investor (or their investments). There can be no basis for comparing treatment that was not accorded in like circumstances. As the *GAMI* Tribunal put it, the question is whether the circumstances were demonstrably so "like" that it was wrong to treat the foreign investor less favourably.

NAFTA: Chapter 15 and State Responsibility

In a submission to a NAFTA tribunal dated 22 June 2005, the government of Canada wrote:

The Claimant seeks to avoid the limitations imposed by Articles 1502(3)(a) and 1503(2) by invoking the principles of attribution in the Articles on State Responsibility prepared by the International Law Commission. The Tribunal should reject the Claimant's attempt to broaden the scope of obligations applicable to Canada Post for two reasons. First, the question of attribution is separate from the question of breach of an applicable obligation resulting in state responsibility. Second, the general rules of attribution cannot be used to circumvent the clear rules established by Parties regarding their responsibility for actions of monopolies and state enterprises.

The Articles on State Responsibility provide that there is an internationally wrongful act of a State when conduct is (a) attributable to the State under international law; and (b) constitutes a breach of an international obligation of the State.

The Articles on State Responsibility, particularly Articles 4 (conduct of organs of State), 5 (conduct of persons or entities exercising elements of governmental authority), and 8 (control directed or controlled by a State), contain rules regarding attribution to a State of certain actions. However, in order to determine whether there is a breach of an international obligation, one must look to the treaty which contains the State's obligations.

In this case, the relevant provisions are those of Chapter 15 of NAFTA, which specify the Parties' obligations with respect to conduct of their monopolies or state enterprises. The Claimant confuses the two elements of state responsibility, attribution and breach of an applicable obligation.

The Articles on State Responsibility do not apply where states have specified in a treaty particular rules governing their responsibility. Article 55 (Lex specialis) provides:

These articles do not apply where and to the extent that the conditions for the existence of an internationally wrongful act or the content or implementation of the international responsibility of a State are governed by special rules of international law.

Contrary to what the Claimant suggests, the Articles themselves provide that if there is a conflict, the special rules provided in the treaty will take precedence. In other words, where, as in the NAFTA, the parties specified what obligations are applicable to state enterprises and government monopolies, and when the actions of monopolies or state enterprises are subject to the same obligations as the State, it is to these provisions that one must turn.

This does not mean the Articles on State Responsibility have no application in the NAFTA context. However, the principles of attribution cannot be used to extend the scope of applicable obligations or the state responsibility for acts of monopolies or state enterprises beyond what is specified in Chapter 15 of the NAFTA.

In any event, if the Articles on State Responsibility were relevant, in light of the fact that Canada Post is a distinct legal entity, the applicable rule would not be Article 4, which deals with organs of the state. Rather, it would be Article 5, which deals with para-statal entities. It may be noted that the rules of attribution contained in Article 5 are not significantly different from those set out in Articles 1502(3)(a) and 1503(2).

Articles 1502(3)(a) and 1503(2) specify that the monopoly or state enterprise will be subject to certain of the State's obligations when it exercises delegated governmental authority. These are self-contained provisions governing the applicability of the Parties' obligations to the conduct of State enterprises and Monopolies. Given that the rules of responsibility for breach of a Chapter 11 obligation by a monopoly or state enterprise are specified in NAFTA, it is those provisions that the Tribunal must apply; there is no need to have recourse to the Articles on State Responsibility. The WTO Appellate Body has followed a similar approach by focussing on the terms of the obligation at issue and not the general rules of attribution.

World Trade Organization (WTO) — Mootness

In a submission to the WTO panel dated 19 July 2004, the Legal Bureau wrote:

In its Responses to Panel Questions, the EC makes a number of assertions with respect to the relevance of the concept of "mootness." Many of these responses are either incorrect as a factual matter, misleading, or do not accurately or completely represent the WTO rules governing dispute settlement, as reflected in the jurisprudence.

In particular, the EC's assertion that, "if a measure is terminated after the establishment of the Panel, the case has become moot in respect of this measure and the Panel is in principle not to rule on it any longer," is simply not supported by the considerable jurisprudence available on this point. To the contrary, the jurisprudence is replete with instances where panels have gone on to make findings with respect to measures that were either removed or modified by the responding party after the terms of reference had been established. For example, in *Chile – Price Band System*, the panel found that, "in our view, Article 19.1 DSU does not prevent us from making findings regarding the consistency of an expired provisional safeguard measure..."

Similarly, in *India – Autos*, a dispute in which the EC, incidentally, was a complaining party, the panel stated that:

> A WTO panel is generally competent to consider measures in existence at the time of its establishment. This power is not necessarily adversely affected simply because a measure under review may have been subsequently removed or rendered less effective. Panels in the past have examined discontinued measures where there was no agreement of the parties to discontinue the proceedings.

In short, a panel's jurisdiction to consider a measure is first determined by its terms of reference (ToR). If the measure falls within its ToR, the panel is to exercise its discretion and make findings on those measures necessary to fulfill the dispute settlement objective of "securing a positive resolution of the dispute."

Canada contests vigorously the EC's assertion that the measures before this Panel never existed or were withdrawn by the EC prior to the establishment of this Panel's terms of reference. The reasons for this are set out in detail in Canada's First Written Submission, its First Oral Statement, in its Answers to the Panel's Questions, and in this Written Rebuttal.

The reliance by the EC on U.S. constitutional law and the practice of the International Court of Justice is misplaced because those sources are not relevant to this issue in the context of the rules of the DSU.

Furthermore, the EC's attempts to support its legal position on the basis of the language found in Articles 3.3, 3.4 and 3.7 of the DSU are misplaced. While it is true that the language in Article 3.3 uses the present tense, it is clear from the remainder of the text and the jurisprudence that the point in time referred to is the point in time at which the terms of reference are established, and not some indeterminate point in time somewhere between the establishment of those terms of reference and the adoption of the panel report by the DSB. Similarly, Article 3.4 is concerned with "recommendations and rulings," which is a different matter from the ability of panels to make findings. Moreover, the use of the phrase "before bringing its case" clearly delimits the scope of Article 3.7 to that time period during which the putative complaining party weighs the costs and benefits of requesting the establishment of a panel. In any event, Canada would not agree with the EC's suggestion that "a case on a measure that is not in existence any longer would be devoid of any practical purpose," especially in a situation where there is a real possibility of the measure recurring.

Finally, the EC points to *Japan – Film* as authority for the proposition that panels must not rule "on measures which have expired or which have been repealed or withdrawn." However, closer scrutiny of that case, and the passage from which the quote is taken, reveals that the panel in that case was considering measures that the responding party argued had "ended years ago," and that, further, the authority for the panel's statement quoted by the EC was a reference to the *U.S. – Gasoline* case. In that case, the panel had observed that:

> [I]t had not been the usual practice of a panel established under the General Agreement [on Tariffs and Trade 1947] to rule on measures that, at the time the panel's terms of reference were fixed, were not and would not become effective.

In contrast, as noted above, in cases where the measure in question existed at the time of the establishment of the terms of reference of the panel, the consistent practice of panels has been to at least make findings on the WTO/GATT consistency of that measure.

INTERNATIONAL ENVIRONMENTAL LAW

Application of the Boundary Waters Treaty / NAFTA to the MNFS Fee Structure

In October 2004, the Legal Bureau wrote:

The focus of our opinion is on the consistency of the fee structure with the 1909 Boundary Waters Treaty (BWT) to the extent that the latter is implemented into Canadian law ...

Boundary Waters Treaty Act Implementation: Before considering the text of Article I, it is first necessary to determine its status in Canadian law, that is to say, is this an obligation owed by Canada at international law, or has it also been implemented into Canadian law. If the former, it may only be useful as a form of statutory interpretation in reading the *Oceans Act* and regulations made under it (including the MNSF); if the latter, it is equivalent in force and status and different tests may be applied to it.

Section 3 of the BWTA purports to implement much of the BWT in Canadian domestic law as follows:

The laws of Canada and of the provinces are hereby amended and altered so as to *permit, authorize and sanction* the performance of the obligations undertaken by His Majesty and in and under the treaty, so as to *sanction, confer and impose* the various rights, duties and disabilities intended by the treaty to be conferred or imposed or to exist within Canada [emphasis added].

Section 3 sets out two levels of "implementation," the first to "permit, authorize and sanction the performance of the obligations undertaken by His Majesty" and separately to "sanction, confer and impose the various rights, duties and disabilities intended by the treaty to be conferred or imposed or to exist within Canada." A preliminary question is whether Article One of the BWT is implemented by the first or second arm of Section 3 of the BWTA.

In our view, the answer to that question is driven by the purposes served by the BWT and to the extent that they are administrative or legal in character. The BWT established, for example, the International Joint Commission, consisting of three commissioners on each side and making it responsible to the respective governments for a variety of tasks. In our view, it is these activities that Section 3 implements in a way to "permit, authorize and sanction." However, the substantive rights created for private individuals, e.g. the "inhabitants, vessels and boats of both countries" in Article I, or access to Canadian courts for USA residents in Article II, are meaningless if not fully implemented and made enforceable in Canadian law. As such, they require the fuller implementation provided in the second arm of Section 3, that is that rights created such as these are implemented by the "laws of Canada ... [being] amended ... so as to sanction, confer and impose the various rights, duties and disabilities intended by the treaty ..." This conclusion not only makes practical sense, it is also consistent with Canadian constitutional practice and statutory interpretation that presumes any implementation of international law obligations into domestic law should be read, if possible, to achieve that result.

As Mr. Justice Gonthier declared in *National Corn Growers Assn. v. Canada (Canadian Import Tribunal)*, 2 S.C.R. 1324:

In interpreting legislation which has been enacted with a view towards *implementing international obligations* [Gonthier's emphasis], as is the case here, it is reasonable for a tribunal to examine the domestic law in the context of the relevant agreement to clarify any uncertainty. Indeed where the text of the domestic law lends itself to it, one should also strive to expound an interpretation which is consonant with the relevant international obligations.

In our view, as the Article I BWT obligations require domestic implementation and Section 3 of the BWTA can be read to achieve that result, as a matter of statutory interpretation and Canadian constitutional practice, we should assume that the implementation is sufficient to meet Canadian international obligations.

Object and Purpose: The object and purpose of the BWT is manifold but can be summarized as follows. The BWT at its heart is a bargain to allocate and prioritize the use of both boundary waters and transboundary waters shared between Canada and the United States. The principal focus was on use rather than transit of waters. In the former context, the bargain was comprehensive, that is applying to all shared water resources. It was traditional, by effectively negotiating a common understanding that would replace the vagaries and uncertainties of applying private common law riparian rights in a transboundary context (e.g. the irrigation allocation in Article VI for the St. Mary and Milk rivers). It was forward looking by allocating water flow for newly discovered hydro-electric generation (Article V) and especially novel in its obligation not to pollute waters flowing into the other country (Article IV). In terms of the transit of waters, it was at once both conservative, creating a treaty obligation of access to both sides of the Great Lakes by both countries for purposes of commerce, yet also progressive by anticipating challenges to access that might arise from regulation and imposing obligations intended to ensure that the flow of water-borne commerce between the countries not be obstructed.

Context: The phrase "Free and open ... equally" utilized at the beginning of Article I is a concept that is well-established in a number of treaties between Great Britain (on behalf of or respecting Canada) and the United States but it is important to note that as both the British Empire and the United States moved from mercantile monopoly to free trade and the need of open and free access lessened, the formulations in successive treaties became more elaborate and, in our view, took on issues beyond mere physical access.

The phrase occurs first in our treaty history in the 1783 *Treaty of Peace* where Great Britain and the United States agreed to free and open navigation but only along the Mississippi River (Article VIII). This access was broadened greatly in the 1794 *Jay Treaty* to allow USA ships to participate in trade with the British colonies in the West Indies.

Thereafter, successive treaties in the 19th century opened up more of Canada and the United States to free and open trade by waterways as the previous regime of mercantile monopolies gradually evaporated. Each treaty utilized the phrase "free and open," though this basic formulation was itself changed to grant access "forever" later in the century.

As between Canada and the United States, several treaties provided for free and open access of waters to the ships of both countries, notably the 1918 *Convention of Commerce* (waters of the North West coast), the 1842 *Webster-Ashburton Treaty* (waters from Lake Superior to Lake of the Woods, the Saint John and Saint Lawrence Rivers), the 1846 *Oregon Treaty* (waters of the Columbia River) and the 1871 *Treaty of Washington* (waters of the Saint Lawrence, Yukon, Porcupine and Stikine rivers).

The basic formulation, "free and open" alone has not been judicially considered to impose any obligations on the two Parties beyond that to allow physical access of one's waters to ships from the other. Instead, courts have paid attention to the tendency late in the 19th century for more elaborate formulations and from them to derive obligations beyond mere physical access.

These additional formulations are comparable to Article I (ii) of the BWT. Most are simpler than that provided in the BWT, e.g. *Webster-Ashburton* is the simplest, providing only for free and open navigation *subject to laws and regulations* while others, notably the *Treaty of Washington,* also has the additional element of being "subject to laws and regulations *not inconsistent with free navigation.*" It must be kept in mind, however, that no other treaty has the benefit of the full formulation or the legislative enactment as has Article I of the BWT.

The phrase "free and open *subject to laws and regulations*" as appearing in the *Webster-Ashburton Treaty* has been subject to interpretation in both Canadian and USA courts, both of which agreed that the imposition of tolls for improvements in navigation, for example, was not inconsistent with free and open navigation (see *Arrow River & Tributaries Slide and Boom Co. v. Pigeon Timber Co.* [1932] SCR 495 and *Pigeon River Improvement, Slide and Boom Co. v. Charles W. Fox, Ltd. S.* Ct 361, 78) ...

Considering now the ordinary meaning of this clause of the BWT, we would make the following further points:

(i) "Laws and regulations" can certainly include the imposition of fees for services rendered by the Canadian Coast Guard.

(ii) Either country may impose its own laws and regulations on navigation. There is no requirement on reciprocity or to agree on identical forms of regulation.

(iii) Equal treatment, while a close kin to "identical" treatment, is not inevitably the same; it is possible, at least hypothetically, for a regime to be applied to USA ships that is different from that of

Canadian, yet not violating the obligation, so long as the different treatment imposed is not otherwise objectively unequal or without discrimination.

Beyond these reasonable conclusions, a real question remains in terms of what the BWT means when it creates a capacity to create regulations so long as they are applied "equally and without discrimination." For it to challenge the MNSF, it must include a concept of "objective" versus "subjective" discrimination and an ability to "pierce" the basic structure of the fees regime to examine underlying inequality and discrimination.

For the first, we are able to conclude that the BWT would set an objective rather than subjective standard of non-discrimination and equal treatment. Looking beyond this Article, the BWT provides a range of obligations, including the very forward-looking obligation not to pollute one's waters to the injury of health or property on the other (Article IV). That provision has been given critical consideration in a range of References to the International Joint Commission, whose Article IX recommendations have always applied an objective standard for pollution and have never considered any *male fides* or intention to pollute as relevant or necessary (see the 1977 *Garrison Diversion Unit Reference*, the 1981 *Poplar River Basin Reference* and the 1988 *Flathead River Basin Reference*). By the BWT itself, these Article IX References are not binding to the parties but that has not prevented them becoming an influential and respected commentary on the meaning of the BWT.

This can be allied with an ability in Article I to pierce a collective standard to find underlying inequality. This is so because a rough collective equality in treatment is not sufficient to meeting the BWT obligation. The BWT requires equality of treatment "to the inhabitants, ships, vessels and boats" of both countries. As such, any individual, on behalf of any vessel, should be able to assert discrimination or inequality of treatment in his case. That he may have been so treated, but that the overall balance between countries is one of rough equality, is insufficient to meet the BWT standard.

"Consensus" in the North American Agreement on Environmental Cooperation

On 8 July 2004, the Legal Bureau wrote:

As the North American Agreement on Environmental Cooperation (NAAEC) provides no written definition of "consensus," the general rule of interpretation prevails. Article 31 of the Vienna Convention on the Law of the Treaties says "a Treaty shall be interpreted in good faith in accordance with the ordinary meaning to be given to the terms of the treaty in their context and in the light of its object and purpose."

Very few international agreements have a written definition of consensus. Two which do are the WTO Agreement and the Convention on the Law of the Sea. The Understanding on rules and procedures governing the settlement of disputes (Annex 2 of the WTO Agreement) specify that the Dispute Settlement Body "shall be deemed to have decided by consensus on a matter submitted for its consideration, if no Member, present at the meeting of the DSB when the decision is taken, formally objects to the proposed decision." And Article 161 of the Convention on the Law of the Sea on the composition, procedure and voting of the Council of the International Seabed Authority indicates that it "means the absence of any formal objection." Therefore, it could be said that a consensus is obtained when none of the Parties formally objects.

With regard to the publication of the report, Article 13.3 indicates that "the Secretariat shall submit its report to the Council, which shall make it publicly available, normally within 60 days following its submission, unless the Council otherwise decides." In Canadian treaty practice, which in this respect is common with most international practice, "shall" is used to express legally binding obligations. Therefore, the Council must make the report publicly available (default position). To preclude this obligation, a decision under Article 9.6 is necessary.

Article 9.6 of the NAAEC says "all decisions and recommendations of the Council shall be taken by consensus, except as the Council may otherwise decide or as otherwise provided in this Agreement." Given that several provisions of the NAAEC explicitly set a different rule by specifying that the Council may decide by a two-thirds vote, it seems that the Parties differentiated between "consensus" and "two-thirds vote." Thus, as the Council is composed of three representatives of the Parties and that "consensus" implies a majority vote without being a two-thirds vote, decisions and recommendations made under Article 9.6 of the NAAEC require the agreement of all three members of the Council (unanimity).

In conclusion, one or two Council members cannot prevent making the report public.

Article II of the BWT: Judicial Reciprocity

On 17 August 2004, the Legal Bureau said:

1. Summary: Article II of the BWT is intended to provide reciprocity of judicial treatment for injuries in one country from interference derived from flows and diversion of waters from the other, but not from pollution created in the other country. While the Article can be utilized to initiate an action in Canada, it offers no assistance in the enforcement of USA court judgements based on USA law in Canadian courts. However, other

and significant options under Canadian law exist for USA litigants to enforce judgements obtained through USA litigation.

2. Issue: We have been asked to consider the possible applicability of Article II of the Boundary Waters Treaty (BWT) to potential litigation with the USA EPA under the "Super Fund" statute (aka CERCLA) in the context of the following questions:

- Can the EPA or private American parties utilize this provision to base a claim in Canadian courts for injury on the pollution of waters or is it limited to injury arising from interruptions to the flow or diversion of waters?
- Can the EPA or private American parties utilize this provision to enforce a judgement of an American court against a Canadian entity?

3. We note that only one prior opinion on Article II is found in the Opinions Index, that of H. Courtney Kingstone, May 21, 1958. His opinion delves usefully in a description of the riparian law of BC that could be applied to a potential USA litigator but does not analyse either of the questions at hand.

4. Article II of the BWT provides as follows (emphasis added):

It is understood, however, that neither of the High Contracting parties intends by the forgoing provision to surrender any right, which it may have, to object to *any interference with or diversions of waters* on the other side of the boundary the effect of which would be productive of material *injury to the navigation interests* on its own side of the boundary.

5. The answer to the first question is bound up in the inherent grammatical uncertainty of the phrase "any interference with or diversion from their natural channel of such waters." Put simply, does this mean:

Any interference with such waters ... or diversion from their natural channel of such waters (thereby implying a possibility that interference might also include pollution),
or
Any interference with...their natural channel ... or diversion from their natural channel of such waters...(thereby limiting the possible injury from interference to impeding, altering or diverting the movement of waters)

6. In our view, the phrase, while grammatically neutral, should be taken to mean the latter and that pollution of waters, unless it also coincidentally leads to interference with the flow or diversion of waters, is not intended to be an injury in the context of Article II. As a result, a suit on that basis would not be given special status in Canadian courts in accordance with Article II.

7. The test that we may apply to the interpretation of Article II is, of course, found in Section 3, Article 31 (1) of the *Vienna Convention on the Law of Treaties* (CTS 1980, No. 37) that provides: "A Treaty shall be interpreted in good faith in accordance with the ordinary meaning to be given to the terms of the treaty in their context and in the light of its object and purpose."

8. In the case of Article II, for several reasons we would conclude that the word "interference" is and should be limited to the *flow* of waters and not the addition of substances that may pollute, but do not effect the flow of such waters. First, the natural or ordinary meaning of "interference" carries with it concepts of collision, opposition to or physical obstruction to the flow of waters, not adulteration of the waters themselves (see *Concise Oxford*). It would require an unnatural stretch of this meaning to include pollution. Secondly, the entire Article is devoted to the state rights, state defences, and in this case, creation of private rights, all structured along slightly differing variations: "the use and diversion ... of such waters" [exclusive jurisdiction of each state], "interference with or diversion from either such waters or their natural channel" [creation of a private right] and reservation by each state to object to interference with or diversions of waters, on the other side [material injury to navigation interests]. The *ejusdem generis* rule provides that where you have created a specific class that form the object of a provision or statute (or in this case a treaty article), that class may be used to limit the meaning to be given to words that are otherwise broader or more general. Here, one can argue that the slightly differing formulations of the rights of states and private parties, as the case may be, create a common class that you wish to regulate, namely, the consequences arising from the diversion or alteration in flow of waters, and such words as interference, that might be construed more generally, should be more narrowly interpreted in accordance with the general extent set out in each of the three instances, all of which appear to deal with the levels, flows and direction of waters, but not their adulteration.

9. Relying upon the well regarded canon of construction *expressio unius est exclusio alterius*, that is to say, "the expression of one thing is the exclusion of the other," it can be argued that the explicit treatment of pollution in the second paragraph of Article IV of the BWT suggests that it is not an element in another article.

10. To these interpretations, flowing from the language of the text of the BWT itself, can be added two distinct further arguments based on the legislative implementation of the Treaty into Canadian law through the passage of the *International Boundary Waters Treaty Act* (R.S., c I-20, s.1) (IBWTA). It may be objected that Canadian implementation of a Treaty

does not constitute an interpretation of that Treaty that is binding at international law; however, since the issue is the practical extent to which public or private American parties might rely upon such implementation in Canada, the language of the statute would be the primary consideration of a domestic tribunal answering the question. I would note at this point that only one case has thus far interpreted Section 4 (which implemented Article II of the BWT) and that it is not on point.

11. While the relevant English language text of Section 4 is faithful to the language of Article II of the BWT and offers no further guidance, the French equivalent departs somewhat: "Toute altération, *notamment* par détournement, des voies navigables du Canada ..."

12. Although it may be argued that "toute altération" is cast broadly to include all interference with waters causing injury, this is fully rebutted because in the French language, the "alteration" is applied to water courses ... ("voies navigables") and not merely waters, strongly establishing that the flow of water and not the water itself, is the object of the provision. In addition, the subsidiary phrase, "*notamment* par détournement," reinforces this interpretation by application once more of the *ejusdem generis* rule, with the result that "all alteration," capable of broad application, should instead be construed narrowly to be consistent with the example given, the diversion of navigable waterways. As an Empire treaty, it should be noted that there is no authoritative French text of the BWT; hence it is especially useful to rely upon the French text of the BWT's statutory implementation, the IBWTA.

13. Secondly, it should be noted that the creation of a private right to sue on a particular basis is explicitly legislated in Section 3 of the IBWTA, but based only on the content of the middle paragraph of Article II of the BWT. Article IV, that mentions pollution, is not implemented into Canadian law at all and is solely retained as an obligation at international law to be owed between the states of Canada and the United States.

14. If a USA litigant cannot use the BWT Article II to launch a suit in Canadian courts based on injury from pollution, how should we approach our remaining question, i.e. can the EPA or private American parties utilize the provision to enforce a judgement of an American court against a Canadian entity?

15. Article II provides a jurisdiction in the Exchequer Court (later the Federal Court) to entertain suits where an American Plaintiff has suffered injury that has taken place in the USA from a Canadian source. The law to

be applied shall be "the same rights and remedies as if the injury took place in the country where such diversion or interference occurs." Section 4 of the IBWTA, which implements the BWT in Canada, provides that the rights and remedies shall be those that would be available "if the injury took place in *that part of* Canada where the interference or diversions occurs.

16. To summarize and distinguish the options: a USA litigant (public or private) can utilize the provisions of the IBWTA to launch a suit in the Federal Court of Canada. However, our interpretation of both the Treaty and Statute suggests that the injury will be narrowly defined and exclude environmental damage from sludge, unless it has also affected the flows of or has diverted water. If instead, a USA litigant initiates a suit in USA Courts and obtains a judgement based on USA law, it is unlikely that they can enforce the judgement so obtained through the Canadian Federal Court by means of the IBWTA, because the Federal Court is explicitly bound to apply Canadian and not foreign law to the controversy. Therefore, USA litigants seeking to enforce a USA judgement must rely on Canadian law and practice *other than the IBWTA* to enforce their judgements through Canadian courts. A very recent Supreme Court Decision, *Beals v. Saldanha* (SCC, delivered December 18, 2003) suggests that while not automatic, Canadian Courts are likely to enforce foreign judgements subject to relatively narrow defences.

Transboundary Pollution and the Effects Doctrine

On 12 January 2005, the Legal Bureau said:

The application of the S*ic utere* principle to cases of transboundary environmental pollution has overwhelming support in international law and is, arguably, the governing USA domestic law. The effects doctrine as originally created in the *Lotus case (France v. Turkey)* 1927 P.C.I.J. (ser. A) No. 9 (September 7, 1927), or as reborn in the competition case law emanating from the USA in the 1940s and thereafter, has not been convincingly demonstrated to support a general application beyond a concurrent criminal jurisdiction (in the case of *Lotus*) or the regulation of economic and market conduct following the USA 1945 *Alcoa case* (*United States v. Aluminium Co. of America*, 148 F.2nd 416 (2nd Cir. 1945).

Analysis
The focus of the paper is on international law as may generally be applied rather than whether USA courts, in applying the effects doctrine as enshrined in the *Third Restatement*, would choose to do so.

(i) Transboundary International Environmental Law

The basic principle, well established in international law and recognized as such by both Canada and the United States, is that of *Sic utere tuo ut alienum non laedas* (use your own property so as not to injure the property of another). This principle was adopted as the basis for the seminal decision in the *Trail Smelter Case* (*Trail Smelter Case*, 1941, 3 R. Int'l Arb. Awards, 1905).

This principle was earlier embedded in Canada/USA treaty law in Article IV of the 1909 *Boundary Waters Treaty* that, we have been suggested to argue, forms the proper USA domestic law applicable to the case:

> It is further agreed that the waters defined herein as boundary waters and waters flowing across the boundary shall not be polluted on either side to the injury of health or property on the other.

The USA *Third Restatement of the Foreign Relations Law of the United States* adopts and extends the *Sic utere* principle. The relevant parts of § 601 read as follows:

(1) A State is obligated to take such measures as may be necessary, to the extent practicable under the circumstances, to ensure that activities within its jurisdiction or control (a) conform to generally accepted international rules and standards for the prevention, reduction, and control of injury to the environment of another state or of areas beyond the limits of national jurisdiction; and (b) are conducted so as not to cause significant injury to the environment of another state or of areas beyond the limits of national jurisdiction.

(2) A State is responsible to all other states (a) for any violation of its obligations under Sub-section 1(a), and (b) for any significant injury, resulting from such violation, to the environment of areas beyond the limits of national jurisdiction.

This principle has been cemented in both arbitral decisions and decisions of the International Court of Justice (ICJ), for example, the *Lake Lanoux Arbitration (France v. Spain)* 24 ILR 100 (Arbitral Tribunal, 1957) and the quite recent 1994 ICJ decision in the Slovak-Hungarian dispute over *Gabčíkovo-Nagymaros.*

The principle has been the basis for a number of recent treaties intended to provide for transboundary environmental assessment (e.g. *Convention on the Law of the Non-Navigational Uses of International Watercourses,* adopted on May 21, 1997 by UNGA Resolution 51/229, and not yet entered into force [neither Canada nor the United States are parties], the *Convention on Access to Information, Public Participation in Decision-Making and Access to Justice in Environmental Matters* (Aarhus, Denmark, June 25,

1998, entered in force on October 30, 2001); [neither Canada nor the United states are parties, but the Convention is heavily subscribed by European states], and the *Convention on Environmental Assessment in a Transboundary Context* (adopted on 25 February 1991 at Espoo, Finland and entered into force on 10 September 1997) [both Canada and the United States have signed the convention, and Canada ratified on 13 May 1998].

Penultimately, it has also been accepted as a fundamental principle in such environmental instruments (highly important, though technically non-binding) as the 1992 *Rio Declaration on Environment and Development.* Principle 2 reads as follows:

> States have, in accordance with the Charter of the United Nations and the principles of international law, the sovereign right to exploit their own resources pursuant to their own environmental and developmental policies, and the responsibility to ensure that activities within their jurisdiction or control do not cause damage to the environment of other States or of areas beyond the limits of national jurisdiction.

Finally, it has been well commented on as forming the basic structure of water law and transboundary pollution (see Gabriel Eckstein, "Application of International Water Law to Transboundary Groundwater Resources and the Slovak-Hungarian Dispute over Gabcikovo-Nagymaros" [(1995) 19 Suffolk Transnat'l L. Rev. 67].

(ii) The Effects Doctrine: Origins

What then is the impact on this well-fortified structure of international law posed by the effects doctrine that, over the course of the 20th century, has emerged as a new source of prescriptive jurisdiction in addition to the then prevailing territoriality and nationality principles.

The effects doctrine, or alternatively the "objective territoriality principle" has had both a former and latter day birth. By former, that is its original application as a clarification of the territoriality principle in the *Lotus* case in which Turkish jurisdiction applied to the acts of a French officer in French territory (i.e. a ship) were held not to conflict with international law because the "effects" of his action were felt in Turkish territory (i.e. a Turkish ship). This branch of international law has been used as justification for concurrent exercises of jurisdiction in criminal law where constituent elements of the offence have been carried out in the territory of two more states.

However, in its extension to civil jurisdiction as applied to economic activity, it is a pure creation of American domestic law and for much of its life, has been substantively limited to justify the extraterritorial application of American competition and anti-trust law (see William K. Walker's article "Extraterritorial Application of U.S. Anti-Trust Laws: The Effect of the European Community-United States Anti-Trust Agreement between with United States of America and the Commission of the European Communities Regarding the Application of Their Competition Laws," 23 September 1991, 30 I.L.M. 1487 (1991) Harvard International Law Journal, Spring, 1992).

The attempt by the United States to do so was bitterly opposed by both Canada and European states, but it must be accepted that the conclusion of agreements by both entities with the United States has substantially ended the dispute on the application of the effects doctrine to anti-trust and competition laws, and arguably more broadly to economic activities. The price paid by the USA for grudging and implicit acceptance of the doctrine has been a collateral application of principles of comity to lessen the impact of the application of USA law to activities in and laws applied by the territorial state (see quite recently the October 5, 2004 *Agreement between the Government of Canada and the Government of the United States on the Application of Positive Comity Principles to the Enforcement of their Competition Laws*).

(iii) The Effects Doctrine generally applied

Typically, the application of the effects doctrine beyond anti-trust and competition activities has been led by the United States. Kathleen Hixson prepared an excellent survey of the amendments to the Second Restatement that led to the adoption of the Third in 1986 (see "Extraterritorial Jurisdiction under the Third Restatement of Foreign Relations Law of the United States," *Fordham International Law Journal*, Fall, 1988). Only at that point was the doctrine's jurisdictional reach stretched beyond economic activities and made a principle of potentially general application.

Since then the doctrine's application within the realm of transboundary environmental law has undoubtedly proceeded in the United States. While the application of the doctrine in the context of the *Comprehensive Environmental Response, Compensation and Liability Act* (CERCLA) is without precedent, there has been more (albeit also recent) activity under the *Resource Conservation and Recovery Act* (RCRA). In that case, suit was brought by the EPA and from its perspective, satisfactorily settled before going to court, against a USA-owned Mexican subsidiary corporation for pollution that entered the USA from its operations in Mexico. Kristi Fettig in her 2002 article "Criminal and Civil Remedies for Transboundary Water Pollution," 15 Tran Nat'l Law 117, enthusiastically argues for a widespread application of the effects doctrine in cases of transboundary environmental pollution. Nevertheless, her argument that the effects doctrine is "Internationally, [a] principle well accepted ..." or "[a] generally recognized principle of jurisdiction" is entirely based on USA sources, invariably the *Third Restatement* and case law applying the Restatement (see footnotes 69 and 71).

Similarly, though less enthusiastically, Austen Parrish argues for the existence and applicability of the effects doctrine, in an article as yet unpublished "Extraterritoriality, International Environmental Law, and the Search for Solutions to Canadian-US Transboundary Water Pollution Disputes." However, in his article, he concludes that bilateral negotiations are a more promising option than the unilateral exercise of USA law to foreign conduct.

The merits of bilateral negotiations notwithstanding, it is apparent that USA courts will apply the effects doctrine as set out in the *Third Restatement* but hopefully subject to the application of principles of comity and a proper weighing of the interests of the territorial state.

Non-American evidence of a general application of the effects doctrine is isolated and fragmentary. There is an older case where a Netherlands plaintiff was successful in obtaining damages for pollution originating upstream from a source in France (see Case No. 21/76, *Handelswerkerig G.J. Bier B.V. v. Mines de Potasse D'Alsace S.A*, Case No. 21/76, 1976 E.C.R. 1735.). However, the court's decision was to enforce a judgment in tort law.

There is lastly the "Opinion of the Inter-American Juridical Committee in Response to Resolution AG/DOC 3375 of the General Assembly of the Organization of American States." In that opinion, speaking to the acceptability of a number of instances of extraterritorial jurisdiction, the Committee states:

B Extraterritoriality and the Limits Imposed by International Law on the Exercise of Jurisdiction

...

(e) A state may justify the application of the laws of its territory only insofar as an act occurring outside its territory has a direct, substantial and foreseeable effect within its territory and the exercise of such jurisdiction is reasonable.

Opinions of the Inter-American Juridical Committee are not binding, though they may be persuasive. Taken together with the Netherlands case, they do not provide convincing evidence of international acceptance that the effects doctrine may be applied routinely beyond economic conduct.

Conclusion

The effects doctrine as evolved from its initial application in anti-trust law in the 1940s has been firmly established in that subject area, not only by the persistence of the USA effort, but more importantly, through the acquiescence of Canada and the European Union by treaties in which implicit acceptance of the doctrine has been bought by the USA acceptance of the importance of comity when the doctrine is exercised. USA extension of the doctrine to other forms of conduct aside from economic has proceeded apace. However, evidence that the doctrine has become one of general application at international law is exceedingly thin and heavily reliant on USA sources.

Parliamentary Declarations in 2004–5 / Déclarations parlementaires en 2004–5

compiled by / préparé par
ALIAKSANDRA LOGVIN

A STATEMENTS MADE ON THE INTRODUCTION OF LEGISLATION / DÉCLARATIONS SUR L'INTRODUCTION DE LA LÉGISLATION

I *Bill S-17: Tax Conventions Implementation Act, 2004 (An Act to Implement an Agreement, Conventions and Protocols Concluded between Canada and Gabon, Ireland, Armenia, Oman and Azerbaijan for the Avoidance of Double Taxation and the Prevention of Fiscal Evasion) / Loi S-17: Loi de 2004 pour la mise en œuvre de conventions fiscales (Loi mettant en œuvre un accord, des conventions et des protocoles conclus entre le Canada et le Gabon, l'Irlande, l'Arménie, Oman et l'Azerbaïdjan en vue d'éviter les doubles impositions et de prévenir l'évasion fiscale)*[1]

Hon. John McKay (Parliamentary Secretary to the Minister of Finance):

Bill S-17 ... addresses fair taxation and good international trade relations ... [It] builds on Canada's well established network of tax treaties with other countries, which happens to be one of the most extensive of any country in the world. At present, we have 83 treaties in effect. The passage of Bill S-17 would make that 87. The new treaties would provide taxpayers and businesses, both in Canada and in these other countries, with more predictable and equitable tax results in their cross-border dealings ...

Tax treaties, or income tax conventions ... are an integral part of our tax system. Basically, they set out the degree to which one country can tax

---

Aliaksandra Logvin is in the Faculty of Law at the University of Ottawa.

1 Editor's note: Bill S-17 was introduced in the House of Commons by Hon. Ethel Blondin-Andrew (for the Minister of Finance) on 9 December 2004. *House of Commons Debates*, 9 December 2004, p. 2488.

the income of a resident of another country. The benefits to Canada having tax treaties in place with other countries are significant ... [Tax treaties] provide certainty on how Canadians will be taxed abroad ... they assure our treaty partners of how their residents will be treated in Canada. Tax treaties also benefit the Canadian economy by contributing to a sound framework for international trade and investment.

There are definite economic disadvantages for countries that do not enter into tax agreements with other countries ... The absence of tax treaties makes the threat of double taxation a great concern to taxpayers ... Without a tax treaty in place to set out the tax rules, the same income can be taxed in both countries without consequential relief. This situation can have a negative impact on the expansion of trade, and the movement of capital and labour between countries ... [F]oreign investors and traders are anxious to know the tax implications associated with their activities in that country. They also want assurances that they will be treated fairly ...

It is important to note the fact that tax treaties are international agreements that require official notice be given before they can be terminated. That in itself adds to a degree of certainty. The tax rules range from an allocation of taxing rights between the two countries to the establishment of a mechanism to resolve tax disputes between those countries.

All these measures promote certainty and stability and help produce a better business climate.

Tax treaties, including the ones enacted in the bill, are especially designed to facilitate trade, investment and other activities between Canada and its treaty partners. They are developed with two main objectives in mind — first ... to avoid double taxation and provide a level of certainty about the tax rules that apply to international transactions; and second, to encourage cooperation between tax authorities in Canada and the treaty countries to prevent tax evasion and tax avoidance. Tax treaties play an important role in protecting Canada's tax base by allowing information to be exchanged between our revenue authorities and their counterparts in countries with which we have tax treaties.

(House of Commons Debates, 14 December 2004, pp. 2737–39)
(Débats de la Chambre des Communes, le 14 décembre 2004, pp. 2737–39)

2   Bill C-4: An Act to Implement the Convention on International
     Interests in Mobile Equipment[2] and the Protocol to the Convention
     on International Interests in Mobile Equipment on Matters Specific
     to Aircraft Equipment[3] / Loi C-4: Loi de mise en œuvre de la
     Convention relative aux garanties internationales portant sur des
     matériels d'équipement mobiles et du Protocole portant sur les
     questions spécifiques aux matériels d'équipement aéronautiques à
     la Convention relative aux garanties internationales portant sur
     des matériels d'équipement mobiles[4]

Hon. Jim Karygiannis (Parliamentary Secretary to the Minister of
Transport):

[A] strong competitive aviation industry is an important underpinning of
Canada's economy today and into the 21st century ... [W]e all recognize
that this sector has faced significant challenges over the past few years ...
[T]he aviation sector is particularly vulnerable to economic shocks and
other world events: 9/11, SARS and record high fuel prices. All have had
a negative effect on the sector ...

  The proposed legislation is one way the government is demonstrating
its commitments to long term viability of the Canadian airline and aerospace industries. Adopting the bill will help these industries compete
more effectively in the global economy by facilitating their access to capital markets ...

  [T]hrough this bill and the ratification of the convention and aircraft
protocol, the Government of Canada will actively support all elements of
Canada's aviation sector.

  Canada played a leading role in the negotiation and the development
of the Cape Town convention and aircraft protocol. The convention and
aircraft protocol represent an unparalleled example of cooperation
between governments and industry in creating an international regime
... The convention and aircraft protocol will establish an international
legal regime that includes remedies to creditors in case of default. New
rules will reduce the risks associated with financing and provide greater

2 Editor's note: Done in Cape Town, South Africa, 16 November 2001, entered into
   force 1 April 2004. Canada has been a signatory to the convention since 31 March
   2004.
3 Editor's note: Done in Cape Town, South Africa, 16 November 2001, entered into
   force 1 March 2006. Canada has been a signatory to the protocol since 31 March
   2004.
4 Editor's note: Bill C-4 was introduced in the House of Commons by Hon. Jean
   Lapierre (Minister of Transport) on 8 October 2004. House of Commons Debates, 8
   October 2004, p. 189.

certainty to creditors and aircraft manufacturers. This will lead to larger amounts of credit being made available to airlines at a lower cost, ultimately generating increased airline earnings and profitability and important spin-off benefits to the broader economy.

The convention and the aircraft protocol will create a [worldwide Internet-based] international registry for rights in aircraft and will set the order of priority among purchasers and creditors. The creation of a single international registry will provide considerable advantage in terms of time, cost savings and improve certainty in resolving questions of priority of interests ... The international registry will be set up and operated by Aviareto, an Irish-based company that was selected through a tendering process supervised by the International Civil Aviation Organization. A permanent supervisory authority will oversee the operation of the registry. It will, among other things, have the authority to appoint and dismiss the registry operator, make regulations dealing with the operation of the registry, establish procedure for receiving complaints, set the fee structure and report to contracting states.

As a signatory party and a key participant to date, Canada will continue to work through ICAO to ensure Canadian interests will be protected throughout this process ... For a country like Canada, the convention contains only a few major innovations. However, it will provide other countries with a considerable measure of legal improvements that may well assist them in getting the most out of their economies while at the same time providing enhanced opportunities for Canadian businesses ...

Implementation of the convention and protocol in Canada will reaffirm Canada's leadership role in international civil aviation. The introduction of this legislation establishes that Canada is taking an important step toward eventual ratification of the convention and aircraft protocol ... [T]he benefits to Canada of implementing the bill and ratifying of the convention and aircraft protocol include: greater security for creditors; increased competitiveness of the Canadian aerospace and airline industries; maintaining jobs in Canada; and spin-off effects for various regions within Canada.

(House of Commons Debates, 18 October 2004, pp. 468–70)
(Débats de la Chambre des Communes, le 18 octobre 2004, pp. 468–70)

3   Bill C-6: *An Act to Establish the Department of Public Safety and Emergency Preparedness and to Amend or Repeal Certain Acts / Loi C-6: Loi constituant le ministère de la Sécurité publique et de la Protection civile et modifiant et abrogeant certaines lois*[5]

Hon. Roy Cullen (Parliamentary Secretary to the Minister of Public Safety and Emergency Preparedness):

[L]'une des toutes premières mesures annoncées par notre gouvernement ... a été la création d'un ministère pouvant mieux assurer la sécurité du Canada et des Canadiens, qui pourrait protéger nos assises économiques solides et qui doterait le Canada d'une place importante dans le monde, une place dont nous pourrions tous être fiers.

With Bill C-6, the Government of Canada is sending a very clear signal that protecting the lives and livelihoods of Canadians is a top priority for our government. The freedom and opportunities we all enjoy depend on the underpinning of a safe and secure society. We recognize that there is no more fundamental role for government than keeping its citizens safe. We also understand that traditional approaches to safety and security no longer apply in the complex environment in which we now live. In the 21st century, threats come in many forms, whether from natural causes, accidents or malicious acts, and from all corners of the globe ... Canadians ... expect the federal government to exercise leadership in resolving any security gaps along our border with the United States, closing it to criminals and potential terrorists while ensuring that Canadians continue to enjoy the benefits of an open society. It is the responsibility of the government to protect the longest undefended border in the world while at the same time facilitating the legal movement of people, goods and services essential to the growth of our economy.

Public Safety and Emergency Preparedness Canada is dedicated to minimizing a continuum of risk to Canadians, from crime to naturally occurring disasters such as floods or forest fires, to threats to national security from terrorist activity. Its mandate is to meet the public safety needs of Canadians and ensure that public safety agencies are equipped to deal with a range of threats to Canadians and our interests abroad.

(House of Commons Debates, 14 October 2004, pp. 402–4) (Débats de la Chambre des Communes, le 14 octobre 2004, pp. 402–4)

---

5   Editor's note: Bill C-6 was introduced in the House of Commons by Hon. Mauril Bélanger (Deputy Leader of the Government in the House of Commons) on 8 October 2004. *House of Commons Debates*, 8 October 2004, p. 189.

4   Bill C-12: Quarantine Act (An Act to Prevent the Introduction and Spread of Communicable Diseases) / Loi C-12: La Loi sur la quarantaine (Loi visant à prévenir l'introduction et la propagation de maladies transmissibles)[6]

Hon. Carolyn Bennett (Minister of State (Public Health)):

[L]e gouvernement du Canada s'est fixé comme objectif de moderniser les lois sur la protection de la santé ... Among the many hard lessons learned from the experience of SARS is the need to strengthen our quarantine legislation to help prevent the introduction and spread of both emerging and re-emerging communicable diseases ...

Now, with Bill C-12, we will replace the outdated quarantine legislation with an improved and modern Quarantine Act so that we can better protect Canadians from the importation of dangerous communicable diseases and ensure Canada can meet its international obligations to help prevent the spread of diseases beyond our borders.

The modernized act we propose has a new focus on airline travel and would provide the Minister of Health with additional abilities. For example, he could divert an aircraft to an alternate landing site if it is necessary to isolate passengers. He can establish quarantine facilities at any location in Canada and order that carriers from certain countries or regions of the world not enter Canada if there are serious concerns that such an arrival may threaten the public health of Canadians. He would be able to close Canadian border points in the event of a public health emergency. The proposed act also lists many more communicable diseases for which Canadian officials could detain departing passengers. While these measures would only be used in rare instances where circumstances warrant, these changes are essential if we are to keep pace with emerging infectious diseases and protect the health of Canadians ...

Canada is a responsible partner of the global public health arena. The updated act is aligned with Canada's obligations under the World Health Organization's international health regulations. The updated act, the creation of the public health agency of Canada, the appointment of the first chief public health officer and the Canadian pandemic influenza plan are all complementary steps in the Government of Canada's strategy for strengthening Canada's public health system. These innovations ensure better communication, collaboration and cooperation among partners.

---

[6] Editor's note: Bill C-12 was introduced in the House of Commons by Hon. Mauril Bélanger (Deputy Leader of the Government in the House of Commons) on 8 October 2004. *House of Commons Debates*, 8 October 2004, p. 190.

(House of Commons Debates, 22 October 2004, pp. 736–38)
(Débats de la Chambre des Communes, le 22 octobre 2004, pp. 736–38)

5   *Bill C-15: An Act to Amend the Migratory Birds Convention Act, 1994 and the Canadian Environmental Protection Act, 1999 / Loi C-15: Loi modifiant la Loi de 1994 sur la Convention concernant les oiseaux migrateurs et la Loi canadienne sur la protection de l'environnement (1999)[7]*

Hon. Bryon Wilfert (Parliamentary Secretary to the Minister of the Environment):

Environment, health and the economy are not mutually exclusive concepts. We should not think of the environment on one hand and the economy on the other ... The source of all our wealth lies in the environment. Those countries who work now to reconcile environmental issues with the need to maintain a competitive economy will become the global economic engines of the 21st century.

Canada, with its rich environment, its wealth of natural resources, and its technological know-how and vigorous economy is well suited to seize the moment and to become a world leader among those that succeed in creating a robust economy based on sound environmental principles ...

In 1916 Canada signed the migratory birds convention with the United States. This historic agreement committed our two nations to ensure the protection of bird species that were threatened by human activity. Since the agreement was signed several Canadian environmental protection laws have been passed, including the Canadian Migratory Birds Convention Act of 1994, the Canadian Environmental Protection Act, 1999, the Fisheries Act, and the Canada Shipping Act, which includes sections relating to the environment ...

Currently, vessels that navigate our waters are subject to Canadian law. Canada has existing laws dealing with the potential environmental effects of ship traffic, including the release of oil into marine waters. These laws include the Migratory Birds Convention Act, 1994, the Canadian Environmental Protection Act, 1999, the Fisheries Act and the Canada Shipping Act. However, recent court cases have revealed ambiguities in two parts of the legislative framework, making enforcement difficult. It is important that these amendments allow us to deal more effectively with law enforcement issues in cases of marine pollution and, in particular, the

---

[7]   Editor's note: Bill C-15 was introduced in the House of Commons by Hon. Jim Peterson (for the Minister of the Environment) on 26 October 2004. *House of Commons Debates*, 26 October 2004, p. 747.

legislative measures that will provide clarity with respect to the new 200 mile exclusive economic zone by affirming that enforcement officers have authority in this area.

Second, we are increasing the fines under the Migratory Birds Convention Act, 1994, to a million dollars with this bill. The increased maximum fine brings the legislation into better conformity with the modern business of shipping, which is big business.

This bill is also aimed at fostering greater collaboration on law enforcement measures and will provide the means to pursue offenders and will provide sentencing guidelines so penalties will be imposed that appropriately reflect the damage done to the environment. The bill does not require us to create a new agency nor does it ask us to develop new policies. It is about saving birds and it is about doing the right thing.

(House of Commons Debates, 2 November 2004, pp. 1047–48) (Débats de la Chambre des Communes, le 2 novembre 2004, pp. 1047–48)

6   *Bill C-17: An Act to Amend the Contraventions Act and the Controlled Drugs and Substances Act and to Make Consequential Amendments to Other Acts / Loi C-17: Loi modifiant la Loi sur les contraventions et la Loi réglementant certaines drogues et autres substances et apportant des modifications corrélatives à d'autres lois*[8]

Hon. Paul Harold Macklin (Parliamentary Secretary to the Minister of Justice and Attorney General of Canada):

Bill C-17 addresses ... the reform of cannabis legislation ... Canadians are ... concerned about the proliferation of commercial cannabis marijuana production operations, commonly known as grow ops. This issue has also become a problem of serious law enforcement concern ... The smuggling of cannabis from Canada to the United States has become a major issue in cross-border law enforcement relations. In spite of considerable amounts of enforcement resources being used to control these grow ops, these efforts have failed to curtail them.

Bill C-17 proposes reforms in respect of two areas, the first dealing with the possession offence regarding small quantities of marijuana and cannabis resin, and the second dealing with the offence of production or cultivation. Under this proposed reform, amendments will be made to the

---

[8]   Editor's note: Bill C-17 was introduced in the House of Commons by Hon. Irwin Cotler (Minister of Justice and Attorney General of Canada) on 1 November 2004. *House of Commons Debates,* 1 November 2004, p. 1012.

Contraventions Act and the Controlled Drugs and Substances Act. In the first instance, the Contraventions Act will be amended so as to permit the act to apply to the new possession offences involving small quantities of cannabis material and to the new cultivation offence involving a very small number of cannabis plants.

Secondly, the Controlled Drugs and Substances Act will be amended to create four new offences of cannabis possession involving small quantities of cannabis material, each with distinct penalties.

(House of Commons Debates, 2 November 2004, pp. 1064–65) (Débats de la Chambre des Communes, le 2 novembre 2004, pp. 1064–65)

Hon. Sarmite Bulte (Parliamentary Secretary to the Minister of Canadian Heritage):

Countries around the world treat cannabis possession in different ways. Some countries tolerate forms of possession and consumption, other countries apply administrative sanctions or fines, while others apply penal sanctions ... [C]ertain states in the United States, notably Alaska, also treat cannabis possession in different ways, although it does vary from state to state. However, despite the different legal approaches toward cannabis, a common trend can be seen, particularly in Europe, in the development of alternative measures to criminal prosecution for cases of use and possession of small quantities of cannabis for personal use. Fines, cautions, probation, exemption from punishment and counselling are favoured by many European justice systems.

En Espagne, en Italie, au Portugal, en Belgique et au Luxembourg, la possession de petites quantités de marijuana n'est pas une infraction criminelle. Aux Pays-Bas, en Allemagne, en Suisse et au Danemark, la possession de petites quantités de marijuana demeure une infraction pénale, mais ne fait jamais l'objet de poursuites. En France, une directive recommande aux juges et aux ministères publics de n'utiliser des sanctions de droit pénal qu'en dernier recours pour les personnes qui n'ont pas commis d'autres infractions que celle qui consiste à consommer des drogues illégales.

Britain recently reclassified marijuana from a class B to a class C drug. Possession will therefore be on a parallel with anabolic steroids and growth hormones, which ... are still illegal but not an arrestable offence ...

Most U.S. states envisage the possibility of imprisonment for the offence of possession of cannabis. However a dozen U.S. states have passed measures decriminalizing possession of small amounts of marijuana. These include California, Alaska, Minnesota, New York, North Carolina, Ohio,

Maine, Nevada, Nebraska, Colorado, Oregon and Mississippi ... Some Australian states and territories have also adopted cannabis decriminalization measures. Some of these measures are similar to what is being contemplated in Bill C-17.

(House of Commons Debates, 2 November 2004, pp. 1086–87) (Débats de la Chambre des Communes, le 2 novembre 2004, pp. 1086–87)

7   *Bill C-19: An Act to Amend the Competition Act and to Make Consequential Amendments to Other Acts / Loi C-19: Loi modifiant la Loi sur la concurrence et d'autres lois en conséquence*[9]

Hon. Jerry Pickard (Parliamentary Secretary to the Minister of Industry):

Bill C-19 would strengthen Canada's competition framework in a global economic partnership to benefit consumers, as well as businesses, both large and small. These amendments would also create a greater symmetry between our competition regime and those of our major trading partners we deal with on a daily basis. That is good for business, which is increasingly multinational, and it is also good for our economy ...

The legislation before us today will strengthen the act by: providing restitution for consumer loss resulting from false or misleading advertising; introducing a general administrative monetary penalty provision for abuse of dominance in any industry; removing the airline specific provisions from the act to return it to a law of general application; increasing the level of administrative monetary penalties for deceptive or misleading marketing practices; and decriminalizing the pricing provisions ...

Bill C-19 balances the interests of businesses and consumers in a number of ways. On the business side, for example, it moves us toward a law of general application by removing the airline specific provisions ... It also decriminalizes the pricing provisions in response to the committee's recommendations and long-standing requests from various business groups. On the consumer side, for example, it ensures that Canadians will have access to remedies similar to those in other states we do business with. When they have lost money as a result of misleading representations, they have a chance to reclaim those losses ...

Bill C-19 would also reform the pricing provisions dealing with price discrimination, geographic price discrimination, predatory pricing and

---

[9] Editor's note: Bill C-19 was introduced in the House of Commons by Hon. Andy Scott (for the Minister of Industry) on 2 November 2004. *House of Commons Debates*, 2 November 2004, p. 1043.

promotional allowances. Bill C-19 would repeal these criminal provisions and bring them under the civil regime under the abuse of dominance provisions ...

Canadians are being well served by our competition regime, which is among the most developed in the world. However, there is always room for improvement. Bill C-19 represents the latest step in an incremental legislative evolution that shows the government is committed to having a modern, effective Competition Act. This legislative package is responsive to the recommendations of Parliament and industry, consumers and businesses. Taken together, these amendments would strengthen the Competition Act. They would effectively deter anti-competitive behaviour that is most harmful to the Canadian economy and Canadian consumers. They would promote legitimate pro-competitive business practices to ensure a competitive marketplace, one where consumers and businesses benefit from competitive practices, product choice and quality service.

(House of Commons Debates, 16 November 2004, pp. 1370–71) (Débats de la Chambre des Communes, le 16 novembre 2004, pp. 1370–71)

8   *Bill C-25: An Act Governing the Operation of Remote Sensing Space Systems / Loi C-25: Loi régissant l'exploitation des systèmes de télédétection spatiale*[10]

Hon. Dan McTeague (Parliamentary Secretary to the Minister of Foreign Affairs):

[T]he proposed remote sensing space systems act is ... important to Canada, to Canadians and to our friends abroad, both in terms of our own security and our international partnerships ...

Canada became a world leader in remote sensing of the earth from outer space when it launched in 1995 its first remote sensing satellite system, the government operated RADARSAT-1. A myriad of civilian applications for remote sensing satellites have since been developed in Canada. These include, for example, those for managing natural resources, monitoring the environment, and providing coastal surveillance and ice mapping services. Today Canadians service about 15% of the world's satellite-derived remote sensing market. ...

In its 10th year of operation, RADARSAT-1 is still the most capable civilian synthetic aperture radar satellite in orbit. When RADARSAT-2, an even

---

[10] Editor's note: Bill C-25 was introduced in the House of Commons by Hon. Joseph Volpe (for the Minister of Foreign Affairs) on 23 November 2004. *House of Commons Debates*, 23 November 2004, p. 1691.

more capable Canadian system is launched by private owners and operators, it will move us that much further ahead of the competition. This proposed legislation seeks to maintain that Canadian leadership position ... The security environment today has ... changed in many different ways. Once, for example, the two rival superpowers observed each other using satellites in outer space. Today Canadians face new asymmetric threats from enemies that might seek to use the commercial availability of satellite imagery. Our security system for satellites must evolve in response to such developments. Furthermore, Canada is a nation that relies on international cooperation to fill the space ambitions of its government and its private citizens. To help the Canadian private sector continue to pursue these important ambitions, a transparent regulatory regime is essential to securing access to sensitive technology and launch services ...

The operation of remote sensing space systems is inherently international in scope. Foreign partners may seek to participate in the operation of a Canadian licensed system. The proposed act makes provision for them to do so, but only in ways that promote and protect, and are consistent with Canada's security, defence and foreign policy interests. This is carried out by setting conditions for a licensee in the conduct of certain sensitive activities.

(House of Commons Debates, 7 December 2004, pp. 2363–64) (Débats de la Chambre des Communes, le 7 décembre 2004, pp. 2363–64)

9   *Bill C-28: An Act to Amend the Food and Drugs Act / Loi C-28: Loi modifiant la Loi sur les aliments et drogues*[11]

Hon. Robert Thibault (Parliamentary Secretary to the Minister of Health):

[T]he proposed amendments will support ongoing work under the North American Free Trade Agreement technical working group on pesticides, through which Health Canada and the United States Environmental Protection Agency have accelerated bilateral harmonization in the registration of pest control products in order to provide faster and simultaneous access to a wide range of newer, safer pest management tools in both countries.

---

[11] Editor's note: Bill C-28 was introduced in the House of Commons by Hon. Ujjal Dosanjh (Minister of Health) on 29 November 2004. *House of Commons Debates*, 29 November 2004, p. 2033.

(House of Commons Debates, 14 December 2004, pp. 2748–49)
(Débats de la Chambre des Communes, le 14 décembre 2004, pp. 2748–49)

10 Bill C-40: An Act to Amend the Canada Grain Act and the Canada Transportation Act / Loi C-40: Loi modifiant la Loi sur les grains du Canada et la Loi sur les transports au Canada[12]

Hon. Carolyn Bennett (Minister of State (Public Health)):

Ce projet de loi vise à modifier la Loi sur les grains du Canada et la Loi sur les transports au Canada, afin de les rendre conformes à la décision d'un groupe spécial de l'Organisation mondiale du commerce, selon laquelle certaines pratiques de manutention et de transfert des grains au Canada vont à l'encontre des obligations du Canada en matière de traitement national, en vertu de l'Accord général sur les tarifs douaniers et le commerce de 1994.

[T]he Canadian grain sector stands out as a great success story … Today Canadian wheat, barley and other grains are known by our customers all over the world for their outstanding quality, consistency, cleanliness and innovation. Each and every year Canada's grain industry does $10 billion worth of business here in Canada and around the world …

Canada's marketing system for wheat has been challenged by the United States on a number of occasions in recent years. Each time the major issue has been the Canadian Wheat Board, and each time the ruling has gone in Canada's favour. Both at NAFTA and the World Trade Organization, panels have consistently upheld Canada's position that the Canadian Wheat Board is a fair trader and that its mandate, structure and activities are consistent with our international trading obligations.

In April 2004 a WTO dispute settlement panel ruled that the Canadian Wheat Board was consistent with Canada's international trade obligations. The U.S. immediately appealed. In August 2004 the appellate body of the WTO upheld the original ruling, namely, that the U.S. had not provided any evidence whatsoever that the Canadian Wheat Board had acted contrary to Canada's international trade obligations. Once again that ruling confirmed that the Canadian Wheat Board operates within the rules. It further supports Canada's position at the WTO negotiating table, namely, the Canadian Wheat Board is a fair trader.

---

[12] Editor's note: Bill C-40 was introduced in the House of Commons by Hon. Andy Mitchell (Minister of Agriculture and Agri-Food) on 11 March 2005. *House of Commons Debates*, 11 March 2005, p. 4324.

The WTO did find against Canada regarding certain grain handling and transportation policies. In response to those findings, Canada decided that changes to Canadian legislation could be made that would both serve to meet our international trade responsibilities and at the same time maintain our world-leading grain quality assurance systems ...

[T]he WTO ruling requires action by Canada on three particular grain policies ... The first is entry authorization requirements ... The second is mixing of foreign grain ... The third is the rail revenue cap program ... To comply with the WTO rulings in these areas, the government is proposing amendments to the Canada Grain Act and the Canada Transportation Act. First, to address the issue of entry authorization requirements, the amendments to the Canada Grain Act remove the requirement that Canadian Grain Commission permission must be sought before foreign grain can enter licensed Canadian elevators. Instead, a regulation will be added requiring licensees operating grain elevators to report to the CGC the origin of all grain.

Second, to address the issue of mixing of foreign grain, the amendments remove the requirement that CGC permission must be sought before foreign grain can be mixed with eastern Canadian grain ...

Further, all licensed elevator operators will be required to maintain the origin of grains at all times to ensure that grain is never misrepresented. It is essential that Canada continue to have the capacity to assure our buyers that they are getting what they pay for, namely, the consistent high quality they have come to expect from Canadian grain ...

[C]hanges to the acts and associated regulations will need to be implemented by August 1, 2005 ... We believe that Canada can conform with the WTO panel findings in a way that will have little practical impact on the Canadian grain handling and transportation system ...

The panel rulings back up Canada's position in the WTO negotiations, namely, that no disciplines on state trading enterprises, like the CWB, are needed beyond those agreed to by the WTO members in the July 2004 framework on agriculture. It also supports our position that CWB is a fair trader ... It is Canada's hope that the decision by the WTO and our compliance in the areas ... outlined will lead other nations to turn the page and put our collective focus where it should be, namely on levelling the international playing field so our producers and processors can compete fairly and effectively in the global marketplace.

(House of Commons Debates, 18 April 2005, pp. 5189–91)
(Débats de la Chambre des Communes, le 18 avril 2005, pp. 5189–91)

B   STATEMENTS IN RESPONSE TO QUESTIONS / DÉCLARATIONS EN RÉPONSE AUX QUESTIONS

1   Environment / Environnement

(a) Arctic / Arctique

Mr. Alan Tonks (York South — Weston):

Last week the Arctic Council released its Arctic Climate Impact Assessment report, which states that the warming of the Arctic is double the earlier projections. The report also states that the warming is a direct cause and effect of the increased concentration of greenhouse gas emissions in the atmosphere ... [What] necessary actions [does] Canada need to take with respect to this profoundly serious environmental problem?

Hon. Stéphane Dion (Minister of the Environment):

I will attend a meeting of the Arctic Council next week, just after the release of the most comprehensive study about the dramatic impact climate change has on the Arctic. We need to act with all our partners on the north. I am very confident that all northern nations will work cooperatively to find solutions to the changing climate for now and in the future.

(House of Commons Debates, 15 November 2004, pp. 1333–34) (Débats de la Chambre des Communes, le 15 novembre 2004, pp. 1333–34)

Ms. Nancy Karetak-Lindell (Nunavut):

[T]he United States senate voted in language in a budget bill that will allow for drilling in the Arctic National Wildlife Refuge in Alaska. This will put at risk the core calving ground of the porcupine caribou herd which migrates between Canada and Alaska. This majestic animal is vitally important to aboriginal and indigenous people on both sides of the border. Will ... our government ... continue to register our concerns?

Hon. Stéphane Dion (Minister of the Environment):

We urge the United States to protect this area, as we have done ... Because we have a sensitive Arctic coastal plain and the impact would be so bad to the calving ground of the porcupine caribou herd, Canada established a national park ...

(House of Commons Debates, 23 March 2005, pp. 4497–98) (Débats de la Chambre des Communes, le 23 mars 2005, pp. 4497–98)

(b) Chrysotile Asbestos / Amiante chrysotile

M. Marc Boulianne (Mégantic — L'Érable):

[L]e Canada a soutenu la décision ... d'exclure de la liste des produits dangereux de la Convention de Rotterdam,[13] l'amiante chrysotile. Maintenant que l'utilisation sécuritaire du chrysotile est reconnue sur le plan international, est-ce que le gouvernement compte amorcer la seconde étape de cette démarche et faire la promotion de l'usage sécuritaire du chrysotile ici même au Canada?

L'hon. Stéphane Dion (ministre de l'Environnement):

[G]râce à notre estimé et ex-collègue, M. Gérard Binet, nous avons pu faire en sorte de protéger la santé ainsi que l'économie ... [C]'est bien l'orientation que nous aurons toujours avec l'environnement et l'économie ensemble, et nous le ferons avec notre futur collègue, M. Gérard Binet.

(House of Commons Debates, 1 December 2004, p. 2132) (Débats de la Chambre des Communes, le 1 décembre 2004, p. 2132)

(c) Great Lakes / Grands Lacs

Mr. Joe Comartin (Windsor — Tecumseh):

[I]n mid-July the Great Lakes provincial and state governments released proposed agreements on diversion of Great Lakes waters. Under the agreement, these states will be able to unilaterally divert water from the Great Lakes without any veto from Canadians. These agreements override treaty arrangements between Canada and the United States that go back 100 years. The legal framework between our countries make it absolutely clear that it is the federal government's responsibility to control the flow of water in the Great Lakes basin ... Will ... [the Government] ... declare ... [its] opposition to these agreements and to the further diversion of water out of the Great Lakes basin?

Hon. Pierre Pettigrew (Minister of Foreign Affairs):

[T]he proposed annex does not affect Canadian and U.S. obligations under the boundary waters treaty. It does not affect levels and flows of the

---

13 Editor's note: Convention on the Prior Informed Consent Procedure for Certain Hazardous Chemicals and Pesticides (Rotterdam, Netherlands, 10 September 1998; *entered into force* 24 February 2004). Canada accepted the Rotterdam Convention on 26 August 2002.

Great Lakes. We are assessing whether the proposed agreements can be implemented in a manner consistent with the treaty, in consultation with the U.S. government, Ontario and Quebec. The Council of Great Lakes Governors has said that it would welcome comments from the Government of Canada after the October 18 deadline.

(House of Commons Debates, 21 October 2004, p. 679)
(Débats de la Chambre des Communes, le 21 octobre 2004, p. 679)

Mrs. Cheryl Gallant (Renfrew — Nipissing — Pembroke):

[S]ince 1993 the Great Lakes Water Quality Agreement commits Canada to reducing the amount of cancer-causing chlorination by-products from entering the Great Lakes watershed. The government ... is spending ... dollars on water treatment systems that use a cancer-causing toxic chemical. Why are they doing so when environmentally friendly alternative water treatment systems are available and have been in use in other countries for years?

Hon. Dan McTeague (Parliamentary Secretary to the Minister of Foreign Affairs):

[T]he Council of Great Lakes Governors has convened on many occasions and is in constant consultation with the provinces and states to ensure that one of the most valuable resources this country has not only remains safe for people to drink but is an asset that generations to come will be able to enjoy.

(House of Commons Debates, 19 November 2004, pp. 1602–3)
(Débats de la Chambre des Communes, le 19 novembre 2004, pp.1602–3)

(d) Kyoto Protocol / Protocole de Kyoto[14]

M. Jack Layton (Toronto — Danforth):

[L]e ministre de l'Environnement a encore mis de l'eau dans le gaz en ce qui concerne l'environnement et les engagements de Kyoto ... Je demande au premier ministre s'il pense que le laisser-faire suffit pour répondre à cette crise de l'environnement.

---

[14] Kyoto Protocol to the United Nations Framework Convention on Climate Change (Kyoto, Japan, 11 December 1997; *entered into force* 16 February 2005), UN Doc. FCCC/CP/1997/L.7/Ad.1, reprinted in (1998) 37 I.L.M. 32. Canada ratified the Kyoto Protocol on 17 December 2002.

Hon. Stéphane Dion (Minister of the Environment):

[L]'engagement du gouvernement du Canada pour Kyoto est de l'ordre de 100 p. 100 … Is it not action when we invest $645 million to improve energy efficiency, or when we include $63 million for energy efficient transportation, $340 million for energy efficient buildings and $240 million for energy efficient manufacturing and industrial processes? The government will work with the planet to fight climate change and to ensure that Canada will always be a good citizen of the world.

(House of Commons Debates, 18 October 2004, p. 485)
(Débats de la Chambre des Communes, le 18 octobre 2004, p. 485)

M. David McGuinty (Ottawa-Sud):

[L]e président russe, Vladimir Poutine, a signé un projet de loi ratifiant le Protocole de Kyoto. Le ministre de l'Environnement peut-il nous faire part de sa réaction face au geste du président russe, geste qui constitue une étape cruciale pour la Russie et qui permettra l'entrée en vigueur du protocole dès l'an prochain?

L'hon. Stéphane Dion (ministre de l'Environnement):

[L]e Canada veut féliciter le président russe. Le Canada a joué un rôle-clé dans la conception et les négociations qui ont mené au Protocole de Kyoto. Le Canada a ratifié le protocole avec fierté, comme un bon citoyen du monde. Maintenant que le protocole a été ratifié par la Russie et qu'il entrera en vigueur sous peu, le Canada est plus résolu que jamais à mettre en œuvre le protocole et à faire sa part pour le bien-être de notre planète et l'avenir de nos enfants.

(House of Commons Debates, 5 November 2004, p. 1275)
(Débats de la Chambre des Communes, le 5 novembre 2004, p. 1275)

(e) Lake Saint-Pierre / Lac Saint-Pierre

M. Guy André (Berthier — Maskinongé):

[N]ous estimons qu'il y a environ 300 000 obus, dont près de 8 000 n'ont pas explosé, qui gisent au fond du lac Saint-Pierre, désigné Réserve mondiale de la biosphère par l'UNESCO. Ces obus s'avèrent une menace environnementale et les citoyens en ont assez d'attendre la décision de les retirer. [Le gouvernement pense-t-il s'engager au sujet de] … la récupération des 300 000 obus qui traînent au fond du lac Saint-Pierre?

L'hon. Bill Graham (ministre de la Défense nationale):

[N]ous sommes très conscients du danger représenté par les engins de guerre qui sont présents depuis la Seconde Guerre mondiale ... Nous travaillons avec les communautés locales, avec Environnement Canada et d'autres. Nous ferons tous les efforts nécessaires pour réduire ce danger. C'est un problème mais nous sommes en train de le régler.

(House of Commons Debates, 18 November 2004, p. 1552)
(Débats de la Chambre des Communes, le 18 novembre 2004, p. 1552)

2   *Foreign Affairs / Les Affaires étrangères*

(a) Afghanistan

Mr. Bernard Patry (Pierrefonds — Dollard):

Knowing the implication of Canada in Afghanistan, not only with troops but also with the first ever recent presidential election, what is the position of Canada given reports of some irregularities during this election?

L'hon. Pierre Pettigrew (ministre des Affaires étrangères):

[L]es premières élections afghanes ont été un grand succès et les informations que nous recevons indiquent un taux de participation élevé, notamment chez les femmes. La journée du vote s'est déroulée sans trop de violence. Ceci reflète manifestement la grande détermination du peuple afghan et de la communauté internationale. L'engagement du Canada et de la communauté internationale aura donc aidé les Afghans à réaliser un gain important en cette période de transition. Some candidates have alleged irregularities and these are being investigated. A Canadian diplomat will be among the three experts on the review panel hearing these complaints. In the meantime, all the signs coming out of the elections are quite positive.

(House of Commons Debates, 12 October 2004, p. 219)
(Débats de la Chambre des Communes, le 12 octobre 2004, p. 219)

(b) Francophonie

M. Jean-Claude D'Amours (Madawaska — Restigouche):

Au Sommet de la Francophonie, le premier ministre a parlé de la responsabilité de protéger. Que fait le gouvernement du Canada pour promouvoir ce concept?

L'hon. Pierre Pettigrew (ministre des Affaires étrangères):

"La responsabilité de protéger" est le titre du rapport final d'un groupe d'experts formés par le Canada, afin d'étudier la question de l'intervention humanitaire. Notre objectif est de veiller à ce que la communauté internationale ait les outils et la volonté pour réagir aux futures tragédies comme celle du Darfour et du Rwanda ... Nous souhaitons maintenant que les Nations Unies adoptent ces principes comme étant les leurs ... [N]ous employons à dégager le consensus nécessaire pour réaliser cet objectif en faveur de la responsabilité de protéger.

(House of Commons Debates, 26 November 2004, pp. 1971–72)
(Débats de la Chambre des Communes, le 26 novembre 2004, pp. 1971–72)

M. Bernard Patry (Pierrefonds — Dollard):

Le Sommet de la Francophonie qui vient de se terminer à Ouagadougou, au Burkina Faso, a vu la Francophonie internationale prendre un virage résolument politique ... [E]n quoi ce virage politique permettra de faciliter la mise en place de solutions efficaces aux problèmes qui affligent entre autres la Côte-d'Ivoire?

L'hon. Jacques Saada (ministre de l'Agence de développement économique du Canada pour les régions du Québec et ministre responsable de la Francophonie):

[A]u Sommet de la Francophonie, plus de 60 pays ont entériné le principe de la responsabilité de protéger, qui est un principe que le premier ministre du Canada met de l'avant aux Nations Unies pour transformer celles-ci et les rendre plus humanistes. Au sommet, la Côte-d'Ivoire a fait l'objet d'une résolution qui confirme la résolution des Nations Unies, en particulier pour l'embargo sur les armes. Nous savons à quel point cette question est importante en Côte-d'Ivoire.

(House of Commons Debates, 29 November 2004, pp. 2031–32)
(Débats de la Chambre des Communes, le 29 novembre 2004, pp. 2031–32)

M. David McGuinty (Ottawa-Sud):

[L]a situation au Togo, pays membre de la Francophonie, est extrêmement préoccupante. À la mort du président Eyadéma, le Togo n'a pas respecté sa Constitution qui prévoyait que dans l'intérim d'une élection le président de l'Assemblée nationale devait exercer ses fonctions présidentielles. Or, les militaires ont mis au pouvoir le fils du président défunt. Cela déstabilise le Togo. Que fait la Francophonie pour dénoncer cette situation?

L'hon. Jacques Saada (ministre de l'Agence de développement économique du Canada pour les régions du Québec et ministre responsable de la Francophonie):

[L]a situation au Togo est effectivement très préoccupante ... [J]'ai personnellement rencontré l'ambassadeur du Togo à Ottawa. Mercredi, la Francophonie, par le truchement du Conseil permanent de la Francophonie, s'est réunie à Paris. Le sherpa canadien y a assisté, et une décision a été prise par le Conseil permanent de la Francophonie de suspendre le Togo des instances de la Francophonie et de suspendre toute aide au Togo provenant par le truchement de la Francophonie internationale, jusqu'à ce que la situation soit corrigée. Nous demandons instamment au Togo de respecter sa propre Constitution et de tenir des élections libres et démocratiques, comme c'est prévu dans cette dernière.

(House of Commons Debates, 11 February 2005, p. 3399)
(Débats de la Chambre des Communes, le 11 février 2005, p. 3399)

(c) Haiti / Haïti

Mme Francine Lalonde (La Pointe-de-l'Île):

[L]e *Washington Post* a dénoncé, le dimanche 5 juin, l'échec de l'ONU et du gouvernement de transition en Haïti, demandant au gouvernement américain d'étudier un nouvel envoi de marines. Les journaux et observateurs haïtiens s'inquiètent aussi de la croissance de l'insécurité, pendant que le Conseil électoral provisoire n'écarte pas l'idée de reporter les élections à une date ultérieure. Quelles mesures le ... [Canada] entend-il proposer, à la Conférence internationale de Montréal sur Haïti, les 16 et 17 juin, pour tenter d'améliorer la situation de ce pays? ... Le ... [Canada] entend-il s'employer à insister auprès des partenaires internationaux pour que s'effectue un désarmement efficace, indispensable à la tenue ordonnée des élections?

L'hon. Pierre Pettigrew (ministre des Affaires étrangères):

Haïti connaît une période extrêmement difficile ... [N]ous nous attendions à ce que l'insécurité augmente à mesure que nous approchions des élections. Notre gouvernement, tout comme les autres membres de la communauté internationale et les gens de l'Organisation des États américains, par le biais de l'Assemblée générale, ont réitéré leur appui au processus électoral que nous souhaitons maintenir ... [N]otre gouvernement souhaite ce désarmement extrêmement important. La MINUSTAH, la mission des Nations Unies, doit voir son mandat renouvelé le 24 juin. Il serait souhaitable que ce mandat soit renforcé. Pour ce qui est du travail de la police, le Canada est heureux de sa propre contribution avec une centaine de policiers. En effet, la MINUSTAH doit faire sa part sur le plan militaire, mais sa mission doit également reposer sur le travail que fait la police. Je crois qu'il s'agit là, en effet, d'une priorité de la communauté internationale.

(House of Commons Debates, 8 June 2005, p. 6821)
(Débats de la Chambre des Communes, le 8 juin 2005, p. 6821)

(d) India / Inde

Ms. Ruby Dhalla (Brampton — Springdale):

[W]hat is the status of the Canada-India bilateral air agreement?

Hon. Jean Lapierre (Minister of Transport):

[T]hese are happy times with Canada-India relations. Last month we celebrated the return of Air-India regular flights to Canada and today we just completed an agreement with India. We are going to increase by fivefold to 35 round trip flights per week for each country. It is going to be a great improvement on Canada-India relations and it is a great agreement for Canada and for India.

(House of Commons Debates, 7 June 2005, p. 6736)
(Débats de la Chambre des Communes, le 7 juin 2005, p. 6736)

(e) Iran

Mr. Paul Forseth (New Westminster — Coquitlam):

[T]he government's relationship with Iran appears muddled and pretty confused. It admits the tragedy of the Kazemi case and then withdraws its ambassador for a while ... Why does the government not have any plan at all to be a leader at the UN with our allies to make human rights mean something and to create a circle of pressure on this rogue state?

Hon. Pierre Pettigrew (Minister of Foreign Affairs):

[T]his is very much what the Government of Canada has been doing. For two years in a row, it has been Canada, at the ... United Nations ... that has been sponsoring a resolution condemning the situation of human rights in Iran. For two years in a row we received the support of the international community. We will continue to put pressure on Iran.

(House of Commons Debates, 5 April 2005, p. 4704)
(Débats de la Chambre des Communes, le 5 avril 2005, p. 4704)

(f) Iraq / Irak

M. Jean-Claude D'Amours (Madawaska — Restigouche):

[L]es Canadiennes et les Canadiens et le monde attendent les résultats définitifs de l'élection qui a eu lieu en Irak, dimanche ... [Quelle est] la réaction du Canada à cette élection historique?

L'hon. Pierre Pettigrew (ministre des Affaires étrangères):

[L]e Canada salue le courage du peuple irakien [qui,] malgré les conditions difficiles et dangereuses, [s'est] ... rendu aux urnes ... Leur détermination et leur attachement au processus démocratique représentent une source d'inspiration pour nous.

(House of Commons Debates, 31 January 2005, p. 2851)
(Débats de la Chambre des Communes, le 31 janvier 2005, p. 2851)

(g) Israel / Israël

Mrs. Carolyn Parrish (Mississauga — Erindale):

According to John Ibbitson of the *Globe and Mail*, large bodies of officials at Foreign Affairs and CIDA are convinced that Canada is about to sacrifice its hard won reputation as an honest broker in the Middle East, a reputation established by Lester B. Pearson in the 1956 Suez crisis. Is the cabinet considering a change in policy in the Israeli-Palestinian conflict?

Hon. Pierre Pettigrew (Minister of Foreign Affairs):

Canada's longstanding Middle East policy is focused on the goal of peace, security and the well-being of Israelis, Palestinians and the other people of the region. It has been endorsed by successive governments over decades. Canada has been a staunch friend and ally of Israel since 1948 ... Our policy in the Middle East reflects our support and concerns, and remains unchanged. Canada's policy remains anchored in our support for international law and our desire to play a constructive role toward peace in the region.

(House of Commons Debates, 21 October 2004, p. 681)
(Débats de la Chambre des Communes, le 21 octobre 2004, p. 681)

Mme Francine Lalonde (La Pointe-de-l'Île):

[L]a décision prise par la Knesset hier de quitter la bande de Gaza sera une bonne nouvelle à deux conditions: d'abord, qu'Israël quitte définitivement la bande de Gaza, où un port et un aéroport pourront alors être construits, et les frontières avec l'Égypte réouvertes; deuxièmement, que, sur la base du tracé des frontières de 1967, reprennent les négociations pour la création de l'État palestinien. Le ministre des Affaires étrangères mettra-t-il tout son poids pour qu'il en soit ainsi?

L'hon. Pierre Pettigrew (ministre des Affaires étrangères):

[M]anifestement, cette initiative prise par Israël de se retirer de la bande de Gaza et d'une partie de la Cisjordanie ne peut être qu'une très bonne nouvelle. Nous l'accueillons bien sûr avec beaucoup de plaisir. Le vote d'hier est donc manifestement une mesure positive. Nous continuons d'appuyer bien sûr le processus de paix. Le Canada appuie depuis longtemps la création de deux États qui pourraient vivre l'un à côté de l'autre en paix manifestement.

(House of Commons Debates, 27 October 2004, p. 829)
(Débats de la Chambre des Communes, le 27 octobre 2004, p. 829)

(h) Middle East / Moyen-Orient

Mr. Stockwell Day (Okanagan — Coquihalla):

[P]rior to his trip to the Middle East, the Minister of Foreign Affairs had requests from Canadian Lebanese organizations to meet with their democratic counterparts in Lebanon. These groups, quite rightly, are opposed to Syria's occupation of Lebanon and they fear the work of groups like Hezbollah ... Why would the minister meet with the dictators of Syria but not meet with these democratic organizations in Lebanon?

Hon. Pierre Pettigrew (Minister of Foreign Affairs):

I[t] ... is important ... to meet these individuals, whether in Lebanon or in Syria, and tell them that Canada supports resolution 1559 which requires Syria to leave the territory of Lebanon. It was easy to meet people who, like Canada, think that Syria should leave the territory, but I prefer to meet the leaders in Syria and Lebanon.

(House of Commons Debates, 14 February 2005, p. 3451)
(Débats de la Chambre des Communes, le 14 février 2005, p. 3451)

(i) North Atlantic Treaty Organization (NATO) / Organisation du Traité de l'Atlantique Nord (OTAN)

Mr. Anthony Rota (Nipissing — Timiskaming):

[F]ormer chief of defence staff General Ray Henault was formally installed as chairman of NATO's military committee on Thursday. What does this mean for NATO and what does this mean for Canada?

Hon. Bill Graham (Minister of National Defence):

[T]he appointment of our former chief of defence staff as the highest ranking military officer in NATO ... will give a chance for Canada's perspective to be brought forward at the highest councils of NATO as it goes forward with its transformation in the hands of a highly professional, dedicated officer ... It is most important to bring a Canadian perspective there at this time. We are grateful he is there.

(House of Commons Debates, 17 June 2005, p. 7374)
(Débats de la Chambre des Communes, le 17 juin 2005, p. 7374)

(j) United Nations / Organisation des Nations Unies

Mr. Stockwell Day (Okanagan — Coquihalla):

[T]he UN is currently facing a serious challenge to its credibility. The Iraqi oil for food scandal investigation is reaching into the highest levels of power in France and Russia, even into the hierarchy of the United Nations itself. As the Prime Minister meets with these very leaders, is he urging them and their ministers to be totally transparent and co-operative with the UN investigation, so that this dark cloud that is presently hanging over the Security Council may be lifted?

Hon. Pierre Pettigrew (Minister of Foreign Affairs):

[T]he Prime Minister uses all opportunities that he has with leaders whether in Paris or Moscow. We think the Prime Minister had a very good visit yesterday in Moscow, where he brought certain elements to the attention of President Putin. On Iraq and the other subjects that the member is raising, we are of course always promoting full support for the work of the United Nations and for transparency on these issues.

(House of Commons Debates, 13 October 2004, p. 319)
(Débats de la Chambre des Communes, le 13 octobre 2004, p. 319)

M. Francis Scarpaleggia (Lac-Saint-Louis):

Les Nations Unies ont dévoilé cette semaine un ensemble de propositions, 101 au total, élaborées par un comité des sages visant la plus profonde réforme de l'organisation depuis sa création en 1945. Le ministre pourrait-il nous dire comment il accueille ce rapport?

L'hon. Pierre Pettigrew (ministre des Affaires étrangères):

[N]ous sommes heureux de ce rapport, qui comporte de nombreuses re-commandations d'intérêt pour le Canada, et nous félicitons le comité des sages pour sa vision et son courage. Nous sommes particulièrement en-couragés ici, au Canada, par le fait que deux initiatives canadiennes im-portantes, soit la responsabilité de protéger et le L-20, c'est-à-dire le G-20 des leaders, aient été incluses dans le rapport. Comme le premier ministre l'a dit hier, il s'agit d'un pas très important pour le Canada, qui travaille activement en faveur d'une politique étrangère dynamique.

(House of Commons Debates, 3 December 2004, pp. 2259–60)
(Débats de la Chambre des Communes, le 3 décembre 2004, pp. 2259–60)

(k) Russia / Russie

Mr. Bill Casey (Cumberland — Colchester — Musquodoboit Valley):

[T]he Russian prosecutor general [has sent a letter] regarding the ille-gally confiscated hotel in Moscow, owned by a Canadian investors, I.M.P., in Halifax ... [I]t says that the prosecutor general of the Russian Federa-tion "is ready to initiate dialogue and cooperation" in this matter. Would the Minister of Foreign Affairs ... put the full weight of his department behind this exercise to get justice for this company and take advantage of this new opening by the prosecutor general of the Russian Federation?

Hon. Pierre Pettigrew (Minister of Foreign Affairs):

[T]his is ... a dossier on which the government has been working very hard over the last few years. [E]very time we have had the opportunity, the [Government] ... have argued strongly that the true judicial system enlightens this thing very well. We very much believe that this is evolving in the right direction.

(House of Commons Debates, 3 December 2004, p. 2260)
(Débats de la Chambre des Communes, le 3 décembre 2004, p. 2260)

(l) Somalia / Somalie

Mr. Alan Tonks (York South — Weston):

As Somalia's new government and newly elected president, Abdullahi Yusuf Ahmed, prepare to restore and return order after years of state collapse, according to a new report by the Norwegian Refugee Council, the country's 400,000 internally displaced people remain in a highly precarious situation. Now that there is a democratic government in place, when will we recognize this government and what actions will our government take to help end the humanitarian crisis in Somalia?

Hon. Pierre Pettigrew (Minister of Foreign Affairs):

[W]e welcome the inauguration of Abdullahi Yusuf Ahmed as transitional president of Somalia. Canada has never stopped recognizing the Somalian state. Canada is committed to addressing the serious humanitarian situation in Somalia. We recently provided a $1 million contribution to the World Food Program. We have provided more than $45 million in humanitarian aid to Somalia since 1991.

(House of Commons Debates, 1 December 2004, p. 2129)
(Débats de la Chambre des Communes, le 1er décembre 2004, p. 2129)

(m) Sudan / Soudan

Mr. Navdeep Bains (Mississauga — Brampton South):

[T]he Prime Minister will be travelling to Khartoum to meet with Sudanese President Omar al-Bashir ... [O]ver 70,000 people have died and over 1.5 million people have been displaced from their homes in the Darfur region of Sudan. Can we be assured that the Prime Minister will confront the Sudanese president about the continuing human rights violations in Darfur?

Hon. Dan McTeague (Parliamentary Secretary to the Minister of Foreign Affairs):

[T]he Prime Minister will continue to press urgently for a resolution to this conflict. This of course will be one of the issues he raises next week when he meets with the Sudanese president ... [W]e have taken a number of initiatives at the United Nations with respect to the Security Council members in support of a resolution that enhanced the African Union mission and $20 million to help in that effort.

(House of Commons Debates, 24 November 2004, pp. 1817–18) (Débats de la Chambre des Communes, le 24 novembre 2004, pp. 1817–18)

(n) Ukraine / Ukraine

Mr. Borys Wrzesnewskyj (Etobicoke Centre):

Ukrainian officials recently summoned Canada's ambassador to Ukraine for publicly raising alarms about the possibility of an undemocratic election in the country's upcoming presidential election ... What is Canada doing to make it clear to Ukrainian authorities that a genuinely democratic political system is a prerequisite for the country's full integration into the western community of nations?

Hon. Pierre Pettigrew (Minister of Foreign Affairs):

[O]n September 21 our ambassador in Kiev declared publicly Canada's serious concern that the elections may fail to meet democratic standards. The Government of Canada is sending about 40 observers, one of the largest contingents ever to observe the election. Our embassy is also leading an informal group of 25 diplomatic missions working together in Ukraine to monitor electoral developments. Canada is actively engaged in efforts to encourage a free and fair election in Ukraine.

(House of Commons Debates, 13 October 2004, p. 317) (Débats de la Chambre des Communes, le 13 octobre 2004, p. 317)

Hon. Stephen Harper (Leader of the Opposition):

[M]illions of people are on the streets of Ukraine ... to protest irregularities in that country's elections ... Is the government willing ... to take action and ... send signals that it will withhold recognition or even assistance to ensure that after a century of struggle against Soviet communism, Ukraine will never again return to undemocratic rule?

Hon. Anne McLellan (Deputy Prime Minister and Minister of Public Safety and Emergency Preparedness):

Considering the allegations of serious and significant electoral fraud from international and Canadian election observers, the Government of Canada cannot accept that the announced results by the central election commission reflect the true democratic will of the Ukrainian people. Therefore Canada rejects the announced final results. The Government of Canada calls for a full, open and transparent review of the election process. Canada will have no choice but to examine its relations with Ukraine if the authorities fail to provide election results that reflect the democratic will of the people of that country.

(House of Commons Debates, 24 November 2004, pp. 1810–11)
(Débats de la Chambre des Communes, le 24 novembre 2004, pp. 1810–11)

Hon. Stephen Harper (Leader of the Opposition):

The Ukrainian Canadian Congress has requested 1,500 observers for elections there. People are also asking for an assurance that there will be no Russian intervention. Has the Prime Minister called in the ambassador of Russia to ensure that elections will be respected, there will be no intervention, and there will be a recognition of a free and fair result?

Hon. Pierre Pettigrew (Minister of Foreign Affair):

[T]he Government of Canada will be ready to send up to 500 qualified observers. We have informed the OSCE to ensure that there will be a fair and transparent election.

(House of Commons Debates, 6 December 2004, p. 2308)
(Débats de la Chambre des Communes, le 6 décembre 2004, p. 2308)

(o) United States of America / États-Units

Mr. John Maloney (Welland):

[We all] know how critical it is that our border with the U.S. remains open to the efficient flow of goods and commerce ... Could the [Government] ... update the House on what [it] ... is doing to ensure access across the Canada-U.S. border?

Hon. Roy Cullen (Parliamentary Secretary to the Minister of Public Safety and Emergency Preparedness):

[T]he Deputy Prime Minister and Secretary Tom Ridge announced today a variety of initiatives to help make border crossing secure and efficient through new fast lanes, integrated border enforcement and, at the Fort Erie border crossing, the examination of options around pre-screening and pre-clearance.

(House of Commons Debates, 14 October 2004, p. 387)
(Débats de la Chambre des Communes, le 14 octobre 2004, p. 387)

Mr. Dave MacKenzie (Oxford):

The United States has now been forced to partner with Sweden in a submarine training program ... [W]hy have we been left behind in submarine warfare capabilities in the Atlantic, Pacific and Arctic waters?

Hon. Bill Graham (Minister of National Defence):

The United States navy partners with lots of other countries. It not only deals with Sweden, it deals with many of our NATO allies. Fortunately I can say that the Canadian navy has one of the best records of working with the United States navy ... and we will continue to do so. We welcome other countries to work with us both together.

(House of Commons Debates, 28 October 2004, pp. 908–9)
(Débats de la Chambre des Communes, le 28 octobre 2004, pp. 908–9)

Mr. Ken Boshcoff (Thunder Bay — Rainy River):

Nearly $1.8 billion in two-way trade across Canada crosses the Canada-U.S. border everyday. About 86% of our exports to the U.S. and 96% of our trade is dispute free, but trade irritants from softwood lumber to the Byrd amendment continue to dominate the headlines. What will the minister do to ease these irritants and improve our trade relations with the United States?

Hon. Jim Peterson (Minister of International Trade):

[T]he U.S. trade relationship is critical to our prosperity. We have opened seven new consulates and we have created the Washington advocacy secretariat. Yesterday, I met in Washington with the new secretary of commerce and I look forward to working with him to resolve our trade disputes, promote North American competitiveness and foster global trade liberalization. On March 1 I will be leading a Canadian advocacy day in Washington, along with the Canada-U.S. parliamentary group who will meet with our American counterparts.

(House of Commons Debates, 15 February 2005, p. 3525)
(Débats de la Chambre des Communes, le 15 février 2005, p. 3525)

3   Health / Santé

(a) Framework Convention on Tobacco Control / La Convention-cadre de l'OMS pour la lutte antitabac[15]

L'hon. Don Boudria (Glengarry — Prescott — Russell):

En mai 2003, l'Assemblée mondiale de la santé a approuvé la Convention-cadre pour la lutte antitabac. Pourquoi le Canada n'a-t-il toujours pas ratifié cette convention, et quand va-t-on le faire?

Hon. Ujjal Dosanjh (Minister of Health):

[T]he framework convention on tobacco control is a very important convention that Canada signed on to last year. It is important that we ratify that convention. We are on our way to very quickly ratifying that convention. We believe in strong tobacco control.

(House of Commons Debates, 18 November 2004, p. 1549)
(Débats de la Chambre des Communes, le 18 novembre 2004, p. 1549)

(b) HIV-AIDS / VIH-SIDA

Mr. David McGuinty (Ottawa South):

[W]hat the government ... ha[s] done to demonstrate empathy for [human suffering caused by HIV-AIDS ...?]

Hon. Aileen Carroll (Minister of International Cooperation):

[T]his morning the United Nations released its report that showed the terrible progression of this crisis. Almost 40 million people are now living

---

[15] Framework Convention on Tobacco Control (Geneva, Switzerland, 21 May 2003; *entered into force* 27 February 2005), reprinted in (2003) 42 I.L.M. 518. Canada has been a party to the convention since 26 November 2004 by ratification.

with AIDS, and the toll on women is horrific. In Africa fully 76% of young people with the disease are women ... [W]e are committed to leading the fight against AIDS. We provided $100 million to the World Health 3 by 5 initiative.[16] The leader of World Health, Dr. Lee, told us that the Canadian lead is a historic ["opportunity we cannot afford to miss."17]

(House of Commons Debates, 23 November 2004, p. 1729)
(Débats de la Chambre des Communes, le 23 novembre 2004, p. 1729)

(c) Human cloning / Le clonage humain

Mr. Paul Szabo (Mississauga South):

Bill C-6 on reproductive technologies passed in the last Parliament and was represented to include a comprehensive ban on human cloning.[18] However, at the same time Canadian representatives before the United Nations were supporting a resolution for only a partial ban, which would permit a form of human cloning called somatic cell nuclear transfer, otherwise known as therapeutic cloning. Will ... our law ... continue to be a comprehensive ban on human cloning by all forms and techniques, including therapeutic cloning?

Hon. Robert Thibault (Parliamentary Secretary to the Minister of Health):

[T]he government's position on human cloning is clear. As of April 2004,[19] under the Assisted Human Reproduction Act, all forms of human cloning are prohibited in Canada for whatever purpose and using whatever technique. Even though therapeutic cloning is now prohibited, important research involving stem cells can still proceed. The Assisted Human Reproduction Act establishes a framework within which research involving in vitro embryos to derive stem cells can be undertaken. Researchers wishing to undertake embryo research to derive stem cells will have to comply with strict regulations.

16 Editor's note: World Health Organization, *The Three by Five Initiative*, "Canada's Landmark Contribution to *Three by Five*," May-June 2004, at <www.who.int/3by5/mediacentre>.

17 Editor's note: *Ibid.*, and WHO, *The World Health Report 2004: Changing History*, Message from the Director-General, at ix; online at <www.who.int/whr>.

18 Editor's note: Bill C-6, An Act Respecting Assisted Human Reproduction and Related Research, was introduced and passed all readings in the House of Commons on 11 February 2004.

19 Editor's note: Bill C-6 received Royal Assent on 29 March 2004.

(House of Commons Debates, 15 October 2004, p. 434)
(Débats de la Chambre des Communes, le 15 octobre 2004, p. 434)

Mr. Rob Merrifield (Yellowhead):

[T]he United Nations General Assembly passed a declaration to ban all forms of human cloning.[20] The margin was 84 to 34, but Canada voted against the ban ... Why has the government gone back on its word?

Hon. Pierre Pettigrew (Minister of Foreign Affairs):

[I]t is very important that we read the resolution as it stands. While important elements of the UN declaration are consistent with Canada's domestic legislation on the prohibition of cloning, the government is unable to support it due to its imprecise drafting, unfortunately ... We could not support the declaration because of the new provisions that were added to the text and expanded its scope beyond cloning. These new provisions were so vague they were raising concerns that they could affect other areas of reproductive health that are quite important for many Canadian families in this country.[21]

(House of Commons Debates, 8 March 2005, p. 4119)
(Débats de la Chambre des Communes, le 8 mars 2005, p. 4119)

(d) Pharmaceutical industry / Industrie pharmaceutique

Mr. Steven Fletcher (Charleswood — St. James — Assiniboia):

Last week the health minister told an American audience in Boston that Internet pharmacies in Canada would not be a drugstore for the United States.[22] Later in the week the Prime Minister said that his government

---

20 Editor's note: United Nations Declaration on Human Cloning, Doc. A/RES/59/280 (8 March 2005).

21 Editor's note: In his explanation after the vote on the declaration, the representative of Canada said reproductive cloning was illegal in Canada in whatever form. The ambiguity of the declaration might give rise to certain political and other concerns. See United Nations, Press Release GA/10333, *General Assembly Adopts United Nations Declaration on Human Cloning by vote of 84-34-37* (8 March 2005), at <http://www.un.org/News/>.

22 Editor's note: See, for example, Christopher Rowland, "Canada Threatens to Halt Shipments of Drugs to US," *Boston Globe*, 11 November 2004, at <www.boston.com/news/globe/>.

had no plans or intentions to shut down Internet pharmacies[23] ... Who should Canadians believe, the Prime Minister or the health minister?

Hon. Ujjal Dosanjh (Minister of Health):

The Harvard University Medical School invited me to speak on the state of health in Canada. I wanted to ensure that I canvassed the issues that were important to both our jurisdictions. One of the issues that has been important for some time is the issue of drug prescriptions. I said then and I say now, and the Prime Minister agrees with me, that a small country like Canada cannot be a drugstore for the United States of America. ... [T]he safety and supply of drugs for Canadians is of utmost importance and we will protect that at any cost.

(House of Commons Debates, 15 November 2004, p. 1330)
(Débats de la Chambre des Communes, le 15 novembre 2004, p. 1330)

(e) Polio

M. Marc Godbout (Ottawa — Orléans):

[N]ous avons récemment appris que de nouveaux cas de polio sont apparus au Yémen et en Indonésie ... [Quelles] mesures ... le Canada et ses partenaires ... [prennent-ils] pour combattre cette terrible maladie?

L'hon. Aileen Carroll (ministre de la Coopération internationale):

[Nous] suivra ... de très près le développement de nouveaux cas de polio. ... Le Canada a investi près de 200 millions de dollars dans cette lutte, et nous continuerons d'appuyer des initiatives afin d'enrayer la polio partout dans le monde.

(House of Commons Debates, 3 June 2005, p. 6609)
(Débats de la Chambre des Communes, le 3 juin 2005, p. 6609)

(f) World Health Organization / Organisation mondiale de la santé

Ms. Beth Phinney (Hamilton Mountain):

[T]here has been considerable talk recently about the risk of a worldwide pandemic and the preparedness of different countries in dealing with such

---

23 Editor's note: Prime Minister Paul Martin denied that Canada was trying to drive Internet pharmacies out of business. See, for example, "Canada Not Trying to Kill Web Drugstores, PM Says," *Reuters*, 13 November 2004, at <today. reuters.co.uk>.

a problem ... [W]hat steps is the government taking to protect Canadians against a potential pandemic?

Hon. Carolyn Bennett (Minister of State (Public Health):

Canada has a comprehensive pandemic influenza plan which the World Health Organization has called a best model for other countries. Today the [Government was] at the WHO in New York to launch the next phase of the global public health intelligence network. This made-in-Canada early warning system gathers and disseminates the reports of public health significance in real time on a 24/7 basis, in seven languages, at the Public Health Agency of Canada.

(House of Commons Debates, 17 November 2004, pp. 1483-84) (Débats de la Chambre des Communes, le 17 novembre 2004, pp. 1483–84)

Mr. Wajid Khan (Mississauga — Streetsville):

[T]he deadly Asian bird flu is poised to trigger a global influenza pandemic. The World Health Organization is urging governments to start manufacturing and stockpiling vaccines to respond to this threat ... [How does the Government] plan ... to answer the WHO's request?

Hon. Ujjal Dosanjh (Minister of Health):

[W]e are actually ahead of the pack on this very issue. Already we have purchased 16 million doses of the anti-viral that is required for this kind of pandemic. The World Health Organization in fact has called Canada's pandemic flu plan a model for other countries and has said, "Canada is more prepared by far than any other country in the world for pandemic influenza."

(House of Commons Debates, 17 February 2005, p. 3651) (Débats de la Chambre des Communes, le 17 février 2005, p. 3651)

Mr. Stockwell Day (Okanagan — Coquihalla):

[L]ast year the foreign affairs committee voted to support Taiwan's request for observer status at the World Health Assembly and then all of Parliament voted to support that also. When it came time to vote at the World Health Assembly, the government instructed our delegates to vote no ... Last week the foreign affairs committee again voted to support Taiwan's request just for observer status ... [W]ill the government ... support Taiwan?

Hon. Pierre Pettigrew (Minister of Foreign Affairs):

Canada has always supported appropriate representation for Taiwan at the World Health Assembly. We have been working quite actively with others toward making that a reality. Canada would most certainly support a World Health Assembly consensus regarding Taiwan's participation in and access to the World Health Organization. We are encouraged by the very fact that our efforts have been noticed and appreciated by Taiwan's representative in Geneva, the vice-minister of foreign affairs and most recent, from Taiwan's minister of health ... [W]e will continue to work with the other members of the World Health Organization to ensure that Taiwan is appropriately represented at these institutions. We will ensure that population benefits from and contributes to the services that the World Health Organization can provide.

(House of Commons Debates, 9 May 2005, p. 5813)
(Débats de la Chambre des Communes, le 9 mail 2005, p. 5813)

4   Human Rights / Les droits de la personne

(a) China / Chine

M. Roger Clavet (Louis-Hébert):

[L]e ministre peut-il nous indiquer s'il a protesté auprès des autorités chinoises, ou s'il s'apprête à le faire, pour sauver la vie du lama tibétain [Tenzin Delek Rinpoche]?

L'hon. Pierre Pettigrew (ministre des Affaires étrangères):

En effet, de hauts représentants du Canada ont d'ores et déjà intercédé à plusieurs reprises auprès des autorités chinoises, à Pékin comme à Ottawa, concernant Tenzin Delek Rinpoche. Des représentants du Canada ont exprimé nos préoccupations à propos de cette affaire, en particulier lors de réunions qui se sont tenues à Pékin cette année, préoccupations quant à l'impartialité de son procès. Nous leur avons demandé d'empêcher cette exécution. Dernièrement, nous nous sommes également efforcés, avec la collaboration d'autres gouvernements étrangers, de porter nos préoccupations à propos de cette affaire à l'attention des autorités chinoises.

(House of Commons Debates, 1 December 2004, p. 2131)
(Débats de la Chambre des Communes, le 1er décembre 2004, p. 2131)

Mr. Stockwell Day (Okanagan — Coquihalla):

[C]ommunist China has demonstrated a horrible record of human rights violations to the people and the territory of Tibet ... [H]ow aggressively [has the Government] raised this specific issue of Tibet with the Chinese leaders?

Right Hon. Paul Martin (Prime Minister):

[I]n addition to having been the only one who met at that time with the Chinese leadership, I am also the first Canadian Prime Minister who had ever met with the Dalai Lama.

Hon. Pierre Pettigrew (Minister of Foreign Affairs):

[R]espect for human rights, including cultural and religious freedoms, minority rights and freedom of expression or association, are important objectives of Canada's views on the situation in Tibet ... It is absolutely part of our foreign policy and of our preoccupations. We will continue to do this ... Canada has consistently spoken out about the human rights situation in China. We have specifically mentioned Tibet in our public statements at the United Nations Commission on Human Rights and at the United Nations General Assembly ... We continue to express Canadian concerns about the human rights situation in China and to Chinese authorities. The Prime Minister, when he met with Prime Minister Wen of China, even gave him a list of cases that preoccupy Canadians ... Th[e] ... Prime Minister signed with Prime Minister Wen a declaration on both sides broadening dialogue between Canadians and Chinese institutions.

(House of Commons Debates, 1 February 2005, pp. 2933–34) (Débats de la Chambre des Communes, le 1er février 2005, pp. 2933–34)

(b) Colombia / Colombie

Mr. Mario Silva (Davenport):

[T]he human rights conflict in Colombia is critical. The internal armed conflict claims the lives of approximately 11 people each day and has created the third highest internally displaced population in the world after Sudan and Angola ... What action is the Canadian government taking to improve the human rights situation in Colombia?

Hon. Pierre Pettigrew (Minister of Foreign Affairs):

[W]e share the concerns ... about the serious human rights situation in Colombia. Our embassy staff in Bogota travels to the conflict areas of Colombia to provide strong and visible support to vulnerable groups and individuals and continually urges the Colombian government, directly and through the United Nations and other organizations, to respect its international human rights obligations. Canada currently chairs a group of 24 donor countries that are working with the Colombian government, United Nations agencies and civil society organizations to promote human rights across the country.

(House of Commons Debates, 31 May 2005, p. 6414)
(Débats de la Chambre des Communes, le 31 mai 2005, p. 6414)

(c) International adoption / Adoption internationale

M. Gilles Duceppe (Laurier — Sainte-Marie):

[A]ttendue depuis deux ans, la signature de l'entente Québec-Vietnam en matière d'adoption internationale est compromise ... [Le gouvernement peut-il nous donner les dernières informations à cet sujet?]

Le très hon. Paul Martin (premier ministre):

[L]e Vietnam ... exige un traité international avec les autres pays afin de permettre les adoptions internationales ... Après un moratoire de trois à quatre ans, l'adoption d'enfants vietnamiens par des Canadiens et des Canadiennes est maintenant permise. C'est une bonne nouvelle et je suis très content que le Canada ait pu signer une entente cadre et que maintenant les provinces, dont le Québec, vont pouvoir négocier à l'intérieur de ce cadre.

(House of Commons Debates, 28 June 2005, p. 7927)
(Débats de la Chambre des Communes, le 28 juin 2005, p. 7927)

(d) International Labour Organization and workers' rights / L'Organisation internationale du travail et les droits des travailleurs

Mme Pauline Picard (Drummond):

[N]os industries font face à des concurrents qui, parfois, pratiquent les pires formes d'exploitation, comme le travail forcé et le travail des enfants. Le Canada ne peut pas travailler à enrayer ces pratiques, puisqu'il n'a pas lui-même ratifié toutes les conventions de l'Organisation internationale du travail qui les interdisent. Qu'attend le gouvernement pour proposer à la Chambre la ratification des traités de l'OIT qui interdisent le travail forcé et le travail des enfants et qui obligent le respect de la liberté syndicale?

Hon. Joe Fontana (Minister of Labour and Housing):

[T]he Government of Canada, through its international labour organization, its membership, its unions and a number of other stakeholder parties, has done some great things around the world in making sure those labour standards, of which the member spoke, are adhered to. Canada has taken a leadership position ... to ensure that Canadian labour standards are upheld not only in Canada but throughout the world.

(House of Commons Debates, 8 October 2004, p. 187)
(Débats de la Chambre des Communes, le 8 octobre 2004, p. 187)

Mr. David Christopherson (Hamilton Centre):

The leadership of UFCW, NUPGE and the Canadian Labour Congress today have pointed out that Canada is a signatory to the United Nations international labour organization. We have ratified ILO conventions that promise to allow freedom of association and the collective bargaining process. The ... [Government] has refused to intervene in Wal-Mart's attack on its unionized workers. How will the government meet Canada's international treaty obligations in the face of Wal-Mart's abusive actions?

Hon. Joe Fontana (Minister of Labour and Housing):

[Canada] takes no back seat in terms of supporting workers' rights around the world. We are working and have adopted five of the eight international labour organizations. We are moving with the provinces to ratify those workers' rights protocols. We are doing everything possible to ensure workers' rights are protected. As for Wal-Mart, that is a provincial jurisdiction. In the provinces of Quebec and Saskatchewan, the provincial ministers are working on those issues right now.

(House of Commons Debates, 24 March 2005, p. 4567)
(Débats de la Chambre des Communes, le 24 mars 2005, p. 4567)

(e) Libya / Libye

Mr. Larry Miller (Bruce — Grey — Owen Sound):

[A] 47 year old man ... is being held in a Libyan prison after receiving a life sentence in 1998 for helping a group that works toward democratic change in Libya, which is under military dictatorship. According to Amnesty International, Libya's human rights record is horrendous, with reports of torture, death in custody and other punishments on political grounds. Will the Prime Minister be raising this issue with Moammar Gadhafi when he visits Tripoli later this month?

Hon. Pierre Pettigrew (Minister of Foreign Affairs):

The Prime Minister uses every opportunity he has to promote human rights on every one of his trips, and ... he will do the same thing when he visits Libya.

(House of Commons Debates, 14 December 2004, p. 2766) (Débats de la Chambre des Communes, le 14 décembre 2004, p. 2766)

(f) Multiculturalism and Cultural Diversity / Le multiculturalisme et la diversité culturelle

M. Maka Kotto (Saint-Lambert):

[L]es pays membres de l'UNESCO avaient jusqu'à aujourd'hui pour faire connaître leur position de négociation dans le cadre du projet de convention sur la diversité culturelle.[24] Or, le gouvernement fédéral n'a pas encore rendu publique sa position sur le projet de convention. Étant donné que le délai expire aujourd'hui même, le gouvernement canadien a-t-il fait connaître sa position à l'UNESCO, et si oui, quelle est-elle?

L'hon. Liza Frulla (ministre du Patrimoine canadien et ministre responsable de la Condition féminine):

Oui, nous allons faire connaître notre position aux autorités de l'UNESCO. C'est une première lecture d'un positionnement. Nous travaillons avec la Coalition pour la diversité culturelle aussi pour que nos positions reflètent celle du Canada, celle de la Coalition pour la diversité culturelle et aussi celle de l'ensemble des provinces.

(House of Commons Debates, 15 November 2004, p. 1332) (Débats de la Chambre des Communes, le 15 novembre 2004, p. 1332)

---

24 Editor's note: Convention on the Protection and Promotion of the Diversity of Cultural Expressions (Paris, France, 20 October 2005, not yet in force), available at <portal.unesco.org/culture/>. Canada has become the first state to ratify the convention on 23 November 2005.

(g) Protecting Canadians abroad / La protection des Canadiens à l'étranger

Ms. Marlene Catterall (Ottawa West Nepean):

Mr. Arar and his family have now lived under a cloud of suspicion for two years due to unproven allegations and independent innuendo by both agencies. Will the minister now insist that these agencies ... either bring forth evidence and lay charges ... or admit they do not have evidence and he is innocent?

Hon. Anne McLellan (Deputy Prime Minister and Minister of Public Safety and Emergency Preparedness):

Indeed, the government has taken this matter very seriously. That is why we established an independent commission of inquiry. Mr. Justice O'Connor is at this time hearing witnesses and reviewing evidence.

(House of Commons Debates, 6 October 2004, p. 34)
(Débats de la Chambre des Communes, le 6 octobre 2004, p. 34)

M. André Bellavance (Richmond — Arthabaska):

Nicolas Royer, de ma circonscription, est disparu dans des circonstances dramatiques au Pérou ... [Le gouvernement] entend-t-il autoriser les soldats volontaires de Valcartier ... pour aller prêter main-forte bénévolement aux recherches ... [et prendre] des dispositions spéciales avec le gouvernement du Pérou afin que ce personnel militaire puisse franchir les douanes péruviennes avec leur équipement spécialisé, et cela, sans aucun problème?

L'hon. Bill Graham (ministre de la Défense nationale):

Nous allons examiner ... de quelle façon nous pourrions aider aux recherches et à son retour ... En ce qui concerne la question d'envoyer présentement des militaires, c'est une question assez complexe. Cependant, nous allons étudier cette possibilité.

L'hon. Pierre Pettigrew (ministre des Affaires étrangères):

Notre ambassadrice à Lima et son personnel ainsi que mes fonctionnaires ici, à Ottawa, effectuent un travail de tous les instants pour coordonner les recherches avec les autorités péruviennes.

(House of Commons Debates, 6 December 2004, p. 2314)
(Débats de la Chambre des Communes, le 6 décembre 2004, p. 2314)

Mrs. Betty Hinton (Kamloops — Thompson — Cariboo):

[I]n June 2003 a Canadian, Zahra Kazemi, was assassinated while in the custody of the Iranian government ... Why did the Canadian government not intervene after her arrest and before her death?

Hon. Dan McTeague (Parliamentary Secretary to the Minister of Foreign Affairs):

[O]ur Canadian ambassador to Iran has taken up the case of Ms. Kazemi ... Canada has renewed its desire to have a trial that is both transparent and fair and which brings those perpetrators of that brutal murder to justice as soon as possible.

Mrs. Betty Hinton (Kamloops — Thompson — Cariboo):

The Iranian ambassador to Great Britain attributed Ms. Kazemi's death to "shrewd security forces," and added, "We're sorry for it." Not sorry enough ... to find her assassins ... What is the government going to do to rectify this situation?

Hon. Dan McTeague (Parliamentary Secretary to the Minister of Foreign Affairs):

[A] couple of months ago we in fact withdrew our ambassador as a most important sign of our condemnation of this act ... The comments of the Iranian ambassador to Britain are the latest in a line of comments from Iranian high officials ... that reflect [Canada's] serious concerns about the circumstances of Ms. Kazemi's death.

(House of Commons Debates, 10 February 2005, pp. 3353-54) (Débats de la Chambre des Communes, le 10 février 2005, pp. 3353-54)

(h) Racial discrimination / Discrimination raciale

Mrs. Susan Kadis (Thornhill):

March 21 marks the International Day for the Elimination of Racial Discrimination. ... [W]hat the [Government] ... plans to do to ensure that Canada continues to be at the forefront of the international struggle to combat racism[?]

Hon. Raymond Chan (Minister of State (Multiculturalism)):

Racism is still a very important issue and it prevents Canadians from participating fully in our society. This morning I was very proud to unveil Canada's first ever action plan against racism. This plan takes a horizontal, coordinated approach and includes new concrete measures in order to achieve an inclusive and equitable society.

(House of Commons Debates, 21 March 2005, p. 4369)
(Débats de la Chambre des Communes, le 21 mars 2005, p. 4369)

(i) Rights of women / Droits des femmes

Mr. Jim Prentice (Calgary Centre-North):

This week Amnesty International issued a ... report highlighting Canada's glaring and obvious inaction over the past decade toward the fact that Canadian aboriginal women face a higher risk of violence than other women in our society. The report states "In every instance, Canadian authorities could and should have done more to" protect these women. Why is the government failing to protect our aboriginal women from violence?

Hon. Andy Scott (Minister of Indian Affairs and Northern Development and Federal Interlocutor for Métis and Non-Status Indians):

On the question of the Amnesty report, I can only go to the Aboriginal Women's Association here in Canada. I have been meeting with them prior to and since the meeting and since the report and we are working on plans right now to deal specifically with that.

(House of Commons Debates, 8 October 2004, p. 188)
(Débats de la Chambre des Communes, le 8 octobre 2004, p. 188)

Mme Françoise Boivin (Gatineau):

[Le gouvernement] s'est rendue à New York, la semaine dernière, pour participer à la convention internationale du statut de la femme, 10 ans après la signature de la Déclaration de Beijing[25] ... [Q]ui a été accompli par le gouvernement du Canada pour promouvoir l'égalité entre les hommes et les femmes?

---

25 Editor's note: Beijing Declaration and Platform for Action, Fourth World Conference on Women, 15 September 1995, Doc. A/CONF.177/20 (1995) and Doc. A/CONF.177/20/Add.1 (1995).

L'hon. Liza Frulla (ministre du Patrimoine canadien et ministre responsable de la Condition féminine):

[L]a semaine dernière, j'ai dirigé la délégation canadienne à la réunion de Beijing +10 aux Nations Unies ... Le Canada a fermement réaffirmé son engagement envers la Déclaration et le Programme d'action de Beijing en matière d'égalité entre les sexes. Nous sommes également fiers, étant donné que nous sommes considérés comme étant un leader en la matière, de certaines réalisations, dont le cadre juridique qui soutient l'égalité entre les sexes et la prolongation de la durée des prestations parentales.

(House of Commons Debates, 8 March 2005, pp. 4118–19)
(Débats de la Chambre des Communes, le 8 mars 2005, pp. 4118–19)

(j) Self-Determination / Autodétermination

Ms. Rona Ambrose (Edmonton — Spruce Grove):

[C]an Quebec speak for Canada at international cultural forums?

Hon. Liza Frulla (Minister of Canadian Heritage and Minister Responsible for Status of Women):

[W]e want the province's voice to concur with our voice and to give it strength on the international level. En fait de diversité culturelle, on sait que le Québec est notre partenaire. On essaye aussi d'avoir un partenariat avec les autres provinces. Il faut dire que le Québec et le Canada s'entendent parfaitement bien sur la position à prendre, c'est-à-dire de signer une convention sur la diversité culturelle avant 2005.[26]

Hon. Pierre Pettigrew (Minister of Foreign Affairs):

[S]peaking on behalf of Canada and speaking on behalf of all Canadians clearly is this government's responsibility. Canada will continue to speak with one voice internationally ... after of course making sure that it is enriched by all of our jurisdictions.

(House of Commons Debates, 14 October 2004, p. 383)
(Débats de la Chambre des Communes, le 14 octobre 2004, p. 383)

---

26 See note 24 in this section.

Hon. Don Boudria (Glengarry — Prescott — Russell):

[O]ur foreign affairs minister urged both sides across the Taiwan Strait to reduce tensions ... [Has] Canada's position regarding this issue remain[ed] as it was?

Hon. Pierre Pettigrew (Minister of Foreign Affairs):

Canada has always maintained that the issue of Taiwan's status should be resolved through peaceful means by China and Taiwan themselves, and that the outcome be acceptable to people on both sides of the Taiwan Strait. Nous restons ... opposés à toute action unilatérale de l'une ou l'autre partie, qui pourrait provoquer une escalade de la tension, ce qui aurait des répercussions négatives sur la stabilité et la prospérité de la région.

(House of Commons Debates, 3 February 2005, p. 3054)
(Débats de la Chambre des Communes, le 3 février 2005, p. 3054)

(k) Social development / Développement social

Mme Françoise Boivin (Gatineau):

[A]ujourd'hui, le ministre du Développement social a signé avec la république d'Estonie un accord concernant la sécurité sociale ... Le ministre du Développement social peut-il me dire qui, exactement, va bénéficier de cet accord?

Hon. Ken Dryden (Minister of Social Development):

[T]oday we are very pleased to have signed a social security agreement with the Republic of Estonia. There are about 23,000 persons of Estonian descent in Canada, many of whom will qualify for pensions as a result of the agreement. The agreement will help enable those who have lived or worked in either of the two countries to receive old age, disability and survivor pensions, recognizing the contributions they have made and telling them that their work is valued and respected.

(House of Commons Debates, 21 February 2005, p. 3758)
(Débats de la Chambre des Communes, le 21 février 2005, p. 3758)

(l) United Nations millennium development goals / Objectifs de développement du millénaire des Nations Unies

Mme Francine Lalonde (La Pointe-de-l'Île):

[L]ors d'une conférence tenue par l'ACDI cette semaine, Stephen Lewis, conseiller spécial de Kofi Annan pour la lutte contre le SIDA et ancien ambassadeur du Canada à l'ONU, a fait un brillant exposé sur l'obligation pour les pays développés de verser le 0,7 p. 100 du PIB s'ils tiennent à atteindre les objectifs du millénaire: réduction de la faim et du SIDA, éducation, accès à l'eau potable. Quand le gouvernement [du Canada] ... décidera-t-il de faire sa ... part pour l'atteinte des objectifs du millénaire?

Hon. Aileen Carroll (Minister of International Cooperation):

[W]e have just received at CIDA an 8% budget increase last year and this year. That means we will be doubling our budget by the year 2010. We have a large and important commitment by the ... government to give us resources to effectively work with other donors, other countries and the UN to achieve the millennium development goals ... [I]n 2003 Canada ranked eighth among OECD members by ODA volume ... [I]t is fourth among G-8 members by ODA GPI, but really I think it is about coherency, effectiveness and our commitment to world poverty.

(House of Commons Debates, 4 November 2004, p. 1228)
(Débats de la Chambre des Communes, le 4 novembre 2004, p. 1228)

Mr. Ken Boshcoff (Thunder Bay — Rainy River):

The international community has launched a series of initiatives to promote financial systems that work for the poor, highlighting microfinance as an important tool for achieving the millennium development goal ...[W]hat Canada is doing to contribute to international developments in microfinance?

Hon. Aileen Carroll (Minister of International Cooperation):

[W]e are ... a strong supporter of microfinance and ... today ...[we are] announcing $4 million in new microfinance initiatives.

(House of Commons Debates, 10 December 2004, p. 2614)
(Débats de la Chambre des Communes, le 10 décembre 2004, p. 2614)

5   *International Criminal Law / Droit pénal international*

(a) Illegal importation / Importation illégale

Hon. Rob Nicholson (Niagara Falls):

[T]hree years after 9/11 our port security is still not adequate ... [The government] said that they would meet International Court security standards by July 1, yet the minister said that the ports were still sieves ... [W]hy has ... [the] government not done more to ensure the safety of Canadians?

Hon. Jean Lapierre (Minister of Transport):

[We are] very worried. Last week, a checker at the port of Montreal pleaded guilty to conspiracy for importing $2.1 billion of drugs: 31 tonnes of hashish and 265 kilos of cocaine ... Mon prédécesseur a annoncé un programme de 115 millions de dollars pour augmenter la sécurité dans les ports. Nous voulons nous assurer de faire des enquêtes sur les antécédents pour ne plus avoir de situations comme celle vécue dans le port de Montréal. Nous allons agir. Nous allons faire la différence. Les ports du Canada seront sécuritaires à l'avenir.

(House of Commons Debates, 12 October 2004, p. 217)
(Débats de la Chambre des Communes, le 12 octobre 2004, p. 217)

(b) Protocol on the sale of children / Protocole concernant la vente d'enfants[27]

Mr. Marc Godbout (Ottawa — Orléans):

Canada has not yet ratified the United Nations optional protocol to the convention on the rights of the child and the sale of children, child prostitution and child pornography. What will the Government of Canada do to address this important question, and thus better protect the rights of children, both domestically and internationally?

Hon. Irwin Cotler (Minister of Justice and Attorney General of Canada):

[T]he protection of children against all forms of sexual exploitation, including child pornography, is a priority of the government ... In the Speech from the Throne, we announced that we would take steps regarding the trafficking in children. We have signed the optional protocol. We are now consulting with the provinces with a view to securing ratification as soon as possible.

(House of Commons Debates, 14 December 2004, p. 2767)
(Débats de la Chambre des Communes, le 14 décembre 2004, p. 2767)

---

[27] Optional Protocol to the Convention on the Rights of the Child on the Sale of Children, Child Prostitution and Child Pornography, GA Res. 54/263, Doc. A/54/49 (25 May 2000); *entered into force* 18 January 2002); at <www.unhchr.ch>. Canada signed the protocol on 10 November 2001. It ratified the protocol on 14 September 2005.

(c) Terrorism / Terrorisme

Mr. Stockwell Day (Okanagan — Coquihalla):

Canada's closest ally, the United States, has banned the terrorist group Tawhid wa'l-Jihad, a group that has claimed responsibility for car bombings, suicide attacks and the deaths of literally thousands of Iraqis. Tawhid wa'l-Jihad is a threat to peace in Iraq, to Great Britain, to the United States and to Israel, and yet we refuse to join our allies in outlawing that offensive killing group, Tawhid wa'l-Jihad. When will Canada outlaw this group?

Hon. Pierre Pettigrew (Minister of Foreign Affairs):

[W]e will continue to pay very close attention to all the groups. We will continue to be absolutely clear that the government will want to promote the peace process ... We will continue to fight terrorism as we have been doing for a number of years by adding $7 billion and $8 billion to our capacity to fight terrorism.

(House of Commons Debates, 1 November 2004, p. 1007)
(Débats de la Chambre des Communes, le 1ᵉʳ novembre 2004, p. 1007)

Mr. Stockwell Day (Okanagan — Coquihalla):

Why is the government [of Canada] maintaining [a] ... go-slow policy when it comes to naming terrorist organizations?

Hon. Anne McLellan (Deputy Prime Minister and Minister of Public Safety and Emergency Preparedness):

We assess the risk on a daily basis in relation to groups who might in fact be carrying on activities in this country that might cause either Canadians or others harm ... [O]n October 18 of this year Canada listed the JTJ, and the appropriate freezing orders to all financial institutions were made. The JTJ was first listed by the United Nations Security Council as being associated with Osama bin Laden. Such measures by the UN are automatically incorporated into Canadian law by virtue of Canada being a member state of the United Nations.

(House of Commons Debates, 2 November 2004, p. 1083)
(Débats de la Chambre des Communes, le 2 novembre 2004, p. 1083)

(d) Trafficking in humans / Trafic de personnes

Mrs. Nina Grewal (Fleetwood — Port Kells):

Many people unwittingly sell themselves into a life of sexual or economic slavery ... Canada can no longer turn a blind eye to this victimization. When will the government ... put a stop to human smuggling?

Hon. Roy Cullen (Parliamentary Secretary to the Minister of Public Safety and Emergency Preparedness):

[T]he attorney general from the United States, Mr. Gonzales, was here in Ottawa and the two governments reaffirmed their commitment to fight this terrible scourge of trafficking in human beings. We are going to build on the cooperative efforts of this government by working with our partners in the United States and internationally on law enforcement issues, including this very terrible and heinous crime of trafficking in humans, which is what we call the new slavery.

(House of Commons Debates, 20 May 2005, p. 6287)
(Débats de la Chambre des Communes, le 20 mai 2005, p. 6287)

(e) War crimes and crimes against humanity / Crimes de guerre et les crimes contre l'humanité

M. Mario Silva (Davenport):

[L]a Commission internationale d'enquête mise sur pied par le Conseil de sécurité de l'ONU pour enquêter sur la violation des droits de la personne et du droit international humanitaire au Darfour a rendu public son rapport hier. Elle recommande vivement au Conseil de sécurité de saisir la Cour pénale internationale de cette question. Le gouvernement du Canada appuiera-t-il cette importante recommandation?

L'hon. Pierre Pettigrew (ministre des Affaires étrangères):

[L]e Canada accueille très favorablement le rapport de la commission ... [L]'été dernier, nous avons déterminé que les atrocités qui se commettaient au Soudan constituaient clairement des crimes de guerre et des crimes contre l'humanité. Dans son rapport, la commission recommande au Conseil de sécurité de renvoyer immédiatement la question du Darfour à la Cour pénale internationale. Nous soutenons sans réserve cette recommandation. Il s'agit d'une mesure concrète pour contribuer à la résolution à long terme de ce terrible conflit.

(House of Commons Debates, 2 February 2005, p. 2978)
(Débats de la Chambre des Communes, le 2 février 2005, p. 2978)

Mr. Stockwell Day (Okanagan — Coquihalla):

[O]ur government and the United Nations [should] ... get the focus back on to Darfur. A genocide continues to unfold there ... Will the government ... take some actions that will give hope to the people in Darfur as they see the horror of another genocide unfolding upon them?

Hon. Pierre Pettigrew (Minister of Foreign Affairs):

We have been very active since October 2003. We have invested $26 million for humanitarian aid, protection and peace building measures. We have given $70 million since 2000 for humanitarian aid in Sudan. We have invested $20 million to help the African Union to do a better job.

(House of Commons Debates, 9 March 2005, p. 4199)
(Débats de la Chambre des Communes, le 9 mars 2005, p. 4199)

6   *International Humanitarian Law / Le droit international humanitaire*

(a) Humanitarian intervention and aid / Aide et l'intervention humanitaire

Mr. Navdeep Bains (Mississauga — Brampton South):

[T]he Prime Minister positioned Canada as an international leader on debt relief ... Could the [Government update Canadians on this issue]?

Hon. Ralph Goodale (Minister of Finance):

Canada ... propos[ed] to eliminate 100% of the debt charges on amounts owed by poor countries to the major international financial institutions. Canada ... has indeed been long regarded as a world leader on debt relief for the poor, shifting money from debt to health and education. This most recent Canadian initiative maintains that leadership as we all go into the G-7 meetings this weekend.

(House of Commons Debates, 3 February 2005, p. 3053)
(Débats de la Chambre des Communes, le 3 février 2005, p. 3053)

(b) Afghanistan

Mr. Wajid Khan (Mississauga — Streetsville):

[I]n early 2006 a brigade HQ and an army task force will be deployed in Kandahar as an ongoing commitment to ISAF in Afghanistan. Given the ongoing grave security situation with regard to the Kandahar region ...what preparations are being taken in the way of equipment and training provision and for force protection for CF units due to be posted to Kandahar?

Hon. Bill Graham (Minister of National Defence):

[O]ur members of the Canadian Forces have extraordinary experience in the country of Afghanistan ... [U]nder the leadership of General Hillier, who was the ISAF commander in Afghanistan and is a recognized expert in the area ... our forces will be trained, they will be equipped and they will acquit themselves well in what will be a dangerous but ultimately successful mission for this country and for the development of peace in the world.

(House of Commons Debates, 23 June 2005, p. 7724)
(Débats de la Chambre des Communes, le 23 juin 2005, p. 7724)

(c) Africa / Afrique

Mr. Rodger Cuzner (Cape Breton — Canso):

[F]or the past year our finance minister has served as a member of Tony Blair's commission for Africa ... Today the commission released its report[28] ... [H]ow this report will set the stage for the African people to finally take charge of their futures? How will it help set the stage for entrepreneurship and growth?

Hon. Ralph Goodale (Minister of Finance):

[Canada] was very honoured to serve on the commission for Africa. It is a United Kingdom initiative that builds upon what Canada began at the Kananaskis summit in 2002. The report is both useful and challenging and covers a broad range of subjects. Canada is responding in many ways. We are leading the world in debt relief proposals. We are increasing Canadian support in the battle against AIDS, malaria, tuberculosis and polio. We are doubling our support for Africa over the next three years.

(House of Commons Debates, 11 March 2005, p. 4320)
(Débats de la Chambre des Communes, le 11 mars 2005, p. 4320)

---

28 Editor's note: G-8, The Commission for Africa, *Our Common Interests*, 11 March 2005, at <www.commissionforafrica.org/>.

(d) China / Chine

Mr. Ted Menzies (Macleod):

China has an active commitment to foreign aid and even has 125 peacekeepers in Haiti, where Canada has none. In 2003 China spent $2.4 billion U.S. on aid to North Korea ... China has a booming economy which is now the number one recipient of private foreign investment in the world, receiving $53 billion U.S. in new money. Canadian companies are ranked among the top 10 investors ... How can the [Government of Canada] ... justify giving aid to China?

Hon. Aileen Carroll (Minister of International Cooperation):

China is changing very quickly. It has the world's largest population and has very uneven social, economic and political development. Having the Chinese build a more democratic and prosperous country is good not only for China, but for the world ... [W]e do not ignore the facts of China. It is important ... [to] understand that 20% of the world's poor live in China ... [T]hrough our development relationship we are able to engage China on many different fronts ... [W]e send experts to China to help at the Supreme Court level and with the legislators ... It is our opportunity to impact China's reform and to be there to assist the Chinese with that. I might add that China frequently looks to Canada in that regard in a manner in which it does not look to other countries.

(House of Commons Debates, 28 October 2004, p. 909)
(Débats de la Chambre des Communes, le 28 octobre 2004, p. 909)

(e) Haiti / Haïti

L'hon. Don Boudria (Glengarry — Prescott — Russell):

[L]'ouragan Jeanne, qui a dévasté les Antilles et les États-Unis, a causé des milliers de pertes de vie et des milliers d'autres personnes souffrent de faim et de manque de logement, notamment en Haïti. Qu'est-ce que le gouvernement du Canada est prêt à faire de plus pour aider le peuple haïtien?

L'hon. Aileen Carroll (ministre de la Coopération internationale):

[J]'offre mes plus sincères condoléances aux victimes de cette catastrophe ... L'ACDI a versé 3,5 millions de dollars pour les secours d'urgence suite à la dévastation causée par l'ouragan Jeanne ainsi qu'une contribution en nature sous forme de feuilles de plastique, de couvertures et d'aide alimentaire. En outre, le Canada versera plus de 180 millions de dollars pour la reconstruction de Haïti.

(House of Commons Debates, 6 October 2004, p. 33)
(Débats de la Chambre des Communes, le 6 octobre 2004, p. 33)

(f) Iraq / Irak

Mr. Larry Miller (Bruce — Grey — Owen Sound):

[T]he government has decided to send ... Canadian [observers] ... to oversee elections in a place that is constantly under fire by insurgents ... What is the government going to do to guarantee the safety of the Canadians he is sending into this international hotbed?

Hon. Pierre Pettigrew (Minister of Foreign Affairs):

[T]his is a government that has contributed substantially to the reconstruction of Iraq already ... [We have been] investing $300 million in the reconstruction of Iraq. We have already disbursed $250 million. We are training Iraqi police in Jordan, contributing to the security of that country. We are doing our share as a member of the international community.

(House of Commons Debates, 6 December 2004, p. 2314)
(Débats de la Chambre des Communes, le 6 décembre 2004, p. 2314)

Mr. Jack Layton (Toronto — Danforth):

[There has been] the proposal from George Bush and others that Canadians should send troops to Iraq ... [W]ould [there] be a vote in the House before troops were sent to Iraq?

Right Hon. Paul Martin (Prime Minister):

[W]e refused to send Canadian troops to Iraq two years ago. That decision stands. Canadian troops will not be going to Iraq.

(House of Commons Debates, 7 February 2005, p. 3151)
(Débats de la Chambre des Communes, le 7 février 2005, p. 3151)

(g) Sri Lanka

Mr. Ted Menzies (Macleod):

[Six] weeks after the tsunami tragedy in southeast Asia ... refugee camps in Sri Lanka are ... waiting for tents and food ... [T]he conflict between the government and the Tamil Tigers is blocking the flow of aid ... [Has Canada] mismanaged this humanitarian crisis?

Hon. Paddy Torsney (Parliamentary Secretary to the Minister of International Cooperation):

Absolutely not ... Canadians can be very proud of the fact that this government has responded with $425 million worth of support. Canadian NGOs, international NGOs and the multinational community are working together to ensure aid is getting into the affected regions.

(House of Commons Debates, 11 February 2005, p. 3399)
(Débats de la Chambre des Communes, le 11 février 2005, p. 3399)

(h) Palestine

Mr. Bill Siksay (Burnaby — Douglas):

[T]oday is the International Day of Solidarity with the Palestinian people, but today stateless Palestinian refugee claimants are facing deportation from Canada. Their deportations will ultimately lead to their return to poverty, violence and severely limited human rights in refugee camps where many have lived their entire lives before escaping to Canada. Could the Prime Minister assure us that Canada will live up to its obligations under the UN Convention on the Reduction of Statelessness[29] and ... ensure that stateless Palestinian refugees are not deported from Canada?

Hon. Pierre Pettigrew (Minister of Foreign Affairs):

[T]his is a day that we have been honouring at the United Nations for 27 years. Our solidarity with the Palestinian people is very important. Canada will continue to promote the security and safety of the Palestinian refugees and to find a solution in the Middle East. [O]ur country [will] ... put forward its very best efforts at this time.

(House of Commons Debates, 29 November 2004, p. 2033)
(Débats de la Chambre des Communes, le 29 novembre 2004, p. 2033)

---

29 Editor's note: UN Convention on the Reduction of Statelessness, done in New York, 30 August 1961, 989 U.N.T.S. 175, *entered into force* 13 December 1975. Canada accessed to the convention on 17 July 1978.

(i) Vietnam

Mr. Ken Epp (Edmonton — Sherwood Park):

Mennonites have an honoured reputation for providing relief and working for peace around the world. There have been recent reports of the arrest and conviction of seven Mennonite workers in Vietnam and reports that Canadian officials are watching the case closely. Is the government pursuing any formal, direct diplomatic initiatives to try to save these individuals from imprisonment and torture?

Hon. Pierre Pettigrew (Minister of Foreign Affairs):

Reverend Quang's case was among several cases that were raised by the Canadian ambassador with high-ranking officials from the Vietnamese ministry of foreign affairs and public security... Our Canadian consulate in Ho Chi Minh City requested and has been denied access to Reverend Quang's trial. The Consulate General sent a representative to the courthouse to ask for permission to observe the trial on November 12 in order to highlight Canadian interest, but was denied entry.

(House of Commons Debates, 15 November 2004, p. 1332)
(Débats de la Chambre des Communes, le 15 novembre 2004, p. 1332)

(j) Landmines / Mines terrestres

Mr. Lloyd St. Amand (Brant):

[O]n December 3, 1997, Canada led the world as the first government to sign, and this House ratified, the mine ban treaty, or Ottawa convention.[30] To date, 152 countries have agreed to ban anti-personnel mines. Sixty-two million stockpiled anti-personnel mines have been destroyed. Working with national governments, the International Red Cross, UNICEF, Mines Action Canada and other dedicated organizations, [could the government update Canadians on the recent developments on this issue?]

Hon. Aileen Carroll (Minister of International Cooperation):

[N]ext week's Nairobi's summit marks the halfway point between the treaty's entry into force and the deadline for the first countries to clear their minefields. At the summit, world leaders, international NGOs, youth

---

30 Editor's note: Convention on the Prohibition of the Use, Stockpiling, Production and Transfer of Anti-Personnel Mines and on Their Destruction (Ottawa, Canada, 18 September 1997; *entered into force* 1 March 1999), *reprinted* in (1997) 36 I.L.M. 1507. Canada signed and ratified the convention on 3 December 1997.

activists and my own parliamentary secretary will measure progress to keep this issue on the international agenda. Canada ... ha[s] been actively involved in the action plan for the implementation of the Ottawa treaty because mine action is a precondition for poverty reduction.

(House of Commons Debates, 19 November 2004, p. 1600)
(Débats de la Chambre des Communes, le 19 novembre 2004, p. 1600)

(k) Military law / Droit militaire

Hon. Stephen Harper (Leader of the Opposition):

[O]ur thoughts and prayers are with the crew of the HMCS *Chicoutimi* and their families.[31] There are apparently nine injured crewmen and the crew remains stranded in the north Atlantic ... Could the Prime Minister ... update us on the condition of the ship and crew and on when we can expect them to be returned safely?

Right Hon. Paul Martin (Prime Minister):

I spoke to Commodore Pile this morning ... [H]e has assured me that in terms of heat and food, which at one point were in doubt, there is no problem. Medical personnel have now arrived on the ship and those who suffered smoke inhalation are being taken care of. A British escort ship is alongside the *Chicoutimi* and as soon as the seas calm down it will be able to undertake the tow back to port.

(House of Commons Debates, 6 October 2004, pp. 26–27)
(Débats de la Chambre des Communes, le 6 octobre 2004, pp. 26–27)

Hon. Bill Blaikie (Elmwood-Transcona):

Is there an intention on the part of the government [of Canada] to go after the British government for having sold us this equipment [the HMCS *Chicoutimi*] in the first place and to go after it for the costs associated with what are obviously inferior submarines?

Hon. Bill Graham (Minister of National Defence):

[T]he present concern of the government is the welfare of the extraordinary men who are serving aboard the submarine under very difficult

31 Editor's note: Updates on the HMCS Chicoutimi tragedy available at <www.forces.gc.ca>.

conditions with tremendous professional capacity. The submarines were acquired by the navy because they will serve Canada well in this program. We of course will be looking at all remedies.

(House of Commons Debates, 6 October 2004, p. 31)
(Débats de la Chambre des Communes, le 6 octobre 2004, p. 31)

(l) Refugees / Réfugiés

Mr. Bill Siksay (Burnaby — Douglas):

[T]he Canadian Council for Refugees stated that Canada's private refugee sponsorship program is in serious trouble. Processing delays mean that many refugees are being put at risk as they wait in situations of extreme insecurity, violence and poverty ... Does the [Government] ... find it acceptable that many of these vulnerable refugees wait for 28 to 32 months for their applications to be processed?

Hon. Judy Sgro (Minister of Citizenship and Immigration):

We need to applaud the many Canadians who are sponsoring refugees from around the world. CIC continues to work with international organizations on uniting people in refugee camps with Canadian families who want to sponsor them.

(House of Commons Debates, 14 October 2004, p. 390)
(Débats de la Chambre des Communes, le 14 october 2004, p. 390)

Mme Raymonde Folco (Laval — Les Îles):

La question des réfugiés paraît régulièrement dans les médias, et les Canadiens se questionnent sur le futur de notre système de protection des réfugiés. La ministre pourrait-elle expliquer ... ce qu'elle compte faire pour répondre aux défis posés par cette situation et qui concernent le pays tout entier? Pourrait-elle également indiquer ce que ce gouvernement fera pour trouver un équilibre entre la protection des vrais réfugiés selon la définition de la convention et ceux qui abusent de notre système?

Hon. Judy Sgro (Minister of Citizenship and Immigration):

[I]t is my government's intention to consult with Canadians, refugee advocates, and other interested parties on how we can better meet the challenges that are facing our government. Canada is well known as a world leader on human interventions. We will deal with the challenges that are facing us. It is time for us to have a system that more appropriately deals with the needs and the realities of the 21st century while at the same time ensuring that we protect those most vulnerable and persecuted across the world.

(House of Commons Debates, 19 October 2004, p. 565)
(Débats de la Chambre des Communes, le 19 october 2004, p. 565)

Mr. Bill Siksay (Burnaby — Douglas):

[O]ver 2,000 Vietnamese boat people remain in the Philippines. These refugees from the war in Vietnam were never resettled and never repatriated and are without status in the Philippines. They receive no support from the UN. Australia, the U.K., Norway and the U.S. are working to close the book on this chapter of world history by resettling some of these stateless refugees. The Canadian Vietnamese community is ready now to do its part to help ... Why has Canada refused to assist with this admirable humanitarian project?

Hon. Joseph Volpe (Minister of Citizenship and Immigration):

Canada played its role and did its part and did it very willingly. Over 50,000 such refugees were welcomed into Canada and integrated into our economy and society. We are proud to have been able to integrate them fully. The situation to which the member refers is one that is resident in the Philippines and that the Philippine authorities are in the process of remedying. The fact that they are stateless creates a little bit of difficulty for all of the nations that have an interest, but the UNHCR is currently involved and engaged.

(House of Commons Debates, 18 February 2005, pp. 3699–700)
(Débats de la Chambre des Communes, le 18 février 2005, pp. 3699–700)

Mrs. Carolyn Parrish (Mississauga — Erindale):

As a signatory to the 1951 Geneva Convention on Refugees,[32] is Canada willing to initiate talks at the UN to ensure Palestinians get the same treatment as convention refugees, guaranteeing basic human rights, adequate funding and international protection?

---

32 Editor's note: Convention Relating to the Status of Refugees (Geneva, Switzerland, 28 July 1951; *entered into force* 22 April 1954) 189 U.N.T.S. 137. Canada accessed to the convention on 4 June 1969.

Hon. Pierre Pettigrew (Minister of Foreign Affairs):

The United Nations Relief and Works Agency for Palestinian refugees, the UNRWA, was established prior to the refugee convention relating to the status of refugees. It was given specific authority to provide assistance to Palestinian refugees. Reflecting this unique political situation of the Palestinian refugees, the international community, through the UN General Assembly, requires UNRWA to continue to provide humanitarian assistance pending a political situation.

(House of Commons Debates, 16 June 2005, pp. 7284–85)
(Débats de la Chambre des Communes, le 16 juin 2005, pp. 7284–85)

(m) Weaponization of space and nuclear disarmament / Militarisation de l'espace et le désarmement nucléaire

Mr. Jack Layton (Toronto — Danforth):

The [Russian] ambassador indicated that he opposed the missile defence plan. One reason he gave was that the plan would involve the weaponization of space and that he had been briefed by American officials accordingly … Does the Prime Minister think that the Russian ambassador was telling the truth about … [the U.S.]'s plans to weaponize space?

Right Hon. Paul Martin (Prime Minister):

[T]he government has made it very clear that we are opposed to the weaponization of space. That is our position and I have made it very clear in discussions with the President, as I know the Minister of Foreign Affairs has with his counterparts and as we have through the defence channels as well … The Americans have told us that the current anti-ballistic system that is under investigation does not involve the weaponization of space.

(House of Commons Debates, 8 October 2004, p. 183)
(Débats de la Chambre des Communes, le 8 octobre 2004, p. 183)

M. Roger Clavet (Louis-Hébert):

[L]a Corée-du-Nord a annoncé hier qu'elle détenait l'arme atomique et qu'elle refusait de reprendre les négociations multilatérales. Les négations à six avec la Chine, la Russie, les États-Unis, le Japon et la Corée-du-Sud doivent reprendre, et la Corée-du-Nord doit renoncer à ses ambitions nucléaires. Le [gouvernement] … peut-il s'engager à intervenir auprès de ses partenaires internationaux pour le redémarrage des négociations et pour inciter la communauté internationale à travailler de concert afin que la Corée-du-Nord revienne à la table des discussions, tout cela, pour éviter une dangereuse escalade entre la Corée-du-Nord et la Corée-du-Sud?

L'hon. Dan McTeague (secrétaire parlementaire du ministre des Affaires étrangères):

[L]es déclarations faites par la Corée-du-Nord sont ... troublant[es] et inquiétant[es] ... [N]ous nous retrouvons dans une position où nous devons relancer tout effort pour avoir une vérification indépendante, afin de s'assurer que le pays ne fonctionne pas d'une manière qui menace la stabilité globale. Nous prenons cette occasion pour nous assurer que c'est vraiment le cas et pour nous assurer qu'il y aura des négociations qui auront comme fin de garder la paix dans cette région.

(House of Commons Debates, 11 February 2005, p. 3401)
(Débats de la Chambre des Communes, le 11 février 2005, p. 3401)

Hon. Stephen Harper (Leader of the Opposition):

[T]he new Canadian ambassador to the United States said that the government is already part of the missile defence program. How could the ... [Government] ... make this decision, so clearly breaking every commitment [it] ... has made ... to Canadians?

Hon. Bill Graham (Minister of National Defence):

We agreed to a NORAD amendment which would allow our American partners, for the security of North America, to obtain the threat assessments and the information they need to make decisions to deploy missiles or other forms of defence ... We have yet to make any decisions in terms of ballistic missile defence. That decision will be made in accordance with Canadian needs and a Canadian appreciation of our strategic interests in support of the defence of North America ... [T]out ce que l'ambassadeur a dit, c'est que nous avons signé l'accord du NORAD.

(House of Commons Debates, 22 February 2005, pp. 3826–29)
(Débats de la Chambre des Communes, le 22 février 2005, pp. 3826–29)

7   *Trade and Economy / Commerce et économie*

(a) Canadian exports / Exports canadiens

Mrs. Diane Finley (Haldimand — Norfolk):

[L]ast Friday the United States department of commerce announced unfair preliminary anti-dumping duties on Canadian hogs. This decision means that Canadian hog producers now have to post potentially crippling bonds on their pork exports to the United States ... [Will this] ... result in U.S. protectionism hurt our farmers once again?

Hon. Jim Peterson (Minister of International Trade):

[T]he U.S. trade dispute is very unfortunate. We have an integrated market in North America and once again the Americans have taken punitive action against our hog producers who can compete with the best in the world. We are going to stand behind them and fight this anti-dumping action with all the resources we have.

(House of Commons Debates, 18 October 2004, pp. 488–89)
(Débats de la Chambre des Communes, le 18 octobre 2004, pp. 488–89)

Ms. Belinda Stronach (Newmarket — Aurora):

Last weekend the governments of the United States and Japan proudly announced the deal to restart trade in beef and set aside BSE concerns ... It has been 525 days since our border was slammed shut ...[W]hat [did] ... the Japanese and Americans [do] to open their border[?]

Hon. Andy Mitchell (Minister of Agriculture and Agri-Food):

When I was in Japan two weeks ago, we received a very firm commitment from the Japanese government that it treated us, Canada and the United States, as an integrated North American beef marketplace. Those arrangements that were being put in place for the United States would also be put in place for Canada in the same time frame. What has taken place is good news for Canadian cattle producers.

(House of Commons Debates, 26 October 2004, pp. 783–84)
(Débats de la Chambre des Communes, le 26 octobre 2004, pp. 783–84)

Ms. Françoise Boivin (Gatineau):

[I]t is evident that the Canadian cattle industry has suffered from the effects of one case of BSE. It has caused distortions in supply, slaughter capacity and trade markets ... [W]hat additional steps ... has [the Government] taken to open our trade markets for Canadian beef?

Hon. Andy Mitchell (Minister of Agriculture and Agri-Food):

[W]e have been making some progress ... [T]here is the move of the rule to the OMB and today President Bush saying that he will direct his officials to expedite that process and progress in the Japanese and Taiwanese markets. Today we were very pleased to hear that Hong Kong is reopening its border to Canadian boneless beef under 30 months of age.

(House of Commons Debates, 30 November 2004, p. 2110)
(Débats de la Chambre des Communes, le 30 novembre 2004, p. 2110)

(b) Imports into Canada / Importations au Canada

Hon. Don Boudria (Glengarry — Prescott — Russell):

Canadian milk producers want better controls at the border on imports of dairy ingredients ... Will the ... [Government] now initiate, under article 28 of GATT, measures that could stop the erosion of our supply management system?

Hon. Jim Peterson (Minister of International Trade):

[T]he [Government] ... will work ... hard ... to protect supply management and our milk producers. The number one thing that we have to get through is the WTO negotiations where we have worked to date, along with the supply management, to protect those industries.

(House of Commons Debates, 15 April 2005, p. 5156)
(Débats de la Chambre des Communes, le 15 avril 2005, p. 5156)

(c) Investment / Investissement

Mr. Brian Masse (Windsor West):

Many Canadians are concerned about the sale of Noranda Inc. to a foreign government that has human rights abuses and environmental and labour practices which are susceptible to all kinds of conditions that are not favourable to Canadian competitors. There are significant employment sovereignty issues with this particular case ... Will the Minister of Industry commit to ... the Canadian public that he will review or delay the sale of Noranda Inc. until the industry committee has had a chance to study this and also the current Investment Canada process?

Hon. David Emerson (Minister of Industry):

The government has an unassailable record of human rights. We will defend it against anyone. The Investment Canada Act requires that we review foreign acquisitions of Canadian companies according to whether it creates net benefits for Canada. We will do that.

(House of Commons Debates, 13 October 2004, p. 317)
(Débats de la Chambre des Communes, le 13 octobre 2004, p. 317)

M. Paul Crête (Montmagny — L'Islet — Kamouraska — Rivière-du-Loup):

Bombardier pourrait choisir de développer son nouvel appareil à l'extérieur du Québec, puisque la concurrence est importante et que d'autres pays et États américains ont déjà présenté des offres à l'entreprise pour l'attirer chez eux ... [L]e gouvernement fédéral veut[-il] faire sa part pour garder le développement de Bombardier au Québec?

Hon. David Emerson (Minister of Industry):

[Y]es ... we are consulting with the aerospace industry across Canada and we are moving to ensure that we have a strategy in place that will benefit the aerospace industry and all of Canada. It will not just be a Bombardier strategy. It will be a Canadian strategy and it will benefit workers across the country.

(House of Commons Debates, 1 November 2004, p. 1006)
(Débats de la Chambre des Communes, le 1er novembre 2004, p. 1006)

(d) Softwood lumber / Le bois d'œuvre

M. Paul Crête (Montmagny — L'Islet — Kamouraska — Rivière-du-Loup):

[O]n apprend aujourd'hui que les Américains vont porter en appel la décision sur le bois d'œuvre que l'ALENA a rendue en faveur du Canada le 31 août dernier.[33] Est-ce que le [gouvernement] ... se rend compte

---

33 Editor's note: On 31 August 2004, the North American Free Trade Agreement (NAFTA) panel ruled that the evidence relied on by the United States International Trade Commission (ITC) did not support the ITC's finding of a threat of material injury to the US softwood lumber industry from Canadian imports. See NAFTA Article 1904 Binational Panel Review, *Certain Softwood Lumber Products from Canada: Final Affirmative Threat of Injury Determination,* Second Remand Decision of the Panel, 31 August 2004, at 7, available at <www.dfait-maeci.gc.ca>.

que ce nouvel appel signifie que la crise du bois d'œuvre va s'étirer encore longtemps et que s'il veut que l'industrie survive à ce nouvel assaut, il faut venir en aide à l'industrie du bois d'œuvre plus que jamais?

L'hon. Jim Peterson (ministre du Commerce international):

[L]es Américains ont indiqué leur intention d'en appeler de la décision. Nous l'avons vu par le passé que, par ce moyen, ils vont faire leur possible pour prolonger la situation. Nous allons continuer à lutter contre cette sorte d'action ... [N]ous avons déjà consacré 356 millions de dollars pour aider à régler la situation de la crise du bois d'œuvre.

(House of Commons Debates, 14 October 2004, pp. 388–89)
(Débats de la Chambre des Communes, le 14 octobre 2004, pp. 388–89)

Ms. Jean Crowder (Nanaimo — Cowichan):

Canada and the U.S. have been without an agreement on softwood lumber for almost four years. NAFTA panels have told the U.S. to halt its duties three times. The minister called the WTO's March 2004 decision on softwood a major victory ... Can the minister tell us why the [two governments] ... cannot get any trade on Canadian softwood? ... [W]ill the minister call for the President to dump the Byrd amendment, immediately remove the illegal duties, and cut a cheque dated Wednesday morning payable to the Canadian softwood industry for $3.7 billion?

Hon. Jim Peterson (Minister of International Trade):

[W]e have incredible trade in softwood, over $7 billion a year going to the United States. The problem is that we have a trade dispute going on with the United States right now ... [W]e keep winning at the WTO ... the NAFTA, and the United States keeps coming back with new measures against us. We are going to continue to fight these measures [and] ...to win. We will also continue to be ready to negotiate a settlement that could lead us to free trade ... [W]e have to fight the Byrd amendment. We have made this very clear to the United States. That is why we have announced retaliatory measures which could total up to $5 billion.

(House of Commons Debates, 29 November 2004, pp. 2029–30)
(Débats de la Chambre des Communes, le 29 novembre 2004, pp. 2029–30)

(e) Trade agreements / Accords commerciaux

M. Pierre Paquette (Joliette):

[L]e ministre du Commerce international négocie un traité de libre-échange avec la Corée du sud et songe à des ententes similaires avec l'Inde et divers pays d'Amérique centrale. Le ministre ne croit-il pas qu'il est temps de s'assurer que, lors de la signature de tels traités, les pays signataires s'engagent à respecter certaines obligations pour que les produits que nous importons ne soient pas le résultat du travail des enfants, du travail forcé ou d'une production qui ne respecte pas les droits humains?

Hon. Mark Eyking (Parliamentary Secretary to the Minister of International Trade (Emerging Markets)):

[T]he minister is in India on a very important trade delegation leading over 65 companies. These are emerging markets. We will be making deals with other countries, so that we increase our trade because we are a trading nation ... Canada has a tremendous record on human rights. Whenever we travel outside the country making deals, like the Prime Minister did when he was in China, we bring up the way we deal with human rights and we expect these other countries to follow suit.

(House of Commons Debates, 6 April 2005, p. 4746)
(Débats de la Chambre des Communes, le 6 avril 2005, p. 4746)

Mr. Stockwell Day (Okanagan — Coquihalla):

Yesterday, the people of France in a no vote rejected the European constitution. Will the government ... admit that areas important to Canada like trade, agriculture ... need to be pursued more on a nation-by-nation basis?

Hon. Jim Peterson (Minister of International Trade):

[T]he vote in France yesterday had absolutely nothing to do with our trading relationship with Europe. We will continue to actively engage with the EU, the proper body. We are now negotiating a trade and investment enhancement agreement and we will continue to act in accordance with the rules established by the EU ... [W]e continue to have numerous bilateral contacts with the 25 members of the EU, but it is the EU that still speaks on issues such as trade.

(House of Commons Debates, 30 May 2005, p. 6336)
(Débats de la Chambre des Communes, le 30 mai 2005, p. 6336)

(f) NAFTA / ALENA

Mr. John Duncan (Vancouver Island North):

Five senators, obviously prompted by the U.S. lumber lobby, recently spoke on the congressional record urging major changes to chapter 19 of NAFTA because of their unhappiness with losing at the NAFTA panel on the softwood dispute. Their statements represent a major threat to NAFTA. Why has the government [of Canada] remained silent to this hostile attack on NAFTA?

Hon. Jim Peterson (Minister of International Trade):

[I]t is quite the contrary. To go back to his speech coming out of Sun Valley, the Prime Minister raised how important it was that the very provisions of NAFTA be respected by all parties ... [We are] advocating throughout the United States that the rule of law be respected.

(House of Commons Debates, 15 October 2004, pp. 436–37)
(Débats de la Chambre des Communes, le 15 octobre 2004, pp. 436–37)

M. Pierre Paquette (Joliette):

[L]'entreprise Gildan a annoncé la fermeture de deux filatures et son déménagement en Caroline du Nord, faisant perdre 285 emplois, dont 115 à Montréal. Tout cela parce que l'ALENA n'assure pas un libre accès au marché américain à tous les vêtements fabriqués à partir de fibres ou de tissus canadiens. Le premier ministre entend-il, lors de sa rencontre avec les présidents Bush et Fox concernant des ajustements à l'ALENA, soulever la question de l'absence d'accès à des vêtements fabriqués avec des tissus canadiens?

L'hon. Jim Peterson (ministre du Commerce international):

[N]ous avons pris des mesures concernant le secteur du vêtement et du textile.

L'hon. Jacques Saada (ministre de l'Agence de développement économique du Canada pour les régions du Québec et ministre responsable de la Francophonie):

En particulier, nous avons lancé un programme de soutien à la diversification de l'industrie textile. Nous avons mis de l'argent dans ce programme, qui a été reconduit en février dernier puis encore plus récemment, avec des fonds supplémentaires d'aide à la productivité du textile et de ces industries, de soutien aux travailleurs, d'initiatives de diversification économique régionale pour les entreprises touchées.

(House of Commons Debates, 3 February 2005, p. 3053)
(Débats de la Chambre des Communes, le 3 février 2005, p. 3053)

(g) World Trade Organization/ Organisation mondiale du commerce

Mr. Russ Powers (Ancaster — Dundas — Flamborough — Westdale):

[T]he corn producers of my riding are economically threatened by the extremely low commodity prices in Ontario as compared to prices paid for U.S. imports and to other Canadian producers ... [W]hat action may be taken to assist the corn producers?

Hon. Andy Mitchell (Minister of Agriculture and Agri-Food):

[W]e are working within the WTO to make sure that our producers are able to compete on a level playing field. That is why collectively in 2003 we provided $4.8 billion of assistance to producers.

(House of Commons Debates, 4 February 2005, p. 3100)
(Débats de la Chambre des Communes, le 4 février 2005, p. 3100)

L'hon. Don Boudria (Glengarry — Prescott — Russell):

Dans les négociations à l'Organisation mondiale du commerce, l'OMC, le gouvernement est-il prêt à protéger le tarif hors contingentement à son niveau actuel pour décourager les importations au-delà du niveau d'accès au marché déjà négocié à l'OMC?

Hon. Andy Mitchell (Minister of Agriculture and Agri-Food):

[I]n our WTO negotiations ... one of the things that we have said clearly is that individual countries need to have flexibility in how they achieve that. That includes allowing our producers to choose their domestic marketing schemes and that includes supply management.

(House of Commons Debates, 16 June 2005, p. 7283)
(Débats de la Chambre des Communes, le 16 juin 2005, p. 7283)

M. Bernard Bigras (Rosemont — La Petite-Patrie):

[L]e Conseil des ministres de l'environnement de l'Union européenne a décidé de maintenir le droit des États membres d'interdire certains maïs et colzas transgéniques, au nom de la protection de la santé de la population et de l'environnement, un droit qui est contesté devant l'OMC. Compte tenu du fait que l'Europe a pris cette décision pour protéger la santé et l'environnement, est-ce que le Canada peut s'engager, aujourd'hui, à retirer sa plainte devant l'OMC?[34] ... Comment le gouvernement canadien peut-il continuer ses poursuites à l'OMC au nom de la liberté du commerce et, du même coup, faire fi des préoccupations légitimes des consommateurs face aux dangers potentiels des OGM?

Hon. Andy Mitchell (Minister of Agriculture and Agri-Food):

[I]n Canada we have a very clear way in which we handle GM products ... We deal with a scrutiny in terms of any product that would come to market ... Before we provide a licence to any product for distribution in this country, we make absolutely certain that we undertake the necessary investigations to ensure it is safe for Canadian consumers.

(House of Commons Debates, 27 June 2005, pp. 7816–17) (Débats de la Chambre des Communes, le 27 juin 2005, pp. 7816–17)

8   Law of the Sea / Le droit de la mer

(a) Fisheries / Les pêches

Mr. Loyola Hearn (St. John's South — Mount Pearl):

[R]ecently, at a United Nations meeting, Canada was one of the sponsors of a resolution recommending action be taken on destructive fishing practices, including bottom trawling ... While such a ban could be tolerated in certain sensitive areas, this one could be interpreted very broadly. Why would Canada and the minister support a resolution that could have a disastrous effect on several of our fisheries, including the shrimp fishery?

Hon. Geoff Regan (Minister of Fisheries and Oceans):

First of all ... the resolution is a non-binding resolution, and as a matter of fact, it talks about sensitive areas ... I said in my address to the UN General

---

34 Editor's note: World Trade Organization, *EC – Measures Affecting the Approval and Marketing of Biotech Products* (Doc. WT/DS292; Request for Consultations, Doc. WT/DS292/1, 13 May 2003). Canada requested consultations with the European Community (EC) concerning certain measures taken by the EC and its member states affecting imports of agricultural and food imports from Canada. The United States (Doc. WT/DS291) and Argentina (Doc. WT/DS293) have also filed their complaints on the same subject matter (at <www.wto.org>).

Assembly earlier this week when I made our position on bottom trawling very clear ... that "Canada's position is that no specific gear type is inherently destructive," depending on how it is used. I said, "From experience we know that all gear types can have negative impacts."

(House of Commons Debates, 19 November 2004, p. 1601)
(Débats de la Chambre des Communes, le 19 novembre 2004, p. 1601)

Mr. Loyola Hearn (St. John's South — Mount Pearl):

Foreign fishing companies continue to break fishing regulations in the NAFO regulated zone ... Canada pays half the cost of operating NAFO ... When will the minister ... [resolve the issue of overfishing]?

Hon. Geoff Regan (Minister of Fisheries and Oceans):

[T]he government ... take[s] this issue very seriously. We have fought hard on the issue of overfishing ... [The Government] ha[s] raised it at the UN. Last year we had more than 240 inspections, an increase of some 50% over the previous year. We saw a drop of about 32% in the number of infractions last year.

(House of Commons Debates, 22 March 2005, p. 4451)
(Débats de la Chambre des Communes, le 22 mars 2005, p. 4451)

Mr. Scott Simms (Bonavista — Gander — Grand Falls — Windsor):

[We are] deeply concerned about the impact of foreign fleets off our shores, and they are doing it illegally ... [W]hat can Newfoundlanders expect coming out of the International Fisheries Governance Conference going on right now in St. John's?

Hon. Shawn Murphy (Parliamentary Secretary to the Minister of Fisheries and Oceans):

[T]his government [is] ... committed to ending the pillage of fish stocks on the Grand Banks and around the world. This conference is just one event in an overall strategy. In the closing ministerial declaration, the minister agreed to strengthen the monitoring supervision regimes, to improve the dispute settlement mechanisms and to deal with countries that opt out of these agreements. The minister has also committed to making it easier to apprehend offenders and to punish them appropriately.

(House of Commons Debates, 5 May 2005, p. 5722)
(Débats de la Chambre des Communes, le 5 mai 2005, p. 5722)

Mr. Scott Simms (Bonavista — Gander — Grand Falls — Windsor):

Regarding the recent incident this weekend involving a Portuguese fishing vessel, would the minister please update the House on that situation?

Hon. Geoff Regan (Minister of Fisheries and Oceans):

[A] Portuguese vessel was arrested in Canadian waters on charges related to fishing inside Canadian waters in 2003. The vessel has been escorted to port in St. John's and the captain will be arraigned this afternoon.

(House of Commons Debates, 30 May 2005, p. 6338)
(Débats de la Chambre des Communes, le 30 mai 2005, p. 6338)

Mr. Scott Simms (Bonavista — Gander — Grand Falls — Windsor):

[T]he government issued citations to a Russian trawler known as the *Odoevsk*. Could the minister please update the House on that situation and the violations made on the Grand Banks of Newfoundland and Labrador?

Hon. Geoff Regan (Minister of Fisheries and Oceans):

Russia has acted responsibly by calling the vessel home and revoking its fishing licence. This is welcome news in the wake of the St. John's conference where all international participants agreed that more must be done to combat overfishing on the high seas.

(House of Commons Debates, 2 June 2005, p. 6564)
(Débats de la Chambre des Communes, le 2 juin 2005, p. 6564)

Treaty Action Taken by Canada in 2004 / Mesures prises par le Canada en matière de traités en 2004

compiled by/préparé par
JAQUELINE CARON

I BILATERAL

Armenia
Convention between the Government of Canada and the Government of the Republic of Armenia for the Avoidance of Double Taxation and the Prevention of Fiscal Evasion with Respect to Taxes on Income and on Capital. *Signed:* Yerevan, 29 June 2004. *Entered into force:* 29 December 2005.

Azerbaijan
Convention between the Government of Canada and the Government of the Republic of Azerbaijan for the Avoidance of Double Taxation and the Prevention of Fiscal Evasion with respect to Taxes on Income and on Capital. *Signed:* Baku, 7 September 2004. *Entered into force:* 23 January 2006.

Belgium
Convention between the Government of Canada and the Government of the Kingdom of Belgium for the Avoidance of Double Taxation and the Prevention of Fiscal Evasion with Respect to Taxes on Income and on Capital. *Signed:* Ottawa, 23 May 2002. *Entered into force:* 6 October 2004.

Bulgaria
Audio-visual Co-production Agreement between the Government of Canada and the Government of the Republic of Bulgaria. *Signed:* Ottawa, 25 April 2002. *Entered into force:* 26 April 2004.

Chile
Third Additional Protocol of the Free Trade Agreement between the Government of Canada and the Government of the Republic of Chile. *Signed:* Santiago, 8 November 2004. *Entered into force:* 24 December 2004.

Exchange of Letters between the Government of Canada and the Government of the Republic of Chile rectifying Annex C-00-B, Annex D-01 and Annex D-03.1 and the Uniform Regulations for Chapter D of the Free Trade Agreement between the Government of Canada and the Government of the Republic of Chile, done at Santiago, on 4 December 1996. *Signed:* Ottawa, Santiago, 25 November 2004, *Entered into force:* 1 January 2005.

Cuba
Agreement between the Government of Canada and the Government of the

---

Jaqueline Caron is Treaty Registrar in the Legal Advisory Division at the Department of Foreign Affairs / Greffier des Traités, Direction des consultations juridiques, Ministère des Affaires étrangères.

Republic of Cuba Regarding the Sharing of Forfeited Assets or Their Equivalent Funds. *Signed:* Havana, 8 July 2003. *Entered into force:* 3 June 2004.

Czech Republic
Exchange of Notes constituting an Agreement amending the Agreement between the Government of Canada and the Government of the Czech Republic on Air Transport, signed at Prague on March 13, 1996. *Signed:* Prague, 28 June 2004. *Entered into force:* 28 June 2004.

Denmark
Exchange of Notes constituting an Agreement to amend the Agreement between the Government of Canada and the Government of the Kingdom of Denmark Relating to the Delimitation of the Continental Shelf between Greenland and Canada done at Ottawa on 17 December 1973. *Signed:* Copenhagen, 20 April 2004.

Estonia
Agreement between the Government of Canada and the Government of the Republic of Estonia on Trade and Commerce. *Signed:* Ottawa, 27 June 1994. *Entered into force:* 10 February 1995. *Terminated:* 20 October 2004. CTS 1995/7.

Audio-visual Co-production Agreement between the Government of Canada and the Government of the Republic of Estonia. *Signed:* Tallinn, 27 May 2002. *Entered into force:* 4 November 2004.

European Community
Agreement between Canada and the European Community on Trade in Wines and Spirit Drinks. *Signed:* Niagara-on-the-Lake, 16 September 2003. *Entered into force:* 1 June 2004.

France
Agreement between the Government of Canada and the Government of the French Republic Concerning Youth Exchanges. *Signed:* Paris, 3 October 2003. *Entered into force:* 1 March 2004.

Germany (Federal Republic of)
Agreement between the Government of Canada and the Government of the Federal Republic of Germany on Audio-visual Relations. *Signed:* Gatineau, 22 June 2004. *Entered into force:* 22 June 2004.

Supplementary Treaty to the Treaty between Canada and the Federal Republic of Germany Concerning Extradition. *Signed:* Mont Tremblant, 13 May 2002. *Entered into force:* 23 October 2004.

Treaty between Canada and the Federal Republic of Germany on Mutual Assistance in Criminal Matters. *Signed:* Mont-Tremblant, 13 May 2002. *Entered into force:* 23 October 2004.

Israel
Agreement on Bilateral Cooperation in Private Sector Industrial Research and Development between the Government of Canada and the Government of the State of Israel. *Signed:* Ottawa, 3 December 2004. *Entered into force:* 3 December 2004.

Kuwait
Exchange of Notes between the Government of Canada and the Government of the State of Kuwait Constituting an Agreement Concerning the Status of Canadian Forces in Kuwait. *Signed:* Kuwait City, 11 May 2004. *Entered into force:* 24 May 2004.

Mongolia
Treaty between the Government of Canada and the Government of Mongolia on the Transfer of Offenders. *Signed:* Ottawa, 20 October 2004. *Entered into force:* 8 June 2005.

Netherlands
Agreement on Social Security between the Government of Canada and the Government of the Kingdom of the Netherlands. *Signed:* Brantford, 27 June 2001. *Entered into force:* 1 April 2004.

Norway
Agreement between the Government of Canada and the Government of Norway Regarding the Sharing of Forfeited or Confiscated Assets or Their Equivalent Funds. *Signed:* Ottawa, 25 March 2004.

Oman
Agreement between the Government of Canada and the Government of the Sultanate of Oman for the Avoidance of Double Taxation and the Prevention of Fiscal Evasion with Respect to Taxes on Income and on Capital. *Signed:* Muscat, 30 June 2004. *Entered into force:* 27 April 2005.

Romania
Convention between Canada and Romania for the Avoidance of Double Taxation and the Prevention of Fiscal Evasion with Respect to Taxes on Income and on Capital. *Signed:* Ottawa, 8 April 2004. *Entered into force:* 31 December 2004.

Russian Federation
Agreement between the Government of Canada and the Government of the Russian Federation Concerning Cooperation on the Destruction of Chemical Weapons, the Dismantlement of Decommissioned Nuclear Submarines, and the Physical Protection, Control and Accountancy of Nuclear and Other Radioactive Material. *Signed:* Sea Island, 9 June 2004. *Entered into force:* 17 August 2005.

Slovak Republic
Audio-visual Co-production Agreement between the Government of Canada and the Government of the Slovak Republic. *Signed:* Ottawa, 5 June 2002. *Entered into force:* 16 July 2004.

South Africa
Audiovisual Co-Production Agreement between the Government of Canada and the Government of the Republic of South Africa. *Signed:* Cape Town, 5 November 1997. *Entered into force:* 19 July 2004.

United Arab Emirates
Convention between the Government of Canada and the Government of the United Arab Emirates for the Avoidance of Double Taxation and the Prevention of Fiscal Evasion with Respect to Taxes on Income and on Capital. *Signed:* Abu Dhabi, 9 June 2002. *Entered into force:* 25 May 2004.

United Kingdom of Great Britain and Northern Ireland
Protocol amending the Convention between the Government of Canada and the Government of the United Kingdom of Great Britain and Northern Ireland for the Avoidance of Double Taxation and the Prevention of Fiscal Evasion with Respect to Taxes on Income and Capital Gains, signed at London on 8 September 1978, as amended by the Protocol signed at Ottawa on 15 April 1980 and as further amended by the Protocol signed at London on 16 October 1985. *Signed:* London, 7 May 2003. *Entered into force:* 4 May 2004.

United Nations High Commissioner for Refugees
Exchange of notes constituting an amendment to the Agreement between the Government of Canada and the Office of the United Nations High Commissioner for Refugees for the Purpose of Deploying Two Royal Canadian Mounted Police Officers to the Republic of Guinea, signed on 7 January 2003. *Signed:* Geneva, 6 January 2004. *Entered into force:* 6 January 2004.

United States of America
Agreement between the Government of Canada and the Government of the United States of America on the Application of Positive Comity Principles to the Enforcement of Their Competition Laws. *Signed:* Washington, 5 October 2004. *Entered into force:* 5 October 2004.

Agreement between the Government of Canada and the Government of the United States of America for Cooperation in Science and Technology for

Critical Infrastructure Protection and Border Security. *Signed:* Washington, 1 June 2004. *Entered into force:* 1 June 2004.

Exchange of Notes between the Government of Canada and the Government of the United States of America concerning Missile Warning and Constituting an Agreement to Amend the North American Aerospace Defence Command Agreement (NORAD). *Signed:* Washington, 5 August 2004. *Entered into force:* 5 August 2004.

Exchange of Notes between the Government of Canada and the Government of the United States of America Constituting an Agreement to Extend the Agreement to Improve Bilateral Security through Enhanced Military Cooperation with Respect to Maritime, Land and Civil Support Functions signed on December 5, 2002. *Signed:* Ottawa, 29 November 2004. *Entered into force:* 29 November 2004.

Exchange of Notes between the Government of Canada and the Government of the United States of America Constituting an Agreement Amending the Treaty on Pacific Coast Albacore Tuna Vessels and Port Privileges done at Washington on May 26, 1981. *Signed:* Washington, 13 August 2002. *Entered into force:* 28 May 2004.

Exchange of Notes between the Government of Canada and the Government of the United States of America Constituting an Agreement Amending the Treaty on Pacific Coast Albacore Tuna Vessels and Port Privileges done at Washington on May 26, 1981. *Signed:* Washington, 10 September 2002. *Entered into force:* 28 May 2004.

Agreement between the Government of Canada and the Government of the United States of America for Cooperation in the Examination of Refugee Status Claims from Nationals of Third Countries. *Signed:* Washington, 5 December 2002. *Entered into force:* 29 December 2004.

Venezuela
Convention between the Government of Canada and the Government of the Bolivarian Republic of Venezuela for the Avoidance of Double Taxation and the Prevention of Fiscal Avoidance and Evasion with Respect to Taxes on Income and on Capital. *Signed:* Caracas, 10 July 2001. *Entered into force:* 5 May 2004.

Vietnam
Agreement between the Government of Canada and the Government of the Socialist Republic of Vietnam on Air Transport. *Signed:* Montréal, 28 September 2004.

II   MULTILATERAL

Agriculture
International Treaty on Plant Genetic Resources for Food and Agriculture. Rome, 3 November 2001. *Signed* by Canada: 10 June 2002. *Ratified* by Canada: 10 June 2002. *Entry into force* for Canada: 29 June 2004.

Aviation
Convention on International Interests in Mobile Equipment. Cape Town, 16 November 2001. *Signed* by Canada: 31 March 2004.

Protocol to the Convention on International Interests in Mobile Equipment on Matters Specific to Aircraft Equipment. Cape Town, 16 November 2001. *Signed* by Canada: 31 March 2004.

Bribery
United Nations Convention against Corruption. New York, 31 October 2003. *Signed* by Canada: 21 May 2004.

Conservation
Convention on the Conservation and Management of Highly Migratory Fish Stocks in the Western and Central Pacific Ocean. Honolulu, 5 September 2000. *Signed* by Canada: 2 August 2001.

Ratified by Canada: 1 November 2005. *Entry into force* for Canada: 1 December 2005.

Defence

Protocol to the North Atlantic Treaty on the Accession of the Republic of Bulgaria. Brussels, 26 March 2003. *Signed* by Canada: 26 March 2003. *Ratification*: 28 March 2003. *Entry into force* for Canada: 27 February 2004.

Protocol to the North Atlantic Treaty on the Accession of the Republic of Estonia. Brussels, 26 March 2003. *Signed* by Canada: 26 March 2003. *Ratified* by Canada: 28 March 2003. *Entry into* force for Canada: 27 February 2004.

Protocol to the North Atlantic Treaty on the Accession of the Republic of Latvia. Brussels, 26 March 2003. *Signed* by Canada: 26 March 2003. *Ratified* by Canada: 28 March 2003. *Entry into force* for Canada: 27 February 2004.

Protocol to the North Atlantic Treaty on the Accession of the Republic of Lithuania. Brussels, 26 March 2003. *Signed* by Canada: 26 March 2003. *Ratified* by Canada: 28 March 2003. *Entry into force* for Canada: 27 February 2004.

Protocol to the North Atlantic Treaty on the Accession of Romania. Brussels, 26 March 2003. *Signed* by Canada: 26 March 2003. *Ratified* by Canada: 28 March 2003. *Entry into force* for Canada: 27 February 2004.

Protocol to the North Atlantic Treaty on the Accession of the Slovak Republic. Brussels, 26 March 2003. *Signed* by Canada: 26 March 2003. *Ratified* by Canada: 28 March 2003. *Entry into force* for Canada: 27 February 2004.

Protocol to the North Atlantic Treaty on the Accession of the Republic of Slovenia. Brussels, 26 March 2003. *Signed* by Canada: 26 March 2003. *Ratified* by Canada: 28 March 2003. *Entry into force* for Canada: 27 February 2004.

Disarmament

Amendment to the Convention on Prohibitions or Restrictions on the Use of Certain Conventional Weapons Which May Be Deemed to Be Excessively Injurious or to Have Indiscriminate Effects. Geneva, 21 December 2001. *Accepted* by Canada: 22 July 2002. *Entry into force* for Canada: 18 May 2004.

Environment

Rotterdam Convention on the Prior Informed Consent Procedure for Certain Hazardous Chemicals and Pesticides in International Trade. Rotterdam, 10 September 1998. *Accession*: 26 August 2002. *Entry into force* for Canada: 24 February 2004.

Stockholm Convention on Persistent Organic Pollutants. Stockholm, 22 May 2001. *Signed* by Canada: 23 May 2001. *Ratified* by Canada: 23 May 2001. *Entry into force* for Canada: 17 May 2004.

Fisheries

Convention for the Strengthening of the Inter-American Tropical Tuna Commission Established by the 1949 Convention between the United States of America and the Republic of Costa Rica. Washington, 14 November 2003. *Signed* by Canada: 22 December 2004.

Health

World Health Organization Framework Convention on Tobacco Control. Geneva, 21 May 2003. *Signed* by Canada: 15 July 2003. *Ratified* by Canada: 26 November 2004. *Entry into force* for Canada: 27 February 2005.

Postal Matters

Acts of the Twenty-third Congress of the Universal Postal Union. Bucharest, 5 October 2004. *Signed* by Canada: 5 October 2004. *Ratified* by Canada: 6 October 2005. *Entry into force* for Canada: 1 January 2006.

Privileges and Immunities

Agreement on the Privileges and Immunities of the International Criminal Court.

New York, 9 September 2002. *Signed* by Canada: 30 April 2004. *Ratified* by Canada: 22 June 2004. *Entry into force* for Canada: 22 July 2004.

Science
Agreement Establishing an International Science and Technology Center. Moscow, 27 November 1992. *Accession:* 26 February 2004.

Taxation
Convention on Mutual Administrative Assistance in Tax Matters. Strasbourg, 25 January 1988. *Signed* by Canada: 28 April 2004.

Telecommunications
Final Acts of the Plenipotentiary Conference of the International Telecommunication Union, Marrakesh (2002). Marrakesh, 18 October 2002. *Signed* by Canada: 18 October 2002. *Ratified* by Canada: 26 April 2004. *Entry into force* for Canada: 26 April 2004.

Trade
Exchange of Letters between the Government of Canada, the Government of the United States of America and the Government of the United Mexican States Amending Annex 401 of the North American Free Trade Agreement. Mexico, Ottawa, Washington, 3 December 2002. *Entry into force* between Canada and Mexico: 15 July 2004.

Trade
Exchange of Letters between the Government of Canada, the Government of the United States of America and the Government of the United Mexican States Constituting an Agreement Amending Annex 401 of the North American Free Trade Agreement. Mexico, Ottawa, Washington, 22 October 2004.

Transnational Crime
Protocol against the Smuggling of Migrants by Land, Sea and Air, supplementing the United Nations Convention against Transnational Organized

Crime. New York, 15 November 2000. *Signed* by Canada: 14 December 2000. *Ratified* by Canada: 13 May 2002. *Entry into force* for Canada: 28 January 2004.

I   BILATÉRAUX

Afrique du Sud
Accord de coproduction audiovisuelle entre le gouvernement du Canada et le gouvernement de la République d'Afrique du Sud. Le Cap, 5 novembre 1997. *En vigueur:* le 19 juillet 2004.

Allemagne (République fédérale d')
Accord entre le gouvernement du Canada et le gouvernement de la République fédérale d'Allemagne sur les relations audiovisuelles. Gatineau, 22 juin 2004. *En vigueur:* le 22 juin 2004.

Traité d'entraide judiciaire entre le Canada et la République fédérale d'Allemagne. Mont-Tremblant, 13 mai 2002. *En vigueur:* le 23 octobre 2004.

Traité complémentaire au Traité d'extradition entre le Canada et la République fédérale d'Allemagne. Mont-Tremblant, 13 mai 2002. *En vigueur:* le 23 octobre 2004.

Arménie
Convention entre le gouvernement du Canada et le gouvernement de la République d'Arménie en vue d'éviter les doubles impositions et de prévenir l'évasion fiscale en matière d'impôts sur le revenu et sur la fortune. Erevan, 29 juin 2004. *En vigueur:* le 29 décembre 2005.

Azerbaïdjan
Convention entre le gouvernement du Canada et le gouvernement de la République d'Azerbaïdjan en vue d'éviter les doubles impositions et de prévenir l'évasion fiscale en matière d'impôts sur le revenu et sur la fortune. Bakou, 7 septembre 2004. *En vigueur:* le 23 janvier 2006.

Belgique
Convention entre le gouvernement du Canada et le gouvernement du Royaume de Belgique en vue d'éviter les doubles impositions et de prévenir l'évasion fiscale en matière d'impôts sur le revenu et sur la fortune. Ottawa, 23 mai 2002. *En vigueur:* le 6 octobre 2004.

Bulgarie
Accord de coproduction audiovisuelle entre le gouvernement du Canada et le gouvernement de la République de Bulgarie. Ottawa, 25 avril 2002. *En vigueur:* le 26 avril 2004.

Chili
Troisième Protocole supplémentaire de l'Accord de libre-échange entre le gouvernement du Canada et le gouvernement de la République du Chili. Santiago, 8 novembre 2004. *En vigueur:* le 24 décembre 2004.

Échange de lettres entre le gouvernement du Canada et le gouvernement de la République du Chili rectifiant l'annexe C-00-B, l'annexe D-01 et l'annexe D-03.1 et le règlement uniforme pour le chapitre D de l'Accord de libre-échange entre le gouvernement du Canada et le gouvernement de la République du Chili, fait à Santiago, le 4 décembre 1996. Ottawa, Santiago, 25 novembre 2004. *En vigueur:* le 1er janvier 2005.

Communauté européenne
Accord entre le Canada et la Communauté européenne relatif au commerce des vins et des boissons spiritueuses. Niagara-on-the-Lake, 16 septembre 2003. *En vigueur:* le 1er juin 2004.

Cuba
Accord entre le gouvernement du Canada et le gouvernement de la République de Cuba concernant le partage de biens confisqués ou des sommes d'argent équivalentes. La Havane, 8 juillet 2003. *En vigueur:* le 3 juin 2004.

Danemark
Échange de notes constituant un accord modifiant l'Accord entre le gouvernement du Canada et le gouvernement du Royaume du Danemark relatif à la délimitation du plateau continental entre le Groenland et le Canada fait à Ottawa le 17 décembre 1973. Copenhague, 20 avril 2004.

Émirats arabes unis
Convention entre le gouvernement du Canada et le gouvernement des Émirats arabes unis en vue d'éviter les doubles impositions et de prévenir l'évasion fiscale en matière d'impôts sur le revenu et sur la fortune. Abu Dhabi, 9 juin 2002. *En vigueur:* le 25 mai 2004.

Estonie
Accord de commerce entre le gouvernement du Canada et le gouvernement de la République d'Estonie. Ottawa, 27 juin 1994. *En vigueur:* le 10 février 1995. *Terminé:* 20 octobre 2004. RTC 1995/7.

Accord de coproduction audiovisuelle entre le gouvernement du Canada et le gouvernement de la République d'Estonie. Tallin, 27 mai 2002. *En vigueur:* le 4 novembre 2004.

États-Unis d'Amérique
Accord entre le gouvernement du Canada et le gouvernement des États-Unis d'Amérique sur la collaboration en sciences et technologies en vue de la protection des infrastructures essentielles et de la sécurité transfrontalière. Washington, 1 juin 2004. *En vigueur:* le 1er juin 2004.

Échange de notes entre le gouvernement du Canada et le gouvernement des États-Unis d'Amérique au sujet de l'alerte antimissile constituant un accord modifiant l'Accord relatif au Commandement de la défense aérospatiale de l'Amérique du Nord (NORAD). Washington, 5 août 2004. *En vigueur:* le 5 août 2004.

Échange de notes entre le gouvernement du Canada et le gouvernement des États-Unis d'Amérique constituant un accord pour prolonger l'Accord concernant l'amélioration de la sécurité bilatérale par une collaboration militaire accrue en ce qui a trait aux fonctions d'appui maritime, terrestre et civil signé le 5 décembre 2002. Ottawa, 29 novembre 2004. *En vigueur:* le 29 novembre 2004.

Accord entre le gouvernement du Canada et le gouvernement des États-Unis d'Amérique concernant l'exercice des principes de courtoisie active dans l'application de leurs lois sur la concurrence. Washington, 5 octobre 2004. *En vigueur:* le 5 octobre 2004.

Échange de notes entre le gouvernement du Canada et le gouvernement des États-Unis d'Amérique constituant un Accord modifiant le Traité concernant les thoniers (thon blanc) du Pacifique et leurs privilèges portuaires fait à Washington le 26 mai 1981. Washington, 13 août 2002. *En vigueur:* le 28 mai 2004.

Échange de notes entre le gouvernement du Canada et le gouvernement des États-Unis d'Amérique constituant un Accord modifiant le Traité concernant les thoniers (thon blanc) du Pacifique et leurs privilèges portuaires fait à Washington le 26 mai 1981. Washington, 10 septembre 2002. *En vigueur:* le 28 mai 2004.

Accord entre le gouvernement du Canada et le gouvernement des États-Unis d'Amérique pour la coopération en matière d'examen des demandes de statut de réfugié présentées par des ressortissants de pays tiers. Washington, 5 décembre 2002. *En vigueur:* le 29 décembre 2004.

Fédération de Russie
Accord de coopération entre le gouvernement du Canada et le gouvernement de la Fédération de Russie relatif à la destruction d'armes chimiques, le dé-

mantèlement de sous-marins nucléaires mis hors service et la protection physique, le contrôle et le dénombrement des matières nucléaires et radioactives. Sea Island, 9 juin 2004. *En vigueur:* le 17 août 2005.

France
Accord entre le gouvernement du Canada et le gouvernement de la République française relatif aux échanges de jeunes. Paris, 3 octobre 2003. *En vigueur:* le 1er mars 2004.

Haut Commissariat des Nations Unies pour les Réfugiés
Échange de notes constituant un amendement à l'Accord entre le gouvernement du Canada et le Haut Commissariat des Nations Unies pour les Réfugiés ayant pour but de déployer deux agents de la Gendarmerie royale du Canada en République de Guinée, signé le 7 janvier 2003. Genève, 6 janvier 2004. *En vigueur:* le 6 janvier 2004.

Israël
Accord sur la coopération bilatérale en matière de recherche et de développement industriels dans le secteur privé entre le gouvernement du Canada et le gouvernement de l'État d'Israël. Ottawa, 3 décembre 2004. *En vigueur:* le 3 décembre 2004.

Koweït
Échange de notes entre le gouvernement du Canada et le gouvernement de l'État du Koweït constituant un accord concernant le statut des Forces canadiennes au Koweït. Koweït, 11 mai 2004. *En vigueur:* le 24 mai 2004.

Mongolie
Traité entre le gouvernement du Canada et le gouvernement de la Mongolie concernant le transfert des délinquants. Ottawa, 20 octobre 2004. *En vigueur:* le 8 juin 2005.

Norvège
Accord entre le gouvernement du Canada et le gouvernement de la Norvège

concernant le partage des biens confisqués ou des sommes d'argent équivalentes. Ottawa, 25 mars 2004.

Oman
Accord entre le gouvernement du Canada et le gouvernement du Sultanat d'Oman en vue d'éviter les doubles impositions et de prévenir l'évasion fiscale en matière d'impôts sur le revenu et sur la fortune. Mascate, 30 juin 2004. *En vigueur:* le 27 avril 2005.

Pays-Bas
Accord sur la sécurité sociale entre le gouvernement du Canada et le gouvernement du Royaume des Pays-Bas. Brantford, 27 juin 2001. *En vigueur:* le 1ᵉʳ avril 2004.

République slovaque
Accord de coproduction audiovisuelle entre le gouvernement du Canada et le gouvernement de la République slovaque. Ottawa, 5 juin 2002. *En vigueur:* le 16 juillet 2004.

République tchèque
Échange de notes constituant un accord amendant l'Accord entre le gouvernement du Canada et le gouvernement de la République tchèque sur le transport aérien, signé à Prague le 13 mars 1996. Prague, 28 juin 2004. *En vigueur:* le 28 juin 2004.

Roumanie
Convention entre le Canada et la Roumanie en vue d'éviter les doubles impositions et de prévenir l'évasion fiscale en matière d'impôts sur le revenu et sur la fortune. Ottawa, 8 avril 2004. *En vigueur:* le 31 décembre 2004.

Royaume-Uni de Grande-Bretagne et d'Irlande du Nord
Protocole modifiant la Convention entre le gouvernement du Canada et le gouvernement du Royaume-Uni de Grande-Bretagne et d'Irlande du Nord tendant à éviter les doubles impositions et à prévenir l'évasion fiscale en matière d'impôts sur le revenu et les gains en capital, signée à Londres le 8 septembre 1978 et modifiée par le Protocole signé à Ottawa le 15 avril 1980 puis par le Protocole signé à Londres le 16 octobre 1985. Londres, 7 mai 2003. *En vigueur:* le 4 mai 2004.

Venezuela
Convention entre le gouvernement du Canada et le gouvernement de la République bolivarienne du Venezuela en vue d'éviter les doubles impositions et de prévenir l'évasion et la fraude fiscales en matière d'impôts sur le revenu et sur la fortune. Caracas, 10 juillet 2001. *En vigueur:* le 5 mai 2004.

Vietnam
Accord sur le transport aérien entre le gouvernement du Canada et le gouvernement de la République socialiste du Vietnam. Montréal, 28 septembre 2004.

II MULTILATÉRAUX

Agriculture
Traité international sur les ressources phytogénétiques pour l'alimentation et l'agriculture. Rome, 3 novembre 2001. *Signé* par le Canada: le 10 juin 2002. *Ratifié* par le Canada: 10 juin 2002. *En vigueur* pour le Canada: le 29 juin 2004.

Aviation
Convention relative aux garanties internationales portant sur des matériels d'équipement mobiles. Le Cap, 16 novembre 2001. *Signé* par le Canada: le 31 mars 2004.

Protocole portant sur les questions spécifiques aux matériels d'équipement aéronautiques à la Convention relative aux garanties internationales portant sur des matériels d'équipement mobiles. Le Cap, 16 novembre 2001. *Signé* par le Canada: le 31 mars 2004.

Commerce (multilatéral)
Échange de lettres entre le gouvernement du Canada, le gouvernement des États-Unis d'Amérique et le gouvernement des États-Unis du Mexique

modifiant l'annexe 401 de l'Accord de libre-échange nord-américain. Mexico, Ottawa, Washington, 3 décembre 2002. *En vigueur* entre le Canada et la Mexique le 22 juillet 2004.

Échange de lettres entre le gouvernement du Canada, le gouvernement des États-Unis d'Amérique et le gouvernement des États-Unis du Mexique constituant un accord modifiant l'annexe 401 de l'Accord de libre-échange nord-américain. *Signature:* Mexico, Ottawa, Washington, 22 octobre 2004.

Corruption
Convention des Nations Unies contre la corruption. New York, 31 octobre 2003. *Signé* par le Canada: le 21 mai 2004.

Criminalité transnationale
Protocole contre le trafic illicite de migrants par terre, air et mer, additionnel à la Convention des Nations Unies contre la criminalité transnationale organisée. New York, 15 novembre 2000. *Signé* par le Canada: le 14 décembre 2000. *Ratifié* par le Canada: le 13 mai 2002. *En vigueur* pour le Canada: le 28 janvier 2004.

Défense
Protocole au Traité de l'Atlantique Nord sur l'accession de la République de Bulgarie. Bruxelles, 26 mars 2003. *Signé* par le Canada: le 26 mars 2003. *Ratifié* par le Canada: le 28 mars 2003. *En vigueur* pour le Canada: le 27 février 2004.

Protocole au Traité de l'Atlantique Nord sur l'accession de la République d'Estonie. Bruxelles, 26 mars 2003. *Signé* par le Canada: le 26 mars 2003. *Ratifié* par le Canada: le 28 mars 2003. *En vigueur* pour le Canada: le 27 février 2004.

Protocole au Traité de l'Atlantique Nord sur l'accession de la République de Lettonie. Bruxelles, 26 mars 2003. *Signé* par le Canada: le 26 mars 2003. *Ratifié* par le Canada: le 28 mars 2003. *En vigueur* pour le Canada: le 27 février 2004.

Protocole au Traité de l'Atlantique Nord sur l'accession de la République de Lituanie. Bruxelles, 26 mars 2003. *Signé* par le Canada: le 26 mars 2003. *Ratifié* par le Canada: le 28 mars 2003. *En vigueur* pour le Canada: le 27 février 2004.

Protocole au Traité de l'Atlantique Nord sur l'accession de la Roumanie. Bruxelles, 26 mars 2003. *Signé* par le Canada: le 26 mars 2003. *Ratifié* par le Canada: le 28 mars 2003. *En vigueur* pour le Canada: le 27 février 2004.

Protocole au Traité de l'Atlantique Nord sur l'accession de la République slovaque. Bruxelles, 26 mars 2003. *Signé* par le Canada: le 26 mars 2003. *Ratifié* par le Canada: le 28 mars 2003. *En vigueur* pour le Canada: le 27 février 2004.

Protocole au Traité de l'Atlantique Nord sur l'accession de la République de Slovénie. Bruxelles, 26 mars 2003. *Signé* par le Canada: le 26 mars 2003. *Ratifié* par le Canada: le 28 mars 2003. *En vigueur* pour le Canada: le 27 février 2004.

Désarmement
Amendement à la Convention sur l'interdiction ou la limitation de l'emploi de certaines armes classiques qui peuvent être considérées comme produisant des effets traumatiques excessifs ou comme frappant sans discrimination. Genève, 21 décembre 2001. *Accepté* par le Canada: le 22 juillet 2002. *En vigueur* pour le Canada: 18 mai 2004.

Environnement
Convention de Rotterdam sur la procédure de consentement préalable en connaissance de cause applicable à certains produits chimiques et pesticides dangereux qui font l'objet d'un commerce international. Rotterdam, 10 septembre 1998. *Adhésion:* le 26 août 2002. *En vigueur* pour le Canada: le 24 février 2004.

Convention de Stockholm sur les polluants organiques persistants. Stockholm, 22 mai 2001. *Signé* par le Canada:

le 23 mai 2001. *Ratifié* par le Canada: le 23 mai 2001. *En vigueur* pour le Canada: le 17 mai 2004.

Imposition
Convention concernant l'assistance administrative mutuelle en matière fiscale. Strasbourg, 25 janvier 1988. *Signé* par le Canada: le 28 avril 2004.

Pêches
Convention relative au renforcement de la commission interaméricaine du thon tropical établie par la Convention de 1949 entre les États-Unis d'Amérique et la République du Costa Rica. Washington, 14 novembre 2003. *Signé* par le Canada: le 22 décembre 2004.

Privilèges et immunités
Accord sur les Privilèges et immunités de la Cour pénale internationale. New York, 9 septembre 2002. *Signé* par le Canada: le 30 avril 2004. *Ratifié* par le Canada: le 22 juin 2004. *En vigueur* pour le Canada: le 22 juillet 2004.

Questions postales
Actes du XXIIIe Congrès de l'Union postale universelle. Bucarest, 5 octobre 2004. *Signé* par le Canada: le 5 octobre 2004. *Ratifié* par le Canada: le 6 octobre 2005. *En vigueur* pour le Canada: le 1er janvier 2006.

Santé
Convention-cadre de l'OMS pour la lutte antitabac. Genève, 21 mai 2003. *Signé* par le Canada: le 15 juillet 2003. *Ratifié* par le Canada: le 26 novembre 2004. *En vigueur* pour le Canada: le 27 février 2005.

Science
Accord portant création d'un Centre international pour la science et la technologie. Moscou, 27 novembre 1992. *Adhésion* par le Canada: le 26 février 2004.

Télécommunications
Actes finaux de la Conférence de plénipotentiaires de l'Union internationale des télécommunications. Marrakech, 18 octobre 2002. *Signé* par le Canada: le 18 octobre 2002. *Ratifié* par le Canada: le 26 avril 2004. *Entrée en vigueur* pour le Canada: le 26 avril 2004.

Cases / Jurisprudence

Canadian Cases in Public International Law in 2004–5 / Jurisprudence canadienne en matière de droit international public en 2004–5

compiled by / préparé par
GIBRAN VAN ERT

*Extradition — proof of treaty before examining judge —
role of extradition judge*

Czech Republic v. Moravek, 2004 M.B.C.A. 174 (8 November 2004),
(Court of Appeal for Manitoba)

The Czech Republic sought extradition of a fugitive, Moravek,
for enforcement of a sentence. Moravek was a Canadian citizen
sentenced to six months imprisonment in the Czech Republic in
1996 after pleading guilty to property offences. He escaped custody en route to prison and returned to Canada. The extradition
judge ordered Moravek discharged. Though the fugitive's identity
and conviction for conduct equivalent to theft were established,
the judge held that the requesting state had not met the onus of
establishing that the extradition treaty, including its amending protocol, applied. The judge also held that Moravek did not have at
least six months remaining to be served on his sentence, as required
by section 3(3) of the Extradition Act.[1]

At the extradition hearing and again on appeal, Moravek argued
that the Czech Republic had not established the Canada/Czech
extradition agreement. Moravek was exploiting what, on its face,
appears to be a typo in the 1997 diplomatic correspondence between Canada and the Czech Republic confirming the latter's succession to treaties to which the former Czechoslovakia was a party.

Gibran van Ert is an associate with Hunter Litigation Chambers in Vancouver.

[1] Extradition Act, S.C. 1999, c. 18, as amended.

611

Among these treaties is the "Treaty between the Czechoslovak Republic and the United Kingdom of Great Britain and Northern Ireland for the Extradition of Criminals, done at London on November 11, 1924, as amended by a Protocol signed at London on June 4, 1936 [sic]." A review of the Canada Treaty Series establishes that the treaty and its 1926 — not 1936 — protocol were in force for Canada as of 1928.[2] Similar correspondence between Canada and Slovakia in 1998 was before the court and cited the amending protocol to 1926. Nevertheless, Moravek persuaded the extradition judge that two protocols were referred to in the record but only one was put before the court, with the result that the requesting stated had failed to prove the extradition agreement.

Moravek was also successful before the extradition judge in arguing that he ought not to be committed because he did not have at least six months remaining on his sentence. Moravek's argument was that the time he spent in police custody — after the pronouncement of his sentence but before escaping the police while en route to prison — must be subtracted from the six-month sentence he was ordered to serve.

Philp J.A. for the Court of Appeal for Manitoba allowed the appeal on both points. He began by reviewing the extradition process. He noted that "Canada's international obligation to surrender a fugitive to another country must be found in a treaty. It is not part of the customary international law."[3] Similarly, he noted that extradition in domestic law is an executive power created by statute, not a power conferred by the common law. The jurisdiction of an extradition judge is therefore not inherent. Rather, it is derived from the Extradition Act and the applicable treaty. Philp J.A. also reviewed case law indicating that extradition is intended to be an expedited process in which the presiding judge plays a modest role in compliance with Canada's international obligations.

Turning to the extradition treaty and its protocol, Philp J.A. noted that section 7 of the act assigns to the minister responsibility for "the implementation of extradition agreements" and that section 8 provides that an extradition treaty, when published in the Canada Gazette or the Canada Treaty Series, must be judicially noticed. Philp J.A. also noted that an extradition agreement is not a

---

2   Treaty between the Czechoslovak Republic and the United Kingdom of Great Britain and Northern Ireland for the Extradition of Criminals, [1928] Can. T.S. no. 8.

3   *Czech Republic v. Moravek* at para. 15.

document required to be included as part of the record of the case at the extradition hearing pursuant to section 33. His lordship went on to cite authorities to the effect that the question of whether a treaty continued to be in force and binding on Canada is one for the minister to determine and not one with the jurisdiction of an extradition judge. In particular, he quoted from a recent BC case, which declined to follow the extradition judge's decision in the present appeal.[4] Philp J.A. concluded that the extradition judge had exceeded his jurisdiction by inquiring into the status of Canada's treaty obligations and concluding that the Czech Republic had not met the onus of establishing that the disputed treaty and protocol applied. Citing *United States of America v. Lépine,* Philp J.A. affirmed that treaty compliance under the Canadian extradition regime is a question for the executive not the courts. Having issued the authority to proceed under section 15 of the act, it must be assumed that the minister concluded that the extradition agreement was the treaty and the amending protocol extended to Canada as of 15 August 1928 and that the difference in the dates in the amending protocol and the diplomatic correspondence was merely a slip.[5]

Philp J.A. also reversed the extradition judge on the duration of Moravek's sentence. His lordship described the argument as "somewhat specious" and noted that there was no evidence of exactly what portion of Moravek's sentence had in fact been served but that it was "less than a day and possibly no more than an hour or two." He held, however, that the question was irrelevant. The Czech Republic's request for extradition stated that the sentence had been rendered but had not become effective for the offender. "That statement dispels any concern that the condition set out in s. 3(3) of the Act — the minimum term of imprisonment remaining to be carried out — had not been met." Philp J.A. agreed with counsel for the republic that the extradition judge had usurped the role of the minister of justice to determine whether or not the minimum sentence requirements under the Act and the treaty had been satisfied.[6] The question of when Moravek's sentence commenced was a question of Czech law, and it was for the minister, not the court, to be satisfied that the requirements of section 3(3) were met.

---

[4] *Ibid.* at paras. 23–6; *Czech Republic v. Ganis,* 2004 BCSC 688.

[5] *Czech Republic v. Moravek* at paras. 27–29; *United States of America v. Lépine,* [1994] 1 S.C.R. 286.

[6] *Czech Republic v. Moravek* at paras. 30–32.

Arbitral awards — North American Free Trade Agreement (NAFTA) —
judicial review

United Mexican States v. Karpa (2005), 74 O.R. (3d) 180 (11 January 2005) (Court of Appeal for Ontario)

This was an appeal from the decision of Chilcott J. in *Mexico v. Karpa* (also known as *Feldman*), a decision considered in last year's *Yearbook*.[7] Chilcott J. rejected an application by Mexico to set aside an arbitral award against it under Chapter 11 of the 1992 NAFTA.[8] The majority of the arbitral tribunal found that Mexico discriminated against an American investor, Feldman, contrary to NAFTA Article 1102 (national treatment). Mexico applied to the Ontario court for judicial review of this award pursuant to Article 34 of the 1985 United Nations Commission on International Trade Law (UNCITRAL) Model Law on International Commercial Arbitration, as implemented in Ontario by section 2 of the International Commercial Arbitration Act.[9] As it had done in the Superior Court, Mexico sought to impugn the NAFTA award on the grounds of Model Law Articles 34(2)(a)(ii) (applicant unable to present his case), 34(2)(a)(iv) (arbitral procedure not in accordance with agreement of parties), and 34(2)(b)(ii) (award conflicts with public policy). The attorney-general of Canada intervened in support of Mexico at first instance but did not participate in the appeal.[10]

Feldman was in the business of exporting cigarettes out of Mexico through his company CEMSA. His main allegation was that Mexico discriminated against CEMSA by failing to extend to it a rebate on export taxes enjoyed by domestic cigarette exporters. To prove this allegation, Feldman sought production by Mexico of the taxpayer records of his competitors. Mexico objected that Article 69 of its Fiscal Code prevented the production of such evidence. Instead, Mexico filed a statement by one of its taxation officials. On the basis of this and other evidence, the tribunal concluded that Feldman had made out a *prima facie* case of discrimination and that Mexico had failed to meet its burden of adducing evidence to show otherwise.[11]

---

7 See [2004] Can. Y.B. Int'l L. 593.

8 North American Free Trade Agreement, [1994] Can. T.S. no 2.

9 International Commercial Arbitration Act, R.S.O. 1990 c. I-9.

10 *United Mexican States v. Karpa* at para. 28.

11 See para. 187 of the tribunal's award, quoted in *United Mexican States v. Karpa* at para. 21.

Armstrong J.A. for the court began by considering the standard of review applicable to the arbitral award. He observed at the outset: "Notions of international comity and the reality of the global marketplace suggest that courts should use their authority to interfere with international commercial arbitration awards sparingly."[12] He next observed that, "[q]uite apart from principles of international comity, our domestic law in Canada dictates a high degree of deference for decisions of specialized tribunals generally and for awards of consensual arbitration tribunals in particular," citing the well-known *Pushpanathan* test for determining the standard of review of Canadian administrative decision-making.[13] Armstrong J.A. went on to apply, in an abbreviated way, the *Pushpanathan* factors. He found that neither the Model Law nor the ICSID Additional Facility Rules (under which the arbitration was conducted) contains a privative clause excluding judicial review, though he briefly noted the constraints on review imposed by section 34 of the Model Law. He observed that there was nothing in the record describing the expertise of the tribunal members but stated: "We do know that the president of the tribunal was selected from a special roster of 45 individuals. The individuals listed on the roster are required, pursuant to NAFTA, article 1124:4, to be 'experienced in international law and investment matters'."[14] Finally, Armstrong J.A. observed that the matters to be decided by the tribunal were "heavily fact laden." On the basis of this analysis, he concluded that "the applicable standard of review in this case is at the high end of the spectrum of judicial deference."[15]

With respect, this analysis is misconceived. The highly deferential result is to be welcomed, but the means employed to reach this result are inappropriate. The Model Law was adopted by UNCITRAL in 1985 to promote uniformity in the law of arbitral procedures around the world. The form of a model law was chosen as a vehicle for international harmonization. This presumably also explains the form its implementation takes in Ontario and other Canadian jurisdictions: a short act declaring the Model Law to be in force in Ontario and appending it as a schedule to the act. One of the aspects of international arbitration that the Model Law seeks

---

[12] *United Mexican States v. Karpa* at para. 34; see also paras. 35–36.

[13] *Ibid.* at paras. 37–38.

[14] In this Armstrong J.A. was mistaken. While NAFTA Article 1124(4) does provide for such a roster, it has never been populated.

[15] *United Mexican States v. Karpa* at paras. 39–43.

to harmonize is judicial review of arbitral awards. It is for this reason that Article 34 sets out the sole grounds for recourse against international arbitral awards, to the exclusion of any other basis of review established under domestic law.[16] Those grounds do not include the fluctuating standard of review derived by application of the pragmatic and functional approach to judicial review elaborated by the Supreme Court of Canada in *Pushpanathan* and other cases. This case law must simply be disregarded in judicial reviews under the International Commercial Arbitration Act and other statutes implementing the Model Law in Canada. The only juridical basis for impugning an international arbitral award in any jurisdiction that has adopted the Model Law is Article 34. To apply the pragmatic and functional approach is not only contrary to the express words of Article 34(1) but undermines the entire purpose of the Model Law, namely the harmonization of arbitral practice around the world.

In spite of his departure from Article 34 in determining the standard of review, Armstrong J.A. was brought back to this article by Mexico's submissions, all of which were framed in terms of Article 34's stated grounds of review. Armstrong J.A. addressed Mexico's first two grounds of appeal together. In the arbitration, Mexico failed to produce certain documents disclosure of which, it claimed, was forbidden by Mexican law. The arbitral award drew an adverse inference against Mexico for this failure to disclose evidence. Mexico challenged this finding as being not in accordance with the agreement of the parties, contrary to Model Law Article 34(2)(a)(iv), and as rendering Mexico unable to present its case, contrary to Article 34(2)(a)(ii). Armstrong J.A. rejected both these grounds of appeal, largely for the reasons given by Chilcott J. below.

Mexico's final ground of appeal was that the award of damages to Feldman was contrary to Ontario public policy and therefore contrary to Model Law Article 34(2)(b)(ii) because the damages were based on the value of tax rebates that were themselves unlawful as a matter of Mexican law. Mexico also relied on the tribunal's finding that Feldman's company, CEMSA, had substantially over-claimed the tax paid and was guilty of tax fraud. Armstrong J.A. rejected these arguments, quoting from Feldman J. in *Schreter v. Gasmac Inc.*:

---

[16] Model Law article 34(1): "(1) Recourse to a court against an arbitral award may be made only by an application for setting aside in accordance with paragraphs (2) and (3) of this article." This article is implemented in Ontario by the schedule to the International Commercial Arbitration Act R.S.O. 1990 c. I-9.

The concept of imposing our public policy on foreign awards is to guard against enforcement of an award *which offends our local principles of justice and fairness in a fundamental way*, and in a way which the parties could attribute to the fact that the award was made in another jurisdiction where the procedural or substantive rules diverge markedly from our own, or where there was ignorance or corruption on the part of the tribunal which could not be seen to be tolerated or condoned by our courts.[17]

Armstrong J.A. found that the tribunal's award of damages was not contrary to public policy, being "rationally connected to the discriminatory conduct found by the tribunal" and "a logical quantification of the harm caused to CEMSA by the discriminatory conduct." Armstrong J.A. also noted that the tribunal had made allowances for Feldman's inflated rebate claims in its assessment of damages.[18]

Like Chilcott J. in the court below, Armstrong J.A. rightly rejected Mexico's attacks on the NAFTA award. However, the judgment's preference for Canadian judicial review jurisprudence over the international standards expressly adopted by the Ontario legislature in the International Commercial Arbitration Act sets a bad precedent.

Criminal law — extra-territoriality — presumption of conformity with international law

R. v. Saunders, 2005 N.S.P.C. 13 (24 March 2005) (Nova Scotia Provincial Court)

The accused was charged with sexual offences committed between 1983 and 1985 in Germany. At the time, the accused was a member of the Canadian Armed Forces and was therefore subject to the Code of Service Discipline. While section 6(2) of the Criminal Code[19] provides in part that no person shall be convicted of an offence committed outside Canada, the Crown argued that the accused was excepted from this provision by section 273 and other sections of the National Defence Act.[20] Section 273 provides in part that where a person subject to the Code of Service Discipline does any act while outside Canada which, if done in Canada, would be

---

17 (1992) 7 O.R. (3d) 608 at 623, quoted in *United Mexican States v. Karpa* at para. 66 (original emphasis).

18 *United Mexican States v. Karpa* at paras. 67–68.

19 Criminal Code, R.S.C. 1985 c. C-46, as amended.

20 National Defence Act, R.S.C. 1985 c. N-4, as amended.

an offence punishable by a civil court, that offence is within the competence of, and may be tried and punished by, a civil court having jurisdiction. Against this, the accused maintained that by virtue of Article VII of the NATO Status of Forces Agreement (SOFA),[21] concurrent jurisdiction over the matters underlying the charges was given to Germany and to the Canadian Armed Forces Service Tribunal, and that the jurisdiction of the latter tribunal ended with the expiry of a three-year limitation period. Read in light of the presumption against the extra-territorial application of legislation, the presumption of conformity with international law, and the provisions of the SOFA, the accused argued that section 273 failed to confer jurisdiction to the provincial court. (It was agreed by the parties that the provisions of Criminal Code section 7(4.1) deeming certain offences to be committed in Canada did not apply retroactively.)

After reviewing at some length the majority and concurring opinions of the Supreme Court of Canada in *R. v. Cook*[22] on the extra-territorial application of Canadian law, Associate Chief Judge Gibson concluded that there are three scenarios in which an extension of Canadian jurisdiction extra-territorially over Criminal Code matters may occur: (1) exceptionally, where there is no Canadian legislation extending the Code's application extra-territorially; (2) where legislation does extend the Code's extra-territorial reach and no treaties define or limit the Code's application in the jurisdiction in which its application is sought; and (3) where legislation extends the Code's application extra-territorially but existing treaties define or limit that extension.

Judge Gibson found that this case presented the latter situation — that is, the Criminal Code's reach was extended beyond Canadian territory by applicable laws but subject to the limits international law places upon Canada's jurisdiction and the presumption that Parliament does not legislate in breach of its treaty obligations.[23] While section 273 of the National Defence Act purports to extend the application of the Criminal Code extra-territorially on the basis of nationality, this provision must be read in the light of the SOFA. In the SOFA, Canada assigned the extra-territorial jurisdiction it acquired by means of that treaty to its military authorities. When the SOFA came into force for Canada in 1953, there was no

---

[21] NATO Status of Forces Agreement, [1953] Can. T.S. no. 13.

[22] *R. v. Cook*, [1998] 2 S.C.R. 597.

[23] *Saunders* at paras. 40–41.

legislation in place giving Canadian civil courts jurisdiction over Criminal Code offences committed by members of the Canadian Armed Forces. To the extent that section 273 purports to extend Canada's extra-territorial jurisdiction, it must be read subject to Canada's treaty obligations, applying the presumption of conformity with international law. By ascribing the jurisdiction granted under the SOFA to its military authorities, Canada chose to limit the exercise of its concurrent jurisdiction with Germany. By imposing a three-year limitation period on military proceedings, Parliament intended matters so prescribed to become matters over which Germany acquired primary jurisdiction under SOFA Article VII at the expiry of the limitation period. Absent an amendment to the SOFA, it was not within the authority of Canada to unilaterally transfer to a civil court the primary jurisdiction it ascribed to its military authorities under the provisions of Article VII.[24]

Judge Gibson acknowledged that Canadian authorities may have a greater interest in proceeding with these charges than their German counterparts, given the nationality of both the accused and the complainants as well as other factors. Yet he rejected the application of a reasonable connection test here, affirming that "the principles of international law require that treaty agreements be followed" and therefore section 273 of the National Defence Act cannot apply until German authorities waive the primary jurisdiction over these offences as provided for by the SOFA.[25]

Judge Gibson's reasons come perilously close to breaching the long-established rule that treaties have no direct legal effect in Canadian law. This is in spite of the learned judge's orthodox invocation of the interpretive presumptions that Parliament intends its legislation to apply territorially and to comply with Canadian treaty obligations. Section 273 of the National Defence Act seems clear that where a person subject to the Code of Service Discipline does any act while outside Canada which, if done in Canada, would be an offence punishable by a civil court, that offence is within the competence of, and may be tried and punished by, a civil court having jurisdiction. Judge Gibson effectively suspends the application of this section on the basis of SOFA Article VII. This may go beyond interpretation. To repeat Lord Diplock's formulation of the presumption of conformity in *Solomon v. Commissioners of Customs and Excise*, "if one of the meanings which can reasonably be

---

[24] *Ibid.* at paras. 48–54.
[25] *Ibid.* at paras. 55–58.

ascribed to the legislation is consonant with the treaty obligations and another or others are not, the meaning which is consonant is to be preferred."[26] The question is whether section 273 can reasonably bear the SOFA-compliant meaning that Judge Gibson ascribes to it. One wonders whether Judge Gibson would have applied this same analysis to Criminal Code section 7(4.1) had that provision applied.

International arbitration — stays of proceedings — UNCITRAL Model Law

Pan Liberty Navigation Co. Ltd. v. World Link (H.K.) Resources Ltd., 2005 B.C.C.A. 206 (8 April 2005) (Court of Appeal for British Columbia)

This was an appeal by the defendant from an order refusing to stay an action on the ground that further proceedings in it should take place in England. The plaintiffs were Cypriot ship owners, two of whose ships were chartered to a company known as Worldlink Transport Company Limited of Beijing (Worldlink Beijing). The charter agreements provided that disputes shall be governed by English law and referred to arbitration in London. The ship owners commenced such arbitrations in 2001 and won default awards when Worldlink Beijing failed to defend. They now sought to enforce the award against the defendant in this action, World Link (HK). The latter denied any relation to or association with Worldlink Beijing.

The matter came before the British Columbia courts when the ship owners' English solicitor learned that a ship under charter to World Link (HK) was headed for the province. The ship owners sought a Mareva injunction against the ship's fuel and bunkers. The style of cause named four defendants, all companies incorporated in Hong Kong or Beijing with names along the lines of "Worldlink Transport." The Mareva injunction was granted *ex parte*. Shortly thereafter, World Link (HK) paid Cdn $850,000 security into court and the ship went on its way. World Link (HK) then sought a stay of the ship owners' action pursuant to the Commercial Arbitration Act,[27] which is the means by which the UNCITRAL Model Law on International Commercial Arbitration

---

[26] *Solomon v. Commissioners of Customs and Excise,* [1967] 2 Q.B. 116 at 143–4; quoted in *Saunders* at para. 31.

[27] Commercial Arbitration Act, R.S.C. 1985 c. 17 (2nd Supp.).

is implemented in Canadian federal law. The chambers judge dismissed the application, holding that the matter was one of enforcement of an award already obtained and therefore fell outside of the arbitration provisions of the charter agreements. Esson J.A. for the court allowed the appeal. He began by agreeing with World Link (HK) that the ship owners' allegations come within the arbitration agreements because the real issue between the parties was a dispute about the identity of the defaulting charterer — that is, was World Link (HK) the same person as Worldlink Beijing? Against the ship owners' argument that the arbitrator, having delivered a final award, lacked any further jurisdiction over the dispute, Esson J.A. held that that was a question of English law to be determined by the English arbitrator.

His lordship then considered whether the chambers judge ought to have granted the requested stay of proceedings under the Commercial Arbitration Act. Section 5(1) of the act gives force of law to the Commercial Arbitration Code as scheduled to the act. The code is based on the UNCITRAL Model Law on International Commercial Arbitration and deviates from the latter in only minor ways. Article 8(1) of the code provides:

A court before which an action is brought in a matter which is the subject of an arbitration agreement shall, if a party so requests not later than when submitting his first statement on the substance of the dispute, refer the parties to arbitration unless it finds that the agreement is null and void, inoperative or incapable of being performed.

Le tribunal saisi d'un différend sur une question faisant l'objet d'une convention d'arbitrage renverra les parties à l'arbitrage si l'une d'entre elles le demande au plus tard lorsqu'elle soumet ses premières conclusions quant au fond du différend, à moins qu'il ne constate que la convention est caduque, inopérante ou non susceptible d'être exécutée.

Esson J.A. noted that the leading authority on Article 8(1) in British Columbia is *Prince George (City) v. McElhanney Engineering Serivces Ltd.*,[28] a decision based on BC's enactment of the UNCITRAL Model Law. In this case, the Court of Appeal adopted the reasons of the Ontario High Court in *Boart Sweden AB v. NYA Stromnes AB*,[29]

---

[28] *Prince George (City) v. McElhanney Engineering Serivces Ltd.* (1995), 9 B.C.L.R. (3d) 368 (C.A.).

[29] *Boart Sweden AB v. NYA Stromnes AB* (1988), 41 B.L.R. 295 (Ont. H.C.).

a judgment arising from Ontario's UNCITRAL statute, to the effect that Article 8(1) gives the courts a clear direction to defer to arbitrators and to hold parties to their arbitration contracts.

To the ship owners' submission that these authorities did not apply where a final award has been issued, Esson J.A. replied that, having regard to the general policy of the law in this area, he would not presume to define the scope of the arbitrator's authority. To this effect, his lordship approved a recent English decision arising from UK legislation implementing the New York Convention on the Recognition and Enforcement of Foreign Arbitral Awards 1958, *Norsk Hydro ASA v. State Property Fund of Ukraine:*

> There is an important policy interest, reflected in this country's treaty obligations, in ensuring the effective and speedy enforcement of such international arbitration awards; the corollary, however, is that the task of the enforcing court should be as "mechanistic" as possible ... [T]he enforcing court is neither entitled nor bound to go behind the award in question, explore the reasoning of the arbitration tribunal or second-guess its intentions.[30]

Esson J.A. therefore allowed the appeal and granted the stay of proceedings.

While the UNCITRAL Model Law is not a treaty, it nevertheless represents a significant multilateral consensus on the principles that should guide domestic courts in their interactions with commercial arbitration proceedings. The Court of Appeal's deferential approach to such proceedings, informed by the judgments of courts in other Model Law jurisdictions, is to be welcomed.

International criminal law — incitement to genocide — crimes against humanity

Mugesera v. Canada (Minister of Citizenship and Immigration), [2005] 2 S.C.R. 100 (28 June 2005) (Supreme Court of Canada)

This appeal arose from a deportation order issued by an adjudicator following proceedings under sections 27(1) and 19(1) of the old Immigration Act.[31] The minister of citizenship and immigration sought to deport the Léon Mugesera, a Rwandan national with permanent resident status in Canada since 1993, on the

---

[30] *Norsk Hydro ASA v. State Property Fund of Ukraine,* [2002] E.W.H.C. 2120 (Comm.) at para. 17.

[31] Immigration Act, R.S.C. 1985 c. I-12, as amended.

grounds of incitement to murder, genocide, and hatred, as well as the commission of a crime against humanity. The minister alleged that Mugesera committed these offences in the course of a violently anti-Tutsi speech he gave in November 1992, more than a year before the beginning of the Rwandan genocide of 1994. The adjudicator's deportation order was upheld by the Appeal Division of the Immigration and Refugee Board (IAD). Mugesera's application for judicial review was dismissed by the Federal Court's Trial Division, but the Federal Court of Appeal set aside the deportation order and reversed several findings of fact made by the IAD.

In joint reasons attributed, unusually, to all of the eight justices who heard the appeal, the Supreme Court of Canada unanimously allowed the minister's appeal and restored the deportation order. The court reviewed at length the law of incitement to murder, incitement to genocide, incitement to hatred, and crimes against humanity, as well as discussing the role of appellate courts at the secondary level of appellate review. This note focuses on the international law aspects of the judgment, namely the offences of incitement to genocide and crimes against humanity.

The court began by reviewing recent events in Rwandan history, including the flight of ethnic Tutsis to Uganda following the establishment of the first republic in 1961, the coming to power of General Juvénal Habyarimana and his hard-line Hutu political party the MRND in 1973, the Tutsi RPF's invasion of Rwanda in 1990, and the conclusion of the Arusha accords in 1993. The court then reviewed the IAD's findings of fact and held that the Federal Court of Appeal "exceeded the scope of its judicial review function" by engaging in "a broad-ranging review and reassessment of the IAD's findings."[32]

The minister alleged that Mugesera's speech incited murder, genocide, and hatred contrary to both Rwandan and Canadian criminal law. Applying section 27(1)(a.1)(ii), the court held that the minister's evidence of these allegations must meet the civil standard of the balance of probabilities. Applying this standard, the court found all three incitement allegations to be well founded. On the specific offence of incitement to genocide, the court observed:

Genocide is a crime originating in international law. International law is thus called upon to play a crucial role as an aid in interpreting domestic law, particularly as regards the elements of the crime of incitement to genocide. Section 318(1) of the *Criminal Code* incorporates, almost word for

---

[32] *Mugesera* at para. 36.

word, the definition of genocide found in art. II of the *Genocide Convention*, and the Minister's allegation B makes specific reference to Rwanda's accession to the *Genocide Convention*. Canada is also bound by the *Genocide Convention*. In addition to treaty obligations, the legal principles underlying the *Genocide Convention* are recognized as part of customary international law: see International Court of Justice, Advisory Opinion of May 28, 1951, *Reservations to the Convention on the Prevention and Punishment of the Crime of Genocide*, I.C.J. Reports 1951, at p. 15. The importance of interpreting domestic law in a manner that accords with the principles of customary international law and with Canada's treaty obligations was emphasized in *Baker v. Canada (Minister of Citizenship and Immigration)*, [1999] 2 S.C.R. 817, at paras. 69-71. In this context, international sources like the recent jurisprudence of international criminal courts are highly relevant to the analysis.[33]

From this propitious beginning, the court went on to observe that section 318(1) of the Criminal Code proscribes the offence of advocating genocide but that there is no Canadian jurisprudence under this provision. To determine the elements of the crime of incitement to genocide, therefore, the court looked to international criminal law, in this case as stated in the jurisprudence of the International Criminal Tribunal for Rwanda (ICTR). The court adopted the ICTR's decision in *Prosecutor v. Akayesu* that a charge of incitement to genocide does not require proof that genocide in fact happened,[34] applying this decision as decisive of the question for the purpose of section 318(1).[35] Likewise, the court applied *Akayesu*, along with Article 3(c) of the Convention on the Prevention and Punishment of the Crime of Genocide,[36] in holding that the criminal act requirement for incitement to genocide under section 318(1) has two elements: the act of incitement must be direct and public. On the meaning of "direct," the court again applied *Akayesu* that the act must specifically provoke another to engage in a criminal act and that the directness of the incitement must be viewed in light of its cultural and linguistic content.[37] The court again relied

---

[33] *Ibid.* at para. 82.

[34] *Prosecutor v. Akayesu* (1998), 9 I.H.R.R. 608 (I.C.T.R.).

[35] *Mugesera* at paras. 84–85.

[36] Convention on the Prevention and Punishment of the Crime of Genocide, [1949] Can.T.S. no. 27.

[37] *Mugesera* at paras. 86–87.

on *Akayesu*, along with the ICTR's decision in the *Media* case,[38] in finding that the guilty mind required for incitement to genocide is an intent to directly prompt or provoke another to commit genocide. The court added that the crime requires specific intent and that such intent may be inferred from the circumstances.[39] Having thus defined the elements of the offence of incitement to genocide, the court went on to affirm the IAD's findings that the offence was made out in respect of Mugesera's speech.

The Supreme Court of Canada also relied heavily on international criminal law jurisprudence and other sources of international law in its consideration of the minister's allegation that Mugesera's speech amounted to a crime against humanity. Section 19(1)(j) of the former Immigration Act provided that persons who there are reasonable grounds to believe have committed a crime against humanity within the meaning of Criminal Code section 7(3.76) shall not be granted admission to Canada. Section 7(3.76) defined crime against humanity as follows:

"crime against humanity" means murder, extermination, enslavement, deportation, persecution or any other inhumane act or omission that is committed against any civilian population or any identifiable group of persons, whether or not it constitutes a contravention of the law in force at the time and in the place of its commission, and that, at that time and in that place, constitutes a contravention of customary international law or conventional international law or is criminal according to the general principles of law recognized by the community of nations.

"crime contre l'humanité" Assassinat, extermination, réduction en esclavage, déportation, persécution ou autre fait — acte ou omission — inhumain d'une part, commis contre une population civile ou un groupe identifiable de personnes — qu'il ait ou non constitué une transgression du droit en vigueur à l'époque et au lieu de la perpétration — et d'autre part, soit constituant, à l'époque et dans ce lieu, une transgression du droit international coutumier ou conventionnel, soit ayant un caractère criminel d'après les principes généraux de droit reconnus par l'ensemble des nations.

This statutory definition of crimes against humanity has now been repealed and replaced by sections 4 and 6 of the Crimes against

---

[38] *Prosecutor v. Nahimana, Barayagwiza and Ngeze*, Case no. ICTR-99-52-T-I, 3 December 2003.

[39] *Mugesera* at paras. 88–89.

Humanity and War Crimes Act,[40] but the court made a point of observing that the differences between the previous and current definitions are not material to the court's discussion of the concept.[41]

The court began its discussion of crimes against humanity by stating that a criminal act rises to the level of a crime against humanity "based on the provisions of the *Criminal Code* and the principles of international law" when four elements are made out:

1. An enumerated proscribed act was committed (this involves showing that the accused committed the criminal act and had the requisite guilty state of mind for the underlying act);
2. The act was committed as part of a widespread or systematic attack;
3. The attack was directed against any civilian population or any identifiable group of persons; and
4. The person committing the proscribed act knew of the attack and knew or took the risk that his or her act comprised a part of that attack.[42]

The court acknowledged "the existence of a great deal of confusion about the elements of a crime against humanity,"[43] and also noted the "vast body of international jurisprudence [that] has emerged" from the ICTR and the International Criminal Tribunal for the Former Yugoslavia (ICTY) since the court's decision in *R. v. Finta* in 1994.[44] The court continued:

These tribunals have generated a unique body of authority which cogently reviews the sources, evolution and application of customary international law. Though the decisions of the ICTY and the ICTR are not binding upon this Court, the expertise of these tribunals and the authority in respect of customary international law with which they are vested suggest that their findings should not be disregarded lightly by Canadian courts applying domestic legislative provisions, such as ss. 7(3.76) and 7(3.77) of the *Criminal Code*, which expressly incorporate customary international law. Therefore, to the extent that *Finta* is in need of clarification and does not accord with the jurisprudence of the ICTY and the ICTR, it warrants reconsideration.

---

[40] Crimes against Humanity and War Crimes Act, S.C. 2000 c. 24 as amended.

[41] *Mugesera* at para. 118.

[42] *Ibid.* at para. 119.

[43] *Ibid.* at para. 125.

[44] *R. v. Finta*, [1994] 1 S.C.R. 701.

Having thus declared its willingness to revise the Canadian law of crimes against humanity in light of recent developments in international law, the court entered into a lengthy consideration of the elements of the crime, focusing particularly on its *actus reus*.

Beginning with the proscribed act, the court considered whether, as a matter of international law, Mugesera's offences of incitement to murder may serve as the "underlying offences" to a crime against humanity. The court found a general equivalency between the Criminal Code concept of "counselling" and the international concept of "instigating," as that term is used in the ICTY and ICTR Statutes.[45] It therefore relied on ICTR and ICTY jurisprudence in finding that instigating/counselling a proscribed act will only satisfy the initial criminal act requirement for a crime against humanity under section 7(3.76) of the Criminal Code where the instigation has led to the actual commission of the instigated offence.[46] The court then considered the same problem in relation to incitement to hatred, looking here to the ICTR and ICTY jurisprudence on persecution. It is here that the court partially overruled *Finta*, following the international jurisprudence establishing that discriminatory intent is only part of the mental element of persecution and is not required for all crimes against humanity.[47] The court went on to find that hate speech, "particularly when it advocates egregious acts of violence, may constitute persecution" and thus serve as the underlying act for a crime against humanity.[48]

The court then turned to the second element of the criminal act requirement for a crime against humanity, namely that the proscribed act contravenes international law. To do so, the court explained that customary international law requires that the proscribed act be committed as apart of a widespread or systematic attack directed against any civilian population or any identifiable group.[49] "Since this requirement is dictated entirely by customary international law, the jurisprudence of the ICTY and the ICTR is again very relevant."[50] Thus, the court considered this requirement as explained in the jurisprudence of the two tribunals and

---

[45] *Mugesera* at para. 134.
[46] *Ibid.* at para. 135.
[47] *Ibid.* at para. 143.
[48] *Ibid.* at para. 150.
[49] *Ibid.* at para. 151.
[50] *Ibid.* at para. 152.

as applicable to the facts of Mugesera's case, finding that it was made out here.[51]

Finally, the court turned to the mental element of crimes against humanity. The court noted that this question was central to *Finta* and that subsequent ICTY and ICTR jurisprudence has borne out the majority finding in *Finta* that the accused must have, in addition to the mental element for the underlying act, an extra mental element consisting of knowledge of the attack and knowledge that his or her acts comprise part of it, or at least that the accused takes the risk that his or her acts are part of it.[52] In the court's judgment, Mugesera possessed the culpable mental state required by section 7(3.76).

The court therefore held that each of the elements of the offence of a crime against humanity contrary to Criminal Code section 7(3.76) was made out. There were reasonable grounds to believe that Mugesera had committed a crime against humanity. He was therefore inadmissible to Canada by virtue of the Immigration Act. The court concluded:

In the face of certain unspeakable tragedies, the community of nations must provide a unified response. Crimes against humanity fall within this category. The interpretation and application of Canadian provisions regarding crimes against humanity must therefore accord with international law. Our nation's deeply held commitment to individual human dignity, freedom and fundamental rights requires nothing less.[53]

Mugesera is a remarkable decision. On occasion, the Supreme Court of Canada or members of it have sought to make room for a "made in Canada" approach to certain international legal questions.[54] Here, however, the court gives unhesitating effect to Parliament's determination that the international law of crimes against humanity should have full force in Canadian law. Indeed, the court goes so far as to partly overrule its own decision in *Finta* to accord with subsequent international developments.

The decision is very much to be welcomed, but with a note of caution. Throughout its reasons the court refers to the customary

---

51 *Ibid.* at paras. 153–70.

52 *Ibid.* at para. 173.

53 *Ibid.* at para. 178.

54 See, for example, the question of refoulement to torture in *Suresh v. Canada (Minister of Citizenship and Immigration)*, [2002] 1 S.C.R. 3 [*Suresh*] or McLachlin J.'s dissent in *R. v. Keegstra*, [1990] 3 S.C.R. 697.

international law of incitement to genocide and crimes against humanity. This emphasis on custom over treaty may be due to the fact that the events at issue in this appeal predate the Rome Statute of the International Criminal Court 1998[55] and other recent attempts to codify international criminal law. While the court speaks of custom in *Mugesera*, it does so without any analysis of its own as to the actual status of the rules of law it describes as forming part of customary international law. It merely applies the jurisprudence of the ICTY and ICTR. In many respects, this is unobjectionable and, indeed, commendable. Some international legal doctrines are so widely accepted as customary that to insist on their proof every time would be pedantic. Furthermore, the court is unlikely to have had before it a sufficient record upon which to make conclusions on state practice and *opinio juris* for itself, even assuming that an appellate court is an appropriate forum to make such decisions (which may be doubted). And as the court rightly noted, a unified response to these international legal questions is eminently desirable. If the ICTY and the ICTR have already reached satisfactory conclusions about the status of certain criminal law doctrines in customary international law, the Supreme Court of Canada need not and perhaps should not do that work over again. And yet domestic courts and lawyers, especially those operating within the common law tradition, must take care not to equate international jurisprudence with international custom. The fact that a decision of the ICTR supports a given interpretation of, or approach to, a legal doctrine does not, in itself, indicate the position of that doctrine in customary international law. Jurisprudence is only a subsidiary means of determining rules of international law; it is not itself a source of international law. Furthermore, international tribunals are not states and therefore their practices cannot contribute to the development of customary international law (at least not as that source of law is currently understood). At points in the court's analysis, one wonders whether it is too willing to find the ICTY and ICTR decisions to represent customary international law. Even if that is not so, some explanation from the court of how it moved from the international jurisprudence of the Rwanda and Yugoslav tribunals to the customary international law incorporated by section 3(7.36) of the Criminal Code would have been helpful.

---

55 Rome Statute of the International Criminal Court, [2002] Can. T.S. no. 13.

Briefly Noted / Sommaires en bref

Certain significant cases decided during the present reporting period (1 July 2004 to 30 June 2005) touching matters of international law have since been appealed. To avoid duplication, I note these lower court decisions briefly here and will note their appeals, as warranted, in subsequent volumes of the *Yearbook*. (Des appels ont été interjetés contres certains jugements importants publiés durant la présente période de rapportage (1ᵉʳ juillet 2004 du 30 juin 2005) et touchants aux questions de droit international. Pour l'instant je note ces décisions de tribunaux inférieurs en bref. Je discuterai leurs appels dans les prochaines éditions de l'*Annuaire*, si jugé nécessaire.)

Immigration and refugee protection — interpretation of act in compliance with international law

De Guzman v. Canada (Minister of Citizenship and Immigration), 2004 F.C. 1276 (20 September 2004) (Federal Court of Canada), appeal dismissed: 2005 F.C.A. 436 (20 December 2005)

The applicant sought judicial review of an Immigration Appeal Division decision denying her sons' permanent residence visas on the ground that she had not disclosed their existence when she immigrated to Canada. The applicant challenged section 117(9)(d) of the Immigration and Refugee Protection Regulations as *ultra vires* the act, contrary to section 7 of the Canadian Charter of Rights and Freedoms, and inconsistent with Canada's international human rights obligations. On the latter point, the applicant relied on several international instruments, notably Article 17 of the International Covenant on Civil and Political Rights 1966,[56] Article 10 of the International Covenant on Economic, Social and Cultural Rights 1966,[57] and Articles 3(1), 9(1), 10(1), and 16 of the Convention on the Rights of the Child 1989.[58]

The application was dismissed. Section 3(3)(f) of the Immigration and Refugee Protection Act[59] provides: "This Act is to be construed and applied in a manner that ... complies with international

---

[56] International Covenant on Civil and Political Rights, [1976] Can. T.S. no. 47.

[57] International Covenant on Economic, Social and Cultural Rights, [1976] Can. T.S. no. 46.

[58] Convention on the Rights of the Child, [1992] Can. T.S. no. 3.

[59] Immigration and Refugee Protection Act, S.C. 2001 c. 27, as amended.

human rights instruments to which Canada is signatory." Kelen J. held that this provision codifies the common law canon of statutory construction that domestic law should be interpreted to reflect "the values contained in international human rights conventions to which Canada has ascribed."[60] Citing *Baker v. Canada (Minister of Citizenship and Immigration)*,[61] Kelen J. found that section 3(3)(f) found that international conventions should "help inform the contextual approach" to statutory interpretation but that it does not "incorporate international human rights conventions as part of Canadian law, or state that they override plain words in a statute." The wording of section 117(9)(d) leaves no room for interpretation consistent with the international instruments cited.

Kelen J.'s order was affirmed by the Federal Court of Appeal on 20 December 2005.[62] On the interpretation of section 3(3)(f), however, the court took a very different view. The judgment will be considered in the next volume of the *Yearbook*.

Immigration et protection des réfugiés — interprétation de la Loi en conformité avec le droit international

Re Charkaoui, 2004 C.A.F. 421 (10 décembre 2004) (Cour d'appel fédérale), demande d'autorisation d'appel à la Cour suprême du Canada accordée le 25 août 2005

L'appelant était résident permanent du Canada lorsqu'il a été arrêté et interdit de territoire en vertu d'un certificat de sécurité émis par les ministres autorisés par la Loi sur l'immigration et la protection des réfugiés (LIPR)[63] et confirmé par le juge désigné de la Cour fédérale. L'appelant a été remis en liberté, avec conditions, en 2005, mais le certificat contre lui est toujours en vigueur. Devant le juge désigné, l'appelant a contesté la procédure canadienne des certificats de sécurité au moyen de pas moins de quarante questions constitutionnelles, y compris des questions soulevant les obligations du Canada resortant du Pacte international relatif aux droits civils et politiques de 1966 et de la Déclaration universelle des droits de l'Homme de 1948.

---

[60] *De Guzman* at para. 53.

[61] *Baker v. Canada (Minister of Citizenship and Immigration)*, [1999] 2 S.C.R. 817.

[62] 2005 F.C.A. 436.

[63] Loi sur l'immigration et la protection des réfugiés, L.C. 2001 ch. 27 tel que modifié.

L'appel a été rejeté. Quant aux questions internationales, la cour ne les a considérées que brièvement. Contre l'allégation de Charkaoui que la procédure d'examen judiciaire prévue aux articles 76 à 85 de la LIPR ne conforme pas aux obligations internationales du Canada, la cour a noté que l'alinéa 3(3)(f) de la LIPR requiert que l'interprétation et la mise en œuvre de celle-ci se conforment aux instruments internationaux sur les droits de l'homme que le Canada a signés, mais n'a trouvé aucune manque de conformité avec les dispositions du Pacte et de la Déclaration. Quant au Pacte, la cour s'est fiée à une communication du Comité des droits de l'Homme des Nations Unies[64] dans laquelle le comité (d'après la cour) a confirmé la conformité de la procédure d'examen judiciaire de l'article 77 de la LIPR avec les dispositions du Pacte. La cour a ajouté, sans plus ample analyse, que:

Sur les plans de l'égalité devant les tribunaux, de l'équité procédurale, de l'indépendance judiciaire ainsi que de l'impartialité des tribunaux, notre Charte n'est en reste avec aucun de ces trois instruments internationaux. Elle confère des droits et des garanties, à toutes fins pratiques, identiques. Nous avons déjà indiqué que la procédure d'examen judiciaire prévue aux articles 77 et suivants s'y conformait. Il en va donc de même pour les trois instruments internationaux.[65]

L'audition de l'appel à la Cour suprême du Canada aura lieu en juin 2006.

Immigration and refugee protection — refoulement *to torture*

Almrei v. Canada (Minister of Citizenship and Immigration) 2005 F.C.A. 54 (8 February 2005) (Federal Court of Appeal), leave to appeal to the Supreme Court of Canada granted 20 October 2005

Almrei was a Syrian citizen detained in Canada since 2001 on a security certificate alleging there were reasonable grounds to believe he was engaged in terrorism. He was ordered deported in 2002. This appeal was from a decision dismissing his application for judicial release from detention.

The appeal was dismissed. Most of the judgment does not directly involve matters of international law. However, Almrei's eighth ground of appeal was that the designated judge was mistaken in concluding that Almrei's continued detention did not violate his

---

[64] *Ahani c. Canada*, communication n 1051/2002.

[65] *Charkaoui* au para. 142.

Charter rights under sections 7 (liberty and security of the person) and 12 (freedom from cruel and unusual treatment or punishment). Almrei argued that the three years he had spent in solitary confinement constituted cruel treatment. The court held that, assuming without deciding that Almrei's detention was cruel and unusual, the remedy of judicial release from detention was inappropriate.

The court went on to consider the English case of *A(FC) and others (FC) v. Secretary of State for the Home Department*,[66] in which the House of Lords addressed the issue of indefinite detention under UK anti-terrorism legislation. The court noted that no provision of the Immigration and Refugee Protection Act (IRPA)[67] authorizes indefinite administrative detention. The court also noted that the English decision involved European jurisprudence regulating deportation to a country in which the detainee faces the prospect of torture and inhuman treatment. On this point, the court noted that while IRPA section 115(1) establishes the principle of non-refoulement to torture in Canadian law, section 115(2)(b) exceptionally authorizes such refoulement on security grounds if the minister is of the opinion that such persons would present a danger to the security of Canada if allowed to remain here. The court then observed that while this latter provision appears clear, section 3(3)(f) subjects the interpretation and application of the IRPA to international human rights instruments to which Canada is a signatory. "This creates an internal contradiction in the IRPA because Canada is a signatory to both the International Covenant on Civil and Political Rights ... and the Convention against Torture."[68] The court observed that the latter treaty absolutely prohibits deportation to torture, without any possibility of derogation, and that the former treaty seemingly does so, too, citing General Comment no. 20 of the UN Human Rights Committee. The court questioned whether these two treaties conflict with Article 33(2) of the Convention Relating to the Status of Refugees,[69] which allows refoulement of refugees whom there are reasonable grounds for regarding as a danger to the security of the country or who, on the basis of criminal convictions for serious crimes, constitutes a danger to the

---

[66] *A(FC) and Others (FC) v. Secretary of State for the Home Department*, 2004 U.K.H.L. 56.

[67] Immigration and Refugee Protection Act, S.C. 2001 c. 27, as amended.

[68] *Almrei* at para. 123.

[69] Convention Relating to the Status of Refugees, [1969] Can. T.S. no. 6.

community of that country. In this connection, the court observed that the Supreme Court of Canada's decision in *Suresh v. Canada (Minister of Citizenship and Immigration)*[70] "did not close the door on a possible deportation to torture" but added that "[t]his issue is the subject of other proceedings."[71]

These comments were *obiter,* and it is far from clear whether the important questions they raise will be taken up on the appeal of this decision to the Supreme Court of Canada, now scheduled to be heard in June 2006.

Extradition — admissibility of evidence

United Mexican States v. Ortega, 2005 B.C.C.A. 270 (17 May 2005) (Court of Appeal for British Columbia), leave to appeal to the Supreme Court of Canada granted 20 October 2005

These were appeals by Mexico and the United States from findings of inadmissibility in respect of evidence presented in support of extradition proceedings in British Columbia. The applicable extradition treaties required that evidence, not just summaries of evidence, be presented at the hearing. However, in neither the Mexican and the US proceedings was there certification by the requesting state that the evidence presented at the extradition hearing would be available at the fugitive's trial. The extradition judge in the Mexican proceeding (*Ortega*) held that to admit the evidence tendered against the fugitive without certification of its availability at trial would unjustifiably infringe section 7 of the Charter. She held that section 32(1)(b) of the Extradition Act[72] should be read subject to section 33(3), thereby reading into the impugned provision an obligation on the requesting state to certify that the evidence presented at extradition is available for trial. The extradition judge in the US proceedings followed *Ortega.*

Section 32(1) provides in part that specified evidence, gathered abroad, that would otherwise be inadmissible under Canadian law, shall be admitted as evidence at an extradition hearing. The specified evidence includes (1) the contents of the documents contained in the record of the case, and (2) the contents of the documents that are submitted in conformity with the terms of an extradition

---

[70] *Suresh, supra* note 54.

[71] *Almrei* at para. 126.

[72] Extradition Act, *supra* note 1.

agreement. In short, the act provides for two novel modes of evidence, the record of the case mode and the treaty mode. The former mode requires certification by an official of the requesting state that the evidence is available for trial (see sections 32(1)(a) and 33(3)). This requirement is absent in respect of evidence admitted by treaty mode. This was the discrepancy the extradition judge identified and sought to correct by her order.

The majority of the Court of Appeal for British Columbia allowed the requesting states' appeals. Smith J.A. (Thackray J.A. concurring) held that the certification requirement in section 33(3) applies only to the record of the case mode because that mode permits the requesting state to enter only a summary of the evidence. Certification serves the purpose of assuring the extradition judge that the evidence so summarized actually exists and is within the control of the requesting state. In the case of extradition proceedings to which the treaty mode applies, certification is unnecessary because the evidence is submitted in support of the extradition request, making its availability for trial plainly obvious.[73] Smith J.A. also held that the reliability of evidence tendered in support of an extradition request is not a principle of fundamental justice for the purpose of section 7 of the Charter.[74] His lordship also rejected the respondents' argument that recent amendments to the Canada-US extradition agreement to require certification of the availability of evidence for trial signify recognition of an international minimum standard on admissibility.[75]

Donald J.A., dissenting, would have upheld the extradition judge's order. He rejected the appellants' concerns that the integrity of Canada's extradition treaty network would be adversely affected by the order, noting that only a few of Canada's fifty extradition treaties have certification provisions and that the more onerous evidentiary standards of the prior Extradition Act did not appear to have affronted our treaty partners. As I write, the appeal is on reserve at the Supreme Court of Canada.

[73] *Ortega* at paras. 74–75.

[74] *Ibid.* at paras. 76–81.

[75] *Ibid.* at paras. 82–84.

Canadian Cases in Private International Law in 2004–5 / Jurisprudence canadienne en matière de droit international privé en 2004–5

compiled by / *préparé par*
JOOST BLOM

A JURISDICTION / COMPÉTENCE DES TRIBUNAUX

I   Common Law and Federal

(a) Jurisdiction *in personam*

Defendant outside the jurisdiction — claim arising out of business, investment, or professional transaction — jurisdiction simpliciter *found — jurisdiction not declined*

UniNet Technologies Inc. v. Communication Services Inc. (2005), 251 D.L.R. (4th) 464, 2005 BCCA 114 (British Columbia Court of Appeal)

The action in this case arose out of a set of transactions relating to the right to use the Internet domain name, "poker.com." ALA, incorporated in St. Vincent and the Grenadines, gave UniNet, a British Columbia company, a 99-year licence to use the domain name. UniNet agreed that it would sublicense the name to a Florida company, Poker.com Incorporated and that the Internet "poker room" would be operated by an Antiguan company. If certain conditions were fulfilled, UniNet would become owner of the name. These transactions were implemented; the actual server used was said to be in Costa Rica. After two and a half very profitable years, UniNet was told that ALA was terminating its licence for breaches of the agreement. UniNet commenced arbitration proceedings against ALA in British Columbia pursuant to the licence agreement, claiming the termination was wrongful. UniNet also commenced the present action against CSI, a Samoan company said to be controlled by the same people as ALA, alleging CSI conspired with

---

Joost Blom is in the Faculty of Law at the University of British Columbia.

ALA to injure UniNet's business or wrongfully interfered with UniNet's contractual relations with ALA. CSI was served *ex juris* on the basis that the claim was for a tort committed in British Columbia. CSI applied for dismissal or a stay on the basis that the court lacked jurisdiction *simpliciter*. (No argument was made on *forum non conveniens*.) The chambers judge held that although the pleadings did not show a tort committed in British Columbia as required for service *ex juris* without leave (rule 13(1)(h) of the Rules of Court), there was a real and substantial connection between the action and British Columbia that established jurisdiction *simpliciter* and thus supported leave, *nunc pro tunc*, to serve *ex juris* under rule 13(3).

The Court of Appeal, whose judgment was given by Newbury J.A., upheld the chambers judge's decision. The Supreme Court of Canada's jurisprudence made it clear that jurisdiction *simpliciter* was to be determined on the basis of a real and substantial connection. The fact that a claim falls within the rules for service of process does not even presumptively establish a real and substantial connection with the province. Conversely, the fact that a claim does not fall within the rules allowing service *ex juris* without leave does not establish the absence of a real and substantial connection. The requisite connection is one between the province and "the action," which includes connections not only with the defendant (who here had no connection with the province) but also with the subject matter of the action. The subject matter of this action has the right to use and eventually to own the domain name as granted by a contract governed by British Columbia law. The dispute between UniNet and ALA was currently the subject of arbitration proceedings in the province. Admittedly, CSI was not a party to the agreement or to the arbitration, but if UniNet's allegations against CSI were true, the litigation was almost a natural continuation of the arbitration proceedings. If UniNet's claim against ALA were being tried in court in British Columbia, CSI would be subject to the court's jurisdiction as a necessary or proper party. The Supreme Court of Canada had said that the values of comity, order, and fairness militated in favour of a flexible approach to determining a real and substantial connection. These values also supported the notion that arbitration rulings should be respected by domestic and foreign courts and enforced when necessary. If UniNet's allegations were true, the use of a sham corporation in a faraway jurisdiction by the alleged conspirators should not preclude UniNet from such remedy as might be appropriate under the laws of the province against both ALA and CSI.

Note. The following decisions also found jurisdiction *simpliciter* to exist and did not decline jurisdiction. *Whirpool Canada Co. v. National Union Fire Ins. Co. of Pittsburgh, Pa.* (2005), 128 Man. R. (2d) 18, 2005 MBQB 205, was a dispute about whether a loss the plaintiff had suffered in Manitoba was covered by an umbrella insurance policy issued in Michigan by a New York-based insurer to a group of companies including the plaintiff. In *R.M. Maromi Investments Ltd. v. Hasco Inc.* (2004), 73 O.R. (3d) 298 (S.C.J.), an Ontario-resident minority shareholder in an Ontario company was suing the Michigan-resident majority shareholder for breach of a shareholders' agreement governed by Michigan law. *Cousin v. Royal Bank of Canada* (2004), 6 C.P.C. (6th) 31 (Ont. S.C.J.) was a claim by Ontario-resident plaintiffs against a Canadian bank for bad investment advice given at its branch in the Turks and Caicos Islands, where the plaintiffs spent their winters.

Two cases involved oppression actions. In *Harbert v. Calpine Canada Energy Finance II ULC* (2005), 235 N.S.R. (2d) 297, 2005 NSSC 211, an investment fund incorporated in the Cayman Islands and managed in Ireland brought an oppression action, as bondholder, against two affiliated Nova Scotia companies and their Delaware parent company, all of whom were liable on the bonds as issuer or guarantor. The Delaware trustee for all the bondholders was also a party. The court found jurisdiction *simpliciter* because the two Nova Scotia companies, jurisdiction over whom was not contested, provided a real and substantial connection with the province and it made no sense to require the American parent to be sued separately in another forum. (*Forum non conveniens* was not argued.) In *Marciano v. Landa* (2005), 1 B.L.R. (4th) 268, 2005 SKQB 59, leave to appeal to Sask. C.A. granted, 2005 SKCA 41, the plaintiff, an Israeli resident, began an oppression proceeding in respect of a Saskatchewan company that was 49 per cent owned by an Israeli company, the shares of which were owned by the plaintiff and two other residents of Israel. The plaintiff also made claims of breach of fiduciary duty and conspiracy against his fellow shareholders in the Israeli company and their brother-in-law, a Saksatchewan resident whose holding company owned the other 51 per cent of the Saskatchewan company. Saskatchewan was *forum conveniens* for the claims against the Israeli defendants because they were necessary parties to the proceeding, the core of which was an oppression claim in respect of a Saskatchewan company.

Smith v. National Money Mart Co. (2005), 8 B.L.R. (4th) 159, 18 C.P.C. (6th) 1 (Ont. S.C.J.), was a class action for charging interest on payday loans that exceeded the limit in the Criminal Code. The action was brought against the Canadian chain that made the loans and against the American company that directed the affairs of the Canadian one. A *forum non conveniens* argument by the American company, which argued that it had no presence and did no business in Canada, was rejected.

Defendant outside the jurisdiction — claim arising out of business, investment, or professional transaction — jurisdiction simpliciter *found not to exist*

Note. Silicon Isle Ltd. v. Cinar Corp. (2005), 3 B.L.R. (4th) 89, 2005 BCSC 401, involved a claim for breach of a confidentiality clause in a settlement agreement that was stated to be governed by British Columbia law, but the subject matter of which was a dispute between an Anguillan and a Québec company, neither of which had any continuing business presence in the province. The court held there was no real and substantial connection with the defendant or the subject matter of the litigation, and the plaintiff was trying to turn a governing law clause into a forum selection clause.

Kuchocki v. Fasken Martineau DuMoulin (2005), 13 C.P.C. (6th) 350 (Ont. S.C.J.), was a decision by an Ontario court that it lacked jurisdiction in a claim by an Ontario resident against a British Columbia lawyer who the plaintiff claimed had agreed to an improvident settlement of her claim arising out of a motor vehicle accident in British Columbia; she lived in that province at the time of the accident and the settlement. Her subsequent move to Ontario, where she had two more accidents, did not supply a real and substantial connection. In *Shekhdar v. K & M Engineering & Consulting Corp.* (2004), 71 O.R. (3d) 475 (S.C.J.), an Ontario resident was held to be unable to bring an action in Ontario for breach of contract and associated torts against American and Bermudan corporations that did business in Washington, DC. The actions against them were stayed (though technically a dismissal would have been more correct) for lack of jurisdiction *simpliciter*. An interesting comment (at para. 30) was that even the parties' consent cannot give jurisdiction to the court of a province that lacks a real and substantial connection with the action. Consent has usually been assumed to give jurisdiction *simpliciter* irrespective of whether there is otherwise a real and substantial connection between the province and the action, although the court has the power to declare that unjustified recourse to the jurisdiction, even if consented to, is an abuse of process and so can refuse to hear the case.

Defendant outside the jurisdiction — claim arising out of supply of goods — jurisdiction simpliciter *found — jurisdiction not declined*

Note. In an action arising out of allegedly defective valves installed in a pipeline in Alberta, orders for service *ex juris* under Rules 30 and 31 of the Alberta Rules of Court were upheld as against a German company that was one of the defendants, all the others being based in Alberta. The province was *forum conveniens* for the claims against the German defendant as well as all those against the Alberta defendants: *Alliance Pipeline Ltd. Partnership v. C.E. Franklin Ltd.* (2005), 46 Alta. L.R. (4th) 106, 2005 ABQB 102.

Defendant outside the jurisdiction — claims arising out of injury to person or damage to property — jurisdiction simpliciter *found — jurisdiction not declined*

British Columbia v. Imperial Tobacco Canada Ltd. (2005), 44 B.C.L.R. (4th) 125, 2005 BCSC 946 (British Columbia Supreme Court)

The province of British Columbia brought an action claiming damages from various tobacco manufacturers and a tobacco trade association pursuant to the Tobacco Damages and Health Care Costs Recovery Act, S.B.C. 2000, c. 30. The act creates a right in the province to recover for health care costs associated with tobacco-related illness. A defendant is liable under the act if it committed a breach of a common law, equitable or statutory duty that induced or encouraged people to consume tobacco products sold in British Columbia. The action was brought against fourteen defendants, eleven of whom were served *ex juris*. Of the latter, four manufactured cigarettes sold in British Columbia and the others, although they did not make cigarettes sold in the province, were said to be liable because of their relationship with one or more of the defendants who did. The statement of claim alleged a number of breaches of duty by some or all of the defendants, including failing to take reasonable measures to minimize the risks of smoking the cigarettes they made or marketed, failing to warn of those risks, making or marketing unduly hazardous products, misrepresenting the risks associated with the products, and conspiring to commit these breaches of duty. The *ex juris* defendants applied for dismissal of the claims on the basis that the British Columbia court lacked jurisdiction *simpliciter* over the claims. They also sought a stay based on *forum non conveniens*.

R.R. Holmes J. rejected the applications. He considered the factors relevant to jurisdiction *simpliciter* (that is, a sufficiently real and substantial connection with the province) as outlined by the Courts of Appeal of British Columbia and Ontario. The government's action was one of a product liability nature, arising out of the sale and consumption of cigarettes in the province. The defendants were alleged to have committed wrongs in British Columbia with respect to cigarettes that were sold there. Foreign manufacturers are properly subject to the jurisdiction of a court in any country where they might reasonably foresee their products would be used or consumed. The defendants who did not manufacture cigarettes sold in the province were alleged to have acted in concert and conspired with those who did, and a conspiracy is a tort committed in the province if the harm is suffered here. Moreover, once jurisdiction over a wrong, including conspiracy, is established, all defendants who are potentially liable may properly be joined in the action. Jurisdiction *simpliciter* being established, the judge went on to hold that no more appropriate forum than British Columbia had been shown. The taking of jurisdiction was not offensive to international standards of judicial jurisdiction. He also rejected the defendants' argument, in relation to both jurisdiction *simpliciter* and *forum non conveniens*, that an eventual judgment in favour of the government would not be enforceable against the defendants in their home jurisdictions. The evidence on that point was inconclusive and, in any event, the enforceability or otherwise of the resulting judgment was not a factor to be taken into account in determining whether there was jurisdiction or whether it should be declined.

Note. The typical personal injury case that raises a jurisdiction *simpliciter* issue is one where a resident of the forum has been injured elsewhere but claims to have suffered loss in the forum as a result of his or her injuries. Jurisdiction *simpliciter* was held to exist and jurisdiction was not declined in *Georges v. Basilique de Sainte-Anne-de-Beaupré* (2004), 7 C.P.C. (6th) 205 (Ont. S.C.J.), where a touristically famous church in Québec was sued by an Ontario resident who was seriously injured in a fall down the church's stairs and was subsequently treated in Québec and Ontario hospitals. The same result was reached in *Kinch v. Pyle* (2004), 8 C.P.C. (6th) 66 (Ont. S.C.J.), in which nine Ontario-resident plaintiffs sued the Florida-resident driver and West Viriginia-resident owner of the car that hit their vehicle while they were driving in Florida. Jurisdiction *simplicter* was based on the defendants' attornment. Ontario was held to be the *forum conveniens* because the principal issues related to quantum, not liability, and most of the witnesses and evidence were in Ontario.

Defendant outside the jurisdiction — claims arising out of injury to person or damage to property — jurisdiction simpliciter *found not to exist*

Note. Where an Ontario resident was injured in an ice hockey game in Québec, his claims against Québec residents for negligent medical treatment were held not to have a real and substantial connection with Ontario: *Deakin v. Canadian Hockey Enterprises* (2005), 7 C.P.C. (6th) 295 (Ont. S.C.J.). Similarly, the mere fact that the victim of a Nebraska automobile accident lived in New Brunswick and was treated there did not constitute a sufficiently real and substantial connection with the province for an action against the US resident, currently serving in Iraq: *MacCallum v. Raspotnik* (2004), 7 C.P.C. (6th) 388 (N.B.Q.B.).

Defendant outside the jurisdiction — claims arising out of injury to reputation —jurisdiction simpliciter *found — jurisdiction not declined*

Burke v. NYP Holdings Inc. (2005), 16 C.P.C. (6th) 382, 2005 BCSC 1287 (British Columbia Supreme Court)

The then general manager of the Vancouver Canucks ice hockey club commenced a libel action in British Columbia against the *New York Post*. He alleged that one of its sports columnists had written defamatory comments about the plaintiff's role in an assault by a Vancouver player against a member of the opposing team, the Colorado Avalanche, that took place during a 2004 Vancouver home game and resulted in serious injury to the Colorado player. The *Post* was based in New York. No copies of the paper were sold in British Columbia, but the story was put on the *Post*'s website, which was, according to the pleadings, read in the province by a radio sports show host who asked the plaintiff about the story on the air. The defendant applied for a stay of proceedings on the grounds that the facts pleaded, if true, did not establish the jurisdiction of the British Columbia courts, and that in any event the court should decline jurisdiction because British Columbia was *forum non conveniens*.

Burnyeat J. dismissed the application. The pleaded facts showed jurisdiction *simpliciter* because there was a real and substantial connection with British Columbia. It was foreseeable to the defendant that the story posted on its website would be read in British Columbia. British Columbia was also *forum conveniens* for the claim. Many witnesses lived in the Vancouver area, and Vancouver was where the plaintiff alleged he suffered substantial damage to his reputation. A New York action would require all the witnesses to the relevant events to travel there. A Vancouver trial would not be substantially unfair to the defendant, which was an internationally known newspaper that presumably expected to have to defend itself in places other than its home state. It would be inordinately expensive for the plaintiff to bring his action in New York, where he had little connection. A British Columbia court would be best suited to assess damage to the plaintiff's reputation. A New York trial would also deprive the plaintiff of a signficant juridical advantage, given the differences that exist between defamation laws in British Columbia and those in New York. It would be unfair to require the plaintiff to clear his reputation by proceeding in a New York court under American defamation standards. There was some evidence that a British Columbia defamation judgment might not be enforced in New York, but the choice of a British Columbia forum, even with that possible outcome, was the plaintiff's to make.

Note. Similar reasons supported British Columbia courts having jurisdiction *simpliciter*, and being the *forum conveniens*, in a British Columbia resident's defamation claim against a Québec resident who had written a federal government report that was posted on a government website: *Wiebe v. Bouchard* (2005), 46 B.C.L.R. (4th) 278, 2005 BCSC 47. It was held appropriate that a defence of fair comment be judged by the standards of British Columbia, where the report was published. It was not a critical disadvantage to the defendant that the trial would be in English.

Defendant outside the jurisdiction — claims arising out of injury to reputation — jurisdiction simpliciter *found not to exist*

Bangoura v. Washington Post (2005), 258 D.L.R. (4th) 341 (Ontario Court of Appeal)

The plaintiff brought an action, framed in terms of a number of intentional torts and negligence, in Ontario against the *Washington Post* and three of its journalists in respect of two articles the newpaper published in 1997 about the plaintiff's activities when he was head of a United Nations drug control program in the Ivory Coast. At the time of publication, the plaintiff was with another United Nations drug control program in Kenya. He lost that job a few days after the articles appeared. He subsequently moved to Canada, living first in Québec and, from 2000, in Ontario. His action was commenced in 2003. Only seven copies were sold in Ontario of the issues of the *Post* in which the articles appeard; the articles were available on the *Post*'s website for free for fourteen days and after that were archived and could be read only by those who paid for access to it. Only the plaintiff's counsel had accessed them in the archive. The motions judge, applying the eight factors for jurisdiction *simpliciter* put forward in *Muscutt v. Courcelles* (2002), 213 D.L.R. (4th) 577 (Ont. C.A.) (noted in "Canadian Cases in Private International Law 2001–2" (2002) 40 Can. Y.B. Int'l L. 583), held the Ontario court had jurisdiction *simpliciter*. He emphasized particularly the fact that the newspaper was internationally known and read, and the fact that the plaintiff would be at a disadvantage suing in the United States because of the "actual malice" requirement that public figures must meet in defamation claims.

The Court of Appeal reversed the motions judge's decision. He had misapplied the *Muscutt* factors; the action had no real and substantial connection with Ontario. (1) Connection between the forum and the plaintiff's claim: the claim had no connection with Ontario at all until the plaintiff moved there some three years after the articles appeared. Whatever damages the plaintiff suffered by losing his position with the United Nations were not suffered in Ontario. (2) Connection between the forum and the defendant: there was no significant connection. Publication in Ontario was minimal. The motions judge's view, that the defendants could foresee that the story would follow the plaintiff wherever he went, would lead to a newspaper being liable to an action in any country to which a plaintiff, long after the initial publication, might decide to move. (3) Unfairness to the defendant in assuming jurisdiction: the motions judge was wrong to refer to the *Post* as being insured against actions anywhere; there was no evidence as to its insurance coverage. (4) Unfairness to the plaintiff in not assuming jurisdiction: this factor only comes into play if there is otherwise a real and substantial connection with the province. (5) Involvement of other parties in the suit: Contrary to the motions judge's view, the fact that two of the defendant journalists now lived in New York and Florida did not favour Ontario as a forum. (6) The court's willingness to recognize and enforce an extra-provincial judgment rendered on the same jurisdictional basis: the motions judge was wrong to suggest that Ontario could be expected to recognize and enforce judgments against Ontario publishers and broadcasters that were sued in any country where the plaintiff chose, after the event, to reside. (7) Whether the case is international or inter-provincial: jurisdiction *simplicier* should be less readily found in international than in inter-provincial cases. (8) Comity and the standards of jurisdiction, recognition and enforcement prevailing elsewhere: the motions judge had wrongly stigmatized the American courts as acting against comity because they refused (as he found) to enforce foreign libel judgments that did not respect the constitutional guarantee of free speech as reflected in the "actual malice" rule. Freedom of speech was a central value in US constitutional law and refusing to recognize a foreign judgment on legitimate grounds of public policy was not contrary to comity. Taking all the factors together, therefore, the Ontario courts lacked jurisdiction *simpliciter.*

Defendant in the jurisdiction — claim arising out of business, investment, or professional transaction — jurisdiction not declined

Note. In *Commonwealth Ins. Co. v. Canadian Imp. Bank of Commerce* (2005), 12 C.P.C. (6th) 1, 12 C.C.L.I. (4th) 226 (Ont. S.C.J.) affd. [2005] O.J. No. 3656 (C.A.), a British Columbia insurer sought to litigate in Ontario issues relating to liability under a policy issued to a Canadian bank, in respect of the loss that the bank had suffered in New York as a result of the 2001 attack on the World Trade Center, where it had offices. Although the bank argued that New York would be a more appropriate forum, given the bank's position that the insurer should be bound by a settlement governed by New York law that the bank had reached with its other insurers, the Ontario court was held to be *forum conveniens*, mainly because the policy in question was governed by Ontario law.

Defendant in the jurisdiction — claim arising out of business, investment, or professional transaction — jurisdiction declined

Note. An action on an insurance policy issued in Québec and covering risks in Québec was stayed in *Majestic Empire Inc. v. Federation Ins. Co. of Canada* (2004), 10 C.C.L.I. (4th) 75 (Ont. S.C.J.), affd. (2004), 16 C.C.L.I. (4th) 45 (Ont. C.A.). There was no reason for an action in Ontario other than the fact that the defendant was a national insurance company. Of relevance was that the claim would be subject to Québec law, which would require expert evidence in an Ontario court.

Defendant in the jurisdiction — claim arising out of employment — jurisdiction simpliciter *found — jurisdiction not declined*

Note. Although his last position had been with the defendants' hotel in Nevada, the plaintiff's wrongful dismissal claim was held within the Ontario court's jurisdiction because the employment contract originated in Ontario and the plaintiff was then a resident there and intended now to return: *Newton v. Larco Hospitality Management Inc.* (2005), 75 O.R. (3d) 42 (C.A.). Some weight was given to the argument that, since Nevada law regarded employment contracts as terminable at will, the plaintiff enjoyed a legitimate advantage if the action was heard in Ontaro. On similar facts and for similar reasons, although without the legitimate advantage factor, jurisdiction was taken in *Lozeron v. Phasecom Systems Inc.* (2005), 50 Alta. L.R. (4th) 152, 2005 ABQB 328.

Declining jurisdiction — parallel proceedings elsewhere (lis alibi pendens)

Ingenium Technologies Corp. v. McGraw-Hill Companies Inc. (2005), 255 D.L.R. (4th) 499, 2005 BCCA 358 (British Columbia Court of Appeal)

Ingenium, a British Columbia developer of web-based software, had made a contract with McGraw-Hill, based in New York, for the distribution and promotion of the software under a McGraw-Hill trademark. The agreement was expressly governed by British Columbia law. Ingenium performed most of its part of the bargain in British Columbia, although the servers on which customers accessed data were currently located in New York. When the agreement was about to expire, a dispute arose about which party had control over the relationship with customers that had acquired and used the software. On 17 January 2005, Ingenium began the present action against McGraw-Hill in British Columbia. On 14 February 2005, McGraw-Hill filed a complaint against Ingenium in federal court in New York covering the same issues. Ingenium applied to the New York court for dismissal on jurisdictional grounds, informing the court that it intended to apply to the British Columbia court for a declaration that the latter had jurisdiction. The New York court refused the application for summary dismissal, after which Ingenium applied to that court for interim injunctive relief against McGraw-Hill. The British Columbia Supreme Court then heard Ingenium's application for a declaration affirming jurisdiction. Ingenium's position was that although it accepted that McGraw-Hill's claims would be heard in New York, it wanted to have its counterclaim against McGraw-Hill determined by a British Columbia court. The British Columbia Court of Appeal, reversing the lower court's decision, held two to one that the British Columbia action should be stayed.

The judge had rightly acknowledged that the existence of parallel proceedings did not trump all other factors and in some instances comity may allow parallel proceedings to continue in both courts. However, in holding in favour of a continuation of the British Columbia action she had overlooked the importance of a positive assertion of jurisdiction by the New York court. In *472900 B.C. Ltd. v. Thrifty Canada Ltd.* (1998), 168 D.L.R. (4th) 602 (B.C.C.A.), a case of parallel proceedings in Ontario and in British Columbia, the court had decided that comity demanded respect for the Ontario court's having already denied an application for a stay. There was no reason why the New York court's assertion of jurisdiction should not be conclusive in this case. It was true that here, unlike in the earlier case, the British Columbia action was commenced first, but that was not a determinative factor, especially because the New York action was filed less than a month after the action was commenced in British Columbia. Nor was it conclusive that the dispute concerned a British Columbia contract and, moreover, there was no evidence that the applicable law was different in New York. Southin J.A. dissented because she thought the parties' agreement that it was a British Columbia contract should be given great weight, and because she saw no reason of comity to defer to the courts of New York when those courts apparently did not defer in return, comity in the Canadian sense not being a doctrine of American law.

Note. Litigants are faced with a complex tactical problem if a "positive assertion of jurisdiction" by the foreign court is now a key to persuading a local court to stay its own proceeding. The party who wants the case heard locally must move as quickly as possible to get the local court to declare that it will take jurisdiction and delay as much as possible the other side's efforts to get the foreign court to do the same. All the while, the opposing party is presumably trying to achieve the opposite. In the British Columbia jurisprudence a "race to a positive assertion of jurisdiction" seems therefore to have replaced to some extent the "race to the courthouse" that was sanctioned in *Westec Aerospace Inc. v. Raytheon Aircraft Co.* (1999), 173 D.L.R. (4th) 498 (B.C.C.A.), affd. (2001), 197 D.L.R. (4th) 211 (S.C.C.).

In *Devon Canada Corp. v. Pe-Pittsfield LLC* (2004), 3 C.P.C. (6th) 54, 2004 ABQB 666, an Alberta action by an Alberta natural gas seller against a Massachusetts buyer was allowed to proceed, notwithstanding a parallel proceeding brought by the buyer against the seller in Massachussetts. The court relied mainly on the gas purchase agreement being made in Alberta, governed by Alberta law, structured to comply with public and regulatory policies of Canada and Alberta, and performed in Alberta because the delivery point of the gas was in the province. The court added that the Massachusetts action was begun only four days before the Alberta one, and an eventual judgment in the Massachusetts action would not be enforceable in Alberta because it was only for declaratory relief. The last factor is of doubtful weight. Even a declaratory judgment from a foreign court can be recognized in Canada as creating a cause of action estoppel or issue estoppel against the losing party.

Proceedings in a claim for damage to cargo were stayed in the Federal Court because the plaintiff had commenced an earlier action in federal court in the United States, where justice could equally well be done and where the plaintiff had not shown it would be at a disadvantage in terms of the applicable law: *Ford Aquitaine Industries SAS v. Canmar Pride (The)*, [2005] 4 F.C.R. 441, 2005 FC 431.

Declining jurisdiction — forum selection clause

Magic Sportswear Corp. v. Mathilde Maersk (The), [2005] 2 F.C.R. 236, 2004 FC 1165 (Federal Court)

The plaintiff, an American company that did business in Ontario, shipped 170 cartons of merchandise by container from New York City to Liberia. The defendant OT Africa Line issued the bill of lading at Toronto, where it had offices and a call centre, and ocean freight was payable there. The contract of carriage contained an exclusive choice of the High Court in London as forum for any dispute arising out of the bill of lading. The plaintiff (actually, its insurer by way of a subrogated claim) commenced an action *in rem* in the Federal Court, claiming Cdn $30,000 damages for partial loss of the cargo. A month later the defendant began proceedings in an English court for a determination that it was not liable for the plaintiff's loss. The plaintiff acknowledged service in the English action and gave notice that it would contest the jurisdiction of the English court, although it had taken no further steps to do so. Meanwhile the defendant obtained, *ex parte*, an injunction against the plaintiff pursuing its action in Canada and, the next day, filed a motion in Federal Court for a stay of that action. The prothonotary referred to *Z.I. Pompey Industrie v. ECU-Line N.V.*, [2003] 1 S.C.R. 450, 224 D.L.R. (4th) 577, 2003 SCC 27 (noted in "Canadian Cases in Private International Law 2002-3" (2003) 41 Can. Y.B. Int'l L. 573), which affirmed the obligation to give effect to a choice of forum clause, subject only to a plaintiff's showing "strong cause" for taking jurisdiction. As the case itself had noted, Parliament had decided, by enacting section 46 of the Marine Liability Act, S.C. 2001, c. 6 (which did not apply to the claim in *Pompey*), to authorize a court to override an exclusive choice of forum clause in a contract for the carriage of goods by water if the actual or intended port of discharge or loading is in Canada, the defendant resides or has a place of business in Canada, or the contract was made in Canada. The prothonotary in the present case held that although section 46 gives the court jurisdiction in the face of the parties' choice of another forum, the provision should not be read as going so far as to preclude the court from declining jurisdiction, in its discretion, if the defendant shows that Canada is *forum non conveniens*. The defendant had not, however, made out the case that the English High Court was a more appropriate forum.

O'Keefe J. dismissed a motion to set aside the prothonotary's order. The judge agreed with her interpretation of section 46 of the Marine Liability Act. The provision removed the court's discretion to stay proceedings because of a forum selection clause, a jurisdiction *simpliciter* issue. It did not remove the discretion to stay proceedings on the ground of *forum non conveniens*. The prothonotary's decision that the Federal Court was the most appropriate forum should not be interfered with. She had taken into account the value of the goods, the plaintiff's presence in Canada, the defendants' having business interests in Canada, and the fact that most if not all the witnesses in the action would come from Monrovia or New York, which factor favoured neither England nor Canada. She had also rightly found that the plaintiff had not attorned to the jurisdiction of the High Court in England.

Note. Although the judge's interpretation of section 46 is a desirable one, it is analytically not quite accurate to base it on the distinction between jurisdiction *simpliciter* and the discretion to decline jurisdiction. The common law rule affirmed in *Z.I. Pompey Industrie v. Ecu-Line N.V.* is not one of jurisdiction *simpliciter*. Rather, it is one of the presumptive effect of a forum selection clause. Under the rule, the clause does not absolutely deprive a court of jurisdiction, but only requires the court to decline jurisdiction unless strong cause is shown to let the action proceed. So perhaps it would be more correct to say that in cases to which section 46 applies, the clause is removed from the discretionary equation but the concept of *forum non conveniens* is not.

In *Ezer v. Yorkton Securities Inc.*, 2005 BCCA 22, leave to appeal to S.C.C. refused, 18 Aug. 2005, a clause in a standard form agreement between a British Columbia client and a stockbroking firm based in Ontario gave exclusive jurisdiction to the courts of the province where the firm accepted the agreement, which was Ontario. The client had not shown "strong cause" why his action for mismanagement of his account should not be heard in Ontario. See also *GreCon Dimter Inc. c. J.R. Normand Inc.*, noted below under 2. Québec, (a) Action personnelle — clause d'élection de for.

Dongnam Oil & Fats Co. v. Chemex Ltd. (2004), 264 F.T.R. 264, 2004 FC 1732 (Federal Court (Prothonotary))

Dongnam owned part of a cargo of edible oil that was carried from New Jersey on board the *Tuapse*, a ship of which Dongnam was the voyage charterer. The oil was transshipped directly from the *Tuapse* to the *Chembulk Clipper* in Nanaimo harbour, British Columbia, without being landed. The *Chembulk Clipper* was to carry the oil to Korea. Dongnam brought an action in the Federal Court for steam and water damage to its cargo and for dilution. The damage had allegedly occurred either on board the *Tuapse* or in the course of transshipment to the *Chembulk Clipper*. The action was against Chemex and Novorossiysk as head charterer and owner, respectively, of the *Tuapse*. The head charter contained a clause requiring all disputes arising out of the contract to be arbitrated in London. The voyage charter to Dongnam was on the Vegoil charter terms, which in their standard form contain a New York arbitration clause, but this clause was amended by the recap fixture to require "[a]bitration, if any, to be settled in London under English law." The bills of lading expressly incorporated the voyage charterparty terms except the rate and payment of freight, but made no mention specifically of arbitration. Chemex brought arbitration proceedings in London against Dongnam and obtained an award for, *inter alia*, dead freight. Dongnam had refused to pay the award. Chemex and Novorossiysk moved for a stay of Dongnam's Federal

Court action in favour of the London arbitration, pursuant to the UNCITRAL Model Law on International Commercial Arbitration as enacted in the Commercial Arbitration Act, R.S.C. 1985, c. 17. In answer to the motion, Dongnam relied on, *inter alia*, section 46 of the Marine Liability Act (see the note of the previous case).

Hargrave, prothonotary, granted the stay in respect of the action against Chemex but refused it in the action against Novorossiysk. Section 46 of the Marine Liability Act was a restriction of freedom of contract and should be interpreted strictly. In this case, none of the parties had any connection to Canada and the contract was not made in Canada. Parliament was aware of the difference between traansshipment and loading. Loading involves a mutuality of enterprise between cargo interests and owner, whereas transshipment generally does not. Parliament did not intend to interfere with the contract just because a legitimate operation took place between vessels in Canadian waters. The contract between Dongnam and Chemex contained a valid arbitration agreement and Chemex was therefore entitled to a stay. Novorossiysk's claim to a stay could only succeed if the London arbitration clause formed part of the bills of lading, which were the only direct connection between Dongnam and Novorossiysk. The bills contained no express arbitration clause. The authorities made clear that a general incorporation of the terms of a charter party was insufficient to incorporate an arbitration clause unless, which was not the case here, the charter party itself stipulated that the clause would apply to disputes under a bill of lading issued pursuant to the agreement.

Note. Although in Canadian law a choice of forum clause is often construed as non-exclusive unless the contrary is expressly stated, a clause in which a marketing agency, working for an American bridal fair organizer, agreed to "submit to the personal jurisdiction of the county or District Courts of Douglas County, Nebraska, for the resolution of any dispute" was interpreted as exclusive in *City Schooner Inc. v. Bridal Fair Inc.* (2005), 2 B.L.R. (4th) 216, 2005 ABQB 155. The judge said the trend in the cases was to assume such clauses were intended to designate an exclusive forum. An exclusive forum selection clause was given effect in *Pickering v. TD Trust* (2005), 16 C.P.C. (6th) 49 (Ont. S.C.J.) (Alberta jurisdiction clause in a bank agreement by which an Ontario resident agreed to lend money to an Alberta business via an Alberta branch of the bank).

(b) Claims in respect of property

Immovable outside the province

Note. The rule that a court has no jurisdiction to make orders directly affecting title to immovable property outside the province was applied in *Loewen v. Loewen* (2004), [2005] 4 W.W.R. 702 (Man. Q.B.), where a wife had sought an order for exclusive possession of a house in British Columbia that she owned jointly with her husband.

(c) Matrimonial claims

Nullity of marriage

Davison v. Sweeney (2005), 255 D.L.R. (4th) 757, 2005 BCSC 757 (British Columbia Supreme Court)

A wife applied for a declaration that a marriage entered into in Nevada was a nullity. She was an Alberta resident and the husband a British Columbia resident at all material times. They obtained a marriage licence and went through a marriage ceremony in Las Vegas after knowing each other for four hours. After the ceremony, they returned to their separate hotel rooms and had not seen each other since. The marriage, which complied with Nevada law as to form, was said to be void for lack of the wife's consent since she was drunk at the time, and voidable for non-consummation. Bernard J. held that according to the authorities the court had jurisdiction to declare a marriage void if either party was domiciled in British Columbia. Now that a married woman had capacity to have a domicile independent of her husband's (Law and Equity Act, R.S.B.C. 1996, c. 253, s. 60(3)(c)), the same jurisdictional rule applied to an application to declare the nullity of a voidable marriage. The court therefore had jurisdiction on both issues based on the wife's domicile in the province. As for choice of law, the issue of consent of a party went to essential validity and so was determined by either party's ante-nuptial domicile. Applying the law of British Columbia, the applicant's intoxication did not deprive her of capacity to give consent. Also applying British Columbia law to the issue of non-consummation, the applicant had not proved that the husband was incapable of consummating the marriage. The marriage was therefore valid.

Divorce — support — division of property — jurisdiction declined

Thor v. Thor (2005), 233 N.S.R. (2d) 266, 2005 NSSC 139 (Nova Scotia Supreme Court)

Haliburton J. held that Sweden was the *forum conveniens* for a divorce proceeding and related matrimonial property and support issues. The wife had filed for divorce in Nova Scotia and the husband, in Sweden. Both parties were Swedish by origin and had lived in Canada for most of the time they were together. Now, however, the husband, who was elderly and frail, had returned to Sweden to be with the children of his first marriage. The marital assets in Canada were known but those in Sweden were not. The husband's Swedish pension could only be divided by a court there. The parties had made two matrimonial property agreements that contemplated that their rights would be those under Swedish law. The wife visited Sweden frequently, and the Swedish courts were in a better position to resolve the issues. The wife would not be at an unfair disadvantage in a Swedish proceeding whereas the husband would be under such a disadvantage in a Nova Scotia proceeding.

Support — jurisdiction declined

Note. In *Kaprzyk v. Birks* (2005), 15 R.F.L. (6th) 221 (Ont. S.C.J.), although the respondent father lived in Ontario, jurisdiction in a child support action against him was declined. The evidence as to the child's needs was in Michigan, where the child and the mother resided and the father still worked. The same result was reached in *Prichici v. Prichici* (2005), 14 R.F.L. (6th) 425 (Ont. S.C.J.), where again the husband was resident in Ontario but the child and mother were resident in Romania. In both cases, the wives wished to take advantage of the Child Support Guidelines that apply in Canadian courts, although in each case neither the claimant nor the child had lived in Canada and the former spouses had made child support agreements that were governed by foreign law. In *G.(A.) v. S.(L.)* (2005), 19 R.F.L. (6th) 244, 2005 ABQB 462, the court did take jurisdiction to award child support against an Alberta-resident father in favour of a mother resident in Kazakhstan with whom he had had a brief relationship while on a trip there. The judge did not, however, apply the Child Support Guidelines, because they were geared to the costs of raising a child in Canada.

Division of property — jurisdiction declined

Note. In *Hunter v. Hunter* (2005), 15 R.F.L. (6th) 183, 2005 SKCA 76, although the Saskatchewan Queen's Bench had jurisdiction to grant a divorce, the court was held not to have jurisdiction *simpliciter* over a matrimonial property claim because it lacked a real and substantial connection with Saskatchewan. The parties' married life had been, and the only marital asset was, in British Columbia. The court applied the rules for territorial competence in the Court Jurisdiction and Proceedings Transfer Act, S.S. 1997, c. C-41.1.

(d) Infants and children

Custody — jurisdiction

Note. The child's ordinary residence is usually the criterion for taking jurisdiction in custody. In *Moggey v. Lawler* (2004), [2005] 3 W.W.R. 124, 2004 MBQB 198, the child was ordinarily resident in Manitoba and the court took jurisdiction over the custody application of the Manitoba-resident mother against a US-resident father. In *Biddlecomb v. Labelle* (2004), 364 A.R. 372, 2004 ABQB 623, the court held it had no jurisdiction to determine custody as between an Alberta-resident father and a New York-resident aunt of the child, because the child was ordinarily resident with the aunt. A clause in the New York court order that granted the aunt custody after the mother's death stated that it was subject to any custody or access order of the Alberta court, but such an order could not confer a jurisdiction on the Alberta court that it did not have.

The British Columbia court refused to decline jurisdiction in an application by a British Columbia-resident father to resume and enhance rights of access under a British Columbia court order, notwithstanding the mother and child having, with permission of the court, become resident in Nebraska some time ago: *L.(S.E.) v. L.(S.J.)* (2005), 15 R.F.L. (6th) 337, 2005 BCCA 102.

Custody — extra-provincial order

Note. In *Cabral v. Cabral* (2005), 17 R.F.L. (6th) 1 (Ont. S.C.J.), the custody and access provisions of a California judgment in divorce were enforced in Ontario under the Children's Law Reform Act, R.S.O. 1990, c. C.12, ss. 41 and 42. The evidence did not indicate a material change in circumstances since the California court had made its order. The father, still resident in California, was therefore subject to the same access limitations in Ontario as in California and also subject to the same restraining order against contacting the children except as permitted under the access provisions.

(e) Adult guardianship

Note. Over the objections of the applicant's brothers, a Saskatchewan court took jurisdiction to appoint the applicant as property guardian for his mother, based on the mother's being domiciled in Saskatchewan although she was now resident in a care facility in Alberta: *Re Hubbard* (2005), 260 Sask. R. 185, 2005 SKQB 130. As it was, the court of the domicile, it expected its order would be recognized in Alberta with respect to the mother's movable assets.

(f) Antisuit injunctions

Note. See *Hollinger International Inc. v. Hollinger Inc.* (2004), 11 C.P.C. (6th) 245 (Ont. S.C.J.), refusing an antisuit injunction because, *inter alia*, the main proceeding sought to be enjoined, which was brought in Illinois, involved a number of defendants and it would be wrong to put the applicant for an injunction in a different position from the other defendants in that proceeding.

2   *Québec*

(a) Action personnelle

Clause d'élection de for

GreCon Dimter Inc. c. J.R. Normand Inc., [2005] 2 R.C.S. 401 (Cour Suprême du Canada)

Le défaut de GreCon, un fabricant allemand, de livrer des pièces d'équipement à Normand, un fournisseur québécois, provoque l'inéxution partielle des obligations de Normand envers Tremblay, qui exploite une scierie au Québec. Tremblay intente une action en dommages-intérêts contre Normand devant la Cour supérieure du Québec. Normand appelle GreCon en garantie. Celui-ci invoque l'exception déclinatoire quant au recours en garantie, en s'appuyant sur une clause d'élection de for contenue dans son contrat avec Normand. Selon cette clause, seul un tribunal allemand serait compétent. Se fondant sur l'article 3139 C.c.Q., la Cour supérieure rejette le moyen déclinatoire en faisant prévaloir l'unité des recours sur le choix contractuel d'un tribunal, prévu par l'article 3148, alinéa 2 C.c.Q. La Cour d'appel confirme le rejet du moyen déclinatoire et résout le conflit entre les articles 3139 et 3148, alinéa 2 par l'application de l'article 3135 C.c.Q., relatif au *forum non conveniens*.

La Cour suprême du Canada a accueilli le pourvoi. Le moyen déclinatoire fondé sur l'absence de compétence des autorités québécoises est accueilli et le recours en garantie devant la Cour supérieure du Québec est rejeté.

La règle substantive fondamentale de l'autonomie de la volonté des parties a préséance sur la règle procédurale supplétive du forum unique. L'article 3148, alinéa 2 C.c.Q. doit prévaloir sur l'article 3139 C.c.Q. dans le contexte d'une action en garantie en présence d'une clause d'élection de for applicable au rapport juridique entre les parties à ce litige si, comme en l'espèce, il ressort de la clause une intention claire d'exclure la compétence des autorités québécoises. Dans ces circonstances, l'autorité québécoise doit décliner compétence. Cette conclusion découle à la fois de l'étude du cadre juridique de ces dispositions et de celle de leur hiérarchie.

Le cadre juridique est celui de la codification québécoise du droit international privé et de ces objectifs propres — soit le principe de l'autonomie de la volonté des parties et la sécurité juridique des transactions internationales. Le législateur québécois, en adoptant l'article 3148, alinéa 2, a reconnu la primauté de l'autonomie de la volonté des parties en matière de conflits de juridiction. Ce choix législatif favorise, par le recours aux clauses compromissoires et d'élection de for, la prévisibilité et la sécurité des transactions juridiques internationales. Ce choix participe également du mouvement d'harmonisation internationale des règles de conflits de lois et de conflits de juridiction. Hormis certaines exceptions, dont l'article 3139 ne fait pas partie et autrement absentes en l'espèce, rien n'indique que le législateur ait voulu limiter les possiblités de dérogation conventionnelle à la compétence des autorités québécoises en matière de conflits de juridiction. L'article 3148, alinéa 2 constitue la pierre angulaire d'une politique législative de respect de la volonté des parties et doit donc recevoir une interprétation large. L'article 3139, qui étend à la demande incidente la compétence de l'autorité québécoise pour entendre la demande principale, vise plutôt l'économie des ressources judiciaires et relève de considérations procédurales d'ordre interne; en tant qu'exception au principe selon lequel le tribunal doit déterminer sa compétence au cas par cas, il doit être interprété de façon restrictive. Une telle interprétation ne contredit pas les principes mis en œuvre par l'article 3139 mais respecte la hiérarchie des normes établies par le Code civil en cette matière.

La hiérarchie des normes entraîne en effet la primauté du principe énoncé à l'article 3148, alinéa 2. L'article 3139 constituant seulement une disposition facultative à caractère procédural, sa portée s'avère limitée et son application est subordonnée à celle de l'article 3148, alinéa 2, lequel reconnaît pleinement l'effet d'une intention claire exprimée dans une clause d'élection de for valide et exclusive. De plus, la nécessité d'interpréter l'article 3148, alinéa 2 en conformité avec les engagements internationaux du Québec vient confirmer le caractère obligatoire des clauses d'élection de for malgré l'existence de dispositions procédurales comme l'article 3139.

Le courant jurisprudentiel retenu par le premier juge, qui écarte les clause d'élection de for dans les cas de recours en garantie, est sans pertinence puisqu'il omet de considérer l'état du droit international privé au Québec depuis la réforme du Code civil, et notamment le principe de la primauté de l'autonomie de la volonté des parties. Quant à l'article 3135 C.c.Q. qui codifie la doctrine du *forum non conveniens* et qui a été utilisé par la Cour d'appel comme moyen de concilier les articles 3148, alinéa 2 et 3139, il n'a aucune application en l'espèce. L'article 3135 a une fonction supplétive et est applicable dans les seuls cas où la compétence du tribunal québécois a été préalablement établie.

Clause d'élection de for — contrat de consommation

Dell Computer Corporation c. Union des Consommateurs, [2005] R.J.Q. 1448 (Cour d'appel du Québec)

L'Union des Consommateurs (l'Union) a présenté une requête afin d'être autorisée à exercer un recours collectif pour le compte d'un groupe de consommateurs qui avaient tenté de se prévaloir d'une offre faite sur le site Internet de Dell relativement à l'achat d'appareils informatiques. Entre le 4 et le 7 avril 2003, Dell a annoncé deux appareils informatiques aux prix de 89 $ et de 118 $ respectivement. Constatant une erreur dans le prix affiché, elle a, le 7 avril, publié un avis de correction et affiché les prix exacts, soit 379 $ et 549 $. Le même jour, un consommateur — Dumoulin — a commandé un appareil au coût de 89 $. Le lendemain, Dell l'a advisé qu'elle ne donnerait pas suite à sa commande au prix annoncé. En première instance, elle a invoqué l'incompétence de la Cour supérieure en raison d'une clause compromissoire contenue au contrat de vente prévoyant que tout litige devait être réglé par voie d'arbitrage obligatoire organisé par le National Arbitration

Forum (NAF). Le premier juge a autorisé le recours collectif et a rejeté le moyen déclinatoire aux motifs que le contrat est de la nature d'un contrat de consommation et qu'une clause d'arbitrage ne peut être opposée à l'Union en vertu de l'article 3149 C.c.Q.

La Cour d'appel a rejeté le pourvoi. Le NAF est un organisme américain spécialisé en matière d'arbitrage qui offre des services de gestion d'arbitrage régis par son code de procédure. Selon ce code, les parties pourraient être entendues au Québec par un arbitre qui doit appliquer le droit québécois. L'arbitrage ne se fera donc pas à l'étranger. Par ailleurs, le contrat de l'appelante contient une clause externe par référence, c'est-à-dire une clause qui renvoie à un document externe, soit les conditions de vente, où l'on trouve la stipulation prévoyant l'arbitrage. Dans ce cas, la clause d'arbitrage devait être portée à la connaissance expresse du consommateur, ainsi que le prévoit l'article 1435 C.c.Q., qui est d'ordre public. Dell ne bénéficie pas d'une présomption de connaissance et devait prouver que le consommateur avait pris connaissance de cette clause, ce qui n'a pas été le cas en l'espèce. Par conséquent, la clause compromissoire de Dell est nulle et inopposable à l'Union. La Cour supérieure est donc compétente pour entendre le litige.

(b) Personnes — protection du majeur

Curatelle — majeure désirant vivre à l'étranger — homologation d'un mandat d'inaptitude — mandataire à l'étranger

Québec (Curateur Public) c. M.G., [2005] R.J.Q. 165 (Cour supérieure du Québec)

La majeure, qui est aujourd'hui âgée de 86 ans et qui présente des symptomes de la maladie d'Alzheimer, est née en Hongrie. En 1956, elle et son mari ont immigré au Canada. Le mari est décédé en 1996 et, selon son désir, il a été inhumé dans son pays d'origine. Le curateur public, qui avait obtenu une ordonnance provisoire pour l'ouverture d'un régime de protection, demande que ce régime soit désormais permanent et que les biens de la majeure lui soient confiés. Aux termes du mandat que celle-ci a donné advenant son inaptitude, Ma. M., en remplacement de son mari, J.F., qui est maintenant décédé, devrait prendre soin de sa personne et administrer ses biens. Cette dernière habite la Hongrie.

La Cour supérieure a décliné compétence en ce qui concerne la requête en ouverture du régime de protection, mais a accueilli en partie la requête en homologation du mandat d'inaptitude. Lors de la signature du mandat, J.F. habitait à Budapest. On peut en déduire que la majeure avait l'intention de retourner dans son pays d'origine. Normalement, la requête du curateur public devrait être accueillie puisque toutes les conditions d'ouverture d'un régime de protection ont été remplies. Toutefois, il lui sera impossible d'exécuter sa charge si la majeure devait retourner en Hongrie. D'autre part, Ma. M. ne pourra s'occuper de la majeure et de ses biens si cette dernière demeure au Québec. Il n'est donc pas possible de se prononcer sur l'une ou l'autre des requêtes telles qu'elles ont été présentées puisque l'on ne peut concilier le droit de la majeure de chosir l'endroit où elle veut résider et les préoccupations légitimes du curateur public et de la mandataire. Compte tenu de ces circonstances exceptionnelles, le tribunal décline compétence quant à la requête du curateur public afin que les autorités hongroises évaluent la situation et tranchent la question (article 3135 C.c.Q.). La majeure est autorisée à retourner en Hongrie, mais elle devra être accompagnée par la mandataire ou par toute personne que celle-ci pourra désigner. Ma. M. devra, dans les plus brefs délais, présenter une requête au tribunal des curatelles de Budapest afin de dénoncer son mandat et demander au tribunal de se prononcer sur la nécessité d'établir un régime de protection ainsi que sur l'opportunité d'établir un plan d'encadrement médical et social. Elle devra également demander des instructions sur la façon de recevoir et gérer les biens actuellement en la possession du curateur public. Celui-ci est autorisé à remettre ces biens après avoir reçu le jugement du tribunal des curatelles de Budapest. Lorsqu'il aura transmis ces biens, la curatelle prendra fin.

B   FOREIGN JUDGMENTS / JUGEMENTS ÉTRANGERS

1   Common Law and Federal

(a) Conditions for recognition or enforcement

Meaning of judgment — non-monetary order

Re Cavell Insurance Co. (Bankruptcy) (2005), 25 C.C.L.I. (4th) 230 (Ontario Superior Court of Justice)

Cavell was a reinsurance company based in England. It had ceased doing Canadian business in 1993 but its obligations to Canadian insurers had an estimated forty-year run-off. As part of bankruptcy proceedings in England the High Court made an order on 20

December 2004 approving Cavell's proposed Scheme of Arrangement under section 425 of the Companies Act (U.K.). Under the scheme an expert Scheme Adjudicator would place a value on all outstanding reinsurance claims against Cavell and the claims would be paid off at once, without a time discount. Known and potential Canadian creditors, mostly insurance companies and financial institutions, made up about 6 per cent of all the creditors entitled to claim under the scheme. On 21 December 2004, Cavell applied to the Ontario court for an order recognizing and implementing in Canada the English High Court's order. An order was also sought staying proceedings in respect of Cavell and its Canadian property.

Farley J. made the orders on 21 December 2004 and confirmed them after a rehearing on 21 February 2005. He held that he had jurisdiction to enforce the UK order, notwithstanding that it was not a monetary order, on either of two grounds. First, the UK order qualified as a "judgment" under the Reciprocal Enforcement of Judgments Convention with the United Kingdom, implemented by the Reciprocal Enforcement of Judgments (U.K.) Act, R.S.O. 1990, c. R.6. Article I(d) referred to "any decision, however described (judgment, order and the like) given by a court in a civil or commercial matter," and there was no reference to the payment of money being a necessary ingredient in the judgment. Only money judgments were entitled to enforcement under Part III of the convention, but the same restriction did not apply to Part V, which included in Article VIII a requirement that a United Kingdom judgment, whether for a payment of money or not, must be "recognised in a court of [Ontario] as conclusive between the parties thereto in all proceedings founded on the same cause of action." Since the common law now permitted the enforcement of non-monetary judgments where that was feasible and appropriate, and since there was a real and substantial connection between the subject matter of the order and the UK court, the judgment should be recognized and given effect by an Ontario order.

The UK order did not fall under the exclusion of judgments that determine "bankruptcy, insolvency or the winding up of companies or other legal persons" in Article II(d)(v) of the convention. The scheme did not deal with the dissolution of Cavell or the distribution of residue assets or net worth to shareholders of Cavell; nor did the scheme adjudicator have any authority to supervise a liquidation of Cavell. There had been no winding-up order in respect of Cavell — all that was proposed was a plan of compromise between

Cavell and (some of) its creditors. The order of the UK court was sufficiently precise to be enforceable. The second ground on which the Ontario court could order the recognition in Ontario of the High Court's order was its inherent jurisdiction to recognize and give effect to a foreign judgment based on the demands of comity.

Farley J. made his order conditional upon the following adjustments to the UK order. First, the UK scheme adjudicator was to reach a commutation valuation based on the rules of the Office of the Superintendent of Financial Institutions of Canada (OSFI), and taking into account the actual considerations of a "mega" claim, subject to the reinsurance policy limits, recognizing that Canada requires such reserves to be in trust whereas the United Kingdom does not. Second, given the uniqueness of the OSFI rules, which would only apply to Canadian carriers being reinsured by Cavell, there was to be a further right of appeal to the Ontario court on this point, recognizing that the scheme adjudicator would lose jurisdiction completely if he did not truly apply the OSFI rules. The affidavit of the scheme adjudicator already reflected these conditions. The precise formulation of these conditions was determined by Farley J. in a subsequent order of 22 April 2005, [2005] O.J. no. 1725. The appeal condition was framed so that an initial appeal would be to the UK court in the first instance but if that court thought the issue would be better dealt with by the courts of another jurisdiction, the UK court would send a letter of request to the foreign court asking it to deal with the issue, and the foreign court's decision would then be binding.

Note. In holding that non-monetary judgments are enforceable at common law, Farley J. relied on *Pro Swing Inc. v. ELTA Golf Inc.* (2004), 71 O.R. (3d) 566 (Ont. C.A.). A non-monetary order made in United States trademark proceedings for an injunction against and an account of profits by a Canadian infringer was held potentially enforceable in Ontario, but for the fact that its terms were not precise enough to permit the Ontario court to give effect to them. The Supreme Court of Canada heard the appeal in December 2005 but had not given judgment at the time of writing.

Although Farley J. held that the UK order was not made in bankruptcy proceedings, his order resembles orders made in such proceedings because it deals with local creditors and assets in such a way as to integrate them into an internationally coordinated process. Interesting also is the dialogue that took place, involving the parties and the courts in both Canada and the UK, on the exact form of the order. The case also illustrates the way the courts are adapting the foreign judgment rules to the exigencies of collective proceedings. For another example, see *Currie v. McDonald's Restaurants of Canada Ltd.*, noted below under *Jurisdiction of the original court — no consent — real and substantial connection with the foreign jurisdiction.*

Finality of the judgment

Note. The rule that a judgment is final notwithstanding that it is under appeal was applied in *Dslangdale Two LLC v. Daisytek (Canada) Inc.* (2004), 6 C.P.C. (6th) 363 (Ont. S.C.J.). Summary judgment to enforce a US judgment was granted, but execution was stayed pending the outcome of the appeal in the United States, and the Ontario judgment would be vacated if the appeal was successful.

Jurisdiction of the original court — no consent — real and substantial connection with the foreign jurisdiction

Currie v. McDonald's Restaurants of Canada Ltd. (2005), 250 D.L.R. (4th) 224, 74 O.R. (3d) 321 (Ontario Court of Appeal)

Currie, as representative plaintiff, commenced a class action against McDonald's for wrongs committed against McDonald's customers in the course of a promotional competition that McDonald's held in Canada and the United States. He alleged, *inter alia*, that those operating the competition had wrongfully diverted prize money away from Canadian contestants. McDonald's argued that Canadian customers' claims had already been the subject of class proceedings in Illinois that had culminated in a final settlement approved by the Illinois court. Canadian customers had been included in the class of plaintiffs in the Illinois proceeding on an opt-out basis. Notice of their inclusion and their right to opt out had been given in Canadian publications as ordered by the Illinois court. A representative plaintiff in a separate Ontario class proceeding had earlier been held bound by the Illinois settlement because he had made submissions to the Illinois court and so had attorned to the jurisdiction: *Parsons v. McDonald's Restuarants of Canada Ltd.* (2004), 45 C.P.C. (5th) 304 (Ont. S.C.J.) (noted in "Canadian Cases in Private International Law 2003-4" (2004) 42 Can. Y.B. Int'l L. 642). The motions judge held that Currie and the class of plaintiffs he represented would have been bound by the Illinois judgment but for a failure of natural justice in the "woefully inadequate" notice given to Canadian class members. Evidence was put before the court that Maclean's magazine, the national publication approved by the Illinois court for the notice to English-speaking Canadian class members, reached less than 30 per cent of Canadian adults who frequent burger restaurants.

The Ontario Court of Appeal, whose judgment was given by Sharpe J.A., affirmed the decision that the plaintiffs were not bound by the Illinois judgment, holding that the inadequate notice not only was a failure of natural justice but also deprived the court of jurisdiction over non-consenting Canadian members of the plaintiff class. The starting point for the latter analysis was the "real and substantial connection" test for the foreign court's jurisdiction, which *Beals v. Saldanha,* [2003] 3 S.C.R. 416, 234 D.L.R. 94th) 1, 2003 SCC 72 (noted in "Canadian Cases in Private International Law 2003-4" (2004) 42 Can. Y.B. Int'l L. 644) confirmed applies to international cases. Ontario courts had authorized national and international classes in certain cases, and there were strong policy reasons favouring the fair and efficient resolution of inter-provincial and international class action litigation. In an action with individual plaintiffs there was no question as to the jurisdiction of the foreign court to bind the plaintiff — the usual issue was jurisdiction over the defendant. Here, however, the question was reversed, because the defendant was seeking to enforce the judgment against the unnamed, non-resident plaintiffs.

To determine whether the assumption of jurisdiction by the foreign court satisfies the real and substantial connection test and the principles of order and fairness, the plaintiff's conduct could be relevant. A Canadian resident who ordered by mail from a foreign country or bought securities on a foreign stock exchange could reasonably expect that legal claims arising from the transaction could be litigated in the country in question. Here, however, the unnamed, non-resident class members had done nothing to invite or invoke Illinois jurisdiction. The principal connecting factors between the cause of action and Illinois were that the alleged wrongful conduct occurred in the United States and Illinois is the site of McDonald's head office. That was perhaps a real and substantial connection, but the principles of "order and fairness" required that careful attention be paid to the situation of ordinary McDonald's customers whose rights were at stake. They would have no reason to expect that any legal claim they might wish to assert against

McDonald's as a result of visiting a restaurant in Ontario would be adjudicated in the United States. Given the substantial connection between the alleged wrong and Illinois, and given the small stake of each individual class member, the principles of order and fairness could be satisfied if the interests of the non-resident class members were adequately represented and if it were clearly brought home to them that their rights could be affected in the foreign proceedings if they failed to take adequate steps to be removed from those proceedings. There might well be cases in which the nature of the rights and interests at stake would make it appropriate to recognize the judgment only if the plaintiff opted in, but in a case like the present one a requirement that the plaintiff have opted in would effectively negate meaningful class action relief.

Thus, provided (1) there is a real and substantial connection linking the cause of action to the foreign jurisdiction, (2) the rights of non-resident class members are adequately represented, and (3) non-resident class members are accorded procedural fairness including adequate notice, it may be appropriate to attach jurisdictional consequences to an unnamed plaintiff's failure to opt out. In such a case, failure to opt out may be regarded as a form of passive attornment sufficient to support the jurisdiction of the foreign court. There was no basis for interfering with the motions judge's finding that the notice given to Canadian McDonald's customers had been inadequate. The Illinois court therefore lacked jurisdiction over unnamed, passive Canadian class members.

The notice had been found inadequate both because it was inadequately circulated and because it was obscurely worded. The judge was entitled to come to those conclusions and, in determining the standard of what was adequate notice, he was entitled to take into consideration the standard of notice the Illinois court applied to US class members. He was not bound to apply the standard that would apply in an Ontario class proceeding. His finding that there was a failure of natural justice was therefore upheld.

Note. The "real and substantial connection" ground for jurisdiction of the foreign court is not available in New Brunswick because the Foreign Judgments Act, R.S.N.B. 1973, c. F-19, reflects the common law as it was understood before the "real and substantial connection" test was adopted: *Pegasus Consulting Ltd. v. OSI Software Inc.* (2005), 9 B.L.R. (4th) 334, 2005 NBQB 368.

Jurisdiction of the original court — consent — submission by the defendant

Note. Although they were refused enforcement on the ground of natural justice, orders of the Saskatchewan Workers' Compensation Board, which by statute had the effect of court judgments, were held otherwise enforceable in Manitoba on the basis that the judgment debtors, who were residents of Manitoba, had attorned to the Saskatchewan courts' jurisdiction by applying for benefits under the workers' compensation scheme: *Saskatchewan (Workers' Compensation Board) v. Bell* (2005), 189 Man. R. (2d) 298, 2005 MBQB 5.

(b) Defences to recognition or enforcement

Fraud

Note. Beals v. Saldanha, [2003] 3 S.C.R. 416, 234 D.L.R. (4th) 1, 2003 SCC 72 (noted in "Canadian Cases in Private International Law 2003-4" (2004) 42 Can. Y.B. Int'l L. 644), clarified that enforcement of a foreign judgment can only be resisted on the ground of fraud if the fraud is proved by new and material facts that the defendant could not reasonably have discovered and brought before the foreign court. This standard was applied in *Zaidenberg v. Hamouth* (2005), 42 B.C.L.R. (4th) 303, 2005 BCCA 356, where the facts allegedly showing fraud not only could have been, but actually were, raised before the foreign court before it gave judgment.

Public policy

Note. In *Re Smith* (2005), 12 C.B.R. (5th) 39 (N.W.T. S.C.), a US court gave judgment in favour of a US bankruptcy trustee against a Canadian resident at a time when the Canadian resident had taken steps that, under Canadian bankruptcy law, imposed a stay of proceedings against him. The US court took notice of the stay but decided it would be helpful to the Canadian trustee to quantify the claim, which was for recovery of payments on a patent. The Canadian court held the judgment was a valid proof of claim in the Canadian bankruptcy and the refusal to abide by the Canadian stay did not offend against Canadian public policy. Canadian courts themselves had a discretion as to whether to respect a foreign stay. *Re Kevco Inc.* (2005), 9 C.B.R. (5th) 230 (Que. S.C.), also involved the enforcement, as a claim in a Canadian bankruptcy, of a US judgment in favour of a US bankruptcy trustee. The court held that since the federal bankruptcy law does not include specific provision for the recognition and enforcement of foreign judgments, the private international law rules of the province where the court sits must be applied.

United States of America v. Shield Development Co. (2004), 74 O.R. (3d) 583 (S.C.J.), affd. (2005), 74 O.R. (3d) 595 (C.A.), was a claim by the US government against two Canadian corporations under the US Comprehensive Response, Compensation and Liability Act (CERCLA) for the costs of cleaning up hazardous substances from a copper processing site in Utah. The defendants argued unsuccessfully that there was a triable issue as to whether the claims offended against Canadian public policy because the US government chose to pursue the defendants, who had ownership interests in the site, rather than the American company that actually operated the site. The defendants had not provided any evidence that they had been improperly targeted.

Another claim of biased justice failed in *Oakwell Engineering Ltd. v. Enernorth Industries Inc.* (2005), 76 O.R. (3d) 528 (S.C.J.). The judgment was from Singapore, and the judgment debtor argued that the close ties between the judiciary and the government in Singapore meant there was a real risk that the judges were biased against him and in favour of the judgment creditor, a Singapore business. The Ontario court held the debtor had presented no cogent evidence of bias, either systemic or particular to this case. Moreover, it had not raised the issue of bias at any stage of the proceedings in Singapore, and the argument by the principal of the debtor company that he could not to do without risking a charge of sedition was unsupported by evidence. Bias was also raised in *Ultracuts Franchises Inc. v. Wal-Mart Canada Corp.* (2005), 196 Man. R. (2d) 163, 2005 MBQB 222, on the ground that two of the Arkansas judges that had given judgment against the defendant in favour of Wal-Mart held shares in Wal-Mart at the time. The contention was rejected. Wal-Mart shares were very widely held and the outcome of the litigation could not affect the value of the shares of such a large company.

In *K.(E.) v. K.(D.)* (2005), 257 D.L.R. (4th) 549, 2005 BCCA 425, a spousal settlement agreement that was approved by a New Jersey court was held not to contravene Canadian public policy by including a provision that a domestic violence complaint against the husband was dismissed. The husband argued the child support obligations in the settlement should not be enforced against him because it was against public policy to stifle the prosecution of a public offence. The court held the impugned provision was considered routine and not contrary to public policy in the jurisdiction where it was agreed to, and did not offend Canadian public policy in the conflict of laws sense.

Natural justice

Note. Judgments consisting of orders of the Saskatchewan Workers' Compensation Board, requiring the defendants to repay benefits they had received, were held to contravene natural justice because the defendants had not been given notices of claim as the act required: *Saskatchewan (Workers' Compensation Board v. Bell* (2005), 189 Man. R. (2d) 298, 2005 MBQB 5. A US judgment given against two men and their marital community was held unenforceable in British Columbia against their wives (one of whom was now divorced from the debtor husband) because they had not been personally served with notice of the proceeding: *Walters v. Tolman* (2005), 47 B.C.L.R. (4th) 140, 2005 BCSC 838. The argument that under US law the wives submitted to the court's jurisdiction by virtue of their marriages was rejected on the ground that such a rule was against Canadian public policy and natural justice.

(c) Effect of recognition or enforcement

Recognition — issue estoppel

CLE Owners Inc. v. Wanlass (2005), 192 Man. R. (2d) 140, 2005 MBCA 32, leave to appeal to S.C.C. refused, 22 August 2005 (Manitoba Court of Appeal)

In 1986, on the basis of an international competition, the plaintiffs, brothers resident in Manitoba, selected Wanlass, a sculptor resident in Oregon, to design the game pieces and game board for a game the plaintiffs had devised, called Capture. The parties entered into an agreement in Oregon by which Wanlass agreed to produce 2,000 sets of the pieces, cast in bronze, in return for 6% of the selling price of the sets. Over the next two years Wanlass designed the pieces and board and made wax models of them, a foundry made moulds from Wanlass's models, and master castings were produced for the plaintiffs' approval. In 1988 the parties made a revised agreement in Winnipeg that included a new company set up by Wanlass and raised the selling price per set from $4,000 to $8,000. The plaintiffs were unsuccessful in marketing the game and had no communication with Wanlass between 1992 and 2002. In 2002, the plaintiffs contacted Wanlass to tell him that they were recommencing their efforts and wanted to confirm his continued participation. Wanlass, who by now was in poor health and living in Utah, refused to have anything more to do with the project. The plaintiffs threatened Wanlass with legal action. In April 2002, Wanlass and his company (the defendants) commenced an action in Oregon for a declaration they had no further obligations to the plaintiffs. In May 2002, having been served with the claim in the Oregon action, the plaintiffs began an action in Manitoba for a declaration as to their rights against the defendants. The plaintiffs took no steps to defend the Oregon action and judgment was given against them in default in July 2002. At the time, the plaintiffs were still negotiating with Wanlass for a settlement. They received no notice of the default judgment until, in November 2002, the defendants filed a defence in the Manitoba action claiming the issues were *res judicata* as a result of the Oregon judgment.

The motions judge ordered the plaintiffs' claims struck out on the ground of *res judicata* and the Court of Appeal affirmed the decision. A default judgment could give rise to *res judicata*. Looking at the pleadings and the history of the proceedings, the Oregon action covered the same issues as the plaintiffs raised in the Manitoba action. The Oregon judgment was entitled to recognition based on the real and substantial connection between the action and Oregon. The original contract was executed there, Wanlass lived there at the time, and his company was registered there. It was immaterial that Wanlass had moved to Utah. Wanlass was not precluded from relying on the default judgment by the fact that he continued to try to reach a settlement with the plaintiffs without telling them he was proceeding to judgment. The plaintiffs had adequate notice of the risk of default judgment and did not take steps to dissuade Wanlass from obtaining it. Nor did they take steps to set the Oregon judgment aside when they learned of it. There was no reason to interfere with the motions judge's refusal to exercise the court's discretion to relieve against the issue estoppel.

c   CHOICE OF LAW (INCLUDING STATUS OF PERSONS) / CONFLITS
    DE LOIS (Y COMPRIS STATUT PERSONNEL)

1   Common Law and Federal

(a) Characterization

Procedure and substance — prejudgment interest

Note. Prejudgment interest, being an issue of substantive rather than procedural law, was awarded according to Pennsylvania law as the law applicable to the plaintiffs' claim for losses suffered as a result of a car accident in that state: *Brown v. Flaharty* (2004), 10 C.P.C. (6th) 361 (Ont. S.C.J.).

(b) Contracts

Formal validity

Canaccord Capital Corp. v. 884003 Alberta Inc. (2005), 46 B.C.L.R. (4th) 64, 2005 BCCA 124 (British Columbia Court of Appeal)

An Alberta company opened a trading account with the plaintiff, a stockbroking firm in British Columbia, which faxed a number of forms to it for the setting-up of the account. The defendant, who was the Alberta-resident principal of the company, signed a personal guarantee for the company's debts to the stockbroker but he did not sign or return a certificate of notarization, which the plaintiff also sent him, without which the guarantee was invalid according to the Guarantees Acknowledgment Act, R.S.A. 2000, c. G-11. When the plaintiff sued the principal on the guarantee, the British Columbia Court of Appeal, affirming the Supreme Court of Canada, held that non-compliance with the Alberta statute was immaterial because the guarantee was governed by British Columbia law as the law that had the closest and most real connection to the contract. The defendant had set up the account in British Columbia and intended to trade there. All of the transactions that were the subject of the guarantee pertained to British Columbia, and the language of the guarantee was appropriate to the law of that province.

Statutory regulation of contract

Williams v. Brown (2004), 282 N.B.R. (2d) 221, 2004 NBQB 385 (New Brunswick Queen's Bench)

At issue here was the right of a Prince Edward Island resident, who was injured in a car accident in New Brunswick, to recover for income loss to the extent that he had already received some Cdn $39,000 in no-fault insurance benefits under his own insurance policy. New Brunswick insurance legislation provided that the recipient of such payments was deemed to release the wrongdoer from liability to that extent. The act also provided that in "an action for damages arising out of an accident," payments received for loss of income must be deducted from a damages award. The court held that the statutory release provision did not apply because the operation of that provision was expressly limited to policies issued in New Brunswick. Moreover, constitutionally, New Brunswick could not legislate in respect of contracts made elsewhere. However, the deduction provision did apply because it was framed in terms of "actions" in the province and the payments the plaintiff had received were payments for loss of income within the meaning of the section. New Brunswick did have jurisdiction to legislate on the recovery of damages in a New Brunswick action.

(c)   Torts

Applicable law

Roy v. North American Leisure Group Inc. (2004), 246 D.L.R. (4th) 306, 73 O.R. (3d) 561 (Ontario Court of Appeal)

The plaintiffs became ill as a result of a virus infection when they were on a Caribbean cruise. More than three years after the cruise, they brought an action in Ontario against Sunquest, the Ontario company that organized the package holiday of which the cruise was a part, and Airtours, a related company, based in the United Kingdom, that operated the cruise ship. In earlier proceedings a motions judge held that Ontario had jurisdiction *simpliciter* over the action against Airtours and was the *forum conveniens*. The present proceeding was concerned with whether the claim against Airtours was statute-barred. The action was brought within the Ontario limitation period but outside the two-year limitation period in the Athens Convention Relating to the Carriage of Passengers and Their Luggage by Sea (1974). The convention was specifically made applicable by the contractual terms in the Airtours cruise brochure, which also specified that English law governed the contract. The Athens Convention was also part of the law of the Bahamas, where the alleged wrongs by Airtours took place. At first instance the judge held that the claim was governed by Ontario law as the law that had the closest and most substantial connection with the issue. The judge attached weight to the injustice that would result from applying the Athens Convention. (Canada became a signatory to the convention after the cause of action in this case arose; see Part 4 of the Marine Liability Act, S.C. 2001, c. 6.)

The Court of Appeal reversed the first instance judge's decision. Issues of limitation were matters of substantive law, as held in *Tolofson v. Jensen*, [1994] 3 S.C.R. 1022, 120 D.L.R. (4th) 289. The fact that the foreign limitation period was shorter than Ontario's was not an injustice so as to warrant a departure from the applicable law, whether English law as specified in the cruise brochure or the law of the Bahamas as the *lex loci delicti*. It might be inconvenient that one law applied to the claim against Sunquest and another to the claim against Airtours, but that did not of itself create a reason to depart from the general rule for choice of law. Finally, the plaintiffs' claim against Airtours was an action arising under the contract and so was subject to English law as provided in the choice of law clause in Airtours' cruise brochure. The brochure provided by Sunquest clearly distinguished between Sunquest as tour operator and the various service providers. The Airtours brochure gave reasonable notice of the limitation period. Moreover, the parties would not reasonably have expected Ontario law to apply to a Caribbean cruise supplied by a British cruise company.

Note. In *Soriano (Litigation Guardian of) v. Palacios* (2005), 255 D.L.R. (4th) 359 (Ont. C.A.), the family of a victim who was struck by a car in Québec brought an action for their losses against the Québec-resident driver and against their own Ontario insurer on their underinsured motorist coverage. Under Québec law, civil actions for injuries stemming from automobile accidents are barred in favour of a no-fault insurance scheme. The court, applying the *lex loci delicti*, held that since there was no claim against the driver under Québec law, there was no basis for a claim against their insurer.

Vicarious liability

Yeung (Guardian ad litem *of) v. Au* (2004), 43 B.C.L.R. (4th) 380, 2004 BCSC 1648 (British Columbia Supreme Court)

The plaintiff was very seriously injured in a collision in British Columbia caused by the negligence of the driver of the other car.

The other car had been leased by the driver's father from a British Columbia car dealer, but the dealer's standard form lease contract (which, by coincidence, was changed a week after the accident) was expressly governed by Ontario law. An issue in the plaintiff's action was whether the lessor of the vehicle was vicariously liable, as owner, under section 86 of the Motor Vehicle Act, R.S.B.C. 1996, c. 318, or whether that issue was to be determined by Ontario law as the proper law of the lease contract. Tysoe J. held that the issue was a tort issue and so was to be decided by the law of the place of the accident, British Columbia. Even if, as the lessor contended, the court was free to apply the law of the province with the most significant relationship to the issue, that still led to the application of British Columbia law. Applying British Columbia law, however, the vicariously liable party was not the lessor but the father, who, as lessee with an option to purchase, was deemed to be the owner for the purposes of section 86.

(d) Marriage and matrimonial causes

Foreign divorce — recognition

Orabi v. El Qaoud (2005), 12 R.F.L. (6th) 296, 2005 NSCA 28 (Nova Scotia Court of Appeal)

The husband and wife were married in Kuwait in 1990, emigrated to Canada in April 2002, and separated in June 2002. In October 2002, the husband obtained a divorce decree in the form of a Revocable Divorce Document from the Shariite Council in Jordan. The wife learned of the divorce for the first time when she received a copy of the decree two months later. Among other matrimonial proceedings, the wife sought a declaration that the Jordanian Revocable Divorce Document was not recognized in Canada. The Nova Scotia Court of Appeal, affirming the court below, held the divorce could not be recognized on the basis of one year's ordinary residence in Jordan by either party (Divorce Act, R.S.C. 1985, c. 3 (2nd Supp.), s. 22(1)) or any other statutory or common law ground. Neither the wife (Divorce Act, s. 22(2)) nor the husband (common law recognition rule) was domiciled in Jordan. There was no real and substantial connection to Jordan (another common law ground for recognition) because everyone in the family was substantially connected with Canada. In addition, the decree violated natural justice because the wife had no notice of the proceedings.

Book Reviews / Recensions de livres

The Rights of Refugees under International Law. By James C. Hathaway.
Cambridge: Cambridge University Press, 2005. 1,184 pages.

In the last fifteen years, there has been a great deal of both academic
and judicial writings interpreting the definition of a convention
refugee as defined in the 1951 Convention Relating to the Status
of Refugees (Refugee Convention). The definition, however, is only
one article in the convention, albeit an important one. There has
been a dearth of analysis — either academic or judicial — on the
other forty-five articles of the Refugee Convention and found within
these articles are an entire set of entitlements for refugees on such
fundamental issues as the rights to work, to education, to health
care, and to freedom of movement. In addition, there are many
entitlements that exist based on other international instruments
such as the International Covenant on Civil and Political Rights
(ICCPR) and the International Covenant on Economic, Social and
Cultural Rights (ICESCR). In today's world, when refugee's entitlements are at risk of being minimized, the comprehensive analysis
provided by James Hathaway in this book is welcomed.

The first three chapters set the stage for the analysis of specific
entitlements that follow. However, these chapters have their own
significance as Hathaway puts forward what he refers to as a "relatively conservative understanding of the sources of both custom
and general principles [of law] premised on a consent-based, modern positivist view of international law."[1] The result of his conclusion for refugee rights is that they must, therefore, be found in
treaty law — either the 1951 Refugee Convention or other international instruments. As noted by Hathaway, he was not aspiring to

[1] James Hathaway, *The Rights of Refugees under International Law* (Cambridge: Cambridge University Press, 2005) at 15.

analyze the issues around sources of international law in depth but rather to give a brief explanation of his reasoning, which he has effectively done by challenging the various arguments in favour of expanding the scope of international law.

The remainder of the book is devoted to analyzing specific entitlements of refugees. The book follows a consistent and coherent methodology throughout. For each entitlement, Hathaway begins by giving some real life recent examples where the entitlement was at issue. These examples are followed by a discussion of the relevant provisions in the Refugee Convention and or other international instruments and an analysis of their content by referring to the drafting history, commentary, and relevant state and treaty body jurisprudence. Subsequently, there is a return to the specific examples to analyze them in light of the discussion on the treaty provisions. Finally, a conclusion on the interpretation that can be given to the entitlement is clearly provided. This is an effective way in which to present the material as there is both the theoretical and the practical application, which not only increases the overall strength of the analysis but will also make this book useful to a larger array of persons — from academics and students, to refugee advocates and other litigants, to judges and to governments seeking to define policies for asylum seekers and refugees.

Within the book, Hathaway has also clearly delineated the entitlements of three different categories of persons in the refugee regime as those categories are understood in the convention — that is, persons who are physically present in a country of asylum, those who are lawfully present, and those who are lawfully staying. Hathaway puts forward a credible analysis that the first category of persons enjoys many rights and entitlements either under the Refugee Convention (for example, the right to enter and remain, *non-refoulement*) or the ICCPR (for example, physical security, *non-refoulement*) or the ICESCR (for example, access to food, shelter, and health care). As the first category has these rights and entitlements, then the other two categories do as well. The importance of this analysis, and the resulting conclusions, cannot be overstated, as many state policies in recent years appear to be based on a premise, or an assumption, that until a person is formally recognized as a refugee, they have minimum rights within a country of asylum. By looking not only at the Refugee Convention but also at the ICCPR and the ICESCR to define the applicable entitlements, Hathaway shows that there is an entire set of rights that accrue to persons once they are physically present in the country of asylum and well before they are either legally present or legally staying.

There can be no doubt as to the contribution that this book should make to the debate about refugee rights. It has breathed life into the convention while, at the same time, putting refugee rights within the broader context of international human rights law. In his epilogue, Hathaway sets forth two challenges for the refugee rights regime — the challenge of enforceability (which he proposes should rest with an independent oversight body) and the challenge of the political will to reconceive the implementing mechanisms of international refugee law in a way that both meets the human rights of refugees and the interests of the governments. Hopefully, the analysis articulated by Hathaway in this book will become the foundation for further discussion, debate, and analysis in this important area of international human rights.

KRISTA DALEY
Senior General Counsel, Immigration and Refugee Board of Canada

The Legislative History of the International Criminal Court. By M. Cherif Bassiouni. Ardsley, NY: Transnational Publishers, 2005. 3 volume set, 1,500 pages.

The International Criminal Court (ICC) finally became a reality with the entry into force of its Statute in 2002. Arguably one of the most significant international organizations to be created since the United Nations, the ICC is the product of many years of work and struggle. The aim of this new collection of materials is to provide readers with a comprehensive legislative history of the ICC by integrating into one publication the documents that constitute the historical and legal foundations of this new world institution.

The collection is edited by M. Cherif Bassiouni, an eminent author and editor of books and articles on international criminal law, comparative criminal law, and international human rights law. Bassiouni is a distinguished research professor of law at DePaul University College of Law and president of the International Human Rights Law Institute. His expertise in international criminal law, particularly when the topic is the ICC, cannot be disputed. He is recognized internationally as one of the driving forces behind the establishment of an international criminal court, having advocated it worldwide for the last thirty years. Bassiouni has served in the United Nations in several capacities: he was the chairman of the Security Council's Commission to Investigate War Crimes in the Former Yugoslavia as well as the vice-chairman of the General

Assembly's Ad Hoc Committee on the Establishment of an ICC. In addition, it is of significant relevance for the collection that Bassiouni also occupied the position of chairman of the Drafting Committee of the 1998 Diplomatic Conference on the Establishment of an ICC. Bassiouni is therefore well positioned to introduce readers to the Statute he helped draft.

The collection is divided into three volumes of commentary, legal documents, reports, and other relevant materials. Volume 1 is divided into two parts with Part I consisting of three chapters. The first chapter provides a historical chronology of events on international criminal justice. This is followed in Chapter 2 by a description of the history and establishment of the ICC. The final chapter outlines the principles of the ICC's operations, including the scope of its jurisdiction, its mechanisms, and its procedural regime. Part II includes a text of the Statute, including elements of crimes and rules of procedure and evidence, a text of the court's regulations, and a comprehensive bibliography. Finally, other relevant documents are included in the appendixes to Volume I, namely the agreements relating to the privileges and immunities and financial regulations of the court and relating to the court's relationship with the United Nations.

Volume 2 contains a legislative history of the Statute from 1994 to 1998. Each article of the Rome Statute is presented along with all its prior versions in a reverse chronological order. So the volume provides the complete textual evolution of each article in the Statute. Reflected in the chronological compilation are the following documents: (1) the texts transmitted between the Drafting Committee and the Committee of the Whole at the Rome Diplomatic Conference; (2) the text proposed by the 1998 Preparatory Committee on the Establishment of an ICC; (3) the text completed by the inter-sessional meeting in Zutphen; (4) the text put forward by the 1995 Ad Hoc Committee on the Establishment of an ICC; and (5) the text proposed by the International Law Commission in 1994. It also contains government proposals made during the 1995–8 sessions of the ad hoc and preparatory committees, most of which have not previously been made available to the public. Volume 3 is made up of the proceedings of the 1998 Rome diplomatic conference. It includes the summary records of the meetings of the diplomatic conference's Plenary meetings, as well as of the meetings of the Committee of the Whole.

Given the proliferation of books published on international criminal law and on the ICC — no other tribunal has had so much published before holding its first trial — is Bassiouni's latest collection of materials a contribution that stands out in the field? Several features do make this collection unique. In contrast with other publications, Bassiouni has merged three of the court's fundamental documents — the 1998 Rome Statute, the Rules of Procedure and Evidence, and the Elements of Crimes — into one integrated document. Therefore, readers benefit from an article-by-article integrated text of the Statute, elements of crimes, and the rules of procedure and evidence. In addition, included in the integrated text are footnotes referencing recently promulgated regulations of the court and decisions of the Assembly of States Parties. This is a unique feature of the collection, one that cannot be found in other publications on the ICC. If a revised edition is planned, the editor would be well advised to further improve the integrated text by also directly inserting the regulations and decisions of the assembly into this article-by-article compilation. The summary records found in Volume 3 are not easily accessible. According to Bassiouni, the United Nations ceased publishing the proceedings in 2004, and the materials are not available electronically. Therefore, the practical value of having included them in this collection cannot be overstated.

The commentaries in the collection are also valuable contributions. Both historical chronologies of international criminal justice found in Volume 1 would be useful resources for the reading lists of any course on international criminal law. The chronologies identify relevant developments throughout history, including civilizations other than Western civilization. The fact that Bassiouni served as the chairman of the Drafting Committee at the Rome conference adds to the uniqueness of the commentaries. Bassiouni states in the introduction to Volume 1 that he has "held back [his] personal views on the interpretation of the statutory provisions" because of the confidentiality of the work of the Drafting Committee.[1] He strays from this stand in Chapter 3, in the section on the ICC's nature, functions, and mechanisms. As he states, "[t]he one exception to this is found in Volume 1, Part 1, Chapter 3, where I describe the ICC's workings. However, my personal views there are limited to issues that are widely debated in academic circles."[2]

---

[1] M. Cherif Bassiouni, *The Legislative History of the International Criminal Court: Introduction, Analysis and Integrated Text* (Ardsley, NY: Transnational Publishers, 2005) at xix.

[2] *Ibid.*

It cannot be denied that Bassiouni's position as chairman of the Drafting Committee significantly colours his commentary on the workings of the ICC. While not presented as such, the commentary is nevertheless an insightful first-hand account of the drafting process both prior to and during the Rome diplomatic conference. Bassiouni is able to provide revealing assessments of the drafting, substantive, and ambiguity problems in the Statute. For instance, readers are informed that some of the drafting problems that have surfaced with the Statute since its adoption in 1998 are the product of instructions received by the Drafting Committee that "the text of articles 5-21 could be read but not altered" due to time constraints.[3] These provisions constitute some of the most contentious issues in the Statute, and Bassiouni's explanation provides a very useful insight indeed.

There are several other reminders that the editor is an interested party, from the fact that Bassiouni concludes Chapter 2 with the speech he gave at the Rome ceremony on 18 July 1998,[4] to the opinions he often states about the intention of the drafters.[5] For instance, Bassiouni comments on the fact that non-states parties can only refer a "crime" to the ICC, while other referrals are to be made for a "situation." This difference in language, Bassiouni worries, "would allow a state to target specific individuals from only one party to a conflict. "[6] He assures the readers that "[s]uch selectivity was never intended by the drafters and there is no doubt in any of the negotiators' minds that referral by a non-state party was to be for a "situation," much like a referral by a state party or by the SC."[7] Likewise, when discussing recent Security Council resolutions, Bassiouni asserts that "providing a blanket prohibition of the ICC's exercise of jurisdiction for a period of time for military and civilian personnel in certain peacekeeping operations ... was not the intent

---

[3] *Ibid.* at 84–85.

[4] *Ibid.* at 120.

[5] For example, Bassiouni inserts his views on the failure to include social and political groups in the definition of genocide — a position for which he advocated strongly before and during the conference. In his view, "[t]he reason why governments in 1998 failed to include these groups within the provision of Article 6 is beyond comprehension." *Ibid.* at 149.

[6] *Ibid.* at 140.

[7] *Ibid.*

of the drafters."[8] Bassiouni also does not shy away from expressing strong opinions about the difficulties created by US opposition to the ICC and analyzes the various measures taken by Washington to obstruct the court.[9] Bassiouni may have been motivated to insert insights and opinions drawn from his experience as a drafter of the Statute in the hopes of influencing future legal interpretations of the Statute. In any case, it provides readers with interesting analytical food for thought.

Unfortunately, the collection suffers considerably from insufficient editing and very poor proofreading, to the extent that it undermines the overall quality of the collection. First, the text has numerous spelling and grammatical mistakes,[10] improper indexing

---

[8] *Ibid.* at 141. He adds: "Probably what is most shocking about resolutions 1422 and 1487 are their promotions of blanket impunity. Only those governments who have a disregard for the international rule of law coupled with the arrogance of power, and more particularly for international humanitarian law, could have led these governments to impose these two resolutions." *Ibid.* at 144.

[9] For example, Bassiouni shares his views on the validity of the bilateral agreements the United States has entered into with other states: "It would be absurd to propose that a state cannot extradite a non-national to another state that has a valid jurisdictional basis to prosecute the requested person." *Ibid.* at 139.

[10] The following list is just a sample of mistakes found in the text: (emphasis added to point out the errors):

- "It may also be *intra vires*, if the SC abuses its authority pursuant to Article 39 of the Charter, though there is no judicial body to review the *legally basis* of that political determination." *Ibid.* at 132.
- "In other words, if a state party resorts to such alternative mechanisms, can that state claim to have satisfied requirements of *complemenarity*, which pursuant to the statute are investigation and if necessary prosecution?" *Ibid.* at 134.
- "Unsettled issues include a state party's inability or unwillingness to prosecute, slow or ineffective national investigations and prosecution, determination not to prosecute, judicial determination of acquittal, or judicial *meeting* of a symbolic sanction." *Ibid.* at 138.
- "Had such an exception to the Court's jurisdiction been formulated in connection with Articles 12-19, *clearly express* opposition to it would have occurred by most of the Diplomatic Conference's *delegation*." *Ibid.* at 144.
- "The Statute does not permit the states parties to ratify the Treaty with any reservations or declarations and understandings [Article 20]. It does, however, allow for amendment and reviewing of the *Statutes*." *Ibid.* at 190.
- "[as corrected by the *procés*-verbaux of 10 November 1998 and 12 July 1999]." *Ibid.* at 201.

and referencing,[11] missing words,[12] incorrect fonts,[13] and incorrectly placed text. For instance, in one of the most confusing mistakes made in the collection, the editor's note, which introduces the integrated text of the Statute, elements, and rules in Part II of Volume I, mistakenly introduces this section as the legislative history of the Statute.[14] In fact, the legislative history is found in Volume II. Second, the commentaries in Volume 1, written by Bassiouni, are filled with awkward sentences[15] and repetitive sections.[16] A reader might be forgiven in thinking that this is an unedited publication, put together quickly in order to reach the academic book market first, given the increasing number of similar collections published by other authors. While perfection cannot be expected, the insufficient editing of this collection warrants that the publisher revise the publication to correct these mistakes (especially given the costs of the collection to the consumer). Otherwise, the reputation of both the editor and the publisher will surely be adversely affected.

---

[11] The index in Volume I incorrectly numbers Chapter 3 of Part I as "Chapter 2." *Ibid.* at vi. There is also an incorrect referral to a document as an appendix to Chapter 2, when, in fact, it is reproduced in Volume III: "The UN, however, issued a publication (reprinted as an appendix to this chapter), which purports to be a record of the Rome Conference prepared by the Office of Legal Affairs. In time, it is likely to become the authoritative diplomatic history of the conference, *faute de mieux.*" *Ibid.* at 76. The index to Volume 2 also contains an error. It mistakenly refers to Article 12 when it means Article 112. M. Cherif Bassiouni, *The Legislative History of the International Criminal Court: An Article-By-Article Evolution of the Statute* (Ardsley, NY: Transnational Publishers, 2005) at vi.

[12] For example: "There is no doubt that only the SC or a state party can refer a "situation" to the ICC *by the.*" Bassiouni, *supra* note 1 at 132.

[13] See the font of footnote 115: *ibid.* at 151. And the font of footnote 207: *ibid.* at 180.

[14] *Ibid.* at 199.

[15] For example, the following sentences could have benefited from some serious editing:
   • "Lastly, with respect to the sources of the law applicable to the interpretation of Article 8, Article 10 controls, subject to Article 9, provided that Article 9 is interpreted as binding with respect to the judicial interpretation of Article 8." *Ibid.* at 164.
   • "Upon the Prosecutor's motion, the Pre-Trial Chamber may issue an arrest warrant if it determines that reasonable grounds that an individual committed a crime within the ICC's jurisdiction exist." *Ibid.* at 169.

[16] For example, a section relating to "unique investigative opportunity" is repeated word for word at both page 169 and 175 of Volume 1 (which led this reader to think she had unknowingly flipped the pages back to the first reference). Several other sections include similar unacknowledged repetitions.

The collection would certainly be a better buy if the publishers had more carefully edited the text. Yet despite these problems, the three volumes taken together provide the essential documentary history of the ICC. This is therefore a valuable resource for academics, jurists, historians, and students of international criminal justice, and the collection deserves to find its way onto the shelves of all academic law libraries.

NICOLE LAVIOLETTE
Associate Professor, Faculty of Law, University of Ottawa

Printsipy mezhdunarodnogo nalogooblozheniia i mezhdunarodnogo nalogovogo planirovaniia. By A.I. Pogorletskii. St. Petersburg: Izdatel'stvo S.-Peterburgskogo gosudarstvennogo universiteta, 2005.

A.I. Pogorletskii of St. Petersburg, who is already known for his writings on taxation and economics,[1] conveys in this work his latest reflections on international tax law and its implications for international tax planning. His reflections gain considerable interest through the substantial changes in the Russian Federation's economy after the Soviet Union collapsed in 1991, combined with the reforms of Russia's tax system.[2] These developments suggest two criteria for appraising the present work: whether Pogorletskii has painted a balanced picture of contemporary international tax law and international tax planning and whether he has conveyed

---

[1] Pogorletskii's earlier treatments of economics and tax law include: A.I. Pogorletskii, *Nalogooblozhenie dokhodov khoziaistvuiushchikh sub'ektov: voprosy teorii i praktiki* (St Petersburg: Izd-vo S.-Peterburgskogo gosudarstvennogo universiteta, 1996); A.I. Pogorletskii, *Ekonomika zarubezhnykh stran* (St Petersburg: Izdatel'stvo Mikhailova V.A., 2000); and A.I. Pogorletskii, *Vneshnie faktory formirovaniia natsional'noi nalogovoi politiki* (St Petersburg: Izd-vo S.-Peterburgskogo gosudarstvennogo universiteta, 2004).

[2] The tax reforms of the Russian Federation's first decade are analyzed in M. Karasseva, *Tax Law in Russia* (The Hague: Kluwer, 2000). Part I of the Russian Tax Code, which introduced changes in personal income tax provisions, took effect in January 1999. *Tax Code of the Russian Federation.* Part 1, translated by W.E. Butler (London: Simmonds and Hill Publishing, 1999). Part 2, which affected the way in which tax is levied upon commercial enterprises operating in the Russian Federation, took effect in January 2001. T. Polivanova-Rosenauer, "Review of the Corporate Income Tax Chapter of the Russian Tax Code" (2002) 42(6-7) Eur. Taxation 228. Supplementary provisions to Parts 1 and 2 have been issued since 2001.

convincingly the extent of the Russian's Federation's integration with the international tax order.

Pogorletskii presents some general reflections on international tax law in his first eight chapters. He treats, *inter alia*, globalization's effects in rendering economic transactions with international tax consequences; the fundamental categories and principles of international taxation; the taxation of persons and corporations according to their place of residence or the sources of their revenues; international double taxation and the ways to eradicate it, most notably tax agreements; the prevention of tax offences; competition among states to create a tax environment conducive to investment; and the harmonization by states of their tax systems, particularly as electronic commerce becomes increasingly ensconced within the international economy. Pogorletskii explains lucidly his reflections on these topics, buttressing his points with various diagrams, tables, and charts. While the reflections themselves might strike Western international tax lawyers as conventional, they are nevertheless significant, since they show that Russian and Western approaches to understanding international tax law are converging.

In nine further chapters, Pogorletskii presents his reflections on international tax planning. He explores, *inter alia*, international tax planning as a legal means to minimize the taxes payable by persons and corporations on their economic activities abroad; forms of taxation of corporations and their tax particularities; ways for corporations to minimize the taxes payable on their foreign revenues; structures that transnational corporations can assume so as to minimize their tax obligations; low-tax jurisdictions and their role in international tax planning; tax havens; special tax regimes in Luxembourg, the Netherlands, Belgium, and Switzerland; and international tax planning's limits. Pogorletskii's reflections on these topics, too, might appear familiar, but they depict Russian approaches to international tax planning as resembling the approaches adopted by Western international tax lawyers.

Thus far, Pogorletskii has presented a good, if conventional, portrait of contemporary international tax law and international tax planning. His portrait reflects broad and careful research, as manifested in a substantial bibliography. The various diagrams, tables, and charts help to clarify the points he makes. Unfortunately, Pogorletskii is less successful in revealing the extent to which the Russian Federation's tax system has become integrated with the international tax order. This deficiency arises primarily through inadequate attention to the legal and factual details of the unfolding Russian tax system. An examination of the more recent tomes of *Tax Notes International, European Taxation,* and other leading international tax journals clarifies precisely how the Russian tax system is changing. Moreover, Russian tax policy furnishes an explanatory context for the measures that the Russian Federation is taking regarding international taxation.[3] If Pogorletskii entered into this degree of detail, he could have illustrated more meaningfully how far the Russian tax system has become integrated with the international tax order. While some integration is implicit in the examples he adduces about the Russian tax system, the existing degree of detail permits no conclusions on its extent.

In sum, Pogorletskii's latest reflections on international tax law and its implications for international tax planning are variable in their quality. His overview of contemporary international tax law and international tax planning — erudite, lucid, and generally persuasive as it is — can be read for profit and pleasure. However, he is less effective in showing how his own country's tax system has become integrated with the international tax order since 1991. This shortcoming is all the more regrettable because it impedes Canadian and other Western tax specialists in engaging in dialogue with their Russian counterparts on how Russia's tax system might be improved. This reviewer can only hope that Pogorletskii will soon strive to remedy it in a companion work.

ERIC MYLES
Adjunct Professor, University of Ottawa

New Wars, New Laws? Applying the Laws of War in Twenty-First Century Conflicts. Edited by David Wippman and Matthew Evangelista. Ardsley, NY: Transnational Publishers, 2005. 308 pages.

The Prosecution and Defense of Peacekeepers under International Criminal Law. By Geert-Jan Alexander Knoops. Ardsley, NY: Transnational Publishers, 2004. 415 pages.

As a result of dramatic changes in the global security environment, particularly since the end of the Cold War, the ongoing threat posed

---

[3] V.A. Kashin, *Obzor fiskal'noi politiki v Rossiiskoi Federatsii i za rubezhom v 2003 godu* (Moscow: Izdatel'stvo ekonomiko-pravovoi literatury, 2004); and A.V. Paskachev and V.A. Kashin, *Obzor fiskal'noi politiki v Rossiiskoi Federatsii i za rubezhom v 2004 godu* (Moscow: Izdatel'stvo ekonomiko-pravovoi literatury, 2005).

by interstate conflict has been joined by major concerns arising from intra-state violence and transnational terrorism. These developments challenge traditional responses to conflict management and pose major dilemmas for proponents of the international rule of law. Further related complications arise from the growing participation of non-state actors and international peacekeepers in hostilities, given the traditional focus of international humanitarian law on the regulation of conflict between state armed forces. Can these new security issues be met effectively within the current framework of international law?

As its title suggests, *New Wars, New Laws? Applying the Laws of War in Twenty-First Century Conflicts* takes a broad approach to this question, assessing the adequacy of international humanitarian law in the context of key contemporary security debates. With this volume, David Wippman[1] and Matthew Evangelista[2] have collected nine essays, plus a substantive introductory chapter, emerging from a 2003 conference at Cornell University, which was held shortly after the American-led invasion of Iraq. Contributors include prominent academics, military lawyers, and non-governmental actors, from within and outside the United States (including two Canadians). *New Wars, New Laws?* is an accessible volume, useful both for students and practitioners. Not intended as a comprehensive treatise, this volume instead illuminates areas of legitimate disagreement, while ultimately emphasizing both the importance and complexity of addressing modern security challenges with existing international legal principles.

Structured around three broad themes, namely the "war on terror," the conduct of hostilities, and military occupation, the essays offer varied, sometimes contradictory, perspectives on the content and application of international humanitarian law. Disagreement is highlighted with competing understandings of the legal regime applicable to the global campaign against terrorism, as contributors struggle with the relationship between law enforcement and armed conflict paradigms. Not surprisingly, problems relating to non-state actors feature prominently throughout many chapters. In particular, the volume offers varied perspectives on legal issues arising from the direct participation of civilians in hostilities, providing insight

---

[1] David Wippman, associate dean and professor, Cornell Law School. David Wippman served as the reviewer's thesis supervisor at Cornell Law School in 2003–4.

[2] Matthew Evangelista, professor and director, Peace Studies Program, Cornell University.

into the nuances of current debates concerning detention and prosecution of "unprivileged belligerents" (or "unlawful combatants")
as well as the very meaning of "direct participation" and its implications for the lawful application of deadly force against non-state actors. "Long-term" foreign military occupation in the Palestinian
territories and Iraq serve to illustrate the practical need for creative,
yet principled, legal responses in areas not directly addressed by
international humanitarian law. Despite their disagreement, contributors to *New Wars, New Laws?* generally agree that a comprehensive redefinition of international humanitarian law is both
unnecessary and unrealistic. While this body of law must continue
to evolve, its current provisions provide a strong and relevant foundation upon which to build effective national security strategies.

While individual states struggle with the legal implications of contemporary challenges, so too do collective security organizations.
The changing nature of modern conflict, particularly the growth
of intra-state ethnic violence, has led to the frequent introduction
of international peacekeepers (and peace enforcers) into failed
and failing states and their more active engagement in military
operations. Worldwide, there are fifteen ongoing UN peacekeeping missions, involving almost 90,000 civilian and military personnel drawn from over 100 countries, continuing a trend begun with
the end of the Cold War. At the same time, other multinational
organizations have also been actively engaged in their own robust
peacekeeping operations, with or without UN authorization. These
operations are increasingly placing peacekeepers in situations involving exposure to international criminal law responsibilities (such
as crime prevention) as well as potential individual liabilities.

Recognizing this reality, Geert-Jan Alexander Knoops[3] addresses,
with *The Prosecution and Defense of Peacekeepers under International
Criminal Law*, the controversial issue of holding wrongdoing
peacekeepers, whether UN "blue helmets" or members of other
forces, accountable for their actions in international fora. This is
not an academic issue. Peacekeepers have committed serious criminal acts in various contexts, both within and outside of UN operations. In Sierra Leone, alleged misconduct of ECOMOG
peacekeepers included war crimes, extrajudicial killings, and
sexual misconduct. Criminal allegations have also undermined
the legitimacy of multilateral peacekeeping operations in, among

---

[3] Geert-Jan Alexander Knoops, professor of International Criminal Law, University of Utrecht; and partner, Knoops and Partners, Amsterdam.

other places, Liberia, Somalia, Bosnia, Kosovo and, recently, the Democratic Republic of Congo.

Knoops begins his original and comprehensive volume with a detailed overview of the evolving nature of peacekeeping operations and its resulting implications for individual criminal liabilities. Intended for a knowledgeable audience, *The Prosecution and Defense of Peacekeepers* presents a methodical and sophisticated legal analysis (undermined slightly by editing concerns). Part 2 assesses the substantive criminal law applicable to peacekeepers, outlining major principles drawn from primary and secondary sources relating to substantive crimes, modes of participation, and available defences. This is followed in Part 3 with an analysis of the significant jurisdictional issues implicated by potential peacekeeper prosecution, concluding that international fora, in particular, the International Criminal Court (ICC), must remain valid options to avoid undermining operational and normative (that is, international criminal law) legitimacy.

Although recognizing the unique political context of peacekeeping, Knoops nonetheless rejects the need for a new, and privileged, legal regime, arguing instead for gradual normative evolution to address its particular challenges. Despite their traditional preferential treatment, Knoops argues that holding peacekeepers criminally accountable for their actions is a "viable and practical concept," and he strongly critiques their (now-expired) Security Council immunity from ICC jurisdiction. If peacekeeping is to be effective, it must set the groundwork for a just and lasting long-term peace, and this should not, and arguably cannot, be built on real or apparent international criminal impunity.

While the evolving nature of modern conflict poses significant national security challenges and raises valid legal debates, *New Wars, New Laws?* illustrates that dismissing the application of international humanitarian law for these reasons is a dangerous and often counter-productive strategy. *The Prosecution and Defense of Peacekeepers* provides a framework within which to ensure that no one is above the law, particularly not the guardians of international peace and security. Both volumes caution against the need for, and wisdom of, a radical redefinition of existing international law, recognizing that the standards we hold ourselves to in meeting modern security threats will inform, to a large degree, the legitimacy and effectiveness of the final result.

CHRISTOPHER K. PENNY
Norman Paterson School of International Affairs, Carleton University

Canada's Offshore: Jurisdiction, Rights and Management. By Bruce Calderbank, Alec M. MacLeod, Ted L. McDorman, and David H. Gray. Victoria: Trafford Publishing, 2006. 3rd edition, 328 pages.

All of the authors have many years of professional experience relating to the jurisdiction and management of Canada's offshore. Bruce Calderback, a professional engineer and chartered surveyor, acted as editor-in-chief of this publication. Alec MacLeod is the legislative advisor to the surveyor general of Canada Lands and monitors the status of inter-provincial boundaries and offshore jurisdictions. Ted McDorman is a professor of law at the University of Victoria and editor-in-chief of the *Ocean Development and International Law: Journal of Marine Affairs.* He has published extensively on subjects pertaining to the law of the sea. David Gray is a professional engineer and has recently retired from the Canadian Hydrographic Service in Ottawa, where he was the Geodesy Radio Positioning and Maritime Boundary specialist for twenty-five years.

The book was published under the auspices of the Association of Canada Lands Surveyors and the Canadian Hydrographic Association. It is divided into eleven chapters, most of which were "a cooperative effort as the revision process progressed,"[1] so that the authors of individual chapters are not identified except for Chapter 10. This special chapter on a "marine cadastre concept" was written by Susan Nichols, Sam Macharia Ng'ang'a, Michael Sutherland, and Sara Cockburn. Nichols is a professional engineer and a professor at the University of New Brunswick, with a long experience in boundary issues, and the other three are involved in various marine research projects. In the words of the preface by Bruce Calderbank, "the objective of this book is to be *the* source of information about Canada's offshore, not only for surveyors, but for everyone with any interest in Canada's offshore. The book goes from international concepts, to Canadian applications, to practical demonstrations."[2]

The first three chapters deal with the basic concepts underlying the discussion in the rest of the book. Chapter 1, "The Surveyor of the Offshore," explains the meaning of the expression "offshore" for the purposes of the book, as referring to "the submerged lands and the subsoil below it, the water column and the air above it,

---

[1] Bruce Calderbank, Alec M. MacLeod, Ted L. McDorman, and David H. Gray *Canada's Offshore: Jurisdiction, Rights and Management* (Victoria: Trafford Publishing, 2006) at iii.

[2] *Ibid.*

seaward from the low water line of the State's mainland and islands."[3] It also describes the functions of a surveyor engaged in
offshore work. Chapter 2, "Maritime International Law Pre-
UNCLOS," contains a good overview of the historical development
of the law of the sea before the Truman Proclamation of 1945 and,
after it, up to the UN Conference on the Law of the Sea. Chapter 3,
"United Nations Law of the Sea, 1982," outlines the basic structure
of the convention and, at first, might appear to bring nothing new
to a law of the sea expert. However, such an expert might well benefit from the section on baselines and how they are drawn. Also
very helpful are the diagrams on international straits, which illustrate the five categories provided for in the convention.

The next two chapters deal with the rules and methods governing bilateral delimitation and seaward limits. Chapter 4, "International Bilateral Offshore Boundaries," reviews several international
decisions and agreements, extracting the main equitable criteria
and methods used in the delimitation of maritime boundaries, as
well as the trends evidenced by a group of cases decided by the
international court.[4] Most helpful are nine figures illustrating the
use of partial effect and enclaves when dealing with offshore islands, taken from international decisions and agreements.[5] Chapter 5, "Determining Offshore Limits and Boundaries," contains
fourteen figures, some of which are crucial for an understanding
of certain maritime limits and boundaries, particularly for some-
one not versed in geometry and geology (like this reviewer). This
applies especially to Figure 5.5 on the seaward limit of the continental shelf, which may extend beyond 200 nautical miles under
Article 76.5 of the 1982 Convention on the Law of the Sea (LOSC).
In addition, this chapter illustrates the seabed features of three
provinces: British Columbia, Nova Scotia, and Newfoundland and
Labrador. The latter figure is of special interest since it depicts the
extension of the continental shelf beyond the Flemish Cap 100
nautical miles seaward of the 2,500-metre isobath.

The following three chapters cover the actual delimitation of
Canada's offshore and related problems. Chapter 6, "Delimitation
of Canada's Offshore," reviews Canada's legislative enactments leading to the Oceans Act of 1996. It shows how Canada's baselines

---

[3] *Ibid.* at 5.

[4] *Ibid.* at 55.

[5] *Ibid.* at 60-70.

were established to determine the limits of Canada's offshore zones of jurisdiction. Again, the numerous figures are most helpful, in particular, Figure 6.10 showing the straight baselines around the Canadian Arctic archipelago as well as the territorial sea, the contiguous zone, and the exclusive economic zone. It is probably the only map in existence illustrating these three offshore zones in the Arctic. Chapter 7, "Canada's Offshore Boundaries," lists all of Canada's offshore boundaries, both resolved and unresolved and discusses briefly the unresolved ones.[6] These boundaries include the Pacific coast, four with the United States; the Atlantic coast, two with the United States; the Arctic, three with Denmark (including the sovereignty dispute over Hans Island), one with the United States, and one with Russia. Chapter 8, "Canada's Offshore Jurisdiction," reviews the Supreme Court of Canada cases on maritime jurisdiction off the coast of British Columbia in 1967 and 1984 and off the coast of Newfoundland and Labrador in 1984. It points to the difference in the extent of provincial jurisdiction between the east and the west coasts — British Columbia's jurisdiction ends at the low water line, whereas Newfoundland and Labrador has a territorial sea of three nautical miles. The reason is that Newfoundland had inherited its own territorial sea from Great Britain and retained it when entering confederation in 1949.

As for the Arctic coast, the book maintains that the waters between the islands of the Arctic archipelago are internal waters of Canada, on the basis of the transfer of Rupert's Land in the Northwest Territories by the British order-in-council of 1870. Although it admits that, in Canada's own order-in-council of 1895 dividing the Northwest Territories into four provincial districts, "there was no specific mention of waters," it concludes that the waters were included as internal waters. Two reasons are given for this conclusion. The first is that, "given the proximity of some islands to the coasts, some of the district islands were in water."[7] The second is that "Canada succeeded to the rights of Great Britain seaward from the low water line" under the Statute of Westminster in 1931, and, "as a result, as of 31 December 2004, all the water areas between the islands beyond the mainland areas of Nunavut and the Northwest Territories, are within the baselines described in the Territorial Sea Geographical Coordinates (Area 7) Order which are 'internal

[6] *Ibid.* at 147.
[7] *Ibid.* at 177.

waters' and belong to the territories."[8] This conclusion raises two objections. First, the simple drawing of provisional district lines could not possibly have vested title in Canada.[9] Second, Great Britain could not have transferred title to the waters enclosed by the 1985 straight baselines, unless it already held such title, which is highly doubtful.

The last three chapters deal with issues pertaining to the implementation of Canada's offshore jurisdiction. Chapter 9, "Administration of Canada's Offshore Oil and Gas Resources," reviews federal legislation for the development of oil and gas resources on the three coasts. It shows how Canada sometimes shares the administration of offshore resources with the provinces or even grants them complete administration. Bilateral agreements in this regard have been concluded with Nova Scotia and Newfoundland and Labrador. Chapter 10, "Marine Cadastre Concept," considers the utility of this concept for registering rights and responsibilities relating to marine resources. It makes numerous suggestions for improving the development of a Canadian marine cadastre. Chapter 11, "Practical Issues Related to Canada's Offshore Oil and Gas Industry," provides examples "to illustrate how international boundary disputes can affect a surveyor's offshore work" and how "the proper use of datum, spheroid and projection information in the delimitation of jurisdictional boundaries can be critical to the completion of offshore work."[10] For instance, the 1982 judgment in the *Tunisia/Libya Continental Shelf Case* "contained two referenced geographical co-ordinates, one was on a Tunisian datum and the other on a Libya datum. The Court did not specify which geographical coordinate was on which datum ... nor the spheroid and projection to be used."[11]

The book ends with a glossary of the more commonly used legal and technical terms, three appendices, and a bibliography. The appendices consist of a list of government departments directly concerned with offshore and related legislation; an enumeration of the Canadian and international decisions mentioned in the text; and a six-page inventory of "significant Canadian offshore oil

---

[8] *Ibid.* at 177–78. For a discussion of the status of the 1895 lines, see Donat Pharand, *Canada's Arctic Waters in International Law* (Cambridge: Cambridge University Press, 1987) at 4-5.

[9] Calderbank et al., *supra* note 1 at 113–14.

[10] *Ibid.* at 241.

[11] *Ibid.*

events," beginning in 1858 when "the world's longest (at the time) gas pipeline was inaugurated to Trois Rivières, Québec."[12] The six-page bibliography includes both legal and technical sources.

By way of final comment, this reviewer has no hesitation in stating that the objective of the book to be the main source of information about Canada's offshore has been fully met. Certainly, this must be the case on the technical aspects. If one wishes to study any Canadian offshore issue, this book is unquestionably the main source to begin with. The twenty-three tables and sixty-four figures, inserted throughout the text, provide the reader with illustrations of physical features that are indispensable for a thorough understanding of the numerous provisions of the LOSC. Good examples are Figures 5.4 to 5.7 on the seaward limits of the continental shelf described in Article 76 of the convention.

In spite of all of its qualities, a few reservations may be justified: one on substance and a couple on form. With respect to substance, the book would have gained in mentioning that it is not universally accepted that the British transfer of the Arctic islands to Canada included title to the waters between the islands. As for the form and given the similarity in the wording of several chapter titles, a grouping of the chapters into three or four parts would have made the book easier to consult. Finally, the errors in the short list of Latin and French phrases should have been corrected. Subject to these few peccadillos, this book is as close to a must read as anyone interested in Canada's offshore could ask for.

A. DONAT PHARAND
Professor Emeritus, University of Ottawa

International Trade in Health Services and the GATS: Current Issues and Debates. Edited by C. Blouin, N. Drager, and R. Smith. Washington, DC: World Bank, 2006. 321 pages.

There is a very polarized debate regarding the impact on health services of commitments to liberalize services trade under the WTO's General Agreement on Trade in Services (GATS).[1] GATS

---

12 *Ibid.* at 317.

1 J.A. VanDuzer, "Navigating between the Poles: Unpacking the Debate on the Implications for Development of GATS Obligations Relating to Health and Education Services," in E.-U. Petersmann, ed., *Reforming The World Trading System: Legitimacy, Efficiency and Democratic Governance* (Oxford: Oxford University Press, 2005) at 167.

proponents emphasize that the agreement's "positive list" approach[2] allows countries to tailor their liberalization commitments in ways consistent with national policy objectives. They point out that there is no obligation on any WTO member to accept the higher tier of GATS obligations, including national treatment and market access, for health services, and the basic obligations applicable to all services, such as most-favoured-nation (MFN) treatment, do not represent any meaningful limitation on regulatory flexibility. In any case, GATS does not apply to most publicly delivered health services. These, they argue, are completely excluded from the scope of all GATS obligations. Most GATS proponents readily admit the fundamental importance of equitable access and other non-commercial goals that inform national policies in health. They assert, however, that GATS commitments to trade liberalization in health services not only can be compatible with such goals but also can make their achievement more likely.[3]

Many GATS critics start from a philosophical objection to a trade regime in which health services are treated like commodities. Trade liberalization commitments are viewed as serious constraints on the ability of governments, especially developing country governments, to achieve equitable access to basic health services and other social objectives of government schemes governing the regulation and delivery of health services. In particular, liberalization commitments are seen as contributing to the development of two-tier markets under which public health services will be undermined and developing country citizens who are the poorest or in rural areas will see a diminution of badly needed health and education services so that already better off and better served urban segments of the population will benefit.[4]

The collection of papers in *International Trade in Health Services and the GATS: Current Issues and Debates,* a book jointly sponsored by

---

[2] The GATS positive list approach allows World Trade Organization (WTO) members to decide whether to undertake the higher tier of commitments under the agreement, including guaranteeing national treatment and market access, for individual sectors by listing them in a national schedule of commitments. Members may also limit the extent of their commitments by limitations they write into their schedules.

[3] For example, R. Adlung, "The GATS Negotiations: Implications for Health and Social Services" (2003) 38 Intereconomics 147.

[4] For example, R. Chanda, "Trade in Health Services" (2002) 80 Bulletin of the World Health Organization 158.

the World Health Organization and the World Bank, is a very useful contribution to this debate in several ways. First, it provides a clear and accessible account of the GATS, a complex and often misunderstood agreement. Second, it provides a balanced discussion of the likely costs and benefits of liberalization of trade in health services and of GATS commitments in health services focusing on the impact on health in developing countries. Third, it provides an accessible and practical guide to the questions that states need to ask themselves in order to formulate a policy on trade in health services and GATS. Fourth, it identifies the substantial gaps in what we know about trade liberalization in health services and about the effects of GATS commitments in this area and so provides a useful guide to future research in this area.

The first substantive chapter in this book sets the stage by identifying the strategic challenges for developing countries in deciding on their position regarding health services commitments under the GATS.[5] The authors begin with an explanation of why the prospect of the application of GATS to health services has sparked such a negative response from stakeholders in national health systems.

The causes of concern are not hard to divine. For every state, health services provision is one way that governments discharge their fundamental responsibility to care for the most basic human needs of its citizens. The delivery of health services cannot be left to the market because health services is an example of market failure. The market place will not supply the minimally necessary quality and quantity of health services at an affordable cost. As a result, there is extensive public sector involvement in regulating, funding, and delivering health services in every state. GATS was the first multilateral agreement dealing with services and marked the first time that most health ministries and the public and private suppliers and professional organizations involved in health services delivery had been required to consider the possible application of trade disciplines to health. As a result of the non-commercial character of national health services supply and regulation, most health stakeholders strongly objected to applying market-based constructs in the GATS, such as MFN treatment, national treatment, and market access, to health services.

---

[5] M. Mashayekhi, M. Julsaint, and E. Tuerk, "Strategic Considerations for Developing Countries: The Case of GATS and Health Services," in C. Blouin, N. Drager, and R. Smith, eds., *International Trade in Health Services and the GATS: Current Issues and Debates* (Washington, DC: World Bank, 2006), 17.

The authors of the chapter go on to point out, however, that for a particular country trade in health services is not simply a question of whether and to what extent to permit foreign suppliers into the domestic market. Some developing countries, such as India and the Philippines, have export interests, in the sense that they would like better opportunities for their health professionals to enter lucrative developed country markets with the hope of securing substantial remittances of foreign earnings, even though in some cases such movement carries with it the risk of losing scarce health professionals to overseas markets and imperiling domestic services. As well, developing countries such as Thailand have sought to market their local health services abroad by offering high quality services to "foreign health tourists" at attractive prices. As these examples illustrate, developing national positions on trade in health services often is not straightforward.

This chapter also provides an introduction to the GATS itself and the ongoing round of services negotiations with an emphasis on the issues for developing countries. Under the architecture of the GATS, certain basic obligations — the most important of which is MFN treatment — apply to all services sectors. The more serious obligations of market access and national treatment apply only to the extent that a WTO member lists a service in its national schedule and then only subject to any limitations that the member has written into its schedule. One of the concerns identified in this chapter is that the GATS exclusion for services supplied "in the exercise of governmental authority" does not clearly exclude what are considered to be public health services in most countries because, typically, such services are delivered through a mix of public and private providers. As well, it is unclear how trade disciplines such as national treatment will apply to health services. Perhaps the greatest concern has been that the regulation and delivery of health services in many countries are in a state of flux, provoking worries that undertaking specific GATS commitments for health services may impose inappropriate limits on the policy space needed for future reforms. While the GATS provides flexibility to WTO members before they list commitments, once commitments are undertaken by a country it is bound to any limitations inscribed in its schedule.[6] Relying on such limitations to preserve adequate policy

---

[6] There is a process under the General Agreement on Trade in Services (GATS) Article XXI that permits a country to withdraw a commitment subject to an obligation to give compensation to other WTO members who claim that their benefits under the agreement are affected.

space, however, is dangerous, especially for developing countries because drafting effective limitations requires being able to predict precisely future medical, technological, demographic, and economic trends related to health care.

Negotiations on new market access commitments and new substantive rules for services trade started in 2000 and now form part of the Doha Round. The authors of this chapter note that, although WTO negotiations are characterized by substantial power imbalances in favour of developed countries, especially the United States and the European Union, there is little pressure in the current round for developing countries to open up their health services markets. At the same time, the authors express concern about potential constraints on domestic regulatory freedom in health services that might result from the negotiation of generally applicable disciplines on domestic regulation.

Finally, the authors discuss the lack of data on the effects of health services liberalization on health care and the effects of GATS commitments. Uncertainty regarding whether commitments will attract foreign investment in health services, combined with uncertainty regarding the scope of GATS and its obligations and continual waves of regulatory reform in health services leads the authors to conclude that, while countries may want to experiment with liberalization, locking in liberalized market access through GATS commitments will be unattractive for most developing countries.

The authors of the next chapter, Rudolf Adlung and Antonia Carzaniga of the WTO Secretariat, describe in detail the existing GATS commitments of WTO members.[7] The authors make clear that, overall, the negotiated level of commitments so far in health services is relatively low. For example, only 42 per cent of all members and about one-third of developing countries have made a commitment in any health sector and most of these simply commit members to provide the level of access already available under their existing regimes. Many developing country commitments guarantee access at a level that is not even as high as the access they grant in fact to foreign health services suppliers. These authors confirm that there has been little interest in the current negotiations in new commitments in health services, though they query whether this makes the negotiations simply a non-event for health services

---

[7] R. Adlung and A. Carzaniga, "Update on GATS Commitments and Negotiations," in Blouin, Drager, and Smith, *supra* note 5, 83.

or a missed opportunity in light of some of the possible benefits of liberalization.[8]

The next chapter synthesizes the detailed information from the preceding chapters into a step-by-step guide for governments regarding how they should develop their policy regarding GATS commitments in health services.[9] The author makes the important point that before GATS commitments need to be considered, states must make prior domestic policy choices about whether and to what extent they will permit private provision of health services. Once they permit private provision, the question becomes whether to permit foreign participation. In this regard, a state must consider the costs and benefits of market access for foreigners, its capacity to regulate foreign service providers, and the scope to use other policy measures, or "flanking measures," to enhance the benefits and mitigate the costs of liberalizing market access. Finally, only after deciding to permit foreign participation does the question of whether to bind access with GATS commitments become relevant. In most cases, the degree to which health services are commercially supplied will make much more of a difference than if they are supplied by foreigners to some extent. In considering GATS commitments, the author emphasizes that, while commitments must be negotiated, there is no requirement in GATS for members to liberalize their existing regime. As discussed earlier, commitments may be undertaken at the level that reflects the existing regime or even at a level that is less liberal than the regime that is presently in place. Finally, the author notes that GATS permits a WTO member to withdraw or modify a commitment, though GATS provides that any member that does so may be required to compensate other WTO members whose service providers are affected as a result.

The following chapter by several distinguished legal experts provides the most extensive and rigorous discussion of GATS legal rules in the book.[10] It focuses on the legal implications of the GATS for health policy. They note that the GATS is not designed to address

---

8 *Ibid.* at 99. The costs and benefits are discussed in another chapter of the book discussed below: C. Blouin, "Economic Dimension and Impact Assessment of GATS to Promote and Protect Health," in Blouin, Drager, and Smith, *supra* note 5, 169.

9 J. Nielson, "Ten Steps to Consider Before Making Commitments in Health Services under the GATS," in Blouin, Drager, and Smith, *supra* note 5, 101.

10 D. Fidler, N. Drager, C. Correa, and O. Aginam, "Making Commitments in Health Services under the GATS: Legal Dimensions," in Blouin, Drager, and Smith, *supra* note 5, 141.

the particular distinctive characteristics of the health sector and that, in the current negotiations, no proposals have been made to create health specific rules regarding domestic regulation. They also conclude, unlike some other authors in the book,[11] that the outcome of the domestic regulation negotiations is unlikely to pose a threat to health policy. They find that the application of the generally applicable disciplines like the MFN is "not particularly troubling."[12] Finally, they conclude that the current rules, including the specific commitments undertaken by WTO members, have so far had little impact on health or, indeed, on liberalization of trade in health services.[13] Nevertheless, they caution that mobilization is required to ensure that health policy concerns are continually voiced at the WTO in light of the commitment in GATS for WTO members to engage in successive rounds of negotiations aimed at progressive liberalization in all sectors, including health services.

In the next two chapters, Chantal Blouin and others examine the economic costs and benefits of liberalization in health services.[14] For each mode of services supply contemplated in the GATS, they review the evidence of trade in health services and its effects as well as the impediments to such trade.

Regarding the cross-border supply of services (GATS mode 1), such as through telemedicine, the authors identify the significant potential for the delivery of a wider range of higher quality services through this mode to under-served areas in developing countries. There are many challenges to such trade, however, including the critical lack of telecommunications infrastructure in many developing countries, the lack of international standards for health services that discourage relying on remote foreign services, and the absence of universally accepted norms for privacy and ethics.

With respect to the export of services to consumers from abroad (GATS mode 2), the authors note the significant potential for at least some developing countries to attract foreign consumers with

[11] Mashayekhi, Julsaint, and Tuerk, *supra* note 5.

[12] *Ibid.* at 156.

[13] The authors cite the conclusion of a joint study by the WTO and the World Health Organization (WHO) that "the overall effect of GATS on trade in health services is negligible to date" (*ibid.* at 163).

[14] C. Blouin, "Economic Dimension and Impact Assessment of GATS to Promote and Protect Health," in Blouin, Drager, and Smith, *supra* note 5, 169; C. Blouin, J. Gobrecht, J. Lethbridge, D. Singh, R. Smith, and D. Warner, "Trade in Health Services under the Four Modes of Supply: Review of Current Trends and Policy Issues," in Blouin, Drager, and Smith, *supra* note 5, 203.

high quality, low cost health services. They also raise the possibility that the development of services for relatively well off foreign patients and some similarly situated local patients may encourage the development of a two-tier health care system with poorer local people being relegated to a lower quality public system. A related concern is that health professionals will abandon the public system in favour of more lucrative opportunities serving wealthy local and foreign patients putting further pressure on public health systems.

The supply of services by foreigners through a commercial presence (GATS mode 3) holds out the promise of foreign capital investment, promoting access to new services, information, and management techniques, though the authors acknowledge that the evidence is weak on the likely significance of such effects. One concern regarding supply through this mode is that foreign investment will not tend to flow to where it is needed most, such as in poor rural areas, but to where the returns are greatest, such as relatively wealthy urban areas. Opening up domestic markets to foreign investment may encourage the development of a two-tier system with some of the negative effects identified earlier. On the other hand, if wealthier patients migrated to private sector suppliers bolstered by foreign capital, permitting foreign investors in health services, it could also result in reduced claims on public sector resources.

Finally, regarding the supply of services by natural persons who have gone abroad (GATS mode 4), the main benefit for developing countries would be the remittances paid by their health professionals working in better paying jobs abroad. From a health policy perspective, one of the challenges associated with remittances is how to channel these payments to private individuals in developing countries into the public health systems in these countries. The main cost associated with the movement of developing country health professionals abroad is the "brain drain" that occurs when migration becomes permanent. In their discussion of trade in health services, the authors note the differential significance of trade in health services for different countries at different levels of development. Most least-developed countries, for example, have no export interests in health but may have substantial interest in attracting foreign investment in health services to supplement meager public resources, whereas some richer developing countries are very interested both in exporting some of their highly skilled health professionals and attracting consumers from other countries. The authors also consider the prospects for developing countries to use "flanking measures" to mitigate the negative effects of liberalization. For example, a state worried about the development of a two-tier system if it permits foreign for-profit hospitals to operate may impose requirements for foreign hospitals to maintain a minimum number of beds for poor patients. The capacity of developing countries to regulate effectively in this way, however, is quite variable.

In the final chapter of this book,[15] the authors conclude that there are many gaps in our current understanding of the impact of trade liberalization in health services on health outcomes and on development and a lack of evidence on whether GATS commitments encourage trade in services. The authors suggest that each government must try to develop a sophisticated understanding of the particular ways in which trade in health services and GATS commitments could affect their country's health system and provide a series of key points and checklists to assist governments in a practical way to do so. This is supplemented by an appendix,[16] which sets out a detailed framework for policy-makers in the form of a questionnaire that identifies the types of information required as well as possible sources of such information. In light of the uncertainties and country-specific effects related to trade in health services, the authors' final recommendation is a simple one: countries may want to "sample" liberalization[17] but should not bind liberalization with GATS commitments.

It is noteworthy that most of the book is about liberalization of trade in health services rather than the GATS. This seems entirely appropriate given the need for a series of prior policy choices before GATS commitments even become a relevant question and the unclear benefits of GATS commitments in this area. Thus, while the core recommendation in the book regarding GATS may be regarded as somewhat tepid — that countries should experiment with liberalization before considering GATS commitments — it is fully supported by the analysis provided. While some have expressed concern about whether countries, particularly developing countries, will be forced into making commitments in the current round of negotiations, several chapters of this book suggest that this concern is exaggerated, noting the absence of negotiating proposals

---

[15] R. Smith, C. Blouin, and N. Drager, "Trade in Health Services and the GATS: What Next," in Blouin, Drager, and Smith, *supra* note 5, 235.

[16] R. Chanda and R. Smith, "Trade in Health Services and GATS: A Framework for Policymakers," in Blouin, Drager, and Smith, *supra* note 5, 245.

[17] *Ibid.* at 243–44.

related to health services and the paucity of requests for market access related to health services.[18]

Nevertheless, as the authors suggest, health policy-makers and trade officials must continue to think about the opportunities and challenges related to trade in health services as the rules of the trading system evolve. In this regard, *International Trade in Health Services and the GATS: Current Issues and Debates* provides a balanced and well-documented overview of current evidence on the implications of the liberalization of health services trade for health, some of the current practices in particular developing countries, and a dispassionate account of the actual and prospective significance of GATS commitments in health services by some of the best people writing on trade in health services from around the globe. Considering the polarized and not always well-informed debate regarding the GATS, this book's sober treatment of the agreement is an especially important contribution.

The practical tools in *International Trade in Health Services and the GATS: Current Issues and Debates* will support trade policy capacity building and facilitate national dialogue among health policy stakeholders regarding what are the best policy options related to health services and trade commitments, including commitments under the increasing number of bilateral and regional trading agreements signed and under negotiation that impose rules relating to services. The template for policy development that is provided is especially important because it may create a common framework for country analyses, facilitating international comparisons and sharing of experience. Use of the template will also encourage more consistent data gathering on health services trade across countries. Existing data gathering on health services trade is quite variable and, in some countries, virtually non-existent.

Finally, the analysis in this book lays the foundation for future research looking beyond health services and international services rules. Future research will need to examine further the impact of

---

[18] Indeed, the nature of the initiatives necessary to facilitate trade in health services will mean that other international organizations, such as the WHO and the UN Conference on Trade and Development (UNCTAD) are likely to play a more important role than the WTO. For example, the development of international quality assurance standards and procedures for assessment by the WHO and other bodies would encourage the international supply of health services in all modes.

other trade rules on health[19] and how trade liberalization in other areas interacts with health services and to locate the discussion of trade in health services within the broader context of international health care governance.[20] Health issues are increasingly global. Addressing them internationally will require diverse approaches that traverse a wide range of disciplines and that are responsive to varying local conditions.[21] *International Trade in Health Services and the GATS: Current Issues and Debates* provides one useful starting point.

J. ANTHONY VANDUZER
Faculty of Law, University of Ottawa

Global Health Governance: International Law and Public Health in a Divided World. By Obijiofor Aginam. Toronto: University of Toronto Press, 2005. 223 pages.

Global health is an issue that has attracted a great deal of attention in recent years as a consequence of the global spread of HIV/AIDS, severe acute respiratory syndrome (better known by its acronym SARS), and other infectious diseases. Obijiofor Aginam's book is a thoughtful and timely study of how the international system in general, and international law in particular, have failed to address effectively the challenges of global health. Aginam starts his analysis from what he identifies as the fundamental paradox in global health today. Increasingly the globalization of commerce and travel as well as other factors have led to the globalization of disease and other health risks. Health problems in any part of the world create health risks everywhere, and, as a result, national solutions cannot be entirely successful. Despite our "mutual vulnerability,"[1] however, the global response so far has been weak and inadequate. Of the efforts that have been undertaken, few have relied on international law. Aginam attributes the existence of this paradox largely to the

---

[19] Some work of this kind has already been done, for example, WHO and WTO, *WTO Agreements and Public Health: A Joint Study by the WHO and WTO Secretariats* (Geneva: WTO, 2002).

[20] For a broad-based discussion of international health governance, see O. Aginam, *Global Health Governance: International Law and Public Health in a Divided World* (Toronto: University of Toronto Press, 2005), which is also reviewed in this volume.

[21] This point is stressed by Aginam, *ibid.* at 90–108.

[1] Obijiofor Aginam, *Global Health Governance: International Law and Public Health in a Divided World* (Toronto: University of Toronto Press, 2005) at 6.

brute fact that, notwithstanding our mutual vulnerability, the burden of disease still falls disproportionately on the developing world. Indeed, because poverty and poor health are directly and intimately linked, this burden is becoming heavier as a consequence of the growing chasm between rich and poor in the world. Aginam makes a carefully crafted and extensively documented argument in favour of new multilateral efforts to address our mutual vulnerability by improving health in developing countries.

In the first substantive chapter of his book, Aginam examines the failure of the international system to address global poverty across the South-North divide and its devastating effects on health. He argues that both states and international institutions, including the United Nations, have marginalized the right to health recognized in the International Covenant on Economic, Social and Cultural Rights both by subordinating it to civil and political rights and by failing to provide mechanisms to give operational effect to it, including refusing to supplement formal legal rights with adequate financial and technical resources from developed countries. He also discusses the "structural adjustment programs" prescribed by the World Bank, which typically involve the removal of barriers to trade and foreign investment and limits on government spending. Aginam characterizes these programs as failing to meet fully their economic growth objectives and, more seriously, leading to worsening health in developing countries by encouraging unsustainable development and cutbacks to health and social programs. In sum, he concludes that the system has succeeded in "globalizing poverty."[2]

Aginam's study is perhaps at its most compelling in demonstrating the frightening and expanding dimensions of mutual vulnerability arising out of deteriorating health conditions in developing countries. He charts the contemporary re-emergence of tuberculosis and the spread of malaria to North America and Europe to show the increasing obsolescence of distinctions between national and international health issues. Outbreaks of these re-emergent diseases as well as new infectious diseases, such as SARS, have been facilitated by a large number of mutually reinforcing characteristics of our globalized world: global trade and travel, globalization of our food supply, centralized processing of food, population growth leading to increased urbanization and crowding, population movement due to wars, famine, and man-made and natural disasters, human

[2] *Ibid.* at 34.

behaviour, including unsafe sex and intravenous drug use, and increased use of anti-microbial agents and pesticides leading to the development of drug resistance.[3]

Next, Aginam exposes the failings of the international system in its efforts to respond to our mutual vulnerability. He refers to these failings as the "vulnerability of multilateralism."[4] While multilateral solutions are essential in a world that is becoming "a single germ pool in which there are no health sanctuaries or safe havens from pathogenic microbes,"[5] international efforts to date have been tepid as a result of developed countries seeking to advance their narrowly conceived self-interest. Aginam shows how early international efforts to address concerns about the spread of cholera were undermined by the economic, strategic, and other interests of European states through an analysis of the succession of international sanitary conferences in the nineteenth century beginning in 1851. Britain, for example, argued against the imposition of quarantines out of concern for its shipping interests. Aginam suggests that the dominance of these kinds of developed country preoccupations remain serious impediments to the development of effective multilateral institutions today. As an example of how such "politicization" has reduced the effectiveness of the World Health Organization (WHO), Aginam describes the failure of the organization to find a way to address the health effects of nuclear weapons testing in the face of opposition from nuclear states.

Aginam provides a specific critique of the limited efforts of the WHO to develop legal instruments to achieve its objectives.[6] He suggests that the WHO has been dominated by an "undue medicalization of public health,"[7] which has discouraged resort to legal solutions in favour of technical medical approaches. In support of this view, Aginam discusses the major legal initiative of the WHO to date, namely the international health regulations (IHRs). In brief, the IHRs oblige member states to advise the WHO of outbreaks of particular diseases, which is followed by WHO notification of all other member states. The IHRs also set constraints on the defensive measures that member states can put in place related

---

[3] *Ibid.* at 56–57.

[4] *Ibid.* at 6.

[5] *Ibid.*

[6] Aginam also characterizes the legacy of the nineteenth-century origins of international law as including an entrenched colonial attitude.

[7] Aginam, *supra* note 1 at 73.

to international travel and traffic. These are designed to protect the country in which the outbreak has occurred from economically damaging restrictions in other states that are out of proportion to the health risk. Aginam characterizes the IHRs as ineffective, attributing this to several causes, including the WHO's lack of familiarity with the creation and enforcement of legal instruments. This has meant, for example, that the IHRs were not accompanied by effective international supervisory mechanisms or incentives to induce compliance. He also notes, however, that legal rules could never be effective on their own. The unwillingness of developed countries to invest in the development of effective disease surveillance in developing countries has reduced the impact of the IHRs. In the final part of this critique, Aginam describes the recent Framework Convention on Tobacco Control, which was adopted by the WHO in 2003, as a possible hopeful signal that the organization has a new interest in the use of legal mechanisms similar to those increasingly resorted to in areas such as the environment.[8]

In the final part of his analysis, Aginam develops a case study of malaria to show another weakness in the current approach to global health care governance — its inappropriate reliance on "globalization from above"[9] in the form of the exclusive reliance on conventional Western medicine over more cost-effective local traditional healing. He documents the utility of traditional medicines and treatments with respect to malaria and describes the failure of WHO programs to recognize them. Based on this case study, Aginam argues for the development of a multilateral approach to disease that is much more inclusive of indigenous knowledge and responsive to input from civil society — an approach he calls "globalization from below."[10]

In light of his analysis, Aginam suggests two possible solutions. First, he proposes partnerships between the World Bank and the WHO and other international agencies concerned with health. One advantage of such partnerships would be to marshal more effectively the financial resources and enormous influence of the bank in developing countries in the interests of health. This would only

[8] Aginam refers, for example, to the Montreal Protocol on Substances That Deplete the Ozone Layer, in force 1 January 1989, (1987) 26 I.L.M. 1550 at 86.

[9] Aginam, *supra* note 1 at 92. Aginam borrows this concept from R. Falk, *Law in an Emerging Global Village: A Post-Westphalian Perspective* (New York: Transnational, 1998) at 29.

[10] *Ibid.*

be successful, in Aginam's view, if the bank moderates its emphasis on neo-liberal economic policies. Aginam suggests that there is scope for such collaboration, identifying existing commonalities between the bank and the WHO.[11]

The second proposal is for a new global health fund targeting the non-proliferation of disease through improved prevention strategies, disease surveillance, and treatments available to vulnerable populations around the world. Such a new financial commitment is necessary in light of declining global health funding for developing countries and official development assistance. Aginam proposes that the new fund operate as a "public-private" partnership independent of existing international institutions. Governance of the new fund would embrace participation from donor and recipient states, civil society organizations, and the private sector following the model of the Global Health Fund to fight HIV/AIDS and other infectious diseases established in 2001.

Aginam's particular focus on the role of international law is a welcome contribution to the literature on global health, providing a useful foundation for future thinking about the existing international rules and how they may be improved. It would have been instructive, however, if Aginam had more clearly pointed to the way forward in the development of international law and institutions in this area. Apart from some references to the utility of looking at international environmental law-making, he does not address international law to any significant extent in the solutions he proposes. Nor does he deal with the issues of how international law in areas such as trade and investment might affect the evolution of global health. Concerns about the possible deleterious effects of trade liberalization itself and liberalization commitments related to goods and services have been loudly expressed in many quarters.[12] As noted, he does critique the World Bank's

---

11 C. Blouin, N. Drager, and R. Smith, eds., *International Trade in Health Services and the GATS: Current Issues and Debates* (Washington, DC: World Bank, 2006), which is also reviewed in this volume, may be an example of the inter-agency cooperation that Aginam is talking about. This study is a joint project of the World Bank and the World Health Organization.

12 There has been significant debate about this in Canada. See, for example, M. Sanger, *Reckless Abandon: Canada, GATS and the Future of Health Care* (Ottawa: Canadian Centre for Policy Alternatives, 2002); and *Building on Values: The Future of Health Care in Canada: Final Report of the Commission on the Future of Health Care in Canada* (Ottawa: Queen's Printer, 2002). Much has been written regarding development implications as well, including Blouin, Drager, and Smith, *supra* note 11, which is also reviewed in this volume.

structural adjustment programs, but the impact of trade liberalization resulting from successive rounds of negotiations in the General Agreement on Tariffs and Trade and the World Trade Organization as well as from the expanding network of regional trading agreements receives only a passing reference.[13]

Overall, however, Aginam's book represents a very significant contribution to our understanding of the complex global nature of health risks, the inadequacy of existing global health governance, and why the law has, so far, played only a marginal role. His study is an excellent example of how a holistic approach employing law, history, international relations theory, and epidemiology can produce an insightful exposition of the contemporary situation. He draws on a wide range of theoretical and empirical scholarship in all of these areas. Aginam also brings to bear his own rich and diverse experience in international health, including a stint as a global health leadership officer at the WHO. In the section of his study on traditional treatments for malaria, Aginam relies on fieldwork and interviews he conducted in eastern Nigeria. Overall, he has provided an eloquent and compelling plea for enhanced multilateral engagement in global health governance.

J. ANTHONY VANDUZER
Faculty of Law, University of Ottawa

---

[13] The first reference to the World Trade Organization does not appear until page 41.

Analytical Index / Indexe analytique

THE CANADIAN YEARBOOK OF
INTERNATIONAL LAW

2005

ANNUAIRE CANADIEN
DE DROIT INTERNATIONAL

(A) Article; (NC) Notes and Comments; (Ch) Chronique;
(P) Practice; (C) Cases; (BR) Book Review
(A) Article; (NC) Notes et commentaires; (Ch) Chronique;
(P) Pratique; (C) Jurisprudence; (BR) Recension de livre

Index of Cases /
Index de la jurisprudence